RIC BAKER  VIVIAN RICHARDI BEITMAN

third
edition

CRITICAL APPROACHES TO
READING, WRITING AND THINKING

Kendall Hunt
publishing company

Cover image © Shutterstock.com

Stoplight on page 239: © ktsdesign/Shutterstock.com

Flag on page 239: © TatjanaRittner/Shutterstock.com

Kendall Hunt
publishing company

www.kendallhunt.com
Send all inquiries to:
4050 Westmark Drive
Dubuque, IA 52004-1840

BRIEF CONTENTS

Preface to the Instructor	xv
Preface to the Student	xix
Acknowledgments	xxi

PART I   Learning to Read, Write, and Think Critically 1

CHAPTER 1	Becoming a Critical Thinker, Reader, and Writer	3
CHAPTER 2	Comprehension	31
CHAPTER 3	Interpretation	61
CHAPTER 4	Inference	111
CHAPTER 5	Self-Monitoring	153
CHAPTER 6	Analysis	187
CHAPTER 7	Evaluation	221
CHAPTER 8	Explanation	263
CHAPTER 9	Problem-Solving	303

PART II   Thinking Critically about Current Issues 329

Putting It All Together	331
Gun Violence and Gun Control	331
Technology Addiction	343
Peace and War	353
Self-Driving Cars	363
Women's Issues	375

Appendix: Word Parts	**387**
Glossary	**391**
Bibliography	**399**
Index	**405**

CONTENTS

Preface to the Instructor   xv
Preface to the Student   xix
Acknowledgments   xxi

PART 1   Learning to Read, Write, and Think Critically   1

CHAPTER 1   Becoming a Critical Thinker, Reader, and Writer   3
SECTION ONE   3
The Meaning of Critical Thinking   3
Thinking Critically   5
  Facts about Critical Thinking   5
The Benefits of Critical Thinking   6
The Critical Thinker's Attitude toward the World   8
  Be Curious (Chapter 2)   8
    Curiosity in Practice   8
  Be Humble (Chapter 3)   8
    Humility in Practice   9
  Be Open-Minded and Flexible (Chapter 4)   9
    Open-Mindedness and Flexibility in Practice   9
  Be Organized (Chapter 5)   9
    Organization in Practice   9
  Be Skeptical (Chapter 6)   9
    Skepticism in Practice   10
  Be Fair-Minded (Chapter 7)   10
    Fair-Mindedness in Practice   10
  Trust in Reason (Chapter 8)   10
    Reason in Practice   10
  Be Persistent (Chapter 9)   10
    Persistence in Practice   10
The Skills of a Critical Thinker   13
  Comprehension (Chapter 2)   14
  Interpretation (Chapter 3)   14
  Inference (Chapter 4)   14
  Self-Monitoring (Chapter 5)   14
  Analysis (Chapter 6)   15
  Evaluation (Chapter 7)   15

Explanation (Chapter 8)   15

Problem-Solving (Chapter 9)   15

Read, Write, and Think Critically: Section One   16

Reading: *Is Anyone Ever Wrong Anymore?,* Mitch Daniels   17

SECTION TWO   18

Things That Can Get in the Way of Critical Thinking   18

Obstacles Caused by the Way We Think   19

Rationalizing   19

Confirmation Bias   19

Memory Errors   20

Obstacles Caused by Our Emotions   22

Attribution Mistakes   22

Wishful Thinking   22

Conformity   23

Defense Mechanisms   23

Chapter Summary   26

Read, Write, and Think Critically: Section Two   26

Reading: *Is Google Making Us Stupid? What the Internet Is Doing to Our Brains,* Nicholas Carr   27

CHAPTER 2   Comprehension   31

SECTION ONE   31

What Is Comprehension?   31

Reviewing the Critical Thinker's Traits: Being Curious   32

Becoming a Better Reader   34

Identifying the Topic   37

Survey and Predict   41

Surveying   41

Use Visual Clues   42

Use Text Features   42

Ask Questions   43

Predicting   43

Read, Write, and Think Critically: Section One   44

Reading: *Interaction with Peers (Student–Student Interaction)*   45

SECTION TWO   47

Developing Vocabulary   47

Context Clues   47

Definitions   48

Synonym Clues   49

Antonym Clues   50

Example Clues   51

Word Parts   52

Glossaries   54

Dictionaries   54

Real-World Mistakes of Comprehension and Their Consequences   55

Chapter Summary   57

Read, Write, and Think Critically: Section Two   57

Reading: *Use All of Your Senses*   58

CHAPTER 3   Interpretation   61

SECTION ONE   61

What Is Interpretation?   61

Reviewing the Critical Thinker's Traits: Humility   61

Determining Significance   64

Identifying Main Ideas and Details   65

Step One: Note the Topic   65

Step Two: Look for Word Clues That the Author Uses
to Organize Ideas and Indicate Importance   66

Transitions   66

Emotive Words   68

Step Three: Look for Details   69

Distinguishing between Major and Minor Details   71

Step Four: Putting It All Together: Identifying Main Ideas   73

Stated and Implied Main Ideas   73

Read, Write, and Think Critically: Section One   81

Reading: *Hormones' Complex Role in Human Sexuality,* David Perlman   81

SECTION TWO   84

Annotating   84

Clarifying Meaning   86

Summarizing and Paraphrasing   86

Summarizing   86

Reading: *The Importance of Critical Thinking,* Lane Wallace   88

Paraphrasing   89

Deciphering Misleading, Unclear, or Ambiguous Language   92

Being Deliberately Vague   92

Ambiguous Terms and Ambiguous Statements   94

Euphemisms and Doublespeak   96

Outlining and Mapping   99

Outlining   99

Mapping   100

Real-World Mistakes of Interpretation and Their Consequences   101
Chapter Summary   102
Read, Write, and Think Critically: Section Two   102
Reading: *5 Things We Know to Be True,* Michael Shermer, Harriet Hall,
    Ray Pierrehumbert, Paul Offit, and Seth Shostak   103

CHAPTER 4 Inference   111
SECTION ONE   111
What Is Inference?   111
Reviewing the Critical Thinker's Traits: Being Open-Minded and Flexible   112
Making Inferences   115
    AIM for Appropriate Conclusions   117
Inferring an Author's Audience   120
Inferring an Author's Purpose   121
Inferring an Author's Tone   123
    Inferring Word Connotation   125
Read, Write, and Think Critically: Section One   135
Reading: *"Black Panther" Hype and Success Shows Importance
    of Representation,* Proma Khosla   135

SECTION TWO   138
Recognizing Assumptions   138
Recognizing Implications   141
Real-World Mistakes of Inference and Their Consequences   143
Chapter Summary   145
Read, Write, and Think Critically: Section Two   145
Reading: *Excerpt from Smile or Die: The Bright Side of Cancer,*
    Barbara Ehrenreich   146

CHAPTER 5 Self-Monitoring   153
SECTION ONE   153
What Is Self-Monitoring?   153
Reviewing the Critical Thinker's Traits: Becoming Organized in Your Life
    and in Your Thinking   154
Recognizing Worldviews   159
Read, Write, and Think Critically: Section One   161
Reading: *Body Ritual among the Nacirema,* Horace Miner   162

SECTION TWO   166
Recognizing Biases   166
    Using the Writing Situation to Determine Bias   168
    Using Language to Determine Bias   168

Monitoring Your Thinking   170
   Metacognition   170
      The Planning Phase   171
      The Control Phase   171
      The Reflection Phase   171
Changing Your Mind   177
Real-World Mistakes of Self-Monitoring and Their Consequences   178
Chapter Summary   179
Read, Write, and Think Critically: Self-Monitoring   180
Reading: *Kids R Not Us: Embracing the Decision Not to Procreate*,
      Katherine Seligman   180

CHAPTER 6   Analysis   187

SECTION ONE   187
What Is Analysis?   187
Reviewing the Critical Thinker's Traits: Being Skeptical   188
Analyzing Arguments   192
   Identifying Arguments   192
Evidence   195
   Kinds of Evidence   196
      Testimony   196
      Facts and Statistics   197
      Analogies   198
      Hypotheticals   198
   Counter-Evidence   199
   Assumptions   199
Read, Write, and Think Critically: Section One   199
Reading: *The Ghosts We Think We See*, Sharon Begley   200

SECTION TWO   202
Logic   202
   Inductive Reasoning   202
   Deductive Reasoning   203
Argument Mapping   204
   Advanced Argument Mapping   206
Analyzing Patterns of Organization   208
   Cause and Effect   208
   Chronological/Process   208
   Classification   209
   Comparison/Contrast   209
   Definition   210

Example   210

Listing   210

Mixed   211

The Scientific Method   212

Steps in the Scientific Method   213

Pseudoscience   214

Real-World Mistakes of Analysis and Their Consequences   215

Chapter Summary   216

Read, Write, and Think Critically: Section Two   217
Reading: *Ghost Hunting Tools of the Trade,* Brian Dunning   217

CHAPTER 7   Evaluation   221

SECTION ONE   221

What Is Evaluation?   221

Reviewing the Critical Thinker's Traits: Being Fair-Minded   222

Evaluating Arguments   226

Evaluating Evidence   226

Determine Relevance   227

Verify Sufficiency   229

Telling Apart Fact, Opinion, and Reasoned Judgment   230

Verify Accuracy   232

Evaluate Source and Author Credibility   233

Evaluating Source Credibility   233

Evaluating Print Sources   233

Evaluating Online Sources   234

Evaluating Author Credibility   235

Reading: *Why So Many Killer Tornadoes?*   236

Evaluating an Organization's Credibility   239

Checklists for Evaluating the Credibility of Organizations   239

Read, Write, and Think Critically: Section One   240
Reading: *On Overconfidence,* James Fowler and Dominic Johnson   240

SECTION TWO   243

Evaluating Assumptions   243

Evaluating Logic   244

Evaluating Deductive Arguments   244

Examples   246

Answers and Explanations   246

Evaluating Inductive Arguments   250
    Recognizing Informal Fallacies   251

Using Argument Maps in Evaluation   256

Real-World Mistakes of Evaluation and Their Consequences   257

Chapter Summary   258

Read, Write, and Think Critically: Section Two   259
Reading: *"Crack Baby" Study Ends with Unexpected but Clear Result,*
    Susan Fitzgerald   259

CHAPTER 8   Explanation   263

What Is Explanation?   263

Reviewing the Critical Thinker's Traits:
    Trusting Your Reasoning   264

Writing to Explain Using the 5 Es   265

Patterns of Development in Writing   268
    Use Graphic Organizers to Organize Your Ideas   269

Writing about Reading   271

Reading: *Mouthing Off in America,* Stephen Randall   271
    Critical Response Writing   272
        Sample Critical Response: "Mouthing Off in America" by Stephen Randall   275
    Critical Analysis Writing   276
        Sample Critical Analysis: "Mouthing Off in America" by Stephen Randall   281
    Journal Writing   283
        Sample Journal Entry: "Mouthing Off in America" by Stephen Randall   284
    Using Sources and Avoiding Plagiarism   285

Oral Communication   286

Real-World Mistakes of Explanation and Their Consequences   287

Chapter Summary   288

Read, Write, and Think Critically: Explanation   289

Adhering to the Standards: Grammar   289
    Significance   290
    Clarity   294
    Accuracy   296
    Completeness   299
    Fairness   300
    Relevance   302
        Titles: Italics or Quotation Marks?   302
        Quotations: Where to Put Punctuation?   302
        First, Second, or Third Person Point of View?   302
        Contractions and Abbreviations?   302

CHAPTER 9   Problem-Solving   303

What Is Problem-Solving?   303

Reading and Writing as Problem-Solving   303

Reviewing the Critical Thinker's Attitude: Being Persistent   305

Describe the Problem   307

   Acknowledge the Problem   307

   Define the Problem   308

   Clarify the Desired Outcome   308

   Describing Reading and Writing Problems   308

   Reading: *The Purpose of Education*, Dr. Martin Luther King Jr.   310

Break Down the Problem   312

   Note the Parts of the Problem   312

   Identify Similar Problems You've Solved in the Past   312

   Identify Theoretical Knowledge   312

   Make a General Plan   313

   Breaking down Reading and Writing Problems   313

Construct Solutions   315

   Do Not Artificially Limit Yourself   316

   Brainstorm Possible Solutions   316

   Consider Advantages and Disadvantages of Solutions   316

   Use the Hypothetical Deductive Method   317

   Constructing Solutions for Reading and Writing Problems   317

Evaluate the Solution   319

   Evaluate the Solution before Implementing It   320

   Evaluate the Solution after Implementing It   321

   Evaluating Solutions for Reading and Writing Problems   321

Real-World Mistakes of Problem-Solving and Their Consequences   323

Chapter Summary   324

Read, Write, and Think Critically: Section One   325

Reading: *Homophobia Doesn't Just Oppress Gay People,
It Affects Us All*, David Hudson   325

PART II   Thinking Critically about Current Issues   329

Putting It All Together   331

Gun Violence and Gun Control   331

   1. "We Can't Stop Mass Murder" *Shikha Dalmia*   332

   2. "Ban Guns" *Paul Waldman*   335

   3. "What Explains U.S. Mass Shootings? International Comparisons
Suggest an Answer" *Max Fisher and Josh Keller*   338

Technology Addiction 343
1. "Why You Can't Stop Checking Your Phone" *Leon Neyfakh* 344
2. "Does Social Media Addiction Really Exist?" *Catherine Knibbs* 348
3. "Google's Former Ethicist Says Better Design Is Key to Tackling Our Tech Addiction" *Jenny Anderson* 350

Peace and War 353
1. "Humans Evolved to Have an Instinct for Deadly Violence, Researchers Find" *Ian Johnston* 354
2. "On Peace" *Daniel Zajfman* 356
3. "On the Perils of Indifference" *Elie Wiesel* 359

Self-Driving Cars 363
1. "Who's Making Sure That Self-Driving Cars Are Safe?" *Ruth Reader* 364
2. "Here's How Self-Driving Cars Could Catch On" *David Roberts* 368
3. "To Get the Most out of Self-Driving Cars, Tap the Brakes on Their Rollout" *Jack Barkenbus* 372

Women's Issues 375
1. "Julia Pastrana: A Monster to the Whole World" *Bess Lovejoy* 376
2. "A Shortage of Women" *Terry L. Jones* 380
3. "Why We Still Need Feminism" *Casey Cavanagh* 382

Appendix: Word Parts 387

Glossary 391

Bibliography 399

Index 405

PREFACE TO THE INSTRUCTOR

Critical Reading, Critical Writing, and Critical Thinking

College reading and writing is challenging. Students must take in a tremendous amount of information, make sense of it, and see how it fits into their understanding of the world. Learning how to approach a reading with the skills and character traits of a critical thinker engages students and makes them more effective readers. Moreover, modern students get their information from a wide variety of sources (Internet, print, media), so now perhaps more than ever they need the ability to read and think critically so that they can evaluate quality and reliability. And they need to be able to critically write about this information so that they can analyze and explain their positions on the material.

Critical thinking, critical reading, and critical writing are intrinsically related to each other. After all, critical thinkers get a large amount of their knowledge from reading; critical reading is simply using the skills and character traits of critical thinkers when approaching texts. Critical writing is also using the skills and mindsets of critical thinkers when writing about texts.

In our experience, reading and writing textbooks often tell students to think critically without specifically explaining to them how to do so or even defining what critical thinking is. Critical thinking is a system of thought used to analyze and evaluate information in order to decide what to believe or what to do. More specifically, a critical thinker is an individual with a set of skills (such as the abilities to analyze, evaluate, make inferences, and so on) and the mindset to apply those skills to their lives. They have character traits (such as open-mindedness, fair-mindedness, skepticism, and humility) that drive them to think critically. Critical thinkers have standards of intellectual integrity that prompt them to care about knowledge and learning—a critical thinker is what every instructor hopes his or her students will become. Critical thinking is important: Critical thinkers are more likely to be successful at school and work, but they are also resilient in the face of adversity and less likely to be taken advantage of.

The Purpose of This Text

This text is designed for students in mid to upper-level reading and writing classes, both at community colleges and four-year institutions. The instruction and exercises are presented in straightforward, direct language, yet they have the depth to allow students to think critically about them, so that both more advanced students and those who might need extra instruction will benefit from them.

This book aims to make students into successful critical readers and writers by teaching them how to apply critical thinking skills to reading and writing. Based on the most current research by scholars such as Facione, Paul, and Van Gelder, *Critical Approaches to Reading, Writing, and Thinking* is designed to create "lifestyle" critical readers, writers, and thinkers rather than just teaching the skills of critical reading, writing, and thinking (although it does that too). We have also personally classroom taught and classroom tested the material in this text, with great success. Its major strength is that it thoroughly explains what is involved in being a critical thinker (in terms of the skills and traits), then it systematically teaches each skill and trait in relation to reading and writing. Our intent is that students will get the big picture and see how these individual skills complement each other to make students into complete critical readers, writers, and thinkers.

We have hand-picked the reading selections for this text so that students from diverse backgrounds and ability levels will find the readings appropriately challenging, and we have given students ample opportunity for practice of skills. At every point, the connection between reading and critical thinking is stressed. Selections such as Dunning's "Ghost Hunting Tools of the Trade" and Fowler and Johnson's "On Overconfidence" give students the opportunity to practice skepticism and think critically about science; Neyfakh's "Why You Can't Stop Checking Your Phone" and Carr's "Is Google Making Us Stupid?" engage students by encouraging them to explore cultural issues surrounding the technologies they are likely using daily. Khosla's "'Black Panther' Hype and Success Shows Importance of Representation" and Lovejoy's "Julia Pastrana: A Monster to the Whole World" allow students to explore the perspective of those from diverse cultures and backgrounds, while Hudson's "Homophobia Doesn't Just Oppress Gay People" and Cavanagh's "Why We Still Need Feminism" give students the opportunity to think critically about current events and issues. Students are further prompted with each reading to critically analyze and write about it.

Content Overview

Critical Approaches to Reading, Writing, and Thinking is organized into two parts. In **Part One, Chapter 1** it thoroughly defines critical thinking, describes the character traits (curiosity, humility, open-mindedness, organization, skepticism, fair-mindedness, trust in reason, and persistence) and skills of a critical thinker (comprehension, interpretation, inference, analysis, self-monitoring, evaluation, explanation, and problem-solving). It then shows how each of these skills and traits relates to reading and writing; for example, students are taught to interpret a text by identifying its main idea and supporting details; they are taught to make inferences about a text by deducing its audience, purpose, and tone; and then they are taught to critically explain their views on the text in writing.

In subsequent chapters, critical thinking, reading and writing skills are introduced in a logical order based on difficulty, each one building on the last, all being reinforced throughout the textbook. Each of these chapters focuses on a single trait and a single skill of critical thinking, teaching each in the context of critical reading. Early chapters focus on developing essential skills such as determining the topic of a reading passage and increasing vocabulary. Later chapters become more challenging as the skills become more sophisticated (evaluation and problem-solving, for instance). This organization is one of the elements that make this text unique.

Part Two is designed to provide students with opportunities to apply all the skills they have acquired as they read and write about a variety of texts, as they will be required to do in their other studies and in their lives. It is organized into five themes that embody topical and controversial issues affecting the United States and the world. Topics include gun control; technology; self-driving cars; women's issues; and peace and war. Each topic includes three readings, each of which presents a different perspective on the issue. The intent here is for students to read and evaluate the different perspectives so that they can think and read critically about the issues and formulate well-developed and defensible positions on them. In this part, students will also be prompted to write about their positions.

Special Features

The following features have been designed to challenge and stimulate students while providing the instructor with an extremely effective method to deliver instruction. As college instructors ourselves, we have written the textbook that we would want for our own students and classrooms; indeed, we have used this textbook and its features in our own classrooms to great success.

- **Preview of Terms.** Each chapter begins with a list of new words that students will encounter in the chapter. This serves as an introduction to the vocabulary and concepts in each chapter and includes page numbers for where the terms are first encountered.
- **Thinkers to Emulate.** This feature introduces students to people who have made an impact on the world through excellent thinking and innovation. They serve as reminders of what amazing feats we can accomplish through critical reading and thinking. The Thinkers to Emulate are diverse, come from a variety of disciplines, and can serve as inspiration to students.
- **Tips for Critical Thinkers.** In every chapter, these boxed, bulleted lists provide students with explicit, step-by-step instructions in how to implement the reading and critical thinking skills they have just read about.
- **Practices.** Each chapter contains a variety of reading and writing-focused exercises, including vocabulary reviews, skills practice, comprehension questions, class discussions, critical writing responses, Internet activities, and extension projects to be done outside of class. Practices are explained using clear directions, and then students are provided with a model that exhibits how the practice can be completed successfully. The practices have been carefully devised to appeal to diverse learning styles and aptitudes and will result in students mastering their goal of becoming critical readers.
- **Read, Write, and Think Critically.** Twice in every chapter, students are provided with a reading selection upon which they can practice the skills they have just learned. These selections have been carefully chosen to be diverse and intellectually stimulating; they are excellent pieces about which to think critically.
- **Expand Your Understanding Boxes.** These appear in every chapter and give students the opportunity to complete advanced research or reading that will take them beyond the textbook so that they can explore how the concepts they are learning in the text relate directly to the real world.
- **Real-World Mistakes of [Skill] and Their Consequences.** Included in every chapter, except for Chapter 1, this feature gives a real-life example of the consequences of not thinking critically. For example, the disaster at Three Mile Island is examined as a failure to analyze. Instructors are encouraged to use these real-world mistakes to stimulate classroom discussion and to ensure that students recognize the importance of critical thinking in their own lives and, by extension, in the world.
- **Real-World Successes.** For each skill, students are introduced to a success of that skill. They are directed to research the success in depth to see what critical reading and thinking can do within fields such as science, environmentalism, and medicine. The juxtaposition of mistakes and failures will make it very clear to students why mastering critical thinking and reading is useful and indeed crucial.
- **Think and Write Critically Marginal Icons.** Specific exercises designed to prompt students to write critically are highlighted with a special icon.
- **Reminder boxes.** Marginal boxes throughout each chapter remind students where concepts are covered more thoroughly in previous chapters.

- **Chapter Summary.** Each chapter concludes with a summary of the main points covered therein; this summary is tied to the learning goals presented at the start of the chapter.
- **Chapter 8: Explanation.** In this chapter, students learn how to critically explain in writing what they have learned through their reading and research. Different forms of written responses and critical analyses are taught in this chapter.
- **Chapter 9: Problem-Solving.** Students learn about the four-step problem-solving strategy: describe the problem, break down the problem, construct solutions, and evaluate solution. Specifically in this chapter, students learn effective strategies for approaching and solving problems they may encounter while reading. They also come to understand explicitly that reading and writing *are* forms of problem-solving.
- **Visuals.** Every chapter contains pictures, graphics, and figures that pique student interest or aid in student understanding.

Supplements for Instructors Offered Online

Annotated Instructor's Edition

PowerPoints

Tests and Quizzes

Practice Activities and Projects

PREFACE TO THE STUDENT

We have three major goals for you as you read this textbook: We want you to *become* a **critical thinker**, a **critical reader**, and a **critical writer**. Becoming a critical thinker is not as simple as just learning the skills. Becoming a critical thinker actually requires a shift in you as a *person* so that you can learn and foster the attitudes—character traits—and skills of a critical thinker. For example, an important **character trait** to develop is *open-mindedness*: the attitude of acceptance and openness to new ideas, even those which you might initially dismiss or dislike. One of the crucial **skills** to cultivate is *inference*: the ability to take in details and come to some conclusions and assumptions about the information. In this text, you will learn about the traits and skills of a critical thinker, learn to apply them to reading texts to become a critical reader (someone who thinks critically about what he or she is reading), and learn to write critically about what someone else has written.

As a critical reader, writer, and thinker, you will be less likely to be taken advantage of and more likely to succeed in your life. Since thinking, reading, and writing are important parts of any career, these will help you make more money and be more successful. In fact, a recent article in *Forbes* magazine listed critical thinking as the skill employers desire most in their employees. Critical thinking will also help you manage your personal problems and relationships. Learning to read, think, and write critically will basically make your life easier and more fulfilling.

Each chapter in *Critical Approaches to Reading, Writing, and Thinking* focuses on a specific character trait and skill, and as you work your way through them, you should find yourself becoming progressively closer to your goal of becoming a critical thinker, reader, and writer. Like becoming a mathematician or a psychologist, becoming a critical thinker is ongoing: You don't stop learning and growing once you are done with a particular math or psychology course, and you can spend the rest of your life honing the skills and dispositions of a critical thinker.

In Part I you will learn skills and strategies that will help you to comprehend, interpret, analyze, and critically evaluate what you read, as well as ways to organize and study what you have learned and write about what you have read. You will also learn about the traits of a critical thinker and how to develop and use them to become a thoughtful and successful critical reader and writer. In addition, Part I contains a chapter on problem-solving that will be very helpful not only in your college classes but in all aspects of your life. Part II of *Critical Approaches to Reading, Writing, and Thinking* consists of longer reading selections about current issues. Five themes are presented, including peace and war, technology, gun control, women's issues, and self-driving cars. This part of the text will allow you to read and think critically to help you formulate your opinions on these issues. It will also provide you with multiple opportunities to practice the skills you have learned.

Throughout the text, specific features have been designed to help make the content clear and easy to follow, aid in studying, and introduce, explain, and illustrate the importance of critical thinking and reading:

- **Preview of Terms:** Each chapter begins with a list of new words and terms you will encounter in the chapter and includes page numbers for where the terms first appear and are defined.
- **Thinkers to Emulate:** This feature introduces you to people who have made an impact on the world through excellent thinking and innovation. They serve as reminders of what amazing feats people can accomplish through critical thinking.

- **Tips for Critical Thinkers:** In every chapter, boxed, bulleted lists provide you with explicit, step-by-step instructions on how to implement the skills you have just read about.
- **Practices:** Each chapter contains a variety of exercises, including vocabulary reviews, skills practice, comprehension questions, class discussions, critical writing responses, Internet activities, and extension projects to be done outside of class. Each practice includes a model that shows how the practice can be completed successfully.
- **Read, Write, and Think Critically:** Two longer reading selections in each chapter provide practice opportunities for the skills you have just learned.
- **Expand Your Understanding Boxes:** These appear in every chapter and provide the opportunity to complete advanced research that will take you beyond the textbook so you can explore how the concepts you are learning relate directly to the real world.
- **Real-World Mistakes of [Skill] and Their Consequences**. Included in every chapter, except for Chapter 1, this feature gives a real-life example of the consequences of not thinking critically. For example, the disaster at Three Mile Island is examined as a failure to analyze.
- **Real-World Successes:** For each skill you learn, you are introduced to a success of that skill in action, and are prompted to research the success in depth to see what critical thinking can do within fields such as science, environmentalism, and medicine.
- **Looking Back:** Marginal boxes remind you where concepts are covered more thoroughly in previous chapters.
- **Chapter Summary:** Each chapter concludes with a summary of the main points covered within it; this summary is tied to the learning goals presented at the start of the chapter.

We know there are multiple demands placed on your time and energy during this challenging time in your life. Our textbook is geared for busy lives: We have aimed to be clear and concise. Not only are we instructors, but we are students ourselves. Both of us have continued our own educations, and we respect your decision to take classes and improve your futures. We are pleased to be a small step in this important endeavor.

ACKNOWLEDGMENTS

We both believe in the power of critical thinking, and we draw inspiration from the critical thinkers who have gone before us and from knowing that future students will benefit from embracing critical thinking, reading, and writing. We are especially grateful to the people who made the hard work of writing a college textbook a little easier.

We would like to thank the excellent faculty at Delaware Technical Community College, particularly those in the English Department, who were continuously supportive of our endeavor. Many people at DTCC provided invaluable assistance in the form of proofreading, providing ideas, supporting improvements to our course, and teaching an early version of the textbook.

We would also like to thank the many reviewers who read the book at various stages and gave us constructive criticism and positive encouragement. We would especially like to thank the staff at Kendall Hunt, who were very helpful, forward-thinking, and enthusiastic about the project.

Ric and Vivian would further like to thank Jeremy Penna, who gave us incredibly astute advice about early drafts.

Ric would like to thank Vivian, whose work ethic and attention to detail are unparalleled. He would also like to thank Jennifer Baker for her unremitting support for and interest in this project. He would like to thank his family and friends for their support. He appreciates every single one of you; even if he has not named you specifically here, he hasn't forgotten you.

Vivian would like to thank her writing partner Ric whose vision and initiative moved this project out of their lunchtime conversations and into publication. She appreciates her sweet and beautiful children who have patiently waited for her to finish this textbook so that they could have more time to spend together: Maddie, Elisabeth, Charlie, and Sammy. Sheer gratitude goes to her wonderful husband Gene, who cooked many delicious meals and kept the kids happy and the house running smoothly while she logged countless hours on this book.

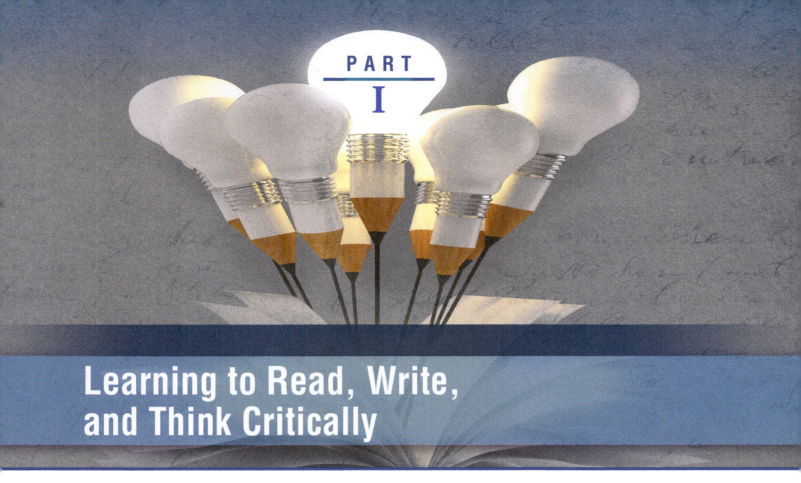

PART I

Learning to Read, Write, and Think Critically

Chapter 1 Becoming a Critical Thinker, Reader, and Writer

Chapter 2 Comprehension

Chapter 3 Interpretation

Chapter 4 Inference

Chapter 5 Self-Monitoring

Chapter 6 Analysis

Chapter 7 Evaluation

Chapter 8 Explanation

Chapter 9 Problem-Solving

Becoming a Critical Thinker, Reader, and Writer

PREVIEW OF TERMS

Critical reading p. 4
Critical writing p. 4
Critical thinking p. 5
Character traits p. 5
Curiosity p. 8
Humility p. 8
Open-mindedness p. 9
Flexibility p. 9
Organization p. 9
Skepticism p. 10
Fair-mindedness p. 10
Trust in reason p. 10
Persistence p. 10
Comprehension p. 14
Interpretation p. 14
Inference p. 14
Self-monitoring p. 14
Analysis p. 15
Evaluation p. 15
Explanation p. 15
Problem-solving p. 15
Obstacles p. 18
Defense mechanisms
 p. 18
Rationalizing p. 19
Reasoning p. 19
Confirmation bias p. 19
Memory errors p. 20
Testimonial p. 20
Attribution mistake p. 22
Wishful thinking p. 22
Conformity p. 23
Denial p. 23
Anger p. 24
Avoidance p. 24
See glossary, pp. 391–397

Learning Goals

In this chapter you will learn about

➤ The Meaning of Critical Thinking   SECTION ONE
➤ The Benefits of Critical Thinking
➤ The Critical Thinker's Attitude toward the World
➤ The Skills of a Critical Thinker
➤ Things That Can Get in the Way of Critical Thinking   SECTION TWO

SECTION ONE

The Meaning of Critical Thinking

Maybe you've opened your email and read something like this:

> Dear friend,
>
> You might be surprised to receive this letter. I am Dr. Dah Emmanuel, a top official in the government of Nigeria. I am requesting your assistance in the sensitive matter of transferring US $4,750,000 out of my bank account. My account has been frozen, and I require the help of a foreign citizen who is legally able to transfer the funds into his account. If you aid me in this matter, I will give you 25% of the funds as your fee, and I will keep 75%. This is an urgent matter, so I ask that you tell no one and act quickly. All you must do is send your bank account number . . .

This letter definitely offers a tempting proposition—more than a million dollars for doing almost nothing—but is it too good to be true? You should read the email carefully and you should think critically, because falling for a scam like this could leave you in financial ruin.

"You should think critically." You've probably heard that before, but no one ever seems to explain how to do it, or even to define what it is. The goal of this book is to do both of those things: to clarify what it means to think critically and to give you the skills you will need so that you can overcome any obstacles in your path to becoming a critical thinker

Critical Reading

Thinking critically about what you are reading in order to determine if it is credible, to decide if it presents a good case, and to avoid being taken in by rhetorical tricks and emotional manipulation.

Critical Writing

Using critical thinking and critical reading skills to analyze and evaluate a text so you can make your own arguments about it. Critical writing is contrasted with descriptive writing, where you just explain what someone else thinks.

(plus, a bonus to being a critical thinker is that you won't be likely to fall for frauds like the Nigerian scam above).

Critical thinking applies to and is useful in all fields. Doctors and nurses, accountants, managers, mechanics, scientists—all have to think critically. Critical thinking can be taught and learned differently depending on what field it is being applied to. This book approaches the task of teaching you to think critically by showing you how to apply the skills and mindsets of critical thinking to reading texts from various disciplines and genres; this text teaches you to think critically by teaching you to read critically. **Critical reading** is thinking critically about what you are reading. It's using the skills of a critical thinker on a text in order to determine if the text is credible, to decide if it makes a good argument or presents a good case, and to avoid being taken in by rhetorical tricks and emotional manipulation. But the critical thinking skills you learn this way won't just make you a *critical reader*; they will also allow you to write critically. **Critical writing** is using critical thinking and critical reading skills to analyze and evaluate a text so you can make your own arguments about it. Critical thinking, reading, and writing skills carry over into other areas of your life, making you a better thinker in general. Critical reading, writing, and thinking open the door to success in college and all other fields and careers.

Complete the following exercise to start you on the path to critical thinking, reading, and writing.

| **PRACTICE 1-1** | **Your Starting Point** |

Directions: Note whether you agree or disagree with the following statements by checking the appropriate box. Be prepared to discuss your answers in class.

Statements	Agree	Disagree
1. If it takes too much effort to learn more about something, I'm okay with not knowing about it.		
2. I don't care what I do or say, as long as I win an argument.		
3. Once my mind is made up, I usually don't change it.		
4. I don't really think there are better or worse opinions; all opinions are equal.		
5. Some beliefs should never be questioned.		

Your answers to these questions will help you determine where your mindset is now as you begin your journey toward becoming a more critical thinker. People who have a natural tendency to think more critically often want to discuss interesting ideas, seem to get obsessed with solving problems, and want proof before believing what other people say. They would tend to disagree with the statements above. In contrast, people who are set in their ways, who aren't too interested in listening to other peoples' points of view, and who don't often bother to look up an unknown word or statement would tend to agree with the questions above. Wherever you fall, everyone needs some training in critical thinking. No one is born a complete critical thinker.

Thinking Critically

> ### Critical Thinking
> A reflective, rational process used to make good decisions or to form beliefs that are more likely to be true.

Often, when people say we are being too critical, they mean we are nit-picking or criticizing. But that's not what the word *critical* in the phrase *critical thinking* means. Instead, it means being careful to use good judgment and consideration. And that's the definition of **critical thinking:** It's a reflective, rational process you can use to make good decisions or to form beliefs that are more likely to be true. In fact, you can use this Likert scale below as you ponder ideas and beliefs. What typically moves your own thinking from a neutral spot on the scale (3) is the presence (or absence) of evidence.

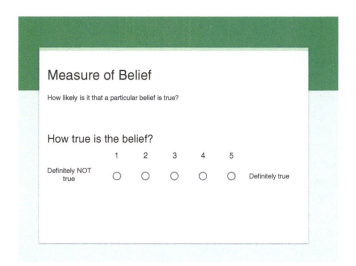

People who can think critically have worked hard to develop key skills; for example, they are good at analyzing arguments and deciding whether information can be trusted. They also try to use critical thinking in all areas of their lives, from their assignments to their home lives and personal relationships. In other words, when they go about their day-to-day business, they have certain essential **character traits**, like *skepticism* and *open-mindedness*, that motivate them to use the skills they have when they need them most. They don't accept *claims* (a claim is a statement that someone declares is true) at face value, and they aren't afraid to question what everyone else accepts as "obviously" true. For example, they are willing to question the belief that certain genders should "naturally" perform certain roles, like women raising the children while men work. Critical thinkers are also aware of the obstacles like innate biases and defense mechanisms that can get in the way of critical thinking, and they make an effort to overcome them.

Because critical thinking is a process, you can't just decide one day that you will be a critical thinker and then suddenly become one. Like keeping yourself in shape, you have to commit to it and continue to work at it. Just like exercising, it will get easier the more you do it, and the benefits you reap from gaining expertise in critical thinking will more than reward the energy you put in.

Facts about Critical Thinking

1. **Critical thinking is not about how smart you are or how much you know.** In fact, lots of smart, educated people are not critical thinkers. So critical thinking is not a subject or a body of knowledge in the same way that biology or history is; critical thinking is using a systematic method to help you employ the knowledge you have, learn new things, and analyze concepts so that by examining your own thinking and using reason, you can arrive at the best conclusion possible.

2. **Critical thinkers are not guaranteed to be right**. Also, because different people have different backgrounds, outlooks, and experiences, two critical thinkers can arrive at different conclusions based on the same evidence. As long as they both approach the evidence with the right attitudes and use the correct skills, they have both thought critically about it.

3. **Critical thinkers are skilled at recognizing when they don't have enough information to make an informed judgment about a situation, and in those cases, they will decide *not* to decide.** But they won't stop there. They will proceed to fill in the gaps in their knowledge until they can make a good decision. For instance, scientists still aren't sure how life first started on planet Earth, so they've withheld judgment on the question. But they are working hard to figure it out. Critical thinkers are driven by intellectual curiosity—they always want to know more and to make the best judgments they can.

4. **Critical thinking has a strong sense and a weak sense**. Critical thinking in the strong sense means thinking critically about *everything*, including beliefs that you agree with or cherish. It means trying to figure out what is true, as opposed to simply trying to prove yourself right. Critical thinking in the weak sense means applying the skills of critical thinking only to ideas that you dislike in order to prove them false. Weak critical thinkers mainly want to win arguments.

5. **Critical thinkers have certain standards**. They care about whether the information or argument they are examining is *accurate* (meaning it is correct), *complete* (meaning all necessary information is included), *fair* (meaning it is free from bias), *relevant* (meaning it applies to the situation), *clear* (meaning it is not vague or ambiguous), and *significant* (meaning it is important). They also hold themselves and their own thinking to these standards, striving to make sure their own reasoning lives up to them. They have intellectual integrity. Each of these standards will be more fully developed in later chapters.

The Benefits of Critical Thinking

Critical thinking has some definite benefits, and they range from very minor to extremely important. Perhaps most obviously, thinking critically helps you do better in school, because you can use the same skills to become a critical reader and writer. And if you can read and write critically, analyze evidence, construct arguments, explain your thoughts, and engage in sound reasoning, you will get better grades. Getting better grades assists you in doing what you want to do after you graduate, whether it is to go on to further education or get a high-paying, satisfying job.

66 No problem can withstand the assault of sustained thinking. 99
—Voltaire

Critical thinking is important to most careers. When doctors and nurses try to determine what is making a patient ill, they need to avoid preconceptions, take all the evidence into account, and analyze it carefully to arrive at the best diagnosis. Managers use critical thinking to figure out what parts of their business models are succeeding and what parts are failing. Detectives need to avoid jumping to conclusions about who is guilty when they investigate a crime scene, and instead follow where the evidence leads. In fact, any job that involves solving problems or coming to conclusions is going to involve critical thinking.

Critical thinkers are more flexible and adaptable than other people when they face problems in their daily lives. They can react better to changing situations and have lots of resources they can use to help them get through difficult times. On the other hand, non-critical thinkers have more trouble reacting to situations, and they can't handle stress as well (Facione et al., 1995).

Critical thinking can also save you time, money, and embarrassment. People who don't think critically are easy to take advantage of. They spend their money on medicines or procedures that aren't proven to work and probably don't, such as magnetic bracelets to cure arthritis. They visit fortune tellers and call psychic hotlines, running up large phone bills. They fall for scams on the Internet, like the Nigerian scam. They even harm or kill other people by trying to use magic or prayer instead of medical treatment to cure sick individuals. Critical thinking will help you to avoid being taken advantage of or making a costly or even deadly error.

The benefits of critical thinking should be clear, but we have to note that thinking critically can have some drawbacks. First, critical thinking and critical reading are hard work. Critical thinking can cause you to decide that what your family, friends, or members of your community believe just isn't true. If you decide not to believe in the religion or political outlook of the people in your social circle, you might suffer social consequences. As a defense mechanism, people might get angry with you or even stop including you in their lives. No one can deny that this is a serious result of thinking for yourself. So being a critical thinker has some risks, and deciding to really pursue critical thinking takes bravery. But people who have decided to become critical thinkers know that the benefits of critical thinking are immense and that rationality and truth are worth the risk.

Critical Thinking	**PRACTICE 1-2**

Directions: On the lines provided, identify the following statements as true (T) or false (F).

_____1. Some people are born strong critical thinkers and don't need training at all.
_____2. Critical thinking is simply finding fault with viewpoints you disagree with.
_____3. Although critical thinking is a difficult process, anyone can be a critical thinker if he or she works at it.
_____4. To be a good critical thinker, you have to know lots of information about lots of different subjects.
_____5. Good thinkers are rarely wrong.
_____6. Good thinkers are more astute readers.

Directions: Answer the following questions on the lines provided.

7. Explain the difference between being critical (nitpicking) and critical thinking.

_____

_____

_____

_____

8. In your own words, explain the difference between a strong and weak critical thinker.

_____

_____

_____

EXPAND YOUR UNDERSTANDING

Directions: In small groups, brainstorm some other examples of the benefits and drawbacks of critical thinking not mentioned above. Try to list at least three more of each. Decide as a group why it is worthwhile to pursue critical thinking as a lifelong goal. Be prepared to explain your answer to the class.

The Critical Thinker's Attitude toward the World

Critical thinkers always strive to think deeply. This broad attitude toward the world can be broken down into several specific *character traits*. Critical thinkers are *curious*, always wanting to know more. Their knowledge that they can make mistakes leads them to be *humble*. They are *open-minded and flexible*, willing to listen to new ideas, and they approach problems in an *organized* way. They are always *skeptical*, but they are also *fair-minded*, treating other people's ideas as they treat their own. They *trust their reasoning abilities* and believe reason and logic can lead them to good conclusions; finally, they remain *persistent*, never giving up just because a problem gets difficult.

Below you will find a short overview of the character traits of critical thinkers, the traits you need to possess in order to be an effective critical thinker, and in turn a critical reader. In each chapter of the remainder of this book, you will find a more detailed discussion of one of these traits, as well as specific tips on how you can work on developing them yourself.

Be Curious (Chapter 2)

Critical thinkers are **curious** *in an intellectual sense; they're hungry for knowledge and information.* They always want to know more and rarely pass up the chance to find out something new. When critical thinkers don't know the answer to a question, they make an effort to find it out. Often this involves reading, so good critical reading skills are essential. They like knowledge for its own sake, although they also want to be able to use knowledge. People who are intellectually curious know that something they learn today might unexpectedly come in handy tomorrow.

Curiosity in Practice   It was intellectual curiosity that led Galileo to improve upon the newly invented telescope so that he could examine the heavens. In doing so, he noticed that other planets had moons, which challenged the established belief that all heavenly bodies orbit the earth. His intellectual curiosity greatly increased our knowledge of the solar system!

Be Humble (Chapter 3)

Individuals who are **humble** *in an intellectual sense know that they don't know everything.* They don't have a problem with being wrong or with admitting when they are wrong. After all, if you don't recognize that you don't know something, how can you learn about it? Sometimes it's hard to stay intellectually humble, especially if you did well in school or have been told by your parents, teachers, or employers that you are smart. When it comes to considering a question or judging an issue, it's a good idea to remind yourself that what you already think about it may be wrong. That way you leave open the possibility of changing your mind so that you can end up being right and, more importantly, learning something new.

Humility in Practice The philosopher Socrates was known for his intellectual humility. His understanding that he lacked true knowledge and his quest to gain it gave birth to Western philosophy and even critical thinking.

Be Open-Minded and Flexible (Chapter 4)

*Critical thinkers are **open-minded** and **flexible:** They are willing to consider new ideas, even if those ideas contradict what they already believe.* It's easy to *say* that you are being open-minded, but a truly open-minded person *genuinely considers* new concepts, allowing him- or herself a fair chance at actually understanding and accepting new ideas. New ideas can be threatening to us, especially if they seem to go against what we already believe, but an open-minded person is brave enough to think about them anyway.

Open-Mindedness and Flexibility in Practice If someone from another culture were to tell you that you are missing out on delicious foods such as snails, frogs, and octopuses, the idea might seem disgusting or even threatening at first, but if you are open-minded and flexible enough to try these foods, you might like them, and your eating options would be greatly expanded.

Be Organized (Chapter 5)

*When critical thinkers have a problem to solve or an issue to consider, they are **organized** in their thinking.* This means they approach the problem according to a system, taking care to determine what the problem involves, what the parts of the problem are, what needs to be done first, second, and last, and how they are progressing in solving the problem or considering the issue. The more complex the issue, the more effort they make to keep their thinking organized.

Organization in Practice Strict organization, combined with precision, allows modern air travel. At any moment, thousands of aircraft are flying across the United States and around the world; since their flight paths cross, a systematic method of organization keeps these planes on time and helps them avoid disaster.

Be Skeptical (Chapter 6)

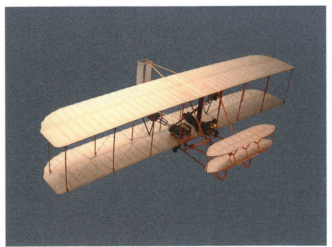

Skepticism is an attitude of doubt toward new, unproven claims. So skeptics are people who won't believe a claim just because they are told it is true. Being **skeptical** is the opposite of being gullible (easily deceived), and skepticism is one of the core attitudes of a critical thinker. After all, one of the main skills of a critical thinker is the ability to examine evidence to decide whether it's convincing. Skepticism is the attitude that motivates the thinker to collect the evidence in the first place. Some people have a negative view of skeptics. They believe that skeptics just refuse to believe anything, but that's not true. Skeptics will believe you if you can give them a good argument or solid evidence; they just take convincing. In fact, skeptics contribute to human advancement.

© Brad Whitsitt/Shutterstock.com

Skepticism in Practice The Wright Brothers were skeptical of the idea that it was impossible for humans to invent heavier-than-air flying machines, so they challenged the idea and proved it wrong. Their skepticism allowed for modern air travel and literally connected all parts of the world!

Be Fair-Minded (Chapter 7)

Being *fair-minded means treating all ideas and arguments with an equal degree of consideration.* To be fair-minded, you have to be open-minded. Open-mindedness allows you to consider ideas in the first place, and fair-mindedness allows those ideas a chance to change your mind if they prove themselves good enough. Fair-minded people look at arguments and ideas they initially disagree with to see what might be good about them. Cultivating this trait allows you to overcome the favoritism you naturally show toward your own ideas, and it therefore enables you to consider ideas in a way that reveals their merits. Being fair-minded doesn't mean being gullible and changing your mind every time a new argument comes along. It just means giving all claims and arguments the chance they deserve. It also involves putting yourself in other people's shoes to see how they arrived at their conclusions.

Fair-Mindedness in Practice If you have ever resisted the urge to declare someone else a bad person because that person was rude to you, you have exhibited fair-mindedness. In this case, fair-mindedness means recognizing that other people have bad days too, and maybe that person didn't mean to act rudely toward you.

Trust in Reason (Chapter 8)

Good thinkers believe that thinking—using **reason**—*can improve their lives.* This belief means that they have faith in themselves and know that the skills they have, combined with their attitude and their persistence, will allow them to solve many problems. But it also means believing that human beings can figure out a great deal about the world around them using only their senses and the power of their own minds.

Reason in Practice We have used our brain power to build vessels like the Mars Rover that have allowed us to explore other planets. We have also used science and reason to learn the age of our universe and even to discover invisible super-massive black holes that lurk at the center of galaxies like our Milky Way! Human reason has discovered and accomplished amazing things.

Be Persistent (Chapter 9)

Finally, critical thinkers are **persistent***: They understand that not giving up is often the key to success.* When problems get hard, critical thinkers settle in for the work they know it takes to be successful. Their trust in reason, combined with their search for truth, gives them determination. Critical thinkers also know how satisfied they feel when they solve a hard problem, analyze a tricky concept, evaluate a difficult text, or make a tough decision. Sometimes, the harder something is, the more satisfaction there is to gain in doing it.

Persistence in Practice Because people like Louis Pasteur and Jonas Salk didn't give up when things got difficult, we have vaccines that protect us against terrible diseases like rabies and polio.

Directions: Read the passage below and answer the questions that follow.

The Englishman Charles Darwin (1809–1882), who eventually became a naturalist, was on track in his youth to be an Anglican preacher. He never considered himself a particularly intelligent child, but he studied diligently and obtained admission to Christ's College at Cambridge University. While there, he developed an amateur's interest in natural history. He decided to embark on a voyage aboard the HMS *Beagle*, which was heading to South America. It was a long voyage—almost five years—but it was fateful indeed. During the trip, he wrote detailed, organized notes on every specimen he studied, from sea plankton to tortoises. On a visit to the Galapagos Islands, he noted that mockingbirds and finches seemed particularly adapted to their roles on the island.

At the time of this voyage, Darwin believed in the traditional view of the Anglican Church, that God had created each species basically as they are now. But he was willing to consider other ideas, and the strength of the evidence in favor of evolution was dawning on him. Before long, he realized that species were not set, and they did more than simply adapt to their surroundings in small ways: Given enough time, they changed into entirely new species. Darwin was at first not sure of the mechanism by which species changed, but he didn't give up trying to discover it. He studied his copious notes and continued to learn as much as he could, and eventually he came up with the theory of *natural selection*, the idea that traits acquired through genetic mutation that make it more likely for an organism to

Thinker to Emulate: Charles Darwin

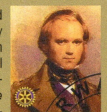

Charles Darwin (1809–1882) was an accomplished biologist and naturalist famous for his theory of evolution, which proved that all life on earth descended from a common ancestor via natural selection. Darwin published multiple books, including *The Descent of Man* and his famous *On the Origin of Species by Means of Natural Selection.* During his lifetime, Charles Darwin worked diligently and displayed courage in challenging established ideas that disagreed with the evidence he uncovered.

© brandonht/Shutterstock.com.

survive and produce offspring become widespread throughout a population of animals. By carefully examining this evidence and contrasting it with the arguments made by those who believed that species were created in their present forms, Darwin became convinced that, through natural selection, "endless forms most beautiful and most wonderful have been, and are being evolved."

Darwin was well aware that many people would not receive the theory of evolution with open arms. He knew they would resist it, because they would see it as an attack on their beliefs, even though Darwin did not intend it as such. So he put off publishing his findings; instead, he sketched out his theory and then worked diligently to fill in with facts and evidence the framework he created. He knew that if the theory of natural selection were to get a fair hearing, it would need to be even more convincing than other scientific theories, because of the resistance it would encounter. Because his wife believed in a literal interpretation of the Bible's Book of Genesis, and because he was sensitive about offending the community, Darwin continued to put off going public with his theory. Finally, he got his courage up and published *On the Origin of Species.*

Charles Darwin was right about the reaction to his theory. In his own day, some people immediately and vehemently criticized it. Although Darwin had anticipated many of these criticisms and was able to respond successfully to all of them, criticism continued. Even in the twenty-first century, many people still deny the theory of evolution. But because Darwin was so careful with his facts and logic, his argument turned out to be strong indeed. It has prompted biologists to test it, and many experiments have confirmed evolution. It is now generally accepted by the scientific community. Charles Darwin has gone down in history as one of the most influential thinkers when it comes to modern science.

Think and Write Critically

1. Explain in your own words why Charles Darwin hesitated before publishing his theory.
2. Which of the character traits of a critical thinker did Charles Darwin possess? Write your answer on a separate sheet of paper and be sure to support your answers with details from the passage.

EXPAND YOUR UNDERSTANDING

Learning More about Darwin While Writing Critically

Directions: Use an Internet search engine such as Google or visit www.aboutdarwin.com/index.html to research further into the life of Charles Darwin. Write an essay that focuses on the details of his illness as well as the resistance he faced from certain religious organizations.

PRACTICE 1-4	**Recognizing the Character Traits**

Directions: Read the anecdotes below. Using the word bank provided, identify the character traits each individual is displaying. Write your answer in the space provided.

> humble   persistent   open-minded   trusting in reason   curious

1. Patrick was never good at math, but he had to pass MAT101 to graduate. This would be the third time he had taken it, and he was determined not to drop the course like times before. He went to class every day, sought out help from the Math center, and eventually passed.

   Patrick is _____.

2. During a movie, Jon heard the main character mention someone named Plato. Jon had no idea who Plato was; he wasn't even sure if it was a person. Jon could have just ignored this reference, but when he got home, he googled Plato and found out that Plato was a Greek philosopher.

   Jon is _____.

3. When the student corrected the teacher on the dates of the battle, the teacher thanked the student for the correction, much to the surprise of the other students.

   The teacher is _____.

4. Rochelle and the other teachers were meeting before the semester to decide what textbook to use for American literature. Rochelle had always used the *Norton Anthology*. She had her reasons and was fairly sure she was right. However, Paul began discussing the merits of the *Heath Anthology*. He made a compelling case, and even though Rochelle had her lesson planned for the *Norton Anthology*, she agreed to give the *Heath Anthology* a chance.

   Rochelle is _____.

5. In chemistry class, the students kept getting results that did not seem quite right. They double-checked the equipment. They ran the experiment again and again. Eventually, after they checked for any variables, they turned in the results even though they seemed surprising. They followed the experiment correctly and accepted that no matter how odd the results were, they must be correct.

The students are _____.

The Character Traits and You   PRACTICE 1-5

Directions: Rate yourself on how much you think you possess of each of the traits by placing a checkmark in the appropriate column. Then answer the following questions on the lines provided.

Trait	Not at all	Not much	Some	A lot	A whole lot
Humility					
Skepticism					
Open-Mindedness					
Fair-Mindedness					
Trust in Reason					
Curiosity					
Organization					
Persistence					

1. Select one character trait that you feel you possess and explain a situation in which you displayed it.

_____

_____

_____

_____

2. Pick one of the character traits that you feel you do not possess. How might you work on developing this trait?

_____

_____

_____

The Skills of a Critical Thinker

So far you've learned what critical thinkers are: People whose mindsets and character traits lead them to use the skills they possess to consider things carefully, systematically, and thoroughly in order to evaluate ideas, form beliefs, and make decisions. Next, let's look at the skills of critical thinkers. Critical thinkers strive to do all of the following:

- *Comprehend* the basic meaning of a text or speech.
- *Interpret* information to make it clearer.

- *Infer* conclusions from evidence.
- *Monitor* their own thinking to see if they are using their skills effectively.
- *Analyze* information, which means they can recognize arguments and see how the individual parts fit together.
- *Evaluate* an argument to determine what's good and bad about it.
- *Explain* their reasoning and their conclusions.
- *Solve problems* using a method that allows them to break the issue into manageable steps and take care of each step.

As mentioned earlier, the following chapters will help you develop the critical thinking skills briefly described below by focusing on how these skills apply to reading texts. Therefore, each skill description defines the skill generally as it applies to all fields, then describes more specifically how it applies to critical reading. Developing these skills and the desire to use them will enable you to be a true critical thinker, reader, and writer.

Comprehension (Chapter 2)

Comprehension *is the skill of making basic sense of a message.* This skill involves understanding the direct, or explicit, information being communicated. Applied to written material, comprehension involves looking over a text to determine what it is likely to be about, so that you can use your prior knowledge about the topic to better understand what you are reading about it. Critical thinkers and readers who possess the skill of comprehension actively seek to improve their vocabularies so they can understand complex words and terms important to understanding what an author is saying. They are skilled at reading actively, annotating a text while they go through it. This first fundamental skill is obviously very important, because if the basic message of a text is misunderstood, it will be hard to use or benefit from the other skills.

Interpretation (Chapter 3)

Interpretation *involves noticing details, identifying relevant information, and clarifying ideas.* If you are good at interpretation, you can discern underlying meanings in what you read, see, or hear. You can recognize what is important. Interpretation also involves categorizing new information to help keep it clear in your mind. When it comes to reading texts, interpretation involves identifying main ideas and details, and clarifying vague, ambiguous, or deceptive language. This skill is important, because it helps you build a clearer, more detailed understanding of what you read.

Inference (Chapter 4)

The skill of **inference** *involves drawing conclusions from the available information.* It means being able to see what is implied by the evidence and follow where a certain train of thought leads. When you are good at making inferences, you can point out likely outcomes, indicate what might happen under certain conditions, and use *inductive and deductive reasoning.* We make inferences all the time, but critical thinkers examine their inferences to make sure they are justified. Applied to reading, this skill involves you inferring tone, audience, and purpose, as well as recognizing what an author is implying.

Self-Monitoring (Chapter 5)

Self-monitoring *means keeping tabs on yourself to see how you are performing.* It involves examining your thought processes, the effort you are putting into a task, and the results you are getting. To monitor yourself, you have to be honest. All people lie to themselves sometimes, but getting good at self-monitoring means having the courage not to lie so you can recognize when you need to work harder or change direction. For instance, if you aren't doing well at the job you are trying to accomplish, you need to admit it. Then you will be able correct yourself. If you have made a mistake, self-monitoring means fixing it. When it comes to reading texts, this skill will allow you to identify your own and the author's worldviews and biases while treating all sides fairly.

Analysis (Chapter 6)

Analysis involves taking something apart, looking at the pieces that make it up, and determining how they work, separately and together. In reading, analysis means you identify an argument and the parts of the argument, such as evidence, logic, and claims, to help you determine whether it is convincing. Thinkers skilled in analysis also know about logic, so they can tell if an argument is sound or contains a *fallacy* (a mistake in reasoning).

Evaluation (Chapter 7)

Evaluation means judging something on its merits in order to determine if it is effective or useful. If you are skilled at evaluation, you can examine information, often gained by analyzing, and determine if it is trustworthy, credible, logical, or valuable. The skill of evaluation involves figuring out what to believe or what to do, which lies at the heart of critical thinking. Applied to reading texts, evaluation means figuring out if an author's sources are credible and if he or she uses good evidence and logic while making an argument.

Explanation (Chapter 8)

The skill of **explanation** *involves putting your own or someone else's thoughts into words so that they are clear and understandable.* It means giving an account of the evidence and logic that back up your arguments, stating your conclusions clearly and concisely, and justifying what you did to arrive at those conclusions. Being able to explain your own or someone else's reasoning is an important skill; if you can explain it, you understand it. If you can't explain something, it usually means you didn't understand it, at least not fully. Therefore, explanation is a skill that lets you know if you have a complete grasp of the concept in question—it helps you figure out if you really know what you think you know. Critical readers are good at explaining their reasoning process in writing. This skill of explanation is a large component of *critical writing*.

Problem-Solving (Chapter 9)

Problem-solving means overcoming challenges by using all the other skills of critical thinking and applying them according to a system. Problem-solving involves breaking a problem down into smaller pieces so that it becomes more manageable. To solve problems, critical thinkers make sure they fully understand the context of the problem, they analyze the problem, and they constructively generate solutions to the problem. Finally, they monitor how well the solutions they came up with are working to overcome the challenge. Being able to solve difficult problems is another one of the major benefits of critical thinking. In a way, reading critically and writing well are forms of problem-solving, so good problem-solvers also tend to be critical readers and good writers.

A portrait of a critical thinker is shown in Figure 1-1.

■ Figure 1-1   Portrait of a Critical Thinker

PRACTICE 1-6   Check Your Understanding

Directions: Read the following statements and write true (T) or false (F) on the lines provided.

1. _____ Self-monitoring involves keeping tabs on yourself in addition to correcting yourself if necessary.
2. _____ People who become skilled at making inferences can always draw the correct conclusion after they have examined the evidence.
3. _____ Thinkers skilled at analysis can identify the different parts of an argument.
4. _____ Being able to explain a concept means that you probably understood it.
5. _____ Noticing details and clarifying information while reading contribute to the skill of interpretation.

Discussion Questions

1. Is it possible to be a critical thinker 100 percent of the time? Why or why not?
2. How could critical thinking help when you read a text?
3. How could having the skills of a critical thinker but not the character traits of a critical thinker be problematic? What would a person with the skills but not the traits be like?

READ, WRITE, AND THINK CRITICALLY: SECTION ONE

Directions: Skim through the following text and answer questions 1–3. Then, read the selection and answer the questions that follow.

1. What do you think the selection will be about?

_____

_____

2. What is your prior knowledge of this topic?

_____

_____

3. The title of the selection is "Is Anyone Ever Wrong Anymore?" Why do you think the author chose this title? What is your own answer to the question posed in the title?

_____

_____

Is Anyone Ever Wrong Anymore?

Mitch Daniels

Mitch Daniels became president of Purdue University in 2013. He served two terms as Governor of Indiana (elected in 2004 and 2008). Prior to leadership roles in higher education and government, Daniels was a successful businessman. His interests include education, healthcare, and conservation. He contributes to the Washington Post, *and he has written three books, notably the best-seller* Keeping the Republic: Saving America by Trusting Americans.

December 6, 2017

1 A recent whim prompted me to reread Stephen Ambrose's "To America," a collection of reflections on the historian's craft and many of the topics and individuals Ambrose wrote about during his prolific career. The book might have been titled "Second Thoughts," because virtually every chapter describes some significant issue on which the author changed his mind over the years: his estimation of presidents such as U.S. Grant, Theodore Roosevelt and Richard Nixon; Harry Truman's decision to use the atomic bomb; the "robber barons" who built the transcontinental railroad; the reality of Soviet tyranny; and several more.

2 In many cases Ambrose relates how he came to dispute conclusions that his university professors and advisers peddled to him in his younger years. Elsewhere, he takes issue with his own previous views. But in each instance, he explains the evolution of his thinking, and the grounds for it, without defensiveness or embarrassment.

3 When the book appeared, early in this century, one would not have found such admissions especially noteworthy. In 2017, they take on a more striking cast, because ours is an era when it seems no one ever confesses to being wrong. Moreover, everyone is so emphatically right that those who disagree are not merely in error but irredeemably so, candidates not for persuasion but for castigation and ostracism.

4 Social historians will need some time and perspective to determine exactly what led to the new closed-mindedness, but some of the causes seem plain. One is the effect of narrowcasting, in which people find the sources of information (or the sources' algorithms find them) that fortify their existing viewpoints and prejudices. "Confirmation bias" has mutated from a hazard of academic research to a menacing political and social phenomenon.

5 Meanwhile, those institutions of higher learning—the adjective now almost needs quotation marks—that should cultivate and model openness to debate and refutation too often have become bastions of conformity and thought control.

6 John Maynard Keynes is frequently credited with the aphorism "When I find I'm wrong, I change my mind. What do you do?" Today, the problem may less be an attitude of stubbornness than that fewer people than ever recognize their mistakes in the first place.

7 In a well-documented fashion, steady doses of viewpoint reinforcement lead not only to a resistance to alternative positions but also to a more entrenched and passionate way in which thoughts are held and expressed. When those expressions are launched in the impersonal or even anonymous channels of today's social—or is it antisocial?—media, vitriol often becomes the currency of discourse and second thoughts a form of tribal desertion or defeat. Things people would not say face to face are all too easy to post in bouts of blogger or tweeter one-upmanship.

8 So honest admissions of error are more eye-catching these days. In recent years, *The Post's* Bob Woodward has recounted how, a quarter-century later, he had come to a very different interpretation of Gerald Ford's pardon of Richard Nixon. And how he wasn't the only one; Sen. Ted Kennedy, who excoriated Ford at the time of his decision, joined Woodward in that assessment, and conferred an award for political courage for the act they had once deemed a corrupt bargain.

9 A few months back, the world lost Jay Keyworth, nuclear scientist and presidential science adviser to Ronald Reagan. Keyworth had assembled the evidence to advocate an anti-ballistic-missile (ABM) system, which establishment opinion of the time relentlessly derided as "Star Wars"—a fanciful and impractical notion, and one in conflict with the then-sacred doctrine of mutual assured destruction.

10 Now, with one rogue nation perfecting both weapons and rocketry capable of annihilating U.S. targets, and another perhaps only years from joining it, the conversation is all about the effectiveness of our ABM system and why the heck the government hasn't made our national safety more certain. We're still waiting for that conversation to include "Thanks, Jay. You were right, and we weren't."

11 Ambrose wrote his book near the end of his life. In fact, it is dedicated to his cancer doctor and nurses. Maybe such honest introspection comes more readily under the imminence of the great event. But our everyday exchanges, and indeed the life of our republic, would be greatly improved by the more common utterance of those three magical little words: "I was wrong."

THINK AND WRITE CRITICALLY

Directions: Answer the prompts below on a separate sheet of paper. Use evidence from the text to support your answers.

4. Why is the author impressed with Stephen Ambrose's thinking and ability to change his mind?

5. Explain what Daniels says about "confirmation bias" in paragraph 4. Is confirmation bias a serious problem? Why or why not?

6. Look up one of the people or historical events mentioned by Daniels, and summarize the legacy or effect.

7. Based on what you've learned so far, do you think a critical thinker would agree or disagree with Mitch Daniels? Why?

SECTION TWO

Things That Can Get in the Way of Critical Thinking

In Section One, you learned what a critical thinker is: a person who has worked hard to gain certain skills, and at the same time developed the desire to use those skills. However, since we all share a common past, and we are all human beings with brains that work in basically the same way, we all have trouble with certain **obstacles** to critical thought. Here you will learn about these obstacles and how to avoid them.

We can group obstacles into two main categories: (1) obstacles caused by the way we think and (2) obstacles caused by our emotions. Besides being prone to these mistakes, we also use **defense mechanisms,** techniques that help us to avoid thinking critically about the beliefs we hold most dear.

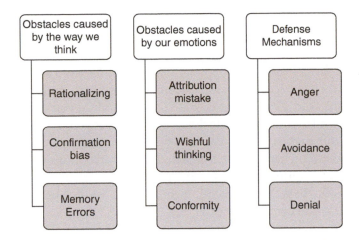

Obstacles Caused by the Way We Think

The way we think can cause us to make mistakes we don't need to make or sometimes don't even realize we are making. Obstacles to clear thought, such as *rationalizing, confirmation bias*, and *memory errors*, can all contribute to our making mistakes. If we aren't aware of these obstacles, we can be tripped up by them.

Rationalizing **Rationalizing** means starting with a conclusion and looking for any excuse to believe it. This process is exactly what you want to avoid, because it is thinking backwards! It is not likely to lead you to a true conclusion, because if you are good at rationalizing, you can support almost any conclusion you want. *Reasoning* is what you want to do to be a good thinker; **reasoning** means that you examine all the evidence fairly, and, using good logic, draw a conclusion from it. So for reasoning, the evidence comes first and the conclusion comes next.

For example, if you want to perform an act you know is wrong—like shoplifting—you can certainly think of reasons why it's okay to do it. You might say to yourself, "This store overcharges anyway, so I am only evening the score. They owe me." But really you are just looking for a reason to back up what you want to believe, which is that stealing is okay in this situation. In this case you are being intellectually dishonest, because you want to steal, and then you lie to yourself to avoid feeling guilty. If you used reason in this situation, it could go like this: "Is it okay for me to steal in this situation? I know that *whom* I am stealing from doesn't matter. It is wrong to steal. I also know I would not like to be stolen from, and I have always believed that stealing is wrong. It is against the law and often results in prices going up so stores can cover losses from thefts. So even though I want to take the merchandise, I won't." Rationalization is very tempting, and everyone engages in it from time to time—even authors of textbooks. But critical thinkers do their best to avoid it as much as possible.

Confirmation Bias **Confirmation bias** occurs when you are trying to judge an argument and only pay attention to the evidence that supports what you already believe, while ignoring or downplaying information that might prove you wrong. If you only pay attention to evidence that seems to prove you right, you will never know when you are actually wrong. For example, if you are annoyed at your roommate because you think she doesn't do enough chores around the apartment, you will take special notice of every time she leaves dishes in the sink and you end up doing them. You won't pay attention to the times that she takes out the trash or does her own dishes, though. This obstacle explains why people can be so stubborn about their beliefs. Even when you present good arguments for alternative points of view, others rarely change their minds

Test Your Memory

Directions: Read the following words and try to remember them.

Sun	Towel
Umbrella	Volleyball
Surf	Shells
Boardwalk	Waves
Sand	Bathing suits
Sunblock	

because they are only paying attention to the information that supports what they believe is right. To think critically, you need to give equal weight to information that might prove you wrong (See attitudes of fair-mindedness and flexibility.)

Memory Errors It might seem like your memory just records everything that happens to you, but that isn't true. Have you ever gone back to a place you remember from your childhood only to find that it looks quite different from what you recalled? This shows that we actually build our memories not only on what happens to us but also on who we are at the moment something happens, on our feelings and perceptions at the time. Have you ever heard a song and started remembering a person or an event that made you sad? Of course, you didn't want to get sad at that moment, but you couldn't help it. Sometimes your memory is outside your conscious control.

Not only are we prone to memory errors, but we are bad at determining which memories are reliable and which are not. Many innocent people have been wrongly convicted based on eyewitness testimony from people who were sure they remembered seeing them committing a crime, and many hours have been wasted searching for accomplices who never existed. For example, in 1995, the FBI put out all-points bulletins and engaged in a nationwide search for Timothy McVeigh's accomplice in the Oklahoma City bombing. Unfortunately, the accomplice was the result of a memory mistake made by a mechanic at the business where McVeigh rented the van he used in the bombing. The mechanic remembered a man he had seen the day before McVeigh came in as being with McVeigh. Although others were involved in the bombing, the mechanic threw the FBI off the trail by giving them an unrelated description of someone who was not involved in the bombing. Memory can be unreliable, and sometimes we remember things that didn't even happen. For these reasons, a critical thinker will be especially skeptical of accepting someone's **testimonial**—his or her personal story about events that happened to him or her—as good evidence for an extraordinary claim without some other form of reliable proof to back it up.

PRACTICE 1-7	Recognizing Obstacles Caused by the Way We Think

Directions: Perhaps you have noticed that one of the quickest ways to lose friends is to lend them money. And, strangely, the people who borrow the money often end up disliking the people who lent them the money. The following passage might explain why. Read it, then answer the questions that follow.

Cassandra needed a car. She had just graduated from college, and money was tight, but luckily her latest interview had gone exceptionally well. She felt as if she and the manager at Adtech had really connected, and she was sure she'd be offered the position. The starting pay was low, but the job came with opportunities for advancement. She just needed transportation.

Immediately, her Uncle Joe came to mind. She and her Uncle Joe had always been fairly close, and after he had gotten divorced, they had grown even closer. Uncle Joe was well off, and she felt comfortable asking for a loan, and even more comfortable that he'd say yes. So without any hesitation, Cassandra called her Uncle Joe and asked him to lend her $5000.00. He agreed. She told Uncle Joe she'd send him $100.00 a week until the loan was paid. The check was soon in the mail, and she quickly had a used Honda that was very reliable.

At first, Cassandra felt gratitude toward her uncle. Every time she got in the car, she thought, "Uncle Joe is a really nice guy." For two months, she made her payments with fidelity, never going back on her promise to send a check every week. But then money got tight. Her starting pay was low, and the opportunities for advancement were slow in coming. She decided to move out of her parents' house—she hadn't been getting along well with them lately, anyway—and rent an apartment of her own. With an apartment came not only rent but utility bills. She needed at least basic cable, and it surprised her how much her first cable bill was. On top of that she had a cell phone bill, her car insurance bill, and her electric bill; plus, she had to eat. And on Fridays she liked to go to the movies or to dinner with her friends. Surely she deserved a little relaxation time? No one could deny that.

The next week, when some of her bills were due, she only managed to send Uncle Joe $50.00. He didn't call or say anything about the smaller amount she sent, so she figured he must not care, and the week after that, she didn't send any money. This time Uncle Joe called.

"Cassandra," he said in a friendly voice, "did you forget to send your payment this week?"

"Sorry, Uncle Joe. I forgot. I'll send it out right away," she replied sweetly, but inside she began to seethe. "Uncle Joe is so greedy," Cassandra thought. "He lives in a giant house. In fact, it's almost a mansion. He's not hurting for money. He might have worked hard when he started out, but now that he owns his own company, he's got people to do his work for him, and all he ever seems to do is lounge around. I think he's not only greedy but lazy, too. Plus, when he got divorced, wasn't I there for him? Didn't I let his dogs out when he had to go to court that time? On top of that, I'm a great listener, and the value of that can't be underestimated. I listened to Uncle Joe on several nights when he was feeling sad about the divorce. He doesn't need the money anyway, and he owes me. If I had to put a monetary value on it, I'd say what he owes me is worth far more than what I borrowed." Cassandra didn't think about the times Uncle Joe had helped her—she only paid attention to when she had helped him. Moreover, she totally forgot how he had nearly gone bankrupt a few years ago and struggled to become solvent again. So Cassandra didn't pay back Uncle Joe, and she started to avoid his phone calls. The more he called and asked for his money, the angrier Cassandra got, and the surer she became that her uncle was just a greedy, selfish man.

1. On a separate sheet of paper, explain how Cassandra's decision not to pay back her uncle is an example of rationalizing, and support your answer with details from the passage.
2. Explain how Cassandra engages in confirmation bias and commits memory errors.
3. For discussion: How could you explain to Cassandra that her behavior is not fair to her Uncle?

THINK AND **WRITE** CRITICALLY

Memory Test   PRACTICE 1-8

Directions: Without looking back at the words in the "Test Your Memory" side box, indicate in the blanks provided whether each of the following words was on the list or not. In the second blank, indicate on a scale of 1–10 (with 1 being very uncertain and 10 being very certain) how sure you are about your answer.

	On the List	**Certainty (1–10)**
1. Sand	_____	_____
2. Beach	_____	_____
3. Surf	_____	_____

4. Sunglasses   _____   _____
5. Shore   _____   _____
6. Sunshine   _____   _____

Now check your answers. On the lines below, indicate what you learned about your memory.

_____

_____

_____

_____

Obstacles Caused by Our Emotions

Our emotions affect the way we think. We are not robots, and we all feel fear, anger, greed, jealousy, sorrow, happiness, love, and joy. The difficult thing for critical thinkers is not to allow how they feel about an issue to affect the way they evaluate it. Obstacles to clear thought that are caused by our emotions include *attribution mistakes, wishful thinking,* and *a desire to conform.*

Attribution Mistakes We tend to believe that the actions of other people are related to the kind of people they are, while we tend to think that our own actions are related to the situation we are in. For example, if someone such as a waiter behaves rudely to you, you might be tempted to say, "Well, he's just a jerk," or worse. But you've certainly been rude to people, too. When you were rude, did you chalk it up to the fact that you simply had a bad day, didn't get enough sleep the night before, or were angry about how your boss had treated you at work that day? You probably didn't say, "Well, I am just a jerk." This is called an **attribution mistake**—because you are unfairly attributing a person's behavior to the wrong cause. If you spend a minute thinking about it, if you were rude because of the situation you were in, isn't it likely that the person you originally wrote off as a jerk was also rude because of the situation? Another example concerns romantic relationships: If your boyfriend or girlfriend breaks up with you to be with someone else, you are probably tempted to think, "What a horrible person! He [or she] is nothing but a jerk." But if the situation were reversed, you would explain your own actions by saying something like, "I can't help the way I feel. I didn't try to fall for someone else; it just happened. It would only make us both unhappy if I stayed in this relationship when my heart is not in it." That's the thing: the attribution mistake is almost always self-serving. We attribute successes to internal causes and failures to external causes when it benefits us, and we refuse to do so for other people. Instead, we attribute their successes to external causes like luck and their failures to character flaws. It's very easy to be harder on other people than we are on ourselves, but it's best to be aware of our tendency to commit the attribution mistake.

Wishful Thinking It might seem that if we believe in something hard enough or want it badly enough, it will be more likely to happen, but the truth is that no amount of wishing causes an event to happen. You are engaging in **wishful thinking** if you say something like, "It would be nice if I got an A on the test I just took. I really want to get an A. I'm a pretty smart person. I probably got an A." Your desire to get an A on the test would cause you to think, without even knowing it, that the chance you had got an A had increased. People even engage in wishful thinking on larger scales. For example, some people don't save or plan for retirement because they just assume that they will somehow have enough money when they reach retirement age. And saving now would be a burden. Therefore, they rationalize, they don't need to save for retirement, because things will just work themselves out. Of course, as much as we'd like it to, wishing for something doesn't make it happen.

Conformity We all want to fit in, but our desire to fit in can also affect the quality of our thinking. If everyone around us believes a certain claim, it is easy to go along with the crowd; this is called **conformity**. When we conform, we fool ourselves into believing what it is popular to believe, even though it may not actually be true. Conformity is a very powerful force. One experiment showed that a majority of people will trick themselves into believing something that is obviously not true—such as that the shorter of two lines is actually longer—just because everyone else around them says they believe it (Wright, 1994). You might have been tempted to do something you knew was not a good idea, like smoking or doing drugs, because you wanted to fit in with your peers. Perhaps you even convinced yourself that what you were about to do wasn't as bad as you first thought—like telling yourself, "Well, if everyone tries smoking, how bad can it really be?" Conformity can be very potent, but very harmful. At one point, many people believed that minorities and women were inferior, not based on evidence, but because others in their society believed it. This belief caused people to oppress or even commit violent acts against innocent individuals because of their desire to conform.

PRACTICE 1-9

Emotional Obstacles

Directions: On a separate sheet of paper, answer the following questions.

1. Consider a time you felt pressured to conform. Did you go along with the crowd? Why, or why not? What were the results of your decision?
2. Think of a time your emotions clouded your judgment. What emotion did you feel, and how did it affect your ability to think straight?
3. Try to identify an example of wishful thinking in yourself or someone else. Explain your example and why it qualifies as wishful thinking.

THINK AND **WRITE** CRITICALLY

Defense Mechanisms

Defense mechanisms are protective strategies our minds use to avoid thinking about ideas that cause us anxiety or challenge our beliefs. They can block us from reaching good conclusions, because we often identify our beliefs as being part of ourselves, and rejecting these core beliefs could mean disrupting our lives; so we hold on to them, despite contradictory evidence. This is especially true when it comes to our religious and political beliefs. A perceived attack on these beliefs can feel like a personal attack. There can also be the fear that changing core beliefs might mean no longer being accepted by people in church, by friends, or by family. Here are three commonly employed defense mechanisms:

1. **Denial**. Individuals who are using *denial* to avoid questioning their beliefs might deny that a valid criticism of their beliefs has been raised at all. They might reject facts, including scientific evidence, that go against their worldview, or they might claim that there is no agreement about the facts and that they are just an "interpretation." People employing denial might also admit that the facts exist but minimize their importance. They might simply be dismissive, brushing aside scientific research as just being

"geeky" or the "product of some egghead." Denial is also very common among drug addicts and alcoholics, who often refuse to admit that they have an addiction at all. Often, denial is engaged in unconsciously or only partly consciously, but it is denial nonetheless.

2. **Anger.** Some people get outraged instead of facing an issue they don't want to deal with. They might claim that it's rude to ask about certain things. They use anger as a way to dismiss troublesome ideas, or to insult the people who are trying to make them think about their ideas (of course, getting angry isn't always a defense mechanism—sometimes anger is justified).

3. **Avoidance.** People using this method simply avoid any discussion that might lead them to think critically about their beliefs. They might change the subject, brush over it, or actually leave the room. They might avoid seeing the people who cause them to question their beliefs.

Whatever the technique used, these defense mechanisms can get in the way of critical thinking.

PRACTICE 1-10   Defense Mechanisms

Directions: Read the *Non Sequitur* cartoon below, and on a separate sheet of paper, answer the questions that follow.

NON SEQUITUR © 2004 Wiley Ink, Inc.. Dist. By UNIVERSAL UCLICK. Reprinted with permission. All rights reserved.

THINK
AND **WRITE**
CRITICALLY

1. What does Danae hope to avoid by handing out her list of things that offend her?
2. Is Danae employing a defense mechanism? If so which one? Explain your answer.
3. Is Danae's strategy helpful or harmful to her personally? Explain your answer.

PRACTICE 1-11   Recognizing Obstacles to Critical Thinking

Directions: Read each of the following scenarios. In the space provided, use the word bank to identify the obstacle or defense mechanism evident in the scenario. Be prepared to explain your answer.

wishful thinking   conformity   rationalization   avoidance   confirmation bias

1. No one in Collin's circle of friends likes rap music. They all say that it sounds like noise; it has no melody and it takes no talent to produce, they claim. Personally, Collin tends to like rap, and he thinks that a lot of skill and knowledge would have to go into producing something that complex. But if everyone else hates it, he reasons that he is probably wrong, so he eventually convinces himself to hate rap too.

   ————————————————————

2. Jeannette has an upcoming exam in anatomy and physiology. It will cover the four chapters read and discussed over the last month. Jeannette hasn't studied. Although there are well over 200 terms she will be expected to remember, Jeannette knows that her memory is great. She will remember the terms just from having heard them mentioned in class. After all, because of her excellent memory, she got through high school without studying. Despite her faith in her memory, her lack of studying results in an F on the exam. ————————————————————

3. Paul's girlfriend goes out of town for the week with her friends. While she is away, Paul runs into Gina, a girl he has had a crush on for several years. Gina asks Paul to "hang-out" on Friday. Paul knows that if he does, his girlfriend will be upset. His girlfriend knows about Paul's crush on Gina. Paul says yes to Gina; after all, if Paul's girlfriend cared, she would have invited him on her vacation. Plus, Paul thinks, she was not nice to him before she left. So, according to Paul, it's really his girlfriend's fault. If his girlfriend had been a better girlfriend, he wouldn't be tempted to hang-out with Gina.

   ————————————————————

4. Jeff finds himself in class with Jose, an acquaintance who knows some of Jeff's friends. His friends don't really like Jose, but Jeff has never met him before. While in class, he notes that Jose raises his hand and confidently answers a few questions. He doesn't pay attention to all the times Jose doesn't raise his hand to answers questions. Jeff concludes that Jose is a know-it-all and so Jeff decides he doesn't like Jose.

   ————————————————————

5. Deondra is terrified (and secretly thrilled) by ghosts. Her friend Cherise tells her that if ghosts are immaterial (can't be touched), then there is no way that they can hurt someone, and if they can be touched, then they can be hurt themselves. So Cherise tells Deondra not to be afraid of ghosts. Deondra tells her that she shouldn't be such a closed-minded skeptic. From that point on, Deondra steers clear of Cherise.

   ————————————————————

EXPAND YOUR UNDERSTANDING

Learning More about Obstacles to Critical Thinking While Writing Critically

Directions: Although the obstacles and defense mechanisms above are important, they aren't the only ones that can keep us from thinking critically. Use your school library, do a Google search for keywords "cognitive biases," or use a website such as www.scribd.com/doc/30548590/Cognitive-Biases-A-Visual-Study-Guide to research two more obstacles or defense mechanisms and explain them in your own words in a short paragraph.

THINK
AND **WRITE**
CRITICALLY

Chapter Summary

- *Critical thinking* is a reflective, rational process used to make good decisions or to form beliefs that are more likely to be true. You have to work to become a critical thinker.

- Critical thinking has lots of *benefits*, including the ability to read and write critically.

- Critical thinkers have the *character traits* of humility, open-mindedness, curiosity, fair-mindedness, skepticism, organization, trust in reason, and persistence.

- The character traits of critical thinkers make them always want to apply the *skills* of critical thinkers, which are comprehension, interpretation, inference, analysis, evaluation, self-monitoring, explanation, and problem-solving. These traits can be developed.

- Critical thinkers have *standards* that they hold themselves and others to.

- Critical thinkers are aware of the potential *obstacles* to clear thinking caused by the way they reason, their emotions, and their defense mechanisms. They strive to avoid them.

READ, WRITE, AND THINK CRITICALLY: SECTION TWO

Directions: Skim through the following text and answer questions 1–2. Then, read the selection and answer the questions that follow.

1. Where do you fall on the measure of belief scale? Do you believe that Google and the Internet are "making us stupid?" Explain in a short answer.

    _____

    _____

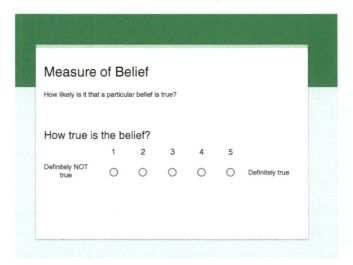

2. What is your prior knowledge of this topic?

    _____

    _____

Is Google Making Us Stupid? What the Internet Is Doing to Our Brains

Nicholas Carr

Nicholas Carr holds a B.A. from Dartmouth College and an M.A., in English and American literature and language, from Harvard University. Carr has been a speaker at MIT, Harvard, Wharton, the Kennedy School of Government, and NASA, as well as at many industry, corporate, and professional events throughout the Americas, Europe, and Asia. He writes on the social, economic, and business implications of technology. He is the author of Does IT Matter *(2004),* The Big Switch: Rewiring the Word, from Edison to Google *(2008), and his latest book* The Shallows: What the Internet Is Doing to Our Brains *(2010). The following essay is an article published in 2008 that was then expanded upon in his book,* The Shallows.

1   "Dave, stop. Stop, will you? Stop, Dave. Will you stop, Dave?" So the supercomputer HAL pleads with the implacable astronaut Dave Bowman in a famous and weirdly poignant scene toward the end of Stanley Kubrick's *2001: A Space Odyssey.* Bowman, having nearly been sent to a deep-space death by the malfunctioning machine, is calmly, coldly disconnecting the memory circuits that control its artificial "brain." "Dave, my mind is going," HAL says, forlornly. "I can feel it. I can feel it."

2   I can feel it, too. Over the past few years I've had an uncomfortable sense that someone, or something, has been tinkering with my brain, remapping the neural circuitry, reprogramming the memory. My mind isn't going—so far as I can tell—but it's changing. I'm not thinking the way I used to think. I can feel it most strongly when I'm reading. Immersing myself in a book or a lengthy article used to be easy. My mind would get caught up in the narrative or the turns of the argument, and I'd spend hours strolling through long stretches of prose. That's rarely the case anymore. Now my concentration often starts to drift after two or three pages. I get fidgety, lose the thread, begin looking for something else to do. I feel as if I'm always dragging my wayward brain back to the text. The deep reading that used to come naturally has become a struggle.

3   I think I know what's going on. For more than a decade now, I've been spending a lot of time online, searching and surfing and sometimes adding to the great databases of the Internet. For me, as for others, the Net is becoming a universal medium, the conduit for most of the information that flows through my eyes and ears and into my mind. The advantages of having immediate access to such an incredibly rich store of information are many, and they've been widely described and duly applauded. "The perfect recall of silicon memory," *Wired's* Clive Thompson has written, "can be an enormous boon to thinking." But that boon comes at a price. As the media theorist Marshall McLuhan pointed out in the 1960s, media are not just passive channels of information. They supply the stuff of thought, but they also shape the process of thought. And what the Net seems to be doing is chipping away my capacity for concentration and contemplation. My mind now expects to take in information the way the Net distributes it: in a swiftly moving stream of particles. Once I was a scuba diver in the sea of words. Now I zip along the surface like a guy on a Jet Ski.

4   I'm not the only one. When I mention my troubles with reading to friends and acquaintances—literary types, most of them—many say they're having similar experiences. The more they use the Web, the more they have to fight to stay focused on long pieces of writing. Some of the bloggers I follow have also begun mentioning the phenomenon. Scott Karp, who writes a blog about online media, recently confessed that he has stopped reading books altogether. "I was a lit major in college, and used to be [a]voracious book reader," he wrote. "What happened?" He speculates on the answer: "What if I do all my reading on the web not so much because the way I read has changed, i.e. I'm just seeking convenience, but because the way I THINK has changed?"

5   Bruce Friedman, who blogs regularly about the use of computers in medicine, also has described how the Internet has altered his mental habits. "I now have almost totally lost the ability to read and absorb a longish article on the web or in print," he wrote earlier this year. A pathologist who has long been on the faculty of the University of Michigan Medical School, Friedman elaborated on his comment in a telephone conversation with me. His thinking, he said, has taken on a "staccato" quality, reflecting the way he quickly scans short passages of text from many sources online. "I can't read *War and Peace* anymore," he admitted. "I've lost the ability to do that. Even a blog post of more than three or four paragraphs is too much to absorb. I skim it."

6   Anecdotes alone don't prove much. And we still await the long-term neurological and psychological experiments that will provide a definitive picture of how Internet use affects cognition. But a recently published study of online research habits, conducted by scholars from University College London, suggests that we may well be in the midst of a sea change in the way we read and think. As part of the five-year research program, the scholars examined computer logs documenting the behavior of visitors to two popular research sites, one operated by the British Library and one by a U.K. educational consortium, that provide access to journal articles, e-books, and other sources of written information. They found that people using the sites exhibited "a form of skimming activity," hopping from one source to another and rarely returning to any source they'd already visited. They typically read no more than one or two pages of an article or book before they would "bounce" out to another site. Sometimes they'd save a long article, but there's no evidence that they ever went back and actually read it. The authors of the study report:

7   It is clear that users are not reading online in the traditional sense; indeed there are signs that new forms of "reading" are emerging as users "power browse" horizontally through titles, contents pages and abstracts going for quick wins. It almost seems that they go online to avoid reading in the traditional sense.

8   Thanks to the ubiquity of text on the Internet, not to mention the popularity of text-messaging on cell phones, we may well be reading more today than we did in the 1970s or 1980s, when television was our medium of choice. But it's a different kind of reading, and behind it lies a different kind of thinking—perhaps even a new sense of the self. "We are not only *what* we read," says Maryanne Wolf, a developmental psychologist at Tufts University and the author of *Proust and the Squid: The Story and Science of the Reading Brain.* "We are *how* we read." Wolf worries that the style of reading promoted by the Net, a style that puts "efficiency" and "immediacy" above all else, may be weakening our capacity for the kind of deep reading that emerged when an earlier technology, the printing press, made long and complex works of prose commonplace. When we read online, she says, we tend to become "mere decoders of information." Our ability to interpret text, to make the rich mental connections that form when we read deeply and without distraction, remains largely disengaged.

9   Reading, explains Wolf, is not an instinctive skill for human beings. It's not etched into our genes the way speech is. We have to teach our minds how to translate the symbolic characters we see into the language we understand. And the media or other technologies we use in learning and practicing the craft of reading play an important part in shaping the neural circuits inside our brains. Experiments demonstrate that readers of ideograms, such as the Chinese, develop a mental circuitry for reading that is very different from the circuitry found in those of us whose written language employs an alphabet. The variations extend across many regions of the brain, including those that govern such essential cognitive functions as memory and the interpretation of visual and auditory stimuli. We can expect as well that the circuits woven by our use of the Net will be different from those woven by our reading of books and other printed works. Never has a communications system played so many roles in our lives—or exerted such broad influence over our thoughts—as the Internet does today. Yet, for all that's been written about the Net, there's been little consideration of how, exactly, it's reprogramming us. The Net's intellectual ethic remains obscure.

10   Google's headquarters, in Mountain View, California—the Googleplex—is the Internet's high church, and the religion practiced inside its walls is Taylorism.* Google, says its chief executive, Eric Schmidt, is "a company that's founded around the science of measurement," and it is striving to "systematize everything" it does. Drawing on the terabytes of behavioral data it collects through its search engine and other sites, it carries out thousands of experiments a day, according to the *Harvard Business Review,* and it uses the results to refine the algorithms that increasingly control how people find information and extract meaning from it. What Taylor did for the work of the hand, Google is doing for the work of the mind.

11   The company has declared that its mission is "to organize the world's information and make it universally accessible and useful." It seeks to develop "the perfect search engine," which it defines as something that "understands exactly what you mean and gives you back exactly what you want." In Google's view, information is a kind of commodity, a utilitarian resource that can be mined and processed with industrial efficiency. The more pieces of information we can "access" and the faster we can extract their gist, the more productive we become as thinkers.

12   Where does it end? Sergey Brin and Larry Page, the gifted young men who founded Google while pursuing doctoral degrees in computer science at Stanford, speak frequently of their desire to turn their search engine

---

*Perhaps a reference to Frederick Winslow Taylor, an inventor known as the father of production management.

into an artificial intelligence, a HAL-like machine that might be connected directly to our brains. "The ultimate search engine is something as smart as people—or smarter," Page said in a speech a few years back. "For us, working on search is a way to work on artificial intelligence." In a 2004 interview with *Newsweek,* Brin said, "Certainly if you had all the world's information directly attached to your brain, or an artificial brain that was smarter than your brain, you'd be better off." Last year, Page told a convention of scientists that Google is "really trying to build artificial intelligence and to do it on a large scale."

13   Such an ambition is a natural one, even an admirable one, for a pair of math whizzes with vast quantities of cash at their disposal and a small army of computer scientists in their employ. A fundamentally scientific enterprise, Google is motivated by a desire to use technology, in Eric Schmidt's words, "to solve problems that have never been solved before," and artificial intelligence is the hardest problem out there. Why wouldn't Brin and Page want to be the ones to crack it?

14   Still, their easy assumption that we'd all "be better off" if our brains were supplemented, or even replaced, by an artificial intelligence is unsettling. It suggests a belief that intelligence is the output of a mechanical process, a series of discrete steps that can be isolated, measured, and optimized. In Google's world, the world we enter when we go online, there's little place for the fuzziness of contemplation. Ambiguity is not an opening for insight but a bug to be fixed. The human brain is just an outdated computer that needs a faster processor and a bigger hard drive.

15   The idea that our minds should operate as high-speed data-processing machines is not only built into the workings of the Internet, it is the network's reigning business model as well. The faster we surf across the Web—the more links we click and pages we view—the more opportunities Google and other companies gain to collect information about us and to feed us advertisements. Most of the proprietors of the commercial Internet have a financial stake in collecting the crumbs of data we leave behind as we flit from link to link— the more crumbs, the better. The last thing these companies want is to encourage leisurely reading or slow, concentrated thought. It's in their economic interest to drive us to distraction.

16   Maybe I'm just a worrywart. Just as there's a tendency to glorify technological progress, there's a countertendency to expect the worst of every new tool or machine. In Plato's *Phaedrus,* Socrates bemoaned the development of writing. He feared that, as people came to rely on the written word as a substitute for the knowledge they used to carry inside their heads, they would, in the words of one of the dialogue's characters, "cease to exercise their memory and become forgetful." And because they would be able to "receive a quantity of information without proper instruction," they would "be thought very knowledgeable when they are for the most part quite ignorant." They would be "filled with the conceit of wisdom instead of real wisdom." Socrates wasn't wrong—the new technology did often have the effects he feared—but he was shortsighted. He couldn't foresee the many ways that writing and reading would serve to spread information, spur fresh ideas, and expand human knowledge (if not wisdom).

17   So, yes, you should be skeptical of my skepticism. Perhaps those who dismiss critics of the Internet as Luddites or nostalgists will be proved correct, and from our hyperactive, data-stoked minds will spring a golden age of intellectual discovery and universal wisdom. Then again, the Net isn't the alphabet, and although it may replace the printing press, it produces something altogether different. The kind of deep reading that a sequence of printed pages promotes is valuable not just for the knowledge we acquire from the author's words but for the intellectual vibrations those words set off within our own minds. In the quiet spaces opened up by the sustained, undistracted reading of a book, or by any other act of contemplation, for that matter, we make our own associations, draw our own inferences and analogies, foster our own ideas. Deep reading, as Maryanne Wolf argues, is indistinguishable from deep thinking. If we lose those quiet spaces, or fill them up with "content," we will sacrifice something important not only in ourselves but in our culture. In a recent essay titled "The Pancake People," the playwright Richard Foreman eloquently described what's at stake:

18   I come from a tradition of Western culture, in which the ideal (my ideal) was the complex, dense and "cathedral-like" structure of the highly educated and articulate personality—a man or woman who carried inside themselves a personally constructed and unique version of the entire heritage of the West. [But now] I see within us all (myself included) the replacement of complex inner density with a new kind of self—evolving under the pressure of information overload and the technology of the "instantly available."

19   As we are drained of our "inner repertory of dense cultural inheritance," Foreman concluded, we risk turning into " 'pancake people'—spread wide and thin as we connect with that vast network of information accessed by the mere touch of a button."

20   I'm haunted by that scene in *2001*. What makes it so poignant, and so weird, is the computer's emotional response to the disassembly of its mind: its despair as one circuit after another goes dark, its child-like pleading with the astronaut—"I can feel it. I can feel it. I'm afraid"—and its final reversion to what can only be called a state of innocence. HAL's outpouring of feeling contrasts with the emotionlessness that characterizes the human figures in the film, who go about their business with an almost robotic efficiency. Their thoughts and actions feel scripted, as if they're following the steps of an algorithm. In the world of *2001*, people have become so machinelike that the most human character turns out to be a machine. That's the essence of Kubrick's dark prophecy: as we come to rely on computers to mediate our understanding of the world, it is our own intelligence that flattens into artificial intelligence.

Discussion Questions

1. Discuss the types of evidence that Nicholas Carr cites to support his contention that the kind of deep reading that used to come naturally has now become difficult. Which type did you find most interesting or convincing? Explain.

2. What abilities does Maryanne Wolf suggest are being lost due to the proliferation of Internet reading and its effect on the brain? Why do you believe these abilities are important or unimportant to retain?

Directions: Answer the prompts below on a separate sheet of paper. Use evidence from the text to support your answers.

3. In what ways are the author's reading habits changing? Do you believe that you read differently than you used to because of the Internet?

4. In your own words, explain the proof the author gives that the Internet is changing our brains.

5. What do you think the author means when he says that Google views "information as a kind of commodity"? Do you agree or disagree with this view? Why?

6. The author gives a rebuttal to his own argument when he mentions how "Socrates bemoaned the development of writing." Explain his rebuttal.

7. Ultimately, do you agree or disagree with the author's view of the impact the Internet will have on our reading and thinking? Why?

Directions: Complete the following critical writing task and bring your findings to class. Be prepared to discuss them.

8. In paragraphs 12 and 13, the author gives one definition of intelligence. Using the Internet or a library, research what "intelligence" is and write a short (three to five paragraphs) essay explaining your findings.

CHAPTER 2

Comprehension

<table>
<tr><td valign="top">

Learning Goals

In this chapter you will learn how to

➤ Comprehend What You Read   SECTION ONE
➤ Be Curious
➤ Become a Better Reader
➤ Identify the Topic of a Reading
➤ Survey and Predict
➤ Develop Your Vocabulary   SECTION TWO

</td><td valign="top">

PREVIEW OF TERMS

Comprehension p. 32
Curiosity p. 32
Topic p. 37
Subject p. 37
Mnemonics p. 39
Relative pronoun p. 39
Antecedent p. 39
Surveying p. 41
Predicting p. 41
Previewing p. 41
Prior knowledge p. 41
Working vocabulary p. 47
Jargon p. 47
Context clues p. 47
Definition p. 48
Synonyms p. 49
Antonyms p. 50
Example p. 51
Root words p. 52
Prefixes p. 52
Suffixes p. 52
Glossary p. 54
Dictionary p. 54
See glossary,
   pp. 391–397

</td></tr>
</table>

SECTION ONE

What Is Comprehension?

In Harper Lee's classic novel *To Kill a Mockingbird*, the main character, Scout Finch, is scolded by her teacher on the first day of school because the teacher isn't happy that Scout's father Atticus has already taught her how to read. Her teacher's inflexible expectation—that children should learn to read only in school under the guidance of a qualified teacher—led Scout to mull over her "crime":

> I never deliberately learned to read, but somehow I had been wallowing illicitly in the daily papers. In the long hours of church—was it then I learned? I could not remember not being able to read hymns. Now that I was compelled to think about it, reading was something that just came to me, as learning to fasten the seat of my union suit without looking around, or achieving two bows from a snarl of shoelaces. I could not remember when the lines above Atticus's moving finger separated into words, but I had stared at them all the evenings in my memory, listening to the news of the day, Bills to Be Enacted into Laws, the diaries of Lorenzo Dow—anything Atticus happened to be reading when I crawled into his lap every night. Until I feared I would lose it, I never loved to read. One does not love breathing (pp. 17–18).

If it could only be as easy for all of us as it was for Scout, who recalls that "reading was something that just came to me." Most of us, however, need to work a bit harder at reading. Scout, an exceptional critical thinker for her age, was open to reading anything and everything, and her willingness to read whatever "Atticus happened to be reading" reveals one of the traits of a critical thinker to be covered in this chapter—curiosity.

In the last chapter, you learned what it means to be a critical thinker, reader, and writer and what character traits and skills are required. In this chapter, the focus is on **comprehension**, especially comprehension of texts. Comprehension is an understanding of information. Grasping information is a vital step toward becoming a critical reader and thinker. Section One of this chapter explores the trait of curiosity and the skills of identifying the topic, surveying, and predicting. Section Two focuses on the skill of developing vocabulary and shows what can happen if you make a mistake in comprehension.

If you were to ask people a simple question, "Why do you read?" you are likely to get a wide range of responses. Likely answers include, "Because I have to read for homework," "Because I like to," "Because I want to learn more," or "Because I need to get specific information." Scout might answer, "Because that's what I do with Atticus." A critical thinker might answer that "reading is one way to learn about the world," revealing a desire to learn and grow intellectually. So, we will look at the trait of *curiosity* in depth in this chapter.

Reviewing the Critical Thinker's Traits: Being Curious

Curiosity—specifically intellectual curiosity—refers to a longing to know more and a desire to seek out opportunities to learn. Another name for intellectual curiosity is inquisitiveness. Inquisitive people are not satisfied with unanswered questions! Instead, they will try to find out the answers to problems or issues. Intellectually curious people recognize that there is no end to the amount of information they can learn, and this fact excites rather than frustrates

> **"** Interest is the mother of intelligence. **"**
> —Dr. Henry Plotkin

them. In addition, inquisitive people realize that they might not need the information right away (or perhaps they will never actually need or use the information), but that does not stop them from still wanting to seek answers and explanations.

In countries across the globe, oppressive governments have denied people opportunities to learn. Imagine how frustrating it would be for an intellectually curious person to be told she was not allowed to learn to read or attend school! Richard Wright, an African American who grew up in the segregated South in the early 1900s, was only able to attend school until ninth grade. As a child, curiosity prompted him to convince his mother to teach him how to read by using old newspapers. In his autobiography *Black Boy*, Wright reveals how a white co-worker helped him defy the law and check out books from the local library. Wright recalls, "I forged more notes and my trips to the library became frequent. Reading grew into a passion. . . . I gave myself over to each novel without reserve, without trying to criticize it; it was enough for me to see and feel something different. And for me, everything was something different. Reading was like a drug, a dope. The novels created moods in which I lived for days." The joy he felt from learning about new subjects in books inspired him to become a writer himself, and he wrote critically acclaimed classics such as *Native Son* and *Black Boy*.

Intellectually curious people obtain pleasure from the ability to read and research the unknown. Try putting yourself in Richard Wright's shoes for a moment, and answer that question again, "Why do you read?"

Thinker to Emulate: Richard Wright

Library of Congress, Prints & Photographs Division, Carl Van Vechten Collection, [LC-USZ62-42502]

Richard Wright, born in 1908 in Mississippi, was an American author and critical thinker who tackled racial issues in his writing. After a difficult childhood marked by poverty and an unstable home life, he moved north, eventually settling in Chicago and New York City. Both his writing and his politics got attention: He wrote through the Federal Writers' Project, became a member of the Communist Party, and explored racial injustice in several books. Notable works include *Uncle Tom's Children*, *Native Son*, *Black Boy*, and *The Outsider*. *Native Son* was made into a play by Orson Welles in 1941 and a movie in Argentina in 1951 (Wright played the protagonist, Bigger Thomas, in the movie). Wright eventually left the Communist Party. A critical thinker who embraced intellectual and personal challenges, he continued to write and settled in Paris, France, where he died in 1960.

Directions: On a separate sheet of paper, answer the following questions. In pairs or small groups, discuss the answers to these prompts.

1. Brainstorm a list of subjects you don't know about but would like to learn more about. Next, make a plan about how you will learn more about the top two subjects on your list. Be specific; write down the steps involved.

2. Can you think of another creative way Richard Wright could have furthered his education?

3. What do you think of the cliché, "Ignorance is bliss"? How might a critical thinker respond to that question?

EXPAND YOUR UNDERSTANDING

Learning More about Intellectual Curiosity While Writing Critically

Use the Internet to research the following people and to see how they, like Richard Wright, sought out learning opportunities (sometimes by breaking or changing the law or by overcoming huge personal challenges).

Linda Brown (of Brown vs. Board of Education)
Frederick Douglass
Helen Keller

THINK AND **WRITE** CRITICALLY

Richard Wright did not shy away from intellectual challenges. He recognized that there was much to learn and was curious enough to look for answers to his questions in newspapers and books. He also recognized that intellectual curiosity was a strength that could lead to a successful career. Here are some tips to help you develop your curiosity:

Tips for Critical Thinkers: How to Be Curious

- **Recognize when you need to learn more.** Acknowledge when you need more information and embrace the challenge of finding it.
- **See curiosity as a strength.** Recognize that intellectual curiosity is often an early, important step toward gaining new knowledge.
- **Begin with a topic that already interests you.** Think of some topics that intrigue you and approach them from a new angle. For example, if you love biking but do not know how to fix a flat tire or how to repair a broken gear, then seek out a way to learn how to perform simple bike repairs.
- **Get creative with research.** You don't always have to conduct your research by reading reference materials in a library or on the Internet. Instead, interview an expert in the field, enroll in a workshop, or find an educational DVD, podcast, or webcast.
- **Fight apathy.** Apathy, indifference or a lack of interest, has a wide variety of causes. While laziness, boredom, or indifference can certainly cause apathy, it can also be the result of health problems, not having enough to eat, depression, and other serious issues. Although we all feel apathetic occasionally, resist the urge to let apathy get in the way of your learning. Become someone who inspires others by your "can-do" approach to unanswered questions and problems. If your intellectual curiosity is being hindered by one of the more serious causes of apathy, seek help first, and then work toward an intellectual goal that inspires you.

- **Follow your interests on the Internet.** The Internet is a haven for the intellectually curious. For example, you can use Google News to keep abreast of recent events. You could also join a site such as http://reddit.com that provides readers with news and items of interest that have been voted upon (by the Reddit community) as being the best on the Internet. Or use the "random article" feature on Wikipedia, which is as easy as going to www.wikipedia.org and clicking on "Random Article" on the left-hand side of the home page.

Becoming a Better Reader

Comprehension—knowledge and understanding of information—is the first important skill of a critical thinker. While having the desire to read is an excellent start, it is not enough. If you expect to satisfy your curiosity through reading, then you need to make sure you fully comprehend what you read.

You are probably one of the many college students who finds reading to be easy in some situations and difficult in others. A history enthusiast breezes through *Guns, Germs, and Steel* yet struggles to get through a chapter on the cardiovascular system; you might find Toni Morrison's novel *Beloved* intensely compelling but yawn while reading your chemistry textbook. Success in college largely depends on how well you master the skills of a critical thinker. As applied to reading, critical thinking involves comprehending and retaining information in textbooks, articles, and other written formats.

As you improve your reading and thinking skills, you are sure to recognize that there are different forms of reading for different tasks. For example, if you are doing research, you might scan for articles that may satisfy your research question. Skimming and scanning for potential texts works just fine when you are in the early stages of research (in the essay that concludes Chapter 1, Carr refers to this as being "a guy on a Jet Ski"). Eventually, however, once you find informative articles, you will want to read and think more deeply and critically (become Carr's "scuba diver in the sea of words").

Frequently students claim to "hate" reading when the actual problem is that they are frustrated with their inability to comprehend what they read. We all tend to enjoy the activities we perform well and to avoid those we aren't so good at. Learning and practicing new skills can sometimes be frustrating, but if you keep the goal in mind—becoming a better thinker and reader—you can keep a positive attitude.

Natalie Goldberg hits upon a common attitude in this excerpt from *Old Friend from Far Away* and gives readers a fresh way of looking at reading:

We start to read *Moby Dick* or *Heart of Darkness*, *Speak! Memory*, *Second Sex*, *Native Son*, *Don Quixote* and ten pages into it, we decide it's too hard, it's boring, we don't like it. I'm sorry to say it does not matter what you think. Your opinion here isn't important. We would be called immature if after ten minutes of meeting someone, we said to him, I don't like you. And yet this is often exactly what we do when we encounter a few pages of a new book. Our job is to stay with the author's words and see what we can learn. Push through. It takes a while to settle into a book's territory.

Carry a book bag with you. Read while you are standing in line at the post office. Snatch a few pages on the bus. You can be transported to India, rather than being irked in the waiting room because your doctor is a half hour late for your exam. When you finally walk into his office, E. M. Forster is filling your lungs. You are in an exotic country as the doctor looks down your throat and into your eyes.

Reading has so many advantages. Not in the least, it is relaxing. You have an experience of spaciousness. Other places and people unfold inside you. Leaning over pages, still and quiet, you are exercising that big muscle in your head. If you keep toning it, it won't become flabby, while all your other appendages hang south. And when you read, you might forget to eat—you are busy rowing up the Nile, crocodiles snapping at your oars. Has anyone before mentioned reading's dietetic benefits?

March off to that library—or bookstore—right now: thousands of adventures and friends await you (pp. 156–157).

While a good attitude is not going to make a beginner golfer into Jordan Spieth, it sure will make golfing lessons more pleasant. The same is true of reading: A positive attitude makes learning the basic skills far more enjoyable. So, take a few moments now to think about your outlook toward reading and answer the following questions. Be honest with yourself.

Think About It: Your Reading Experience

The Past

1. What were your experiences with reading as a small child?

2. Did your parents, siblings, other family members, or caregivers read to you regularly? If so, when, and what kind of books (picture books, children's books, comics, newspapers, etc.)?

3. What was your favorite book as a child?

4. Did you read as an adolescent? Yes/No

5. What would you choose to do during your leisure time as an adolescent or teenager?

6. Did you have a lot of reading materials in your home? If so, what kind?

7. Did you read newspapers or magazines? If so, which ones?

8. How were your grades in reading classes?

9. Did you like reading about subjects such as science or history? Yes/No

10. Did comprehension problems keep you from getting the grades you felt you were capable of getting? Yes/No

11. Did you go to a public library and/or to your school library? How often?

12. What genres did you read? Realistic fiction? Science fiction? Fantasy? Mythology? Poetry? Historical fiction? Nonfiction? Other?

13. Did you largely have positive or negative experiences with reading?

The Present

1. How do you feel when an instructor assigns a large amount of reading?

2. Where do you read?

3. Do you have a library card? Yes/No

4. Do you go to the school or public library frequently? Yes/No

5. How do you prefer to get your news?

   _____

6. If you see something interesting on TV or online, do you follow up by reading about or researching the topic? Yes/No

7. Do you subscribe to any newspapers or magazines? Yes/No

8. Do you read with other family members? Yes/No

9. How do you approach a textbook chapter? Do you use any pre-reading techniques? If so, list them below.

   _____

   _____

   _____

10. If you do not understand something that you have read, what do you do?

    _____

    _____

11. Does the idea of spending an afternoon with a book sound appealing to you? Yes/No

---

PRACTICE 2-2	Expand Your Understanding through Discussion

Directions: In pairs or small groups, discuss several of your answers to the above questions. As a group, pick one question from either "The Past" or "The Present" and assign one student to jot down your individual answers to share with the whole class later.

Because every student is unique, there is no "one-size-fits-all" solution to all challenges. You may find some strategies more useful to you than another student might, and you may find inspiration in unexpected places. No matter what your experiences with reading have been up to this point, you can always try something new that will help to turn you into a more effective, enthusiastic reader. Based on your answers above, think about some ways you could improve your attitude toward reading and become more successful at comprehending what you read. Then read the suggestions in the following box.

Think About It: How Can You Become a Better Reader?

The Future

1. **Look through the Table of Contents of this book.** Identify several concepts that you would like to learn more about or would consider implementing in your reading assignments this semester.
2. **Consider subscribing to a newspaper or periodical.** (You can also subscribe online.)
3. **Subscribe to an online service** like www.dictionary.com or www.wordsmith.org that delivers a new vocabulary word to your email inbox every day.
4. **Read more.** The more you practice reading, the better you will get at it.

While being open to change and embracing the challenges of comprehension can certainly help, many students share similar concerns when they face a challenging reading. In the following chart, some typical student concerns are listed along with potential solutions to them.

Student Comments	Possible Solutions
"Reading puts me to sleep."	• Make sure you are getting 7 to 8 hours of sleep per night. • Become more engaged in the reading by relating it to your life and your chosen career. • Change your location or position. • Read out loud. • Annotate (p. 84).
"There are too many words I have to look up in the dictionary."	• Improve your working vocabulary (p. 47). • Jot definitions in margins. • Use context clues (p. 47).
"I don't get it. I just don't understand."	• Survey the text before reading and make predictions. • Read out loud. • Check your predictions as you read (p. 43).
"I can't remember any-thing after I put the book down."	• Make connections to your own life and interests. • Outline or map the information after you are done (p. 99).

Expand Your Understanding through Discussion — PRACTICE 2-3

Directions: Do you recognize yourself in any of the above comments? In pairs or small groups, discuss these comments and solutions. Assign one student to jot down a list of which strategies group members have found to be useful and which techniques they might want to try in the near future.

If you want to improve your comprehension, you will benefit from learning many skills and drawing upon a repertoire of strategies. Even people who read for a living (lawyers, editors, teachers, among others) use different strategies when they have problems with a particular text. A strategy as simple as slowing down and reading out loud might be enough in some reading situations. If one strategy does not work for you, try another.

In this chapter, we review several skills necessary to achieve reading success: identifying topic, surveying, and predicting (all in Section One), and building vocabulary (in Section Two). Take the time to learn these strategies, which will enable you to achieve what is really important: *comprehension* of what you read.

Identifying the Topic

You will have a hard time with comprehension if you do not recognize the **topic** of a reading. The topic, also known as the **subject,** is what the reading is about. Read the following paragraph, and see if you can figure out the answer to the question, "What is it about?"

First, Anne tried moving the piano into the kitchen, but it did not fit. While she liked the look of the sofa in the master bedroom, it was really better suited for the baby's room, so she moved it as well. It was frustrating to her that the water in the sink and bathtub did not work, but she tried all of the faucets again anyway to no avail. The colors pink and purple were dominant in every room. In Anne's humble opinion, the pink shutters did nothing for the exterior of the house, but that was nothing a little crayon couldn't help.

Difficult, right? If you knew what the paragraph was about, the topic, then the details would make sense. (The topic is identified at the end of the chapter on p. 57; see for yourself if knowing it helps your comprehension.)

The paragraph about Anne lacks the clues we expect from a writer that help to indicate the topic or subject of a text. Specifically, it lacks two clues: title and repetition of key words. As a rule, the topic of a paragraph or longer reading can be stated in one word or a short phrase. The topic is often the quick and simple answer to the question, "Who or what is it about?"

As you will learn in the next section, when you survey you can easily identify the topic (see pp. 41–44 for more detailed information about surveying). In textbooks, for example, the topic is frequently included in the title of the chapter. Subtopics are smaller topics within the general subject, and, in textbooks, they often appear as subheads. A biology textbook, for instance, might have *cells* as the topic of a chapter, and a likely subtopic would be *cell mitosis*, which would appear in a subhead.

Another way to identify the topic is by annotating the text (see pp. 84–86 for more detailed information about annotating). Often the topic, or synonyms for the topic, will be used several times throughout the course of a paragraph, chapter, or article. If you are underlining or highlighting key terms, then you should notice if the same words or phrases keep appearing.

A common mistake many students make when identifying the topic is picking a word or short phrase from the text that is either *too broad* or *general* or *too specific* or *detailed* to accurately describe the topic. Much like Goldilocks, you don't want a topic that is "too big" or "too small": You want to pinpoint the topic that is "just right."

Say you are trying to rent an apartment and seek help from a realtor. You would neither tell the realtor you are looking for "a dwelling" (too broad/general), nor that you need "an apartment with 8.5' ceilings, oak hardwood floors, and tan tiles in a diamond shape on the kitchen floor" (too specific/detailed); "a two-bedroom apartment" would suffice and get you the assistance you needed.

PRACTICE 2-4   Identifying the Topic

Directions: Read the following paragraphs to determine the topic of each by underlining key terms (or their synonyms) that are used more than once. Then look at the list of possible topics that follows each one and indicate which one is too broad (TB), too specific (TS), and just right (JR).

Here's a model

In order to reconstruct human evolution, human paleontologists search for and study the buried, hardened remains or impressions—known as **fossils**—of humans, prehumans, and related animals. Paleontologists working in East Africa, for instance, have excavated the fossil remains of human-like beings who lived more than 3 million years ago. These findings have suggested the approximate dates when our ancestors began to develop two-legged walking, very flexible hands, and a larger brain.

From *Human Evolution and Culture* by Ember, Ember, and Peregrine

_TB_   a. Fossils
_JR_   b. Fossils of human-like beings
_TS_   c. East African fossils

Now you try

1. We all have had experience with acids and bases, whether we've called them by these names or not. Acidic substances tend to be a little more familiar: lemon juice, vinegar,

tomatoes. Substances that are strongly acidic have a well-deserved reputation for being dangerous: The word *acid* is often used to mean something that can sear human flesh. It might seem to follow that bases are benign, but ammonia is a strong base, as are many oven cleaners. The safe zone for living tissue in general lies with substances that are neither strongly acidic nor strongly basic. Science has developed a way of measuring the degree to which something is acidic or basic—the pH scale. So widespread is pH usage that it pops up from time to time in television advertising ('It's pH-balanced!').

From *Biology: A Guide to the Natural World* by Krogh

_____ a. Acids and bases

_____ b. pH-balanced

_____ c. Substances

2. Another memory-enhancing option is to draw on special mental strategies called *mnemonics* (from the Greek word meaning 'to remember'). **Mnemonics** are devices that encode a long series of facts by associating them with familiar and previously encoded information. Many mnemonics work by giving you ready-made retrieval cues that help organize otherwise arbitrary information.

From *Psychology and Life* by Gerrig and Zimbardo

_____ a. Memory

_____ b. Mnemonics

_____ c. Retrieval cues

3. Agreement with relative pronouns relies on identifying the relationship among a **relative pronoun** (a pronoun such as *that, which, who,* and *whom* that introduces a dependent clause), its **antecedent** (the word the pronoun refers to), and its verb. When a relative pronoun refers to a plural antecedent, it requires a plural verb. When a relative pronoun refers to a singular antecedent, it requires a singular verb. Note that relative pronouns signal a dependent clause. The antecedent for the relative pronoun is often found in the independent clause.

From *Writing for Life: Paragraph to Essay* by Henry

_____ a. Relative pronoun and antecedent agreement

_____ b. Parts of speech

_____ c. Plural and singular antecedents

4. In contrast with panic disorder, phobias involve a persistent and irrational fear of a specific object, activity, or situation—a response all out of proportion to the circumstances. (These are sometimes called *specific phobias,* as contrasted with the broader fears found in agoraphobia.) Many of us respond fearfully to certain stimuli, such as spiders or snakes—or perhaps to multiple-choice tests! But such emotional responses only qualify as full-fledged phobic disorders when they cause substantial disruption to our lives.

From *Psychology: Core Concepts* by Zimbardo, Johnson, and McCann

_____ a. Disorders

_____ b. Phobias

_____ c. Emotional responses

5. Usually, students treat the meanings of words as "subjective" and "mysterious." I have my meanings of words, and you have your meanings of them. On this view, problems of meaning are settled by asking people for their personal definitions. What do *you*

mean by "love," "hate," "democracy," "friendship," etc.? Each of us is then expected to come forward with a "personal definition." *My* definition of love is this . . . *My* definition of friendship is that. . . .

From *Critical Thinking* by Paul

_____ a. Definitions of love and friendship

_____ b. Personal definitions

_____ c. Words

6. The only thing that flowed more than tea in those aisles was Afghan gossip. The flea market was where you sipped green tea with almond *kolchas*, and learned whose daughter had broken off an engagement and run off with her American boyfriend, who used to be *Parchami*—a communist—in Kabul, and who had bought a house with under-the-table money while still on welfare. Tea, Politics, and Scandal, the ingredients of an Afghan Sunday at the flea market.

From *The Kite Runner* by Hosseini

_____ a. Afghan gossip

_____ b. Afghan food and customs

_____ c. A broken engagement

7. Maycomb was an old town, but it was a tired old town when I first knew it. In rainy weather the streets turned to red slop; grass grew on the sidewalks, the courthouse sagged in the square. Somehow, it was hotter then: a black dog suffered on a summer's day; bony mules hitched to Hoover carts flicked flies in the sweltering shade of the live oaks on the square. Men's stiff collars wilted by nine in the morning. Ladies bathed before noon, after their three-o'clock naps, and by nightfall were like soft teacakes with frostings of sweat and sweet talcum.

From *To Kill a Mockingbird* by Lee

_____ a. Maycomb

_____ b. How heat affected people in Maycomb

_____ c. Maycomb as a hot and tired town

8. Wade Boggs was one of the most proficient hitters in the history of baseball. He won the batting title five times and had a lifetime batting average of .363. He is also highly superstitious. Early on in his career he formed the belief that he could hit better after eating chicken. For that reason, he ate chicken almost every day for twenty years when he played baseball. He is not alone in his superstitious behavior. Wayne Gretzky, the great hockey star, always tucked in the right side of his jersey behind his hip pads. Jim Kelly, the Buffalo Bills quarterback, forced himself to vomit before every game. Bjorn Borg did not shave after he began to play in a major tennis tournament. Bill Parcells would buy coffee from two different coffee shops before every game when he coached the New York Giants.

From *Don't Believe Everything You Think* by Kida

_____ a. Superstitions

_____ b. Superstitions in sports

_____ c. Wade Boggs' superstitions

9. Scientists have never been good about explaining what they do or how they do it. Like all human beings, though, they make mistakes, and sometimes abuse their power. The most cited of those abuses are the twins studies and other atrocities carried out by

Nazi doctors under the supervision of Josef Mengele. While not as purely evil (because almost nothing could be) the most notorious event in American medical history occurred not long ago: from 1932 to 1972, in what became known as the Tuskegee Experiment, U.S. Public Health Service researchers refused to treat hundreds of poor, mostly illiterate African American sharecroppers for syphilis in order to get a better understanding of their disease. Acts of purposeful malevolence like those have been rare; the most subtle scientific tyranny of the elite has not been.

From *Denialism* by Specter

_____ a. Scientific experiments

_____ b. The Tuskegee Experiment

_____ c. Abuses of scientific power

10. As a society, we largely avoid political discussions in polite conversation, reserving them for relationships that can withstand a knock-down-drag-out fight—or with people whom we are actively working to alienate. If you're like us, you learned this lesson slowly and still forget it occasionally. You have also undoubtedly left an animated political "discussion" thinking two things about people at the other end of the political spectrum. The first is: Can they really believe that? The bad thinking behind others' beliefs often dismays us. How can they be so blind to the obvious? Their beliefs are clearly not rational, not logical, and perhaps not even sane.

From *The Time Paradox* by Zimbardo and Boyd

_____ a. Beliefs in political discussions

_____ b. Politics

_____ c. Fighting in politics

Survey and Predict

Many students approach a textbook chapter or an academic article with one goal in mind: *to finish it*. Unfortunately, rushing through a chapter about skeletal muscle fibers or the medieval philosophies of Thomas Aquinas will not help you understand the material; complex ideas require and deserve more time and attention.

Think about other academic endeavors that require your concentration and inspire your intellectual curiosity, such as completing a chemistry lab, solving a math problem, or playing a musical composition. Do you just dive into the activity without any advance preparation? No, probably not. Rather, in chemistry, you read the lab directions and get the necessary equipment and materials; in math, you scan the problem and see if you can break it down into smaller parts; and in music, you tune your instrument and look over the notes, determine the key, and set the tempo. Taking steps to prepare for these tasks is similar to **surveying** and **predicting** during the reading process.

Surveying

Surveying, also known as **previewing**, is a strategy for getting an overview of a reading selection. It only takes a few moments, but surveying gives you a general idea of the material, sparks your curiosity about what you are going to read, and helps activate your **prior knowledge**, the information you already know through learning and experience.

If you take the time to survey, you can probably identify the topic before you start reading (since the topic often appears in the title or is mentioned several times throughout the passage). When you have a sense of the topic and the organization of the text, you are more likely to anticipate what will be discussed and to make connections to what you already know about the subject. This will help you to understand and remember the content. Think back to the chemistry lab, math problem, and musical performance examples: Students who know that they will need to mix a solution, solve for *x*, or play an allegro mentally prepare for those steps.

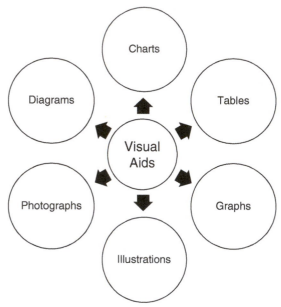

Use Visual Clues

Textbook authors and publishers are aware of the benefits of surveying. As a result, you can expect that a good textbook will make it easy for you to survey by including visual cues that you should notice as you survey each chapter:

- Items in **bold**
- Items in *italics*
- Items in larger fonts
- Ideas in different colors
- Vocabulary in boxes, highlighted, or in a different font
- Bulleted or numbered lists
- Visual aids

Use Text Features

In addition to these visual cues, textbook authors often include textual features that are intended to help you make sense of the material. Take advantage of these features by reading them prior to reading an entire chapter. Here is a list of what to look for when you are previewing.

What to Look for When Previewing

- **Title:** The title of the chapter almost always provides you with the topic
- **Subheadings:** Subheadings are printed in bold font larger than the rest of the text (although smaller than the title) and will give you the subtopic of each section
- **Introduction:** Authors may provide a section titled "Introduction;" if not, you can read the first paragraph of the chapter or article to get an overview of what the author plans on covering
- **Chapter objectives:** *Objectives* are the learning goals the author intends you to achieve by reading the chapter (usually found on the first page); looking over these objectives will tell you what the focus of your learning will be
- **Text boxes:** Authors often provide important supplemental information in boxes within the text or in the margins
- **Biographical notes:** Authors may give you a brief biography of a person who figures prominently in a chapter so that you will have a sense of the person's life and accomplishments prior to reading the chapter; these notes are common in fields such as literature, philosophy, and history
- **Historical notes:** The author may need to give you a brief overview of a country, an event, or an era in history in order for you to understand the context of the new information you are about to read
- **Summaries:** A summary will tell you what information in the chapter the author considers to be significant and especially important to your comprehension; if there is not a summary, then you can read the last paragraph of the chapter
- **End-of-chapter questions:** Questions at the end of the chapter indicate how the author would "test" your understanding of the main points; reading end-of-chapter questions ahead of time will allow you to identify and formulate answers as you read the chapter itself

Ask Questions

Formulating your own questions will also help you comprehend a text. An excellent strategy for formulating questions is to take the items in bold, italics, and larger fonts and turn them into questions. For example, say your geology textbook has a subheading "Igneous Rocks." You could draw on your prior knowledge about rocks by remembering that igneous rocks are a type of rock along with sedimentary and metamorphic rocks. With this in mind, you could come up with a few questions: What exactly are igneous rocks? How are they formed? How are they different from sedimentary and metamorphic rocks? Where can igneous rocks be found? If you take a few moments to ask questions while you survey, then you will have set a concrete goal for yourself to achieve while you read: You want to find the answers.

Tips for Reading Comprehension: Surveying

- Read the title to learn the topic of the text.
- Look at the subheadings to identify the subtopics of each section.
- Activate your prior knowledge by asking yourself, "What do I already know about this topic? How do the subtopics fit into the chapter?"
- Look at any visual aids.
- Read textual features provided by the author.
- If the author does not include an introduction or a summary, then read the first and last paragraphs of the chapter.
- Pay particular attention to items in bold, italics, and larger fonts and ask questions that you expect to be answered by the chapter's contents; for example, if a heading in the chapter is "The Importance of Cloning," your question might be "Why is cloning important?" Write these questions in the margin and, later, when you read, highlight or underline the answers.

Surveying the Chapter	PRACTICE 2-5

Directions: Go back to the beginning of this chapter and survey it. Use the Tips for Reading Comprehension: Surveying. Turn headings into questions; write down two questions that you expect will be answered in section two of this chapter.

1. _____

2. _____

Predicting

It is easier to acquire new knowledge when you are actively engaged with the information. When you apply critical thinking to a text, you can stay interested and engaged in the reading by predicting. *Predicting* is an active mental process that requires you to speculate and hypothesize about what might happen next in the reading. Even if some of your predictions are wrong, the act of predicting keeps your mind engaged with the reading. You can even start with the questions you posed while you surveyed the text; predict what some of the answers will be and see if you are right or not.

What you predict depends largely on what it is that you are reading. For example, if you are reading a novel for entertainment, you might make predictions about the plot or about relationships among characters. In a romance novel, you could predict what obstacles will prevent the main character from finding true love until the last few pages; in a war story, you can predict what tactics the desperate general will try next.

Prediction is a useful tool for studying. When you predict, you have to pay attention to what you are reading and begin seeing the information as a whole instead of separate parts. For example, suppose you are reading about cloning in your biology textbook. After starting with a definition of cloning (copying a single gene), you expect the text will elaborate on how cloning has advanced knowledge in the field of biology. As you read about early efforts to clone bacteria cells, you predict that the text will build up to reproductive cloning within more complex organisms, maybe even in animals and humans. You have some prior knowledge, so you predict that the text will cover some well-known cloning endeavors such as Dolly the sheep, cloned in 1997. Sure enough, the text does explain how Dolly the sheep was cloned, so you make further predictions about what other species have been useful in cloning research. You expected that other barnyard animals would be cloned after Dolly, and you find out that a dog has already been cloned and that people can pay large sums of money to have favorite pets cloned! Finally, you predict that the section will end with a discussion about human cloning, specifically the technical and ethical issues surrounding the concept. Through predicting, you can better recognize the connections among the topic (cloning) and subtopics (such as bacterial cloning, reproductive cloning, Dolly the sheep, and human cloning).

READ, WRITE, AND THINK CRITICALLY: SECTION ONE

Directions: Survey this selection from a study skills textbook and make predictions. Do not actually read the selection yet. Answer the five questions below in complete sentences.

1. What is the title? What does it suggest about the selection?

   _____

   _____

   _____

2. Are there any visual cues (bold, italics, larger font, charts, etc.)? What are they?

   _____

   _____

   _____

   _____

3. Read the first paragraph and make a prediction about what the authors want you to take away from this selection.

   _____

   _____

4. What is your prior knowledge about this topic?

   _____

   _____

5. Use one of the subheadings in the Abraham Maslow figure and formulate a question that you expect will be answered in the visual or text.

   _____

   _____

Interaction with Peers (Student–Student Interaction)

Studies of college students repeatedly point to the power of the peer group as a source of social and academic support (Pascarella, 2005). One study of more than 25,000 college students revealed that when peers interact with one another while learning they achieve higher levels of academic performance and are more likely to persist to degree completion (Astin, 1993). In another study that involved in-depth interviews with more than 1,600 college students, it was discovered that almost all students who struggled academically had one particular study habit in common: They always studied alone (Light, 2001).

Peer interaction is especially important during the first term of college. At this stage of the college experience, new students have a strong need for belongingness and social acceptance because many of them have just left the lifelong security of family and hometown friends. As a new student, it may be useful to view your early stage of the college experience and academic performance in terms of the classic hierarchy model of human needs, developed by American psychologist Abraham Maslow (See **Figure 2-1**).

According to Maslow's model, humans cannot reach their full potential and achieve peak performance until their more basic emotional and social needs have been met (e.g., their needs for personal safety, social acceptance, and self-esteem). Making early connections with your peers helps you meet these basic human needs, provides you with a base of social support to ease your integration into the college community, and prepares you to move up to higher levels of the need hierarchy (e.g., achieving educational excellence and fulfilling your potential).

Studies repeatedly show that students who become socially integrated or connected with other members of the college community are more likely to complete their first year of college and continue on to complete their college degree (Tinto, 1993). (See below effective ways to make these interpersonal connections).

Take Action!

Top Strategies: Making Connections with Key Members of Your College Community

Here is a list of 10 tips for making important interpersonal connections in college. Start making these connections now so that you can begin constructing a base of social support that will strengthen your performance during your first term and, perhaps, throughout your college experience.

1. Connect with a favorite peer or student development professional that you may have met during orientation.
2. Connect with peers who live near you or who commute to school from the same community in which you live. If your schedules are similar, consider carpooling together.

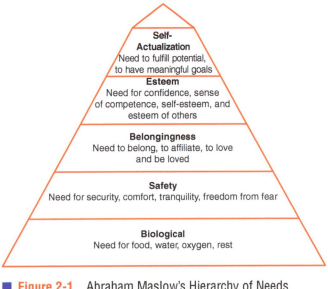

■ **Figure 2-1** Abraham Maslow's Hierarchy of Needs Resembles a Pyramid

3. Join a college club, student organization, campus committee, intramural team, or volunteer-service group whose members may share the same personal or career interests as you.

4. Connect with a peer leader who has been trained to assist new students (e.g., peer tutor, peer mentor, or peer counselor) or with a peer who has more college experience than you (e.g., sophomore, junior, or senior).

5. Look for and connect with a motivated classmate in each of your classes and try working as a team to take notes, complete reading assignments, and study for exams. (Look especially to team up with a peer who may be in more than one class with you.)

6. Connect with faculty members in a field that you're considering as a major by visiting them during office hours, conversing briefly with them after class, or communicating with them via e-mail.

7. Connect with an academic support professional in your college's Learning Center for personalized academic assistance or tutoring related to any course in which you'd like to improve your performance.

8. Connect with an academic advisor to discuss and develop your educational plans.

9. Connect with a college librarian to get early assistance and a head start on any research project that you've been assigned.

10. Connect with a personal counselor or campus minister to discuss any college adjustment or personal-life issues that you may be experiencing.

Getting involved with campus organizations or activities is one way to connect you with other students. Also, try to interact with students who have more college experience than you. Sophomores, juniors, and seniors can be valuable social resources for a new student. You're likely to find that they are willing to share their experiences with you because you have shown an interest in hearing what they have to say. You may even be the first person who has bothered to ask them what their experiences have been like on your campus. You can learn from their experiences by asking them which courses and instructors they would recommend or what advisors they found to be most well informed and personable.

Remember

Your peers can be more than competitors or a source of negative peer pressure; they can also be collaborators, a source of positive social influence, and a resource for college success. Be on the lookout for classmates who are motivated to learn and willing to learn with you, and keep an eye out for advanced students who are willing to assist you. Start building your social-support network by surrounding yourself with success-seeking and success-achieving students. They can be a stimulating source of positive peer power that drives you to higher levels of academic performance and heightens your motivational drive to complete college.

Directions: Now, go back and read the selection and answer the following three questions, using the information you learned from surveying and predicting.

6. You made a prediction about what you would learn in this selection in question 3. Was your prediction correct? Yes/No
   If not, then what did you learn instead?
   _____

7. Which of the strategies in the "Take Action!" box would you be willing to try?
   _____

8. What is the answer to the question you came up with in question 5?
   _____

SECTION TWO
Developing Vocabulary

In Section One you learned some helpful strategies for comprehension: identifying the topic, surveying, and predicting. When you read a passage, you will find it much easier to comprehend if you have a strong vocabulary, so Section Two focuses on ways to develop your vocabulary.

An important goal as a college student is to develop your vocabulary. While there is not a single, foolproof way to do this, the best advice is to *read*. Avid readers tend to have the best vocabularies. As college students, you are likely to have a heavy reading load, so if you have not been a voracious reader up to this point, that is probably about to change! Earlier you learned that sometimes there is no apparent reason to learn new information, but curious people want to learn it anyway. Vocabulary development is a good example of this: You might not use a new word today or tomorrow or even next semester, but intellectual curiosity prompts you to learn new definitions that might come in handy today or years down the road.

It is not enough to be exposed to new vocabulary words, learn the definitions for a quiz, relearn them for an exam, and then promptly forget them, as tempting as that may be. As you learned in Chapter 1, we are all susceptible to memory errors, so we need to put some extra effort into committing new vocabulary words to our memories. Try to make the new words part of your **working vocabulary**—the words that you are comfortable utilizing on a daily basis. To do this, make a concentrated effort to use new words when you speak and write; perhaps you can set a goal to practice the new words you encounter in your college courses by putting them on index cards. If you are reluctant to use a new word in conversation, you can become more comfortable using it by accessing an online dictionary that has audio, such as www.merriam-webster.com or www.dictionary.com, listening to how it is pronounced, and saying the word until it rolls off your tongue.

As you take more advanced courses within your chosen major, the vocabulary you need to know will become more specialized. Part of succeeding in your major is learning **jargon**, the vocabulary that will be part of your future career. Until this specialized vocabulary becomes second nature to you, there are several techniques you can use to decode unfamiliar words:

- **Use context clues:** Look for hints within the sentence a word appears in, or in surrounding sentences, that suggest its meaning
- **Use word parts:** Use the meanings of prefixes, roots, and suffixes to figure out the meaning of a word
- **Use the glossary:** Look for a list of key words and their definitions as they are used in the textbook or field of study at the back of the book
- **Use a dictionary** (hard copy or online): Consult a reference book or website that provides an alphabetical listing of words with their meanings and other useful information such as how to pronounce them, their part of speech, and origin
- **Use a subject area dictionary:** See, for example, *Taber's Medical Dictionary* and *Hawley's Condensed Chemical Dictionary*

Context Clues

Many students use context clues to figure out the meanings of words without being aware they are doing so. **Context clues** are the hints about meaning that exist within a sentence, usually close to the word in question. For example, when you read the first paragraph in this section, did you stop and tell yourself to use context clues? Probably not, yet you still got a sense of what the paragraph was all about. Reread these sentences:

> Avid readers tend to have the best vocabularies. As college students, you are likely to have a heavy reading load, so if you have not been a voracious reader up to this point, that is probably about to change!

Did you get out your dictionary and look up the words *avid* and *voracious*? If not, how did you figure out the meaning of these sentences with those words? Chances are you unconsciously used context clues to figure out that *avid* and *voracious* mean being eager and enthusiastic readers; experience tells you that people who are willing to read a lot will have stronger vocabularies than those who shy away from reading.

Context clues give you the general idea of what new words mean. What is your mind doing when you use context clues? Your mind is making connections and filling in the blanks created by unknown vocabulary words with whatever fits to help the sentence make sense. Being aware of the cognitive process behind using context clues should help you build your working vocabulary. Try to slow down your thinking and become familiar with these common types of context clues: *definitions, synonyms, antonyms,* and *examples.*

Definitions

Definitions are the most obvious of the context clues because frequently an author will provide the definition close to the word in question. If the word being defined is not in bold, as it frequently is in textbooks, then the author might set it off with commas or dashes. Another method authors use to make a definition stand out is to introduce it with words such as *means, or, in other words,* and *that is* as in the following sentence:

> An *anecdote*, that is, a short story used to entertain or to educate, is a clever way to start out a college essay.

A critical reader will recognize that the definition of *anecdote* is "a short story used to entertain or educate." You would not need to consult a dictionary if you use the context clue within the sentence.

PRACTICE 2-6	Identifying Vocabulary Using Definitions

Directions: Read the following sentences and underline the word or phrase that defines the word in italics.

1. A sign that a person is not thinking critically is an *obstinate* clinging to an opinion that does not have good evidence to support it; in other words, exhibiting a stubborn adherence to beliefs lacking support.
2. *Altruism,* that is, a selfless devotion to the welfare of others, is an admirable quality.
3. While people may think the word *cupidity* has something to do with Valentine's Day and love, in reality it means a strong, greedy desire, often for wealth.
4. Miranda was known for her *capricious* behavior, meaning she would often do impulsive and unpredictable things.
5. The formerly successful stockbroker never expected to be *destitute* or suffering from extreme poverty.
6. Ari's professor told him that his research paper was *vacuous*; Ari thought it was a compliment until he looked up "vacuous" in the dictionary and learned that it meant stupid.
7. Seeing a shooting star on New Year's Eve was, to Andrea, an *auspicious* beginning to the new year; in other words, she saw it as a favorable sign.
8. The *clandestine* meetings between the spy and his informant, held in secret for several months, came to an abrupt end when they were discovered by a counter-spy.

9. Many religious people say that they experience a feeling of *sanctity* or state of holiness within their place of worship.
10. The problem gambler was in a *quagmire*, meaning that he was in quite a predicament after losing all of his money on a risky bet.

Synonym Clues

Synonyms are words that have meanings identical or close to that of another word, for example, synonyms for the word *cold* include *arctic, frigid, below zero, frosty, frozen,* and so on. A synonym clue works by providing another, more familiar word with a similar definition in the same sentence as the new word. Often, the word *or* will signal that a synonym is being provided. Punctuation also signals synonyms; frequently, readers will encounter a new word or its synonym set off by commas such as in this example:

> Garrett's suggestion that he save money by moving in with his brother was *preposterous*, ridiculous, in fact, because the two young men had not spoken in years.

Identifying Vocabulary Using Synonyms	**PRACTICE 2-7**

Directions: Read the following sentences and underline the word or phrase that is a synonym for the word in italics. Then define the word in italics using your own words. The first one is done for you as an example.

> Even at a young age, Jonathan had the sense that life was *ephemeral* or short-lived; his beloved grandmother's death was probably the cause of his understanding of mortality.

<u>   fleeting, not lasting   </u>

1. Upon reaching the *summit* of the mountain, Alaina triumphantly put the Italian flag on the top with other countries' flags.

   _____

2. Marita believed that it was pure *serendipity* that caused her to sleep through her alarm and miss the bus; by luck she wasn't on the bus when it was involved in an accident.

   _____

3. People who suffer from mental illness have the added challenge of overcoming the *stigma* or shame that some societies associate with illnesses such as depression, schizophrenia, and addiction.

   _____

4. Sheila marveled at the new student's brilliant, *luminous* eyes.

   _____

5. Danielle was a *precocious*, advanced child, and her parents worried that her behavior made people think she was much older than she was.

   _____

6. Sometimes criminals are ordered to pay *restitution* or repayment to their victims.

   _____

7. The *loquacious* host was upstaged by an even more talkative guest at the party.

   _____

8. Many people who lived through the Great Depression developed *frugal* or thrifty habits that lasted a lifetime.

   _____

9. The *brazen*, bold teenager sprayed graffiti on the overpass in the vicinity of the police station and didn't seem to care whether he got caught.

   _____

10. Typically Lynn was a careful skier who avoided *precipitous* slopes, but she decided to take a risk and try the steep run at the top of the mountain.

    _____

Antonym Clues

Antonyms are words that have the opposite meaning to another word. An example of an antonym exists in this sentence:

> Angelo's willing *acquiescence* to his ex-wife's demands made her suspicious; it was in sharp contrast to his usual disagreeable resistance to every one of her requests.

How would you define *acquiescence*? Well, you could recognize the antonym clue later in the sentence: "it was in sharp contrast to his usual disagreeable resistance . . . ." This phrase suggests the *opposite* of acquiescence, namely, *resistance*; therefore, you can work out that *acquiescence* means *not* being resistant, *going along with*. Words such as *unlike, opposed to, rather*, or *in contrast* can suggest an antonym clue is being provided.

PRACTICE 2-8   Identifying Vocabulary Using Antonyms

Directions: Read the following sentences and underline the word or phrase that is an antonym for the word in italics. Then define the word in italics in your own words (answers may vary slightly). The first one is done for you as an example.

A *novel* solution to the problem proved hard to find; the students kept coming up with the same old ideas.

Novel: <u>new, fresh</u>

1. Plants *flourished* in Dana's garden unlike the dying specimens in her neighbor's yard.

   Flourished: _____

2. Once Rodrigo *ventured* his controversial opinion, he wondered if he should have held back and kept quiet instead.

   Ventured: _____

3. When Danica finally admitted that she *loathed* Bart, he was relieved that she no longer pretended to like him.

   Loathed: _____

4. Andrew's *candid* observations were in stark contrast to his brother's guarded and veiled opinions.

   Candid: _____

5. The *profundity* of the graduation ceremony was quite unlike the shallow and silly antics that followed the formal ceremony.

    Profundity: _____

6. Erin's logic was shown to be *erroneous*, and she was especially perturbed that her husband was praised for his correct reasoning.

    Erroneous: _____

7. Strangers meeting each other on a deserted road should ask "Friend or *foe*" to judge whether the stranger might prove to be a threat.

    Foe: _____

8. Mr. Chen's *acumen* in his business dealings was a welcome change from his predecessor's ignorance and lack of ability.

    Acumen: _____

9. Barton's *churlish* behavior was in sharp contrast to his brother's gracious way of handling himself during social events.

    Churlish: _____

10. The students thought their teacher was being serious when she said she was going to fail every student who neglected to bake a batch of chocolate chip cookies for her, but then she explained that she was just being *facetious*.
    Facetious: _____

Example Clues

Example context clues provide you with an idea of what a word means by giving you examples of things that could fall into the class to which the word refers. Consider the following sentence:

Some *genres*, like comedy and action, are more popular with younger moviegoers.

When trying to figure out what the word *genres* means, you can use the examples provided in the sentence—*comedy* and *action*—to determine that it most likely means *categories* or *types of* film. Certain words or phrases in a sentence signal that examples are about to follow. *For instance, for example, like,* and *such as* are often used to indicate an example clue is being provided.

Identifying Vocabulary Using Examples	PRACTICE 2-9

Directions: Read the following sentences and underline the examples that help you determine the meaning of the word in italics. Then write a definition of the word in your own words. The first one is done for you as an example.

Some *eccentricities*, such as saving one's fingernail clippings or bodily waste, might well be viewed as signs of a developing mental disorder.

Definition: _____ unusual behaviors _____

1. Shakespeare and Jane Austen, among the most famous of the *literati* of Europe, have inspired and impressed other scholars for generations.

   Definition: _____

2. *Invocations* like the Lord's Prayer and Psalm 23 have provided people with comfort for ages.

   Definition: _____

3. The *epithets* "feminine" and "girlish" are now unfairly considered insults even when applied to women.

   Definition: _____

4. The name Mark Twain is an example of a *pseudonym* that has become better known than the author's real name, which was Samuel Langhorne Clemens.

   Definition: _____

5. Going on a budget means cutting back on *superfluous* expenses such as subscribing to hundreds of TV channels in addition to belonging to several movie services.

   Definition: _____

6. CEOs who cut jobs and salaries to save the company money and then award themselves huge bonuses are perfect examples of *hypocrites*.

   Definition: _____

7. Brandon was prone to *vehement* outbursts; for instance, he once screamed at a grocery store clerk for moving the mayonnaise.

   Definition: _____

8. Tess was often described as being *diffident* because she could hardly shake hands with new people and she was unable to speak up in class.

   Definition: _____

9. Jacqueline acted as a *liaison* between the teachers' union and her high school; for example, she was the person who would share important information and keep the lines of communication open between the two groups.

   Definition: _____

10. Anthropologists study *indigenous* people such as Native Americans in the United States and the Inuit in Canada.

    Definition: _____

Word Parts

Recognizing root words, prefixes, and suffixes can help you improve your vocabulary, which will improve your comprehension of everything you read. A **root word**, the most basic form of a word, can be modified by adding prefixes and suffixes. **Prefixes** are word parts put at the beginning of a root word to make a new word, and **suffixes** are the word parts added to the end of a root word to create a new word by changing its part of speech or tense.

For the sake of pronunciation, sometimes a combining vowel, *o*, joins the word parts. Also, a word can be formed by using more than one root word, prefix, or suffix, and some words can be built by combining prefixes and suffixes (without any root word). Some words do not include a prefix or suffix, and sometimes a group of letters that spell a common prefix or suffix do not have the same meaning (such as *ped*, meaning either foot or child). See the appendix for some common word parts not listed below.

<table>
<tr><td>**Identifying Word Parts**</td><td>**PRACTICE 2-10**</td></tr>
</table>

Directions: Select the word in the word box below that best completes each of the following sentences. Refer to the partial tables of common root words, prefixes, and suffixes below to help you choose the correct words.

Common Root Words		
Root	**Meaning(s)**	**Example(s)**
ben(e)	Good	Benefit
Bio	Life	Biosphere
Chron(o)	Time	Chronological
Fact	make or do	Factory
Log	speech, words, or the study of	dialogue, terminology, psychology
Viv	Life	Viable

Common Prefixes		
Prefix	**Meaning(s)**	**Example(s)**
De	opposite of, away from; down	Decline
Mal	Bad	Malpractice
Re	back, again, anew	Revert

Common Suffixes			
Part of Speech	**Suffix**	**Meaning(s)**	**Example(s)**
Adjective	*ous*	having, full of, characterized by	Harmonious
Noun	*ation, tion, sion*	the act of	Subtraction
Noun	*er, or*	one who does	teacher, doctor
Noun	*ic*	the art or science of or actions or qualities of	Economics
Verb	*fy*	to make or cause	Horrify

Source: *Building an Active College Vocabulary* by Licklider

Benediction	Malefactor
Benefactor	Malicious
Bionic	Revive
Chronobiology	Vivacious
Deface	Vivify

1. Jasmine was a lively and _____ addition to parties on campus.
2. Advancements in technology have made it possible for _____ replacement parts to seem even more life-like.
3. Seeming to enjoy causing pain and distress, Malcolm was arrested several times for his _____ behavior.
4. At the end of religious services, pastors typically bestow a _____ on their congregations to wish them well.
5. An interesting specialty within the field of science is _____, the study of the effects of time on biological rhythms.
6. Soon after graduating from a prestigious business school, Armando was fortunate to secure a _____, a wealthy financier who wanted to give him a good start toward making an ambitious business plan a reality.

7. Anyone in the medical field must know how to _____ an unconscious person.
8. A _____ is someone who makes or does evil.
9. After a long day at an amusement park, Aunt Wendee thought a nap and an ice cream cone would _____ three-year-old Caroline.
10. To _____ property means doing damage to it.

Glossaries

If you encounter a new word while you are reading a textbook, you are in luck. Most quality textbooks contain a **glossary**—a concise list of key words and their definitions in the back of the book. The advantage of using a glossary before turning to a dictionary is twofold: (1) It is convenient; and (2) it will define the word as it is being used in the field of study.

PRACTICE 2-11	Using a Glossary

Directions: Use the glossary provided at the back of this book to define the following terms introduced in this chapter.

1. **Comprehension:** _____

   _____

2. **Surveying:** _____

   _____

3. **Jargon:** _____

4. **Context clues:** _____

Dictionaries

Dictionaries, both online and in print, contain lists of words and their meanings organized alphabetically. Besides providing information on correct spelling, pronunciation, and definitions, they also include the following features to provide a more accurate and thorough understanding of words:

- **Guide words.** These are words at the top of each page of a print dictionary that indicate the range of words located on that page.
- **Information on etymology.** Details about the origins and history of words.
- **Information about syllabification.** Dots, dashes, or slashes are used to show how words break down into units or syllables.
- **Information on part of speech.** Abbreviations are used after words to show their part of speech, for example, noun (n.), verb (v., vt.), adjective (adj.), etc.
- **Spelling modifications.** Changes in spelling are often included to show what happens when a suffix is added to a word: for example, the plural of *puppy* is *puppies*.

Here is an example of a dictionary entry from Merriam-Webster's Collegiate® Dictionary, 11th Edition, www.m-w.com.

gap
Pronunciation: \gap\
Function: *noun*

Etymology: Middle English, from Old Norse, chasm, hole; akin to Old Norse
gapa to gape
Date: 14th century
1 a: a break in a barrier (as a wall, hedge, or line of military defense) **b**: an assailable position
2 a: a mountain pass **b**: Ravine
3: Spark Gap
4 a: a separation in space **b**: an incomplete or deficient area <a *gap* in her knowledge>
5: a break in continuity: Hiatus
6: a break in the vascular cylinder of a plant where a vascular trace departs from the central cylinder
7: lack of balance: Disparity <the *gap* between imports and exports>
8: a wide difference in character or attitude <the generation *gap*>
9: a problem caused by some disparity <a communication *gap*> <credibility *gap*>

Using a Dictionary	**PRACTICE 2-12**

Directions: Use the example dictionary entry to answer the following questions about the word *gap*, as it is used in the passage below.

Women received about three-fifths of what men received for similar work. However, as we mentioned previously, the **gap** is closing as more women attend college and abandon lower-paying professions (such as teaching) for more lucrative employment in business, engineering, and the sciences.

1. What part of speech is the word *gap*? _____
2. What is known about the etymology of the word *gap*?

   _____

3. How many meanings are given for the word gap? _____
4. Which definition of *gap* explains the meaning of the word as it is used in the example sentence? _____

Real-World Mistakes of Comprehension and Their Consequences

In Chapter 1, you read that failing to think critically could result in serious consequences. When people are unable to apply critical thinking skills to a reading, a misunderstanding or failure to comprehend could result. Most of us have heard of real-world consequences of poor comprehension. Perhaps you have gotten a question wrong on an important exam because you neglected to read the directions carefully. Or you got involved in a house project and had to stop in the middle to run out to a hardware store because you did not realize what tools were required to complete it. Some incidents involving people misunderstanding directions are more serious than others, and errors in comprehension can cost time and money and could put you or others in danger. Even the small amount of reading required to decipher the label on a medicine bottle can pose alarming challenges.

A study by Dr. Michael Wolf revealed that nearly half of the study participants did not understand at least one out of five prescription labels. Even more distressing were those with low literacy rates who were unable to comprehend instructions on four out of five labels on medication bottles. Wolf believes some patients mix up the numbers on the label (reversing, for example, the number of doses per day with the number of days the medicine should be taken). The problem is significant: In July 2006, the Institute of Medicine stated that 1.5 million patients suffer some injury each year due to medication mistakes.

As might be expected, patients for whom English is a second language are especially vulnerable to these types of comprehension errors. A survey of 592 ESL speakers revealed some worrisome statistics: Almost 10 percent incorrectly gave medication to their children; one-third acknowledged confusion due to the language barrier that existed between themselves and their doctors; 17 percent performed an activity that should have been avoided while they were on medication; and 28 percent literally guessed at the dosage amount because they could not read the prescription label.

A well-meaning attempt to improve comprehension of pharmaceutical labels resulted in the creation of colorful warning labels consisting of both text and images. However, studies have shown that these, too, can be misunderstood. In *The New York Times*, Deborah Franklin writes, "You might see, for example, a red sticker depicting a gushing faucet, with a message in fine print that reads, 'MEDICATION SHOULD BE TAKEN WITH PLENTY OF WATER.' But, how much is plenty? Would a cup of coffee be acceptable instead?" The vague phrasing might not be enough to help patients who already have questions about administering medication. Yet another example mentioned in Franklin's article refers to a common warning sticker: "The 'FOR EXTERNAL USE ONLY' sticker stumped 25 percent of even those who could read every word, and misled 90 percent of the adults in the lowest literacy group."

Medication mistakes can occur during any step of the process (prescribing, dispensing, and administering). In other words, it is not just the patient who is to blame for comprehension errors; medical professionals, pharmacists, and caregivers, too, can misunderstand directions. These lapses in comprehension could, in part, be prevented through the use of some of the strategies mentioned in this chapter such as reading aloud and developing vocabulary, not to mention recalling that comprehension requires careful attention and time.

For Discussion

1. Explain how the mistakes discussed above qualify as a failure of comprehension.
2. What actions could doctors, pharmacists, patients, and caregivers take to minimize the likelihood of these mistakes?

*The topic of the paragraph you encountered earlier in the chapter (in "Identifying the Topic") was unclear because it lacked a title and key words. The topic is *playing with a Barbie dollhouse*. Reread the paragraph in the shaded box below and see if it now makes sense.

First, Anne tried moving the piano into the kitchen, but it did not fit. While she liked the look of the sofa in the master bedroom it was really better suited for the baby's room, so she moved it as well. It was frustrating to her that the water in the sink and bathtub did not work, but she tried all of the faucets again anyway to no avail. The colors pink and purple were dominant in every room. In Anne's humble opinion, the pink shutters did nothing for the exterior of the house, but that was nothing a little crayon couldn't help.

Real-World Successes of Critical Thinking

Helen Keller

You just read about a serious result of failing to think critically, but people who succeed at thinking critically can achieve great success. An example of a person who mastered comprehension despite seemingly insurmountable obstacles was Helen Keller (1880–1968), who was both blind and deaf.

Directions: Using the Internet or a library, research Helen Keller in depth. Prepare a detailed description of how Helen Keller achieved comprehension of the world around her and what she was able to accomplish as a result. Include an explanation of any skills, character traits, and standards of critical thinking that contributed to her success. Get ready to share your findings with the class.

Chapter Summary

- **Comprehension** is a knowledge and understanding of information. Grasping information is a vital step toward becoming a critical reader and thinker.

- The trait of **curiosity** is defined as inquisitiveness: the desire to learn more and to seek new learning opportunities.

- Becoming a better reader involves thinking about your reading experiences and figuring out what strategies work best for you.

- The **topic** is the subject or general idea of a book, story, conversation, article, movie, and so on. Typically, the topic can be stated in a word or short phrase; in a text, the topic is frequently identified in the title or in key terms that are repeated throughout the reading.

- The strategy of **surveying** aids comprehension by activating your prior knowledge and giving you an overview of what to expect in a reading. *Surveying* involves looking over the text for visual cues and textual aids, reading portions of the text such as introductions and summaries (if provided), and formulating questions that you expect the reading will answer. **Predicting** is a strategy that helps to ensure comprehension by keeping you engaged in the text; when you predict, you make guesses about what may come next in the text.

- There are several ways you can develop your vocabulary. Using **context clues**, **word parts, dictionaries**, and **glossaries**, you can learn new words which will help you become a more effective reader. Context clues include **definitions, synonyms, antonyms**, and **examples**; word parts include **roots, prefixes**, and **suffixes**.

READ, WRITE, AND THINK CRITICALLY: SECTION TWO

Directions: Survey this selection from a human development textbook. Do not read the selection yet. Instead, answer the questions below prior to reading the text.

1. What is the topic?

   _____

   _____

   _____

2. What is your prior knowledge about this topic?

   _____

   _____

   _____

3. Make a prediction about the content.

   _____

   _____

   _____

4. Read the first paragraph, and write a question that you expect will be answered in the text that follows.

   _____

   Now, read the selection and be prepared to answer additional questions once you are done reading.

Use All of Your Senses

When studying, try to use as many different sensory channels as possible. Research shows that information that's perceived through multiple sensory modalities or channels is remembered better (Bjork, 1994; Schacter, 1992) because it forms more interconnections in long-term memory areas of the brain (Zull, 2002). When a memory is formed in the brain, different sensory aspects of it are stored in different areas. For example, when your brain receives visual, auditory (hearing), and motor (movement) stimulation that accompany with what you're learning, each of these associations is stored in a different part of the brain. See **Figure 2-2** for a map of the surface of the human brain; you can see how different parts of the brain are specialized to receive input from different sensory modalities. When you use all of these sensory modalities while learning, multiple "memory traces" of what you're studying are recorded in different parts of your brain, which leads to deeper learning and stronger memory (Education Commission of the States, 1996).

Listed here are some major channels through which learning occurs and memories are stored, along with specific strategies for using each of these channels while studying.

Visual Learning

The human brain consists of two hemispheres (half rounds): the left and the right hemispheres (See **Figure 2-3**).

Each hemisphere of the brain specializes in different types of learning. In most people, the left hemisphere specializes in verbal learning, dealing primarily with words. In contrast, the right hemisphere specializes in visual–spatial learning, dealing primarily with images and objects that occupy physical space. If you use both hemispheres while studying, you lay down two different memory traces (tracks) in your brain: one in the left hemisphere, where words are stored, and one in the right hemisphere, where images are stored. This process of laying down a double memory trace (verbal and visual) is referred to as dual coding (Paivio, 1990). When this happens, memory for what you're learning is substantially strengthened, primarily because two memory traces are better than one.

To capitalize on the advantage of dual coding, use any visual aids that are available to you. Use the visual aids provided in your textbook and by your instructor, or create your own by drawing pictures, symbols, and concept maps, such as flowcharts or branching tree diagrams. See **Figure 2-4** for a concept map that could be used to help you remember the parts and functions of the human nervous system.

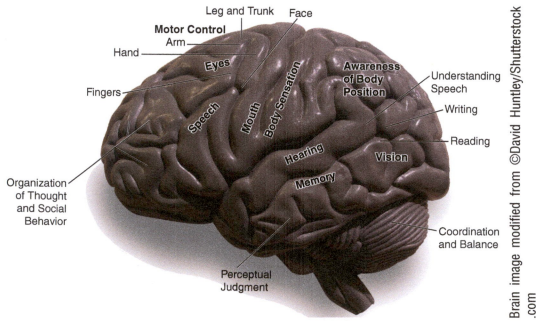

■ **Figure 2-2**   A "Map" of the Functions Performed by the Outer Surface of the Human Brain

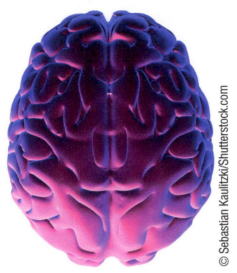

■ **Figure 2-3** The Human Brain Consists of Two Halves, Known as the Left Hemisphere and the Right Hemisphere

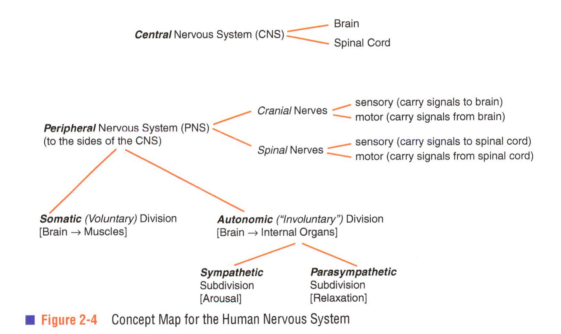

■ **Figure 2-4** Concept Map for the Human Nervous System

Drawing and other forms of visual illustration are not just artistic exercises; they also can be powerful learning tools (i.e., you can draw to learn). Drawing keeps you actively involved with the material you're trying to learn. By representing the material in visual form, you're able to dual-code the information you're studying, thus doubling its number of memory traces in your brain. As the old saying goes, "A picture is worth a thousand words."

Directions: Answer the following questions, using information you learned from surveying and predicting.

5. You made a prediction about what you would learn in this selection in question 3. Was your prediction correct? _____ (yes/no) If not, then what did you learn instead?

_____

_____

6. What did you learn from the first visual aid (Figure 2-2)?

_____

_____

_____

7. What is the answer to the question you came up with in question 4?

_____

_____

8. Define these words from the selection by using context clues or a dictionary.
   Perceived (para. 1) _____
   Stimulation (para. 1) _____
   Modalities (para. 1) _____
   Substantially (para. 3) _____
   Capitalize (para. 4) _____

CHAPTER 3

Interpretation

Learning Goals

In this chapter you will learn how to

➤ Interpret What You Read   SECTION ONE

➤ Be Intellectually Humble

➤ Determine Significance

➤ Identify Main Ideas and Details

➤ Annotate Readings   SECTION TWO

➤ Clarify Meaning

➤ Decipher Ambiguous Language

➤ Outline and Map

PREVIEW OF TERMS

Interpretation p. 61

Humility p. 62

Significance p. 64

Relevance p. 64

Main idea p. 65

Major detail p. 65

Minor detail p. 65

Thesis p. 65

Topic sentence p. 65

Transition p. 66

Emotive words p. 68

Details p. 71

Stated main idea p. 73

Implied main idea p. 73

Annotating p. 84

Clarifying meaning p. 86

Summarizing p. 86

Paraphrasing p. 89

Vagueness p. 93

Simile p. 93

Metaphor p. 93

Ambiguity p. 94

Equivocation p. 94

Euphemism p. 96

Irony p. 96

Doublespeak p. 96

Framing p. 96

Outline p. 99

Formal outline p. 99

Informal outline p. 100

Mapping p. 100

Webbing p. 100

See glossary, pp. 391–397

SECTION ONE

What Is Interpretation?

You are probably familiar with the role of an interpreter (for a hearing-impaired person or for someone who speaks another language, for instance): a person who has the job of making meaning clear so that effective communication can take place. **Interpretation** means taking in information, identifying what is most important, working out what is confusing, and verifying that you have grasped the author's or speaker's message. When, in your role of critical reader, you apply the skill of interpretation to written texts, you will make sense of information by identifying main ideas and details, by annotating, by making language clearer, and by putting material into categories. Before you learn how to interpret, though, it's important to remember to be intellectually humble.

Reviewing the Critical Thinker's Traits: Humility

Complete the following exercise to see how much you know.

PRACTICE 3-1   **Test Your Knowledge**

Directions: On a sheet of paper, answer the following questions. Don't look up the answers; use your own knowledge.

1. Why does sugar make children "hyper"?
2. Why are there more crimes during a full moon?
3. Why does reading in dim light ruin your eyesight?
4. Why is it necessary to wait 30 minutes after eating before you go swimming?
5. Why does shaving make hair grow back darker and thicker?
6. Why do you get sleepier after eating turkey than you do after eating other foods?
7. Why was Christopher Columbus brave enough to try to sail around the world when the other educated people of his day believed the world was flat?

Thinker to Emulate: Socrates

© Stefanel/Shutterstock.com

The Greek philosopher Socrates was born around 470 BCE. Socrates didn't write anything himself; we only know of him through various writers of his day, the most famous of whom was Plato. Possibly working as a stonemason, Socrates spent his entire life in the city of Athens. He only left for a brief time to serve in the military, where he distinguished himself for bravery. He continued to display bravery over the years, twice risking his life to resist unlawful demands from those in power. He spent most of his time discussing philosophy, seeking truth, and goading the Athenians about what he saw as their immoral lifestyle. He was ultimately brought to trial for corrupting the youth (by teaching them to think critically) and was sentenced to death. Socrates decided to drink poison rather than flee or be exiled from Athens in 399 BCE.

> **❝** I know nothing except the fact of my ignorance. **❞**
>
> —Socrates

Here's a riddle: When does not knowing anything make you the smartest person around?

Answer: When you are aware of your lack of knowledge.

In ancient Greece, the philosopher Socrates was pronounced the wisest of all human beings by an oracle (a priest that the gods were said to have spoken through). This puzzled Socrates, because he had spent his whole life developing his *intellectual* **humility**, an awareness of how much he *didn't know* and how often he was actually wrong when he thought he was right. So Socrates set off to discover what the oracle truly meant. He questioned the famous people of Athens, the city he lived in, to discover if anyone was wiser than he was. To his surprise, he discovered that, paradoxically, the oracle was right. None of the people he questioned seemed to know what they said they knew. So Socrates really was the wisest, because he had one advantage that was both small and incredibly significant at the same time: While he didn't know anything either, he at least *knew that he didn't know.* The other prominent citizens of Athens weren't aware of their own ignorance. They didn't know that they didn't know.

Discussion Questions

1. Is Socrates' wisdom a true kind of wisdom?
2. What advantage did Socrates have over the other citizens of Athens? Did Socrates do the other citizens a favor by showing them their lack of knowledge, or was he merely being a nuisance?

THINK AND WRITE CRITICALLY

EXPAND YOUR UNDERSTANDING

Learning More about Socrates while Writing Critically: Many scholars consider Socrates to be the father of critical thinking. Using the library or the Internet, find out more about Socrates; focus on *Socratic Irony*, the *Socratic Method*, and Socrates' death. Why might people consider Socrates so important to the history of critical thought? Write an essay that details your findings.

Although it doesn't hurt to know lots of information, being a critical thinker is not really about how much you know. The wisest people are aware of where their expertise lies, and just how much they don't know. With the vast amount of knowledge that exists today, no single person can possess even a small portion of it.

Measure of Belief

How likely is it that a particular belief is true?

How true is the belief?

	1	2	3	4	5	
Definitely NOT true	○	○	○	○	○	Definitely true

Remember the Likert scale introduced in the first chapter as a way to measure your level of belief in a claim? If you do not know much about the topic, you simply won't know whether or not you believe in it! Intellectually humble thinkers are comfortable with admitting they do not know and cannot commit to the extremes of saying the claim is *definitely true* or *definitely not true* (perhaps putting themselves at a "3" on the scale). They can then research to find out more and see where the evidence leads.

Now stop and review your answers to Practice 3-1. Did you spend time trying to explain why any of the assertions are true? Actually, every single statement is false. These are common myths, and you have probably heard one or all of them expressed as a fact at some point in your life. The point of the exercise is to show that, in many cases, what you think you know is simply wrong. A lot of false information is out there, and thinking critically is the only way to sort out what is true from what isn't.

People who are intellectually humble are not afraid to admit when they don't know something or to admit when they are wrong. They appreciate it when someone else corrects their mistakes. After all, even though it can be hard to find out you are wrong, the person who corrects your mistakes does you a great favor—gets you closer to the truth.

Tips for Critical Thinkers: How to Be Intellectually Humble

- **Start by reminding yourself of times you have been wrong in the past.** This should help you remember that you might be wrong in the current situation.
- **Think about how much false information is out there, and how difficult it is to separate truth from falsehood.** Think about something you once believed that you no longer do.
- **Be aware of how your worldviews, experiences, and upbringing can cloud your judgment.** It's hard to see past our own worldviews, so we need to work to keep them from getting in the way of our reasoning.
- **Resist the urge to claim knowledge that you don't have.** There's no shame in not knowing something. If you don't have enough information, reserve judgment until you find out what you need to know.

- **Don't be afraid of being wrong and admitting it.** Remember that admitting you are wrong provides you with the opportunity to learn what is true.
- **Make sure your conclusions are tentative.** Be flexible (as we will discuss in Chapter 4); leave open the possibility of changing your conclusions when you learn new things.

PRACTICE 3-2	Displaying Intellectual Humility

Directions: Respond to the following prompts on a separate sheet of paper.

THINK
AND **WRITE**
CRITICALLY

1. Write down all of the classes you have taken in the last year. Now rank them in order of your personal expertise: First, list the subject you know the most about, and last, the subject you know the least about. In what way could believing that you're an expert cause you to do badly in your best subject? Could your awareness of your weakness in your worst subject actually help you? If so, how?
2. Have you ever known you were wrong during an argument but refused to admit it? Explain the situation, including what you were wrong about. How might the situation have ended differently if you had admitted your error up front?

Spotlight on Standards: Significance

Critical thinkers have certain standards when they look at information. In other words, it matters greatly that the information under consideration is accurate, complete, fair, relevant, clear, and significant. In this chapter on interpretation, in which we look at ways to pull out the most important information from the text, we will focus on **significance**. Obviously, when you are trying to arrive at a belief that is more likely to be true or to make a good decision, some pieces of information are more important (or significant) than other pieces of information. The evidence that is more significant should carry more weight than the evidence that isn't as important. For example, say you are trying to decide which car to purchase. You have narrowed your choice down to two vehicles made by two different automobile makers. You remember that your parents always buy cars made by the first automobile maker, and you want to please your parents. However, you read an article published by AAA (which you know strives to give accurate and balanced information about automobiles and traveling) that cites a study of thousands of cars, and, unfortunately, the study brings to light some serious safety concerns regarding the cars made by the company favored by your parents. Which piece of information is more significant: your parents' opinion or the study reported on by AAA? A critical thinker will recognize that the study done on thousands of vehicles is more significant than loyalty to the parents' favored automobile maker. In this case, the critical thinker will chose the second car or will continue to research other models.

Determining Significance

Determining significance is a large part of interpretation. **Significance**, one of the standards that you learned about in Chapter 1, refers to how important something is to a discussion, a text, an issue, or an argument. You've heard of a "significant other"—a person intimately close to another person—so if something is *significant*, it means that it is extremely close and central to the subject. Depending on the context, some information will not be important and other information will be essential; by thinking critically, you can figure out what is important and what isn't.

Related to significance is **relevance**—how closely related the information is to the issue at hand. You also learned about relevance in Chapter 1 when you found out what standards critical thinkers will use to evaluate information. For instance, if an author is trying to prove that a flu vaccine is safe to give to the public, only certain information will help her do that. Types of side effects and kinds of potentially toxic chemicals included in the vaccine would be relevant. If she includes details about the cost of the vaccine, you would label that information irrelevant. When it comes to critically reading texts, determining significance and relevance involves figuring out the main idea of a text, and determining which details are more important and which are less important.

Identifying Main Ideas and Details

On p. 37 of Chapter 2, you saw how recognizing the topic of a selection helps with comprehension. Identifying the topic of a selection also helps lead you to other essential parts of the reading: the *main idea, major details*, and *minor details*.

The **main idea** is the most significant idea in a paragraph, article, or textbook chapter, and understanding the main idea is essential to comprehension and interpretation. Another way to think of the main idea is that it is the *claim* that the author makes about the topic. A **claim** is an assertion or statement that might be open to challenge or disagreement. The main idea is the most general idea in the piece or passage. **Major and minor details** are specific ideas that support, explain, and elaborate on the main idea, and as you will see, some details are more significant and relevant than others.

The main idea of a longer piece of writing (two or more paragraphs) is generally called a **thesis**. If the main idea of a paragraph is expressed directly, it is called a **topic sentence**. Not every paragraph will have a main idea, however; some paragraphs simply develop a description or idea established in a preceding paragraph. In fact, certain longer works, such as novels or plays, will not have a thesis. You will generally find a thesis in a piece of informative or persuasive writing.

To identify the main idea of a selection, follow these four steps:

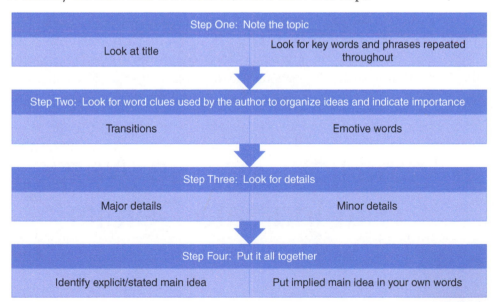

Step One: Note the Topic

In Chapter 2, you learned that the topic is the subject of the passage and is typically stated in a short word or phrase. Now, your main goal is to find out what it is that the author is claiming or stating about the topic. This is also known as the *controlling idea*, what everything in the piece relates to both directly and indirectly.

Reminder

See Chapter 2, pp. 37–41 to practice identifying the topic of a selection. Ideally, you will be able to state the topic in a short word or phrase, and it will be neither too broad nor too specific but will be "just right."

To help you understand what a main idea is, keep in mind that various authors might write about the same topic but will have different opinions about it and, therefore, express different main ideas. Here is an example:

Topic: *Reality television shows*

Author 1: "Reality television shows reflect what is wrong with society; people are narcissistic and attention-seeking."

Author 2: "Reality television shows are inspirational in their portrayal of real people experiencing real challenges."

Author 3: "Reality television shows have many benefits over scripted dramas and comedies."

Author 4: "Reality television shows are damaging to children who expect to acquire fame despite having little to no talent."

So, in step one you should be able to state the topic of a passage clearly and concisely. Remember, the topic should be a word or short phrase that is neither too general or broad nor too specific or narrow. In the example above, the stated topic is "reality television shows" (just right), whereas "television shows" would be too broad and "reality TV stars' fame" would be too specific. In this first step, you may also start to get a sense about how the author treats the topic throughout the passage. You might, for example, get a general sense about whether the author is approving, disapproving, or neutral toward the topic.

Step Two: Look for Word Clues That the Author Uses to Organize Ideas and Indicate Importance

Transitions and emotive words will give you clues as to what authors judge to be important and how they organize their thoughts.

Transitions **Transitions** are words that suggest the level of importance of what is being discussed or indicate an author's shift in direction or focus. Transitions, both within individual sentences and within entire paragraphs, assist the reader in comprehension and interpretation.

Authors often make a point to use transition words that will direct the reader to the significant details in a passage. Transitions help to establish organizational patterns such as

Transitions or Cue Words That Indicate Details

Chronological Order:	Comparison:	Contrast:	Classification:	Examples or illustration:	Listing:	Cause and Effect:
First, second, last, finally, later, soon, next, afterwards, subsequently, when, during, eventually, since	In comparison, like, similar, as, in much the same way, both	But, in contrast, unlike, different, instead, on the other hand, however	Categorize, characteristics, types, traits, classes	One reason, another point, for example, in this case, to illustrate, including, to explain, in such instances, specifically, especially, such as, some, few, one, many	Also, in addition, another, moreover, furthermore, besides	Causes, reasons, effects, results, happens, because, since, source, becomes, consequence, outcome

■ **Figure 3-1** Transitions That Indicate Details

chronological order, comparison/contrast, classification, examples or illustration, and *listing.* See Figure 3-1 for a list of commonly used transitions that tend to indicate details.

Sometimes authors will even use transitions that act as arrows pointing directly to main ideas. These types of transitions signal *emphasis or level of importance.* When you come across a transition that indicates a conclusion, claim, main idea, or thesis (such as *in conclusion* and *therefore*), take note: The statement that follows such a transition is likely to be the main idea. See Figure 3-2 for transitions indicating main ideas.

Keep in mind, however, that authors will exhibit personal preferences regarding how few or how many transitions they like to use. Some details and main ideas are simply mentioned in a reading without any introduction by a transition.

Transitions or Cue Words That Indicate Main Ideas

Emphasis: Above all, in fact, without a doubt

Conclusions: In conclusion, in summary, therefore

■ **Figure 3-2**   Transitions That Indicate Main Ideas

Recognizing Transitions   PRACTICE 3-3

Directions: Underline the transitions in the following sentences. Above the transition, write what type of transition it is.

Here's a model

example
You ought to be more conscientious; <u>specifically</u>, you should always be punctual.

Now you try

1. Unlike previous wars, the Gulf War was not a long conflict.

2. Another short engagement was the 1983 Lebanon conflict.

3. It was not, however, technically a war, since war was never declared.

4. One reason war was not officially declared is that the U.S. forces were there to assist the Lebanese.

5. The Lebanese conflict started small, but eventually 1,200 Marines were deployed.

6. The 1983 invasion of Grenada was without a doubt the result of Cold War politics.

7. The invasion of Grenada was heavily criticized by the United Nations, but the action was heavily supported by the U.S. population.

8. Moreover, the invasion of Grenada represented the first time that a government had returned to democracy after going communist.

9. Since friendly fire killed U.S. troops during this conflict, some changes were made in defensive policy.

10. Afterwards, the U.S. Special Operations Command was formed.

Emotive Words Like transitions, emotive words can serve as clues to the author's attitude toward the topic. **Emotive words** are words that express opinion, judgment, or emotion. An examination of the emotive words selected by an author provides readers with clues into an author's opinion or claim about a topic. (See Figure 3-3 for a list of commonly used emotive words.)

Similar to transitions, emotive words give you an insight into the thinking process of the author. When an author uses a *superlative* like "best," an *aesthetic* word like "attractive," a word expressing *judgment* like "bad," or a word making a *recommendation* like "should," you should recognize these words for what they express: opinions.

Superlatives	Most, least, best, worst, highest, greatest
Aesthetic	Beautiful, lovely, ugly, hideous
Judgment	Poor, pathetic, amazing, important, bad, good, advantages, disadvantages
Recommendation	Must, should, might, can, ought to, obliged to, could

■ **Figure 3-3**   Common Emotive Words

PRACTICE 3-4   Recognizing Emotive Words

Directions: Underline the emotive words in the following sentences. Above the emotive word, write what type of emotive word it is.

Here's a model

                                        aesthetic
The Wicked Witch of the West is actually not that <u>ugly</u>, if you look closely.

Now You Try

1. Traveling the world is definitely something you should do.

2. You will see some of the most beautiful, breathtaking sights you will ever behold.

3. The Great Pyramid of Giza is an amazing landmark that has existed for thousands of years.

© Dan Beckwoldt/ Shutterstock.com

4. If you visit it, you should go inside the pyramid to see the incredible passages dug in it.

5. Another one of the best places to visit is the lovely city of Paris in France.

6. This city has too many sights to name, and one disadvantage to the city is that it would take many trips to see it all.

7. But if you can only go to Paris once, you must see the Eiffel Tower and the Louvre.

8. The Eiffel Tower is amazingly tall, and when it is lit up at night, it looks glorious.

9. The Louvre is an important museum that houses many stunning pieces of art, such as the Mona Lisa.

10. No matter where you go, you ought to make it a point to see the world.

Step Three: Look for Details

Authors use **details** to support, develop, and elaborate upon the main idea. They answer the reporter's questions (who, what, where, when, why, and how) and come in a variety of forms:

Form of Detail	Definition	Example
Anecdote	Short story—often an interesting incident; can be biographical	"Trying out for *The Voice* was both the best and worst experience of my life! Besides meeting judges Christina Aguilera and Blake Shelton…." (story continues)
Example	A situation, occurrence, or item that is representative of the subject being discussed	"Some reality TV show stars disappear after the season ends, yet others become hugely successful. As examples of the hugely successful sort, imagine the bank accounts of former *American Idol* contestants Kelly Clarkson and Carrie Underwood!"
Fact	Information that can be objectively verified	"*The Real Housewives* franchise started in 2006 in Orange County, California and has spread far beyond the borders of the United States with such international locations as Athens, Melbourne, and Vancouver."
Figure	Quantifiable number, statistic	Over 90% of television viewers have watched some sort of reality TV programming."
Quotation	Words spoken or written by someone else	"An expert in media studies claims, 'Today's adolescents, unfortunately, shape their career aspirations after the popular reality shows of the day.'"
Reason	Something offered in explanation	"One reason viewers watch reality TV is because they enjoy having people to root for as well as people to hate."
Result	A consequence or effect of a given cause	"A positive result of watching reality TV occurs when viewers become inspired to make a change in their lives."

The form that some details take can depend on the role they are serving in the selection. For example, the sentence "Ninety percent of people who smoke develop some health problem" could be a statistic, or it could be a reason why the person writing the sentence chooses not to smoke.

| **PRACTICE 3-5** | **Determining the Form of Details** |

Directions: Read the following paragraph. The main idea is double-underlined for you, and the remaining sentences each contain a detail that supports the main idea. For each of the details listed below the paragraph, write which form they take: *anecdote, example, fact, figure, quotation, reason,* or *result*. Each form is used only once.

Today I went to my mailbox, sorted through the bills and the catalogs, and was pleasantly surprised to find something quaint and old-fashioned: a hand-written thank you note. I turned it over, examined the hand-writing in blue ink that spelled out my name and address, and felt instantly cherished. People just don't seem to send hand-written letters anymore, so receiving one is an occasion to be noted. <u><u>Many changes have occurred in communication from the early days of the U.S. Postal Service to the electronic means of communication we favor today.</u></u> In the 21st century, email has definitely surpassed the hand-written letter as the major means of written communication. An obvious reason people prefer email over so-called snail mail is convenience. Often, those who will bother to write an actual letter will be a bit old-fashioned themselves; for example, your grandmother and your next-door neighbor are more likely to take pen to paper than to log on and send a hasty email. We take for granted that we can get an email almost instantaneously from across the globe and almost forget how times have changed. The U.S. Postal Service was started in 1792, and the Pony Express ran from 1860–1861. From 2011 to 2012, revenue earned by the U.S. Postal Service for delivery of first-class mail declined 3.1% during its first quarter. This decrease is largely due to the popularity of email. My own mailman recently said, "Don't tell anybody, but I prefer email myself!"

1. Today I went to my mailbox, sorted through the bills and the catalogs, and was pleasantly surprised to find something that seemed quaint and old-fashioned: a hand-written thank you note. I turned it over, examined the hand-writing in blue ink that spelled out my name and address, and felt instantly cherished.

   _____

2. An obvious reason people prefer email over so-called snail mail is convenience.

   _____

3. Often, those who will bother to write an actual letter will be a bit old-fashioned themselves; for example, your grandmother and your next-door neighbor are more likely to take pen to paper than to log on and send a hasty email.

   _____

4. The U.S. Postal Service was started in 1792, and the Pony Express ran from 1860–1861.

   _____

5. From 2011 to 2012, revenue earned by the U.S. Postal Service for delivery of first-class mail declined 3.1% during its first quarter.

   _____

6. This decrease is largely due to the popularity of email.

   _____

7. My own mailman recently said, "Don't tell anybody, but I prefer email myself!"

   _____

As noted in Step Two, many transitions specifically point you in the direction of details: *first reason, second point, one fact, another result, an important detail*. As you look for the main idea, you want to identify the details in the following two ways:

1. Notice information that comes in the form of an anecdote, example, fact, figure, quotation, reason, or result.
2. Look at the information that follows transitions that tend to introduce details. Authors purposefully select details that support and develop their main idea. Once you identify the details, you can see how they start to add up to give you an overall impression that the author wants you to get about the topic.

Distinguishing between Major and Minor Details

Once you have identified the details, determining which details are most significant and relevant in supporting the author's message will help you identify the controlling idea. There are two kinds of details: *major details* and *minor details*. If the most general statement or idea in the passage is the controlling or main idea, then the major details have a moderate level of specificity—they are medium-specific. The minor details tend to be very specific—in fact, they are sometimes too specific to be particularly relevant or significant to the larger message as a whole. They merely develop the major details or make the writing more interesting. Consider the following example passage:

> Without a doubt, an irony of a vacation is that it is frequently planned as a way to relieve stress, but, unfortunately, it often becomes its own tremendous source of stress. Vacations are costly and difficult to arrange for most working families, and they are fraught with unexpected hassles. A one-way ticket to Florida often costs more than $300, and one has to pay to check bags these days.

The first sentence is the most general sentence in the passage. You might already be forming the notion that it is the main idea. The second sentence is more specific than the first sentence, but it is not as specific as the third. The third sentence is very specific, mentioning place names and prices. To understand and remember this passage, you need to note the major detail it gives—that vacations are expensive hassles—because this detail will be most relevant to establishing and supporting the controlling idea. You do not need to remember, though, that a ticket to Florida costs $300. That's a minor detail.

Distinguishing between Major and Minor Details   PRACTICE 3-6

Directions: In the following passages, sentences are numbered (and, in some cases, portions of a sentence are numbered). The main idea is double-underlined for you. Circle the transitions and emotive words. On the lines below each passage, write the number(s) corresponding to the sentence(s) that contain major details. Then, write the number(s) that correspond to the sentence(s) that contain minor details.

Here's a model

> [1]Without a doubt, an irony of a vacation is that it is frequently planned as a way to relieve stress, but, unfortunately, it often becomes its own tremendous source of stress. [2]One source of stress is due to expectations because the image of an idyllic vacation day quickly degenerates into reality. [3]For instance, the land breeze brings horseflies onto the beach, and the city is ridiculously crowded and expensive. [4]The commercials that advertise cruises and Disney vacations always show smiling, relaxed families sharing good food and good times, but the reality is that

the commercials don't show people getting seasick on the cruise or standing in the inevitable long lines at Disney's theme parks. [5]Another source of stress is that vacations are costly and difficult to arrange for most working families. [6]The average family spends about $3,500 on vacation, and even if they try to resist the pull of the BlackBerry or the laptop, vacationers cannot fully relax knowing that work is piling up for them in their absence. [7]When I asked a frazzled traveler on the plane what her favorite part of the vacation was, she honestly responded, "Going home."

Major details: 2, 5

Minor details: 3, 4, 6, 7

Now you try

1. [1]A fortunate dog owner is the one who recognizes the many ways in which dogs enrich our lives. [2]First, dogs encourage us to get out and get fresh air and exercise. [3]While you may think you are just making your dog happy by going for a walk and throwing a Frisbee, in truth you are both benefitting from the cardiovascular workout. [4]If you have a dog that loves water like Labrador Retrievers do, you can spend happy hours throwing sticks along the beach for your pet to fetch. [5]In addition to the benefit of encouraging exercise, dogs are also famous for accepting us just as we are. [6]After spending all day trying to impress the boss, to keep up with the emails and phone calls, and to maintain peace with family members, it is wildly refreshing to have that wagging tail tell us that we can just be ourselves.

    Major details: _____

    Minor details: _____

2. [1]People can control illusions to achieve desired effects. [2]Architects and interior designers use principles of perception to create objects in space that seem larger or smaller than they really are. [3]A small apartment becomes more spacious when it is painted with light colors and sparsely furnished with low small couches, chairs, and tables in the center of the room instead of against the walls. [4]Psychologists working with NASA in the U.S. space program have researched the effects of environment on perception in order to design space capsules that have pleasant sensory qualities. [5]Set and lighting directors of movies and theatrical productions purposely create illusions on film and on stage.

    From *Psychology and Life* by Gerrig & Zimbardo

    Major details: _____
    Minor details: _____

3. [1]An *epithelium* (ep-i-THĒ-lē-um; plural, *epithelia*) is a sheet of cells that covers an exposed surface or lines an internal cavity or passageway. [2]Each epithelium is a barrier with specific properties. [3]Epithelia cover every exposed surface. [4]The surface of the skin is a good example, but epithelia also line the digestive, respiratory, reproductive, and urinary tracts—passageways that communicate with the outside world. [5]Epithelia also line internal cavities and passageways, [6]such as the chest cavity, fluid-filled chambers in the brain, eye, inner ear, and the inner surfaces of blood vessels and the heart.

    From *Human Anatomy* (6th ed.) by Martini et al.

    Major details: _____
    Minor details: _____

4. ¹Being able to fix cars is an incredibly useful skill with several benefits. ²The first of many benefits is the fact that, over the course of your lifetime, this skill will save you a great deal of money. ³A brake job can run upwards of $600, while the parts alone might only total $200. ⁴Second, if you can diagnose the problems with your own car, you can avoid being ripped off by unscrupulous mechanics. ⁵Who's to say that your car's Fram-shaft isn't broken, if you have no idea that such a thing doesn't even exist? ⁶Finally, you can use this skill to help others. ⁷When your favorite cousin or your best friend needs an oil change, you will feel good about being able to lend a hand.

Major details: _____

Minor details: _____

Step Four: Putting It All Together: Identifying Main Ideas

Recognizing the topic (Step One) is a good start toward identifying the main idea of a passage. Paying attention to transitions (Step Two), emotive words (Step Two), and details (Step Three) will help you determine what significant point the author is making about that topic. Step Four is when you put all this information together and clearly identify the main point an author is making about a topic. A good way to do this is to ask yourself the following questions and answer them based on what you have learned in steps one to three.

Questions to Ask to Identify Main Idea

- If I could only take away one piece of information from this passage, what would the author want it to be?
- What is the most important point the author makes about the topic?
- What is the author's attitude or approach toward the topic?
- What should I remember about this passage?

The most significant point of the piece is what the author wants you to remember, and that point is undoubtedly the main idea. After having gone through Steps One through Three, use the above questions as the final step in order to identify the main idea of a passage.

Stated and Implied Main Ideas   A **stated** or **explicit main idea** is a thesis that the author just comes out and says. In other words, when you can point to a single sentence in a paragraph or essay that functions as the main idea, it's a stated main idea. Remember, in a single paragraph, the stated main idea is called a topic sentence. In a longer passage (two or more paragraphs), it is referred to as a thesis statement.

In contrast to a stated main idea, an **implied main idea** is not written out in one clear, direct sentence. The author of a paragraph with an implied main idea (or a longer essay with an implied thesis) leaves it to you, the reader, to figure out the main idea by examining the major and minor details of the piece and the words the author has chosen. In particular, you should focus your attention on transition words, emotive words, and details in your attempt to identify an implied main idea.

In those pieces of writing with an implied main idea (or thesis if it is a longer passage), you can try to write the main idea (or thesis) in your own words in a single sentence in the margin of the text while you annotate the passage. Start with the topic, and then add to the topic a concise thought that establishes the author's opinion or attitude toward that topic.

Implied main idea

Although not everyone agrees on how to define reality television, it has undeniably made an impact on the culture.

Example of a Paragraph with an Implied Main Idea

What was the first reality television show? Some people might answer, *The Adventures of Ozzie and Harriet*. Others may say, *Candid Camera*. Still others might tell you, *The Real World*. How people define the term "reality TV show" varies considerably, but most people agree that it is a show featuring real people as opposed to professional actors and it is not scripted by writers. A history of reality television shows suggests that people enjoy watching average folks in funny or dramatic situations. Some people find reality TV to be shallow; others see it as harmless entertainment. These types of shows have become hugely popular and have made stars out of their participants. While people might not agree about which show was the first official reality TV show, most people will agree that reality TV is here to stay.

Use the following tips to help you identify the main idea of a paragraph or longer passage.

Tips for Critical Thinkers: How to Identify the Main Idea

Step One   Identify the topic in a word or short phrase.

Step Two   Highlight any transitions or emotive words: Pay special attention to transitions and emotive words that may suggest the author's attitude toward the topic.

Step Three   Look for details: Carefully examine the major and minor details that the author has included. Ask yourself how these details add up to an overall claim that the author wants convey.

Step Four   Put it all together by doing the following:

1. **Reread the paragraph and see if there is a topic sentence that explicitly states the main idea.** Topic sentences are frequently at the beginning and/or end of the paragraph, but they can also appear anywhere within the paragraph. If you locate the stated main idea in the form of a topic sentence, underline or highlight it.

2. **In a longer passage or essay, look for the main idea in the form of a thesis statement.** If it's a stated main idea, the thesis statement often appears at the end of the first, or introductory, paragraph but, like a topic sentence, it can appear anywhere throughout the passage. If the author states it directly, then underline or highlight it.

3. **Look for the most general idea or statement in the passage or piece;** this will likely be the stated main idea.

4. **To find the implied main idea, ask yourself questions** such as What is the most important thing to remember? and What does the author think or feel about the topic?

5. **If the main idea is implied**, write the claim the author is making about the topic in a concise sentence in the margin of your text.

Identifying the Stated Main Idea

Directions: Read the following paragraphs. Circle transitions and emotive words. Notice details. On the line next to each paragraph, identify which of the numbered sentences directly states the main idea.

Here's a model

__2__ [1]Typical American parents run their children to and from their multiple activities all week long, barely pausing for family dinners and leisurely play in the backyard. [2]Busy family members feel the effects of decreased family time. [3]Whereas kids used to be content to play, at most, a fall sport and a spring sport, it is not unusual now for them to squeeze soccer practice in after baseball practice all in a jam-packed Saturday afternoon. [4]These activities are not limited to sports: Children today have an array of after-school choices that include art, music, Scouts, chess, cooking, and foreign languages. [5]Some kids may not have the chance to get bored, which sounds like a good thing, yet the result is actually a decreased ability to be creative and make their own fun. [6]Given a free afternoon, some children don't know what to do with themselves without direction from their parents, teammates, or coaches. [7]Therefore, while there are advantages to giving children the opportunities to try new things, the distinct disadvantages of these over-scheduled lives are serious.

Now you try

1. _____ [1]Not everyone who is convicted of a crime and sentenced ends up in prison. [2]Some offenders are ordered to prison only to have their sentences suspended and a probationary term imposed. [3]They may also be ordered to perform community-service activities as a condition of their probation. [4]During the term of probation, these offenders are required to submit to supervision by a probation officer and to meet other conditions set by the court. [5]Failure to do so results in revocation of probation and imposition of the original prison sentence.

From *Criminal Justice Today* by Schmalleger

2. _____ [1]Throughout history, religion has been used to justify committing acts of extreme cruelty and violence against human beings. [2]Religious terrorism, especially that of al-Qaeda and other Islamic extremists, is widely perceived to be the most dangerous kind of terrorism, one that results in more destructive acts of indiscriminate violence. [3]There are four basic reasons for the extreme violence of religious terrorism:
   1. [4]Violence is believed to be a sacramental act or divine duty in accordance with theology;
   2. [5]Religious terrorists view large-scale and indiscriminate violence as necessary for achieving their goals;
   3. [6]Religious terrorists do not feel constrained by public opinion or a need to gain popular support because they are engaged in a total war; and
   4. [7]Religious terrorists generally believe that modifying the system is insufficient; they seek fundamental changes in the existing order.

From *Global Issues: Politics, Economics, and Culture* by Payne

3. _____ [1]Do you know anyone who has polio? [2]Rubella? [3]Tuberculosis? [4]Me neither. [5]We can thank vaccines for that. [6]Vaccines have been developed to protect people from diseases by increasing our immunity to them. [7]In the United States, vaccines have fortunately eradicated (did away with completely) a large number of diseases that at one time posed terrible threats to people. [8]For instance, polio used to cause significant suffering to people, including former President F.D. Roosevelt, yet the United States

has been polio-free since 1979 thanks to the vaccine created in 1955. [9]Once the deadliest of childhood illnesses, measles is considered eliminated in the United States, although people can still contract the disease if they travel to foreign countries and should, therefore, be properly vaccinated. [10]As yet another example, diphtheria used to cause breathing problems, comas, and death, yet the vaccine introduced in the 1920s has made it virtually unheard of in modern-day America.

4. _____ [1]Another memory-enhancing option is to draw on special mental strategies called mnemonics (from the Greek word meaning 'to remember'). [2]*Mnemonics* are devices that encode a long series of facts by associating them with familiar and previously encoded information. [3]Many mnemonics work by giving you ready-made retrieval cues that help organize otherwise arbitrary information.

—From *Psychology and Life* by Gerrig and Zimbardo

5. _____ [1]Today, unlike in the sport's early days, participants in Mixed Martial Arts (MMA) need to have both boxing and grappling skills. [2]Fast hands are extremely important, because one punch can knock out a competitor as he shoots in for a takedown. [3]Moreover, good footwork will ensure that he maintains good ring position. [4]But if he does not have grappling skills and is successfully taken down (as is likely to occur), he will be as helpless as a fish out of water if his opponent is a skilled grappler. [5]Woe to the competitor who steps into the ring only having mastered one of these skill sets.

6. _____ [1]A much more plausible explanation [than poverty] for the absence of baseball in Haiti is that Haitians developed lasting antipathy to this very American sport during the U.S. occupation of their country from 1915 to 1934, an "intervention" designed to protect America's interest in the recently opened Panama Canal. [2]According to Paul Farmer, historians estimate that 15,000 Haitians, most of them insurgents, were killed by American troops during this highly unpopular occupation, which lasted much longer than any other in Latin America, so Haitian resentment toward the United States and all things American ran deep for many years. [3]As a result, one might conclude, Haitians have never embraced baseball.

From "The Sports Dominance Mystery" by Stephen Sniderman

7. _____ [1]Most chess books teach that pawns are worth 1 point, knights and bishops 3, rooks 5, and the queen 9. [2]This point value is often accurate, but the skilled player knows that their worth actually varies depending on the state of play. [3]For example, in the early game, knights may be more valuable than bishops, because they are more maneuverable. [4]A pair of bishops in the endgame, with their ability to control both colors, becomes more valuable than a pair of knights. [5]In some instances, a queen should even be sacrificed if doing so puts one's opponent in a position from which he cannot recover.

8. _____ [1]Ancient people believed that the universe was born because of conflicts between various mythological deities. [2]Many modern folk ascribe the creation of the universe to their respective god; Christians, Jews, and Muslims believe that god created the universe in six days and then rested on the seventh day (although they don't always believe that these are literal 24-hour days). [3]Some modern scientists, such as Stephen Hawking, believe that the universe came to be literally out of nothing as the result of quantum fluctuations, a natural occurrence. [4]The actual cause behind the origin of the universe remains an open question.

9. _____ [1]Some people rely on clichés when they are communicating with others, yet the use of clichés that are no longer commonplace may cause confusion. [2]" A bird in the hand is worth two in the bush" may just elicit a raised eyebrow or a puzzled, "Huh?"

when you suggest that your friend take the first decent parking spot she can find in a crowded lot. [3]Answering your sister when she asks you if you want to go bowling or to the movies with "Six of one, half-dozen of the other" is also bound to result in a funny look. [4]"Measure twice and cut once" makes perfect sense, but you still might confuse your buddy who only wanted to know if he should look up the recipe for daiquiris or if he should just wing it.

10. _____ [1]A major reason for this [an increase in narcissism], the authors argue, is the exploding number of vehicles our culture provides to promote feelings of entitlement and habits of self-regard. [2]We have an entertainment industry that promotes the Kardashians as much as it does Meryl Streep, which disentangles success from talent and suggests we are all potential celebrities. [3]We have all manner of personal broadcasting systems at our disposal—Twitter, Facebook, YouTube—which lead us to believe that whatever we have to say has value. [4]For years, we've lived off unlimited credit, believing that we're entitled to things we can't afford and that the value of whatever we own—homes, 401(k)s, derivatives—can only go up. [5]We have customized entertainment (My.nbc, My.nytimes, My.yahoo), which makes us see the world as a child does, a place that curves to fit our needs and desires and opinions; the Internet has become less a portal into other worlds than a mirror of our own, or what Nicholas Negroponte at the MIT Media Lab famously calls 'The Daily Me.'

From "The Benjamin Button Election" by Jennifer Senior

Identifying the Implied Main Idea   PRACTICE 3-8

Directions: Read these paragraphs (some of which are from *Practice 2-4 Identifying the Topic*). Notice transitions, emotive words, and details. On the lines provided, write the implied main idea in your own words in a single sentence.

Here's a model

In order to reconstruct human evolution, human paleontologists search for and study the buried, hardened remains or impressions—known as *fossils*—of humans, prehumans, and related animals. Paleontologists working in East Africa, for instance, have excavated the fossil remains of human-like beings who lived more than 3 million years ago. These findings have suggested the approximate dates when our ancestors began to develop two-legged walking, very flexible hands, and a larger brain.

From *Human Evolution and Culture* by Ember, Ember, and Peregrine

Fossils show paleontologists how humans evolved and when they developed certain traits.

Now you try

1. In contrast with panic disorder, phobias involve a persistent and irrational fear of a specific object, activity, or situation—a response all out of proportion to the circumstances. (These are sometimes called *specific phobias*, as contrasted with the broader fears found in agoraphobia.) Many of us respond fearfully to certain stimuli, such as spiders or snakes—or perhaps to multiple-choice tests! But such emotional responses only qualify as full-fledged phobic disorders when they cause substantial disruption to our lives.

From *Psychology: Core Concepts* by Zimbardo, Johnson, and McCann

_____

_____

_____

2. Usually, students treat the meanings of words as "subjective" and "mysterious." I have my meanings of words, and you have your meanings of them. On this view, problems of meaning are settled by asking people for their personal definitions. What do *you* mean by "love," "hate," "democracy," "friendship," etc.? Each of us is then expected to come forward with a "personal definition." *My* definition of love is this . . . *My* definition of friendship is that. . . .

From *Critical Thinking* by Paul

_____

_____

_____

3. The only thing that flowed more than tea in those aisles was Afghan gossip. The flea market was where you sipped green tea with almond *kolchas*, and learned whose daughter had broken off an engagement and run off with her American boyfriend, who used to be *Parchami*—a communist—in Kabul, and who had bought a house with under-the-table money while still on welfare. Tea, Politics, and Scandal, the ingredients of an Afghan Sunday at the flea market.

From *The Kite Runner* by Hosseini

_____

_____

_____

4. Maycomb was an old town, but it was a tired old town when I first knew it. In rainy weather the streets turned to red slop; grass grew on the sidewalks, the courthouse sagged in the square. Somehow, it was hotter then: a black dog suffered on a summer's day; bony mules hitched to Hoover carts flicked flies in the sweltering shade of the live oaks on the square. Men's stiff collars wilted by nine in the morning. Ladies bathed before noon, after their three-o'clock naps, and by nightfall were like soft teacakes with frostings of sweat and sweet talcum.

From *To Kill a Mockingbird* by Lee

_____

_____

_____

5. Wade Boggs was one of the most proficient hitters in the history of baseball. He won the batting title five times and had a lifetime batting average of .363. He is also highly superstitious. Early on in his career he formed the belief that he could hit better after eating chicken. For that reason, he ate chicken almost every day for twenty years when he played baseball. He is not alone in his superstitious behavior. Wayne Gretzky, the great hockey star, always tucked in the right side of his jersey behind his hip pads. Jim Kelly, the Buffalo Bills quarterback, forced himself to vomit before every game. Bjorn Borg did not shave after he began to play in a major tennis tournament. Bill Parcells

would buy coffee from two different coffee shops before every game when he coached the New York Giants.

From *Don't Believe Everything You Think* by Kida

_____

_____

_____

6. Scientists have never been good about explaining what they do or how they do it. Like all human beings, though, they make mistakes, and sometimes abuse their power. The most cited of those abuses are the twins studies and other atrocities carried out by Nazi doctors under the supervision of Josef Mengele. While not as purely evil (because almost nothing could be), the most notorious event in American medical history occurred not long ago: from 1932 to 1972, in what became known as the Tuskegee Experiment, U.S. Public Health Service researchers refused to treat hundreds of poor, mostly illiterate African American sharecroppers for syphilis in order to get a better understanding of their disease. Acts of purposeful malevolence like those have been rare; the most subtle scientific tyranny of the elite has not been.

From *Denialism* by Specter

_____

_____

_____

7. As a society, we largely avoid political discussions in polite conversation, reserving them for relationships that can withstand a knock-down-drag-out fight—or with people whom we are actively working to alienate. If you're like us, you learned this lesson slowly and still forget it occasionally. You have also undoubtedly left an animated political "discussion" thinking two things about people at the other end of the political spectrum. The first is: Can they really believe that? The bad thinking behind others' beliefs often dismays us. How can they be so blind to the obvious? Their beliefs are clearly not rational, not logical, and perhaps not even sane.

From *The Time Paradox* by Zimbardo and Boyd

_____

_____

_____

8. Many people enjoy taking a leisurely stroll through a brightly colored garden teeming with flowers. Annuals, such as marigolds and petunias, are plants that bloom for only one season. In contrast to perennials, annuals will not come back year after year but must be replanted. While it is a bit labor-intensive to plant annuals each year, the advantage is that they tend to be vivid in color and can last the entire season if the blooms are pinched off periodically. Perennials such as delphiniums and daisies will return each year so long as the growing conditions remain good. Perennials tend to grow taller than annuals but do not last as long within the single season as annuals do.

_____

_____

_____

9. To Sherlock Holmes she is always THE woman. I have seldom heard him mention her under any other name. In his eyes she eclipses and predominates the whole of her sex. It was not that he felt any emotion akin to love for Irene Adler. All emotions, and that one particularly, were abhorrent to his cold, precise but admirably balanced mind. He was, I take it, the most perfect reasoning and observing machine that the world has seen, but as a lover he would have placed himself in a false position. He never spoke of the softer passions, save with a gibe and a sneer. They were admirable things for the observer—excellent for drawing the veil from men's motives and actions. But for the trained reasoned to admit such intrusions into his own delicate and finely adjusted temperament was to introduce a distracting factor which might throw a doubt upon all his mental results. Grit in a sensitive instrument, or a crack in one of his own high-power lenses, would not be more disturbing than a strong emotion in a nature such as his. And yet there was but one woman to him, and that woman was the late Irene Adler.

From *The Adventures of Sherlock Holmes* by Sir Arthur Conan Doyle

_____

_____

_____

10. It had always been a bit of a game—a game with no winners, but at least most people knew the rules. Officially, you were on your own. A mandatory evacuation meant just that: Get out. Drive if you have a car—do whatever it takes if you don't: Call a friend or someone from church. The city wasn't safe. Even the Red Cross had pulled back a few years earlier and announced that ahead of a hurricane it would no longer deploy volunteers and resources south of Interstate 12. There were New Orleanians who had to look at a map to even know where Interstate 12 was located. The answer: far away—across the causeway, the twenty-four-mile bridge over Lake Pontchartrain, and then nearly that far again into the northern wilds of St. Tammany Parish. With no Red Cross shelter, refugees running for cover were left with a collection of schoolhouses of dubious fortitude, and then, the Superdome. Maybe. Here the game got as intricate as poker, with city officials signaling as sternly as they could that even the Dome might not be available this time. That was partly to scold Dome refugees for what they had done to it a storm or two ago: seats and plumbing fixtures ripped out; walls defaced with graffiti; fights; filth. Wherever culpability for that mess lay, the reference carried an ulterior message for anyone who needed reminding: You don't want to be Domed. The Dome is a drag. Make your own plans. Get out.

From "Real Ugly, Real Fast," by Jed Horne

_____

_____

_____

READ, WRITE, AND THINK CRITICALLY: SECTION ONE

Directions: Skim through the following text and answer questions 1–3. Then, read the selection and answer the questions that follow.

1. What do you think the selection will be about? *Answers will vary.*

_____

_____

_____

2. Read the first two paragraphs. Are people most likely to fall in love in springtime? Explain.

_____

_____

_____

3. What do you already know or can quickly find out about oxytocin?

_____

_____

_____

Hormones' Complex Role in Human Sexuality

David Perlman

David Perlman (b. 1918) is the science editor for The San Francisco Chronicle. *His career has spanned over 70 years and has taken him around the world to research and report on scientific advances. Notable articles include one of the first articles about AIDS ever published before the disease even had a name, an article entitled "Astounding Undersea Discoveries" about hot water geysers in the sea west of Ecuador, and research on a pre-human skeleton found in Ethiopia known as Ardipithecus ramidus. A Columbia University graduate, Perlman has won several journalism awards from prestigious science-based organizations and served as president of the National Association of Science Writers as well as the Council for the Advancement of Science Writing. The following piece was published in* The San Francisco Chronicle *on January 8, 2009.*

1 In the spring a young man's fancy lightly turns to thoughts of love . . . but whither when the year is young?

2 It matters not, for as long as the hormones are in tune, love can bloom at any time, say scientists who study the genetics and neurobiology of animals whose family lives shed new light on human sexuality.

3 Larry J. Young, a Georgia neurobiologist, studies the genes and hormones of the cute but often **pestiferous** little beasts called prairie voles, which mate and bond for life.

4 Those genes and hormones exist in humans, too, and in a uniquely literate essay in today's issue of the journal *Nature*, Young points to the role they play in animals and humans.

5 "Poetry it is not. Nor is it particularly romantic. But reducing love to its comprehensive parts helps us understand human sexuality and may lead to drugs that enhance or **diminish** our love for another," he said.

6 Young, a professor in the psychiatry department at Emory University in Atlanta and the Yerkes National Primate Research Center there, has discovered that two closely related peptide hormones called oxytocin and vasopressin play powerful roles in both animal and human sexuality.

7   "I call oxytocin the motherly hormone," Young said in an interview, "because its release in the body of female voles is involved in uterine contractions, in lactation and in the mother's early bonding with vole babies. It's also the hormone responsible for lifelong pair bonding between males and females.

8   "Vasopressin is closely related to oxytocin, but it's dependent on testosterone—so it's the macho version of oxytocin."

9   In the Bay Area, scientists say Young's research of togetherness in prairie voles is proving valuable to understanding many disorders in the human condition.

10 "Oxytocin is the hormone of monogamy," said neuropsychiatrist Louann Brizendine, who directs the Women's Mood and Hormone Clinic at UCSF which also takes male patients. "If you give men nasal squirts of oxytocin, it increases their trust in others, their ability to be affectionate—it brings out their feminine side, is how I'd put it.

11 "Years ago a man I was seeing said to me, 'Give me some of that oxytocin—I just want to love someone!'"

12 Because **monogamy** and love are examples of powerful human interactions, Brizendine believes the hormones involved could also prove important for people with disorders like **autism**, Asperger's syndrome and even schizophrenia, because the symptoms mean they can rarely find close relationships.

13 Young's primary research shows the effects of the hormones on prairie voles, but he also discovered that oxytocin has similar effects on mountain voles, a different species that are not monogamous and do not pair-bond for life. When mountain voles are exposed to doses of oxytocin in the lab, the males will bond with females in a close and sometimes lifetime relationship like their cousins, Young said.

14 The varied genes that trigger the release of oxytocin and the testosterone-dependent vasopressin in both voles and humans, Young said, have obviously had a long evolutionary history, as it is also found in other, more primitive pair-bonding animals—even though monogamy is extremely rare throughout the animal kingdom.

15 "In all my work," Young said, "I'm trying to understand how we humans interact with each other—to understand the genetics and biochemistry of the social brain, and how it may go wrong in **profound** disorders like autism and schizophrenia."

16 Brizendine called Young's work "deeply important because it clearly **correlates** the phenomenon of pair-bonding in his voles with monogamous relations in humans."

17 As for the vasopressin, Brizendine said, one variation in the gene that controls the hormone can make a man "more **prone** to long-term bonded relationships," while a man with another variation of the gene "will be **prone** to infidelity."

18 Dacher Keltner, a psychologist and director of the Berkeley Social Interaction Laboratory at UC Berkeley, calls Young's vole research—along with work by Sue Carter at the University of Maryland and Thomas R. Insel at the National Institute of Mental Health—"unbelievably influential in showing us that there's a physical, biological basis to long-term monogamy, love, devotion and feelings of trust with each other."

19 The new awareness of the role of hormones in human relations is **underscored** in new books being published this year by both Keltner and Brizendine. "Born to Be Good: The Science of a Meaningful Life" by Keltner is out next week, and "The Male Brain" by Brizendine will be published in September.

20 Oxytocin, meanwhile, is sold commercially as a "trust hormone" to be used in nasal sprays. One ad claims it can "produce significant increase in **charisma**, which creates a highly trustworthy appearance," while another calls its brand "a great female seducer."

21 But all three scientists—Young, Brizendine and Keltner—agree that it's much too early to be **peddling** the hormones that way.

22 "We're only at the beginning of our laboratory studies, and people should be extremely careful," Young said.

---

4. Use context clues and/or a dictionary to define the following words (marked in bold in the reading).

a. pestiferous (para. 3): _____

b. diminish (para. 5): _____

c. monogamy (para. 12): _____

d. autism (para. 12): _____

e. profound (para. 15): _____

f. correlates (para. 16): _____

g. prone (para. 17): _____

h. underscored (para. 19): _____

i. charisma (para. 20): _____

j. peddling (para. 21): _____

5. In your own words, explain the role of oxytocin in maternal bonding.

_____

_____

_____

_____

6. Identify three major details from the essay.

_____

_____

_____

_____

_____

_____

7. Identify three minor details from the essay.

_____

_____

_____

_____

_____

_____

_____

8. Chose a detail from the essay and identify what type of detail it is.
   Detail: _____
   Type: _____

9. What is the main idea of this article?

_____

_____

_____

_____

_____

SECTION TWO

Annotating

You learned in section one how to identify the main idea and the details in a selection, so in section two you are ready to learn to annotate, clarify meaning, and outline.

Annotating means to mark up documents that you read, noting what's important. Annotating will greatly aid your comprehension and interpretation by allowing you to keep track of what is significant.

Many people develop their own personal style of annotating, but here are some useful general tips.

Tips for Critical Thinkers: How to Annotate

- Underline the topic
- Put two lines underneath the main idea, if stated explicitly
- Write the main idea in your own words, if implied
- Put checkmarks next to important supporting details (and label type of detail—reason, example, fact, and so on)
- Number examples or items in a list
- Number steps in a process
- Circle transitions (and label them cause/effect, comparison/contrast, etc.)
- Circle emotive words (and label them superlative, aesthetic, judgment, or recommendation)
- Label critical information (or information with which you strongly agree or disagree) with an asterisk or exclamation point
- Place a question mark next to information you do not understand or write a question in the margin
- Mark facts "F" and opinions "O"
- Jot down definitions of new vocabulary words
- Record any predictions you make in the margin
- Write thoughtful reflections and connections in the margin
- Draw arrows to connect ideas

Some students use differently colored highlighters and pens to indicate different things, like topic, main idea, or details. Be careful not to go overboard and develop such a complicated system that you cannot distinguish between the most important points in the text and the minor supporting details.

PRACTICE 3-9	Annotating

Directions: Annotate the following passage. The first four paragraphs are done for you.

Implied MI: A desert is difficult to imagine and, despite having some areas consisting of water, a desert is terribly hot, windy, and hard to inhabit safely.

Description of a desert

By Ann Plato

" They wandered in the wilderness in a solitary way. Thirsty, their souls fainted in them."—

Psalms   *From Psalm 107:4*

Annotations (handwritten):
- judgment / Topic
- def. - placed at intervals
- def. - green growing with plants
- superlative / aesthetic / located in Northern Africa / Contrast
- Topic / addition transition
- Comparison
- def. - in the middle of
- Topic / 5 Details about oases: ① ②
- ③ def. - having live people there ④
- Why aren't all 32 of them inhabited?
- [Oases]
- So sometimes even the oases cannot be counted on as a source of water!
- time transition / superlative / judgment / effect
- Prediction: the rest of the essay will focus on these "disastrous consequences."

It is difficult to form a correct idea of a desert, without having seen one. It is a vast plain

of sands and stones, interspersed with mountains of various sizes and heights, without roads or

shelters. They sometimes have springs of water, which burst forth, and create verdant spots.

The most remarkable of deserts is the Sahara. This is a vast plain, but little elevated

above the level of the ocean, and covered with sand and gravel, with a mixture of sea shells, and

appears like the basin of an evaporated sea.

Amid the desert there are springs of water, which burst forth and create verdant spots,

called Oases. There are thirty-two of these which contain fountains, and Date and Palm trees;

twenty of them are inhabited. They serve as stopping places for the caravans, and often contain

villages.

Were it not for these no human being could cross this waste of burning sand. So violent,

sometimes, is the burning wind that the scorching heat dries up the water of these springs, and

then frequently, the most disastrous consequences follow.

In 1805, a caravan, consisting of 2,000 persons and 1,800 camels, not finding water at the usual resting place, died of thirst, both men and animals. Storms of wind are more terrible on this desert than on the ocean. Vast surges and clouds of red sand are raised and rolled forward, burying everything in its way, and it is said that whole tribes have thus been swallowed up. The situation of such is dreadful, and admits of no resource. Many perish victims of the most horrible thirst. It is then that the value of a cup of water is really felt.

In such a case there is no distinction. If the master has not, the servant will not give it to him; for very few are the instances where a man will voluntarily lose his life to save that of another. What a situation for a man, though a rich one, perhaps the owner of all the caravan! He is dying for a cup of water—no one gives it to him; he offers all he possesses—no one hears him; they are all dying, though by walking a few hours further, they might be saved.

In short, to be thirsty in a desert, without water, exposed to the burning sun, without shelter, is the most terrible situation that a man can be placed in, and one of the greatest sufferings that a human being can sustain; the tongue and lips swell; a hollow sound is heard in the ears, which brings on deafness, and the brain appears to grow thick and inflamed. If, unfortunately, anyone falls sick on the road, he must either endure the fatigue of traveling on a camel (which is troublesome even to healthy people) or he must be left behind on the sand, without any assistance, and remain so till a slow death comes to relieve him. No one remains with him, not even his old and faithful servant; no one will stay and die with him; all pity his fate, but no one will be his companion. (1841)

Compare your annotations to the annotations in the sample paragraph. Did you write thoughtful reflections and connections in the margin? Did you remember to mark the following items?

- Topic
- Information that seems important
- Ideas that seem difficult
- Places where you had questions
- New definitions
- Main idea and major details

Clarifying Meaning

Once you've recognized what's significant and relevant in a text you're reading or an argument you're analyzing by identifying the main ideas, major details, minor details, and by annotating, it's time to **clarify meaning**: to make sure you understand exactly what the author or speaker of a text intends to say. You can use three strategies to clarify meaning:

- Summarizing
- Paraphrasing
- Deciphering misleading or ambiguous language

Summarizing and Paraphrasing

Summarizing and paraphrasing, besides being useful for preparing for exams and writing research papers, are perfect for figuring out if you've "gotten" what an author is saying. You won't be able to summarize or paraphrase if the meaning of a text isn't clear to you.

Summarizing **Summarizing** is giving a concise overview of a longer selection. A summary includes the most important information (main idea plus major details) of an article or chapter and is written using your own words. A summary is *always* shorter than the original and rarely contains minor details. A summary is *not* a personal reflection on a work. In addition, a summary is *not* an evaluation of the author's work.

Depending on the length of the original passage, the length of your summary will vary. If you read a 40-page chapter, then your summary is likely to consist of multiple paragraphs. If you read a short article, you can expect to write a few sentences or a paragraph. Many summaries are around 10 percent of the length of the original, but do not get hung up on the length of the summary; rather, focus on capturing the central theme and the major details as succinctly as possible.

A good summary has five traits:

1. *Accuracy*: Your summary correctly conveys facts and details.
2. *Completeness*: Your summary covers everything that is significant, and nothing that is not (i.e., it includes main idea and major details but leaves out minor details). To

capture all of the major details, answer the reporter's questions (who, what, where, when, why, and how.)

3. *Conciseness*: Your summary is brief *but* comprehensive.
4. *Objectivity*: Your summary does not include your personal opinions on the subject matter. It is not a review.
5. *Originality of expression*: Your summary uses language that is original to you. You will learn to paraphrase ideas in your own words.

Only when you fully understand material can you write a summary of it. If you read a text yet struggle with writing a summary, it is an indication that you did not understand the passage. Writing a summary, therefore, can serve as an excellent "test" to see whether you interpreted an author's meaning correctly.

Tips for Critical Thinkers: How to Summarize

1. **Read and annotate**. Pay careful attention to the topic, emotive words, major details, and important examples.
2. **Identify the main idea (of a paragraph) or thesis (of a longer passage).** If the main idea or thesis is stated explicitly by the author, underline it or highlight it. If the main idea or thesis is implied, write it in your own words in the margin: topic + assertion about the topic = main idea/thesis.
3. **Start your summary by listing the identifying information**: the author's name, the title of the work, the source, and its copyright date.
4. **Put the main idea in your own words,** then give major details as necessary so readers can understand your summary.
5. **Check to make sure that your summary is accurate, complete, concise, and objective.**
6. **Insert transitions to make sure your summary flows smoothly**.
7. **Reread to make certain you have included all of the necessary information from the text without echoing the language and without including personal opinion.**

PRACTICE 3-10   Writing a Summary

Directions: Read the following selection entitled "Importance of Critical Thinking" by Lane Wallace. Annotate it and look up any words you do not know. Reread and then cover up the text in order to write a concise summary in your own words. Use the tips on pp. 86–87 as a guide.

Here's a Model (which summarizes Plato's "Description of a Desert" from pp. 85–86)

Ann Plato's "Description of a Desert" (1841) gives the impression of a desert as being a huge, hostile area of sand which may also consist of shells, stones, mountains, and gravel. The Sahara is an impressive desert in Africa. In some places, oases give relief from the heat to caravans by being a source of water, living things, and villages; however, even an oasis that at one point had fountains and trees can become dried up by the wind and heat. An example from 1805 illustrates the horror that a caravan of people and animals faced when the oasis they expected to provide water had dried up. Also, the wind can become destructive and can blow enough sand to bury entire tribes of people. In the face of certain death, even the richest man (perhaps the owner of the caravan) cannot hope to buy a drink of water from a servant because no one would want to endure the swelling of tongue and lips, deafness, and brain damage that precedes an agonizingly slow death on the desert.

The Importance of Critical Thinking

Lane Wallace

Lane Wallace is a prolific author, journalist, speaker, and researcher. She is passionate about diverse topics, notably aviation, education, psychology, and healthcare. Wallace encourages people to find and use their voices to improve their communities and lives. The first female columnist at Flying *magazine, Wallace was also one of its editors for 12 years. This article is one of over 150 articles she published in* The Atlantic.

May 29, 2009

1 In a column that came out yesterday in the *New York Times*, Nicholas Kristof explored some of the emotional "hot buttons" that separate the thinking of "liberals" and "conservatives." (The column was a follow-up to an earlier column he wrote about how people tend to use the internet to seek news and information that reinforces already-held positions.) Part of the reason the two groups have difficulty engaging in meaningful discussion, Kristof said, was that the two camps don't just think differently. They *feel* differently. They react strongly, and in different ways, to different scenarios and cues.

2 No big news flash there. What any of us hold as core values . . . emotional or otherwise . . . informs our worldview, and influences how we interpret information or events.

3 More interesting to me was Kristof's take on a solution to the impasse. "How do we discipline our brains to be more open-minded, more honest, more empirical?" Kristof asked. How, indeed?

4 A prerequisite for any progress, he acknowledged, is an admission that the "other" side of an argument has at least some legitimate concerns. But Kristof also quoted University of Virginia psychology professor Jonathan Haidt, who said that "our minds were not designed by evolution to discover the truth; they were designed to play social games." Therefore, according to Haidt, "the best way to open the mind is through the heart." Kristof expanded on this to suggest finding moderates on the "other" side and eating meals with them to build emotional bonds that allow a differing point of view to make it through to the other side.

5 I'm not sure I agree with Haidt about our minds being designed solely (if, in fact, he meant that) for social games. Our ability to reason is as legendary as our ability to manipulate. By the same token, the number of people who like me very much but won't for two seconds entertain a discussion point that challenges a position they hold is legion. Which means . . . what?

6 Well, for one thing, it means that I'm not sure lunches or emotional bonds alone . . . while certainly helpful additions to the equation . . . are enough to tip the balance, or create suddenly-improved communication between opposing camps.

7 In my experience, there are two factors that seem to make the biggest difference as to whether or not two people can have a meaningful and productive discussion from different points of view (assuming both are fairly self-assured and reasonable beings):

8 1. The first factor is whether the people involved see the world in black-and-white terms, or in more complex shades of gray. For those who see the world in absolute terms of black and white (on the left or the right), the only choice of movement is all the way to the other side. Which is an awfully long distance to move an opinion. People who are more inclined to see the world in nuanced shades of gray, on the other hand, can consider a slightly different shade without feeling their basic values threatened. The options for movement, and therefore their potential willingness to consider another perspective, are far greater.

9 2. The second factor is how skilled, practiced, and comfortable both participants are in the art of critical thinking. The website criticalthinking.org offers more definitions of what critical thinking consists of than anyone probably needs. But at its most exemplary, the site says, critical thinking is based on "clarity, accuracy, precision, consistency, relevance, sound evidence, good reasons, depth, breadth, and fairness." Critical thinkers "avoid thinking simplistically about complicated issues and strive to appropriately consider the rights and needs of relevant others." And "they realize that no matter how skilled they are as thinkers . . . they

will at times fall prey to mistakes in reasoning, human irrationality, prejudices, biases, distortions, uncritically accepted social rules and taboos, self-interest, and vested interest."

10   Which is to say, people skilled in the art of critical thinking make a practice of questioning everything. Even their own opinions. They don't necessarily sit in the middle ground of any debate, but they understand the potential fallibility of sources, and acknowledge the legitimate existence of other points of view . . . subject to examination, along with their own. Meaningful exploration and discussion of issues, therefore, becomes possible. Even productive.

11   In theory, this is the strength and purpose of a liberal arts education (one intended to provide general knowledge and foster intellectual capabilities and reasoned, rational thought). And to the degree that this teaching happens, I think it *is* a strong and important argument for a liberal arts education.

12   But here's the bad news. How many of us actually put our "gut" opinions or the information that comes at us daily through the rigorous filters of a critical thinker? I don't have the answer to that, but the results of a 1995 study done by the Center for Critical Thinking aren't encouraging. In a study of 140 professors at 66 public and private universities in California, the researchers found that while an overwhelming majority (89%) claimed that critical thinking was a primary objective of their instruction, only a small percentage (19%) could give a clear explanation of what critical thinking was. And from the respondents' answers, the researchers concluded that only 9% were teaching with a view toward critical thinking on a typical day in class. And that's professors tasked with *teaching* the subject. How must the rest of us fare?

13   Granted, that's only one study. And clearly, there's a lot more to the subject than one column or post can cover. Like so many issues in the world, it's complex. But developing the ability to step back a step and question where opinions come from; objectively consider and dissect an argument for its strengths and flaws, look at what the source of any information is and through what biases, values, assumptions, or lenses we or others are filtering that information, consider what other information might exist to counter or support any given "fact" . . . and, yes, consider that we, too, might have to adjust our views or thinking in the end . . . is central to upgrading both the level and of productivity of discourse in this country.

14   Critical thinking acumen doesn't get mentioned as often as the other skills we test for or examine in education debates. But it's essential if we want to "discipline our brains to be more open-minded, more honest, more empirical." And it's every bit as important as math, science, reading or writing in terms of being an informed, discerning citizen in an increasingly complex world.

_____

_____

_____

_____

_____

_____

Paraphrasing   **Paraphrasing** is putting an author's specific ideas into your own words in order to make sense of them. You can paraphrase any idea expressed by an author—a main idea, a major detail, or a minor detail—although paraphrases almost always contain both the main ideas and the major details from the original, especially if you are writing a summary. You only paraphrase short passages or paragraphs. A paraphrase is usually close in length to the original material but may be slightly shorter or longer.

A good paraphrase retains the meaning of the original but expresses it in a new way. Well-written paraphrases don't simply swap out some of the words used in the original passage; they express the idea using a different sentence structure than the original author used.

Paraphrasing comes in handy as you conduct research. Academic and professional writers tend to use **jargon**—technical language specific to their fields— that might be difficult for students and other non-experts to decipher, so it is useful to be able to rephrase it in a way that makes it easier to understand. Use quotations sparingly in a paraphrase (the goal is to use your own words) and only quote those sentences that are exceptionally well written, are difficult to paraphrase without losing some of the author's original intent, or are unusually creative or profound.

Tips for Critical Thinkers: How to Paraphrase

1. **Read and annotate**. Pay careful attention to the topic, emotive words, major details, and important examples.
2. **Identify the main idea and the major details of the paragraph or excerpt** and underline or highlight them.
3. **Shut the book or minimize the computer program on your screen**. That way, you won't be tempted to use words or phrases too close to the author's original.
4. **Write your paraphrase using a different sentence structure than the original author used, and different words where appropriate.** Change what words you can, but leave names, dates, and numbers the same so that you don't change the meaning of the original. You may also wish to combine sentences or divide sentences. For example, if the original passage was two sentences, make your paraphrase one or three sentences. If you can do so without altering the original meaning, change the order in which information is presented.
5. **Make sure you have identified the major details** that answer the important questions about the main idea/thesis: *who, what, where, when, why*, and *how*.
6. **Include an attributive tag.** An attributive tag consists of the author's name and a signal verb. For example: "Delaney's research shows that…" or "Delaney argues…" or "Delaney explains…" Be sure to use a verb that accurately characterizes the author's intent (*argues* suggests a far different intent than *explains*).
7. **Insert transitions to make sure your paraphrase flows.**
8. **Put quotation marks around any phrases that are impossible to reword without losing the original meaning**. You don't need to quote individual words.
9. **Reread** to make certain you have included all of the necessary information from the text without echoing the language. Make sure your paraphrase means the same thing as the original passage but is expressed in an original way. Your paraphrase should also sound natural.
10. **Give a source reference to avoid plagiarism.** Use the method your professor specifies.

Some Common Mistakes in Paraphrasing

Which of the following is the best paraphrase of this sentence that you read earlier in this chapter (in the subsection entitled *Stated and Implied Main Ideas*)?

Original text: "In those pieces of writing with an implied main idea (or thesis if it is a longer passage), you can try to write the main idea (or thesis) in your own words in a single sentence in the margin of the text while you annotate the passage."

Paraphrase A: In those sections of writing with a suggested main idea (or thesis if the passage is longer), you can attempt to write the main idea (or thesis) in an individual sentence in your own words in the blank space around the text as you mark up the piece of writing.

Paraphrase B: Baker and Beitman (2019) explain that you could try to write the thesis or main idea in your own words in a single sentence within the margin of the passage while annotating, if the piece of writing has an implied main idea or thesis.

Paraphrase C: Baker and Beitman (2019) explain that when the main idea is not explicit, we would say it is implied, and if it is from a longer passage, the main idea is referred to as a thesis.

Paraphrase D: Baker and Beitman (2019) explain that sometimes main ideas are hinted at (or suggested by) the author rather than written out explicitly, and if the text is a longer passage, the main idea is called a "thesis." When that is the case, the student should use his or her own words to express the main idea/thesis in a single sentence and jot it down in the margin.

Remembering that a good paraphrase must not echo the original author's words and syntax, you likely identified Paraphrase D as being the best paraphrase of the original text. Notice how the writer of Paraphrase A merely subs in synonyms for the words used in the original (e.g., "pieces" becomes "sections" and "try" becomes "attempt") and fails to use an attributive tag to identify the original authors. Passage B is slightly better due to the addition of authors' names and copyright date; however, the wording is too similar to the original and essentially flips the first half of the sentence with the second half. Paraphrase C includes the attributive tag but leaves out the important point about writing the implied main idea as you annotate. Finally, in Paraphrase D, we have an attributive tag, natural language, and complete inclusion of all significant ideas.

Writing a Paraphrase	**PRACTICE 3-11**

Directions: Read the following sentences from the passage in Practice 3-10. Annotate them and look up any words that you might not know. Reread them, and then cover up the text in order to write a paraphrase using your own words.

Here's a model

"Which is to say, people skilled in the art of critical thinking make a practice of questioning everything. Even their own opinions."

    Wallace (2009) stresses that critical thinkers question **all** beliefs and ideas, and this habit includes questioning their own ideas as well.

Now you try

1. "What any of us hold as core values…emotional or otherwise…informs our worldview, and influences how we interpret information or events."

    _____

    _____

    _____

    _____

2. "Well, for one thing, it means that I'm not sure lunches or emotional bonds alone… while certainly helpful additions to the equation… are enough to tip the balance, or create suddenly-improved communication between opposing camps."

    _____

    _____

    _____

3. "The first factor is whether the people involved see the world in black-and-white terms, or in more complex shades of gray. For those who see the world in absolute terms of black and white (on the left or the right), the only choice of movement is all the way to the other side. Which is an awfully long distance to move an opinion. People who are more inclined to see the world in nuanced shades of gray, on the other hand, can consider a slightly different shade without feeling their basic values threatened. The options for movement, and therefore their potential willingness to consider another perspective, are far greater."

_____

_____

_____

_____

4. "But developing the ability to step back a step and question where opinions come from; objectively consider and dissect an argument for its strengths and flaws, look at what the source of any information is and through what biases, values, assumptions, or lenses we or others are filtering that information, consider what other information might exist to counter or support any given 'fact'... and, yes, consider that we, too, might have to adjust our views or thinking in the end... is central to upgrading both the level and of productivity of discourse in this country."

_____

_____

_____

_____

5. "Critical thinking acumen doesn't get mentioned as often as the other skills we test for or examine in education debates."

_____

_____

_____

Deciphering Misleading, Unclear, or Ambiguous Language

It is important to be able to recognize when an author is using potentially misleading language so that you can decode his or her message. Be on the lookout for the following ways in which authors can use language to obscure meaning:

- Being deliberately vague
- Using ambiguous language and making ambiguous statements
- Using euphemisms and doublespeak

Being Deliberately Vague

You hear people say vague things all the time, such as,

"Back in the day..."
"That movie was interesting."
"She's attractive."
"That's not too bad."

Some words do not have precise meanings, and this is fine in everyday speech. For example, if your friend tells you his grade on the last test was "decent," you get his general idea: He didn't score an extremely high grade, but he also didn't fail, and he's not unhappy with how he did. But when his professor is trying to calculate his final grade for the class, she had better have recorded his grade as a specific number; if she wrote "decent" in her grade book, no one is going to be happy. The word "decent" does not have a precise meaning; it is *vague*.

Often words are vague because they are "borderline cases"—it isn't clear whether they belong to one group or another. For example, is a man who is 5'10" tall, of medium height, or short? Where does the group "short" end and the group "tall" begin? **Vagueness** often happens because authors or speakers use comparisons without specifying *to what they are comparing their subject*.

Sometimes speakers and authors are intentionally vague, either to appeal to a wide audience or because they don't want to be pinned down. Politicians do this frequently. For example, President Barack Obama, in his inaugural speech on January 20, 2009, said:

> The success of our economy has always depended not just on the size of our gross domestic product, but on the reach of our prosperity; on the ability to extend opportunity to every willing heart—not out of charity, but because it is the surest route to our common good.

President Obama intended primarily to inspire people, but what specifically does he mean by the words *success, prosperity, opportunity*, and *common good*?

> ### Advanced Language Concept: Similes and Metaphors
>
> **Similes** are comparisons using the words *like* or *as*. As an example, consider the simile, "Adam felt as unwanted and useless as an old, broken chair left in the attic." Often used for poetic or literary effect, similes draw unexpected comparisons (usually you don't think of a person as being like a piece of furniture).
>
> **Metaphors** are also comparisons, but they do not use the words *like* or *as*. Whereas similes most often are contained in one line of text, a metaphor may take up extended space (several lines or an entire passage). An example of a brief metaphor is "Lyla's eyes were snuffed out candles." This metaphor suggests that her eyes lack light or spirit.
>
> Both similes and metaphors pose additional challenges to critical thinkers. As you interpret the author's message, you should determine what subjects are being compared and why.

Discussion Questions

1. Do you think President Obama was being intentionally vague? If so, why do you think he might have chosen to be vague?
2. Do the vague terms in the excerpt above have clear definitions? Can you define them specifically?
3. If these terms cannot be specifically defined, what influence should they have on you?

EXPAND YOUR UNDERSTANDING: *POLITICAL SPEECH*

Directions: Use Google to find and read both of President Obama's inaugural addresses (January 20, 2009 and January 21, 2013). See if you can identify in the speeches any other examples of vagueness, specifically pointing out words and phrases that are vague.

Tips for Critical Thinkers: How to Clarify Vague Language

- **Ask questions to determine the specific meaning of a term.** When you encounter the vague word, ask the "reporter's questions": *Who, what, where, when, why*, and *how*. Answering these questions will help you pin down the meaning of words.
- **If the term is a comparison, see if the vagueness can be eliminated by determining what the term is being compared to.** For example, if someone is described as "short," try to find out if the author has a reference that indicates what he or she considers "tall."
- **Determine if it is even possible for the term to have a specific meaning.** If the vagueness can't be eliminated by using the strategies above, set aside the part of the text or argument that is vague and don't allow it to influence your judgment.

Ambiguous Terms and Ambiguous Statements

A term is **ambiguous** if it can have two or more specific meanings, and the meaning the speaker or writer intends isn't clear. For example, in the sentence, "He's seeing her," the word *see* is ambiguous, because it has more than one meaning. *See* can mean "perceive with the eyes," but it can also mean "date." You can't tell from the sentence alone what the author means to express. Often, the more generalized a word is—the less it refers to something concrete—the more chance it has of being ambiguous. Take the word *honor*, as expressed in the sentence, "It was his honor that compelled him to donate money to the orphanage." You can't be sure if his great personal integrity caused him to give to charity or if a judge told him to do it; in fact, these are only two of the many possible definitions of *honor*.

Entire sentences can also be ambiguous, either because of grammatical mistakes—some quite comical, such as, "Wearing nothing but diapers, we watched the baby toddle across the room"—or because of the structure of the sentence. Nothing is grammatically incorrect about the sentence, "She touched the man with the hat," but it isn't clear whether she touched a man who was wearing a hat, or whether she used a hat to touch a man.

Ambiguity can lead to **equivocation**: a situation in which a speaker or writer uses different meanings for the same term in the middle of an argument. Consider the argument: "All men have a right to pursue their own happiness. But women are clearly not men, so women do not have a right to seek their own happiness." The writer here equivocates when he uses the term *men*. In the first sentence, *men* is used in the archaic sense of *humankind*. But suddenly the author begins to use *men* in the specific sense of "persons of the male gender." He wasn't logically entitled to make that tricky switch mid-argument, so the conclusion that women don't have a right to try to be happy is faulty. It's pretty obvious that the person making this argument has an agenda, isn't it?

Tips for Critical Thinkers: How to Clarify Ambiguity

- **First, be aware of whether a speaker or writer has an agenda that might cause him or her to be purposefully ambiguous.** Is the person trying to avoid giving a specific meaning so that he can appeal to as wide an audience as possible, or so he can later deny what he originally meant you to believe?
- **Look for the key terms or sentences in the text or argument.** Which terms or sentences are important to the author's goal of persuading you to accept his or her point? That's where you need to look out for ambiguity.
- **See if you can use context to clarify the ambiguity.** For example, is the sentence, "He's seeing her," given as part of a discussion of who is dating whom? If so, that will make the meaning clear: He is going out with, or dating, her.
- **Consider if knowledge of the intended audience of the piece can clarify the ambiguity.** If the ambiguity is unintentional, it might be because the author assumes his or her audience shares a common understanding of the definition of the ambiguous word. For instance, if a speaker addressing an audience of economists says, "the market needs to be free," you can probably figure out that *free* is intended to mean "without regulations," as opposed to "not incarcerated."
- **Look to see if the author stipulates (or specifies specifically) what she means.** Sometimes honest authors will clarify ambiguity if you read further.
- **Replace the ambiguous word in the sentence or argument with a synonym for the meaning you think the author intends.** If you are trying to figure out what *chair* means in the sentence, "More than $150,000 was set aside to pay the salary of the new chair," if you substitute *object upon which people sit* for *chair*, the sentence makes no sense, so you can rule out that meaning.

"Are you smoking or jumping?"

www.CartoonStock.com

Analyzing Ambiguity	PRACTICE 3-12

Directions: Answer the following questions about the cartoon above.

1. Even situations can be ambiguous. Explain the ambiguity in the cartoon. Why is the man in the window apparently having trouble understanding the situation?

   _____

   _____

   _____

   _____

2. What recent cultural changes in the United States motivated the cartoonist to draw this cartoon?

   _____

   _____

   _____

3. Does it seem like the cartoonist has an agenda? With which figure in the cartoon does he seem to sympathize?

   _____

   _____

   _____

   _____

Advanced Language Concept: Irony

Irony involves words or a situation in which what seems to be the case and what is actually the case are sharply different. Irony may pose some additional challenges as readers work on interpreting the author's message.

Authors use *verbal irony* when what they say is intentionally very different from what they mean—and usually the opposite meaning is meant. For example, in Shakespeare's *Julius Caesar*, the character Mark Antony gives a famous funeral oration for the slain Caesar wherein he calls Caesar's assassins "honorable men."

Another common form of irony is *dramatic irony*, when the readers or viewers of a work have knowledge that the characters do not, and this knowledge causes great tension. For example, if while watching a horror film, you have ever screamed at the television "don't open the door!" because you knew that the main character was about to encounter the monster, you have felt the tension of dramatic irony.

Situational irony happens when what one expects to happen in a situation and what actually happens contrast. In the ancient play *Oedipus Rex*, the king causes his own son to kill him by trying to make sure he doesn't. He sends his son out of the kingdom, and not knowing his origin, the son (Oedipus) ultimately kills his own father.

Euphemisms and Doublespeak

A **euphemism** is a word that is used to replace another more offensive or disagreeable word. Often euphemisms are used to smooth over difficult subjects in a polite way. For example, rather than tell someone that a beloved relative has died, one might say that he has "passed away" or "gone to a better place." Or instead of saying that we have to eliminate bodily waste, we say "use the bathroom" or "go to the restroom." Often euphemisms refer to subjects that are culturally taboo, or off-limits, such as excretion and sex. If you say you want to "sleep with" someone, you aren't really saying you want to lie down and sleep next to him or her.

Doublespeak is a special form of euphemism that is used to disguise or distort meaning. Often doublespeak is designed to make something unpleasant seem good or make something negative into something positive. Doublespeak gets in the way of honest communication. Frequently associated with politics, the military, or corporations, doublespeak is often used to **frame** an issue—to cast it in a certain light in order to influence the way you think about it—to the benefit of the person or agency doing the doublespeaking. Think about the following examples of doublespeak.

> Would you vote for a *death tax*? How about for an *inheritance tax*?
> Would it be acceptable to *assassinate* a *freedom fighter*? How about taking *executive action* against a *terrorist leader*?
> Should we use *rubber bullets and tear gas* against *rioting civilians* or should we *pacify* an *incident of civil unrest*?

Tips for Critical Thinkers: How to Detect Euphemisms and Doublespeak

- **Be aware of the context of the situation.** Is a "taboo subject" (like sex or excretion) under discussion? Has a situation occurred (like a firing, a death, a breakup) that would offend one of the parties involved in the discussion? Does one of the parties have a possible interest in disguising the truth or in making it difficult for the other parties to understand what is being said? Is one of the parties a political, military, or corporate organization?
- **Look for framing.** Are any words or phrases intended to cast a situation, concept, individual, or organization in an unduly positive or negative way?
- **Try to determine what concepts or ideas are being specifically expressed.** This will help you hone in on the concepts being hidden by the euphemisms or doublespeak.
- **Try to imagine how "the other side" or someone in disagreement with the statement would express it.** This will show you exactly which part of the statement is a euphemism or doublespeak. For example, if a corporate president says, "We are downsizing to enhance liquid assets," one of the workers might phrase that statement as, "They are firing me in order to make more money for the stockholders."

Clarifying Language

PRACTICE 3-13

Directions: Underline the word or phrase in each of the following sentences that is hindering clear communication. If the entire sentence is unclear, underline all of it. In the space labeled "type," identify whether the offending language is *vague*, *ambiguous*, *euphemistic*, or *doublespeak*. Then, in the space marked "clearer," rewrite the sentence to express the meaning clearly.

Here's a model

She was <u>quite tall</u>.
Type: _____vague_____
Clearer: _____She was 6'3" tall._____

Now you try

1. Patient: My left ear hurts.
   Nurse: Okay, so you have ear pain, right?

   Type: _____
   Clearer: _____

2. The meeting we had to go to this afternoon was really long.

   Type: _____
   Clearer: _____

3. Max captured a video of an eagle taking flight after school today.

   Type: _____
   Clearer: _____

4. Check your tire pressure frequently.

   Type: _____
   Clearer: _____

5. I need to tell you, I haven't been entirely forthcoming with you.

   Type: _____
   Clearer: _____

6. Hanging on as long as he could, he finally went to a better place.

   Type: _____
   Clearer: _____

7. Regrettably, there was collateral damage in our troop's latest action.

   Type: _____
   Clearer: _____

8. I promise you, I will give you exactly what you deserve.

   Type: _____
   Clearer: _____

9. I know a thing or two about running a company.

   Type: _____
   Clearer: _____

10. Our company will undergo a headcount adjustment to meet cost-revenue guidelines.

Type: _____

Clearer: _____

PRACTICE 3-14   Interpreting Unclear Communication

Directions: Read the following passage, which is an example of unclear communication, and answer the questions that follow. Use evidence from the passage to support your responses.

Complete Venture Services is pleased to announce a sizable revenue enhancement in this quarter's earnings statements. It is true that all profit enhancement goals were not exceeded, but shortfalls will be compensated for by a rightsize implementation. Excess resources will be reduced, and the corporation will make good use of this opportunity to engage in further realignment to bring it more closely in line with its vision.

Employees will be happy to note that the realignment will result in further career flexibility and will open subsequent opportunities for advancement and/or lateral movement. Employees who aren't amenable to realignment will also be given their appropriate due. The board is confident that all of these steps will help Complete Venture Services exceed enhancement goals in the next quarter and continue our uncompromising approach to customer service.

1. Identify examples of vague language and doublespeak in this passage.

_____

_____

_____

_____

2. Identify examples of ambiguous language in this passage and indicate what the ambiguous words could possibly mean.

_____

_____

_____

_____

3. The author of this passage is intentionally impeding communication. Why is he or she doing so, and what is the author really saying?

_____

_____

_____

_____

Outlining and Mapping

Outlining and mapping are the final strategies you should use to help you interpret what you read. The advantage of outlining or mapping after you read a long text, such as an article or a chapter, is that you create a visual representation of the material that is quick and easy to use. It helps you to comprehend and study what you have read and to interpret what is most significant about what you read.

Outlining

An **outline** is a method of organization used to indicate the different levels of importance and relationships between ideas on a given topic. There are two types of outlines, formal and informal. Both types of outlines are useful for organizing information you have read.

A **formal outline**, often required in academic and professional settings, has a structured format that makes use of letters, numbers, and indentation. Use the tips in the following box to guide you in creating a formal outline. Also, see Figure 3-4 for an example of the format of a formal outline and Figure 3-5 for a sample topic outline of Chapter 2.

Tips for Critical Thinkers: How to Outline

- A formal outline is the preference for academic and professional work.
- Depending on the directions of your instructor, you can write either a topic outline (where you list the ideas as phrases) or a sentence outline (where you write the ideas as complete sentences); the key, however, is to be consistent throughout the outline.
- In Figure 3-4, notice how Roman numerals, capital letters, Arabic numbers, and lower-case letters as well as indenting or tabbing are used to show levels of comparable importance.
- Outlining is a process of division, so you always need at least two parts for each section of your outline (because you cannot divide something into one part). If you have an "A" you also need a "B." Word processing software includes automatic outlining, but be aware that the results are not always correct.

```
Thesis: State the thesis in a complete sentence.
  I. First major support for thesis
    A. Minor support for first major support
      1. Explanation or support for minor support
        a. Detail about the above support
        b. Detail about the above support
      2. Second explanation or support for minor support
        a. Detail about the above support
        b. Detail about the above support
    B. Minor support for first major support
      1. Explanation or support for minor support
        a. Detail about the above support
        b. Detail about the above support
      2. Second explanation or support for minor support
        a. Detail about the above support
        b. Detail about the above support
  II. Second major support for thesis
  III. Third major support for thesis
```

■ **Figure 3-4** Format of a Formal Outline

Thesis: Chapter 2, "Comprehension," is a review of the strategies you need to improve your reading comprehension.
  I. Comprehending What You Read
  II. Reviewing the Critical Thinker's Trait: Curiosity
  III. Becoming a Better Reader
  IV. Identifying the Topic
  V. Surveying and Predicting
  VI. Developing Vocabulary
      A. Context Clues
          1. Definition
          2. Synonyms
          3. Antonyms
          4. Examples
      B. Word Parts
          1. Root Words
          2. Prefixes
          3. Suffixes
      C. Glossaries
      D. Dictionaries

■ **Figure 3-5**   Sample of a Formal Outline—Topic Outline of Chapter 2

- Comprehending What You Read
- Reviewing the Critical Thinker's Trait: Curiosity
- Becoming a Better Reader
- Identifying the Topic
- Surveying and Predicting
- Developing Vocabulary
  Context Clues
  Word Parts
  Glossaries
  Dictionaries

■ **Figure 3-6**   Sample of an Informal Outline of Chapter 2

You are better off learning and following the format established by this text or by your professor and not relying on software to do the work for you.

Informal outlines indicate organization more casually. You do not need to worry about the strict format of a formal outline. Instead, you can skip lines or use bullets, dashes, letters, numbers, asterisks, and other symbols to indicate level of importance. Like a formal outline, the key to making an informal outline more effective is to be consistent. If you use a dash to indicate your first major detail, then you should use a dash for every subsequent major detail, and remember that if you divide an idea, you must have at least two subdivisions (see Figure 3-6).

Mapping

A *map* uses geometric shapes and lines to indicate the organization of material. **Mapping** is less formal than outlining, but the goal is the same—to show the different levels of importance and relationships among ideas. Do not include insignificant or irrelevant information.

Depending on the course requirements, you may opt for the flexibility of mapping rather than outlining. If you appreciate visual learning aids, you will find mapping an excellent addition to your study techniques. Have you been in a writing class in which you needed to brainstorm ideas for an essay? If so, there is a good chance your instructor taught you to map your ideas. One method of mapping is to put the topic in the center of the page in a circle and then branch off with smaller circles until you have a clear picture of the topic. This is also called **webbing**. Another method is to place the topic at the top of the page in a rectangle, and then draw lines to the smaller rectangles placed below to include the major and minor details. With a little creativity, you can map an entire textbook chapter and give yourself a head start in studying for exams and mastering the material (see Figure 3-7).

Real-World Mistakes of Interpretation and Their Consequences

Learning to interpret can mean the difference between keeping your home or losing it. In 2007, the United States entered its worst recession since the Great Depression of the 1930s. More than 80 percent of the home mortgages in the United States were subprime mortgages: loans to people who had bad credit scores and who were bad credit risks.

To make up for the risk they were taking, banks charged higher interest rates for these loans, and they often made loans that were known as adjustable-rate-mortgages, or ARMs. These types of mortgages have interest rates that are frequently adjusted based on a variety of reasons; most often the interest rates go up. Because these mortgages were written in a confusing fashion, many of the borrowers had trouble understanding the terms of the loans they were signing. Lenders did nothing to explain the mortgages to the borrowers: "When I asked to go over the loan application, they said, 'You don't need to. All you need to do is sign it,'" explained one unfortunate borrower. So they had to make sense of the loans on their own—but they couldn't interpret them. Many of these mortgages were known as 2-28 loans, meaning they had a low interest rate for the first two years, but after that the interest rate and therefore the cost of payments jumped drastically. A borrower's payments could go from $1,000 a month during the first two years to more than $3,000 in the third year! And with the interest rate being adjustable, the payments could potentially climb even higher.

Undoubtedly, predatory lending (lending designed to take advantage of the vulnerable) played a big part in the troubles in which these poor homeowners found themselves. It was in the interest of the lenders to make sure that the borrowers did not understand the contracts they were signing, so they made certain that the language was not easy to understand. This is a point that's been stressed in this chapter: Sometimes people will intentionally make language vague, ambiguous, or deceptive in order to confuse the reader. You have to watch out for yourself. If the borrowers of these loans had had better interpretation skills, they might have been able to understand their contracts better, or they might have been able to make sense of the government literature that warns people away from predatory lending. Many of them lost their homes. And the problem did not end there. Because the lenders had bundled these subprime loans into mortgage-backed securities, when the borrowers began to default (stop paying) on their mortgages (combined with other complex issues affecting the economy), it drew the entire country into a deep downturn. Maybe you too felt the effects of the recession that started in 2007, a recession that began in part because of the use of deceptive, manipulative language by lenders and the poor skills of interpretation of borrowers.

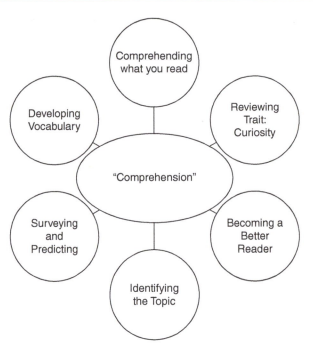

■ **Figure 3-7**   Sample map of Chapter 2 "Comprehension"

For Discussion

1. Explain how the mistakes discussed above qualify as a failure of interpretation.

2. What actions could lenders and borrowers have taken to avoid these mistakes?

Real-World Successes of Critical Thinking

Navajo Code Talkers

You just read about the cost of failing to think critically, but people who succeed at thinking critically can achieve great success. During World War II, Native Americans of the Navajo tribe successfully used their language as an unbreakable code, stymieing the efforts of the Japanese to decrypt American communication.

Directions: Using the Internet or a library, research Navajo Code Talkers in depth. Prepare a detailed description of how the Code Talkers succeeded during World War II, including an explanation of any skills, character traits, and standards of critical thinking that contributed to their success. Get ready to share your findings with the class.

Chapter Summary

- *Interpretation* is the skill of making sense of information by noticing details, making ideas clearer, and putting material into categories. In critical reading, interpretation involves recognizing main ideas and details, annotating, clarifying meaning, and outlining.

- Being *humble,* specifically being intellectually humble, means having an awareness of how much you don't know.

- *Significance* means that something is important to the subject. Determine it by telling the difference between main ideas and details.

- *Main ideas* are the primary point in a reading. *Details* support or clarify the main ideas. Find the main idea by noting the topic, looking for word clues, identifying major and minor details, and then putting all of those things together.

- *Annotating,* making marks on documents you are reading, will help you keep track of what is significant in a reading.

- Good strategies for *clarifying meaning* include summarizing, paraphrasing, and deciphering misleading language.

- *Decipher unclear language* by recognizing when authors are being vague, using ambiguous words or sentences, or employing euphemisms or doublespeak.

- *Outlining and mapping* allow you to represent visually the information you have gained by interpreting the text.

READ, WRITE, AND THINK CRITICALLY: SECTION TWO

Directions: Skim through the reading "5 Things We Know to Be True" by Shermer, Hall, Pierrehumbert, Offit, and Shostak and answer questions 1–3. Then, read the selection and answer the questions that follow.

1. Select one of the subsections (evolution, homeopathic medicine, climate change, vaccines, or alien visitation) and write a brief journal entry about your current level of belief in the topic.

2. What is your prior knowledge of any of the five subtopics?

   _____

   _____

3. How much do you know about these topics? Does this reading make you feel intellectually humble? Why or why not?

_____

_____

5 Things We Know to Be True

Michael Shermer, Harriet Hall, Ray Pierrehumbert, Paul Offit, and Seth Shostak

Michael Shermer is the founder and publisher of Skeptic Magazine. *He is a regular contributor to* Time Magazine, Scientific American, the Los Angeles Times, *and* Nature. *Shermer is a prolific author, having written such titles as* The Believing Brain: From Ghosts and Gods to Politics and Conspiracies—How We Construct Beliefs and Reinforce Them as Truths, The Mind of the Market, *and* Why Darwin Matters: Evolution and the Case Against Intelligent Design.

Harriet Hall is a retired Air Force Colonel and physician. She writes frequently about pseudoscience and dubious medical practices, especially for Science-based Medicine, Skeptic Magazine, *and her own website* The Skepdoc.

Ray Pierrehumbert is a physics professor at Oxford University and was formerly at the University of Chicago. He has published a considerable body of research in the following fields: climate dynamics, planetary dynamics, climate and ocean physics, Early Earth, and atmospheric dynamics. He contributes to the body of scientific knowledge in such publications as Science, Astrophysical Journal, Nature Climate Change, *and* Journal of Geophysical Research.

Paul Offit is a pediatrician and an award-winning, best-selling author of multiple books about medical concerns, including Pandora's Lab: Seven Stories of Science Gone Wrong, Autism's False Prophets: Bad Science, Risky Medicine, and the Search for a Cure, Bad Faith, *and* Deadly Choices: How the Anti-Vaccine Movement Threatens Us All. *He is a co-inventor of a life-saving rotavirus vaccine, RotaTeq. Director of the Vaccine Education Center at the Children's Hospital of Philadelphia, Dr. Offit has published over 160 articles and is a professor at the Perelman School of Medicine at the University of Pennsylvania.*

Seth Shostak, Director of the Center for SETI research, is a senior researcher and writer looking for evidence of extraterrestrials. He has written hundreds of articles in diverse fields: astronomical, film/video, science, and technology. Shostak also authored two books about astronomy and contributed to six additional books.

Evolution Is the Only Reasonable Explanation for the Diversity of Life on Earth

Michael Shermer

1 On January 14, 1844, Charles Darwin wrote a letter to his friend Joseph Hooker, recalling his voyage around the world on the HMS *Beagle*. After five years at sea and seven years at home thinking about the origin of species, Darwin came to this conclusion: "At last gleams of light have come, & I am almost convinced (quite contrary to opinion I started with) that species are not (it is like confessing a murder) immutable."

2 *Like confessing a murder*. Dramatic words. But it doesn't take a rocket scientist—or an English naturalist—to understand why a theory on the origin of species by means of natural selection would be so controversial. If new species are created naturally—not supernaturally—what place, then, for God? No wonder that more than a century and a half later people of some religious faiths still find the theory so terribly threatening. But in those intervening years scientists have found so much evidence in support of the theory that it would be truly astonishing if it turned out not to be true—as shocking as if the germ theory of disease fell apart or if astrophysicists were forced to abandon the big bang model of the universe. Why? Because of a convergence of evidence from many lines of inquiry.

3 For example: Comparing data from research in population genetics, geography, ecology, archaeology, physical anthropology and linguistics, scientists discovered that Australian Aborigines are genetically more closely related to South Asians than they are to African blacks—which makes sense from an evolutionary perspective because the migration pattern of humans out of Africa led them to Asia and then to Australia.

4   The consistency of dating techniques also gives us confidence that the theory is true. Uranium-lead, rubidium-strontium and potassium-argon dating, for example, are all reasonably consistent in their determination of the age of rocks and fossils. The ages are given in estimates, but the margins of error are in the range of 1 percent. It is not as if one scientist finds that a fossil hominin is 1.2 million years old while another one finds it is 10,000 years old.

5   Not only are the dates consistent, but the fossils also show intermediate stages—something antievolutionists still insist don't exist. There are now at least six intermediate fossil stages in the evolution of whales, for instance, and more than a dozen fossil hominins, several of which must have been intermediate with humans since the hominins branched off from chimpanzees six million years ago. And geologic strata consistently reveal the same sequence of fossils. Trilobites and mammals are separated by many millions of years, so finding a fossil horse in the same geologic stratum as a trilobite—or even more drastically, a fossil hominin in the same stratum as a dinosaur—would prove problematic for the theory of evolution, but that has never happened.

6   Finally, vestigial structures are signs of evolutionary history. The Cretaceous snake *Pachyrhachis problematicus* had small hind limbs, which are gone in most of today's snakes. Modern whales retain a tiny pelvis for hind legs that existed in their land-mammal ancestors. Likewise, flightless birds have wings. And of course, humans are replete with useless vestigial structures—a distinctive sign of our evolutionary ancestry—such as wisdom teeth, male nipples, body hair, the appendix and the coccyx.

7   As the great geneticist and evolutionary theorist Theodosius Dobzhansky famously noted, "Nothing in biology makes sense except in the light of evolution."

Homeopathy Has No Basis in Science

Harriet Hall

8   Homeopathy is a system of medicine that purports to treat disease with minute doses of substances that in a healthy person would produce symptoms of that disease. It is based on the unscientific thinking of a single misguided individual, a German doctor named Samuel Hahnemann, who invented it in the early 1800s.

9   Homeopathy not only doesn't work; it couldn't possibly work. It is inconsistent with our basic knowledge of physics, chemistry and biology. Oliver Wendell Holmes thoroughly debunked it in 1842 with his essay "Homeopathy and Its Kindred Delusions." He would have been appalled to think anyone could still believe it in 2016.

10   Few users of homeopathy have bothered to inform themselves about what they are taking or the wacky ideas behind it. The simplest way to explain homeopathic theory is with this example: If coffee keeps you awake, dilute coffee will put you to sleep—the more dilute, the stronger the effect. If you dilute it until there isn't a single molecule of coffee left, it will be even stronger. (The water will somehow remember the coffee that is no longer there.) If you drip the coffee-free water onto a sugar pill and let it evaporate, the memory of coffee will be transferred to the sugar pill, and the pill will relieve insomnia.

11   If any of that makes sense to you, you should be worried.

12   You wouldn't think anyone would buy a medicine that contained no active ingredient, but they do. A product called Oscillococcinum is sold in most American pharmacies, bringing in an estimated $15 million a year from customers hoping to relieve the symptoms of flu and colds. The name is that of the oscillating bacteria that a French physician, Joseph Roy, imagined he could see in the blood of flu victims and in duck liver; no one else ever saw them. The box says the active ingredient is *Anas barbariae* 200 CK HPUS. That means Muscovy duck (the heart and liver), and it means they diluted it 1:100 and repeated that process 200 times, "succussing" it after each dilution (it is shaken, not stirred). Any chemistry student can use Avogadro's number to calculate that by the 13th dilution, there is only a 50–50 chance that a single molecule of duck remains, and by the 200th dilution the duck is history. All that remains is the quack.

13   Homeopaths' prescribing methods are unbelievably silly. They ask a laundry list of irrelevant questions (What color are your eyes? What foods do you dislike? What are you afraid of?). They consult two books. The first is a *Repertory* listing remedies for every possible symptom—for example, clairvoyance (yes, it considers this a symptom), dental caries and "tearful" (sic). The second is a *Materia Medica* listing the symptoms associated

with each remedy ("dreams of robbers" are linked to table salt!). Yes, dilute table salt and pretty much anything imaginable can be a remedy. Some of my favorites: Berlin wall, eclipsed moonlight, dog's earwax and the south pole of a magnet. It's absurd, but an estimated five million adults and one million children use homeopathic remedies every year in the U.S., mostly self-prescribed and purchased in a pharmacy.

14 Even though there are published studies claiming that homeopathy works, you can find a study to support almost anything, and rigorous scientific reviews of the entire body of research have consistently concluded that it works no better than placebos. As Edzard Ernst, emeritus professor of complementary medicine at the University of Exeter in England, and author Simon Singh have written, "The evidence points towards a bogus industry that offers patients nothing more than a fantasy."

15 The FDA allows the sale of homeopathic remedies under a "grandfather" clause exempting them from the requirement to demonstrate effectiveness, but it is considering changes in regulation. I wish they would require a label stating, "Contains no active ingredient. For entertainment purposes only." The persistence of homeopathy demonstrates the inability of the general public to think critically. People have used homeopathy instead of effective drugs, vaccines and malaria prophylaxis, with disastrous results. People have died.

16 Homeopathy was bunk in 1842, and it remains bunk today. By now we ought to know better.

Climate Change Conspiracy Theories Are Ludicrous

Ray Pierrehumbert

17 I am always baffled that some people have convinced themselves that the scientific consensus underpinning anthropogenic global warming is a vast conspiracy to destroy the American way of life, foist socialism on the unsuspecting masses, or. . . insert your favorite gripe here.

18 If it is a conspiracy, it is a truly remarkable one, spanning nearly two centuries and the scientific communities of dozens of nations. The foundations of our understanding of planetary temperature begin with the work in the 1820s of French physicist Joseph Fourier, who established that a planet's temperature is determined by the balance between energy received from the sun and infrared radiation emitted back into space. Quantification of Fourier's basic idea depended on the development of blackbody radiation theory by Austrian Ludwig Boltzmann in the mid-1800s and his German contemporary Gustav Kirchhoff. Irish-born physicist John Tyndall brought carbon dioxide into the picture in the late 19th century by showing that it traps infrared radiation, and Swedish chemist Svante Arrhenius put it all together shortly thereafter.

19 There were many later developments in the 20th century, culminating in a quite complete theory incorporating both carbon dioxide and water vapor feedback, which Syukuro Manabe developed while working at NOAA's Geophysical Fluid Dynamics Laboratory in the 1960s and 1970s. We have learned plenty since then, but Manabe basically nailed it. Our understanding of the connection between greenhouse gases and global warming rests on the same principles that underlie heat-seeking missiles, weather satellites and infrared remote controls. It would take quite a conspiracy to fake all that.

20 It would take an even greater conspiracy to fake the changes in Earth's climate that theory predicts and scientists have observed, including higher global average temperatures, rising sea levels, dwindling ice in the Arctic and Antarctic, melting glaciers, increases in the intensity and duration of heat waves, and more. The cabal would also have to fake all the data from past climates that tells us there is no magic mechanism (clouds or otherwise) that will save us from the well-established warming effects of carbon dioxide acting in concert with water vapor. It would have to fake the observations that tell us that subsurface ocean waters are warming—evidence that the energy that is heating the planet's surface is not coming from the oceans. (Energy is conserved, so if the oceans were causing surface warming, then they would be cooling down in response. Conservation is not just a personal virtue—it's the law!) Likewise the carbon isotope and carbon budget data that prove that the carbon dioxide accumulating in the atmosphere really does come from deforestation and burning fossil fuels. It would have to fake the observed conjunction of stratospheric cooling with tropospheric warming, which is characteristic of the influence of carbon dioxide and other long-lived greenhouse gases on the atmosphere.

21 And so on and so forth. It adds up to an awful lot of stuff to fake and makes faking the moon landing look like a piece of cake.

22   Science rewards those who overturn previous dogma (think quantum theory versus classical mechanics), so the fact that the basic theory of anthropogenic global warming has weathered all challenges since appearing in its modern form in the 1960s is saying a lot. Global warming is a problem, and we caused it. That's still true even if Donald Trump disagrees. Arguing about the basic existence of the problem has no place in a sane discourse.

Vaccines Do Not Cause Autism

Paul Offit

23   It has been almost 20 years since a paper published in the *Lancet* gave birth to the notion that vaccines caused autism. Since then, more than two dozen studies have refuted the claim, and the original paper has been retracted.

24   For the most part, the money and time devoted to studying the vaccine-autism hypothesis have been worth it. First, media outlets no longer carry this story under the false mantra of balance, telling two sides when only one is supported by the science. Now the story is one of a disproved claim proposed by a discredited doctor. Second, most parents no longer believe that vaccines cause autism. A recent study showed that 85 percent of parents of children with autism do not believe that vaccines were the cause.

25   Unfortunately, despite the mountain of evidence refuting the association, a small group of parents still believe that vaccines might cause autism. Their failure to vaccinate their children not only endangers the children but also weakens the "herd immunity" that keeps disease outbreaks contained. There are several plausible reasons why they feel this way.

26   One possibility is that the cause or causes of autism remain unknown—the same situation that applied to diabetes in the 1800s, when no one knew what caused it or how to treat it. At the time, people proposed a variety of crazy causes and heroic cures. Then, in 1921, Frederick Banting and Charles Best discovered insulin, and all these false beliefs melted away. Until a clear cause and cure for autism emerge, the vaccine hypothesis will be hard to put completely to rest.

27   Another possibility is that the notion that vaccines cause autism is comforting—certainly far more comforting than studies that have shown a genetic basis. If autism is caused by events occurring outside the womb, then parents can exercise some form of control. If the disorder is genetic, there is no control.

28   And everyone loves a bogeyman. It is nice to be able to point a finger at an evil force causing autism, especially if it is big pharma or big government. Conspiracy theorists argue that the only reason studies have shown that vaccines do not cause autism is that a vast international conspiracy is hiding the truth. Although only a small group of parents hold this belief, their voices are disproportionally represented on the Internet.

29   Finally, parents of children with autism often perceive them as developing normally up to about 12 months of age. Then, after receiving a series of vaccines, the child misses speech, language, behavior and communication milestones typically seen in the second year of life. In fact, several studies examining videotapes taken in the first year of life show that these children were not developing normally. But from the parents' perspective, they were.

30   The most encouraging aspect of the vaccine-autism controversy has been the emergence of academics, clinicians, public health officials and parents who have taken to the Internet, the airways and the print media to represent the science that has exonerated vaccines. As a consequence, the tide has turned. We now hear the voices of parents who are angry that other parents, by choosing not to vaccinate, have put all children at risk.

31   This societal outcry in favor of vaccines was made all the more immediate by the 2015 measles outbreak, which began at the Disney theme park in southern California and spread to 189 people, mostly children, in 24 states and the District of Columbia. Unfortunately, nothing educates better than the virus. Invariably, it is the children who suffer our ignorance.

No Credible Evidence of Alien Visitations Exists

Seth Shostak

32   Millions of people in the U.S. claim they have been abducted by aliens, according to a 2013 story in the *Washington Post*. That's an impressive tally for the aliens. And yet the government's response has been tepid. That should tell you something: either the Feds think it's not happening, or they're part of the problem.

33 Many people believe the latter. They say that the government knows the aliens are here but keeps the evidence under wraps at Area 51 or some other top-secret venue.

34 But hold on.

35 Unless extraterrestrials prefer Americans (and exceptionalism aside, why should they?), then the rate of abduction worldwide shouldn't be terribly different from what it is here. Assuming an aliens-without-borders effort, tens of millions of folks around the world have been grabbed by the grays. I think the United Nations would notice. I think you'd notice.

36 Abductions, of course, are only one component of the so-called UFO phenomenon. The majority of the evidence is composed of sightings—eyewitness accounts, photos and videos. Most of these can be explained as aircraft, rockets, balloons, bright planets or, occasionally, hoaxes. Some remain unexplained—but that only means they're *unexplained*, not that they're flying saucers, no matter how convinced the people who report them might be. There remains no scientifically validated evidence that extraterrestrials have been here, either recently or in the distant past. The pyramids, the Nazca lines in Peru and all the other artifacts that have been ascribed to ancient astronauts can be straightforwardly explained by human activity.

37 In fact, few scientists or science museum curators feel that the claim we're being visited is even plausible. Even aside from the formidable technical challenges of interstellar travel, ask yourself this: Why are they here now? *Homo sapiens* has only been broadcasting its presence to the universe since the advent of television and radar. Unless the extraterrestrials come from a very close star system, there has not been adequate time for them to learn of our existence and fly to Earth. Even if they could get here at the speed of light (which they couldn't), they'd have to live within 35 or so light-years of us—and there aren't all *that* many close stars. Besides, high-speed space travel takes an enormous amount of energy. Would you pay a gargantuan utility bill just for a little "catch and release" sport-fishing for hominins?

38 Nevertheless, for decades polls have shown that roughly one third of the populace believes our world is host to cosmic visitors. If despite the lack of good evidence, you insist on believing this is true, you also have to admit they are the best guests you could ever have. They don't kill us, they don't foment unrest, they don't steal the silverware. The Roswell incident was nearly 70 years ago. If aliens have been here since, they deserve good conduct medals.

---

4. Did the reading confirm or contradict your prior knowledge of each of the subsections? Select one subsection and explain how it compared to what you already knew about the topic.

_____

_____

_____

5. Select one unfamiliar word from each of the subsections of the article. Define these words from the selection using context clues or a dictionary, and then use each one in an original sentence.

"Evolution" subsection:

a.   Word: _____

b.   Definition: _____

c.   Original sentence: _____

_____

_____

"Homeopathy" subsection:

a. Word: _____

b. Definition: _____

c. Original sentence: _____

_____

_____

"Climate Change" subsection:

a. Word: _____

b. Definition: _____

c. Original sentence: _____

_____

_____

"Vaccines" subsection:

a. Word: _____

b. Definition: _____

c. Original sentence: _____

_____

_____

"Alien Visitation" subsection:

a. Word: _____

b. Definition: _____

c. Original sentence: _____

_____

_____

6. Put the main idea (claim) of each of the sections in your own words.

"Evolution" main idea:

_____

_____

_____

"Homeopathy" main idea:

_____

_____

_____

"Climate Change" main idea:

_____

_____

_____

"Vaccines" main idea:

_____

_____

_____

"Alien Visitation" main idea:

_____

_____

_____

7. Identify a major detail from each of the subsections and determine type of detail.

"Evolution" subsection:

a. Detail: _____

b. Type of detail: _____

"Homeopathy" subsection:

a. Detail: _____

b. Type of detail: _____

"Climate Change" subsection:

a. Detail: _____

b. Type of detail: _____

"Vaccines" subsection:

a. Detail: _____

b. Type of detail: _____

"Alien Visitation" subsection:

a. Detail: _____

b. Type of detail: _____

8. Clarify Hall's language in the following sentence: "All that remains is the quack" (para. 12). What does she mean?

_____

9. Paraphrase what Pierrehumbert writes in the first sentence of "Climate Change Conspiracy Theories are Ludicrous."

_____

_____

_____

10. In your own words, explain the comparison that Offit makes between the cause(s) of autism and the cause(s) of diabetes (para. 26).

_____

_____

_____

CHAPTER 4

Inference

Learning Goals

In this chapter you will learn how to

➤ Draw Inferences While Reading   SECTION ONE
➤ Be Open-Minded and Flexible
➤ Aim for Appropriate Inferences
➤ Infer an Author's Intended Audience
➤ Infer an Author's Purpose
➤ Infer an Author's Tone
➤ Recognize an Author's Assumptions   SECTION TWO
➤ Recognize the Implications of an Author's Assumptions

PREVIEW OF TERMS

Inference p. 111
Imply p. 111
Open-mindedness p. 113
Flexibility p. 113
Communal reinforcement p. 113
Defense mechanisms p. 113
Denial p. 113
Anger p. 113
Avoidance p. 113
Status quo bias p. 113
Conclusion p. 115
Completeness p. 117
Appropriate conclusion p. 117
Audience p. 120
Purpose p. 121
Tone p. 123
Denotation p. 125
Connotation p. 125
Images p. 125
Assumptions p. 138
Implication p. 141
See glossary, pp. 391–397

SECTION ONE

What Is Inference?

On your way home from classes, you pass your neighbor's house and see brightly colored balloons on the mailbox and lamppost. A dozen cars are packed into their driveway. You notice one of the drivers coming out of her car, and she's carrying a present and a stack of pizza boxes. You smile and think to yourself, "The Nelsons are having another party!" What you have done on that ride home through your neighborhood is *inferred*—you took in some information, thought about how the details fit what you already know and understand, and reached a logical conclusion.

Critical thinkers are skilled at **inference**—coming to a justifiable conclusion based on the information available. Critical readers apply the skill of inference to a text. An author or speaker will often **imply** (hint or suggest) ideas rather than state every idea explicitly. Critical thinkers recognize when an idea is being implied and can draw conclusions based on what is indirectly suggested by the author. They use the information provided by the author as well as their own prior knowledge and experience to arrive at a reasonable conclusion.

Inferences are important in our daily lives (for example, we might see flashing emergency lights while driving on the highway and infer that we should slow down) and also in our attempt to gain knowledge through reading, listening, and watching for information (for instance, we may glance at the television, see a phone number listed at the bottom of the screen, and infer that a TV program is attempting to sell us something). The skill of inference is recognizing what *is not* being said or written directly. The attitude of open-mindedness and flexibility should help you recognize indirect messages.

Reviewing the Critical Thinker's Traits: Being Open-Minded and Flexible

Dan was the happiest he had ever been in his entire life: He had just proposed to his long-time girlfriend Alicia and she accepted! Recent community college graduates, Dan and Alicia were excited to start their life together. Both had gotten jobs in their chosen fields; Dan was working for a small marketing firm, and Alicia was an automotive technician at a successful car repair shop. Dan was proud of the fact that Alicia's career wasn't traditional for a female, and Alicia thought that Dan looked so handsome in the suits and ties she picked out for him as his graduation gift. They were starting to hunt for a small house. Life seemed perfect—perfect, that is, until one morning before work when Dan brought up what he thought was a joke.

"Hey, Alicia, when we get married, I suppose you will cut the grass in addition to keeping our cars running smoothly."

"Well, yeah, why?" Alicia asked.

"Actually I was kidding. I know you'll keep our cars running but I figured I'd be the one to handle any lawn-care jobs."

"Hmmm . . . Why? You have seasonal allergies! Why would you even *want* to cut the grass?"

"That's one of the jobs my dad always did. I don't know. I guess I never thought about it before. I kind of figured we'd run the household similar to how my parents ran theirs while I was growing up. They are still happily married; it must work!"

Alicia didn't say anything for a few minutes. Then she took a deep breath and said, "So, are you telling me that you expect *me* to cook all the meals and do all the laundry while you do all the outdoor work? And, are you telling me that we'll do it this way just because that's how your parents did things? I didn't think you were so sexist and old-fashioned." She crossed her arms in front of her and stared at him.

"I'm not sexist, and I'm not old-fashioned! Wasn't I your biggest supporter when you decided to change your major from ultrasound technician to automotive technician? How can you say that about me?"

"If you think I am going to live in a house that is just like your parents' 1950s-inspired marriage, then you are dead wrong!" Alicia had tears in her eyes as she yelled at Dan. This was turning into their worst fight ever.

Dan stammered, "Alicia, calm down. How did you think we'd split up the chores?"

Alicia answered, "I thought we could make a list of all the chores that have to be done and pick the ones we don't mind doing, and then the ones that are left we could take turns doing or even tackle them together. Remember, you always told me that you love to cook but that your mom never let you experiment in the kitchen. Well, now it's your time to experiment!"

Even though her plan sounded reasonable, Dan wasn't so sure. What would his parents say if they came to visit and he was in the kitchen and Alicia was outside pushing a lawnmower? What would his friends say? He told Alicia he'd have to think about it and left for work.

>> Education's purpose is to replace an empty mind with an open one. "

—Malcolm S. Forbes

Alicia fumed. She twisted the engagement ring on her finger and wondered why she never noticed before how close-minded Dan was.

In the meantime, Dan thought about Alicia and their fight all day long. He was distracted and unhappy at work and couldn't wait to talk to her in person and try to resolve their issue. The way he saw it, Dan could either dig in his heels and insist on splitting up chores along gender lines, or he could change some of his beliefs that were, he had to admit, a little old-fashioned. If he chose the first option, he might end up losing Alicia AND having his seasonal allergies flare up every Saturday when he had to cut the grass! If he chose the second option, he could prove to Alicia and to himself that he was not sexist (plus, there was a great new steak marinade he wanted to try to make!).

Decision made, Dan picked up steaks and ingredients for the marinade on his way home from work and surprised Alicia by showing off his culinary skills and his enlightened attitude!

In the situation above, Dan displays two very important traits of a critical thinker: *open-mindedness and flexibility.* **Open-mindedness** is the tendency to consider ideas, even ideas that are contrary to what you already believe, with a spirit of openness and willingness to learn something new or to see them from a fresh perspective. **Flexibility** is the ability to change your thoughts and belief systems based on new information. Being flexible can help you make good inferences as you take in additional information and evaluate how the new ideas fit with your prior knowledge.

Remember in Chapter 1 when you learned about how hard it is to be a critical thinker? One reason it can be difficult to be open-minded and flexible is communal reinforcement. **Communal reinforcement** is the tendency of people to believe what they hear, often repeatedly, within their communities. A community can include your peer group, family, school, religious affiliation, political party, clubs, and sports teams, as well as people who listen to the same types of radio and television programs as you do or who seek the same types of Internet sites. Communal reinforcement can hinder critical thinking because an idea that gets repeated within a community gains strength, even if there isn't adequate evidence to support it. As you work toward being a critical thinker, you will need to remind yourself to stretch your thinking beyond what your community believes and repeats.

You also learned about **defense mechanisms** in the first chapter. Sometimes your mind tries to protect itself from new, unfamiliar, or uncomfortable information if that information might contradict what you already believe. As a result, people often use **denial**, **anger**, or **avoidance** to keep themselves from dealing with difficult ideas.

Another obstacle to flexible thinking is the status quo bias. The **status quo bias** is a preference for the existing state of affairs. In other words, people like things the way they are, and they prefer

Thinker to Emulate: Robert Byrd

Source: Congress.gov

Robert Byrd (born Cornelius Calvin Sale, Jr.; November 20, 1917 – June 28, 2010) was a United States Senator from West Virginia from 1959 to 2010. He has the distinction of being the longest-serving member of the U.S. Congress.

While he originally exhibited some strong biases (probably due to communal reinforcement) that led to his opposition of the 1964 Civil Rights Act, he later apologized for his intolerance and voted in favor of the Civil Rights Act of 1968. Other notable stances include Byrd's changing opinion about war: While Byrd supported the Vietnam War, he was strongly against the war in Iraq.

For his ability to be open-minded and flexible, he is a thinker to emulate. Byrd frequently and publically expressed his regret that he was not immediately supportive of civil rights; this demonstrates his humility and his ability to learn from his mistakes, as evidenced by his eventual endorsement of Barack Obama for president.

not to change unless they have a very, very good reason or unless they have to. This can be a dangerous bias, because people will continue to perform the same acts even when they do not produce effective results, just because they are used to doing them. Or they will cling to the same thoughts and hold the same views, even if reality has shown them that those views are not true. We are all susceptible to the status quo bias. To be an effective critical thinker, you have to learn to guard against the status quo bias in yourself. Like Robert Byrd, you have to learn not to value your conclusions and viewpoints solely because you are used to them.

EXPAND YOUR UNDERSTANDING

Learning More about Robert Byrd While Writing Critically

Read Robert Byrd's obituaries on the Internet and answer the following questions. Here are two links to obituaries, but you are encouraged to find your own to read as well.

www.nytimes.com/2010/06/29/us/politics/29byrd.html

www.washingtonpost.com/wp-dyn/content/article/ 2010/06/28/ AR2010062801241.html

THINK AND WRITE CRITICALLY

1. What would a critical thinker think of some of Byrd's decisions?
2. What other decisions show Byrd's ability to be open-minded and flexible (in addition to Byrd's changing opinions regarding civil rights and war)?
3. Review the character traits of a critical thinker (Chapter 1). What other character traits does Byrd exemplify?

Tips for Critical Thinkers: How to Be Open-Minded and Flexible

- **Remember the attitude of intellectual humility.** Be aware of the tremendous amount of knowledge in the world that you have not yet tapped into and stay open-minded to new ideas and possibilities.
- **Engage with the material.** As you read or listen to information, be aware of when you strongly agree or disagree with it. Make notes to yourself and conduct further research to see if your response is justified.
- **Brainstorm.** Rather than settling on the first idea that comes to your mind, brainstorm for additional possibilities.
- **Be aware of communal reinforcement.** Reading widely, watching and listening to a variety of information sources, and surrounding yourself with people who have experienced other cultures and lifestyles are all ways to open your mind to new perspectives.
- **Recognize use of defense mechanisms.** While it is easy to notice *others'* use of defense mechanisms, it is much harder to recognize it in ourselves. If you tend to deny information ("No, I don't believe it!") or get angry ("I am sick of having to listen to your opinions all the time!") or attempt avoidance ("Let's change the subject"), then you might be allowing your defense mechanisms to get in the way of seeing an issue in a new light.
- **Guard against the status quo bias**. Be aware of when you might be giving preference to your current ways of doing things or thinking because that is easier and more comfortable than considering new ideas. Making changes and being flexible can lead you to unexpected and wonderful new insights.

Discussion Questions

1. Have you ever been in a situation like Dan's situation? How did you react?

2. If Dan's or Alicia's beliefs make you uncomfortable, ask yourself why. Can you identify any of the obstacles to critical thinking in your own reaction?

Making Inferences

Whereas in Chapters 2 and 3 you were focusing on what the author states directly, in this chapter you will pay particular attention to the subtleties of *how* the author says it as well as what he or she *doesn't* say.

As a critical thinker, one of your goals is to draw inferences. An *inference* is a reasonable and logical judgment based on evidence. Another word for inference is **conclusion**. Drawing accurate conclusions requires you to be aware of the messages that are indirectly implied by an author.

We make inferences all of the time in our daily lives. When a classmate walks into the classroom, takes off her sunglasses, and reveals a black eye, your curiosity and concern prompt you to make inferences. You may not want to ask her directly and she might not want to announce to the class what happened, so you take the available information, combined with your own knowledge and experience, and come to the logical conclusion that she bumped into something. Could you also infer that she was hit in the eye? Sure, you could. Could you infer that she is wearing makeup for a part in a school play? Yes, but that conclusion does not make as much sense and would therefore require more information from the student to confirm that she came straight from the theater and didn't have time to remove her makeup before biology lab.

Frequently, you need more information in order to come to the best possible conclusion. Perhaps you overhear this classmate saying how clumsy she can be, which would point to the conclusion that she bumped into something or fell. Or perhaps you hear her muttering to her best friend that she is never going out with her ex-boyfriend again because he lost his temper and got physical with her, which would suggest that he hit her in the eye. New information has to be integrated with the evidence already provided, so you can either come to a tentative conclusion or wait until you get additional facts.

As you read texts, listen to speeches, or watch films or shows, keep the above example in mind: Making inferences requires you to be observant and logical in order to arrive at a justifiable conclusion. Oftentimes, however, you need to be flexible; as more information becomes available to you (for instance, as you read further or when a speaker says something to contradict your initial conclusion), you may need to modify your first conclusion. At this point it helps to be flexible and open-minded to other possible explanations, and it would be useful for you to get in the habit of annotating inferences in the margin.

Tips for Critical Thinkers: How to Make Inferences

- **Verify your comprehension**. Be sure you understand the author's or speaker's explicitly stated message by identifying the topic, activating your prior knowledge, asking questions, and defining unknown vocabulary words.
- **Consider your interpretation**. Clarify meaning and determine significance by annotating, summarizing the main idea and details, and creating an outline or map if necessary.
- **Observe carefully**. Notice what is and what is not being stated.
- **Be creative**. Don't censor yourself as you brainstorm possible inferences. While the most logical conclusion is often the most obvious one, this is not always so.

- **Return to the text or situation to verify information**. Try not to let your own experiences and knowledge take you in a different direction than the available information is actually leading. Annotating the text (jotting down inferences in the margin) should help keep you on track.
- **Do research.** Acknowledge when you need to get more information *before* you come to a final conclusion. Do the necessary background reading and research.

PRACTICE 4-1   Making Inferences about Scenarios

Directions: Read the following scenarios and make at least three inferences about each one. Put a check mark next to the inference you believe is the most likely, based on the information provided to you. The first one is done for you.

Here's a model

Scenario: You are home alone late at night and hear strange noises coming from outside. As you don't want to go outside to investigate, you stand by an open window and hear a low moan, a throaty mew sound, and scuffling noises coming from underneath your front porch.

Inferences: <u>There is an unfriendly ghost trying to scare you by making noises outside the house.</u>
<u>A burglar got hurt while trying to break into your house.</u>
✓ <u>Neighborhood animals (possibly the two cats you frequently see wandering around) are fighting under your front porch.</u>
_____

Now you try

1. Scenario: One of your co-workers puts in longer work hours than the rest of the employees working in the same position.

   Inferences: _____
   _____
   _____
   _____

2. Scenario: You are shopping in your college bookstore and see a classmate returning a large pile of textbooks.

   Inferences: _____
   _____
   _____
   _____

3. Scenario: You are meeting a friend at the movies. This friend prides herself on being punctual and considerate, yet she is already a half-hour late.

   Inferences: _____
   _____
   _____
   _____

AIM for Appropriate Conclusions

When you draw conclusions, you aim to follow the author's message carefully to arrive at inferences that are likely and reasonable. An **appropriate conclusion**, therefore, is one that is logical and likely to be accurate given your prior knowledge and the information provided by the author. Not all conclusions will be appropriate, however. Sometimes, even when you are reading critically, you can infer too much and draw an inappropriate or wrong conclusion. Because you are using your own experience and knowledge in addition to the clues the author gives you, your own ideas may prevent you from accurately concluding what the author is implying. (By the way, an inappropriate conclusion might just happen to be correct, but it would be correct out of luck or coincidence, not out of the process of carefully fol-

> ### Spotlight on Standards: Completeness
>
> As you are aware, critical thinkers pay attention to whether information adheres to the standards. In this chapter on inference, we will focus on **completeness**. If you are trying to draw logical conclusions, it is important that you have as much information as possible to consider. Remember that drawing an inference requires observing both what the author says as well as what an author implies. In addition, you need to incorporate your own prior knowledge, experience, and powers of logic. If you do not have enough information—that is, if there are gaps in your knowledge or if the author does not provide enough evidence, then we could say the information is incomplete and you might have to hold off drawing a reasonable inference. For example, say you are reading an article about an upcoming political election in an attempt to determine which candidate you want to vote for. The article includes a lot of information about both candidates' stances regarding many important topics: education, abortion, the economy, taxes, the environment, and international relations. You notice, however, that the author leaves out a topic that is important to you: gun control. Before you make a decision about whom you will vote for on election day, you decide you need more complete information, and you search other political articles and news programs in an attempt to find out each candidate's position on gun control. In this way, you have assured yourself that you have a complete picture and can infer which person would be best for the job.

lowing the author's implied message.) Other times you may not have enough information to draw a conclusion. In that case, you need to read further or do some outside research in order to get more complete information. Use the acronym AIM to remind you of what the potential conclusions could be:

A   Appropriate: Conclusion fits logically with the details and evidence available

I   Inappropriate: Conclusion is not backed up by the information provided

M   More information required: Conclusion could work, but the details don't give you quite enough to be certain; more research or reading is necessary

Let's look at the model scenario again from Practice 4-1 to see how, as a critical reader, you would apply AIM to possible conclusions.

Scenario: You are home alone late at night and hear strange noises coming from outside. As you don't want to go outside to investigate, you stand by an open window and hear a low moan, a throaty mew sound, and scuffling noises coming from underneath your front porch.

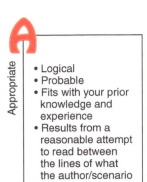

Appropriate
- Logical
- Probable
- Fits with your prior knowledge and experience
- Results from a reasonable attempt to read between the lines of what the author/scenario suggests

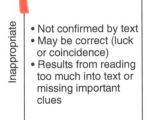

Inappropriate
- Not confirmed by text
- May be correct (luck or coincidence)
- Results from reading too much into text or missing important clues

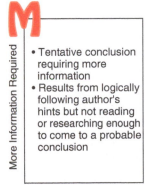

More Information Required
- Tentative conclusion requiring more information
- Results from logically following author's hints but not reading or researching enough to come to a probable conclusion

■ **Figure 4-1**   AIM

Possible Inferences	AIM	Student's Thought Process
Neighborhood animals (possibly the two cats you frequently see wandering around) are fighting under your front porch.	**A** **Appropriate** • Logical • Probable • Fits with your prior knowledge and experience • Results from a reasonable attempt to read between the lines of what the author/scenario suggests	*This inference seems logical and probable. Animals certainly do fight sometimes. It fits with my prior knowledge and experience. I have seen two cats wandering around my yard almost every day for months. The front porch would make a good hiding place for them. I believe this conclusion is reasonable and is suggested by the details in the given scenario, especially the mewing sound.*
There is an unfriendly ghost trying to scare you by making noises outside the house.	**I** **Inappropriate** • Not confirmed by text • May be correct (luck or coincidence) • Results from reading too much into text or missing important clues	*There aren't any details that suggest the sounds are being made by a ghost. I doubt that this would be correct (even by luck or coincidence) because there isn't any scientific evidence proving ghosts exist. This conclusion would be inappropriate and would result from letting my imagination get the best of me.*
A burglar got hurt while trying to break into your house.	**M** **More Information Needed** • Tentative conclusion requiring more information • Results from logically following author's hints but not reading or researching enough to come to a probable conclusion	*This conclusion could be appropriate but only if I could get more information to support it. For instance, if the very next day the police interview neighbors about a string of burglaries, then that new information would need to be incorporated into the scenario.*

Always revisit the text! When you draw a conclusion, ask yourself what exactly in the text gave you that impression. If you cannot pinpoint what the author or speaker said that made you draw a potentially inappropriate conclusion, then you will need to reread and try again or reserve judgment until you have additional information.

PRACTICE 4-2   Drawing Appropriate Conclusions

Directions: Read the following selections and label the conclusions that follow as appropriate (A), inappropriate (I), or more information necessary (M). The first one is done for you.

Here's a model

Anatole wrote in his note that here [Nelson] was his best student and we would soon see why. We did. The day Nelson came to us he only spoke, "How are you, thank you, please," for English, but after a few weeks he could say about anything that mattered, without turning it all on its head the way Mama Tataba used to. I would say Nelson is gifted. But I'll tell you what, gifted doesn't count for a hill of beans in the Congo, where even somebody as smart as Nelson isn't allowed to go to college, any more than us Price girls are. According to the Underdowns, the Belgians are bent on protecting against independent thought on native ground.

From *The Poisonwood Bible* by Kingsolver

Possible conclusions:

   __A__ a. The narrator lives in the Congo, in which the Belgians exert control and the natives face discrimination.

   __I__ b. Mama Tataba and the Underdowns are sympathetic to the Belgians' cause in the Congo.

   __M__ c. Nelson, Anatole, and the Price girls become close during their time together in the Congo.

Now you try

1. To demonstrate, let me ask you a question that you can answer objectively—but only if you kept all of your old report cards. Here it is: How'd you do in high school?

   The answer is: probably not as well as you remember—at least not if the students at Ohio Wesleyan are any guide. In one study, students at OW were asked to recall their high school grades. Then the researchers checked the students' responses against the actual transcripts. No less than 29 percent of the recalled grades were wrong. (This, at least, was better than German students. Given a similar test, they did even worse: 43 percent wrong.) Keep in mind, this is not ancient history the students are being asked to recall; these are college freshmen and sophomores being asked about their grades in high school just a few years earlier.

   What's more, the students' errors weren't neutral. Far more grades were shifted up (recalling an A instead of a B) than down. Not surprisingly, perhaps, students had a better memory for good grades than for bad. The recall accuracy for As was 89 percent; for Ds it was 29 percent. (Researchers threw out the Fs.) Nor were the errors isolated. Overall, seventy-nine of the ninety-nine students inflated their grades. (Too few students deflated their grades to allow meaningful generalizations.)

From *Why We Make Mistakes* by Hallinan

Possible conclusions:

   _____ a. If students were asked to recount their accomplishments in sports, the results would be similar (they would inflate their successes).

   _____ b. Germans are more arrogant than Americans.

   _____ c. Our memories are not perfect.

2. There were two striking things about the servicemen and servicewomen I met on the trip to Afghanistan. First, their morale was incredibly high. There was a real sense of mission among these soldiers. A story I heard from a young major from Delaware sort of encapsulated the spirit of our forces there. A pediatric hospital in Kabul lost power when its generator broke down, and the needed parts could not be purchased. Neither the Karzai government nor the U.S. Embassy could figure out how to come up with the $320 they needed to buy the replacement part. So while the patients in the hospital suffered, the Marines passed the hat, raised the money, got the part, and fixed the generator. They saw a problem and remedied it the quickest way they could.

From *Promises to Keep* by Biden

Possible conclusions:

   _____ a. Biden strongly admires the Americans serving in the military in Afghanistan.

   _____ b. Biden has taken more than one trip to Afghanistan.

   _____ c. The Karzai government and the U.S. Embassy could have easily come up with the money to buy the replacement part for the hospital, but they just didn't want to.

3. Plagiarism, as we have seen, includes a variety of very different behaviors: buying papers (a rare but dramatic instance); using a friend's paper; falsifying a bibliography; wholesale copying into one's own paper without citation; and borrowing a phrase or an idea without crediting the originator, whether intentionally or inadvertently. Although about 60 percent of college students report that they have engaged in one form or another of plagiarism, only 2 percent admit to buying a paper. Given the range of practices lumped together as "plagiarism," it is difficult to generalize about students' motives. Some express supreme disrespect for institutional guidelines, while others simply haven't mastered the conventions of citation.

From *My Word! Plagiarism and College Culture* by Blum

Possible conclusions:

_____ a. Most college instructors would frown upon incidents of plagiarism.

_____ b. Students who plagiarize are also likely to cheat on tests.

_____ c. The 2 percent who admitted to purchasing a paper possibly bought the papers on the Internet.

Because making inferences can be tricky even for the best critical readers and thinkers, it helps to examine as much information as possible. Considering an author's or speaker's intended audience, purpose, and tone allows you to make inferences about what he or she is saying. In fact, the skill of inference assists you in determining the author's audience, purpose, and tone in the first place; you can then use what you learned from each of these to make further inferences about the text.

Inferring an Author's Audience

Knowing the author's or speaker's audience can assist you in making reasonable inferences. The **audience** is the group of people that the author (or speaker) has in mind when writing. In most instances, an author wants to reach a particular audience and will appeal to the audience's background, characteristics, prior knowledge, assumptions, and values. For example, an anatomy and physiology text aimed at college freshmen will be written differently than a text intended for medical doctors already practicing in the field.

Sometimes authors are clear and obvious about whom they intend to reach, but more often than not, the reader must use inference to figure out their intended audience. Here are some tips you can use to infer an author's intended audience.

Tips for Critical Thinkers: Inferring an Author's Audience

- **Identify the source of the information.** Is it from a textbook, an academic journal, a popular periodical, a newspaper, or a trade book?
- **Recognize the occasion.** Was the work published in response to a specific event? For example, was an author writing in response to research done by another expert in the field? Was a candidate delivering a politically motivated speech during an election year?
- **Identify the level.** Are the word choices, concepts, and sentence structures difficult, average, or easy? Does the author use technical jargon that would suggest that he or she has a particular audience in mind that is already educated and experienced in a specific field? You should annotate the text as you notice clues to the author's target audience.
- **Think about audience characteristics.** What do audience members have in common? Do they belong to the same profession, political group, religion, nationality? Do they have similar experiences, attitudes, values, and needs?

- **Look up other works by the author.** In your local or college library catalog or on a site such as Amazon.com, you can look up an author's other works and see if they give you clues into the author's typical audience.
- **Conduct research.** In many instances, you will need to conduct a quick Internet search to find out more about source and occasion.

Inferring the Author's Audience
PRACTICE 4-3

Directions: Reread "5 Things We Know to Be True" by Shermer, Hall, Pierrehumbert, Offit, and Shostak on p. 103. Identify the following information and then write a short paragraph explaining whom you think the author was addressing.

Source:

_____

_____

Occasion:

_____

_____

Level:

_____

_____

Audience Characteristics:

_____

_____

Authors' other works:

_____

_____

Audience:

_____

_____

_____

_____

_____

THINK AND WRITE CRITICALLY

Inferring an Author's Purpose

Purpose is the reason an author writes (or a speaker speaks). Writers and speakers have goals that they want to accomplish by reaching out to an audience. To list just a few examples, a textbook author's goal would be to educate; a humorist (such as Dave Barry or Amy Sedaris) would have the goal of using funny situations to make readers think; and a newspaper columnist's purpose could be to relate the day's news in a concise and informative fashion. At the most basic level, the purpose is usually *to inform, to persuade*, or *to entertain*. However, within each of those classifications, there are underlying and more focused goals that the writer is apt to have. See Figure 4-2 for some typical purposes.

To inform	To persuade	To entertain

• To explain
• To clarify
• To show
• To introduce
• To provide
  background
• To describe
• To give directions
• To define
	• To convince
	• To recommend
	• To suggest
	• To argue
	• To express an
	  opinion
	• To take a political
	  stance
	• To sell
		• To be funny
		• To tell a story
		• To frighten
		• To inspire
		• To shock
		• To connect
		  emotionally
		• To excite
		• To reminisce

■ **Figure 4-2**   Purposes for Writing or Speaking

Identifying the intended audience for a reading and the connotations of the language used in it can help you infer an author's purpose. For example, if the audience is college students in an introduction to anthropology course, then you can expect that the purpose of the text is to inform. If a writer uses words with strong connotations to get the intended audience to desire and therefore purchase a product, then you would be safe in inferring that his or her purpose is to persuade (much like the names of the Benjamin Moore paint colors in Practice 4-6 are designed to attract buyers).

Authors also sometimes try to obscure their purpose. Not all audiences will respond positively to a direct sales pitch, for example, so an author might attempt to make it appear that his or her purpose is something else, perhaps to inform.

Losing weight is one of the most difficult things a person can do, but science has shown that certain things can make it much easier. The key is to establish good habits and to have good nutrition.

Establishing good habits can be as simple as making sure that you don't snack and that you don't eat more than you need to. In the United States, we often have overly large portion sizes during our meals. It's also helpful not to have snack foods around your house. That way, when you get the urge, the junk food is too much trouble to acquire. Good nutrition primarily means getting the nutrients you need and expending more calories than you take in. Some recent scientific studies have shown that weight loss supplements can be beneficial in helping you burn calories. One particularly excellent supplement, in this author's experience, is *Fit Fast*, a delicious low-calorie shake that comes pre-packaged and is chock full of vitamins and nutrients. It will definitely help you lose weight, and you may want to look into purchasing it, as it will help you achieve your weight loss goals.

At first glance, the reader might think the purpose is to inform by giving objective information on the topic of weight loss. A closer look, however, reveals the hidden purpose: trying to persuade readers to purchase dietary supplements, and *Fit Fast* in particular, through the use of words with strong connotations like *excellent, delicious,* and *definitely*.

Knowing an author's purpose helps you target what the author is indirectly implying. For instance, if an author writes a persuasive article about having pets spayed and neutered, then you might determine that the author is implying that people who neglect to spay and neuter their pets are being irresponsible. The author might not choose to come right out and say this, but reading critically you would infer that the author is saying these pet owners are negligent.

Tips for Critical Thinkers: Inferring Purpose

- **Examine details**. Details reveal a lot about purpose. An author whose purpose is *to inform* will use facts and objective information. An author trying *to persuade* readers will use details that are more subjective and opinionated. An author who employs engaging and imaginative details is trying *to entertain*.
- **Look at the source of the information**. A textbook or newspaper will aim to inform, whereas campaign literature is meant to persuade, and popular magazines are intended to entertain.
- **Read the foreword or preface**. If the author chooses to include a foreword or preface, it will be located in the first few pages of a book and it might tell you exactly what the author's purpose is.
- **Utilize connotations**. As you read, annotate words that have strong connotations that imply the author's purpose.
- **Be open-minded and flexible**. You may need to change your first impression if you come across information that contradicts it. Also, authors frequently have multiple purposes in mind. Their major goal may be to persuade, but they might need to give you enough information about the issue first as background, which could lead you to believe their purpose is to inform.
- **Annotate**. Any clues to the author's purpose should be circled, underlined, highlighted, or otherwise marked in the text.

Determining the Author's Purpose	PRACTICE 4-4

Directions: Revisit the reading "5 Things We Know to Be True" by Shermer, Hall, Pierre-humbert, Offit, and Shostak on pp. 103–107. What is the authors' purpose? Explain your reasoning (what specific information in the text led you to your conclusion?).

General purpose (to inform, to persuade, or to entertain):

_____

Specific purpose: _____

_____

Explanation: _____

_____

_____

_____

_____

Inferring an Author's Tone

Like audience and purpose, tone is another facet of an author's work that can help you infer his or her message. **Tone** is the attitude or feeling conveyed in a piece of writing. Tone can be revealed through subject matter, word choice (connotations), sentence structure, punctuation, and emotion.

Authors take into account both purpose and audience when using certain tones. For example, if an author is writing to persuade an audience of 18-year-olds to register to vote, then an angry or disgusted tone will not be as effective as an informative or inspired tone. If a neuroscientist is writing to an audience of colleagues in the same field to inform them of a new discovery in brain research, then readers would expect an academic tone.

Think about how you can infer a friend's mood or tone when you are face to face. Not only does his voice convey emotion, but his facial expressions, body language, and choice of words contribute to the overall impression he projects. The same is true on the written page, but since you cannot actually hear or observe the author face to face, you need to look at other information such as word choice and sentence structure. There are as many possible tones for a piece of writing (or a speech or other creative work) as there are adjectives to describe someone's personality. Figure 4-3 lists some words that indicate emotion and are commonly used to describe an author's tone.

Use the following tips to infer an author's tone.

Tips for Critical Thinkers: Inferring Tone

- **Pretend the author is in front of you, speaking.** Can you detect an attitude or feeling? Ask yourself what emotion or attitude the author's voice projects.
- **Notice sentence structure and punctuation.** Short, clipped sentences might suggest an angry or rushed tone. Long and complex sentences might suggest an informative tone. Note how the use of all-caps or multiple exclamation points can convey powerful emotions such as anger or excitement. Mark your text to show where sentence structure and punctuation reveal possible shifts in tone.
- **Recall what you learned about audience.** Authors want their audience to keep reading and to be informed, persuaded, or entertained by their writing. Make a note in the margin about whom you think the audience is and infer how the author's tone would affect these likely readers.
- **Remember the author's purpose.** Ask yourself what tone would best accomplish the author's purpose. If the author strays from the tone you would expect, try to determine why. How does the author's tone enhance the purpose of the text?

Academic	Admiring	Argumentative
Arrogant	Belligerent	Bitter
Calm	Concerned	Condescending
Cynical	Demanding	Disgusted
Gregarious	Hesitant	Humorous
Informative	Inspired	Intimate
Ironic	Irritated	Nostalgic
Playful	Reflective	Sarcastic
Sentimental	Sympathetic	Remorseful
Troubled	Unsettled	Wistful

■ **Figure 4-3** Tone Words

Discussion Questions

1. Which tone words in Figure 4-3 are unfamiliar to you? Look them up in a dictionary, and then, in small groups, discuss what an author using these tones might sound like.

2. When you are face to face with a person, how do you read his or her tone? How does it differ when you are inferring an author's tone from the written page?

3. Pretend you must write a letter to your roommate explaining why you don't want to live with her next semester. Pick three different tones you could use, and share in pairs or small groups how the letters would differ depending on each tone.

4. Brainstorm some additional adjectives that could describe an author's tone or attitude. Add to the table; define if necessary.

THINK
AND **WRITE**
CRITICALLY

Inferring Word Connotation

Much of the tone projected by an author comes through word choice. The connotations of the words used in a piece of writing strongly project the author's message and attitude. **Denotation** simply refers to the dictionary definition of a word; **connotation**, on the other hand, refers to the feelings associated with the word. In fact, some connotations (and their associated emotions) are strong enough to create **images** (mental pictures) in the minds of audience members. An example is the word *home*: the denotation of *home* as defined by www.m-w.com is "one's place of residence." The connotations of the word *home*, however, are far richer—just ask any soldier or college freshman who longs to be *home* for the holidays. The connotations include the feelings associated with *home* such as warmth, security, and familiarity as well as the images associated with *home* such as loved ones gathered around the kitchen table.

Skilled writers deliberately use some words that provoke negative emotions and others that bring forth positive emotions. Annotate the passage to identify which words have positive or negative connotations. Use a thesaurus to look up synonyms and see how changing the word choices might affect the tone. Using inference, you can read between the lines and recognize when an author has consciously selected a word with a strong connotation in order to elicit a desired emotional response from their audience members and create a specific mental image in their minds.

Here are some useful tips for inferring when a word has strong connotations.

Tips for Critical Thinkers: Inferring Connotations

- **Use a dictionary**. Clarify the denotative (dictionary) meaning of the word first.
- **Look at the context**. Take a closer look at the words and ideas surrounding the word in question so that you are aware of context. A word that could have a negative connotation in one context might be positive in another.
- **Consult a thesaurus**. Make a list of synonyms that could have been used by the author. What emotional connotations do they have?
- **Substitute synonyms**. Try substituting a few synonyms for the word in question and see how that changes the feeling of the sentence.
- **Identify the image**. When you annotate, write any strong images that come to mind in reference to a specific word in the margin next to it.

PRACTICE 4-5   The Effect of Connotation

Directions: Read the following passage, paying attention to the underlined words. Then answer the questions that follow.

As the reporter saw the politician for the first time, she sized him up. He was <u>slim</u>, with short <u>salt-and-pepper</u> hair framing a <u>rugged</u> face. His custom-tailored suit fit his <u>slender</u> <u>physique</u> well, seeming to advertise both physical and mental <u>efficiency</u>. His <u>countenance</u> bore an <u>amused</u>, slightly <u>curious</u> look, as if he were <u>contemplating</u> what her first question to him would be. Yes, she thought to herself, he was one <u>cool</u> fellow.

1. List the words that connote physical attractiveness. _____

   _____

   _____

2. List the words that give an impression of competency. _____

   _____

   _____

3. What overall impression does the author want you to have of the politician? _____

   _____

   _____

   _____

   _____

4. Change the overall impression of the politician to the opposite of what you noted in question 3 by filling in the blanks in the passage below with words that have the same denotation (meaning) as the original words but different connotations.

   As the reporter saw the politician for the first time, she sized him up. He was _____, with short _____ hair framing a _____ face. His custom-tailored suit fit his _____ well, seeming to advertise both physical and mental _____. His _____ bore an _____, slightly _____ look, as if he were _____ what her first question to him would be. Yes, she thought to herself, he was one _____ fellow.

Like authors who make deliberate word choices by taking into account connotations, advertisers know how to sell products by using words with particular connotations. A product that has a name that is alluring to the audience is more likely to sell than a product that sounds unappealing. Notice, for example, how many cleaning products have cheery names, perhaps to offset the drudgery of cleaning! A critical thinker might ask if consumers were being swayed by these laundry products' names: *Bold*, *Cheer*, and *Fab*. Would you expect *Timid*, *Depress*, or *Awful* to fare as well, even if they had the exact same ingredients and cleaning power? To avoid potential negative connotations, many companies make up product names (more cleaning examples: *Clorox* and *Lysol*).

Noticing Connotations

Directions: Look at this swatch of paint colors and answer the questions that follow.

© Kitch Bain/Shutterstock.com

1. Who is the likely intended audience?

   _____

   _____

   _____

2. Do the names of these colors have positive or negative connotations? Explain.

   _____

   _____

   _____

3. What images might the audience picture for each of the following paint names?

   a. Antarctic Glow: _____

   b. Aqua Delight: _____

   c. Precision: _____

   d. Evening Shadow: _____

  e. Solitary Swirl: _____

  f. Bobbin Head Blue: _____

4. Select one of the colors in the paint swatch and brainstorm two new names for it. One name should have a more positive connotation; the other name should have a more negative connotation.

Original color name: _____

  a. Positive Connotation: _____

  b. Negative Connotation: _____

PRACTICE 4-7   Inferring Audience, Purpose, and Tone in Reading Passages

Directions: Read and annotate Passages 1–10 to determine audience, purpose, and tone. The model is done for you.

Audience: Consider the source, occasion, and level. You might need to do a quick Internet search to learn more about the author and the source. Write a sentence or two explaining whom you believe the author is addressing and why.

Purpose: Determine the authors' most likely overall purpose: to inform, persuade, or entertain. Then, using Figure 4-2 on p. 122, try to identify the author's specific goal within those categories.

Tone: Pick the words from the chart in Figure 4-3 (p. 124) that best sum up the tone of each of the passages. Pay particular attention to connotations; you may wish to circle or highlight words that have strong positive or negative connotations. There may be more than one answer, or you may come up with a new tone word to describe the author's attitude.

Here's a model

Thus, Americans who live in the North and West learn about the Civil War as a matter of ancient history, in which our brave Union troops forced the South to abandon the ugly institution of slavery, we defeated the traitor Jefferson Davis, and the country remained united. (We'll just draw a veil over our own complicity as perpetrators and abettors of slavery; that was then.) But most white Southerners tell a different story, one in which the Civil War is alive and kicking; then is *now*. Our brave Confederate troops were victims of greedy, crude Northerners who defeated our noble leader, Jefferson Davis, destroyed our cities and traditions, and are still trying to destroy our states' rights. There is nothing united about us Southerners and you damned Yankees; we'll keep flying our Confederate flag, thank you, that's *our* history. Slavery may be gone with the wind, but grudges aren't. That is why history is written by the victors, but it's victims who write the memoirs.

From *Mistakes Were Made (but not by me)* by Tavris and Aronson

Audience: <u>The audience is an educated audience who has some background in American history.</u>

Purpose: General purpose: ____<u>to persuade</u>

Specific purpose: <u>to express an opinion, to take a political stance</u>

Tone: ___<u>sarcastic, irritated</u>

Now you try

Passage 1

Thanks to my complete lack of office skills, I found it fairly easy to avoid direct contact with the new technology. The indirect contact was disturbing enough. I was still living in Chicago when I began to receive creepy Christmas newsletters designed to look like tabloids and annual reports. Word processors made writing fun. They did not, however, make reading fun, a point made painfully evident by such publications as *The Herald Family Tribune* and *Wassup with the Wexlers!*

Friends who had previously expressed no interest in torture began sending letters composed to resemble Chinese takeout menus and the Dead Sea Scrolls. Everybody had a font, and I was told that I should get one, too. The authors of these letters shared an enthusiasm with the sort of people who now arrived at dinner parties hoisting expensive new video cameras and suggesting that, after dessert, we all sit down and replay the evening on TV. We, the regular people of the world, now had access to the means of production, but still I failed to see what all the fuss was about. A dopey letter is still a dopey letter, no matter how you dress it up; and there's a reason regular people don't appear on TV: we're boring.

From *Me Talk Pretty One Day* by Sedaris

Audience:

_____

_____

_____

Purpose: General purpose: _____

Specific purpose: _____

Tone: _____

Passage 2

This bookish inclination at length determined my father to make me a printer, though he had already one son (James) of that profession. In 1717 my brother James returned from England with a press and letters to set up his business in Boston. I liked it much better than that of my father, but still had a hankering for the sea. To prevent the apprehended effect of such an inclination, my father was impatient to have me bound to my brother. I stood out some time, but at last was persuaded, and signed the indentures when I was yet but twelve years old. I was to serve as an apprentice till I was twenty-one years of age, only I was to be allowed journeyman's wages during the last year. In a little time I made great proficiency in the business, and became a useful hand to my brother. I now had access to better books. An acquaintance with the apprentices of booksellers enabled me sometimes to borrow a small one, which I was careful to return soon and clean. Often I sat up in my room reading the greatest part of the night, when the book was borrowed in the evening and to be returned early in the morning, lest it should be missed or wanted.

From *The Autobiography of Benjamin Franklin* by Benjamin Franklin

Audience:

_____

_____

_____

Purpose: General purpose: _____

Specific purpose: _____

Tone: _____

Passage 3

Within [the castle doors], stood a tall old man, clean shaven save for a long white moustache, and clad in black from head to foot, without a single speck of colour about him anywhere. He held in his hand an antique silver lamp, in which the flame burned without a chimney or globe of any kind, throwing long quivering shadows as it flickered in the draught of the open door. The old man motioned me in with his right hand with a courtly gesture, saying in excellent English, but with a strange intonation.

"Welcome to my house! Enter freely and of your own free will!" He made no motion of stepping to meet me, but stood like a statue, as though his gesture of welcome had fixed him into stone. The instant, however, that I had stepped over the threshold, he moved impulsively forward, and holding out his hand grasped mine with a strength which made me wince, an effect which was not lessened by the fact that it seemed cold as ice, more like the hand of a dead than a living man. Again he said,

"Welcome to my house! Enter freely. Go safely, and leave something of the happiness you bring!" The strength of the handshake was so much akin to that which I had noticed in the driver, whose face I had not seen, that for a moment I doubted if it were not the same person to whom I was speaking. So to make sure, I said interrogatively, "Count Dracula?"

From *Dracula* by Bram Stoker

Audience:

_____

_____

_____

Purpose: General purpose: _____

Specific purpose: _____

Tone: _____

Passage 4

We went down the hill and found Joe Harper and Ben Rogers, and two or three more of the boys, hid in the old tanyard. So we unhitched a skiff and pulled down the river two mile and a half, to the big scar on the hillside, and went ashore.

We went to a clump of bushes, and Tom made everybody swear to keep the secret, and then showed them a hole in the hill, right in the thickest part of the bushes. Then we lit the candles, and crawled in on our hands and knees. We went about two hundred yards, and then the cave opened up. Tom poked about amongst the passages, and pretty soon ducked under a wall where you wouldn't 'a' noticed that there was a hole. We went along a narrow place and got into a kind of room, all damp and sweaty and cold, and there we stopped. Tom says:

"Now, we'll start this band of robbers and call it Tom Sawyer's Gang. Everybody that wants to join has got to take an oath, and write his name in blood." Everybody was willing. So Tom got out a sheet of paper that he had wrote the oath on, and read it. It swore every boy to stick to the band, and never tell any of the secrets; and if anybody done anything to any boy in the band, whichever boy was ordered to kill that person and his family must do it, and he mustn't eat and he mustn't sleep till he had killed them and hacked a cross in their breasts, which was the sign of the band. And nobody that didn't belong to the band could use that mark, and if he did he must be sued; and if he done it again he must be killed. And if anybody that belonged to the band told the secrets, he must have his throat cut, and then have his carcass burnt up and the ashes scattered all around, and his name blotted off the list with blood and never mentioned again by the gang, but have a curse put on it and be forgot forever.

Everybody said it was a real beautiful oath, and asked Tom if he got it out of his own head. He said some of it, but the rest was out of pirate-books and robber-books, and every gang that was high-toned had it.

From *The Adventures of Huckleberry Finn* by Mark Twain

Audience:

_____

_____

_____

Purpose: General purpose: _____

Specific purpose: _____

Tone: _____

Passage 5

Bulging like a gigantic hornet's nest against the shores of the Red Sea, Sudan has rarely known stability. Civil war erupted even before the nation gained independence from Britain in 1956. (A frail peace lasted between 1972 and 1983.) The roots of the violence have never changed: British-ruled Sudan wasn't a country; it was two. The south is tropical, underdeveloped, and populated by Dinkas, Nues, Azandes, and some hundred other ethnic groups of African descent. The north, by contrast, is drier, and wealthier—a Saharan world with strong links to the Muslim Middle East. Shackled together by lunatic colonial borders, these two groups—northern Arabs and southern blacks—have been at odds since the 19th century, when northern slave raiders preyed on the tribes of the south.

From "Shattered Sudan" by Salopek

Audience:

_____

_____

_____

Purpose: General purpose: _____

Specific purpose: _____

Tone: _____

Passage 6

Philosophers have explained space. They have not explained time. It is the inexplicable raw material of everything. With it, all is possible; without it, nothing. The supply of time is truly a daily miracle, an affair genuinely astonishing when one examines it. You wake up in the morning, and lo! your purse is magically filled with twenty-four hours of the unmanufactured tissue of the universe of your life! It is yours. It is the most precious of possessions. A highly singular commodity, showered upon you in a manner as singular as the commodity itself!

For remark! No one can take it from you. It is unstealable. And no one receives either more or less than you receive.

Talk about an ideal democracy! In the realm of time there is no aristocracy of wealth, and no aristocracy of intellect. Genius is never rewarded by even an extra hour a day. And there is no punishment. Waste your infinitely precious commodity as much as you will, and the supply will never be withheld from you. No mysterious power will say:—"This man is a fool, if not a knave. He does not deserve time; he shall be cut off at the meter.". . . Moreover, you cannot draw on the future. Impossible to get into debt! You can only waste the passing moment. You cannot waste to-morrow; it is kept for you. You cannot waste the next hour; it is kept for you.

From _How to Live on 24 Hours a Day_ by Arnold Bennett

Audience:

_____

_____

_____

Purpose: General purpose: _____

Specific purpose: _____

Tone: _____

Passage 7

Take a moment to evaluate your financial picture. Note the dollars coming in and those going out, and prioritize how those dollars are best spent. Most people fail to take a clear look at their expenses. Examine fixed costs such as car and rent or mortgage payments over adjustable ones such as gifts, clothes, private schools, kids' activities, meals out, entertainment, and so on. Getting a true handle on your financial needs allows you to set goals and make better career and life choices.

Acknowledge one fact: You can't have it all. Each person has only twenty-four hours in any one day. You must set limits. The reality is that, over the last twenty years, both men and women have increased the number of hours they work at their full-time jobs. Women average forty-three hours of work per week, while men average fifty, and when you add on commute time it is clear that our work weeks are long. Sixty percent of all employees would like to work less, according to the Work and Family Institute.

From *What to Do with the Rest of Your Life* by Ryan

Audience:

_____

_____

_____

Purpose: General purpose: _____

Specific purpose: _____

Tone: _____

Passage 8

Tom [In response to his mother's suspicions that he is not actually going to the movies]: I'm going to opium dens! Yes, opium dens, dens of vice and criminals' hangouts, Mother. I've joined the Hogan Gang, I'm a hired assassin, I carry a tommy gun in a violin case! I run a string of cat houses in the Valley! They call me Killer, Killer Wingfield, I'm leading a double-life, a simple honest warehouse worker by day, by night a dynamic *czar* of the *underworld, Mother.* I go to gambling casinos, I spin away fortunes on the roulette table! I wear a patch over one eye and a false mustache, sometimes I put on green whiskers. On those occasions they call me—*El Diablo!* Oh, I could tell you many things to make you sleepless!

From *The Glass Menagerie* by Williams

Audience:

_____

_____

_____

Purpose: General purpose: _____

Specific purpose: _____

Tone: _____

Passage 9

Our decisions can be quite complex. In fact, if we wanted to maximize the accuracy of our judgments, we would have to gather an enormous amount of information. Just consider the decision to get a new job. To maximize the enjoyment, fulfillment, and financial rewards from a new position, we would need to gather data on the type of work involved in a variety of different careers, the educational requirements for those careers, the salaries offered, and on and on. After we picked a career, we would have to investigate all the companies in the field that we could work for. As you can gather, if we did a thorough search to maximize our decision accuracy, we'd spend more time deciding where to work than actually working. We can't live our lives like that. Thus, we use heuristics when we make our decisions.

Heuristics are general rules of thumb that we use to simplify complicated judgments. These simplifying strategies can be quite beneficial: they reduce the time and effort required to make a decision, and they often result in reasonably good decisions. While heuristics give approximate, rather than exact, solutions to our problems, approximate solutions are often good enough. The problem is, heuristics can also lead to systematic biases that result in grossly inaccurate judgments. So let's look at a few of the heuristics we commonly employ, and the biases that arise from their use.

From *Don't Believe Everything You Think* by Kida

Audience:

_____

_____

_____

Purpose: General purpose: _____

Specific purpose: _____

Tone: _____

Passage 10

Writers who seriously intend to influence others have to keep their audience firmly in mind. It's all too easy to forget the audience as we sit alone at a desk scribbling away (well, these days also tapping away). But experienced writers learn that they must always write with the intended readers in mind. Past failures—having had manuscripts rejected, severely criticized, or simply passed over by others—motivate them to figure out who they are writing for and how best to engage the interest of that particular audience.

From *Logic and Contemporary Rhetoric* by Cavender and Kahane

Audience:

_____

_____

_____

Purpose: General purpose: _____

Specific purpose: _____

Tone: _____

READ, WRITE, AND THINK CRITICALLY: SECTION ONE

Directions: Survey the following text and answer the questions below. Then, read and annotate the selection, and answer the questions that follow.

1. What is your prior knowledge of this topic?

   _____

   _____

2. Read the title and first paragraph and make a prediction about the content of the article.

   _____

   _____

   _____

   _____

"Black Panther" Hype and Success Shows Importance of Representation

Proma Khosla

Proma Khosla is an entertainment reporter in the greater New York area. She has worked as a dance teacher, a translator, and a freelance writer and has published pieces in Teen Vogue *and* Glamour. *Now she works for* Mashable, *where the following article appeared in 2018.*

1 Contrary to the Gill Scott Heron/Vince Staples track scorching the *Black Panther* trailer, this movie's revolution *will* be televised. It will be broadcast in movie theaters, on TV screens, and in the hearts and minds of audiences around the world who flocked to theaters to watch Hollywood's first black superhero in action.

2 Until an embarrassingly recent time (and still in this moment, if we're being realistic), Hollywood bigwigs hesitated to bet on women and people of color, especially in **tentpole** franchises like the Marvel Cinematic Universe.

3 They were mistaken.

4 *Black Panther*'s massive success did not arrive in a vacuum. It is the product of decades of the film industry hindering visibility and representation of minority actors and characters. Audiences who craved to see themselves on-screen—who perhaps didn't even know this was possible—grew slowly stronger and louder, until a deafening declaration (as loud as $218 million) showed we want and deserve more.

5 Black Panther is the Marvel Cinematic Universe's first black superhero, but crucially, he's the first non-white (or at least white-passing) superhero headlining his own movie *period*. In its two years of building hype, *Black Panther* became a **bastion** of **inclusivity** and empowerment for people of all colors in the audience.

6 Kayla Sutton, of the website Black Girl Nerds, started the viral hashtag #WhatBlackPantherMeansToMe, a prompt based on a conversation she'd had with her young son.

7 "Whenever the promo or the trailer would come on for the movie itself he would get visibly excited," Sutton recalled in a phone interview with Mashable. Her son is a fan of the comics and TV shows, but his final reason for loving Black Panther was "he's black like me."

8 "It's also been very humbling to see that and to put out there the thirst for more representation, not just for those in the black community but for any other community that is underrepresented as well," Sutton said.

9 According to a 2017 study, roughly 30 percent of speaking roles in film were given to people of color (13.6 percent black, 5.7 percent Asian, 3.1 percent Hispanic, and 7 percent other). The numbers are worse for LGBTQ+ roles.

10   In 2015, writer Dylan Marron began taking stock of the dialogue spoken by people of color in popular films. Most of the dialogue totals per film—including Oscar darlings and major franchises *Lord of the Rings* – are under a minute. Marron specifically chose films that weren't about race and that dealt with universal themes. They just happened to default to white characters.

11   "When you're younger," Marron said in 2015, "you don't really have the tools to wonder why, or you don't think to ask why. You just accept it as truth."

12   Sutton is Afro-Latina, so she's experiencing the *Black Panther* hype as part of the black community and as a Latina woman to whom this film represents the opportunity for more rich, diverse stories on screen. She cried when she saw the trailer in theaters (received with raucous applause)—the only other time she did that was for *Coco*.

13   To that end, film execs are taking notice. IMAX C.E.O. Greg Foster told The Hollywood Reporter this weekend: "Representation matters. *Get Out, Wonder Woman, Coco* and now *Black Panther* show Hollywood that **authenticity** and inclusiveness wins." *Black Panther*'s audience was widespread and diverse, and many of them may return for more diverse Marvel fare.

14   One Marvel fan, Marissa Tinsley, grew up a fan of the X-Men, so it was only through his MCU debut that *Black Panther* got her attention.

15   "It thrills me that BP brings us a movie where the cast isn't all or majority white," she told Mashable via email. "Makes for a sweet, long overdue change."

16   As a non-black person of color, Tinsley said it "warms my little heart" to see widespread enthusiasm for the film. "We've always been required to insert ourselves into white narratives when it comes to mainstream cinema (or mainstream anything). It's a nice change for others to have an opportunity—and not be scared—of experiencing other narratives and POVs."

17   With *Black Panther* in such a **pivotal** position, the film is attracting viewers of all kinds—including those with no prior interest in superheroes or the MCU—like Brandon Jordan, whose sister works at Black Girls Create. Jordan only got into Marvel movies a few years ago and previously felt "out of place" when he couldn't join in excitement for something like *The Avengers*.

18   "What this movie means to me personally is a sense of community throughout black culture," Jordan told Mashable via email. "I always wondered if black music could go mainstream why couldn't black movies and TV shows."

19   Tinsley hopes that *Black Panther* "hits it out of the park." As she pointed out, this isn't a niche film.

20   "It's a huge, big budget superhero movie filled with actors—who although they may not look like me—actually represent a more accurate reflection of my world and environment."

21   While some say that *Black Panther* is just a movie, that it isn't a tool of resistance or **deus ex machina** that will solve all Hollywood's problems. And while that may be true, it would be a mistake for the film industry to return to its established status quo after such a colossal, if temporary, shift.

22   "Maybe this is opening the doors for people to come in, characters that are of Latin descent or Asian descent—that for me has been the biggest response that's what we feel like *Black Panther* is gonna do," Sutton said. "That to me has been more meaningful to people; seeing that this is not just for the black community, [but] for anyone that is not white, really. This is huge for all of us because we're getting that door open."

23   While the average movie audience is about 50 percent white, *Black Panther*'s opening weekend numbers were 65 percent of people of color (black viewership alone was up more than 20 percent). The audience breakdown was more equal than ever—37 percent black, 35 percent white, 18 percent hispanic—proving that *everyone* shows up for what is ultimately just a damn good movie.

24   "It also makes me think that perhaps maybe more POC will have the opportunities to not only star in films, but also take the lead in their everyday sphere, inspire future generations, and just . . . be who they are," Tinsley said. "Living their lives and stories and knowing that they're universal and valuable."

3. Use context clues and/or a dictionary to define the following words (marked in bold in the reading).

   a. Tentpole (para. 2): _____

   b. Bastion (para. 5): _____

   c. Inclusivity (para. 5): _____

   d. Authenticity (para. 13): _____

   e. Pivotal (para. 17):): _____

   f. Deus ex machina (para. 21): _____

4. Who is the likely audience? What does the audience need to know to fully understand this piece?

   _____

   _____

   _____

5. What is the author's general purpose? What is her specific purpose? How do you know?

   _____

   _____

   _____

6. What is the tone of the essay? How did you figure it out?

   _____

   _____

   _____

7. List four words that have strong connotations (either positive or negative). How do these words affect the tone of the essay?

   a. _____ b. _____ c. _____ d. _____

   _____

   _____

   _____

8. On another sheet of paper, respond to the following prompt in a short essay: Do you agree with the author about the value of inclusivity and representation? Explain your response in detail.

SECTION TWO
Recognizing Assumptions

Once you understand an author's direct and indirect messages, the next important step is to identify an author's assumptions. **Assumptions** are beliefs that an author takes for granted as being true. You can recognize an assumption because it is something an author generally doesn't give any explanation for—he or she just assumes that it is true (hence the word *assumption*). Often assumptions are sweeping statements that ground an author's point of view. For example, we all tend to share certain basic assumptions—that other people exist, that the sun will rise tomorrow as it has always done in the past, that we aren't living in a dream world or in the matrix, and so forth. But authors also often have more specific assumptions that come from their upbringing, their culture, their religion, or their own personal history. For example, someone born in the United States might hold the basic assumption that men and women are equal, that personal and financial freedom is desirable, or that each person should decide for him/or herself how to live. But someone born in a different culture might assume that men and women have very different roles and purposes in life, that following state institutions without question is the best way to live, and that tradition deserves great respect. Here is an example:

> I believe my family has my best interests at heart, always. My grandparents in particular have gone through so much that I can't help but listen to their advice even when it seems to contradict more modern advice. Both of them are in their 90s, and they have hardly gone to any doctors! They are in excellent health, so I figure if I do what they've done, I should live into my nineties also.
>
> When my grandmother was younger, she wasn't able to have another baby after having my mother, and she was sure that it had something to do with an infection she got soon after my mom's birth. Ever since then, she has distrusted the medical profession and urged all of her loved ones to depend on home remedies whenever possible. Although over fifty years have passed since she was given the news that she would never have any more children, she remembers that day like it was yesterday.
>
> My husband and I have been trying to conceive a baby for several years now, and we aren't having any luck. He wants to go to a fertility doctor, but, at my Grandma's insistence, I have decided to try some natural remedies like drinking grapefruit juice and raspberry tea. I think we will eventually be successful!
>
> —Lacey, Age 36

Here, the author makes certain basic assumptions that you have to accept if you are to agree with her. She assumes that the medical profession—notably in the field of fertility—hasn't changed much since her grandmother's child-bearing years. She also assumes that her grandmother attributed the cause for her inability to have another child to the correct cause (her infection) rather than to another possible cause. Finally, she assumes that her family's advice is better than the advice of medical professionals. If you share her assumptions, you might find the passage very convincing, but if you don't, you might be very skeptical about what she's saying.

Notice that Lacey never comes out and says what her assumptions are, and often authors don't. If an author believes that her audience shares basic assumptions, she won't feel that she needs to make them explicit. Inferring an author's audience will allow you to figure out what unstated assumptions an author is making.

Understanding an author's assumptions will help you evaluate an author's argument, which you will learn to do in Chapter 6. You also have your own set of assumptions, as you will explore in Chapter 7 when you learn about worldviews.

The following tips will help you recognize implicit assumptions made by authors.

Tips for Critical Thinkers: Recognizing Assumptions

- **Infer the author's audience and think about what you know about the audience**. For example, if the author is writing to doctors, you know that most doctors assume that science is effective and that bacteria and viruses cause disease.
- **Try to find out about the author's biography.** Is the author a member of a certain cultural tradition, professional organization, political party, or religious sect? If so, the author might share the basic beliefs of this organization—but be careful not to infer too much.
- **Think about what has to be true if the author's statements are to be believable.** For example, if an author says that we should pass stricter environmental protection laws, he is assuming that protecting the environment is a good thing.

Recognizing Assumptions in Short Passages   PRACTICE 4–8

Directions: Read the following short paragraphs. Use the tips above to figure out the assumptions that underlie the passages and write them on the lines provided.

Here's a model

Standing up straight will make you look more confident, and hence will make you more attractive.

    <u>Other people find confidence attractive. You want to be found attractive.</u>

Now you try

1. More funding for education would help students do better.

   _____

2. Let's increase the penalties for animal cruelty.

   _____

3. Having a national Smoke Out day will help raise smoking awareness and help people quit smoking.

   _____

4. Raising the minimum wage by $.50 would help keep people out of poverty.

   _____

5. Marijuana might not be as harmful as alcohol, but unlike alcohol, it is illegal, so you should not use it.

   _____

Recognizing Assumptions in Longer Passages   PRACTICE 4–9

Directions: Read the following short selections. Using all of the tips above, identify any assumptions made by the authors and write them on the lines provided.

1. Since the five undergraduate degrees that will earn you the most money are all in the field of engineering, you will certainly want to major in engineering. Petroleum engineering is the degree that will cause you to be the richest, so perhaps you should

set your sights on that. Child and family studies, followed by elementary education, are the lowest-paying undergraduate degrees, so you definitely won't want to major in those. I've heard people tell me that those two degrees involve very important work, and that they lead to jobs that, while not necessarily lucrative, are very fulfilling, but let's get real. "Life satisfaction" won't pay the mortgage.

Assumptions _____

_____

_____

_____

_____

2. When you think of Stella McCartney, Betsey Johnson, and Sarah Burton, what comes to mind? Obviously, you answered something to the effect of "cutting-edge fashion" or "women designers." Like so many professions, the world of fashion design used to be dominated by men, but these three designers have proven that women can be equally driven, equally inspiring, and equally successful. Men and women alike should take note of their new collections if they hope to look current (without looking trendy). While many of their designs are classics and can be worn year after year, investing in a few new pieces shows that you laugh in the face of the recession. A favorite of celebrities worldwide, Stella McCartney can make the average vacationer in the Hamptons look like a Hollywood star. McCartney's handbags typically run $1,000–$2,000, but you cannot put a price tag on your image. One of Betsey Johnson's charming sheath dresses (retailing for only $300–$500) can give your summer wardrobe a lift that you will not regret. Finally, Sarah Burton, the Alexander McQueen designer who was the talk of the fashion world after creating Kate Middleton's wedding dress, appeals to princesses and commoners alike by using colors and shapes found in nature.

Assumptions _____

_____

_____

_____

_____

PRACTICE 4-10   Recognizing Assumptions in a Visual

Directions: Answer the following questions about the cartoon.

1. Who is the likely audience for this cartoon?

   _____

   _____

   _____

2. What is the artist's purpose?

   _____

   _____

   _____

3. What is the assumption that underlies this cartoon about the state of truth in today's society?

   _____

   _____

4. What is being implied by the sign and comment in the cartoon? In drawing this cartoon, is the artist trying to get you to understand something or get you to do anything?

   _____

   _____

   _____

Recognizing Implications

After inferring the author's assumptions, you should go a step further and recognize their **implications**—the consequences or possible effects of these ideas. To recognize implications, you need to ask additional questions as you think about and respond to a text.

- **What has the author directly stated?**
- **What has the author implied?** What logically follows from the available information or current situation? (i.e., if you were to follow the author's logic, then what could you expect to believe or understand?)
- **What would happen if x were true? (x = implication)** In other words, if the author's conclusion is true, what effect would it have on your life or the world? For example, if an author is arguing that abortion should be illegal, would more women go to prison?
- **What are some other options or alternatives to the author's viewpoint or argument?** What might someone with different assumptions believe about the issue?

Look back at the passage that Lacey wrote about dealing with her infertility (p. 138). Reread it looking for direct messages, indirect messages, and consequences.

a. What has been directly stated?
   This personal story directly states that Lacey is taking the advice of her grandmother to drink grapefruit juice and raspberry tea rather than consulting with a medical professional about her infertility.

b. What is being implied? What logically follows from the available information or current situation? (i.e., if you were to follow the author's logic, then what could you expect to believe or understand?)
   What is being implied by the story is that the medical profession is to blame for the grandmother's inability to have a second child. What logically follows from this

information is that other people should distrust the medical profession and should, instead, rely on old wives' tales and old-fashioned remedies to tackle health concerns.

c. What would happen if x were true? (x = implication) In other words, if the author's conclusion is true, what effect would it have on your life or the world?
If it were true that the medical profession should not be relied upon for fertility help, then this information would transform the way infertile people are treated. It is likely that fewer people will be able to conceive if they no longer consult with doctors who can perform in vitro fertilization or who can connect patients with surrogates or sperm donors. It is also possible that serious health issues might be missed (Lacey might have a cyst or tumor or her husband might have a low sperm count for some reason that should be addressed). These implications could lead to worrisome consequences.

d. What are some other options or alternatives to the author's viewpoint or argument?
Other options or alternatives to consider include the possibility that Lacey is misinformed and that her grandmother has unfairly biased her against doctors, and there might be medical reasons for her/her husband's infertility that should be dealt with.

The act of asking and answering these questions will require you to be open-minded— as you consider ideas from a fresh perspective—and flexible—as you work your way through information and adjust your initial impressions.

PRACTICE 4-11   **Recognizing Implications**

Directions: Reread the two passages from Practice 4-9. Answer the following questions in order to explore potential consequences.

1. Paragraph about picking your college major
   a. What has been directly stated?

   _____

   _____

   _____

   _____

   b. What is being implied? What logically follows from the available information or current situation? (i.e., if you were to follow the author's logic, then what could you expect to believe or understand?)

   _____

   _____

   _____

   _____

   _____

   _____

   c. What would happen if x were true? (x = implication) In other words, if the author's conclusion is true, what effect would it have on your life or the world?

   _____

   _____

   _____

   d. What are some other options or alternatives to the author's viewpoint or argument?

_____

_____

_____

2. Paragraph about fashion

   a. What has been directly stated?

_____

_____

   b. What is being implied? What logically follows from the available information or current situation? (i.e., if you were to follow the author's logic, then what could you expect to believe or understand?)

_____

_____

_____

   c. What would happen if x were true? (x = implication) In other words, if the author's conclusion is true, what effect would it have on your life or the world?

_____

_____

_____

   d. What are some other options or alternatives to the author's viewpoint or argument?

_____

_____

_____

_____

Real-World Mistakes of Inference and Their Consequences

Because inferences can be subtle and tricky, people make mistakes of inference quite easily. The severity of the mistakes vary from mildly embarrassing to excruciatingly painful. We have heard of tragedies such as the medical professional who misdiagnoses a patient, assuming he has heartburn when in fact he is experiencing a heart attack or the general who minimizes the enemy's threat, resulting in numerous deaths within his unit.

You have probably heard of incidents involving a police officer who shoots, assuming someone is reaching for a weapon when it is actually only a cell phone or wallet. This mistake in inference involves misjudging the victim's attitude (tone) and intention (purpose). In Malcolm Gladwell's book *Blink*, he recounts the mistakes of inference that led to the shooting in the Bronx in 1999 by four police officers of 22-year-old Amadou Diallo as he pulled out his wallet. Gladwell points to the officers' errors in drawing conclusions: "The officers made a series of critical misjudgments, beginning with the assumption that a man getting a breath of fresh air outside his own home was a potential criminal" (p. 194). Furthermore, Gladwell explains the reason behind the incident as a failure in mind-reading, which he defines as "This practice of inferring the motivations and intentions of others.... picking up on subtle, fleeting cues in order to read someone's mind" (p. 192). One of the officers, Sean Carroll, tried to explain, "My prior experience and training, my prior arrests, dictated to me that this person was pulling a gun" (p.190). You have learned in this chapter that sometimes prior experience and knowledge are not enough to make valid inferences and that sometimes another person's purpose and tone are not what they first appear to be. Unfortunately, a potentially treacherous situation such as the Diallo shooting "brought out the absolute worst in [the officers'] decision making" (p. 264).

Another example of an officer mistakenly inferring danger, perhaps subconsciously, when danger did not exist, is the case of the shooting of an off-duty officer, Omar J. Edwards, in New York by another officer, Andrew P. Dunton. According to the article, "New State Panel to Study Police Shootings,"

> The May 28 shooting underscored the problems of officers of different units— and particularly those in plain clothes—colliding in heightened street situations. According to officials, Officer Edwards was off duty and in civilian clothes, chasing a man he believed had just broken into his car, when a team of plainclothes officers from an anticrime unit in the 25th Precinct saw him running with his gun drawn, and confronted him.
>
> In a matter of seconds, one of the anticrime officers, Officer Dunton, shouted a command at Officer Edwards, then opened fire, striking him three times and killing him, officials said. Officer Edwards was 25; his funeral was Thursday in Brooklyn.*

This particular shooting and others like it have raised the concern that a disproportionate number of black and Latino officers are the victims of shootings by other officers. The panel mentioned in the article will study "perception and bias" to investigate whether subtle racial tensions are partially responsible for these errors in inference. Is it possible that communal reinforcement and other biases caused Officer Dunton (who is white) to perceive a black man holding a gun as a greater threat than he would have done if Officer Edwards had also been white?

As you have learned, conclusions can be appropriate, inappropriate, or in need of more information. Critical thinkers follow the evidence, examine what is expressed directly and what is implied, and attempt to come to a justifiable conclusion. Police officers are often in dangerous situations, and there have been many cases in which quick actions (and even quicker inferences) have saved lives. However, these examples focus on how difficult it is to make inferences, especially when more information is needed or when the parties involved are frightened, confused, and armed. When a police officer suddenly shoots someone in the middle of a heated incident, it is quite possible that he or she has jumped to an inappropriate or hasty conclusion based on emotion rather than logic.

For Discussion

1. Explain how the mistakes discussed above qualify as a failure of inference.
2. Think of other stories you have heard of or read about involving police officer(s) inferring and reacting quickly. Discuss whether the officer(s) made good inferences or not and how any mistakes of inference could be avoided.

> ## Real-World Successes of Critical Thinking
>
> ### The Capture of BTK
>
> You just read about the cost of failing to think critically, but people who succeed at thinking critically can achieve great success. Police officers used inference and other critical thinking skills in their identification and arrest of the BTK ("bind, torture, and kill") serial killer, Dennis Rader, in 2005.
>
> *Directions*: Using the Internet or a library, research the investigation into Dennis Rader. Prepare a detailed written description of how the police officers succeeded at finding and capturing Rader, including an explanation of any skills, character traits, and standards of critical thinking that contributed to their success. Get ready to share your findings with the class.

THINK
AND **WRITE**
CRITICALLY

Chapter Summary

- *Inference* is the skill of recognizing what an author or speaker implies or suggests.

- Having an attitude of *open-mindedness and flexibility* helps you make good inferences. Open to new ideas and flexible enough to follow where the evidence leads, a critical thinker can examine both what is stated explicitly by an author and what is suggested by an author.

- When making *inferences*, you will consider the author's direct and indirect messages. When you draw inferences/conclusions, AIM for appropriate inferences. Remember that even when you think critically, you can draw conclusions that are not supported by the text. Potential conclusions can be *appropriate, inappropriate,* or they can *require more information.* A critical thinker will aim for appropriate conclusions and will do more reading or research when necessary.

- Authors write with a particular *audience* in mind and take into account that audience's characteristics and values when making decisions about what to say and how to say it.

- The author's (or speaker's) *purpose* is the goal that he or she hopes to accomplish by writing or speaking. The three general purposes are *to inform, to persuade,* and *to entertain,* and within each of these purposes you can infer a more specific goal.

- *Tone* is the author's attitude toward the subject and can help reveal inferences. *Connotation* refers to the emotions and images associated with word choice; authors selectively choose words that give negative or positive impressions and, therefore, affect the tone.

- Authors base their arguments on *assumptions,* which you need to uncover.

- Recognizing *implications* means that you explore consequences. You do this by asking critical questions of the text to determine what the author's message (both implied and explicit) means for the reader.

READ, WRITE, AND THINK CRITICALLY: SECTION TWO

Directions: Survey the following text and answer the questions below. Then, read and annotate the selection and answer the questions that follow.

1. What is your prior knowledge of this subject? _____

_____

_____

_____

2. Make a prediction about the article based on the subtitle ("What pained her were the teddy bears.") _____

_____

_____

_____

Excerpt from Smile or Die: The Bright Side of Cancer

Barbara Ehrenreich

Barbara Ehrenreich, a prolific author who has published Bait and Switch *and* Nickel and Dimed, *among many other works, is also a political activist and democratic socialist. She holds a PhD in cellular biology. The following selection is excerpted from the first chapter in her book* Bright-sided: How the Relentless Promotion of Positive Thinking has Undermined America, *published in 2010.*

1 The first attempt to **recruit** me into positive thinking occurred at what has been, so far, the low point of my life. If you had asked me, just before the diagnosis of cancer, whether I was an optimist or a pessimist, I would have been hard-pressed to answer. But on health-related matters, as it turned out, I was optimistic to the point of **delusion**. Nothing had so far come along that could not be controlled by diet, stretching, Advil, or, at worst, a prescription. So I was not at all alarmed when a mammogram—undertaken as part of the routine cancer surveillance all good citizens of HMOs or health plans are expected to submit to once they reach the age of fifty—aroused some "concern" on the part of my gynecologist. How could I have breast cancer? When the gynocologist suggested a follow-up mammogram four months later, I agreed only to placate her.

2 I thought of it as one of those drive-by mammograms, one stop in a series of mundane missions, but I began to lose my nerve in the changing room, and not only because of the kinky necessity of baring my breasts and affixing tiny X-ray opaque stars to the tip of each nipple. The changing room, really just a closet off the windowless space that housed the mammogram machine, contained something far worse, I noticed for the first time—an assumption about who I am, where I am going, and what I will need when I get there. Almost all of the eye-level space had been filled with photocopied bits of cuteness and **sentimentality**: pink ribbons, an "Ode to a Mammogram," a list of the "Top Ten Things Only Women Understand" ("Fat Clothes" and "Eyelash Curlers," among them), and, **inescapably**, right next to the door, the poem "I Said a Prayer for You Today," illustrated with pink roses.

3 It went on and on, this mother of all mammograms, cutting into gym time, dinnertime, and lifetime generally. In the intervals while she [the technician] was off with the doctor, I read *the New York Times* right down to the personally irrelevant sections like theater and real estate, eschewing the stack of women's magazines provided for me, much as I ordinarily enjoy a quick read about sweatproof eyeliners and "fabulous sex tonight," because I had picked up this warning vibe in the changing room, which, in my increasingly anxious state, translated into: femininity is death. Finally there was nothing left to read but one of the free local weekly newspapers, where I found, buried deep in the classifieds, something even more **unsettling** than the growing prospect of major disease—a classified ad for a "breast cancer teddy bear" with a pink ribbon stitched to its chest.

4 Yes, atheists pray in their foxholes—in this case, with a yearning new to me and sharp as lust, for a clean and honorable death by shark bite, lightning strike, sniper fire, car crash. Let me be hacked to death by a madman, was my silent supplication—anything but **suffocation** by the pink sticky sentiment embodied in that bear and oozing from the walls of the changing room. I didn't mind dying, but the idea that I should do so while clutching a teddy and with a sweet little smile on my face—well, no amount of philosophy had prepared me for that.

5   My official induction into breast cancer came about ten days later with the biopsy, from which I awoke to find the surgeon standing perpendicular to me, at the far end of the gurney, down near my feet, stating gravely, "Unfortunately, there is a cancer." It took me all the rest of that drug-addled day to decide that the most heinous thing about that sentence was not the presence of cancer but the absence of me—for I, Barbara, did not enter into it even as a location, a geographical reference point. Where I once was—not a commanding presence perhaps but nonetheless a standard assemblage of flesh and words and gesture—"there is a cancer." I had been replaced by it, was the surgeon's implication. This was what I was now, medically speaking.

6   Fortunately, no one has to go through this alone. Forty years ago, before Betty Ford, Rose Kushner, Betty Rollin, and other pioneer patients spoke out, breast cancer was a dread secret, endured in silence and euphemized in obituaries as a "long illness." Something about the conjuncture of "breast," signifying sexuality and nurturance, and that other word, suggesting the claws of a **devouring** crustacean, spooked almost everyone. Today, however, it's the biggest disease on the cultural map, bigger than AIDS, cystic fibrosis, or spinal injury, bigger even than those more prolific killers of women—heart disease, lung cancer, and stroke. There are roughly hundreds of websites devoted to it, not to mention newsletters, support groups, a whole genre of first-person breast cancer books, even a glossy upper-middlebrow monthly magazine, *Mamm.*

7   The first thing I discovered as I waded out into the relevant sites is that not everyone views the disease with horror and dread. Instead, the appropriate attitude is upbeat and even eagerly acquisitive. There are between two and three million American women in various stages of breast cancer treatment, who, along with anxious relatives, make up a significant market for all things breast cancer related. Bears, for example: I identified four distinct lines, or species, of these creatures, including Carol, the Remembrance Bear; Hope, the Breast Cancer Research Bear, which wore a pink turban as if to conceal chemotherapy-induced baldness; the Susan Bear, named for [the woman who inspired the Susan G. Komen Foundation]; and the Nick and Nora Wish Upon a Star Bear.

8   And bears are only the tip, so to speak, of the cornucopia of pink-ribbon-themed breast cancer products. You can dress in pink-beribboned sweatshirts, denim shirts, pajamas, lingerie, aprons, loungewear, shoelaces, and socks; accessorize with pink rhinestone brooches, angel pins, scarves, caps, earrings, and bracelets; brighten up your home with breast cancer candles, coffee mugs, pendants, wind chimes, and night-lights; and pay your bills with Checks for the Cure.™ "Awareness" beats secrecy and stigma, of course, but I couldn't help noticing that the existential space in which a friend had earnestly advised me to "confront [my] mortality" bore a striking resemblance to the mall.

9   This is not entirely, I should point out, a case of cynical merchants exploiting the sick. Some breast cancer accessories are made by breast cancer survivors themselves, such as "Janice," creator of the Daisy Awareness Necklace, among other things, and in most cases a portion of the sales goes to breast cancer research. Virginia Davis of Aurora, Colorado, was inspired to create the Remembrance Bear by a friend's double mastectomy and told me she sees her work as more of a "crusade" than a business. When I interviewed her in 2001, she was expecting to ship ten thousand of these teddies, which are manufactured in China, and send part of the money to the Race for the Cure. If the bears are infantilizing—as I tried ever so tactfully to suggest was how they may, in rare cases, be perceived—so far no one has complained. "I just get love letters," she told me "from people who say, 'God bless you for thinking of us.'"

10 The ultrafeminine theme of the breast cancer marketplace—the prominence, for example, of cosmetics and jewelry—could be understood as a response to the treatments' disastrous effects on one's looks. No doubt, too, all the prettiness and pinkness is meant to inspire a positive outlook. But the **infantilizing trope** is a little harder to account for, and teddy bears are not its only manifestation. A tote bag distributed to breast cancer patients by the Libby Ross Foundation (through places such as the Columbia-Presbyterian Medical Center) contained, among other items, a tube of Estée Lauder Perfumed Body Crème, a hot pink satin pillowcase, a small tin of peppermint pastilles, a set of three small, inexpensive rhinestone bracelets, a pink-striped "journal and sketch book," and—somewhat **jarringly**—a box of crayons. Marla Willner, one of the founders of the Libby Ross Foundation, told me that the crayons "go with the journal—for people to express different moods, different thoughts," though she admitted she has never tried to write with crayons herself. Possibly the idea was that regression to a state of child-like dependency puts one in the best frame of mind for enduring the prolonged and toxic treatments. Or it may be that, in some versions of the prevailing gender ideology, femininity is by its

nature incompatible with full adulthood. Certainly men diagnosed with prostate cancer do not receive gifts of Matchbox cars.

11 But I—no less than the bear huggers—needed whatever help I could get and found myself searching obsessively on-line for practical tips on hair loss, how to select a chemotherapy regimen, what to wear after surgery and eat when the scent of food sucks. There was, I soon discovered, far more than I could usefully absorb, for thousands of the afflicted have posted their stories, beginning with the lump or bad mammogram, proceeding through the agony of the treatments, pausing to mention the sustaining forces of family, humor, and religion, and ending, in almost all cases, with an upbeat message for the terrified neophyte. I couldn't seem to get enough of these tales, reading on with panicky fascination about everything that can go wrong.

12 But, despite all the helpful information, the more fellow victims I discovered and read, the greater my sense of isolation grew. No one of the bloggers and book writers seemed to share my sense of outrage over the disease and the available treatments. What causes it and why is it so common, especially in industrialized societies? Why don't we have treatments that distinguish between different forms of breast cancer or between cancer cells and normal dividing cells? In the mainstream of breast cancer culture, there is very little anger, no mention of possible environmental causes, and few comments about the fact that, in all but the more advanced, metastasized cases, it is the "treatments," not the disease, that cause the immediate illness and pain. In fact, the overall tone is almost universally upbeat. The Breast Friends website, for example, featured a series of inspirational quotes: "Don't cry over anything that can't cry over you"; "When life hands out lemons, squeeze out a smile."

13 The cheerfulness of breast cancer culture goes beyond mere absence of anger to what looks, all too often, like a positive embrace of the disease. As a "Mary" reports, on the "Bosom Buds" message board: "I really believe I am a much more sensitive and thoughtful person now. It might sound funny but I was a real worrier before. Now I don't want to waste my energy on worrying. I enjoy life so much more now and in a lot of aspects I am much happier now." Or this from "Andee": "This was the hardest year of my life but also in many ways the most rewarding. I got rid of the baggage, made peace with my family, met many amazing people, learned to take very good care of my body so it will take care of me, and reprioritized my life." Cindy Cherry, quoted in *the Washington Post,* went further: "If I had to do it over, would I want breast cancer? Absolutely. I'm not the same person I was, and I'm glad I'm not. Money doesn't matter anymore. I've met the most phenomenal people in my life through this. Your friends and family are what matter now."

14 The effect of all this positive thinking is to transform breast cancer into a rite of passage—not an injustice or a tragedy to rail against but a normal marker in the life cycle, like menopause or grandmotherhood. Everything in mainstream breast cancer culture serves, no doubt inadvertently, to tame and normalize the disease: the diagnosis may be disastrous, but there are those cunning pink rhinestone angel pins to buy and races to train for. Even the heavy traffic in personal narratives and practical tips that I found so useful bears an implicit acceptance of the disease and the current clumsy and barbarous approaches to its treatment: you can get so busy comparing attractive head scarves that you forget to question whether chemotherapy is really going to be effective in your case.

15 As an experiment, I posted a statement on the [Susan G. Komen Foundation's] message board, under the subject line "Angry," briefly listing my complaints about the **debilitating** effects of chemotherapy, **recalcitrant** insurance companies, environmental carcinogens, and, most daringly, "sappy pink ribbons." I received a few words of encouragement in my fight with the insurance company, which had taken the position that my biopsy was a kind of optional indulgence, but mostly a chorus of **rebukes**. "Suzy" wrote to tell me, "I really dislike saying you have a bad attitude toward all of this, but you do, and it's not going to help you in the least." "Mary" was a bit more tolerant, writing, "Barb, at this time in your life, it's so important to put all your energies toward a peaceful, if not happy, existence. Cancer is a rotten thing to have happen and there are no answers for any of us as to why. But to live your life, whether you have one more year or 51, in anger and bitterness is such a waste. . . . I hope you can find some peace. You deserve it. We all do. God bless you and keep you in His loving care. Your sister, Mary."

16 "Kitty," however, thought I'd gone around the bend: "You need to run, not walk, to some counseling. . . . Please, get yourself some help and I ask everyone on this site to pray for you so you can enjoy life to the fullest." The only person who offered me any reinforcement was "Gerri," who had been through all the treatments and now found herself in terminal condition, with only a few months of life remaining: "I am also angry. All the

money that is raised, all the smiling faces of survivors who make it sound like it is o.k. to have breast cancer. IT IS NOT O.K.!"

17 There was, I learned, an urgent medical reason to embrace cancer with a smile: A "positive attitude" is supposedly essential to recovery. During the months when I was undergoing chemotherapy, I encountered this assertion over and over—on Web sites, in books, from oncology nurses and fellow sufferers. Eight years later, it remains almost axiomatic within the breast cancer culture, that survival hinges on "attitude." One study found 60 percent of women who had been treated for the disease attributing their continued survival to a "positive attitude."

18 The link between the immune system, cancer, and the emotions was cobbled together somewhat imaginatively in the 1970s. It had been known for some time that extreme stress could debilitate certain aspects of the immune system. Torture a lab animal long enough, as the famous stress investigator Hans Selye did in the 1930s, and it becomes less healthy and less resistant to disease. It was apparently a short leap, for many, to the conclusion that positive feelings might be the opposite of stress—capable of boosting the immune system and providing the key to health, even if the threat is not a microbe but a tumor.

19 But where were the studies showing the healing effect of a positive attitude? Could they be duplicated? One of the skeptics, Stanford psychiatrist David Spiegel, told me he set out in 1989 to refute the popular dogma that attitude could overcome cancer. But to his surprise, Spiegel's initial study showed that breast cancer patients in support groups—who presumably were in a better frame of mind than those facing the disease on their own—lived longer than those in the control group. Spiegel promptly interrupted the study, deciding that no one should be deprived of the benefits provided by a support group. The dogma was affirmed and remained so at the time I was diagnosed.

20 The dogma, however, did not survive further research. In the 1990s, studies began to roll in refuting Spiegel's 1989 work on the curative value of support groups. The amazing survival rates of women in Spiegel's first study turned out to be a **fluke**. A few months later, a team led by David Spiegel himself reported in the journal *Cancer* that support groups conferred no survival advantage after all, effectively contradicting his earlier finding. Psychotherapy and support groups might improve one's mood, but they did nothing to overcome cancer.

21 It could be argued that positive thinking can't hurt, that it might even be a blessing to the sorely afflicted. Who would begrudge the optimism of a dying person who clings to the hope of a last-minute remission? Or of a bald and nauseated chemotherapy patient who imagines that the cancer experience will end up giving her a more fulfilling life?

22 But rather than providing emotional sustenance, the **sugarcoating** of cancer can exact a dreadful cost. First, it requires the denial of understandable feelings of anger and fear, all of which must be buried under a cosmetic layer of cheer. This is a great convenience for health workers and even friends of the afflicted, who might prefer fake cheer to complaining, but it is not so easy on the afflicted. Two researchers on benefit finding report that the breast cancer patients they have worked with "have mentioned repeatedly that they view even well-intentioned efforts to encourage benefit-finding as insensitive and inept. They are almost always interpreted as an unwelcome attempt to minimize the unique burdens and challenges that need to be overcome." One 2004 study even found, in complete contradiction to the tenets of positive thinking, that women who perceive more benefits from their cancer "tend to face a poorer quality of life— including worse mental functioning—compared with women who do not perceive benefits from their diagnoses."

23 Whether repressed feelings are themselves harmful, as many psychologists claim, I'm not so sure, but without question there is a problem when positive thinking "fails" and the cancer spreads or eludes treatment. Then the patient can only blame herself: she is not being positive enough; possibly it was her negative attitude that brought on the disease in the first place. Clearly, the failure to think positively can weigh on a cancer patient like a second disease.

24 Breast cancer, I can now report, did not make me prettier or stronger, more feminine or spiritual. What it gave me, if you want to call this a "gift," was a very personal, agonizing encounter with an ideological force in American culture that I had not been aware of before—one that encourages us to deny reality, submit cheerfully to misfortune, and blame only ourselves for our fate.

3. Who is the likely audience?

_____

_____

_____

4. Use context clues and/or a dictionary to define the following words (marked in bold for this exercise).
   a. Recruit (para. 1): _____
   b. Delusion (para. 1): _____
   c. Sentimentality (para. 2): _____
   d. Inescapably (para. 2): _____
   e. Unsettling (para. 3): _____
   f. Suffocation (para. 4): ___ _____
   g. Devouring (para. 6): _____
   h. Infantilizing (para. 10): _____
   i. Trope (para. 10): _____
   j. Jarringly (para. 10): _____
   k. Debilitating (para. 15): _____
   l. Recalcitrant (para. 15): _____
   m. Rebukes (para. 15): _____
   n. Fluke (para. 20): _____
   o. Sugarcoating (para. 22): _____

5. Write what kind of connotation (negative or positive) you think each of the following words has and the image or impression each one creates in your mind.

Word	Positive or Negative Connotation?	Image or Impression
Recruit		
Delusion		
Sentimentality		
Inescapably		
Unsettling		
Suffocation		
Devouring		
Infantilizing		
Trope		
Jarringly		
Debilitating		

Recalcitrant		
Rebukes		
Fluke		
Sugarcoating		

6. What is Ehrenreich's purpose?

_____

_____

_____

7. What is Ehrenreich's tone? _____

8. What does Ehrenreich directly state in the article?

_____

_____

_____

9. What is being implied?

_____

_____

_____

_____

_____

_____

10. What do YOU think? Measure your current belief on the Likert scale. Write a **journal entry** about your level of belief in the following claim: *Positive thinking can cure cancer.*

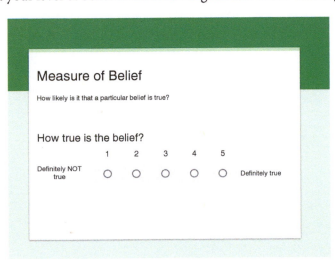

CHAPTER 5

Self-Monitoring

Learning Goals

In this chapter you will learn how to

➤ Monitor Your Skills and Mindset   SECTION ONE

➤ Be Organized

➤ Acknowledge and Examine Worldviews

➤ Recognize Bias in Yourself and Others   SECTION TWO

➤ Monitor Your Thinking

➤ Change Your Mind Based on Evidence

PREVIEW OF TERMS

Self-monitoring p. 154

Worldview p. 159

Bias p. 166

Writing situation p. 168

Loaded language p. 168

Monitoring p. 170

Metacognition p. 170

Fairness p. 171

Cognitive dissonance p. 177

See glossary, pp. 391–397

SECTION ONE

What Is Self-Monitoring?

Many authors understand the necessity of a bad first draft that can, with a little revision, become an excellent piece of writing. Consider the following passage wherein a writer describes how she goes about starting a project:

> What I do at first is procrastinate. After all, I have a vision in my head of what I want to write, and, though it is vague and fuzzy, it is also undoubtedly a masterpiece. So if I actually start writing, I know that I can only disappoint myself. Nothing I write can live up to the imaginary model I hold. Plus, I know how difficult writing actually is. And who wants to put herself through a process that is bound to be disappointing and difficult?

> But eventually the time comes when I know that I have to start my project. As most authors know, few things are more daunting than that unspoiled, virgin-white piece of electronic or real paper. *Just do it*, I tell myself. *But once you get started the imaginary vision will disappear like a puff of smoke and all you will be left with is gritty reality*, my own voice answers back. *I don't want to*. I then have to get forceful with myself. *What are you, a coward, afraid of a little toil and frustration?* So with no excuses left, I force myself to write that opening section.

> And let me tell you, it is almost always as bad as I feared it would be. The writing is strained, forced, and it doesn't hold to the outline I have already developed for myself. It belabors points that don't need to be belabored, and it brushes over parts

that need in-depth explanation. The vision I held in my head has been proved wrong, as always, and it is frustrating indeed.

But then I go back to my internal discussion. *Well, that is definitely a start, if nothing else,* I encourage myself. *I don't know if this writing can be salvaged, but I damn sure am not going to give up. Now how can I make this better?* And slowly but surely, laboriously, I set about trying to make my terrible first draft into a quality finished product. I make hard decisions about what can be cut. I add details or support where necessary. I move things around. And almost always, though it could never match the unrealistic vision I had in my head, I end up through the virtue of my own hard work with a finished product I can be proud of.

What this author is modeling is the internal conversation she holds with herself as she works through her writing. An important part of critical thinking is **self-monitoring**—keeping tabs on yourself as you write or as you think about a text or an argument. This writer, for example, is aware of the quality of her work, of when she needs to do better, and of what is working well.

Self-monitoring also requires that you recognize whether you have the proper mindset prior to tackling an intellectual challenge. First, you need to make sure that you are organized. That way you can be as effective as possible in the tasks you undertake. You will need to account for your own and the author's worldviews and biases. Then, you need to keep track of how well you are accomplishing your task. None of these things are easy, but this chapter will guide you through how to accomplish them.

Reviewing the Critical Thinker's Traits: Becoming Organized in Your Life and in Your Thinking

You know how hard it can be to accomplish something when you can't find the things you need. Have you ever needed a tool from the basement or garage, but had no idea where to look for it because there was no rhyme or reason to how the tools were stored? Maybe the screwdrivers were scattered around in several drawers, and the hammer was in a container with the paint supplies. Or perhaps you had your heart set on wearing a particular piece of clothing but just had to give up because you couldn't find it in your dresser? Of course, the problem in both examples is *organization,* or lack thereof. Because no system was used to categorize or store similar tools or pieces of clothing, everything got mixed together and lost.

> Organizing is what you do before you do something, so that when you do it, it is not all mixed up.
> —A. A. Milne

Similarly, if you have a project to complete, you need to approach it in a systematic fashion, or it will be very difficult to finish it. In the first example above, once you found the hammer and screwdriver, maybe intending to put together your dresser, would you just randomly start driving in screws and banging together pieces of wood, or would you approach the project one step at a time, doing the basic tasks first and the more advanced tasks later? It's a safe bet that you would use some system, or else you'd probably end up totally frustrated, with a piece of furniture that wouldn't quite fit together.

You should try to be organized in both your life and your thinking. Organization needs to become a habit, not only because it will increase your productivity, but because it will make you a more systematic thinker, thus making you better at analysis. Good organization is often the key to success, as typified in the case of chess grandmaster Xie Jun.

Tips for Critical Thinkers: How to Be Organized in Your Life

- **Keep your living space neat and structured.** Pick up clutter, clean up your messes immediately after you make them, do the dishes after you cook, etc. Also, decide where you will store your belongings according to categories and make sure to always return your stuff to its proper place. Strangely, having a clean, structured environment will make you feel more inclined to do the work you need to do.

- **Develop a routine.** Get up and go to bed at the same time every day, do your homework at a designated time, exercise a certain number of times per week at a set time, do your laundry on Sundays, and so forth. That way, daily tasks won't build up, making you feel overwhelmed. Plus, you will maintain your physical health (and your mental health, since your mind and body are connected).
- **Keep a to-do list.** Write down the things you need to do today in the order you need to do them and get into the habit of doing so every morning. Then check off the tasks as you complete them. You will free up your imperfect memory and have more brain power at your disposal to actually accomplish the jobs you need to do, as opposed to simply trying to remember what those things were in the first place.
- **Set long-term goals and steadily work toward them.** Like driving without having a road map or GPS, you'll never get anywhere if you don't know where you're going. So decide where you want to be one, five, and ten years from now. Then list the steps you will need to take to accomplish each goal and when you need to take those steps. Check up on your progress and never get discouraged. As long as your goals are realistic in the first place, planning and determination will take you a long way toward accomplishing them.

> **Thinker to Emulate:**
> **Xie Jun**
>
> Xie Jun, born in China in 1970, is a chess grandmaster. She was Women's World Chess Champion on two occasions and is only the second woman in history to accomplish this feat.
>
> To become a chess grandmaster, Xie Jun displayed great persistence and organization. She began studying to master chess at the age of six. Even though she did not have much support in doing so, as she grew older she nevertheless developed a system by which she could advance in her chess skills until she accomplished her goal of becoming a champion. She was rated second or third in the world for most of her career (when she wasn't champion), and she was instrumental in helping her team win the gold medal in the 1998 Chess Olympiad.

Once your life is organized, work on approaching your thinking in an organized fashion. Organizing your thoughts is similar to organizing your life: Here are some tips for how to do so.

Tips for Critical Thinkers: How to Be Organized in Your Thinking

- **Think about one thing at a time.** When you have a mental problem to solve, try to clear your mind of distracting thoughts that aren't related to the task at hand. If something is bothering you, try to take care of that problem first.
- **When considering an argument or problem, break it down into its component pieces, and then group the pieces together in your mind using categories based on similarity.** For example, all information relating to the background or origin of the problem should be grouped together, all information relating to details about the problem should go together, and all information relating to solutions of the problem should be grouped together.
- **Use maps, outlines, or tables to keep information straight.** If you have a great deal of complex information that you can't categorize in your head, use the tools you've already learned to keep track of it. For example, create a map or outline (see Chapter 3, p. 99) to represent how all the pieces of an argument go together. Or create a table to allow easy comparison of details.
- **Think systematically.** Develop a system for approaching your issue and go step by step when you think about it. Your system will depend on what you are thinking about and what you hope to accomplish.

One system you can make good use of is known as Bloom's (Revised) Taxonomy, which will help you think about an issue and determine if you have mastery of it. If you can answer questions about a specific concept that are based on each level of the Taxonomy, then you know you're getting a good understanding of it. Figure 5-1 outlines Bloom's Taxonomy and the questions to systematically ask yourself when thinking about an issue. The column to the right gives example questions that you might ask yourself when learning about Bloom's Taxonomy.

Level	Definition	Questions to Ask	Examples
Remembering	Recalling basic facts about a subject	What are the basic details of the problem? Do I remember the facts?	What is the exact definition of Bloom's Taxonomy?
Understanding	Showing comprehension of the facts and concepts	Can I restate the facts/concepts in my own words?	Can I explain Bloom's Taxonomy in my own words?
Applying	Using the information to perform a task	What could I do with the information I have learned?	How can I use Bloom's Taxonomy to help me study what I'm learning in school?
Analyzing	Breaking the concept into its component pieces	What are the parts or steps involved in what I'm thinking about? What are different ways this problem could be approached?	What are the steps in using Bloom's Taxonomy that help me study? What are the parts of the Taxonomy?
Evaluating	Judging the truth, effectiveness, or worth of the information or concept	Is this information useful to me? Is it convincing? Is it a good argument?	How useful is Bloom's Taxonomy in helping me understand what I'm studying? In what ways could it be more useful?
Creating	Combining or relating information to form a new concept	How does what I'm thinking about relate to what I already know? Can I connect these facts to other facts in order to create a new idea?	How does Bloom's Taxonomy relate to critical thinking? Does what I've learned about critical thinking help me understand Bloom's Taxonomy better?

■ **Figure 5-1**   Bloom's Taxonomy

The Taxonomy was actually designed by Bloom to help educators challenge their students, to get them to do more with the material than simply repeat word-for-word what they were taught. Since many professors use Bloom's Taxonomy when developing questions and exercises in your class, knowing about it will also help you in answering those questions. For example, if you can recognize that a question you've been asked corresponds to the evaluating level of Bloom's Taxonomy, you know your professor is requiring you to judge how effective something is, and you can answer accordingly.

PRACTICE 5-1   Organize Your Life

Directions: Respond to the following prompts on a separate sheet of paper.

1. Name two categories of items (like DVDs, books, or clothes) you own that could benefit from better organization. What system could you use to organize these items? Explain your systems in detail.
2. Jot down the tasks you need to accomplish over the next three days. Prioritize them by number: write a "1" next to the one that needs to be finished first, a "2" next to the one that needs to be finished second, and so forth. Get into the habit of crossing off each item as you complete it. Check your list and add to it every morning.
3. Write down a goal you want to accomplish in the next five years. Next to your goal, list the date by which you want to have it accomplished. Then list the steps you will need to take to complete your goal; next to each step, list when you need to have completed it. If necessary, do some research to figure out what steps you need to take to achieve your goal.

THINK AND WRITE CRITICALLY

Organize Your Thinking

Directions: Read this passage and on the lines provided answer the questions that follow it. The questions correspond to the levels of Bloom's Revised Taxonomy and serve as examples of the kinds of questions you could ask yourself when thinking about an issue.

We are not good random number generators. This human tendency is known as the gambler's fallacy: the belief that independent events can influence each other's probabilities. It is aptly named, for casinos make millions of dollars each year because of it. People who reason that a coin which has come up heads ten times in a row is "due" to come up tails are committing this fallacy; so are people who reason that a roulette wheel which has landed on red several consecutive times must be on a "hot streak" upon which they can capitalize. These are independent events with no "memory" of what preceded them.

But the gambler's fallacy has more subtle effects than roulette wheels. Due to the human reluctance to infer randomness, people often conclude that events which coincide must be causally connected. Sometimes this is a valid assumption; other times, it almost certainly is not:

The maths tells us that in respect of probability, people are much like tosses of a coin: we will see occasional clusters, even of cancer.

Tell that to the residents of Wishaw near Sutton Coldfield where a huge mobile phone mast overshadowed 35 of the houses, until someone pulled it down one bonfire night.

. . . "I was going through chemotherapy," she says, "when I started meeting my neighbours in the hospital.

"It was then we started looking at the mobile phone mast and now we know for certain that it is responsible."

In any random sample of data, we will inevitably see coincidental clustering. And the larger the pool of data is, the larger the clusters will tend to be. In a country the size of the U.K., it is very likely indeed that cancer cases, even rare forms of cancer, may cluster together purely by chance in at least a few places. Of course, it is certainly possible that a local cluster of cancer cases may have a common cause, and that possibility should not be overlooked.

The problem arises when detailed scrutiny turns up no common cause, yet sufferers understandably in search of an answer persist in believing there must be one, refusing to consider the possibility of random chance. The result, as we see here, is that innocent parties often get blamed by people who believe there simply must be some connection—such as concluding that cell phone towers cause cancer, despite the fact that these towers do not emit ionizing radiation which can damage DNA. A similar explanation was probably at play in medieval witch trials, where any unusual run of bad luck would often be blamed on black magic practiced by the town outcast. It is also seen today in so-called "healing" shrines, where the few spontaneous recoveries among vast crowds of suffering pilgrims are attributed to the miraculous powers of the shrine, rather than the inevitable occasional chance event.

Human beings are often brought to grief by inferring hidden causes when we should infer random chance. Our inability to innately comprehend statistical principles causes us to commit this fallacy. By treating chance as the default explanation, which it should always be, and learning to ask for evidence of an underlying cause before dismissing randomness as an explanation, we could shed many unnecessary superstitious hindrances.

Reprinted by permission of Adam Lee.

1. (Remembering): Find the definition of the Gambler's Fallacy in the text and write it down exactly as it appears.

_____

_____

_____

2. (Understanding): Explain the Gambler's Fallacy in your own words.

_____

_____

_____

3. (Applying): How could you use this information in a Las Vegas casino?

_____

_____

_____

_____

4. (Analyzing): What examples does the author give of people falling victim to the Gambler's Fallacy?

_____

_____

_____

5. (Evaluating): Does the author provide enough detail and evidence so that you understand the Gambler's Fallacy and how to avoid it? Why or why not?

_____

_____

_____

_____

6. (Creating): How does the Gambler's Fallacy relate to your life? If you've never experienced it directly, how does it relate to a subject you've learned about in school?

_____

_____

_____

_____

Recognizing Worldviews

Once you are sure your thoughts are organized, it is time to consider how your worldviews and biases might affect your interpretation of what you read, see, hear, or write.

To start thinking about your worldview, consider the tradition of a "Sky Burial." Read the passage below and then answer the questions that follow.

> In Tibet, corpses are often given a "Sky Burial." When a loved one dies, his or her body is ritually "disassembled"—the flesh is stripped from the bones and the bones are broken with a mallet. The body is then left on the side of a mountain so that birds and other wild animals can eat it. Whatever remains is left to the elements. The Buddhist practitioners of Sky Burial view it both as a reminder of the impermanence of life and as an act of generosity, of giving back to nature.

1. What are your initial reactions to this Tibetan funeral practice?

   _____

   _____

   _____

2. Based on this practice, what judgments have you made about its Tibetan practitioners? Do you find them barbaric, savage, or disgusting? Why or why not?

   _____

   _____

   _____

3. What do you believe the practitioners of Sky Burial would think about your own mourning practices?

   _____

   _____

   _____

4. If the practice of Sky Burial is offensive to you, why do you think you feel that way?

   _____

   _____

   _____

The last question above is probably the hardest to answer. The difficulty is that our reactions and thoughts stem from our individual worldview. A **worldview** is a framework of values and beliefs by which you understand the world and navigate your way through it. Essentially, a worldview is what you use to comprehend the world and how you fit into it. You can think of worldview as a pair of prescription glasses; worldviews cause us to see people, situations, and events around us in a certain way. If you put on someone else's prescription glasses, the world could look very different.

What was the first thing you saw when you looked at this picture? Did you see an old woman or a young woman?

Look again; both a young and old woman are in the picture, but until this is pointed out to you, you probably won't be aware that there is more than one person in the picture. This illusion is a graphic illustration of what a worldview is like. Until you have an experience that shocks you and jars your worldview, or until you meet someone with a radically different worldview, you might not even be aware that you have a worldview at all. The way you view the world seems to be just the natural way the world is, but, as with the picture above, there are multiple ways in which the world can be viewed.

Library of Congress, Prints & Photographs Division, [LC-DIG-ds-00175].

Your worldview helps you answer the following questions:

- What is true about the world?
- How did the world get here?
- How did I get here?
- What matters most in life?
- What should I strive to do or be?
- How do I attain my goals?

Everyone has a worldview; it would be impossible not to. Having a worldview can be a good thing; it can help make the world less confusing and scary; it can also provide a sense of connection with others who share your worldview.

So how can worldviews be a problem? After all, everyone is a product of his culture and background. The problem is not so much that worldviews are the lens through which we see and interpret the world, but that worldviews often remain unexamined. We should base our judgments on objective reasoning and critical thinking; however, if we never acknowledge our worldview and never critically examine it, we might make decisions based on what we assume to be true rather than what the evidence suggests is true. This is because every worldview contains certain weaknesses, biases, and blind spots. The world is so complex and contradictory that no single worldview can account for it.

Another problem with worldviews is that they can cause us to be *ethnocentric*, which means believing that our ethnicity or culture is superior to others' ethnicities or cultures. They can also make us think that our particular influences (like our religion, the traditions of our family, the politics we favor) are better than the things that have influenced others. Recognizing this tendency can make you more sensitive to other people who have different backgrounds, traditions, ethnicities, cultures, and politics; it makes you get along better with people who have different worldviews.

Being more understanding of different worldviews is very important, since people base their values and behaviors on their worldviews, and, unfortunately, differing worldviews lead to conflict. When worldviews are different enough, they can lead to issues that are almost irresolvable. For example, the worldviews of some fundamentalist Muslims—that Islam should be the official religion of a state, that Islam is destined to be the dominant religion in the world, and that extreme means of conversion are warranted—is incompatible with the worldviews of many Westerners—that the state should not support a religion, that everyone should be free to choose his or her own religion, and that extreme means of conversion are never okay. This clash of worldviews explains a great deal about the conflicts in which Europe and the United States have been involved in the 21st century.

For these reasons, it is important that every critical thinker try to become aware of his or her worldview and strive to be more understanding and tolerant of the worldviews of others. As you examine your worldview and assumptions more closely, you may find that some beliefs need to be abandoned if they do not stand up to your critical thinking. Other times you may find that your beliefs hold up to critical scrutiny, but you might need to explain them in a clearer, better way to people who have different assumptions.

PRACTICE 5-3   Writing about Worldviews

THINK
AND **WRITE**
CRITICALLY

Directions: On another sheet of paper, explore the following questions so that you can better understand your own worldview.

1. How did the universe get here?
2. How did human beings get here?
3. If you could choose any country or culture to live in, which would it be and why?

4. If you could choose any profession, what would you choose? What do you think this says about your values?

5. What is the worst thing a human being could possibly do? Why?

THINK AND WRITE CRITICALLY

For Further Thought

1. Examine your answers to the questions above. Why did you answer them the way you did? Did you arrive at your beliefs using reason, logic, and evidence, or did you gain your beliefs because you were told they were true or because you were raised to believe in them?

2. Choose a worldview that is very different from your own. Research that worldview. Pretend you are someone who holds that worldview and answer the questions in Practice 5–3.

Worldviews and Texts   PRACTICE 5-4

Directions: Read the following scenarios and answer the questions that follow.

Case 1

You are reading an opinion piece in your local newspaper about terrorism and the Middle East. The American author of the piece proclaims that the U.S. government should use whatever means necessary to keep America safe, including torture of captured terrorists, drone strikes against enemy fighters when they are at home with their families, and midnight raids into enemy villages.

1. What can you tell about the worldview of the author? What does he value?
2. How do you feel about the author's opinion? Do you agree or disagree? Why?
3. How do you imagine someone with different worldviews and values might respond to the piece in the newspaper?

Case 2

You are having a discussion with a friend, Jane. She tells you that she plans to put off going to college immediately after high school. Instead, she is going to join the Peace Corp and go to a country in Africa. She states that she couldn't feel good about herself if she didn't help those who are less fortunate. She says that she knows she was lucky to be born into a developed country to well-off parents, but some people aren't so lucky, and their unfortunate situation in life is not their fault.

© leonello calvetti/Shutterstock.com.

1. In Jane's worldview, what is one of the most important things that accounts for a person's situation in life? In your opinion, is Jane right or wrong about this?

2. Do you agree with Jane that a person has an obligation to help the less fortunate? Why or why not?

READ, WRITE, AND THINK CRITICALLY: SECTION ONE

Directions: Survey the following text and answer the questions below. Then, read and annotate the selection, and answer the questions that follow.

1. What do you predict the selection will be about? What is the topic?

_____

_____

2. What is your prior knowledge of this topic?

_____

_____

Body Ritual among the Nacirema

Horace Miner

Horace Miner (1912–1993) was a professor of anthropology and sociology at Wayne State University. He was a Fulbright scholar and published many works over the course of his prestigious career. The following piece appeared in American Anthropologist *in 1956.*

1 The anthropologist has become so familiar with the diversity of ways in which different peoples behave in similar situations that he is not apt to be surprised by even the most exotic customs. In fact, if all of the logically possible combinations of behavior have not been found somewhere in the world, he is apt to suspect that they must be present in some yet undescribed tribe. This point has, in fact, been expressed with respect to clan organization by Murdock. In this light, the magical beliefs and practices of the Nacirema present such unusual aspects that it seems desirable to describe them as an example of the extremes to which human behavior can go.

2 Professor Linton first brought the ritual of the Nacirema to the attention of anthropologists twenty years ago, but the culture of this people is still very poorly understood. They are a North American group living in the territory between the Canadian Cree, the Yaqui, and Tarahumare of Mexico, and the Carib and Arawak of the Antilles. Little is known of their origin, although tradition states that they came from the east. . . .

3 Nacirema culture is characterized by a highly developed market economy which has evolved in a rich natural habitat. While much of the people's time is devoted to economic pursuits, a large part of the fruits of these labors and a considerable portion of the day are spent in ritual activity. The focus of this activity is the human body, the appearance and health of which loom as a dominant concern in the ethos of the people. While such a concern is certainly not unusual, its ceremonial aspects and associated philosophy are unique.

4 The fundamental belief underlying the whole system appears to be that the human body is ugly and that its natural tendency is to debility and disease. Incarcerated in such a body, man's only hope is to avert these characteristics through the use of the powerful influences of ritual and ceremony. Every household has one or more shrines devoted to this purpose. The more powerful individuals in the society have several shrines in their houses and, in fact, the opulence of a house is often referred to in terms of the number of such ritual centers it possesses. Most houses are of wattle and daub construction, but the shrine rooms of the more wealthy are walled with stone. Poorer families imitate the rich by applying pottery plaques to their shrine walls.

5 While each family has at least one such shrine, the rituals associated with it are not family ceremonies but are private and secret. The rites are normally only discussed with children, and then only during the period when they are being initiated into these mysteries. I was able, however, to establish sufficient rapport with the natives to examine these shrines and to have the rituals described to me.

6 The focal point of the shrine is a box or chest which is built into the wall. In this chest are kept the many charms and magical potions without which no native believes he could live. These preparations are secured from a variety of specialized practitioners. The most powerful of these are the medicine men, whose assistance must be rewarded with substantial gifts. However, the medicine men do not provide the curative potions for their clients, but decide what the ingredients should be and then write them down in an ancient and secret language. This writing is understood only by the medicine men and by the herbalists who, for another gift, provide the required charm.

"Body Ritual Among the Nacirema" by Horace Miner, originally published in *American Anthropologist*, June 1956, pp. 503-507.

7   The charm is not disposed of after it has served its purpose, but is placed in the charm-box of the household shrine. As these magical materials are specific for certain ills, and the real or imagined maladies of the people are many, the charm-box is usually full to overflowing. The magical packets are so numerous that people forget what their purposes were and fear to use them again. While the natives are very vague on this point, we can only assume that the idea in retaining all the old magical materials is that their presence in the charm-box, before which the body rituals are conducted, will in some way protect the worshipper.

8   Beneath the charm-box is a small font. Each day every member of the family, in succession, enters the shrine room, bows his head before the charm-box, mingles different sorts of holy water in the font, and proceeds with a brief rite of ablution. The holy waters are secured from the Water Temple of the community, where the priests conduct elaborate ceremonies to make the liquid ritually pure.

9   In the hierarchy of magical practitioners, and below the medicine men in prestige, are specialists whose designation is best translated "holy-mouth-men." The Nacirema have an almost pathological horror of and fascination with the mouth, the condition of which is believed to have a supernatural influence on all social relationships. Were it not for the rituals of the mouth, they believe that their teeth would fall out, their gums bleed, their jaws shrink, their friends desert them, and their lovers reject them. They also believe that a strong relationship exists between oral and moral characteristics. For example, there is a ritual ablution of the mouth for children which is supposed to improve their moral fiber.

10   The daily body ritual performed by everyone includes a mouthrite. Despite the fact that these people are so punctilious about care of the mouth, this rite involves a practice which strikes the uninitiated stranger as revolting. It was reported to me that the ritual consists of inserting a small bundle of hog hairs into the mouth, along with certain magical powders, and then moving the bundle in a highly formalized series of gestures.

11   In addition to the private mouth-rite, the people seek out a holymouth-man once or twice a year. These practitioners have an impressive set of paraphernalia, consisting of a variety of augers, awls, probes, and prods. The use of these objects in the exorcism of the evils of the mouth involves almost unbelievable ritual torture of the client. The holymouth-man opens the client's mouth and, using the above mentioned tools, enlarges any holes which decay may have created in the teeth. Magical materials are put into these holes. If there are not naturally occurring holes in the teeth, large sections of one or more teeth are gouged out so that the supernatural substance can be applied. In the client's view, the purpose of these ministrations is to arrest decay and to draw friends. The extremely sacred and traditional character of the rite is evident in the fact that the natives return to the holymouth-men year after year, despite the fact that their teeth continue to decay.

12   It is to be hoped that, when a thorough study of the Nacirema is made, there will be careful inquiry into the personality structure of these people. One has but to watch the gleam in the eye of a holymouth-man, as he jabs an awl into an exposed nerve, to suspect that a certain amount of sadism is involved. If this can be established, a very interesting pattern emerges, for most of the population shows definite masochistic tendencies. It was to these that Professor Linton referred in discussing a distinctive part of the daily body ritual which is performed only by men. This part of the rite involves scraping and lacerating the surface of the face with a sharp instrument. Special women's rites are performed only four times during each lunar month, but what they lack in frequency is made up in barbarity. As part of this ceremony, women bake their heads in small ovens for about an hour. The theoretically interesting point is that what seems to be a preponderantly masochistic people have developed sadistic specialists.

13   The medicine men have an imposing temple, or latipso, in every community of any size. The more elaborate ceremonies required to treat very sick patients can only be performed at this temple. These ceremonies involve not only the thaumaturge but a permanent group of vestal maidens who move sedately about the temple chambers in distinctive costume and headdress.

14   The latipso ceremonies are so harsh that it is phenomenal that a fair proportion of the really sick natives who enter the temple ever recover. Small children whose indoctrination is still incomplete have been known to resist attempts to take them to the temple because "that is where you go to die." Despite this fact, sick adults are not only willing but eager to undergo the protracted ritual purification, if they can afford to do so. No matter

how ill the supplicant or how grave the emergency, the guardians of many temples will not admit a client if he cannot give a rich gift to the custodian. Even after one has gained admission and survived the ceremonies, the guardians will not permit the neophyte to leave until he makes still another gift.

15 The supplicant entering the temple is first stripped of all his or her clothes. In everyday life the Nacirema avoids exposure of his body and its natural functions. Bathing and excretory acts are performed only in the secrecy of the household shrine, where they are ritualized as part of the body-rites. Psychological shock results from the fact that body secrecy is suddenly lost upon entry into the latipso. A man, whose own wife has never seen him in an excretory act, suddenly finds himself naked and assisted by a vestal maiden while he performs his natural functions into a sacred vessel. This sort of ceremonial treatment is necessitated by the fact that the excreta are used by a diviner to ascertain the course and nature of the client's sickness. Female clients, on the other hand, find their naked bodies are subjected to the scrutiny, manipulation and prodding of the medicine men.

16 Few supplicants in the temple are well enough to do anything but lie on their hard beds. The daily ceremonies, like the rites of the holymouth-men, involve discomfort and torture. With ritual precision, the vestals awaken their miserable charges each dawn and roll them about on their beds of pain while performing ablutions, in the formal movements of which the maidens are highly trained. At other times they insert magic wands in the supplicant's mouth or force him to eat substances which are supposed to be healing. From time to time the medicine men come to their clients and jab magically treated needles into their flesh. The fact that these temple ceremonies may not cure, and may even kill the neophyte, in no way decreases the people's faith in the medicine men.

17 There remains one other kind of practitioner, known as a "listener." This witchdoctor has the power to exorcise the devils that lodge in the heads of people who have been bewitched. The Nacirema believe that parents bewitch their own children. Mothers are particularly suspected of putting a curse on children while teaching them the secret body rituals. The counter-magic of the witchdoctor is unusual in its lack of ritual. The patient simply tells the "listener" all his troubles and fears, beginning with the earliest difficulties he can remember. The memory displayed by the Nacirema in these exorcism sessions is truly remarkable. It is not uncommon for the patient to bemoan the rejection he felt upon being weaned as a babe, and a few individuals even see their troubles going back to the traumatic effects of their own birth.

18 In conclusion, mention must be made of certain practices which have their base in native esthetics but which depend upon the pervasive aversion to the natural body and its functions. There are ritual fasts to make fat people thin and ceremonial feasts to make thin people fat. Still other rites are used to make women's breasts larger if they are small, and smaller if they are large. General dissatisfaction with breast shape is symbolized in the fact that the ideal form is virtually outside the range of human variation. A few women afflicted with almost inhuman hyper-mammary development are so idolized that they make a handsome living by simply going from village to village and permitting the natives to stare at them for a fee.

19 Reference has already been made to the fact that excretory functions are ritualized, routinized, and relegated to secrecy. Natural reproductive functions are similarly distorted. Intercourse is taboo as a topic and scheduled as an act. Efforts are made to avoid pregnancy by the use of magical materials or by limiting intercourse to certain phases of the moon. Conception is actually very infrequent. When pregnant, women dress so as to hide their condition. Parturition takes place in secret, without friends or relatives to assist, and the majority of women do not nurse their infants.

20 Our review of the ritual life of the Nacirema has certainly shown them to be a magic-ridden people. It is hard to understand how they have managed to exist so long under the burdens which they have imposed upon themselves. But even such exotic customs as these take on real meaning when they are viewed with the insight provided by Malinowski when he wrote:

> Looking from far and above, from our high places of safety in the developed civilization, it is easy to see all the crudity and irrelevance of magic. But without its power and guidance early man could not have mastered his practical difficulties as he has done, nor could man have advanced to the higher stages of civilization.

3. The author claims that "The fundamental belief underlying the whole system appears to be that the human body is ugly and that its natural tendency is to debility and disease" (para. 4). What evidence does Miner give to support this claim?

_____

_____

_____

_____

4. What is the author's tone?

_____

_____

_____

5. What is the connotation of the following words, and why do you think the author chose them?
   Exotic (para. 1, 20); extremes (para. 1); loom (para. 3); unique (para. 3); incarcerated (para. 4); natives (para. 5, 6, 7, 14); charm (para. 6, 7); magical (para. 7, 10, 11); maladies (para. 7); ablution (para. 8, 9, 16); exorcism (para. 11, 17); barbarity (para. 12)

_____

_____

6. Have you ever met someone from Nacirema? What questions would you want to ask someone from Nacirema in order to better understand their culture?

_____

_____

_____

7. What are some assumptions that Miner makes about the habits of the Nacirema? Does he approve or disapprove of their rituals?

_____

_____

_____

_____

SECTION TWO

Recognizing Biases

The inability of a worldview to account for the complexity of the world may lead to bias. **Bias** is commonly defined as an unfair judgment or an unreasonable point of view that is resistant to change. When we are biased, we judge arguments without looking fairly at the reasoning or evidence given to support them. It is much like having sunglasses on, for just as sunglasses block certain light rays from the eyes, biases block certain claims from our minds. We just don't see the value of some arguments when we have a bias against them. Our biases affect the most common daily experiences such as trying to decide where to eat to important issues such as voting for the next president. As you are reading a text, if you notice bias in yourself or in the author, be sure to annotate the word, phrase, or sentence that identifies the potential bias.

PRACTICE 5-5	Bias

Directions: Read the following example of everyday bias, then complete Practice 5–6 to better understand how bias can cause us to react without thinking.

> Leighton goes to her doctor for her annual checkup, but this year she gets some unwelcome news. Her doctor says that Leighton's cholesterol level is elevated, her blood pressure is worrisome, and her BMI (body mass index) is too high. Her doctor says that Leighton needs to eat less red meat and less junk food. Having always been a fan of processed foods and steak, Leighton isn't too happy about this. "Well, if I can't eat my normal foods," she says with some irritation, "what can I eat?" Her doctor stifles a smile. "Have you ever heard of tofu?" he asks. "Let's start with that." Leighton frowns. "Ewww," she moans. "I don't even want to try that. That sounds disgusting."

Now, suppose your doctor tells you that you must cut red meat and processed foods out of your diet for health reasons, and your doctor suggests that, instead of red meat and processed foods, you should be eating more of the following:

Tofu
Soy burgers
Flax seeds
Agave (in place of honey)
Kale
Seaweed

How would you react to your doctor's suggestion? Did you say the foods are unappetizing? Was your opinion based on experience or on your worldview? Would you say it would be impossible for you to give up red meat? If you reacted in disgust to the idea of eating seaweed or tofu but have not tried them, how do you compare with Leighton? You are both passing up the chance to improve your health by making changes to your diet. Remember that, as a critical thinker, you are trying to form beliefs that are more likely to be true and to make better decisions. Bias often prevents you from forming beliefs and making decisions that conflict with your worldview.

It is important as a critical thinker to be aware of your worldview and what potential biases you have.

Even though there is not a quick and easy way to discover your worldview, you can get a working idea of what it is by answering certain "big" questions, like what is most important to you.

A. *Directions:* Read the following statements and note whether you agree (A) or disagree (D) with them.

_____ 1. The sexes are naturally better at performing different jobs and tasks.

_____ 2. I should be proud of my country simply because it is mine.

_____ 3. Social classes are a natural feature of society.

_____ 4. People are poor because they are lazy or have failed in some way.

_____ 5. A person's sexual orientation is something he or she is born with.

_____ 6. Different races are naturally better or worse at certain things.

_____ 7. It is better to be religious than not to have a religion.

_____ 8. People who live in a country should speak the language of the majority of the residents of that country.

_____ 9. Having a diverse population in terms of race, culture, and religion makes a nation stronger.

_____10. Animals deserve certain rights and should be protected.

After you have noted your initial reactions to each of the statements, take a look at several of your responses and try to think why you responded the way you did. Was your reaction to a statement based on a reasoning process (can you support your response with specific evidence) or was your response the "natural" one (your "gut reaction")? If a response does not arise from reasoning, it is a biased judgment and is likely the product of a worldview.

B. *Directions:* Now choose one of your responses to the statements above. On another sheet of paper, answer the following questions in relation to the response you chose.

1. What evidence supports your response?
2. What assumptions are your responses based on?
3. How would you explain your answer to someone who holds the opposite opinion?

THINK
AND **WRITE**
CRITICALLY

EXPAND YOUR UNDERSTANDING: DEFENDING YOUR POSITIONS

Directions: Your instructor will split you into groups according to your responses to one of the above statements. As a group, prepare an argument to support the position your group has chosen. After the groups have prepared their respective arguments, your instructor will moderate and evaluate a debate between the groups.

As you probably realized, the hardest part of the exercise was justifying your responses. Responses come quickly, as they are the products of worldviews; supporting them is more difficult, since you have to use critical thinking skills.

As we said earlier, bias is the inability to see the full spectrum of evidence concerning an argument or issue. A biased individual cannot see the objective worth of an argument. While it is essential for a critical thinker to recognize his or her biases, it is also important to be able to spot bias in texts. To find bias in a text, it can be helpful to look at the writing situation and language used.

Using the Writing Situation to Determine Bias

The **writing situation** refers to the author's background and biography, the event that prompted the author to write, the author's purpose, and the author's audience. Examining these things will help you notice potential bias on the part of an author. To investigate the writing situation, ask yourself the following questions:

- **Who is the writer and what are his or her credentials?** Is he or she a member of a certain organization, profession, religion, political party, etc.? What is the author's professional background? Does the author have a degree or expertise in the subject that he or she is writing about?
- **What event happened to prompt the author to write?** Was there a situation in the world that caused the author to write the text?
- **Where was the text published?** What do you know about the publisher? What is the reputation of the publisher? What sort of thing does the publisher usually publish?
- **Who is the text intended for?** Who is the audience? What assumptions does the audience make? What worldview does the audience hold?
- **What is the purpose of the piece?** What is the author hoping to accomplish by writing the piece?

By understanding the situation in which the author wrote, you should be able to say whether the author is potentially biased. For example, suppose you are assigned to read an article for a social science class. The article is concerned with the question of whether the minimum wage should be raised. The author is a small business owner, is against unions, and the article has been published on a website that is strongly politically conservative. Being aware of these facts about the writing situation, you should be on the lookout for bias. You should also know, however, that it's possible for a biased author to still make a valid argument.

> **For Further Thought**
>
> Find a recent article that pertains to a controversial topic. Determine whether the author is potentially biased by figuring out the writing situation surrounding the article. Should you expect to find bias in the article or not? Explain your response.

Using Language to Determine Bias

The words a writer chooses to use can also tell a reader what bias may be operating in a text. For instance, consider the following statement:

> Malevolent oil companies want to rob the country of its most precious resource: the splendor of the Alaskan wilderness.

> **Reminder**: Tone and word connotations were covered in Chapter 4, pp. 123–125.

The words used here have been purposefully chosen to create an impression in the reader's mind without the use of argumentation. For instance, the statement compares oil companies to robbers. This comparison will most likely lead the reader to think negatively of the companies; on the other hand, stating that the wild land is beautiful and is the country's most precious resource will probably create a positive response to the wilderness. This statement then has no support aside from the impression created by the words chosen to express it. Writers often use their choice of words to influence readers to accept a claim rather than providing reasons and evidence to support it. When a writer uses word choice in an attempt to persuade the reader without evidence or argumentation, the writer is using what is called **loaded language.**

What do you know about the author and what are the author's credentials?	Investigate his or her background.
What is the outside event?	Determine if an event in the world caused the author to produce the piece.
Where was the text published?	See if the place of publication provides a clue to potential bias.
Who is the author's audience?	Investigate the assumptions and shared beliefs of the audience.
What is the author's purpose?	Figure out what the author is trying to accomplish.

■ **Figure 5-2**   The Writing Situation

Ask yourself the following questions when thinking about the language used in a text.

Tips for Critical Thinkers: How to Evaluate Word Choice

- **Examine connotations.** Does the wording used create a positive or negative impression in the reader? What images (mental pictures) do the words elicit in the reader?
- **Experiment with different word choices.** If the information were expressed in a different manner, would the reader's response change? Use a dictionary or thesaurus to examine word choices more closely. What other words could have been selected that would have changed the impression without changing the overall message?

Loaded Language	PRACTICE 5-7

Directions: Read the following statements and identify the bias in each by underlining examples of loaded and biased language. Look back at the section on deciphering misleading, unclear, or ambiguous language on p. 92 of Chapter 3 if you need some help.

1. Bums are homeless because they are lazy.
2. Every doctor knows how to treat his patients.
3. The zealotry of animal activists knows no bounds.
4. Corrupt politicians want to raise taxes on honest, hard-working Americans.
5. Greedy corporations simply want to make a quick buck.

EXPAND YOUR UNDERSTANDING

Directions: Review various media (TV, Internet, or newspapers, for instance) to find five examples of loaded language. Then bring these examples to class and present your findings.

Here is a checklist you can use to assess bias in written material:

Bias Checklist

Before Reading:

- Know the topic.
- Know your own thoughts or biases concerning the topic.
- Be aware of the writing situation.

While Reading:

- Determine if opinions are supported by evidence.
- Determine if the author has overlooked or purposefully omitted information that does not support his or her opinion.
- Make sure the author is not trying to manipulate the emotions of the reader.
- Note the use of loaded language.

After reading:

- Note your reaction.
- Note any change the piece has had on your opinion of the topic.
- Determine how the text changed your opinion.

Monitoring Your Thinking

When you examine a text critically, you are approaching it with certain traits and are utilizing a lot of skills, often simultaneously. This can get complicated! Monitoring can help with this complex process. **Monitoring** is the practice of checking your thinking throughout any mental task (reading a text, looking at a visual, solving a problem, or analyzing an argument, just to name a few). What exactly does this mean?

On the sitcom *Friends* (1994-2004), Matt LeBlanc's character Joey Tribiani would often approach a potential date by asking, "How YOU doin'?", and he didn't need to communicate much more than that in order to land a date. We all run into acquaintances in the cafeteria or parking lot who will casually ask, "How are you?" to which we answer, "Fine," without actually giving our response any serious thought. We move rapidly from one activity to the next; we run errands, attend classes, and hang out with friends, without taking the time to think about how we are truly doing until some crisis—a break-up, the death of a close friend, a health scare, or an accident— forces us to stop what we are doing and think about the internal state of our bodies and minds.

In a similar fashion, a hasty reading of a text can lead us from one paragraph to the next with the words making hardly any impact on us. Just as we give the thoughtless reply, "Fine," to an acquaintance at the cafeteria, we may see the words on the page but not mull them over enough to gain a deeper, more critical understanding of the text. In contrast, as a critical thinker you can practice an internal conversation called monitoring as you read. Recall that the introduction of this chapter included an author monitoring herself as she wrote ("And let me tell you, it is almost always as bad as I feared it would be . . ."). Think of monitoring as your chance to ask yourself, "How YOU doin'?" and to give yourself the chance to answer thoughtfully.

Metacognition

Closely connected to monitoring is metacognition. **Metacognition** means, essentially, thinking about thinking. In other words, as you are reading and processing new information, you should make the extra effort to be aware of your brain's thought processes along the way. Throughout a cognitive task, like reading a difficult text or critically writing an essay, you should get in the habit of pausing regularly to check in with yourself and assess how well (or not) you are learning and thinking critically about the new information.

Keeping tabs on yourself in this way during the completion of a task is a process with three phases: planning, control, and reflection. See Figure 5-3 for a visual representation of this process.

The Planning Phase

During the planning phase, you will decide what needs to be done and how you will go about doing it. Ask yourself the following questions to help you with this phase:

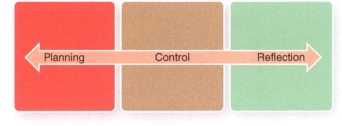

1. What exactly do I need to accomplish?
2. What are the steps in accomplishing my goal?
3. What do I already know about this task?
4. What do I need to learn? How can I go about learning it?
5. How do I feel about completing this task? Does it conflict with my worldviews or values?

■ **Figure 5-3** The Three Phases of Self-Monitoring

Answering these questions will give you a clear idea of what you have to do and what you have at your disposal to help you.

The Control Phase

The control phase is where you make sure that you are completing your task correctly and well. Ask yourself the following questions to help with this phase:

1. Am I putting in enough effort?
2. Am I taking too much time to do my task or am I rushing through it?
3. Do I need to seek help with my task?
4. Am I allowing my worldviews or biases to cloud my judgment of how effectively I am completing this task?
5. Am I allowing any of the obstacles to critical thinking to get in the way of my completing this task well?
6. Am I being a good critical thinker while accomplishing this task? Am I displaying the character traits and using the skills of a critical thinker effectively?

Your answers to these questions will help you do your best at the task. When your answers reveal to you a problem with your work or effort, make the necessary adjustments or corrections.

The Reflection Phase

This phase comes when the task is finished. During this phase you make sure that you are satisfied with the job you have done. Ask yourself these questions during this phase:

1. Did I accomplish the goals I set for myself during the planning phase?
2. Did my work measure up to the standards of critical thinkers (accuracy, completeness, fairness, relevance, clarity, and significance)?
3. How do I feel about the work I have done? Am I satisfied with it and with myself?

If you are not happy with your answers to any of these questions, go back and make changes to your work until you are certain that you have done your best.

Spotlight on Standards: Fairness

Fairness is the ability to give equal consideration to every argument by putting aside personal feelings and biases. As you are monitoring your thinking, you may find that you can ask yourself such questions as "Is this fair?" or "How can I analyze this information fairly when I don't like what the author has to say?" As you read a text, be conscious of your own defense mechanisms—they may be trying to tell you that you feel so strongly about the topic that you will have to make an extra effort to be fair. You should also make note of when you read something that doesn't sound fair and recognize that the author might be biased; in that case, you need to do more research to make certain that you are getting a fair and balanced view of the issue. Especially during the control and reflection phases of the monitoring three-step process, you should attempt to answer the crucial question, "Is my assessment of the information fair?" Only when you can unequivocally answer "Yes!" to that answer will you be able to say you are done with your work!

When you first practice engaging in self-monitoring, you will need to keep these questions in front of you and be sure to ask them as you work through your project. But as you become more skilled at monitoring, you will begin to work your way through the three phases naturally. It will become habitual, you will be better at completing your work, and you will produce better products.

THINK AND WRITE CRITICALLY

EXPAND YOUR UNDERSTANDING

Practice Monitoring while Writing Critically

Directions: The next time you are assigned an essay or a project for another class, keep a journal wherein you answer each of the questions in the three phases above. Keep a detailed record of your progress through the task and finish by writing a short reflection on how the questions in each phase helped or did not help you complete your task.

PRACTICE 5-8	Monitoring

Directions: Read and annotate the following passage from "As the World Watches: Media Events Are Modern Holy Days," by Rosalind Silver, and then do the tasks and answer the questions that follow.

1. Use the three phases of monitoring that you learned above. Answer the questions in each phase as you work through the piece and the questions below.
2. What is your prior knowledge of the content in this selection?

   _____

   _____

3. What needs additional clarification?

   _____

   _____

4. If you knew you were having a quiz today on this material, what grade would you expect to receive?

   _____

   _____

5. In the first paragraph, the author mentions several historical events. Pick one of the following events and explain on another sheet of paper what you learned about it over the course of your academic career. How did you learn about it? Was your education on this topic sufficient? If not, how could it have been improved?

   a. The 1961 space launch
   b. The assassination of John F. Kennedy
   c. The marriage of Prince Charles and Princess Diana
   d. Watergate

(Continued)

As the World Watches: Media Events Are Modern 'Holy Days'

How television's coverage of extraordinary events creates meaning for our lives.

Rosalind Silver

That bright morning in 1961 should have been a normal commuting day. But police monitoring the early morning traffic in California became more and more puzzled by a break in the pattern. Instead of proceeding to work, an ever- growing number of commuters slowed down, pulled off the road and parked. They were listening to the radio.

Since the patrolling officers did not have AM radio, it took them a while to realize the cause of this phenomenon. The bemused drivers were merely joining the workers, housewives and students who were already gathered around television sets in homes, offices, and classrooms all over the country. The first American astronaut was going into space. Ordinary activities were irrelevant. The whole world was watching. The absorbed witnesses to the happenings of that day have been joined since then by the multitudes of mourners at Kennedy's funeral, the half-a-world-away celebrants who got up in the middle of the night to attend Charles and Diana's wedding, and the countrywide citizen-judges of the Watergate hearings.

Journalist Tom Wolfe, who described the astronaut launching in his book *The Right Stuff*, likened the astronauts to medieval knights who were doing single combat for their society. Since their role appealed to the nation's need for a way to fight the Cold War, their actions and fate assumed an overarching importance that transcended the events themselves.

In fact, this centrality of importance in which television provides a ritual outlet for the whole society is the crucial characteristic of what are often called "media events," or what communications researcher Elihu Katz calls "the high holidays of television." Katz, Director of the Communications Institute at the Hebrew University, Jerusalem, and Professor at the Annenberg School of Communications at the University of Southern California, is involved in a systematic study of this phenomenon. He proposes that "media events" are a specifically delimited kind of happening which may be easily distinguished from ordinary news and entertainment by the application of proper criteria. Their study sheds light on the events, ceremonies and values which depend on television to help make life meaningful in our society.

Being There

To begin with, true media events are broadcast live, taking full advantage of the excitement inherent in being present when something important occurs. Although they must be preplanned in some sense, they are not set up by the networks and they exist for a higher purpose than hype. That is, they are not publicity-created "pseudo-events."

In some ways "media events" share a number of the characteristics of news. They are tied to specific events that have a beginning and an end. They depend on a combination of visual transmission and factual commentary. They usually take place in public and are acknowledged as possessing common interest for the society as a whole. And they are extremely dependent on television's often-noted capacity for making the grandiose and complex, intimate and personal.

But unlike the news of the day, media events reach far beyond the day-to-day round of misfortune and circumstance to create compelling sense of occasion that transfixes viewers. Watching them often becomes a communal outlet transformed into a participatory requirement — a kind of sacred obligation (holy day of obligation?) for complete society membership.

As Katz points out, special television happenings are one of the few types of programming that transform TV watching into an occasion instead of a casual everyday experience. People get dressed up and visit each other' homes to celebrate the Superbowl; the whole world watched the moon landings.

6. Based on the title of this article and the short selection from it that you just read, what would you infer to be Silver's major claim in the entire essay?

   a. That a compelling drama or television reality show can cause people to interrupt their lives, no matter what they are doing, to watch it.

   b. That modern media events have taken the place of religious holidays, and participation in them seems more and more necessary for membership in society.

   c. That historical events must be covered by the news media to have any impact on society.

   d. That only media events that are broadcast live can take the place of outmoded societal celebrations.

7. Did you feel yourself losing your concentration at any time during your reading? If so, why do you think it happened when it did, and what strategies did you use or could you have used to regain your concentration?

   _____

   _____

   _____

8. Infer the author's worldview from this passage; specifically how does she feel about television and media in general? Does she hold a positive, negative, or neutral view of these things?

   _____

   _____

   _____

9. Did the three phases of self-monitoring, and the questions in each phase, help you complete this task? Which questions were the most helpful?

   _____

   _____

   _____

PRACTICE 5-9   Monitoring your Understanding of the Chapter

Directions: Identify each of the following statements as true (T) or false (F). Use the context of the word or term as it is used in the chapter to help you. You may use a dictionary if you need to.

_____ 1. To be organized, you need to organize both your environment and your thoughts. (p. 154)

_____ 2. *Worldview* is another word for *bias*. (p. 166)

_____ 3. When considering the writing situation, the first step is to determine the audience. (p. 168)

_____ 4. The problem with worldviews is they often remain unexamined. (p. 160)

_____ 5. A person's worldview could cause him or her to be ethnocentric. (p. 160)

_____ 6. You don't have to worry about obstacles to critical thinking when you are monitoring your thinking. (p. 171)

_____ 7. Metacognition is closely related to monitoring your thinking. (p. 170)

Self-Monitoring and Controversial Issues

Directions: Read the scenarios below and answer the questions that follow them.

Here's a model

Controversial Issue: Benefits/Drawbacks of Facebook or other social networking sites.

Brandon enjoys connecting with his friends on Facebook. On a daily basis, in fact, he spends hours playing games, sending messages, looking at photos, and taking part in polls. Recently, he ran into a former girlfriend, Dianna, and asked her why he hadn't seen her profile on Facebook. Dianna replied that she did not see the point of spending all that time cultivating online friendships when she barely had time to visit her friends in "real life." She also claimed that Facebook is not so far off from the concept of "Big Brother" and that she did not want her privacy compromised by advertisers and by the creators and shareholders of Facebook.

a. Put the claim in your own words. Do you understand the issue? Decide if you need to do more research and monitor your comprehension as you do research.

   I think the claim is about how Facebook might be sort of "spying" on users and then tailoring advertisements to users' particular interests. I'm not sure if this is true or not. More research would be helpful.

b. Identify the biases (yours and the author's or speaker's). Might your worldview prevent you from being fair?

   The speaker in this case, Dianna, might be biased against Facebook because she knows that her ex-boyfriend spends a lot of time on it. As for myself, I think Facebook is fun but also a little silly. What I haven't thought about much is how it might be harmful and might be an invasion of privacy.

Now you try

1. *Controversial Issue:* Prayer in public schools

   Juan is a public school student who attends religious services regularly on the weekends with his family. In his public school, he has several friends who complain that prayer is "not allowed" and that they could get in "serious trouble" if they pray in school. Juan's best friend Martin is the most vocal of these friends; he is trying to convince Juan that banning prayer in school has led to America's demise.

   a. Put the claim in your own words. Do you understand the issue? Decide if you need to do more research and monitor your comprehension as you do research.

   _____

   _____

   _____

   b. Identify the biases (yours and the author's or speaker's). Might your worldview prevent you from being fair?

   _____

   _____

   _____

(Continued)

2. *Controversial Issue:* Alternative medical treatment

Anna's grandmother Nana suffers from respiratory problems, but Nana has recently heard from several people that if she tries aromatherapy, she is sure to be cured by a restoration of balance and harmony to her body. Nana is tired of using prescription medication and of trying to eat right and exercise; she claims that the healing properties of oils such as tea tree oil, lavender, and eucalyptus will be better for her. Anna worries about her grandmother but doesn't know if she should interfere.

a. Put the claim in your own words. Do you understand the issue? Decide if you need to do more research, and monitor your comprehension as you do research.

_____

_____

_____

b. Identify the biases (yours and the author's or speaker's). Might your worldview prevent you from being fair?

_____

_____

_____

3. *Controversial Issue:* Cell phones linked to cancer

Like most teenagers, Dominique loves to keep in touch with her friends by using her cell phone. However, her father forbids her to use it and took it away when he read that cell phones might cause cancer, though the evidence that they do is lacking. Dominique does not know how to convince him that using the cell phone is certainly no more dangerous than many other risks we take in modern life, such as driving cars or using other electronic devices. Her father is adamant in his claim that cell phone usage causes cancer.

a. Put the claim in your own words. Do you understand the issue? Decide if you need to do more research, and monitor your comprehension as you do research.

_____

_____

_____

b. Identify the biases (yours and the author's or speaker's). Might your worldview prevent you from being fair?

_____

_____

_____

Changing Your Mind

Another skill you need to master in order to be good at monitoring yourself is the ability to change your mind. Once you have accounted for your own and the author's worldviews and biases, you may find that the author makes a good point. You may find, if you are being honest with yourself, that the author has convinced you, and it might be time to change your mind about something you previously believed. For many people, changing one's mind is considered to be a sign of weakness or confusion. Famous thinker Ralph Waldo Emerson, however, considered changing one's mind to be a sign of intelligence, and he expressed this sentiment when he said, "A foolish consistency is the hobgoblin of little minds." What Emerson meant by a "foolish consistency" is stubbornly sticking to a conclusion in the face of evidence that it is wrong.

Admitting when you are wrong is often very hard. Many intelligent people are particularly afraid of admitting error, because their self-image involves their being viewed as smart, and they unconsciously think that admitting mistakes will make them seem less intelligent to other people (and possibly to themselves). This is ironic, because studies have shown that intelligence is something that can be developed, and people who identify themselves as intelligent are actually harming their intellectual development when they refuse to admit to themselves and others that they are wrong (Dweck, 2002). By refusing to change their minds, they are giving up the chance to move forward and to grow.

Another reason that admitting error is difficult involves our worldviews, as we discussed on p. 159. Some of our most cherished beliefs about the way the world works are so fundamental that we don't make a distinction between these beliefs and our actual identify. For example, someone who has a firm belief in God might identify herself first and foremost as a religious person, or someone who is a staunch Democrat might view his liberal political outlook as crucial to his life. But you are more than your political, religious, ethnic, or cultural identity, and changing your mind actually won't kill you (although sometimes it might seem like it will). It may well be a life-shaking experience, and as we mentioned in Chapter 1, being a critical thinker takes courage. Ultimately, though, changing your mind about views you have come to regard as mistaken can be liberating. In any case, it will free you from **cognitive dissonance**, a stressful feeling that comes from trying to hold two contradictory ideas at the same time or from trying to deny what you have already admitted to yourself is true. J. D. Vance, author of *Hillbilly Elegy: A Memoir of a Family and Culture in Crisis* (2016), memorably describes cognitive dissonance:

> We choose not to work when we should be looking for jobs. Sometimes we'll get a job, but it won't last. We'll get fired for tardiness, or for stealing merchandise and selling it on eBay, or for having a customer complain about the smell of alcohol on our breath, or for taking five thirty-minute restroom breaks per shift. We talk about the value of hard work but tell ourselves that the reason we're not working is some perceived unfairness: Obama shut down the coal mines, or all the jobs went to the Chinese. These are the lies we tell ourselves to solve the cognitive dissonance—the broken connection between the world we see and the value we preach (p. 147).

Here are some tips for how to change your mind if you find you have good reason to:

Tips for Critical Thinkers: How to Change Your Mind When It Is Warranted

- **Start by making a conscious effort not to identify yourself with your beliefs**. This is probably impossible to accomplish entirely, since your beliefs can influence you so much, but it can help to continuously remind yourself that you and your self-image would ultimately remain intact if your beliefs were to change.
- **Remind yourself that being wrong is not a sign of weakness, nor is it a sign of stupidity**. Everyone makes mistakes and is wrong at some point. In fact, admitting errors and changing your mind is an indication of maturity, intelligence, and critical thinking ability.

- **Identify yourself as a critical thinker and commit to searching for the truth in every situation.** In this way, making mistakes and changing your mind will not be so threatening to your identity.

THINK AND WRITE CRITICALLY

EXPAND YOUR UNDERSTANDING:

Consider a Time You Changed Your Mind

Directions: In a short essay, recount a time when you changed your mind about a belief or a value that mattered to you. Explain your original position, the process through which you came to change your mind, and the conclusion at which you finally arrived. End your essay with a discussion of how the change made you feel and how it affected your life. If you can't think of anything important about which you changed your mind, pick a position that you currently feel strongly about and imagine what could cause you to change your mind about it and how changing your mind would make you feel. You might wish to look ahead at the "Practicing Being Fair-Minded" exercise (p. 224) for topics.

Real-World Mistakes of Self-Monitoring and Their Consequences

To conclude our consideration of self-monitoring, let's look at some actual examples of what can happen if we don't regulate our own thinking:

Ava Worthington. Madeline Neumann. What tragic thread ties these girls together? Their senseless deaths in March 2008. Ava and Madeline are dead, in part, because their parents relied on prayers rather than medical treatment. These children had treatable illnesses, but their parents' adherence to certain extreme religious practices led to fatal consequences and subsequent criminal investigations.

Fifteen-month-old Ava Worthington of Oregon City, Oregon, had bronchial pneumonia and a blood infection that could have been treated with antibiotics; Madeline Neuman, a Weston, Wisconsin, 11-year-old girl had an undiagnosed but treatable form of diabetes (diabetic ketoacidosis). Whereas Ava's family belonged to a small fundamentalist sect, the Followers of Christ Church, which has come under some scrutiny for a disproportionately high number of infant and child deaths, Madeline's parents did not belong to any organized religion. In both cases, however, the parents believed that God would heal their children through the power of their prayers.

While it is impossible to know all of the details surrounding these cases, nor do we propose to know the mindsets of the parents, it is not such a stretch to say that these senseless deaths may have been avoided if the parents had been armed with the attitude and skills of critical thinkers as they relate to self-monitoring. These parents accepted all of the teachings of their particular religion (without questioning whether or not the medical advice of that religion—"pray"—was adequate); they clearly did not question worldviews. They should have sought out other viewpoints, even viewpoints that did not conform to their pre-existing biases, and treated those other viewpoints in a fair way.

No topic should be off limits to critical thinkers. Critical thinkers should apply respectful scrutiny to all areas, even their cherished worldviews, especially when those worldviews conflict with life-saving advancements in medical science. So it's clear that examining your own thinking is very important—indeed, it can be crucial.

For Discussion

1. Explain how the mistakes discussed above qualify as a failure of self-monitoring.

2. How could people of deep religious faith avoid these types of serious mistakes yet still honor the teachings of their religions?

EXPAND YOUR UNDERSTANDING

Advanced Research

Use the Internet to research studies that investigate whether prayers aid in healing. A study conducted by Herbert Benson, Jeffery A. Dusek, Jane B. Sherwood, Peter Lam, Charles F. Bethea, William Carpenter, Sidney Levitsky, Peter C. Hill, Donald W. Clem, Manoj K. Jain, David Drumel, Stephen L. Kopecky, Paul S. Mueller, Dean Marek, Sue Rollins, Patricia L. Hibberd et al. (April 2006) and published in the American Heart Journal (www.ahjonline. com/) would be a good starting point. Begin with the following articles, and expand your search as necessary to get a clear understanding of the issue introduced in "Real-World Mistakes of Self-Monitoring":

- www.nytimes.com/2006/03/31/health/31pray.html
- www.msnbc.msn.com/id/12082681/ns/health-heart_health/t/ power-prayer-flunks-unusual-test/
- www.christianitytoday.com/ct/2009/may/27.43.html?start=1

Real-World Successes of Critical Thinking

Wendy Kopp of Teach for America

You just learned about tragic failures of critical thinking, but critical thinking can also be used to succeed. Wendy Kopp, the creator of Teach for America, is an example of a creative and effective critical thinker.

Directions: Using the Internet or a library, research Wendy Kopp and Teach for America in depth. Prepare a detailed description of how Kopp succeeded in her conception of this approach to education, including an explanation of any skills, character traits, and standards of critical thinking that contributed to her success. Get ready to share your findings with the class.

THINK AND **WRITE** CRITICALLY

Chapter Summary

- *Self-monitoring* is a skill of critical thinkers that involves noticing the thinking process and making adjustments as necessary to ensure mastery of material.

- *Organizing* your thinking and your life will make you a better critical thinker. Organize your life by keeping your living space neat and structured, developing a routine, keeping a to-do list, and setting and working toward long-term goals. Organize your thinking by thinking about one thing at a time, categorizing information, using maps and charts, and thinking systematically.

- *Worldviews* are frameworks that are made up of our basic assumptions about how the world works. They color the way we view the world. Misunderstandings and misconceptions arise when people approach an issue from divergent worldviews. Becoming aware of your worldview and how it might affect your perception of the people and issues around you is part of self-monitoring. Acknowledging different worldviews may help you consider points from various perspectives other than your own.

- *Bias* is a tendency to view material in an unfair way; bias often stems from our prejudices or our worldviews. Holding strong biases may prevent people from recognizing good evidence if it conflicts with their cherished beliefs. An examination of the writing situation and author's use of language often gives away an author's bias.

- *Monitoring* means using metacognition to keep track of your comprehension and concentration, your use of critical thinking skills and character traits, and your own worldviews and biases as you examine a text. It can be helpful to view monitoring as a three phase process (planning, control, reflection); asking yourself specific questions during each phase can help you do your best during a project. To be a critical thinker, you have to cultivate the skill of *changing your mind* when the situation warrants it or when an argument has proven your previous opinion wrong.

READ, WRITE, AND THINK CRITICALLY: SELF-MONITORING

Directions: Survey "Kids R Not Us: Embracing the Decision Not to Procreate" by Katherine Seligman and answer questions 1-2 below. Then, read and annotate the selection, and answer the questions that follow it.

1. What do you predict the selection will be about? What is the topic?

   _____

   _____

2. What is your prior knowledge of this topic?

   _____

   _____

Kids R Not Us: Embracing the Decision Not to Procreate

Katherine Seligman

Katherine Seligman is a freelance writer, reporter, and special contributor to national magazines and newspapers. She has written for the San Francisco Chronicle, *the* San Francisco Examiner, *the* Sacramento Bee, *and* USA Today. *The following piece was published in* The San Francisco Chronicle *in 2007.*

1   It was time for the "Childfree Landslide News." Christine Fisher leaned forward and announced this in a soft voice that would sound surprisingly strong when it aired as part of her weekly (at least on Mars, she says, where weeks are 13 days) online show, the "Adult Space Child Free Podcast." She had just put in a day at the pharmaceutical company where she works and was home in her Newark apartment, shoes off, with her husband flopped on a sofa reading in the next room and her two cats roaming underfoot.

2   She started the podcast, a **medley** of commentary, news and personal narrative, to reach an audience outside "diaperland" about a year ago. Fisher knew as early as third grade that she did not want children. She had no interest in games that involved playing house or cooing over babies. In the world of childfree men and women, she is what's known as an "early articulator." Now 32, she has had her share of friends who became temporarily unavailable or disappeared when they had lads. Even in the Bay Area, which Fisher finds one of the better places for childfree mingling because of its cultural diversity—San Francisco has one of the lowest ratios of kids of any U.S. city—it can be hard for the childfree to connect.

3   Her listeners are a far-flung **demographic**, with a few hundred of various ages mostly in the United States, but also scattered as far away as the United Arab Emirates, Norway and Uruguay. The topics are almost as varied. On this winter Tuesday, Fisher reviewed medical news (part of the landslide) about hospital admissions from unsafe abortions in developing countries and hormone-related skin cancer risk, responded to listener feedback (someone named Snerdie wanted to know whether strollers are really allowed in casinos), listed her New Year's resolutions, and gave a "shout-out" to a friend who was ill. Then, in what's become her signature end to the show, she leaned into the microphone and said, "This is Chris the Fixed Kitty saying, 'Keep from breeding!'"

4   "It's very difficult to find other childfree people," said Fisher, who works part time as a quality assurance associate. "We tend to be a very quiet, closet-type group. When I mention I'm not having kids, I get a few specific reactions. Either someone tells me I will change my mind, which is probably more frequent with the older generation, or they try to persuade me. Or I get this really strange reaction, which is, 'You are so nice.' When you realize there is this public perception that you're cold or not caring, you learn to be quiet about it."

5   Childfree organizations have been around for a few decades, but new social groups, books, an online magazine, unscripted: the childfree life, and **myriad** Web sites (Childfree by Choice alone links to 20 other resources) have sprung up in the past few years, their visibility fueled by the Internet but also by changing attitudes. In the 1950s, there was an assumption that everyone would get married, then have children. Family life "proceeded in lockstep," said Stephanie Coontz, a professor at Evergreen State College in Washington and director of research and public education at the Council on Contemporary Families. As many as 80 percent of people thought that staying single and childless was "deviant or abnormal," she said. But in the 1970s, amid turbulent social change, the availability of the birth control pill and public debate about population growth, those assumptions were challenged. These days, the "vast majority" of people think it is acceptable not to have kids or marry, said Coontz.

6   "My generation was looking at whether we could have careers and keep our own names," said Coontz. "The next generation was not as interested in that and not as defensive. A lot of these strong feelings are part of the process of sorting out how we deal with this changing world."

7   Personally, Coontz takes a "middle-of-the-road approach," she said. She has kids but supports the decision of those who choose not to. The childfree often spend more time caring for aging parents or relatives and also end up, through taxes, supporting the next generation. "It's the younger generation that is going to pay for our Social Security and foot some of the bills," she said. "We do owe parents who raise kids a debt."

8   Even so, the stigma remains. "We're seen as threatening institutions," said Teri Tith, an East Bay woman with a Web site called Purple Women & Friends. Jennifer L. Shawne, author of the 2005 tongue-in-cheek book "Baby Not on Board," was **inundated** with responses from readers—and people who just heard about it. Many but not all thanked her, said Shawne, who lives in San Francisco. To some, a decision not to have lads is tantamount to a stand against religious or American values. "I did a lot of radio call-in shows where I was called names," she said. "One man in Beaumont, Texas, said my husband and I deserved to die alone."

9   Several people interviewed for this story wanted to be known by a first name only or not identified at all because they were not, as one woman put it, "out." The woman said she was worried about her boyfriend, who is still uncertain about fatherhood. Would her feelings be a deal-breaker? It has happened before.

10   "There is still a public-policy and religious and cultural stigma," said Elaine, a Southern California blogger known as AlphaGirl, who is unapologetic about the **adversarial** tone of her Web site—Childfree: Uncut. Unedited. Uncensored—but didn't want to use her last name. "For some reason when someone comes forward and says, 'I want to have kids,' no one comes forward and says, 'You will change your mind.' But when I was younger and said kids weren't on the docket, people felt free to question the decision."

11   Some statistics suggest more women now are childless by choice, but it's hard to come up with a firm estimate because women, on average, are having children older, and demographers don't usually ask why they don't have them. The National Center for Health Statistics confirms that 6.6 percent of women between the ages of 15 and 44 called themselves voluntarily childless in 1995, up from 2.4 percent in 1982. And according to 1998 U.S. Census Bureau statistics, 19 percent of women 40 to 44 were childless, compared with 10 percent in that age group in 1976.

12 As a group, the childfree are no more **homogenous** than parents. They include gay and lesbian and single men and women who all, these days, face the same kind of question: Why don't you want kids? Some grappled with infertility, then embraced the childfree life. Others never had the urge to procreate, grew out of it or decided against kids because of a mate who didn't want them. And there are those who say they just can't afford it, especially in San Francisco.

13 "For us, it's well thought out," said Teresa Marchese, a fitness trainer, whose husband, Jay Mercado, is an artist. "It's the whole financial aspect. Neither of us has the option of quitting work. We rent and we have a fluctuating income. The people I know who are having kids, they're moving back to Oklahoma. We don't want to leave the city."

14 In one survey of childfree couples, most ranked independence, marital satisfaction and the lack of desire to have kids as top reasons not to have them. To them, the decision was not a "lifestyle" choice, said Laura Scott, a Virginia writer who's surveyed more than 170 childfree couples about their decision for a project on the subject. Being able to travel or sleep late were benefits, not motivations, for most, she said.

15 Attitudes about kids also vary. There are childfree people who are annoyed by what they see as a kid-centric society, where they are constantly forced to listen to people talk about their children's schools, precious achievements or poop. They resent employee benefits that are offered only to parents, or what they see as the burden of doing more than their share of work while people with kids rush off to pick them up. "Work-family benefits?" writes AlphaGirl. "Yeah, right. Lactation rooms in the workplace? Oh, please." She once confronted the human resources department at the large bank where she worked to demand the same flexibility given her co-workers who were parents. The bank didn't make a policy change, and Elaine said she is disappointed in the lack of progress toward treating all employees equally. "I don't think one group should come before any other," she said.

16 Many childfree people want to spend time around children, the kind who can be handed back. They just want to find a social universe that doesn't revolve around children.

17 "We're getting harder to ignore," said Tith. "We're controversial whether we mean to be or not." Even the term childfree can be **contentious**. There are people who prefer a hyphenated child-free or childless, names that, to others, imply that something is missing.

18 Tith joined No Kidding!, a social club founded by a Toronto teacher in 1984, after moving from the Bay Area to Canada because of her husband's job. Through No Kidding! she joined a poker group, worked on the organization's annual convention and made friends who didn't have kids. When she returned to live in a rural East Bay town, she co-founded the San Francisco Bay Area Childfree Meetup, a group that gets together for dinner and winetasting, and started her blog, where she posts her own comments and links to other childfree bloggers—even some who are not, including a Silicon Valley moms group, that also links to her. ("They found my blog to be an even and reasonable voice, and I was terribly flattered," she says of the moms group).

19 "Some of us do hate kids, but that makes me uncomfortable because I don't," she said. Tith came to her childfree decision by circumstance, after a medical condition made it clear she couldn't **conceive**. Married at 22, she and her husband split up, partly, she said, because of the strain of fertility issues. "To me, I would always be one half of an infertile couple," she said. Nine years ago she remarried. Her husband, who thinks that the world is crowded enough, did not want kids.

20 "I assumed I would want kids," she said. "I had to accept that I couldn't and I made a choice to. But every woman's story is different. You hear all different ones."

21 Lingba, a Potrero Hill lounge, is crowded and noisy on a winter night when the members of the newly formed San Francisco Childfree Meetup find one another at a corner table. There are about a dozen this time, more than at the previous month's inaugural event. There are several couples, two married women who came without their husbands and many single people. Most are from San Francisco, but a few live other places, including Novato, where, one woman said, "Yuppies go to breed."

22 "When I said I was happily childfree I might as well have said I was a serial killer," she said.

23 "I just never realized I did want kids," said Valerie Francescato, the group's founder, who works for a furniture manufacturer. What stops the rude questions, she said, is to say she can't have kids.

24 "I had a hysterectomy, but that's not related to why I don't want kids," said another woman, who is from Australia, where she felt as if being childfree wasn't such an issue. After moving to the Bay Area, she said, she

finds it hard to socialize with people in her apartment building because they all have kids and they leave her and her husband out of their social plans.

25 "I said we'd have to rent a couple of kids," she said. "Then I ran across this group and said, 'Thank God.'"

26 An Iranian American woman who is a financial analyst said she'd been asked if she didn't want kids because she'd been abused or neglected. "They assume something is wrong with me," she said. "I'm 35. I won't change my mind. I hang out with a lot of Europeans who are a lot more accepting of it. Why do I have to explain myself? It happens so much I'm angry."

27 "Your best friends disappear. They fall off the end of the earth when they have kids," said Rick, a scientist whose best friend moved to Palo Alto to be closer to work, then became unavailable.

28 Rick said he's "child **neutral**" but is leaning toward not wanting them. "I would have to be crazy about someone, then it would have to be financially right." His decision has prompted colleagues to assume he's gay, since he lives in San Francisco and isn't coupled up, with kids. "Whatever," he said. "Some people are so narrow-minded." Men face many of the same stereotypes that women do, he said. People think it's a selfish decision or that there is something wrong with him.

"Do you notice kids in strollers?" asked Rick, as Meetup members sipped their drinks.
"I don't," said the financial analyst.
"I'll stop and pet a dog, but I won't stop and say, 'That's so cute,' to a baby," said Rick.
"I just like peace and quiet," said the analyst.
"I can't imagine waking up four or five times a night," Rick said.
"Friends ask me, 'How's your fabulous life?'" said the analyst. "And I say, 'Fabulous!'"

29 Most of the talk was not about children, or a lack of them, but about hobbies and recent trips and interests. Like people on a first or second date, the childfree were trying to figure out where and if their lives intersected.

30 Chris Fisher first got involved in the childfree world as a college student in Toledo, Ohio, by joining a mailing list. She was too busy in graduate school—a stint in medical school before finding her way to a graduate program in biology—to look for other childfree people. But she was settled enough in her decision by her mid-20s to undergo a tubal ligation.

31 "I need to do an episode about that saga," she said, in a phone interview during her commute home from work, a time she uses to record her thoughts on an MP3 or return calls. "I was 25 and had known I was going to have my tubes tied eventually."

32 The time was right because she had health insurance and was about to move. The problem: Her doctor was hesitant because of her age and childless status. "I could have gotten a handgun faster," she said. Eventually the doctor was "worn down," she said, but only after he saw in her medical records that she'd been stating her intention not to have kids for years. She had to sign a consent form and wait for 30 days to undergo the procedure, guidelines that exist in many states.

33 "I'm set," she said. "I got a doctor to agree to do this, but it's difficult for women across the country."

34 She met her husband at a fencing club. She mentioned she didn't want to be a mother, but was looking forward to being an aunt. "He said he wanted to be an uncle," she said. "That was very interesting, in my eyes." Her parents have accepted the couple's decision not to have kids, although they initially thought their only child would change her mind, Fisher said. "They have to settle for grand-kitties," she said.

35 She and her husband moved from the Midwest to the Bay Area in 2005 for work. He is a physicist in Silicon Valley. "It's hard to express how different this place is," she said. "There is an understanding here that there are many things people devote their lives to. . . . It's not the mommies and the non-mommies. We all live in the same world. There is a lot more we have in common than we don't have in common."

36 Fisher recently scaled back to part-time work so she'd have more time for other pursuits—photography, writing, podcasting, reading (especially science fiction and horror) and spending time with her husband, who arrived home one Tuesday as she was podcasting and sat in the next room reading. He sometimes makes sound effects, but leaves the content to her. It was while talking to him one day that she came up with the nickname Fixed Kitty. "We were talking about some comment and I said, 'That's why I'm not a parent. I'm fixed. I'm a fixed kitty.'"

37 "This is where I get to look like Carrie Fisher instead of Chris Fisher," she said, as she put on her headphones, which did make her look a little like the "Star Wars" actress, if you ignored the long pony tail hanging down her back. At various times she had to fend off a cat, which wanted to jump on her lap, then went to sit in an empty box left out for his benefit.

38 She talked about her New Year's resolution to come up with a better response to people who don't understand her decision. Why is it people feel they can ask if she has kids? Would they come up and ask if she were gay?

39 "When someone asks why you don't have lads, it gets very personal," she said. "They need to rethink the assumption that there is something wrong if you don't."

3. Use context clues and/or a dictionary to define the following words
    a. medley (para. 2): _____
    b. demographic (para. 3): _____
    c. myriad (para. 5): _____
    d. inundated (para. 8): _____
    e. adversarial (para. 10): _____
    f. homogenous (para. 12): _____
    g. contentious (para. 17): _____
    h. conceive (para. 19): _____
    i. neutral (para. 28): _____

4. What problems are faced by the people in the article who choose not to have children?

    _____

    _____

    _____

    _____

5. Review the obstacles to critical thinking in Chapter 1. What might be some of the barriers that people who have children would need to overcome in order to understand people who choose not to have children?

    _____

    _____

    _____

6. In paragraph 8, the author says that some people view the decision not to have children as "tantamount to a stand against religious or American values." Explore this worldview in detail. What assumptions underlie it? What biases could it lead to?

    _____

    _____

    _____

    _____

    _____

7. Explain how this essay fits into the writing situation:

_____

_____

_____

_____

_____

_____

8. What do you believe? Measure your belief in the claim that having children will (or will not) make people happier. Critically write an essay in which you argue either that having children will generally make people happier or that people should not be socially pressured to have children. As you write, keep a journal in which you answer the questions in the three phases of self-monitoring (p. 171).

THINK
AND **WRITE**
CRITICALLY

CHAPTER 6

Analysis

PREVIEW OF TERMS

Analysis p. 187
Skepticism p. 188
Extraordinary claim p. 188
Empirical evidence p. 188
Testimonial p. 188
Argument p. 192
Premise p. 192
Proof p. 192
Evidence p. 192
Rhetorical question p. 193
Accuracy p. 196
Expert testimony p. 197
Fact p. 197
Statistics p. 197
Analogy p. 198
Hypothetical example p. 198
Counter-evidence p. 199
Assumption p. 199
Logic p. 202
Inductive reasoning p. 202
Cogent p. 202
Deductive reasoning p. 203
Syllogism p. 203
Valid p. 203
Argument mapping p. 204
Pattern of organization p. 208
Cause and effect p. 208
Chronological p. 208
Process p. 209
Classification p. 209
Comparison/contrast p. 209
Example pattern p. 210
Listing p. 210
Mixed pattern p. 211
Science p. 212
Scientific method p. 213
Scientific theory p. 213
Scientific fact p. 213
Pseudoscience p. 214
See glossary, pp. 391–397

Learning Goals

In this chapter you will learn how to

➤ Analyze What You Read   SECTION ONE
➤ Be Skeptical
➤ Analyze and Identify Arguments
➤ Recognize and Evaluate Evidence
➤ Use Logic in Inductive and Deductive Reasoning   SECTION TWO
➤ Map Arguments
➤ Analyze Patterns of Organization
➤ Understand the Scientific Method

SECTION ONE

What Is Analysis?

The ancient philosopher Socrates (whom you learned about in Chapter 3) famously said, "The unexamined life is not worth living." Socrates meant that in order to be the best person you can possibly be, you have to analyze your actions and behavior to figure out what is working and what isn't. In fact, analysis is one of the best tools to learn about things, whether related to your own life or the world around you. **Analysis** is the process of breaking something into pieces and examining how those pieces function alone and together. The point of analyzing is to understand your subject better, whether it's a car engine, the plot of a movie or book, or an argument you are reading and preparing to write critically about.

Every field uses analysis differently. Engineers, when trying to isolate why something they've built won't function, might carefully check every piece of the system until they can isolate and fix what doesn't work. In chemistry, a scientist will break apart a chemical reaction so that he or she can understand what elements cause specific reactions. In forensic science, a CSI will study every part of a crime scene, separating out DNA evidence from fiber evidence, in the hopes of learning who committed the felony. These are all different methods of employing the critical thinking skill of analysis.

When reading, you primarily use analysis to break down and understand an author's arguments. It is crucial to understand an author's argument so that you can later critically evaluate it and explain your judgments about it in writing. Arguments are everywhere, and you probably encounter them every day in newspapers and magazines, conversations with friends, on the radio, and in television news and commentary. For that reason, this chapter focuses on how to analyze arguments. Specifically, in this section you will learn to recognize arguments and the evidence used to support them. In Section Two, you will learn how to recognize the logic of an argument, how to map an argument, and how to determine the pattern the author uses to organize the argument.

First, though, let's look at a mindset that's crucial to learning to both analysis and organization: being skeptical.

Reviewing the Critical Thinker's Traits: Being Skeptical

Being skeptical is important to your mindset as you work toward becoming a critical thinker. **Skepticism** means having a "prove it" attitude. To understand skepticism, it might help to see what a person who isn't skeptical looks like. Consider the following example:

> Whenever times got difficult for Wyatt or he felt stressed, he would visit a psychic. Sure, it could get expensive, but he valued the advice. It always seemed to apply so well to him; his psychic advisor really seemed to know things about him that no one else knew. True, Wyatt sometimes found it difficult to implement the psychic's advice, and though his friends said it was because the advice was just too vague, Wyatt knew that it was his own fault. He just wasn't trying hard enough, wasn't quite sharp enough. Anyway, he was only spending a few dollars here and there. Then his psychic suggested he invest in the psychic's company. . . .

In the above example, Wyatt lacked skepticism. Skepticism involves asking for proof. It means demanding that those who make extraordinary or dubious (doubtful) claims provide evidence for them; they need to make a good argument. *Being skeptical does not mean doubting everything.* A critical thinker is entitled to "stand on the shoulders" of those who have gone before him or her. Other things, such as what your friend's favorite movie is, simply do not matter enough for the skeptic to demand evidence or to investigate them. To be a skeptic, you must withhold belief until adequate evidence has been provided to support an extraordinary claim.

> ❝ Men become civilized, not in proportion to their willingness to believe, but in their readiness to doubt. ❞
>
> —H.L. Mencken

Guidelines for Evaluating Whether a Claim Is Extraordinary

1. **If the claim involves the supernatural, it can generally be considered an extraordinary claim.** Ghost stories, tales of ESP, and similar yarns require special evidence. Many times, there is no *empirical evidence* (**empirical** means that the **evidence** can be tested with experiments or by observation) for supernatural claims. Instead, the evidence exists solely in the form of **testimonials**; people claim that they have seen a ghost, or even more dubiously, someone they know has seen one. As noted later in this chapter, testimonials can be very unreliable. If testimonials are the only evidence supporting an extraordinary claim, that claim is poorly supported.

Other times, evidence for the supernatural, if it takes a tangible (physical or substantial) form such as pictures or recordings, cannot be reproduced by other researchers and is ambiguous. For example, consider the following picture. Is that figure on the staircase a

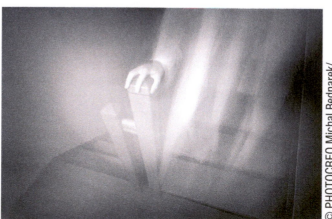

© PHOTOCREO Michal Bednarek/Shutterstock.com

ghost, a double exposure, or a fraud inserted with Photoshop or more old-fashioned methods? Which of these explanations is most likely? Most pseudoscientific claims, which you will learn about later in this chapter, are extraordinary claims.

Thinker to Emulate: Harry Houdini

Harry Houdini, born Erik Weisz in Austria-Hungary in 1874, was a famous escape artist and magician during the early part of the 20th century. Known as the "Handcuff King" because he could purportedly get free from any cuffs, Houdini wowed audiences with illusions and daring escapes from dangerous predicaments.

But Houdini was also a committed skeptic, and he spent a good deal of his time debunking spiritualists and mediums who claimed to be able to use magic or contact the dead. Before he died, he told his wife that if he were able, he would return as a spirit and utter a phrase that only she would know. He never returned and the phrase was never spoken.

Library of Congress, Prints & Photographs Division, [LC-USZ62-112419].

2. **If something seems too good to be true, it probably is**. Does the claim miraculously solve a difficult problem in a very easy way, or does it appeal because it is something we would like to be true? For example, consider the claim that the only thing we need to do to bring down high gas prices is not to buy any gas during a single day of each year. This statement presents an overly easy solution to a difficult problem; one day of lower sales wouldn't be enough to impact the bottom line of most oil companies.

3. **If the claim seems to have far reaching consequences to daily life, it is probably extraordinary.** An example of this type of claim is the assertion, made by many people in 1999, that most of the computers in the world would crash at the turn of the millennium. The more parts of life and the world that a claim seems to affect, the stronger the evidence supporting it needs to be for a skeptic to believe it.

4. **If the claim seems like it is merely meant to manipulate or scare you, withhold belief unless you are provided with compelling evidence.** Stories about people hiding under cars in mall parking lots, waiting to slash your ankles and rob you, fall into this category. All of these claims require extraordinary evidence, and the skeptic is better off withholding belief until such evidence is provided. Remember also that it is up to the person making the argument to provide evidence for it; it is not up to the skeptic to prove the argument wrong.

Being a skeptic means being willing to research or test some claims for yourself. Certain beliefs are so widespread in society that no single individual is advocating them or arguing for them; everyone simply accepts them as true. Yet if they are supernatural or too good to be true, they still merit investigation. The Internet makes it easier to research ideas, but it takes skill to determine which sites are reliable, as you will see later in this chapter (p. 192). A trip to the local library or an interview with an expert might still be necessary.

Here are some tips for how to adopt a skeptical attitude:

Tips for Critical Thinkers: How to Adopt a Skeptical Attitude

- **Consider whether a claim is dubious or extraordinary**. If it is, ask or look for empirical evidence that supports it and check that the evidence is specific and accurate. When analyzing texts, look in the text to see if the claims are backed up with evidence. Evaluate the evidence, as you will learn to do in the next chapter.

- **Be open-minded and do not commit yourself to believing, or not believing, a claim before you investigate it**. Making up your mind about something before analyzing the evidence is a recipe for being wrong.

- **Try to read between the lines**. Consider whether the person making a claim stands to benefit from your believing it.

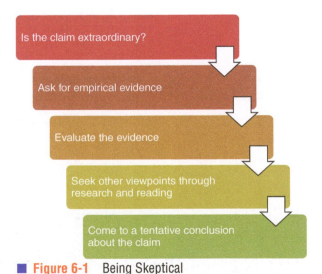

Is the claim extraordinary?

Ask for empirical evidence

Evaluate the evidence

Seek other viewpoints through research and reading

Come to a tentative conclusion about the claim

■ **Figure 6-1** Being Skeptical

- **Try to stay informed.** Read, listen to, and watch a variety of news sources.
- **Remember that it is very possible and even likely that your own beliefs are wrong or lack adequate supporting evidence.** The next chapter will develop the concept of fair-mindedness, the trait of looking fairly at the quality of your own beliefs.

PRACTICE 6-1   Being Skeptical about Claims

Directions: Consider the following claims. For each claim, identify whether it qualifies as extraordinary (for example, does it involve the supernatural or is it too good to be true?) and explain your answer. For each extraordinary claim, on a separate sheet of paper, list specific evidence that you think could be used to prove the claim true beyond a reasonable doubt.

Here's a model

Use this model as a reference, but don't copy the wording in your answers.

Microsoft Corporation will give you a dollar for each time you forward a particular email.

This claim is extraordinary, because it seems too good to be true. It appeals to something I wish was true, the idea that with almost no effort I could make money. This claim seems doubtful, because even a company as rich as Microsoft could go broke if it had to pay everyone who forwarded an email. Evidence that could convince me that this claim was true would be a press release from Microsoft indicating it as a fact. The press release would have to be printed in a reputable source.

Now you try

1. Dreams can predict the future.
2. Certain mystics can levitate themselves.
3. Bigfoot exists.
4. The average cereal contains more carbohydrates than proteins.
5. Humans evolved from ape-like ancestors.
6. Aliens visit earth and abduct people.
7. The stars (and their corresponding astrological symbols) predict people's destiny.
8. Ghosts are real.
9. Hypnosis can be used to get someone to stop smoking.
10. People can take an inactive substance as medicine and actually recover from a disease (the placebo effect).

PRACTICE 6-2   Being Skeptical about Texts

THINK AND WRITE CRITICALLY

Directions: Read the following passage and answer the questions that follow on a separate sheet of paper.

What Is Astrology?

Astrology dates back to ancient Sumer, and probably earlier. It is more than 2000 years old, and humans have been relying on it and finding wisdom in it for all of that time. By definition, astrology is the practice of finding meaning in the stars. With a little background information, such as your birthday (preferably the exact minute you were born), a skilled astrologer can tell you a great deal about your personality, where you have been, and where you are going.

An astrologer looks at more than just the stars, though; astrology also takes into account the position of the moon, sun, and planets, their locations relative to each other, and what part of the sky they are currently in (their "house"). By looking closely at this important information, an astrologer can tell you whether you are adventurous, cautious, energetic, lethargic, passionate, or reserved, for example. She can also tell you if you are going to be changing careers and what type of career you would be more suited to. She can also tell you if you are in the right romantic relationship. For thousands of years, people have been using this information to make life changes, and it has been proven time and time again to help. Astrology works!

But perhaps you are doubtful. How could the planets and stars influence me, you might be asking yourself. This is an extremely complicated question, but at least an initial answer can be given in simple terms. Everything in the universe is connected, and each thing influences everything else. Perhaps you have heard the expression that a butterfly that flaps its wings in Japan can cause a hurricane in Hawaii. Well, how much influence do you think things as large and majestic as the planets and their movements can have on something as small and insignificant as an individual human and his or her personality and destiny? If you look inside your heart, you will find that you already intuitively know that this is true. Just gazing at the night sky and its firmament of glorious stars allows you to feel this certainty for yourself.

Maybe you have a scientific mind and you need more evidence. Consider the story of William Smith. Not generally a gullible person, William never believed in astrology. But, like all of us, he found himself going through a difficult time. He had recently been through a major break up, was dissatisfied with his job, and to make matters worse, his doctor had recently diagnosed him with a possible health problem that could be extremely serious, although the tests had not yet come back. Not knowing where to turn, William took the plunge and called one of our expert astrologists. Knowing his birthday and time of birth, our astrologist consulted the Zodiac charts and helped William come to some realizations: he was better off without his former paramour, she said. Since Leo, his birth sign, was passing through the sixth house, it meant that he would ultimately have well-being in his place of employment, so she told him to stay at his job, because things would get better. And the stars indicated that his health issue was nothing serious. Still doubtful, William decided to give it some time and see what happened. He cut off ties with his ex, stayed at his job, and waited for the test results. And as countless people found before him, the stars didn't lie. He soon met a new girlfriend, his job got better, and indeed, the doctor called and told him his tests came back negative. He was healthy.

So if you are passing through a rough patch in your life, or if you just want to learn more about your personality or your destiny, you should call one of our expert astrologers now.

Now you respond

1. Is this an extraordinary claim? Why or why not?
2. Does the author use evidence to back up the claim? If so, what evidence?
3. Is evidence lacking, and if so, how could it be improved?
4. Why do you think someone might pay for the type of services described above?

EXPAND YOUR UNDERSTANDING

Skepticism and the Internet

THINK AND WRITE CRITICALLY

Directions: Visit the following websites to research the term skepticism for yourself. Then, on another sheet, answer the questions that follow.

- www.skeptic.com
- www.skepdic.com
- www.skeptic.com/about_us/manifesto.html
- www.randi.org

Questions to Think Critically About

1. What have you learned about skepticism that this chapter did not teach you?
2. What particular subjects or topics do these websites find particularly dubious? Choose one and briefly explain why these websites find it doubtful.
3. Are there any topics that are off limits to skeptics, or anything that you shouldn't be skeptical about? Why or why not?
4. Why was Harry Houdini especially qualified to debunk paranormal claims?

Analyzing Arguments

Once you've gotten yourself in a skeptical mindset, you're in a position to analyze ideas and arguments effectively. As a critical reader and writer, it's especially important to learn how to analyze arguments, to recognize their different parts and determine what role those parts play. An **argument** is a claim backed up by one or more reasons offered in its support. When you hear the word *argument*, the first thing that might come to your mind is people angrily yelling at each other, but that's not how *argument* is used here. Individuals, newspapers, television shows, and advertisements are constantly trying to convince you that what they are saying is accurate and that there are good reasons for believing their claims. In that sense, arguments are everywhere, and if you don't know how to recognize them and analyze them, you're at a disadvantage.

Identifying Arguments

Even when you know what an argument is, it's not always easy to recognize one. The key is to remember that the claim of an argument has to be supported. The statements that provide support for the claim of an argument are known as **premises, proof,** or **evidence**. When an argument's claim has support and is intended to follow logically from that support, it is called the argument's *conclusion*. If no evidence is offered for the claim, all you have is an assertion, not an argument. You might hear someone say:

> **Reminder**
> Claims were defined on p. 5 of Chapter 1.

"You should follow politics."

All this person is doing is giving an unsupported opinion. He needs to provide evidence to support his opinion if he wants to make an argument. So, if he says the following, he *has* made an argument:

"You should follow politics, because voting for an inferior candidate can harm the economy."

The statement "you should follow politics" is the conclusion and the statement "voting for an inferior candidate can harm the economy" is the evidence. Whether it is a good argument, though, depends on the strength of the evidence and the logic connecting the evidence to the conclusion, which you will learn how to determine in Chapter 7, Evaluation.

An argument's evidence needs to consist of statements that it is possible to agree or disagree with and that it is possible to prove true or false (see Kinds of Evidence on p. 196). **Rhetorical questions** (questions with obvious answers or ones that are simply used for effect) are often equivalent to statements and can sometimes be used as evidence in arguments. For example, asking the rhetorical question "Who doesn't want to be happy?" is essentially the same as making the statement "Everyone wants to be happy."

Questions, commands, and exclamations *can't* serve as the evidence of an argument, however. For example, it wouldn't make sense to say, "I disagree" in response to the question "Did you do your homework?" It would also be pretty nonsensical to say that the command "Do your homework!" is false. Finally, "Oh wow!" isn't something that can be disagreed with or proven true or false. You can ignore these three types of statements when trying to determine if something is an argument. If the only statements in a passage are like these, you can be sure that no real argument is being made.

In some cases, certain cue words or phrases indicate that an argument is being presented. Look for cue words or phrases that either indicate the presence of a conclusion or the presence of support for a conclusion. Some of the more common cue words and phrases are shown in Figure 6-2.

Often, perhaps even most of the time, when an author is making an argument, you won't find these cue words at all, though. You will have to recognize the argument by the context (the situation in which it is presented). For example, if you are reading an article that is critical of Facebook, you might see the following passage:

Social networking sites like Facebook are major distractions for students. Facebook makes it very difficult for students to concentrate on their school work, sucking up inordinate amounts of time. It is also easy for one student to slander another on Facebook, and the site administration itself is not responsive enough to handle such situations. Facebook should be banned on college campuses.

None of the cue words are present in the passage above, yet you shouldn't have much trouble recognizing that the passage is making an argument. The fact that the text is criticizing Facebook should help you realize that the last sentence of the passage serves as a conclusion that is supported by the evidence given earlier in the passage. Indeed, you may find that the author or speaker uses a word of recommendation (review emotive words in Chapter 4) such as "should," "must," or "ought to" when making an argument as in the case of the last sentence in the Facebook example above.

Conclusion Cue Words	Support Cue Words
Accordingly	Because
Consequently	For example
Hence	In addition
In conclusion	Moreover
So	Namely
Thus	Since
Therefore	The reasons are

■ **Figure 6-2**   Argument Cue Words and Phrases

Tips for Critical Thinkers: How to Identify Arguments

- **Make sure that at least two separate statements are made.** An argument must have a conclusion and at least one reason that the conclusion is true (called a premise or evidence). However, a single sentence can contain both evidence and a conclusion. Annotate or label the parts of the argument.
- **Ignore questions, commands, and exclamations.** Since you can't disagree with them or prove them true, they can't serve as the basic statements in an argument. Rhetorical questions, however, can count as evidence.
- **Look for cue words or phrases that indicate the presence of evidence or conclusions.** These hints will make identifying arguments easier.
- **Consider the context of the situation.** Use the skills you learned in Chapter 4 to consider the connotation of the words used or the tone of the overall piece. A confrontational or critical tone will often accompany an argument.

PRACTICE 6-3	Identifying Arguments

Directions: Read each of the following statements. Underline cue words that indicate the presence of evidence and circle cue words that indicate the presence of a conclusion. Write an A besides those that contain an argument and an N beside those that don't.

Here's a model

___A___ John was incredibly rude to Sara at her last party. People should not be rude to the hosts of parties they are invited to. (Therefore) John should not be invited to any more of Sara's parties.

Now you try

_____ 1. Since you studied really hard for your anatomy final, you should be able to pass without a problem.

_____ 2. Man, the latest Marvel movie was really cool. I really liked it.

_____ 3. Have you considered studying abroad? Studying in Europe or Asia is a great experience.

_____ 4. A national healthcare system will simply make healthcare more expensive, so you shouldn't support it.

_____ 5. You should get your children vaccinated, because scientific studies have shown that the risk posed by vaccination is far outweighed by its benefits. The anti-vaccination movement won't seem to acknowledge this fact.

_____ 6. Make sure you give me back the DVD you borrowed. I promised I'd lend it to my friend Joe. He really likes action movies.

_____ 7. Exercising regularly keeps you healthy. And who wouldn't want to be healthy? Therefore you should exercise regularly—at least three times per week.

_____ 8. Many people have gotten rich by coming up with a product that fulfills a need that many people have.

_____ 9. You're telling me that I shouldn't smoke. So what? I've heard how bad smoking is for you, but I just don't care. Everyone has to die sometime.

_____ 10. Cursing blatantly on prime-time television offends a good segment of the viewing public, plus it interferes with the ability of parents to raise their children the way they think best. The FCC has the responsibility to protect children and to shield people from offense. The FCC should fine stations that allow blatant cursing.

Evidence

Evidence (or *premises*) consists of the statements that provide support or *proof* for a conclusion. These statements must have a *truth value* (the ability to be judged true or false) to count as evidence. For example, "Joseph was doing 79 in a 55 mile-per-hour zone" could be declared true or false: Either Joseph was traveling that speed or he wasn't. But a statement such as "Coors has captured the essence of the Rocky Mountains" isn't true or false; it's simply a poetic expression that sounds attractive but doesn't mean anything specific. Many poetic statements, such as metaphors, can't be given a simple truth value and therefore can't be used as evidence. Is the statement "The yellow smoke [rubbed] its muzzle on the window-panes" true or false?

As indicated above, evidence must be presented in the form of a statement. It can't be an exclamation, a command, or a question (unless it's a rhetorical question). Moreover, you can't reasonably declare an exclamation, command, or question true or false, so these types of utterances don't have a truth value. Consider the following two arguments.

> Bigfoot exists, because DNA evidence pointing to a new North American ape species has been found.
> Bigfoot exists. I know it, because I saw one.

Both offer reasons to believe that Bigfoot exists, so they count as evidence. Whether they are convincing arguments has to be evaluated. You will learn to evaluate arguments and the reliability of the evidence used to support them in Chapter 7.

Evidence also can't simply be an affirmation of belief (a statement of how much the person believes the conclusion) or an explanation of how the belief was acquired. If instead of the arguments about Bigfoot given above, the writer had said the following, she would not have given any evidence to support her point:

> Bigfoot exists. I know it, because I was raised to believe in him.

Even though the cue word *because* hints that the speaker of the argument intends her conclusion—"Bigfoot exists"—to be supported by the statement "I was raised to believe in him," the statement doesn't actually give someone else reason to believe that Bigfoot exists; it's just an explanation of how she got the belief. The speaker hasn't offered any proof of Bigfoot's existence. Similarly, if she had said, "I know Bigfoot exists, because I really, really believe in him," she wouldn't be doing any better, because she would simply be affirming her belief.

Tips for Critical Thinkers: How to Recognize Evidence

- **Look for reasons offered in support of a claim.** Make sure the reasons provide proof for the claim. As you annotate a text, clearly mark these reasons.
- **Disregard questions, commands, and exclamations.** They can't be evidence.
- **Make sure the statement can be proven true or false.** If you can't assign it a truth value or if it's a poetic statement, it doesn't count.
- **If the speaker simply affirms his or her belief or tells how he or she got the belief, it's not evidence.** Such statements aren't proper support.

Spotting Evidence	PRACTICE 6-4

Directions: Indicate which of the following statements could function as evidence in an argument by writing an E next to them. Write an N next to each statement that does not provide evidence. If you write N, explain why the statement is not evidence by identifying it as a question, a command, an exclamation, an affirmation of belief, an explanation of how the belief was acquired, or a statement that cannot be proved to be true or false.

_____ 1. The current proposal will raise taxes 2.5 percent. _____

_____ 2. It would make me happy if Bigfoot were real. _____

_____ 3. How could you not believe in psychics? _____

_____ 4. What the world wants today is the real thing: Coca-Cola. _____

_____ 5. A majority of people believe in ghosts. _____

_____ 6. I've always believed that aliens abduct people. _____

_____ 7. Astrophysics is truly amazing. _____

_____ 8. The defendant was in New York the day of the crime. _____

_____ 9. Tell me where you were last night. _____

_____ 10. He is 6'1" tall. _____

PRACTICE 6-5   Recognizing Conclusion and Evidence

Directions: Underline the premises in the following passage. Double underline the conclusion. Circle any cue words that indicate the presence of evidence or a conclusion.

Religion is a force for good in the world. For example, the Jewish religion places a good deal of emphasis on scholarship, impressing on its adherents the importance of academic study. Christianity emphasizes the virtues of charity and nonviolence. And Islam teaches self control and the benefit of daily ritual to those who practice it. It is true that much violence has been committed in the name of religion, but the real fact of the matter is that those who committed such violence did so out of a perverse, mistaken interpretation of their religion. My religion means a great deal to me.

Spotlight on Standards: Accuracy

As you recall, one of the standards of critical thinkers is **accuracy**. Critical thinkers care whether information or evidence they are using is correct. They will take efforts to double-check accuracy. For example, if a critical thinker is trying to make an argument against implementing new gun control laws, and he finds a statement on a website that gun control laws have not lowered the murder rate in the UK, he will take pains to check to see if that statement is true. If he finds it is not, he will refuse to use the inaccurate statement, even if it supports his argument. Because of their standards, strong critical thinkers would rather be accurate than win arguments.

Kinds of Evidence

Most evidence fits into four main categories: *testimony, facts and statistics, analogies*, and *hypotheticals*. Each category lends itself to certain uses and has its own strengths and weaknesses.

Testimony   *Testimony* is proof that hinges on what a person says. It generally takes two forms: *testimonials* and *expert testimony*. *Testimonials*, or *anecdotes*, are short, usually vivid personal recollections of events. However, because of the problems with memory and sense perception, and because of the biases humans are prone to, testimonials are usually not strong enough forms of evidence to prove extraordinary claims. While testimonials are usually sufficient to support everyday claims, the only claims they can absolutely support are claims about someone's feelings or internal state. If a friend says that she felt lonely yesterday, this testimonial probably ought to be all the evidence you need to believe her. But if she tells a story about how she was abducted by an alien, her claim is not sufficiently supported by her anecdote alone. An argument supported by a testimonial might look like this:

I didn't use to believe that a spirit world existed, but then my friends and I played with a Ouija board. That thing was eerie! It knew things it shouldn't, and it moved by itself. At least I know I wasn't moving it, and I don't think my friends were either.

The second form of testimony is expert testimony. **Expert testimony** is distinguished from an anecdote because it's not a personal story; instead it's an expert's interpretation of facts that relate to his or her field of expertise. The strength of evidence of this kind relies on the reputation of the expert giving the testimony. If the testimony of the expert agrees with the consensus of other experts in the field, that lends it even more strength. It's important to remember, though, that expert testimony is still an opinion, even if it is an educated opinion.

Here's an example of an argument supported by expert testimony:

Khalid Alvani, noted expert in Middle Eastern strategic and international studies, questioned the Obama administration's decision to provide further arms to Syrian rebels. "While it is true that President Bashar al-Assad is a tyrant who has used chemical weapons against his people, will providing arms to insurgents ultimately produce a theocratic regime that is equally tyrannical and hostile to the U.S.?" he questioned.

Facts and Statistics   A direct or documented observation about the world is called *empirical evidence* or, more simply, a *fact*. A **fact** is something that can be easily checked by independent observers; it's something that no one (at least no one without an agenda) would deny. Some examples of facts are statements like

- The hardness of a diamond on the Mohs Scale is 10.
- Abraham Lincoln was killed in 1865.
- It takes Mars 687 days to orbit the sun.
- The octave on a piano keyboard is the eight-note interval between notes.

Facts are strong forms of evidence, and if you are fortunate enough to have them on your side, they tend to offer direct proof of a claim.

Statistics are numbers calculated from sets of data. You are undoubtedly familiar with statistics. During election years, the nation is bombarded with statistics predicting the outcome of the race. Statistics are derived in multiple ways: by analyzing scientific experiments, by asking people their opinions on social issues, by looking at profit margins, or by making observations about the weather, to name just a few. Statistics can never predict with absolute certainty, though; they only deal in probability. This is because statistical reasoning is a form of induction (see p. 202 for more on inductive reasoning).

Since many statistics are used to explain a fact or make a prediction about a population (for example, a given statistic might state that 16 percent of American men get prostate cancer), the population sample from which the statistic is derived must meet certain characteristics in order for the statistic to be trustworthy.

- *It must be sufficiently large.* If a sample is too small, you might see odd events occurring. For example, although you would expect a flipped coin to turn up heads 50 percent of the time, this is only really true if you flip the coin numerous times. If you only flip it 5 or 10 times, it wouldn't be that unusual to get heads more than 50 percent of the time.
- *It must be representative.* This means it has to accurately reflect the makeup of the target population. For instance, if you are trying to find out who is likely to be elected president, you need to know who is likely to vote in the election. If most

of the people who vote in the election are white seniors, your results won't be very reliable if you poll only young African Americans.

- *It must be randomized.* This doesn't mean that members of the population are just picked haphazardly; it means that every member of the target population has an equal chance of being chosen. This helps reduce any bias from the sample. To illustrate, if a scientist wants to see how effective a new cancer treatment drug is, but only health-conscious people volunteer for the study, she won't know if her drug is entirely effective, because her sample might get better partly because they exercised and ate right.

Here's an example of a short argument that uses statistics as evidence:

The U.S. Census Bureau indicates that as of 2010, 16% of citizens in the United States lacked medical insurance. The U.S. lagged behind other developed countries in insuring its citizenry; only 2% of citizens in developed countries besides the United States lacked health insurance. In 2013, they reported that 25% of seniors who declared bankruptcy did so because of medical bills. Almost 50,000 deaths per year in the United States are caused because people do not have adequate medical insurance.

Analogies An **analogy** is a comparison between two subjects. The purpose of an analogy used as evidence is to suggest that what is true of one of the subjects is probably true of the other subject. The following argument uses an analogy as evidence.

Current attempts to negotiate a peace deal between the Israelis and the Palestinians are bound to fall apart. After all, the current deal is very similar in terms to the attempted 1993 agreement, which also fell through.

The argument is comparing the two peace deals and using their similarities to make a prediction that one agreement will end up like the other agreement. Analogies can be strong forms of evidence, but they can't ever prove anything with certainty, since the first subject is never identical to the second subject.

Hypotheticals A **hypothetical example** is a piece of evidence that is based not on hard facts but on imagined possibilities. Hypotheticals can be useful pieces of evidence, because they prompt audiences to consider situations they might overlook or help them to see the logical outcome of their arguments. The effectiveness of hypothetical evidence hinges on its believability; if the hypothetical example could possibly come true, it will be much more compelling. Can you see how the following argument based on a hypothetical example could be effective?

We should install smoke detectors in our apartment. Imagine that one night a burner on the stove is accidentally left on. Smoke would fill the house before we could wake up, and we might die. And you've been known to leave the burners on, haven't you?

You will learn how to evaluate each of these types of evidence in Chapter 7.

PRACTICE 6-6   Finding Evidence

Directions: Search through various media outlets (like newspapers or magazines) or use the Internet to find an example of each kind of evidence. Bring your evidence to class and be prepared to explain it.

Counter-Evidence

Counter-evidence is a particular type of evidence given in opposition to the claim of an argument. Counter-evidence comes in the same types as the general evidence you just learned about, because it is the same. The only difference is that counter-evidence is intended to oppose the primary evidence in an argument. You need to pay attention to counter-evidence, because when you evaluate an argument, good objections to a point can cause you to disregard that point. Another name for counter-evidence is *objections*. Here is an example of counter-evidence given in opposition to an argument making the biased (and untrue) claim that females don't have an aptitude for higher education:

> While it may be true that males earn more doctorates than females, females earn more bachelors and masters degrees than males.

Assumptions

As you learned on pp. 138–139 of Chapter 4, **assumptions** are beliefs that an author takes for granted as being true. Assumptions often underlie arguments and provide the basis from which they are made. In this case, they serve as a form of evidence. They are, however, evidence that the author takes for granted as true or that the author makes no attempt to support. You should note the assumptions an argument makes when you identify the argument's evidence. For example, the claim "Nevada should outlaw prostitution" contains the assumption "What is morally wrong should be outlawed." You will learn to evaluate assumptions in Chapter 7 when you learn to evaluate evidence.

READ, WRITE, AND THINK CRITICALLY: SECTION ONE

Directions: Skim through the following text and answer questions 1–3. Then, read the selection and answer the questions that follow.

1. Do YOU believe in ghosts? Measure your belief, and write a brief paragraph about what you think.

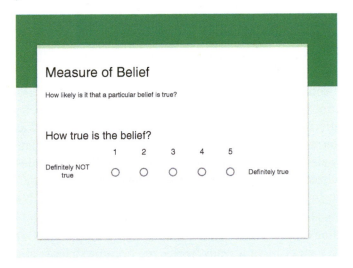

_____

_____

2. What is your prior knowledge of this topic?

_____

_____

3. The title of the selection is "The Ghosts We Think We See." What does this suggest about what the author will claim about ghosts?

_____

_____

The Ghosts We Think We See

Sharon Begley

Sharon Begley has been science columnist at various prestigious outlets and publications, such as Reuters, Wall Street Journal, *and* Newsweek, *where she was also the science editor. She has authored* Train your Brain, Change your Brain, *and co-authored multiple books including* The Emotional Life of Your Brain *and* The Mind and the Brain. *The following piece appeared in* Newsweek *in 2007.*

1 Bruce Hood usually conducts experiments under much more **rigorous** conditions than this, but since he had a large audience one recent evening in London, the University of Bristol psychology professor figured he'd seize the opportunity. Holding up an old cardigan, he asked if anyone would be willing to wear it if he paid them $40. Every hand shot up. Then Hood added that the sweater had been worn by a notorious murderer. All but a couple of hands disappeared. "People view evil as something physical, even **tangible**, and able to infect the sweater" as easily as lice, Hood says. That idea helps explain a number of supernatural beliefs, he argues: "The idea of spirits and souls appearing in this world becomes more plausible if we believe in general that the nonphysical can transfer over to the physical world."

2 And believe it we do. A Gallup poll found that only 7 percent of Americans do *not* believe in telepathy, deja vu, ghosts, past lives or other supernatural phenomena, which may have more than a little to do with the soaring popularity of Halloween. Even **eminent** rationalists such as Alfred Russel Wallace, who discovered natural selection (prompting Darwin to speed up his own work), believed in ghosts, haunted houses, levitation and clairvoyance. But "supernatural"—anything that cannot be explained by laws of physics or biology—also encompasses more **mundane** phenomena. It includes the belief that you can feel someone staring at you from behind, and that if you think about someone he is more likely to phone you (this doesn't work for getting first dates to call you for a second, however). Far from being pathological, the ubiquity of such beliefs is actually a clue to how the normal mind works, cognitive scientists now realize, for belief in the supernatural arises from the same mental processes that underlie everyday reasoning and perception.

3 Chief among those normal processes is our neurons' habit of filling in the blanks. The brain takes messy, incomplete input and turns it into a meaningful, complete picture. Visualize four Pac-Man-like black shapes arranged so that the wedge removed from each seems to form a corner of a white square. Neurons in the brain's visual regions, whose job is to fire when the eyes see a square's edges, do fire—even though there are no edges to see. The mind also sees patterns in random data, which is why the sky is speckled with bears and big dippers. This drive to perceive patterns—which is very useful in interpreting experimental data as well as understanding people's behavior—can also underlie such supernatural beliefs as seeing Jesus in the scorch marks and flecks of grain on a grilled-cheese sandwich. "If a stain looks like the Virgin Mary," says Hood, "then it is a divine sign and not a coincidence. If the wind in the cave sounds like a voice, then it is a voice."

4 Patterns can be in time as well as space. Hence such superstitious rituals as wearing the same shirt when you compete in a sports event, or not standing on the white lines of a tennis court, as John McEnroe refused to do. If you depart from the ritual to prove to a skeptic that it really works, you become so tense about the loss of the magic **talisman** that you're indeed likely to lose. Game, set and match for superstition.

5 The mind also tends to **impute** consciousness to inanimate objects (ever yell at a balky computer?). This leads us to believe that natural phenomena are "purposeful, caused by agents with sentient minds," says Hood, whose book "The Supernatural Sense" is due next year. It's only a short step to thinking that " 'things that go bump in the night' are the result of some spirit or agent," not branches brushing against your drainpipe.

6 The belief that minds are not bound to bodies reflects a dualism that shows up in children as young as 2. "This is universal, seeing minds as separate from bodies," says psychologist Paul Bloom of Yale University. "Kids have no trouble believing stories in which people exchange bodies, for instance. And since supernatural beings like ghosts are without material bodies but with minds, our belief in **dualism** makes them totally plausible."

7 And the belief that you can feel someone staring at you from behind? Someone who sees you suddenly pivot is likely to return your stare, leading to the false conclusion that you did detect the gaze. Thanks to "confirmatory bias," people tend to remember every time a hunch like this—or like the idea that the phone rings after you think about someone—is borne out. We forget all those times it isn't.

8 As scientists probe deeper into the brain for what underlies superstition, they have found a surprising suspect: dopamine, which usually fuels the brain's sense of reward. In one study, two groups of people, either believers in the supernatural or skeptics, looked at quickly displayed images of faces and scrambled faces, real words and nonwords. The goal was to pick out the real ones. Skeptics called more real faces nonfaces, and real words nonwords, than did believers, who happily saw faces and words even in gibberish. But after the skeptics were given L-dopa, a drug that increases dopamine, their skeptical threshold fell, and they ID'd more faces and words as real. That suggests that dopamine inclines the brain to see patterns even in random noise. Boo!

4. Use context clues and/or a dictionary to define the following words (marked in bold in the reading).

   a. Rigorous (para. 1): _____
   b. Tangible (para. 1): _____
   c. Eminent (para. 2): _____
   d. Mundane (para. 2): _____
   e. Talisman (para. 4): _____
   f. Impute (para. 5): _____
   g. Dualism (para. 6): _____

5. Would you wear an article of clothing worn by a serial killer? Why or why not?

6. Identify the claim and evidence of the argument given by the author.

7. In paragraph 5, the author says, "the mind also tends to impute consciousness to inanimate objects." Explain in your own words what the author means. How could this tendency lead us to believe in ghosts?

8. Do you agree or disagree with the author's dismissal of the supernatural? Critically write an essay explaining your stance. Use evidence in your essay.

SECTION TWO

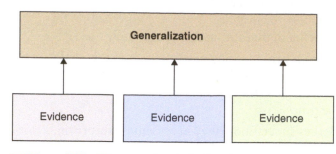

■ **Figure 6-3** Diagram of an Inductive Argument

Logic

Now that you can identify arguments and recognize assumptions, evidence, and conclusions, you need to be able to analyze an argument and recognize its **logic**, the reasoning that links the evidence to the conclusion. Then you will be able put all this knowledge together to map arguments and recognize patterns of organization. Logic is at the heart of critical thinking: it helps you to form beliefs that are likely to be true and to make good decisions!

There are two major forms of logic used in arguments: *inductive reasoning* and *deductive reasoning*.

Inductive Reasoning

Inductive reasoning involves drawing a general conclusion from specific pieces of evidence. The more pieces of evidence from which the conclusion is drawn, the more *probable* (or likely) the conclusion is (see Figure 6-3).

For example, if you want to know whether you are better off buying your electronics from stores or from the internet, you have to look at the prices and availability of merchandise in both brick-and-mortar stores and on various websites to draw a conclusion. If you look at several stores and several websites and find that more products are available cheaper from online stores, you would have used induction to conclude where to buy your electronics. Your reasoning might look like this:

Evidence   The electronics store at the mall has a fair selection but high prices.
The big box electronics store near my house has a larger selection but even higher prices.
Three websites I checked have an extremely large selection and lower prices than either store.

Conclusion   Therefore, I am better off buying my electronics online.

Induction, however, can never lead to certainty. To be certain that you are better off buying your electronics online, you would have to actually look at the selection and prices of electronics in every store there is, both in the real world and online, which is, of course, impossible. An inductive argument that leads to a conclusion that is highly probable is **cogent** (You will learn more about cogency in Chapter 7).

Induction is useful because it allows you to use your experience to increase your knowledge about the world. It allows you to generalize about the world, which is how you learn new things. It is quite useful to know where to buy your electronics, because knowing that can save you money. If you didn't use induction to come to general conclusions, then every time you wanted to buy electronics, you'd have to do the entire search all over again. That wouldn't be very practical.

Some unscrupulous people or organizations exploit the fact that the general public isn't aware of the nature of inductive argument. For example, in the past, cigarette companies made the claim that because we weren't 100 percent certain that cigarette smoking caused cancer, we shouldn't assume that it does, and therefore the government should not take any action to regulate the sale of cigarettes. Many scientists, however, agreed that the probability that cigarettes cause cancer was very, very high. The scientists' conclusion was cogent, and the cigarette companies were being deceptive.

Deductive Reasoning

Deductive reasoning involves drawing specific conclusions from generalizations. For example, the following argument is deductive:

All sporting events have rules. Therefore football, which is a sport, has rules.

The generalization that all sports have rules allows us to figure out that any particular sport must have rules. The classic form of a deductive argument is known as a *syllogism*. A **syllogism** has two premises and a conclusion; the first premise is the generalization, and the second premise is a specific fact or observation to which the generalization is to be applied (see Figure 6-4).

The example argument is actually a syllogism. If you break it down, it looks like this:

Generalization	All sports have rules.	**Major Premise**
Specific Fact	Football is a sport	**Minor Premise**
Conclusion	Football has rules.	**Conclusion**

We should note, though, that not all deductive arguments are syllogisms, nor do they all have two premises.

A deductive argument that uses good logic is called **valid**, meaning that if the premises are true, the conclusion must be true (you will learn more about validity in Chapter 7). This means that a good deductive argument leads to a conclusion that is not just probably true; it is definitely true. For example, the argument "Steve committed the crime, so he will be found guilty" is not valid. It is not certain he will be found guilty based only on the statement that he committed the crime. Sometimes the guilty go free.

Inductive reasoning and deductive reasoning work together. Deductive reasoning allows you to draw conclusions that are certain, but to use deduction, you need to start with generalizations. And where do you get those generalizations? From inductive reasoning. For example,

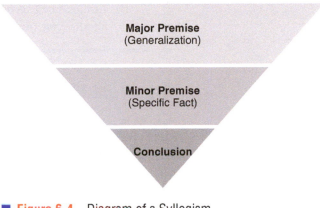

■ **Figure 6-4**   Diagram of a Syllogism

the generalization that begins the deductive syllogism above—"All sports have rules"—was derived from thinking inductively about sports (in other words, if you noticed that badminton has rules, golf has rules, volleyball has rules, through inductive reasoning you can come to the general conclusion that "All sports have rules"). In turn, deductive reasoning helps you organize and categorize knowledge, making your inductive reasoning more effective.

| Logic and Evidence | PRACTICE 6-7 |

Directions: For each of the following mini-arguments, underline the statements that serve as evidence. Double underline the conclusion. Circle any cue words that indicate the presence of evidence or conclusions. Then, indicate whether the argument is inductive (I) or deductive (D) on the line provided.

Here's a model

__D__   The only birds that sit on power lines are crows. I saw a bird on a power line yesterday on my way home. (Hence) it must have been a crow.

Now you try

_____   1. My dog and my friend's dog love apples. I bet most dogs would love apple-flavored treats.

_____ 2. Students who regularly attend their college courses get passing grades. Oliver never skips a class (he attends regularly). Therefore, we can conclude that Oliver will get passing grades.

_____ 3. Stealing is wrong, but Britta's friends have been shoplifting from local stores. Therefore, Britta should try to dissuade her friends from stealing.

_____ 4. Former President Richard Nixon had the Watergate scandal, Bill Clinton went through the Monica Lewinsky scandal, and Donald Trump has faced various scandals, both personal and professional. History 101 students conclude that American Presidents are vulnerable to scandals.

_____ 5. Since the fact that germs cause illness is well-founded, and since Carl is ill, doctors ought to find germs in his body.

_____ 6. Students who plagiarize get sent to the Dean. Johan plagiarized, so he will get sent to the Dean.

_____ 7. People who get their work done before the deadline deserve praise. Susan should be praised, because she completed her work early.

_____ 8. I looked at 100 sheep, and they were all white. All sheep are white.

_____ 9. When traffic cameras were installed at the intersection of Rts. 4 and 273, the number of accidents increased. Traffic cameras increase accidents.

_____ 10. Bullies need to be punished. Nelson bullies Bart; therefore Principal Skinner should give him detention.

Argument Mapping

So far, you've learned about simple arguments, and it's pretty easy to figure out the evidence, conclusions, and logic in a simple argument. But arguments in the real world get far more complex, and it's easy to lose track of them. **Argument mapping**, a way to visually analyze an argument, will help you keep the relation between the evidence and conclusions clear in your mind. Here are some tips for how to make a simple argument map.

Tips for Critical Thinkers: How to Make a Simple Argument Map

- **Identify the conclusion, write it at the top of the page, and draw a box around it.** Shade or color the box to distinguish it as the conclusion.
- **Identify the evidence, write it down under the conclusion, and draw a box around it.**
- **Draw lines from the evidence (or premises) to the conclusion.** These lines represent the connection between the evidence and the conclusion.
- **If pieces of evidence are linked together, draw a line connecting them together before you connect them to the conclusion.** Evidence is linked if two or more pieces of evidence are needed to support the conclusion, and none of them can support it independently.
- **Label as "inductive" or "deductive" the main line linking each piece or group of evidence to the conclusion.**

Figure 6-5 shows a map of the argument, "Bigfoot exists, because DNA evidence pointing to a new North American ape species has been found."

Figure 6-6 illustrates a map of an argument with linked premises. The argument is "Since all sports have rules, and football is a sport, football has rules."

■ **Figure 6-5** Map of Bigfoot Exists Argument

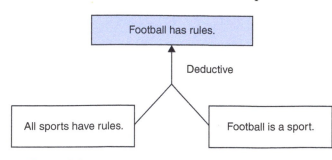

■ **Figure 6-6** Map of Football has Rules Argument

Simple Argument Mapping

PRACTICE 6-8

Directions: Map the following simple arguments in the boxes provided. For question 5, create your own map on another sheet of paper.

1. Overeating is bad for you, since it causes obesity. It also causes cardiovascular disease.

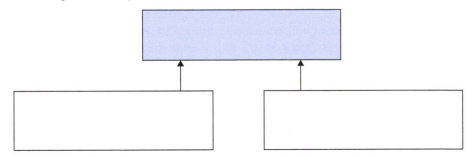

2. If it rains, then the ground gets wet. It rained, so the ground is wet.

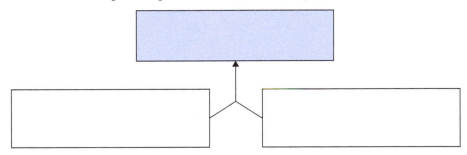

3. It's wrong to spend more on wars than on education. Per budget period, the United States spends $618 billion on war and defense and only $200 billion on education. Even though that's an increase over previous years, the priorities of the United States need to be reevaluated.

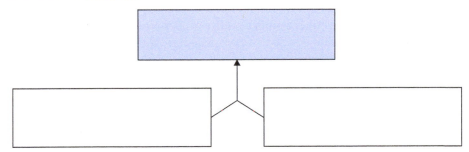

4. Because plants need light to grow and my new hibiscus is a plant, it will need light to grow.

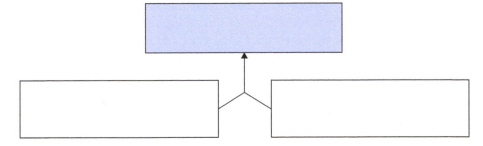

5. Because tracking systems are so helpful in recovering stolen vehicles, anyone who owns an expensive car should get one. These systems are also nice because they lower insurance rates.

Advanced Argument Mapping

Most real arguments are more complex than those in Practice 6-8. In order to analyze them, it is even more important to keep all the relationships straight. Luckily, you can use the strategies for mapping simple arguments to map complex arguments. Often you will find that complex arguments are actually a series of mini-arguments that support a primary conclusion. So a complex argument map will look like a tree made out of simple argument maps.

You will also have to keep track of any counter-evidence, as defined on p. 199. You need to catalog the objections, so that when you are evaluating the argument, you can weigh the pros and cons and decide if the evidence given is outweighed by the objections.

Here are some tips for creating advanced argument maps.

Tips for Critical Thinkers: How to Make an Advanced Argument Map

- **Identify all the statements that affect the argument.** Ignore statements that can't serve as evidence. Keep the concept of relevance in mind (discussed on p. 64 of Chapter 3). If the author digresses into irrelevant statements or asides, ignore those too.
- **Identify the primary conclusion of the argument and write it at the top of your page.** Draw a box around it and shade it in. It is possible for an argument to have more than one primary conclusion.
- **Identify the main evidence (premises) used to support the primary conclusion.** Box them and draw lines and arrows to indicate their relationship to the conclusion.
- **If these premises are the conclusions of mini-arguments, identify the premises that establish them.** Box the supporting premises and draw lines and arrows to indicate their relationship to their conclusions.
- **Identify any objections to evidence or conclusions and write them next to the statement they are objecting to.** Circle the objections and put a minus sign next to them.
- **Label as "inductive" or "deductive" the main line linking each piece or group of evidence to its conclusion.**

Figure 6-7 shows an advanced map for the following argument:

Men tend to like video games more than women do. This is because these games simulate advancing one's station in life and defeating one's enemies, which men enjoy. Males are especially rewarded by gaining a higher social station. Scientists have provided proof that men get a larger dopamine reward than women do when they achieve a higher social station. Men also especially enjoy violently defeating their enemies. That's pretty obvious, since even though most men are not violent, most fights involve men, and people who fight obviously want to defeat whomever they're fighting. Since video games simulate raising one's social station in life and beating one's enemies, men tend to like them more than women do.

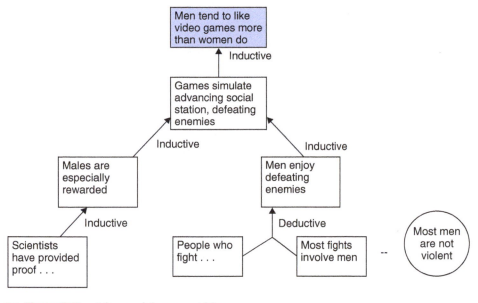

■ **Figure 6-7**   Advanced Argument Map

Advanced Argument Mapping   PRACTICE 6-9

Directions: Map the following advanced arguments. For question 1, fill in the boxes provided with the statements from the argument. For questions 2 and 3, create your own maps on a separate sheet of paper.

1. Companies that don't pay attention to the health of the environment certainly tend to pay attention to their bottom lines. Fines compel these companies to consider their impact, especially if the fines are heavy. So companies that don't worry about the environment should be heavily fined. BP clearly did not consider how its actions would affect the environment. We know this because BP cut corners when it came to ordering environmental impact studies. The company also fought against environmental regulations (even though this is typical for oil companies). For all of these reasons, BP should get fined a substantial amount for the 2010 Gulf Oil Spill.

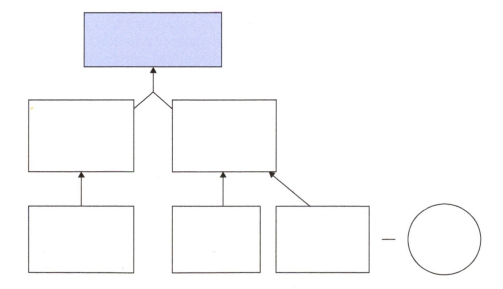

2. Although women may not be physically as strong as men, they equal men in all other areas, and even in jobs that require physical strength, they more than make up for their lack of brute strength in other ways. Therefore, women should receive equal pay. Another reason women deserve the same pay as men is that they have proven themselves equally valuable in crisis situations, and value should be rewarded. Moreover, paying women better wages leads to an improved economy, because they will spend their higher wages on goods and services.

3. The war on drugs has been a dismal failure. As many people in the United States use drugs as ever, as shown by the latest Office of National Drug Control Policies report. This fact is also pretty obvious if you just ask around. Some more proof that the war on drugs has failed so terribly is that our prisons are overcrowded with nonviolent drug offenders, and police officers waste valuable time arresting small-time drug users when they could be pursuing violent offenders. Moreover, the war on drugs has deprived our country of a valuable medicinal herb called marijuana. Even though drug war proponents claim marijuana is a gateway drug, doctors use it to help AIDS patients maintain their weight. It's also useful for managing glaucoma.

Analyzing Patterns of Organization

Now that you have learned about evidence and logic, you are in a position to analyze a reading for its pattern of organization. A **pattern of organization** (also known as a thought pattern) is the method the author uses to present the evidence and to arrange it logically so as to support his or her claim most effectively. Recognizing the pattern of organization will help you remember the details and understand the argument. It will also help you understand the author's purpose (review purpose on p. 121) and study for tests. While authors use many patterns of organization, seven patterns are most common: *cause and effect, chronological/process, classification, comparison/contrast, definition, example*, and *listing*. Authors can use one of these patterns as their primary means of organization, or they can use a mixed pattern consisting of two or more of them. As you annotate a text, notice (and mark) transition words that suggest pattern of organization.

Cause and Effect

A **cause and effect** pattern means that an author details a cause, or more than one cause, and then discusses the effect, or effects, that could result. To help recognize cause and effect patterns, look for words like *because* and *therefore*. (Look back at Figure 3-1 on p. 66 for more cause and effect transition words.) Cause and effect is a common pattern in history and science courses. If you recognize that textbook material is in the cause and effect pattern, you can study the material more effectively, perhaps by creating a visual or outline (i.e., outline the causes of a military conflict). The following paragraph uses a cause and effect pattern of organization:

> Why does it rain? Rain formation is a complex process, with many causes, but the major causes are water-saturated air and coalescence. Processes like evaporation or wind will cause water vapor to build up in the atmosphere. Water will generally start to condense around a small particle in the air. As long as the air is warm enough (so that snow or ice doesn't form), turbulence in the air will eventually cause water vapor to coalesce, or fuse, into a large droplet. Once the droplet gets large enough to overcome air resistance, it falls. We call the result rain.

Chronological/Process

Writers use a **chronological** pattern to show the order in which events occurred. A chronological pattern is common in narratives (stories), processes, directions, and historical information. Words like *before, after,* and *soon* are often clues that an author is using this pattern. (See Figure 3-1 for more transition words that might indicate a chronological pattern.) As you study, if you notice that the material is in chronological order, create a time line for review. The following paragraph illustrates a chronological thought pattern:

> The first Battle of Bull Run, the first major conflict in the Civil War, was a disaster for the Union. The Union troops began the attack with some initial shelling, pretended to attack one flank of the Confederate troops, and then attacked the other flank. At this point the rebel troops seemed to be facing defeat, and their lines broke; they retreated to Henry House Hill. There the Confederates regrouped, though, and through a brave attack, managed to capture the bulk of the Union's artillery guns. The Union forces eventually retreated.

A special kind of chronological pattern is known as a process pattern. Authors employ a **process** pattern when they want to show how to complete a task, or how a task was completed, and when the order of the steps matters. Words like *first, second,* and *last* are often hints that an author is using this pattern. The following paragraph illustrates a process pattern of organization:

> Changing the oil in your car is a very easy process. First, gather all the necessary supplies, including the right kind of new oil filter. Second, open the oil filler cap to allow the oil to drain more easily. Third, loosen and remove the oil plug. Fourth, take out the oil filter, which may require a special wrench. Fifth, replace the plug. Sixth, put on the new filter. Seventh, put in the proper amount of oil. Finally, clean up, check the oil pressure, and fill as needed. You're done!

Classification

The **classification** pattern is used to divide broad subjects into categories and to show what specific ideas or objects belong within those categories. Words like *types* or *traits* could show that an author is using a classification pattern of organization. (See Figure 3-1 for more transition words that might indicate a classification thought pattern.) Common in such courses as sociology, biology, geology, and psychology, the classification pattern lends itself well to charts and tables. If you encounter text in the classification pattern, create a chart or table to bring attention to traits. The following paragraph illustrates a classification pattern:

> Experts have identified many different styles of leadership. Three of the most important types of leadership styles are the authoritarian style, the collaborative style, and the laissez-faire style. The authoritarian style means that the leader keeps all   the decision-making powers to him- or herself. The traits of this type of leader tend to be bossiness and self-importance. The collaborative style involves seeking input from the group, helping to reach a consensus, and then guiding the group as they act on the consensus. This kind of leader tends to be very open-minded. The laissez-faire style means that the leader allows almost all decisions to be made by the group. The laissez-faire leader tends to be easy-going.

Comparison/Contrast

The **comparison/contrast** pattern is employed by a writer to show how ideas are similar or how they are different. When an author shows how ideas are similar, she is comparing, and when she shows how they are different, she is contrasting. Of course, an author may both compare and contrast. Words such as *like, as,* and *both* might indicate that an author is comparing, and words such as *unlike* and *instead* could mean that an author is contrasting. (Figure 3-1 gives more comparison/contrast transition words.) Textbook authors frequently employ the comparison/contrast pattern, and students could create a Venn diagram as a way to study the concepts. The following paragraph illustrates a comparison/contrast pattern of organization:

> Reading and watching movies share many similarities, but ultimately they are different at their core. Both often revolve around a compelling narrative; the more interesting the story, the more likely you are to continue reading or watching. When movies and stories contain lots of action and descriptive scenes, they also tend to hold your attention. On the other hand, movie watching can be quite passive. You can just sit back and allow the director of the movie to entertain you and create the meaning. When you read, you need to be active and construct the meaning in conjunction with the author. That is a fairly substantial difference.

Definition

When a writer needs to define terms or ideas in order to make sure that the reader is not confused, he might use a *definition* pattern of organization. Often the definition pattern involves giving the basic meaning of the term early in the passage, then giving defining characteristics. Words like *means, refers to, consists of, is characterized by,* or *is defined as* could give you a clue that the author is defining something. The following paragraph illustrates a definition pattern:

> **Histrionic personality disorder** is a type of disorder distinguished by more than the usual expression of emotion and need for attention. A histrionic personality is a person who would be defined as "dramatic" by friends, but it goes much deeper than that. The person afflicted with this disorder is constantly showing off, quickly changes his or her mood, and often acts as if friendships are deeper or more intimate than they actually are. The sufferer of this disorder is very sensitive to criticism and needs to be the center of attention.

Example

To make a concept or definition more clear, authors will sometimes provide cases or illustrations. This is known as an **example pattern**. Examples make it far easier to understand a difficult concept, because they make it more concrete and help you picture it. Words like *for example* or *such as* could give you a clue that the author is providing examples. (See Figure 3-1 for more example words.)

The following paragraph illustrates an example pattern:

> The history of warfare has revolved around an arms race. Each weapon is designed in response to a new type of defense, which prompts a new defense to be designed, which in turn prompts a new weapon. For instance, the advent of chainmail made it more difficult for a cutting weapon, such as a knife or a light sword, to injure the wearer. To answer chainmail, people constructed heavier bludgeoning weapons, like maces (a club with a metal ball on the end) or morning stars (spiked maces). If a soldier was hit with a mace, his bones would be broken even if he were wearing chainmail. To respond to the heavier bludgeoning weapons, people made heavier armors, like plate mail.

Listing

The **listing** pattern is employed when a writer wants you to know that multiple points are important or that there is more than one factor to be considered in the issue under discussion. This type of pattern is known as *addition* when the author uses it to add more evidence, and it is known as *enumeration* when the author lists steps and numbers them. Words such as *furthermore* might indicate a listing pattern. Words such as *also* and *another* point toward an addition pattern. *Also* and *next* indicate an enumeration pattern, as does the use of numbered or bulleted lists. The following paragraph illustrates a listing pattern:

> Many factors must be considered when engaging in a job search after graduation. For one thing, you need to think seriously about what you want to do. If you pick a profession that you dislike, you will not have the motivation to get good at it. You will also need to consider if you are willing to relocate, because the jobs you want may not be located in your area. It can be difficult leaving friends and family, but it may be necessary. Another point to consider is if previous experience is required to break into the field. If so, an internship may be necessary before you can land a job in your chosen field.

Mixed

A **mixed pattern** of organization is when an author uses more than one pattern in a paragraph or text. Since authors have various purposes, even within the same text, they will often employ mixed patterns of organization in order to most effectively make their point. For example, when discussing dogs, an author may define what a canine is generally, then give examples of different breeds, comparing and contrasting the breeds as she goes. If you notice clue words from more than one pattern of organization contained in the same paragraph or passage, the author may be using a mixed pattern. The following paragraph illustrates a mixed pattern. It uses both the definition and example patterns.

> The word *genre* refers to a broad category within music, literature, film, or some other artistic field. Each genre usually has its own style, themes, and content. For example, in film, some of the genres are action, comedy, drama, horror, and suspense. Movies within each genre tend to be similar to each other and different from movies in another genre. Action movies are characterized by shallow dialogue, chases, and explosions, while horror movies are characterized by startling shots, gore, and gratuitous titillation, for instance.

Identifying Patterns of Organization	PRACTICE 6-10

Directions: Read each of the following paragraphs. Circle any clue words you find (see Figure 3-1 for clue words). Then write the type of pattern in the blank provided. Each pattern is used once.

1. _____ Cardiac arrhythmia refers to a medical problem wherein the electrical activity in the human heart is not normal, meaning that the heart could be beating too slowly, too quickly, or irregularly. This issue can be fairly harmless, or it could lead to death. Many different reasons exist for why one may have a cardiac arrhythmia, and only a doctor can diagnose such a condition.

2. _____ The movie *Friends with Benefits*, released in 2011, is exactly the same as *No Strings Attached*, also released in 2011. Both feature a young couple who attempt to have a casually intimate relationship with no rules or commitment. Both young couples discover this is impossible, however, as they grow increasingly jealous of possible romantic rivals. At the end of both movies, the young couples mature into a committed relationship. Why does Hollywood release identical movies at the same time?

3. _____ Multiple aspects play into being in tip-top physical shape. First, you need a healthy body fat ratio. This depends on your age and gender. Second, you need to be strong, meaning your muscles need power. Third, you need muscle endurance; you need to be able to use your muscles for extended periods. Fourth, you need to be cardiovascularly fit. Last—and this is not to be overlooked—you need to be flexible. This will help you resist injury.

4. _____ The solar system began as a cloud of spinning dust, known as a nebula. At first, gravity was responsible for the condensation of the cloud, but then conservation of angular momentum made the cloud spin faster and faster. Next, the center of the cloud heated up, and then the disk began to flatten out. After that, gravity began to draw parts of the flattened disk into clumps, which later formed into planets, a process known as accretion. Finally, the sun ignited because of the density at the center of the disk, and the solar system as we know it was born.

5. _____ There were many reasons for the Great Depression of 1929. The causes are also complex and varied. The banks failed in huge numbers, while the stock market simultaneously crashed. At the same time, the Federal Reserve reduced the country's money supply, while foreign countries enacted unfavorable monetary policies. This was a perfect storm of problems that all together contributed to the Great Depression that is so famous; at least some scholars believe that these are the causes.

6. _____ Some books can change your life. For religious people, books such as *The Purpose-Driven Life* and, of course, *The Bible*, can cause a great spiritual awakening. For others, famous works of literature, such as those of Shakespeare or Homer, can lead to an artistic epiphany. Even a book like *Harry Potter* can instill a love of reading and lead you into a whole new world.

7. _____ Four major types of gamblers have been identified: social, frequent, problem, and compulsive. Social gamblers view gambling as entertainment and do it occasionally. In no way is it a problem for these kinds of gamblers. Frequent gamblers gamble more often but gambling is still not the focus of their lives and is not a problem for them. Problem gamblers gamble with money they should use for other things, like living expenses, and these gamblers may "chase losses" (keep gambling when they lose). The last category is compulsive gamblers. These kinds of gamblers have a major issue with gambling. They may go bankrupt or get divorced over gambling, but they still cannot stop.

8. _____ A twelve-step program is defined as a method of recovering from addiction, and usually consists of a group of principles and a defined course of action. The most famous is Alcoholics Anonymous. The twelve steps in this program are (1) admit to being powerless over alcohol, (2) believe that a higher power can fix it, (3) make a decision to turn to the higher power, (4) make a moral inventory of oneself, (5) admit to all one's wrongs, (6) be ready for a higher power to remove these failings, (7) ask the power to remove the failings, (8) make a list of persons wronged, (9) make amends where possible, (10) continue moral inventory and admit wrongdoing, (11) seek to improve contact with a higher power, (12) strive to practice these principles on daily affairs forever.

The Scientific Method

So far, you've learned how to understand texts better by analyzing the arguments they make and by recognizing the thought pattern(s) the author uses. Scientists also use a method of analysis to understand the world better: the scientific method. Critical thinking and scientific thinking are very similar and are based on the same principles (and scientists/critical thinkers alike embrace the standards of accuracy, clarity, completeness, fairness, relevance, and significance). So it's useful to learn something about science.

Science is a system by which we discover truths and laws about the material world. Although science is a large and varied discipline, it generally has the following characteristics:

• *It uses only natural explanations*, accounts that only make use of physical processes and laws. Magic and the supernatural, not being measurable or predictable (or even able to be proven real), are never used as explanations.

- *It uses peer review.* Scientists submit their work to other scientists to be checked.
- *It is self-correcting.* While scientists are human and prone to bias and error, scientists are praised for finding scientific errors during the peer review process or through further experiments.
- *It operates according to a system called the scientific method.*

The **scientific method** is a method of analysis that has proven to be especially good at generating new knowledge and separating what's true from what's false. Although its application differs somewhat depending on the field, it generally consists of six steps.

Steps in the Scientific Method

1. *Observation.* A scientist looks around and notices something interesting about the world. Perhaps she notices strange organisms in the blood of a sick animal.
2. *Questioning.* The scientist asks herself why what she observes happens. Continuing our example above, she might say, "What is the connection between these organisms and the animal's illness, if there is one?"
3. *Proposal of hypothesis.* The scientist makes an educated guess to answer the question she just formulated. In our example, she could propose that the new organisms cause illness.
4. *Prediction.* She says, "If my hypothesis is true, certain events ought to take place." For instance, she might say, "If these organisms cause illness and I inject them into healthy animals, they ought to get sick too."
5. *Experimental testing.* The scientist devises a way to test whether her prediction is correct. The scientist from our example then injects the organisms into healthy animals and carefully watches and records what takes place.
6. *Revision of the hypothesis* or *tentative acceptance.* If the prediction is proven false—for example, if the healthy animals stay healthy—the scientist needs to go back to the hypothesis and figure out why she was wrong; she'll make a new guess and test that guess. If her prediction is correct—and the animals get sick—she won't stop, though; she'll make more predictions and test them, too. So really step six could be called *lots more testing.*

A hypothesis scientists are able to use to make predictions and which has survived many attempts to prove it false (what scientists call *falsifying*) is incredibly useful for science. It can explain much about the world or the universe, and becomes a *scientific theory.* A **scientific theory** is a wide-ranging explanation of events we observe. The results of experimental testing could be called **scientific facts.** When the animals in the example above got sick, their observed illness after being injected was a scientific fact. When scientists do enough of these experiments and figure out that certain tiny organisms called germs or bacteria make creatures sick, they then have a framework to explain all their experiments, and they might call it the "Germ Theory of Disease."

Once you understand this, you'll see that a scientific theory is not the same thing as an everyday theory. In your daily life, if someone tells you he has a theory about why your car keeps breaking down, he just means that he has an idea. In science, the term *theory* is far stronger—in a way, scientific theories are more useful than scientific facts. Some of the most valuable and long-standing explanations in science are "only" theories: the germ-theory of disease, the theory of evolution, atomic theory, the heliocentric theory (the idea that the sun is at the center of the solar system), and the theory of gravity are just some examples. Although all of these theories faced some resistance at first, their usefulness and value are no longer in doubt.

Science uses deduction, but induction is especially important in science. Experimenting is a form of induction. Because of what you have learned about induction, you can understand why scientific theories can never be proven 100 percent true. They just get more and more probable the more they survive falsification. The theories named above, which have never yet been falsified, are considered extremely probable, so much so that most scientists doubt they will ever be proven false.

PRACTICE 6-11   Understanding Science

Directions: Answer the following prompts on a separate sheet of paper.

1. In your own words, explain the difference between a *scientific fact* and a *scientific theory.*
2. Use the library or the Internet to discover and research another scientific theory similar to the ones listed above. Name some of the observations (scientific facts) it explains.

Pseudoscience

Science and the scientific method led directly to the invention of computers, antibiotics, and space flight, just to scratch the surface. For this reason, people have a great deal of respect for science, and some people want a share of its glory. Some people want their personal beliefs to be considered scientifically based. Unfortunately, their beliefs aren't scientific—they are pseudoscientific. **Pseudoscience** is a theory or system that claims to be scientific but isn't. Usually a theory or system is considered a pseudoscience for one (and usually more) of the following reasons:

- It can't be tested scientifically or proven false.
- It doesn't progress as a field, meaning it doesn't make new discoveries or discard unproven ideas.
- Its practitioners don't do real experiments, or if they say they do, they avoid peer review.
- It often involves the supernatural or the occult.
- Practitioners look for evidence that it is true and avoid or ignore evidence that it's false.

> **Reminder**
>
> You learned about the strong and weak sense of critical thinking and about rationalization in Chapter 1.

Believers in a pseudoscience are usually weak critical thinkers, meaning that they think critically about information that casts doubt on their pseudoscientific beliefs, but they are gullible when it comes to their own beliefs. They tend to rationalize away evidence that falsifies their beliefs, and they often claim that scientists are involved in a big conspiracy to suppress the fact that their beliefs are scientifically based.

It is not always easy to tell pseudoscience from science, but the skill of analysis (as well as the other skills you are learning in this book) will help you to do so. Some beliefs and practices have been generally recognized and agreed upon as being pseudoscience by prestigious scientific bodies like the National Academy of Sciences. You're pretty safe in regarding alien abduction, astrology, ESP and psychics, facilitated communication, Scientology, Scientific Creationism, and Intelligent Design Creationism as pseudoscientific. Moreover, certain popular materials in the media are also pseudoscientific, including programs like *Ghost Hunters* and *Psychic Detectives*, as well as books like *The Secret*.

If a belief does not claim to be science, though, then it is not fair to label it pseudoscience. Most mainstream religious or spiritual beliefs like Buddhism, Protestant or Catholic

Christianity, Hinduism, Islam, and Judaism are not pseudoscientific, because they don't declare that they can be proven scientifically, even though they admit to being concerned with spirituality or the supernatural.

Directions: Answer the following prompts on a separate sheet of paper.

1. In your own words, explain the difference between science and pseudoscience.
2. Using the Internet, research either *Homeopathy* or *Facilitated Communication*. Determine whether to classify the one you choose as pseudoscience or science. Explain your decision.

Real-World Mistakes of Analysis and Their Consequences

Now that we've learned what it means to analyze, let's take a look at the very real dangers of failing to analyze.

On March 28, 1979, the entire northeastern seaboard of the United States came within half an hour of becoming a radioactive wasteland. It started as a normal day at Three Mile Island in Harrisburg, Pennsylvania, and because the reactor operators had no reason to suspect anything, they were running the nuclear reactor in Unit 2 at 97 percent of full power. Then the problems began. Two maintenance men accidentally allowed water to seep into the condensed air lines, causing the system to automatically shut the valves that let coolant through to the reactor. This caused the reactor to begin to overheat, and the water already inside the reactor, cooling it, turned to steam, increasing the pressure in the pipes. A failsafe mechanism designed to vent the steam and head off an explosion inexplicably got stuck open. Steam began gushing out of the tank, and with it, the water intended to cool the reactor. However, the rising steam, because of a technical malfunction, caused the gauges in the reactor control room to indicate that the coolant level in the reactor was rising when in fact it was falling. Fighting to prevent a steam explosion, the operators began to shut off some of the emergency coolant supply to the reactor. Of course, the reactor then got hotter, creating more steam, and thus causing the water level to appear even higher.

Now the operators were panicking. It seemed that the reactor was growing hotter and hotter, approaching a melt-down, while the coolant level went higher and higher. It didn't make sense. So they shut off the coolant entirely—the worst possible thing they could have done. And of course the problem got worse. Instead of taking the time to stop and analyze the clues they had, the TMI operators doggedly maintained their conclusion that the reactor was going to explode because it had too much coolant. At one point, at least fifty engineers stood in the control room, all trying to keep the reactor from getting more coolant—coolant that, in reality, it desperately needed. A disaster potentially as large as Chernobyl was minutes from occurring.

That's when a shift supervisor named Brian Mehler arrived on the scene. He used a technique the other fifty managers weren't using—calm analysis. He took a few minutes to examine the clues he had. He saw that it was getting hot in the containment building, which would indicate a steam leak. He also saw that the line temperature near the valve was higher than it should be. And he noticed that the pressure in the system was abnormally low, which shouldn't be the case if the coolant level was rising. Because he studied these subtle hints, he was able to reach the correct conclusion: That the reactor was actually very *low* on coolant. He ordered that the tank with the leaking valve be closed and

isolated from the piping. Some much needed coolant water was thereby able to accumulate, and the disaster was partially prevented, though the reactor still melted halfway down, releasing dangerous radiation and ultimately costing more than $975 million dollars to clean up.

Luckily for those who live on the East Coast, the incident at Three Mile Island did not lead to a total failure of analysis. One person successfully analyzed the situation. However, it does illustrate the potentially horrifying costs of not analyzing a dangerous situation correctly, and it also demonstrates the power of intelligent, thoughtful analysis.

For Discussion

1. Explain how the incident at Three Mile Island discussed above qualifies as a failure of analysis.

2. What actions could the plant operators have taken to analyze the situation better and solve the problem earlier?

Real-World Successes of Critical Thinking

The Apgar Score

You just learned about a near-catastrophic failure of critical thinking, but critical thinking can also be used to succeed. Dr. Virginia Apgar, an anesthesiologist, invented the Apgar Score, a method to assess the overall health of newborns.

Directions: Using the Internet or a library, research the Apgar Score in depth. Prepare a detailed description of how Dr. Apgar succeeded in developing the Apgar Score, including an explanation of any skills, character traits, and standards of critical thinking that contributed to her success. Get ready to share your findings with the class.

THINK AND WRITE CRITICALLY

Chapter Summary

- *Analysis* is the process of breaking something into pieces and examining how those pieces function alone and together. Applying this skill to reading texts generally involves identifying arguments and then analyzing them based on the evidence provided, the conclusions reached, and the strength of the logic used to tie the evidence to the conclusions.

- Being *skeptical* is necessary when evaluating arguments. Skepticism means having doubt and reserving judgment about a claim until you have looked at the evidence in support of it. Notably, you should be skeptical when evaluating *extraordinary claims*.

- An *argument* is a claim backed up by one or more reasons for believing the claim to be true.

- *Evidence* is support offered for a conclusion. The four main *types of evidence* are analogies, facts and statistics, testimony, and hypotheticals.

- There are two major forms of *logic* (the reasoning of an argument): *Inductive reasoning* involves drawing a general conclusion from specific pieces of evidence; *deductive reasoning* involves using a generalization to draw a specific conclusion; syllogisms are the classic form of deductive reasoning.

- *Argument mapping* is a way to graphically represent how the premises support the conclusion of an argument.

- *A pattern of organization* is the method the author uses to present the evidence and to arrange it logically so as to support the claim most effectively. The major patterns are cause/effect, chronological, classification, comparison/contrast, definition, example, listing, and mixed.

- *The scientific method,* a system by which scientists test and reject hypotheses, is how scientists discover truths and laws about the material world. *Pseudoscience* is a belief or endeavor that pretends to be scientific but isn't.

READ, WRITE, AND THINK CRITICALLY: SECTION TWO

Directions: Survey the following text and answer the questions below. Then, read and annotate the selection, and answer the questions that follow.

1. What is your prior knowledge of this topic?

   _____

   _____

   _____

2. Read the title and first paragraph and make a prediction about the content of the article.

   _____

   _____

   _____

Ghost Hunting Tools of the Trade

Brian Dunning

Brian Dunning is an author, writer, and skeptic. He has produced two films about critical thinking and science, but he is primarily known for the website Skeptoid, *where the following article appeared in 2008.*

1 Television shows about ghost hunting have been popular for over 50 years, and though the basic concept is the same, recent decades have seen the hunt become less about psychics and **séances** and more about electronic detection gear. Just about every TV show about ghost hunting sends a crew of investigators into a building, armed to the teeth with all sorts of equipment.

2 The use of any kind of measuring equipment to detect ghosts is fundamentally, and completely, bogus. How can I make a blanket statement like that? Measuring equipment detects what it is designed to detect, whether that's light, heat, **electromagnetism**, or whatever. Thus it will only detect things that emit measurable amounts of those energies. For us as viewers to accept that some piece of handheld measuring equipment has a useful function in detecting a ghost, we must base our acceptance on the premise that ghosts are known to emit those types of energies in measurable amounts. If there were any truth to this, science would have discovered it long ago. Hospital operating rooms would have ghost detection equipment built in. Mortuaries and crematoriums would have ghost detection equipment at the top of their list. Search and rescue crews would use ghost detection equipment. If ghosts did exist and were detectable, you can bet that there would be huge industries behind it. I can't think of anything that would attract more venture capital dollars from Silicon Valley. However, no **rigorous** research has ever shown that ghosts can be reliably detected with hardware. It's easy to disbelieve me, but it's much harder to disbelieve the lack of interest from greedy corporate America.

Dunning, B. "Ghost Hunting Tools of the Trade." *Skeptoid Podcast*, Skeptoid Media, 1 Jan 2008. Web. 14 May 2018. <http://skeptoid.com/episodes/4081>. Reprinted by permission.

3   So now let's look at the popular tools of the trade of ghost hunting. The important takeaway is to understand what these devices are actually detecting when the ghost hunters point them around the room, and why their crazily jumping needles and indicators are perfectly consistent with, and explained by, the *absence* of ghosts.

4   **Infrared thermometers** are the most blatantly misused of the ghost hunting tools, so are a great place to start. These handheld devices measure the temperature of the object they are pointed at. They work exactly like your vision, except that they are sensitive to far infrared instead of the visible spectrum. They measure surface temperatures, just like your vision measures surface colors. If you can see something, an IR thermometer can measure its temperature. However, ghost hunters use these devices to detect what they believe are cold spots in rooms. IR thermometers are not capable of detecting something without a visible surface. In fact, an IR thermometer is even less likely than your vision to see a hazy apparition. Firefighters use infrared because the longer wavelengths of **infrared** penetrate smoke more effectively than the shorter wavelength of visible light; so if there *were* a hazy invisible apparition floating in the middle of the room, infrared is perhaps the *worst* technology to detect it. Variations of IR readings inside a room are merely showing temperature gradations on the walls, caused by heating and AC, insulation variances, studs, wiring, or pipes behind the wall, radiant heat, recent proximity of another ghost hunter, sunlight, temperatures in adjacent rooms, or countless other causes.

5   **Infrared motion detectors** work on the same principle. If the amount of IR radiation striking the sensor changes, an alarm can be activated. Such a change is caused by a sudden change in temperature within the detector's field of view, or a significant movement by an object with a visible IR signature. A ghostly cold spot moving within a room could not be detected, unless it also cooled the walls or floors enough to trip the activation threshold.

6   **Particle detectors** are devices that measure ionizing radiation. The most common particle detectors are Geiger counters, also called halogen counters. These work by measuring cascade effects caused by incoming particles that strike molecules of halogen gas inside the detection chamber. Typically, alpha, beta, and gamma particles are detected by these. It's not the most common of ghost hunting tools, but occasionally you will see someone pointing a Geiger counter around the room, though you may hear them describe it by any of several fancier and more high-tech sounding names. It's a Geiger counter. For a ghost to emit ionizing radiation, it would have to be an awfully sick ghost; or be composed largely of unstable radioactive metals. Ionizing particles don't just appear out of thin air, they are emitted by the decay of unstable isotopes that are typically heavy and have significant mass.

7   **EMF meters** are perhaps the favorite tools. EMF meters detect electromagnetic fields, and are used in ghost hunting on the premise that ghosts emit electromagnetism, though this claim is rarely supported by any suggestion of what the power source might be. There are many different types of EMF meters. More affordable units, such as those typically used by television performers, need to be held precisely for a period of time at each of the three axis to get a reading, and so they are clearly not used on television in a manner that would produce any useful result. When they are, or when a more expensive three-axis meter is used, they are designed to detect the operation of electrical appliances or wiring. Ghost hunters are usually thoroughly accessorized with every electronic gizmo under the sun: radios, cell phones, flashlights, cameras, TV cameras, and other ghost hunting accessories; and all of these will produce a result on the EMF meter. Building wiring or appliances will also be detected. But, even in an environment with no electrical devices at all, the presence of the TV camera alone renders the EMF readings totally useless. Even without ghost hunting equipment, electrical wiring, or a TV camera, a sensitive meter can even detect the oscillation of a steel filing cabinet vibrated imperceptibly by footsteps. In the midst of all the absurd amounts of EMF pollution on a TV ghost hunting set, the pretense that the alleged EMF field of a ghost (who's not carrying any batteries) can be identified, is foolish.

8   **Ion detectors** are interesting animals. The few commercially available ion detectors are available online almost exclusively through ghost hunting and alternative wellness websites, which gives some clue of how useful they actually are. Ions occur naturally in the atmosphere from a variety of sources: solar radiation and weather being the main ones. Also, if you go to a part of the country where radon gas is an issue, an ion detector taken into the basement can go crazy sensing airborne ions created by radon decay. Ghost hunters prefer to regard this reading as indicative of the presence of a ghost. Ion detectors can also sense the presence of static

electricity, so if your ghost is carrying a large static charge, you ought to be able to see it scuffing its shoes across the carpet.

9   **Cameras** of different types are used by ghost hunters. Sometimes they'll take a conventional visible spectrum camera and snap away, in the hope that spirit orbs or other manifestations will appear on the processed film. Since this phenomenon has already been thoroughly discussed in our episode on orbs, there's no need to repeat it here. Suffice it to say that all such images are well established artifacts of photography and of cameras, and well understood by knowledgeable photographers. They happen every day in photographs that have nothing to do with ghosts. Near infrared photography is the **monochromatic** "night shot" video that you see all the time, and that your home video camera probably offers. The light source is an infrared bulb on the camera, similar to the invisible light source inside your TV remote. These cameras record only what near infrared light is reflected from the subject, and of course they also record other near infrared sources, which are relatively common. Far infrared photography is the thermal imaging discussed previously. It's simply a visual display of the same heat sources detected by IR thermometers and motion detectors.

10   **Dowsing rods** are probably the least controversial of ghost hunting tools, in that increasingly few people accept that they have any useful function. Yet ghost hunters still employ them. And why not? A self-described psychic's untestable verbal reports are under the psychic's complete control. They cannot be tested, measured, or duplicated by others—they say only exactly whatever the psychic wants to say. **Dowsing** rods simply give the dowsers another way to communicate whatever they choose to communicate. Since the rods are held in the dowser's own hand, they move only when the dowser wants them to move, and do not move when the dowser doesn't want them to. No form of dowsing has ever passed any type of controlled test, and no dowser has ever proposed any plausible hypothesis suggesting that dowsing might be an actual phenomenon. It is among the most childish of pretended ghost detection methods. The only thing you can learn from dowsing is which way the dowser wants to swing his dowsing rods.

11   **Audio recording gear** is used when the ghost hunter hopes that EVP, or electronic voice phenomena, will appear on the recording. EVP's are discussed often enough to warrant their own Skeptoid episode, and we'll be discussing them in detail in the future. An EVP is said to be the voice of a ghost, and the claim is that ghosts can talk perfectly well but can only be heard on an electronic recording. This means that recording gear has the ability to convert inaudible frequencies into audible ones. Engineers do not design this capability into most recording gear, since a change of frequency of perhaps tens of thousands of hertz would render all recordings completely useless and horrible to listen to. So, like they tend to do with all the electronic gear they carry, ghost hunters completely misunderstand, misuse, and mischaracterize the functions of these instruments.

12   When you turn on the television and you watch people pointing their gizmos around the room, acting all dramatic and pretending to detect ghosts all around them, any intelligent adult should laugh out loud. Or better yet, change the channel. Of course an intelligent adult should be free to watch whatever they want, and that's fine—but one place I will draw the line is the point where you let your children watch one of those shows and allow them to accept the silly claims as fact. Watch it and enjoy it as entertainment, if you find those people truly engaging and clever enough to be entertaining; but please, explain to your kids the science behind what they're seeing. Or, as the case may be, the lack of science behind it.

3. Use context clues and/or a dictionary to define the following words (marked in bold in the reading).

a. Séances (para. 1): _____

b. Electromagnetism (para. 2): _____

c. Rigorous (para. 2): _____

d. Infrared (para. 6): _____

e. Monochromatic (para. 9): _____

f. Dowsing (para. 10): _____

4. What is the author's claim? How do you know?

_____

_____

_____

5. Does anything about this passage (i.e., language, tone) indicate bias on behalf of the author?

_____

_____

_____

6. What evidence does the author give to support his claim? For each piece of evidence you identify, indicate its type.

_____

_____

_____

7. What assumptions underlie the author's arguments?

_____

_____

_____

8. Do you find the author's argument convincing? Why or why not?

_____

_____

_____

CHAPTER 7

Evaluation

Learning Goals

In this chapter you will learn how to

➤ Define Evaluation   SECTION ONE
➤ Be Fair-Minded
➤ Evaluate Arguments
➤ Evaluate Evidence
➤ Evaluate Source and Author Credibility
➤ Evaluate Assumptions   SECTION TWO
➤ Evaluate Logic of Deductive and Inductive Arguments
➤ Use Argument Maps in Evaluation

PREVIEW OF TERMS

Evaluation p. 221
Fair-mindedness p. 222
Counter-argument p. 226
Relevance p. 227
Irrelevance p. 227
Sufficiency p. 229
Fact p. 230
Opinion p. 230
Personal opinion p. 230
Reasoned judgment p. 231
Accuracy p. 232
Antecedent p. 247
Consequent p. 247
Modus ponens p. 247
Modus tollens p. 247
Fallacy p. 251
See glossary, pp. 391–397

SECTION ONE

What Is Evaluation?

Have you ever walked out of a movie or turned one off because it was bad? Why was it so bad? Was it full of plot holes, cheesy dialogue, or cheap special effects? How did you decide you didn't like it? You evaluated it according to the standards set by movies you've liked in the past.

When you use the skill of **evaluation,** you judge something to see if it is worthwhile, good, or effective. Your professors evaluate you when they grade your work, for example. Evaluation is one of the most important skills in critical thinking—in fact, it lies at the heart of critical thinking, because critical thinking is a process used to make good decisions or to form beliefs that are more likely to be true; in other words, critical thinking is a way to evaluate beliefs and decisions.

Much like analysis, evaluation is used differently depending on the field. Electrical engineers need to evaluate plans and equipment to make sure that they are safe and won't break down, military personnel need to judge whether their plan of attack or defense is likely to work, and doctors and nurses need to appraise their treatment options to determine which will be most effective in making their patients healthy. Critical readers, of course, need to use the skill of evaluation to determine if authors and evidence are credible and if the arguments they read are good or bad; critical writers are engaged in a process of evaluation when they are writing essays.

Remember that the skill of evaluating arguments is not just useful when you're reading a text or writing an essay. As we noted earlier in the book, arguments are everywhere (salespeople try to convince you to buy products by making an argument, politicians try to persuade you through argumentation to vote for them, and your friends present arguments to you about how you should spend your time). So learning to evaluate arguments is crucial. First, though, you need to know about an important attitude that relates to the skill of evaluation: fair-mindedness.

Reviewing the Critical Thinker's Traits: Being Fair-Minded

Context Clues

If you do not know what the word *gullibility* means, use the vocabulary skills relating to context clues that you learned in Chapter 2 to figure out its meaning.

In Chapter 6, you read about Wyatt, who lacked skepticism. Meet Nicole. Unlike Wyatt, who was gullible, she has no problems with gullibility and considers herself a skilled evaluator.

Nicole rarely believes anything without extensive proof. In fact, she has strong views on most subjects, and she finds the arguments of her opponents fairly easy to pick apart. For example, Nicole enjoys smoking, and she hates to be told where to smoke. Her family and friends have repeatedly asked her not to smoke in their presence, but they cannot convince her that passive smoking is unhealthy. Even though she has read many scientific studies that concluded it is, Nicole is very skilled at finding fault with them. Woe to the person who tries to argue with her or defend such research, because Nicole can cite several studies favorable to her position that conclude that second-hand smoke is harmless. Knowing these studies inside and out, Nicole believes they are nearly flawless in terms of logic and method. Never mind that her friends can point out what seem to be statistical errors or that her favorite studies were sponsored by cigarette companies. No, Nicole "knows" herself to be a logical thinker, so she continues to smoke around her family. . . .

> "Fairness is what justice really is."
>
> —Potter Stewart

In Chapter 6 you learned how to be skeptical about what other people write or say (see pp. 188–190). To be a successful critical thinker, you need to apply the same standard of skepticism to your own views. This is called being fair-minded. **Fair-mindedness** (treating all ideas and arguments with equal consideration) helps you to come to good conclusions, gives every argument a decent chance at gaining your approval, helps you evaluate texts fairly and write fairly, and helps keep your worldview and biases from clouding your judgment. Fair-mindedness is what Nicole *lacks* in the above example.

Did you ever notice that if a stranger cuts you off in traffic, you think that person is a real jerk, while if you or a friend of yours cuts someone off in traffic it is simply a mistake that anyone could make? Similarly, it is common practice, and very human, to "go easy" on those arguments that support ideas you want to believe, while applying a more rigorous and critical standard to those arguments you do not want to be true.

Being fair-minded is related to being open-minded, but there are some

Thinker to Emulate: Sonia Sotomayor

An effective judge must put personal biases aside while weighing evidence and abiding by the law. Supreme Court Justice Sonia Sotomayor (b. 6/25/54) achieved the highest position in the U.S. judiciary system in part due to being a critical thinker. Her career included work as a prosecutor and Assistant District Attorney in Manhattan, and the challenging cases she presided over demanded fair-mindedness.

Source: Congress.gov

One of her most famous rulings came after being appointed to the U.S. District Court for the Southern District of New York by President George H.W. Bush when she essentially ended the Major League Baseball strike of 1995. In 1998, appointed to the U.S. Court of Appeals by President Bill Clinton, Sotomayor was known for her fair and practical application of the law. On May 26, 2009, Sotomayor was nominated to the Supreme Court by President Barack Obama, and she was confirmed on August 6, 2009.

definite differences. As discussed in Chapter 4, *open-mindedness* involves a willingness to consider other people's ideas; *fair-mindedness* means treating other people's ideas the same way you treat your own. To be fair-minded, you have to control some of those things that tend to get in the way of critical thinking, such as confirmation bias (see Chapter 1). Typically, once people have a point of view, they tend to twist new evidence to fit that point of view and ignore or discount evidence that proves them wrong. Since these kinds of biases are common to everyone, they can be very difficult to overcome, but critical thinkers like Supreme Court Justice Sonia Sotomayor are committed to fair-mindedness. Here are some tips.

> ### Confirmation Bias
> Confirmation bias is the tendency to pay attention to information that supports what we already believe and to ignore or downplay information that might prove us wrong.

Tips for Critical Thinkers: How to Be Fair-Minded (as illustrated in Figure 7-1)

- **Accurately restate the other person's viewpoint using neutral language**. Do not make value judgments at this point. State the viewpoint in such a way that you feel the person expressing the view would not object to your characterization of what he or she has said. This step will help you make sure you understand what is actually being said. You cannot accurately criticize something unless you understand it.
- **When considering an argument or viewpoint that you disagree with, start by looking for its strong points**. Note good points it makes, good evidence it provides, and good logic it employs.
- **Try to place yourself in the mindset of the person expressing the viewpoint**. Ask yourself what could cause a person to hold such a view. Don't distort or misrepresent his or her beliefs and desires. Don't minimize his or her experiences and views. Your goal here is to identify with the person stating the argument—to empathize with him or her.
- **Stay humble by reminding yourself of the times you have been wrong in the past**. Think of things that you were sure about that you later found out were wrong. Doing this will help you keep in mind that it is quite possible that the person on the other side of the issue could be right in the current situation, or at the very least could have some valuable insights into the issue at hand.

> ### Straw Man
> The straw man **fallacy** (mistake in an argument) involves distorting an opponent's argument in order to make it easier to disprove. See p. 254.

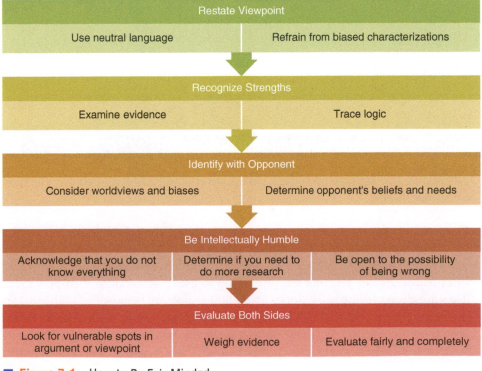

■ **Figure 7-1**   How to Be Fair-Minded

- **Be prepared to look for weak spots in the opposing viewpoint or argument using the evaluation skill you will learn in this chapter.**

Another way to develop a more fair-minded attitude is to practice adopting viewpoints you disagree with and attempting to argue in favor of them. When you do this, remember to argue fairly and logically, as you would expect those who actually advocate a particular viewpoint would do. The following two exercises provide practice in fairly treating claims and arguments that you might disagree with, rather than rejecting them out of hand.

PRACTICE 7-1   Practicing Being Fair-Minded

Directions: Choose one of the following topics. Then critically write an essay in which you accurately and fairly state one of the main arguments people who advocate the opposite position to yours on the topic would make to support their position. Finally, give one or more good reasons why their argument could be correct. Complete this exercise on another sheet of paper.

Here's a model
Euthanasia

I am personally inclined to think that euthanasia is wrong. Those who feel it is right, however, argue that a terminally ill patient should be able to end his or her own life. They feel that every individual should be free to choose whether his or her life is worth living and that free choice is what a democracy is based on. They also state that the suffering undergone by people with terminal illnesses might be so bad that forcing them to continue living is like torturing them. Their argument could be correct, because it might be impossible to know the intense pain these people are in, and that might make it morally wrong for someone who is not in such pain to dictate anything to a person who is.

Now you try

1. Gun-control
2. Abortion
3. Using torture to extract information from suspected terrorists
4. Prayer in schools
5. Mandatory vaccinations

PRACTICE 7-2   Detecting Problems with Fair-Mindedness

Directions: This passage provides a biased viewpoint. Read it and answer the questions that follow.

Gun control advocates say they simply want society to be safer, but that's a lie. What they really want is to take firearms away from decent, honest citizens and leave the guns in the hands of criminals. They won't stop until the entire world is at the mercy of armed bad guys. The tool they are trying to use to accomplish their goal is fear. They are always telling scary stories about how people are being killed with guns and how a gun in the home actually makes you less safe because an angry spouse or careless child might find it. But make no mistake, if you gave up your guns, these control fanatics would want you to give up axes, hedge trimmers, and kitchen knives next.

Gun control advocates have mastered the art of twisting words around to make them fit their agenda. That's clear, because they are so great at twisting words and manipulating language. It's what they use to get what they want. They are always upset about something, and they twist their opponents' words into gibberish. And they are totally unreasonable. Trying to reason with a gun control advocate is like trying to negotiate with a rabid dog.

Gun control advocates have it out for honest gun owners. They have made it such that going hunting or taking your firearm to an indoor gun range for an afternoon of relaxing target shooting is dangerous. They will call you a "gun nut" and tarnish your reputation so that people start giving you dirty looks. Then they will start spouting off stupid statistics about how the murder rate is lower in countries with stricter gun regulations or some such nonsense, and if you try to calmly talk to them about how disarming this country would simply take the guns away from good people and leave them in the hands of bad people, they will probably start shouting at you and questioning your intelligence.

Maybe we should just give the gun control people what they want and pass laws so that no one can own guns. And then we can sit back and watch the country fall apart as more people start getting robbed and killed by the criminals who didn't give up their guns. On second thought, scratch that. They would just start saying it was somehow our fault for not keeping them safer.

Now you respond

1. What characteristics of the passage indicate unfairness? For example, what specific words and phrases suggest the author is biased?

   _____

   _____

   _____

   _____

2. Put yourself in the mindset of the author. What worldview do you imagine might have prompted the author to make such an argument? Does that worldview excuse the author's bias?

   _____

   _____

   _____

   _____

Internet Activity

Research the Thinker to Emulate Sonia Sotomayor on the Internet and then answer the questions below. You can start your search on the following websites:

   www.loc.gov/law/find/sotomayor.php
   http://www.supremecourt.gov/about/biographies.aspx

1. What does her biography suggest about what may have influenced her worldview?
2. Pick one of her court rulings to research in-depth. What do you think of the ruling? Was she fair-minded? Explain your answer.

Evaluating Arguments

Once you've committed to being fair-minded, you are in a position to evaluate an argument according to the standards of critical thinkers to determine if it is strong or not. A strong argument must have the following characteristics:

- **It uses good evidence**. Often knowing about the source of the evidence will help you determine if it's good or not.

Reminder: Evidence typically fits into one of these four categories: (1) testimony, (2) facts and statistics, (3) analogies, and (4) hypotheticals; each type requires careful evaluation.

  - **It is based on warranted assumptions**. The beliefs underlying the argument have to be plausible.
  - **It uses good logic**. If it's a deductive argument, it must be valid; if it's an inductive argument, it should avoid inductive fallacies.
  - **It isn't proved wrong (refuted) by any counter-arguments**.

A **counter-argument** is an argument used to refute another argument. There is no real difference between an argument and a counter-argument, except in the way a counter-argument is used—it is designed to prove the original argument wrong. If a counter-argument is presented, you need to evaluate both the initial argument and the counter-argument to determine which one is stronger. Remember that just because a counter-argument is given, it doesn't mean that the original argument has been refuted; a challenge is not a refutation.

As you measure your belief in various claims, strong, logical evidence is what should move your thinking away from a neutral "3." If the claim lacks evidence, then you might measure the belief as being "definitely not true." On the other hand, if you read or hear compelling evidence, then your own thinking might move closer to believing the belief is "definitely true."

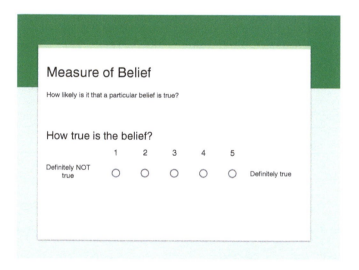

In the remainder of this chapter, you will learn to evaluate arguments by determining if the evidence given to support them is strong enough, if the source the evidence comes from is reliable, if the assumptions are warranted, and if the logic used is good.

Evaluating Evidence

As you learned in Chapter 6 (see p. 192), an *argument* is a conclusion backed up by evidence, and evidence comes in many forms and from many sources. Evaluating the reliability of evidence allows you to evaluate the reliability of an entire argument.

When you evaluate evidence, you need to take a close look at the following considerations:

- Is it relevant?
- Is it sufficient?
- Is it made up primarily of facts, opinions, or reasoned judgments?
- Is it accurate?

Determine Relevance

Evidence should be **relevant** to the conclusion—meaning that it closely and directly relates to and supports the conclusion. When evidence is **irrelevant**, it's unimportant and unrelated. Sometimes authors will introduce irrelevant evidence, either on purpose to throw their readers off track (see red herring fallacy on p. 254) or by accident because they are unsure about what constitutes good, logical, relevant evidence.

Consider the following argument:

You go to your boss to ask for a raise. The reasons (evidence) you give for deserving a raise include improved sales figures since you started, several letters from both customers and managers that praise your performance, and a list of classes you have attended on your own time. Just as you see your boss nodding approvingly, you blurt out, "Plus, the rent is going up at my apartment complex!" His expression changes and, suddenly, your formerly solid argument falters. You have introduced irrelevant evidence, which has caused your boss to think you are only providing reasons for a raise because you need the money, not because you deserve one based on your job performance.

In addition to evaluating an argument to see if it includes irrelevant evidence, as a critical thinker you need to recognize when an argument has *left out relevant evidence*. This can happen when the person making an argument does not want to include evidence that might weaken his or her case. Seeking out opinions from assorted sources can help you verify that an argument neither includes irrelevant evidence nor omits relevant evidence.

Each type of evidence—*testimonials, facts and statistics, analogies*, and *hypotheticals*—can have problems related to relevance, as you can see below and as you will see later in the chapter as you learn about logical fallacies.

> ### Spotlight on Standards: Relevance
>
> **Relevance** is an important standard of critical thinkers. Critical thinkers always ask themselves how what they are reading, writing, or evaluating is logically connected to the issue or argument at hand. Critical thinkers refuse to allow themselves to be distracted from important issues by information that has no bearing on it. If you have ever asked someone, "How does that relate?" or declared, "I don't see why that matters," you have shown yourself to be concerned with relevance.

- **Testimonials.** Advertisements that use testimonials depend on the audience being swayed by the image of a celebrity, yet the celebrity's success in sports, movies, or music is usually irrelevant to the quality of the product being sold.
- **Facts and Statistics.** As you learned in Chapter 6, facts and statistics can be quite compelling, but if they are irrelevant to the argument they will not be persuasive. For example, a real estate agent could try to convince a home buyer to purchase a particular house by quoting the local school system's strong test scores, but if the home buyer doesn't have children, then that evidence is irrelevant to the buyer's decision.
- **Analogies.** An analogy draws comparisons between two subjects, so if the similarities are irrelevant or insignificant, then the analogy should fail to convince you. If you tried to make the argument that cats should be walked like dogs, since cats are four-legged, furry house pets just like dogs are, you would be leaving out the significant differences between cats and dogs. The analogy would be weak.
- **Hypotheticals.** Hypotheticals can also include irrelevant information or omit relevant information. Imagine you are considering cheating on a math test, but one of your friends gives you lots of reasons not to do it. Hypothetically, he says, you could get caught, fail the class, and lose the teacher's respect. Plus, he says, you

wouldn't know how to do the problems when you got to a higher level math class. If, however, you didn't plan on taking any more math classes, then that hypothetical reason is irrelevant to your decision.

PRACTICE 7-3   Determining Relevance

Directions: The conclusions below are followed by four pieces of evidence, but only three pieces of evidence are actually relevant to the conclusion. Put an X next to the evidence that is irrelevant.

Here's a model

Conclusion: People probably do not have paranormal abilities.

_____ Evidence 1: James Randi's challenge (now promising to award $1,000,000) has been in existence since 1964, yet still no one has been able to prove that he/she has paranormal powers.

__X__ Evidence 2: The majority of people report that they believe in ESP and other paranormal abilities.

_____ Evidence 3: One of the most famous psychics, Uri Geller, claimed to have proof of his abilities but was actually shown to be a fraud.

_____ Evidence 4: Most people who claim to have paranormal abilities will flat-out refuse even to try to prove it: instead, they get out of proving their claims by saying that their "gifts" are "beyond scientific study" or are "above scrutiny" and that believers simply "must have faith."

Now you try

1. Conclusion: Scientific illiteracy is a serious problem in the United States.

_____ Evidence 1: The vast majority of high school graduates do not understand how the word *theory* in science differs from the casual use of the word *theory*, and this can cause them to misunderstand the importance of such theories as the Big Bang Theory and the Theory of Evolution by Natural Selection.

_____ Evidence 2: A recent poll shows that the number of graduates who feel that they have a "good" or "excellent" grasp of science has plummeted in the last decade.

_____ Evidence 3: Studies show that not only is scientific illiteracy a problem but so is math illiteracy.

_____ Evidence 4: Adults who do not have a good grasp of scientific topics may make dangerous decisions such as the decision not to vaccinate their children or the decision to rely on alternative or dubious medicine.

2. Conclusion: Social media sites help users feel a greater connection with their peers.

_____ Evidence 1: An interesting point to come out of a 2010 study is that a large percentage of Facebook users will log on first thing in the morning, even before using the bathroom or getting a cup of coffee!

_____ Evidence 2: Teens report a lower incidence of depression and loneliness after spending time on a social media site.

_____ Evidence 3: Among teenagers and adults who were polled about their Facebook habits, the vast majority said that they felt the site fostered a sense of community.

_____ Evidence 4: Family members and friends who move far away value the ability to stay connected to loved ones back home, even if it just means seeing photos and postings from them online.

3. Conclusion: Everyone should learn a second language.

_____ Evidence 1: Dr. Andrew Weil's book *Healthy Aging* looks at how learning a foreign language could decrease your chances of suffering from Alzheimer's disease and other memory loss.

_____ Evidence 2: Children who learn another language perform markedly better in all academic areas.

_____ Evidence 3: Lots of famous people know more than one language.

_____ Evidence 4: Knowing a second language can increase your chances of getting into college or landing your dream job.

EXPAND YOUR UNDERSTANDING

Directions: With a partner, look at item 3 from exercise 6–9 on p. 208. Identify each piece of evidence in the argument, then evaluate each piece to see if it is relevant, noting the type of evidence and any problems with relevance.

Verify Sufficiency

Sufficiency means having enough evidence to successfully support a particular argument. As a critical thinker, you must ask yourself if there is enough evidence to support a specific conclusion. There is no magic number; some arguments are compelling with just one or two reasons; others require dozens of reasons to be convincing. You need to evaluate every argument individually to see if it has enough evidence to be convincing.

As you just learned, extraordinary claims require extraordinary evidence. That means the more unusual or spectacular the claim, the more evidence you should demand to support it. If a friend claims to have lost 10 pounds, a pretty ordinary claim, then you would not need a lot of evidence (at most, if you were really skeptical, you might want to see his "before" and "after" weight totals on a scale, or it might be enough evidence to see that his clothes are fitting loosely). If a friend claims to have been abducted by aliens and subjected to bizarre reproductive experiments, you would require a lot of evidence before you would be able to believe such an extraordinary story.

On p. 253, you will read about the fallacy of hasty generalization, which is a mistake in reasoning that occurs when you jump to a conclusion from a small sample of evidence. For example, if you only ever owned one laptop and its hard drive crashed six months after purchase, you would not have enough evidence to conclude that "all laptops are a waste of money": This would be a hasty generalization. You would need a much larger sample size before you could make a conclusion about laptops in general. The fallacy of hasty generalization is committed when you draw a conclusion from evidence that is not sufficient to support it.

Remember to be fair when judging sufficiency: It is not fair to demand a tremendous amount of evidence to support a conclusion you don't agree with yet require very little evidence for a conclusion that you believe is correct.

EXPAND YOUR UNDERSTANDING

Write Critically about Claims

Directions: With a partner, consider the claim that "the Loch Ness Monster is real." Write an essay wherein you explain what evidence would be sufficient to prove this claim.

Telling Apart Fact, Opinion, and Reasoned Judgment

Reminder: In Chapter 3 you learned to highlight emotive words in a passage to gain insight into the author's opinion (see p. 68).

Crucial to your ability to evaluate evidence is your ability to distinguish facts from opinions. When making an argument, authors and speakers rely on both facts and opinions to gain agreement from their audience. A **fact** is a statement that can be objectively verified, meaning that it can be checked out and found to be true by anyone, whatever their personal feelings or biases about it. Here is a list of facts:

- The kelvin is a unit of temperature; 0 kelvin is −273.15 degrees Celsius and −459.4 degrees Fahrenheit.
- John Keats, one of the Romantic poets, only lived to age 25.
- The U.S. Census takes place every 10 years in order to allocate congressional seats, electoral votes, and federal funds to government-run programs.

Each of these facts can be objectively verified in a variety of reference resources. They were derived from observation, experimentation, and historical documentation. Personal feelings about the kelvin, John Keats, or the U.S. Census will not affect the truth of each of these statements.

Reminder: Facts are defined on p.197 of Chapter 6 as one type of evidence.

An **opinion** is a judgment about something. There are two kinds of opinions: personal opinions and informed opinions. A **personal opinion** is a statement that other people might disagree with, meaning that others may apply their own personal interpretations and come to varied conclusions about the same information. Often personal opinions deal with matters of taste. Consider these personal opinions:

- Learning about kelvins in high school science classes was just a big waste of time.
- John Keats was a better poet than Lord Byron.
- The U.S. Census is an underhanded ploy to learn private information about American citizens, so you should consider ignoring it.

Each of these opinions expresses a personal interpretation. Other people thinking about kelvins, Keats, and the Census might have different feelings, beliefs, and attitudes about these topics. The opinions expressed above cannot be verified objectively, nor would they appear in reputable reference sources.

Something else to notice about personal opinions is that they often contain emotive words (see Figure 3-2 on p. 67). Emotive words take the following forms: superlatives (most, best), aesthetic (wonderful, fine), judgment (good, wrong), and recommendation (should, ought to). In the examples above, emotive words and phrases include "big waste of time," "better," "underhanded," and "should."

Sometimes it's difficult to tell a fact from a personal opinion. Skilled writers can make personal opinions sound like facts simply by claiming that they are ("It's a fact that baseball is more entertaining than football") or by using a very decisive tone ("It's undisputed that rap is better than rock"). Also, sometimes part of a sentence may contain a fact and another part of the same sentence might include a personal opinion (example: "The U.S. Civil War cost Americans the greatest number of casualties, and it inspired the best movie ever made,

Gone With the Wind"). It can be tricky to tell facts from personal opinions, yet evaluating evidence effectively will depend on it.

Directions: Use the phrases below to fill in the following chart to identify the differences between fact and personal opinion.

- Allows for personal judgment
- Can be objectively verified
- Consistently noted in multiple references
- May be confirmed through observation, experimentation, or historical documentation
- Open to subjective interpretation
- Various sources may provide contradictory ideas

Fact	Personal Opinion

The second type of opinion is **reasoned judgment** (also called *informed opinion*)—an opinion resulting from the research and experience of an expert in the field. This can also be referred to as *expert testimony* (see Chapter 6, p. 197). When you evaluate evidence, an informed opinion should carry more weight than the opinion of a non-expert. And often, informed opinions are necessary to help us understand what a body of facts means. For example, when Ben Bernanke, who served as Chairman of the Federal Reserve from 2006 to 2014, offers his opinion about the U.S. economy, you should take his statement quite seriously, more seriously than the opinion of a casual acquaintance who rants about finances whenever you run into him at the grocery store. Bernanke's expertise allowed him to examine the facts—that unemployment was increasing and the stock market falling, along with other data—and determine that the economy was heading toward a recession.

Tips for Critical Thinkers: Telling Fact from Opinion

- **Investigate potential "facts."** If an author uses a phrase like, "It's a proven fact that . . ." then you should research and see if that is, indeed, true.
- **Look for words that signal emotions**. Highlight or underline words that signal strong feelings such as superlatives, aesthetic values, judgment, and recommendation, but remember that the presence of these types of words does not guarantee a statement is an opinion.
- **Check reference books**. Facts can be easily accessed in a range of reference books whereas opinions cannot.
- **Carefully consider informed (expert) opinions**. An expert's opinion should be weighed more heavily than that of a non-expert. As with all evidence, evaluate the author and the source of the informed opinion to verify that it is, indeed, from a credible expert in the field.
- **Annotate the passage.** Label facts (F) and opinions (O). If a particular sentence includes both fact and opinion, label both parts accordingly.

PRACTICE 7-5   Identifying Facts and Opinions

Directions: Annotate the following statements and then label each F (fact), O (opinion), or B (both).

1. _____ The Pittsburgh Steelers have won the most number of Super Bowls as of 2015.
2. _____ An American city with considerable charm, Savannah, Georgia, was established in 1733.
3. _____ Michael Jackson's death on June 25, 2009, was the most devastating celebrity death since Elvis died August 16, 1977.
4. _____ Canada stretches from the Atlantic to the Pacific and shares a border with the United States.
5. _____ Everyone should try to visit at least one country in Asia such as Indonesia.
6. _____ The periodic table of elements is confusing unless you are an aspiring chemist.
7. _____ You would be better off downloading podcasts on iTunes than wasting time downloading music all day.
8. _____ Andrew Wyeth's paintings perfectly capture life in Pennsylvania.
9. _____ The children's program *Sesame Street* started running in 1969.
10. _____ Founded by Bill Gates, the Microsoft Corporation is more impressive than any of the other computer companies.

PRACTICE 7-6   Expand Your Understanding through Discussion

Directions: In pairs or small groups, discuss the following statements regarding "opinions." Focus on what you think a critical thinker would believe about each statement.

1. "Everyone is entitled to his or her opinion."
2. "That's just your opinion."
3. "Everyone's opinion is equal."
4. "Inconsistencies of opinion, arising from changes of circumstances, are often justifiable." (Daniel Webster, 1846)
5. "There never was in the world two opinions alike, no more than two hairs or two grains; the most universal quality is diversity." (Michel Eyquem, seigneur de Montaigne, 1533-1592)

Verify Accuracy

Accuracy means how correct information is. Evidence is not acceptable if it is inaccurate, so you will often need to double-check information in other sources to ensure it is true. Two types of evidence, *statistics* and *testimonials*, are especially vulnerable to inaccuracies.

Statistics can be misunderstood, manipulated, and falsely reported. When the pharmaceutical company Merck faced allegations that its drug Vioxx increased chances of having a heart attack, it instructed its salespeople to give concerned doctors a card "which claimed—falsely—that Vioxx was eight to eleven times safer than other similar painkillers" (Specter, 2009, p. 41). What makes statistics so difficult to evaluate is that different experts can look at the results of the same study and come up with different interpretations. Also, most of us do not have the ability or the means to replicate studies for ourselves (such as the alarming studies that resulted in Vioxx being pulled off the market), so we are at the mercy of the professionals and the companies that are responsible for such studies and statistics. What can you do in a situation like this? Well, you can look for statistics, or interpretations of statistics, from neutral parties—people and organizations that do not stand to lose or gain anything by the information they provide.

Testimonials, too, are subject to inaccuracies. Take, for example, a 1998 study about whether childhood vaccines caused autism. Dr. Andrew Wakefield's study supposedly identified a causal connection between the MMR vaccine and autism; however, "The study was severely flawed, has been thoroughly discredited, and eventually ten of its thirteen authors retracted their contributions" (Specter, 2009, pp. 61-62).

Many times, your best tool in evaluating accuracy is knowledge of the source's credibility.

EXPAND YOUR UNDERSTANDING

Directions: Using your library or the Internet, research the claim that aliens abduct humans. Find evidence provided by proponents of the claim. Now research further to see if the evidence given by alien abduction proponents is accurate. Prepare to share your findings with the class.

Evaluate Source and Author Credibility

Personally, academically, and professionally, you frequently need to "consider the source." As you evaluate information, how reliable it is will depend on how trustworthy its source happens to be. Both individual authors and organizations are sources of information. This section will explain how to evaluate the credibility of sources in general, and will then specifically focus on authors and organizations.

Evaluating Source Credibility

Authors and organizations spread information using two primary methods: print and online (since this is a reading textbook, we will focus on these methods, but obviously there are other ways to share information such as through television, film, billboards, commercials, and speeches). Print materials such as books, periodicals, and newspapers are reviewed by multiple people prior to publication. Online materials, on the other hand, may or may not be similarly reviewed by editors or peers, which makes it important that you check them carefully.

Evaluating Print Sources Despite the popularity of online sources, print sources are still very useful. In fact, serious researchers depend on print sources because, in most cases, they have gone through a more vigorous review process prior to publication that includes review by editors and fact-checkers. Another advantage of print sources over online sources is that certain important information is made obvious in print, including the author's name and background, the references he or she consulted, and publication information, while often this same information is difficult to locate or verify online.

Despite these advantages over online sources, print sources also need to be evaluated for quality and reliability. Use the checklist below to evaluate some specific issues relevant to print sources.

Checklist for Evaluating Print Sources

- **Quality**. *Does the source contain the features common to quality sources?* These include a bibliography (list of references used in the text), in-text citations, a table of contents, and an index. While the inclusion of these features does not guarantee quality, their omission could indicate problems with the source.
- **Currency**. *Check the date of the text.* Some fast-moving fields, such as medicine and computer science, require that you access the most current information, as there can

be rapid changes in information due to ongoing research and scientific discoveries. Other disciplines, such as literature and history, do not change over time in the same way, so older references may still be useful and acceptable. Use the most current edition for the most up-to-date information.

- **Review**. *Determine whether the information has been reviewed by other people.* If it has been *peer-reviewed*, the work has gone through a process of careful review by other experts in the field; this is a rigorous process that dramatically increases its trustworthiness. If it has been *edited*, then it has been proofread and edited for clarity and grammatical errors; editors can also make recommendations about content, but they might not be experts in the field.

  Usually, a text published in print form has been peer-reviewed or edited, unless it is self-published. If it is self-published, check if the author mentions editors or reviewers in the acknowledgments, preface, or conclusion.

- **Publisher**. *Check whether the publisher is reputable.* You can look up information about the publisher online or in a reference book such as the *Writer's Market*. As a general rule, sources published by university presses and professional organizations are reputable.

Evaluating Online Sources

If you have spent any time at all on the Internet, you have probably uncovered your fair share of both useful and useless information. Anyone with Internet access can post ideas for free or at little cost, which makes it especially important for you to learn how to separate reliable information from questionable information.

In some cases, the extension on the website address (URL) will tell you something about the site: .edu (education), .gov (government), or .mil (military). However, you still have to be aware that all organizations, like people, have specific outlooks, so don't depend on the ending of a website's address to tell you much about the content of the site.

Most colleges and universities subscribe to databases that allow you to search and retrieve full-text documents from reputable sources. Databases provide documents from news sources, journals, and reference publications and can specialize in fields such as medicine, law, business, education, international studies, history, sociology, and psychiatry. Whenever possible, use research generated from databases rather than from websites, because database sources are more likely to have been peer-reviewed or fact-checked.

Here are a few special considerations as you evaluate online sources:

Checklist for Evaluating Online Sources

- **Currency**. *Does the site appear to be frequently and consistently updated*, or does it look like it was uploaded a while ago with no apparent attempt to keep it current? Is the site unfinished or under construction? Are the links to other websites in good working condition?

- **Accuracy**. *Can you verify facts and figures in other sources?* Use several sources from a combination of print and online references when learning about a topic. Moreover, if an idea seems to contradict what you already know about a topic, cross-check the information in assorted references. You can always ask a professional in the field to take a look at the website and offer an informed opinion.

- **Access**. *Can you contact the author?* Is there an address, phone number, or email address that would permit you to get additional information if necessary? Can you clearly identify who contributes to and maintains the site?

Evaluating Author Credibility

If the source of information is an author (as opposed to an organization), then evaluating that information requires you to learn a bit about him or her so that you can determine if he or she is a credible source. Sometimes authors have their own homepages that you can check, but you have to be on the lookout for bias when an author writes about him- or herself. You can access quick information about authors on sites such as www.amazon.com, the author's publisher's website, www.biography.com, and www.wikipedia.org (but be aware that authors can edit their own Wikipedia pages to include only the most favorable information). Knowing about the author can help you to judge for yourself if the information is likely to be credible or not. Use the following checklist when evaluating an author.

Checklist for Evaluating an Author's Credibility

1. **Does the author seem knowledgeable?**

   - **Education.** *Verify that the author's education is relevant to his or her chosen field.* Do not be overly impressed with a title such as "doctor" or "professor," but make certain that the author is, indeed, educated in the field that he or she writes about.
   - **Experience.** *Check to see that experience contributes to the author's expertise in the particular field you are researching.* Where has the author worked? Is the author considered a leader in the field? Has the author published other writings? When possible, access these other publications, especially if they are relevant to the research you are conducting because that would increase your understanding of the issue.
   - **Reputation.** *Research the author's reputation in the field.* You can conduct a quick Internet search to see what reviewers or other professionals in the field have written or said about the author.

2. **What are the circumstances surrounding the author and the text?**

   - **Intent.** *Determine the author's purpose.* Evaluating an author requires you to determine his or her motives for writing. Use what you learned in Chapter 4 to infer the author's intentions (to inform, persuade, or entertain). Is the author responding to a political event? Is the author trying to sell you on an idea or a product? Does the author propose a solution to a problem?
   - **Discipline.** *Consider the discipline you are researching in; some fields inspire more controversy than others.* If an author writes about a discipline that is especially controversial, then you may need to conduct some additional research. For example, a field like chemistry embraces tried-and-true research methods, has a strong, fact-based background, and does not incite as many strong emotions as a more subjective field like sociology or criminal justice. If one author's opinion seems to deviate widely from other research in the field, then that author might be either on the cutting edge of the field or on the outskirts of it. Either way, you need to investigate further.

3. **Does the author sound biased?**

   - **Language.** *Evaluate the type of language an author uses.* Chapters 4 and 5 discuss ways to evaluate an author's use of language. In particular, you should carefully examine emotive language and loaded language. Moreover, Chapter 3 explores how to clarify the meaning of vague or misleading language (*equivocation, euphemisms,* and *doublespeak*). An author who is deliberately vague or ambiguous is typically not as credible as a direct, upfront author.
   - **Bias.** *After closely examining language, see if you can identify biases and recognize when you need to conduct additional research.* A strong bias might limit the author's

ability to treat the topic fairly, and your own biases can interfere with your ability to be a critical thinker. You can certainly still learn something from a biased author, but you will need to balance out your research by seeking out alternative viewpoints.

An author does not have to have perfect credentials in each of these areas in order to be a credible source. It is entirely possible that an author may be new to a field and lacking some experience, but that doesn't mean you should automatically discredit his or her information. Instead, you should weigh the author's credentials overall. Lack of experience or education, for example, might be a red flag but not necessarily a disqualifier. Look at the big picture.

Even if you find that the author is quite trustworthy, try not to get stuck using research generated by only one author. A comprehensive review of a topic requires the use of a number of sources.

PRACTICE 7-7   Source and Author Credibility

Directions: *The Week* article "Why So Many Killer Tornadoes?" introduces some differing opinions that attempt to answer the question posed in the title. First, you will read "Why So Many Killer Tornadoes" to get some background information. Then, you will read two of those opinions referenced in *The Week*, Gregg Easterbrook's and John Hayward's, and evaluate them for source and author credibility. Refer to the "Checklist for Evaluating Online Sources" on p. 234 and the "Checklist for Evaluating an Author's Credibility" on p. 235. Finally, on a separate sheet of paper, write a paragraph about both sources, both authors, and which opinion you are more likely to agree with and why.

Why So Many Killer Tornadoes?

After a brutal one-two punch of twisters, the debate over a possible link between climate change and deadly weather begins anew. To view this article, go to http://theweek.com/article/index/215596/why-so-many-killer-tornadoes

What's Causing the Tornado Tsunami
Gregg Easterbrook

May 24, 2011

"Tornadoes are currently on a frightening upswing." That could have been written yesterday—but was written 12 years ago, by your columnist, in the November 8, 1999 issue of *The New Republic*.

The onslaught of tornadoes is not some sudden, unexpected bolt out of the blue. I wrote about tornadoes a dozen years ago because 1998 and 1999 were terrible years for tornadoes. Now three of the last 12 years have been terrible for tornadoes, and the 1950-2010 trend isn't so great either.

This spring's tornado activity has been awful. At least 116 people died in Joplin, Missouri, on Sunday during an unusually strong and large tornado. A portion of Tuscaloosa, Alabama was destroyed by a

The Tornado Year
Struggling to understand an awful tragedy
John Hayward

May 24, 2011

CNN has an oddly phrased sub-head for today's story about the unusual number of killer tornadoes we've seen this year:

The tornado that killed 117 people in Missouri this week puts the U.S. on track for a record-breaking year, **despite** improved forecasting and warning systems. *[emphasis mine]*

"Despite?" Why would "improved forecasting and warning systems" reduce the number of tornadoes? They don't *control* the weather, they predict it.

One gathers from reading the whole story that they're talking about a record-breaking year for tornado *fatalities*. The Joplin tornado is the latest in a string of

tornado last month. Many tornadoes hit the Ozarks region in April. There were 875 confirmed tornadoes in April, triple the previous April high of 267, in 1974. So far 481 Americans have been killed by tornadoes this spring.

In recent decades, the installation of a Doppler radar warning system in tornado-prone areas has tended to reduce fatalities—sirens get people's attention. But even 24 minutes of warning, which Joplin received on Sunday, may not be sufficient for a tornado that was a hard-to-believe half a mile across. (The touch-down part of a tornado is rarely more than 100 yards wide.) More disturbing tornado facts are here.

Weather patterns include random variation: some recent years have been mild for tornadoes. Before this spring, the worst tornado sequence in U.S. annals came in 1953, when atmospheric greenhouse gas levels were lower than today. Nevertheless, there are reasons to think tornadoes are a harbinger of climate change.

For years, pundits and politicians have claimed that strong hurricanes prove global warming. In this 2005 speech, Al Gore asserted, "The scientific community is warning us that the average hurricane will continue to get stronger because of global warming." Gore went on to compare hurricanes to al qaeda. But not only have four of the last five Atlantic hurricane seasons been quiet, the 20th century showed no trend of rising Atlantic hurricane frequency or intensity.

Pundits and politicians attach significance to hurricanes because they are visual events—hurricane courses can be predicted, and their arrivals on shore televised. Tornadoes come and go so quickly, they are almost impossible to catch on film. But their comings and goings may be warnings of climate malfunction.

What's causing the tornado tsunami of 2011? This spring, the jet stream has shifted south and east of its typical position. That brings the cold, dry air on the north edge of the jet stream into more contact with the warm, moist air masses on its south edge, around the Gulf of Mexico. The result is rotating thunderstorms—sometimes, as happened in the Ozarks in April, forming day after day in succession.

Surely there have been times in the past when the jet stream shifted east and south: this may or may not be related to greenhouse gases. But greenhouse gas levels in the atmosphere are rising, and weather variations are rising—not just tornadoes, but droughts

tragedies, which meteorologist Greg Carbin told ABC News leaves us "approaching 500 fatalities for the year to date," when "the average annual death toll from tornadoes has been around 60 to 70 people."

"That is something we have not experienced in this country in over 35 years," Carbin continued, "and it still looks like we're still around the number nine as far as the deadliest year on record. So there have been many years in the past over the past couple of generations in which we've exceeded 500 fatalities in a year, it's just that they haven't occurred recently."

In fact, overall tornado deaths have been slowly declining over the past three decades, both in absolute numbers and as a percentage of a growing population. They dipped sharply after the 1970s, most likely as a result of improved forecasting and construction technology. They've held fairly constant, with a very slight decline, in each succeeding decade. An article at BrainPosts.com provides these totals:

Decade	Total Deaths	Deaths per Million
1950s	1419	8.6
1960s	942	4.9
1970s	998	4.7
1980s	522	2.2
1990s	579	2.2
2000s	556	1.9

The total for the 2010s, of course, are very high because of the horrific tragedies over the past couple of months. There's little doubt this will go down as the worst decade in a long time, unless we're extraordinarily fortunate over the next nine years.

"Fortune" is the key factor in understanding the Joplin disaster. It was a twist of incredible bad luck that such a powerful tornado rolled through the middle of a populated area, and chanced to destroy the local hospital. As a general trend, an increasingly large and centralized population produces greater odds that a tornado will hit a heavily developed area.

Also, according to an article in the *International Journal of Epidemiology* cited by the BrainPosts essay, one of the primary risk factors for injury or death in a tornado is "advanced age." Medical science has given us an aging population, with more people enjoying longer lives, and more elderly citizens capable of living on their own. This could be a factor in paving the way for more injuries and deaths when a tornado smashes through an area with many elderly residents.

Of course, you just *know* another explanation for the killer tornadoes will be offered. You probably thought of

and deluge rains. Chances are two plus two equals four.

It is important to bear in mind that climate change, not global warming, is the threat. They seem like the same thing but are not. The mild warming of the past 100 years—about 1 degree Fahrenheit globally averaged—was good for crop yields, and moderated demand for energy. (Power use for warming on cold days exceeds power use for cooling on hot days). If all that happens is continued mildly rising temperatures, that might be beneficial.

Changing climate is another matter altogether. Climate change can bring more tornadoes, increase droughts in some places while increasing floods in other places—all three impacts are being observed. Long-term shifts in rainfall patterns might turn breadbasket regions into crop-failure regions. Our increasingly globalized economy is dependent on air travel and air cargo. What if storms and turbulence begin to make flying conditions unfavorable not once in a long while, but often?

Despite what the talk radio and Tea Party types say, there is strong scientific consensus that human activity has begun to alter Earth's climate. Here is the latest statement on this matter, from the National Academy of Sciences last week.

The United States Congress—dedicated to its twin goals of doing nothing, while collecting campaign contributions—needs to act on greenhouse gases. These tornadoes are not originating from Oz.

it the moment you began reading this article. The *UK Daily Mail,* which once again collects some of the most remarkable images of the devastation in Joplin today, asserts that "Many weather experts are blaming global warming."

Hilariously, they explain why any such "weather expert" would be a complete idiot or a deluded fanatic *in the very next paragraphs*—because "twisters generally occur when cold air hits warm air and, because it is almost summer, the air is warm over much of the U.S.," while "Unusually cold air is pushing down from the north, contributing to major storm activity." So global warming causes cold air?

No, wait, I forgot, it's "climate change" now, and by definition, that can produce both cold *and* warm air. I don't know why the *Daily Mail* used the archaic "global warming" terminology. Do the fanatics still call it that over in England? If so, they really should take a cue from their American comrades and start using the more supple "climate change" formulation.

It is natural for us to try understanding a horrible disaster, and challenge ourselves to find ways we might prevent the next one. Much good has come from human ingenuity rising to meet that challenge. We nevertheless find ourselves rendered humble and speechless by the ruins of Joplin, and the knowledge that fate defeated science with a pillar of howling wind last Sunday night.

Update: Oh, for crying out loud. Looks like Al Roker is on the "global warming causes tornadoes" bandwagon.

"We have had these tornadoes and earlier this week we had a tornado in Philadelphia. And so, you know our weather, or climate change is such now that we are seeing this kind of weather not just in rural parts of our country, but in urban centers as well."

From "What's Causing the Tornado Tsunami" by Gregg Easterbrook. Reprinted by permission of Gregg Easterbrook.

"The Tornado Year: Struggling to Understand an Awful Tragedy" by John Hayward, in *Human Events,* 5/24/2011. Reprinted by permission.

THINK
AND WRITE
CRITICALLY

EXPAND YOUR UNDERSTANDING

Write Critically about Source and Author Credibility

Read the third article referenced in *The Week*: Alok Jha's "Are Tornadoes More Common Because of Climate Change?" from Britain's *Guardian.* Assess source and author credibility (again using the checklists in the chapter). Finally, write an essay that explains which of the three opinions you find to be most credible and why.

Evaluating an Organization's Credibility

If a work is not credited to a specific author, it often comes from an organization. Like authors, organizations also have biases that need to be considered when you evaluate them as sources. There are a huge number of organizations that share information with the public in both print and online formats. Also similar to authors, some organizations are more credible than others.

Many professions have national and local organizations that provide a means for sharing information with people in the same field. As a rule, these are credible starting places for your research. Many organizations are nonprofit but will charge membership dues in order to support their research, conferences, and publications. Typically, these professional organizations publish periodicals and online articles to share current information in their respective fields. Often the websites for these organizations will end in *.org* but not always. Some examples of professional organizations are the National Society of Professional Engineers, the International Literacy Association, the American Historical Association, and the National Council of Teachers of English.

Other organizations exist to promote a certain issue or ideology (way of thinking about a particular subject). These organizations are characterized by a strong focus and often a strong bias for their pet topic. Sometimes, their names will sound a lot like the professional organizations mentioned above; for example, the American Association of Professional Psychics (www.certifiedpsychics.com) sounds good, but a quick glance at the website reveals little more than the fact that they charge $3.99 per minute for a psychic reading. Many pseudoscientific beliefs are promoted through websites such as this one.

Use the general tips for evaluating sources on pp. 233–236 as well as the specific tips included in the following checklists when evaluating the credibility of organizations. Characteristics of reputable organizations are in the "green light" checklist; characteristics of questionable organizations are in the "red flag" checklist.

Checklists for Evaluating the Credibility of Organizations

Characteristics of Reputable Organizations

- **Mission Statement.** Does the organization have a clearly defined mission statement that explains its purpose and agenda?
- **Research.** Does the organization include research by professionals in the field and encourage diversity of topics and viewpoints?
- **Membership.** Are the costs and benefits of membership clearly established? Benefits typically include print publications, discounted fees to attend conventions, and professional development opportunities.

Characteristics of Questionable Organizations

- **Testimonials.** Does the organization use testimonials? Questionable organizations may post testimonials from "real people" on their websites in an attempt to lure more followers.
- **Costs.** Are any costs clearly stated? It may be difficult to gain access to information without paying some dollar amount that isn't clearly established from the onset.
- **Identification.** Can you identify the people in charge of the organization? Sometimes the people contributing to the organization are only identified by first names or initials.

EXPAND YOUR UNDERSTANDING

Evaluating Organizations on the Internet

Research these organizations on the Internet using the websites below. Use the General Checklist for Evaluating Sources as well as the green light and red flag checklists above to consider how credible each organization might be. Write a short paragraph evaluating each organization on a separate piece of paper.

American Society of Civil Engineers—website www.asce.org and American Association of Psychics—website www.americanassociationofpsychics.com

READ, WRITE, AND THINK CRITICALLY: SECTION ONE

Directions: Skim through the following text and answer questions 1–3. Then, read the selection and answer the questions that follow.

1. What do you think the selection will be about?

   _____

   _____

2. What is your prior knowledge of this topic?

   _____

   _____

3. The title of the selection is "On Overconfidence." Why do you think the authors chose this title?

   _____

   _____

On Overconfidence

James Fowler and Dominic Johnson

James Fowler is a published author and political scientist working at the University of California, San Diego. Dominic Johnson is associated with Edinburgh University, Scotland, and works as a reader in politics and international relations. The following piece was originally published January 2011 in Seed *magazine.*

1 Imagine a world where people lacked confidence. We would scarcely be able to face a new day, struggling to summon the courage to show our work to our bosses or apply for a new job. Surgeons would be **racked** with doubt about upcoming operations. Military commanders would hesitate at key moments when decisiveness was essential. Politicians would be unable to defend their views against the constant hail of personal and intellectual criticism.

2 Confidence is so vital even for the mundane activities of everyday life that we take it for granted. But it also looms large whenever we try to explain achievements that are out of the ordinary. Confidence is widely held to be an almost magic ingredient of success in sports, entertainment, business, the stock market, combat and many other domains—would Donald Trump, Muhammad Ali, and General Patton have risen to fame without their sizzling confidence? No way.

3   At the same time, confidence can be dangerous. Like fire, it can be extremely useful in controlled amounts, but confidence in excess—overconfidence—can easily burn out of control and cause costly decision-making errors, policy failures, and wars. For example, overconfidence has been blamed for a string of major disasters from the 1990s dotcom bubble, to the 2008 collapse of the banks, to the ongoing foot-dragging over climate change ("it won't happen to me"). These events are no blip in the longer timeline of human endeavor. Historians and political scientists have blamed overconfidence for a range of **fiascos**, from the First World War to Vietnam to Iraq.

4   We may be surprised by the recurring problem of overconfidence—why don't people learn from their mistakes? As the archetypal self-doubter Woody Allen suggested, "Confidence is what you have before you understand the problem." But the recurrence of overconfidence is no surprise to psychologists.

5   All mentally healthy people tend to have so-called "positive illusions" about our abilities, our control over events, and our vulnerability to risk. Numerous studies have shown that we overrate our intelligence, attractiveness, and skill. We also think we have better morals, health, and leadership abilities than others. A survey of 1 million high school students showed that 70 percent think they are above-average leaders (only 2 percent rated themselves below average). In another study 94 percent of college professors claimed that their research was above average. We believe we will live longer than others, and we will avoid common calamities like car accidents, crime, earthquakes, and major illness. Like the children in Garrison Keillor's Lake Wobegon, we are all above average.

6   Positive illusions appear to be undergirded by many different cognitive and motivational biases, all of which converge to boost people's confidence. This is dangerous because people are more likely to think they are better than others, which makes aggression, conflict, and even war more likely. As psychologist Daniel Kahneman put it: "The bottom line is that all the biases in judgment that have been identified in the last 15 years tend to bias decision-making toward the hawkish side."

7   Confidence thus poses a major puzzle. On the one hand, overconfidence appears to be a widespread and powerful feature of human **cognition**, but on the other hand it appears to cause faulty assessments and major disasters. That makes little sense. Why would this kind of false belief survive in competition with accurate beliefs? How could it even have evolved in the first place?

8   The beginnings of a solution suggest themselves at the point where we started, with the good things that confidence brings. As Michael Jordan said, "You have to expect things of yourself before you can do them." If confidence allows us to set expectations, then overconfidence might work as a kind of self-fulfilling prophecy, helping us to achieve even more. Consider the fantastically self-confident Muhammad Ali, who said he "never even thought of losing" and even at school "boasted weekly—if not daily—that one day I was going to be the heavy weight champion of the world .... When I proclaimed that I was the Greatest of all Time, I believed in myself. And I still do."

9   Overconfidence may therefore be advantageous because it increases ambition, resolve, and persistence in many of life's tasks—even if the price of maintaining this overconfidence is occasional disasters. Just as successful poker players must sometimes bluff the strength of their hand if they are to win, overconfident individuals may be able to outperform their rivals if they believe in themselves enough to keep going when others would give in.

10   The idea that overconfidence is advantageous is interesting. But it has remained just that—an idea. There always lurks a compelling alternative hypothesis: While overconfidence might indeed encourage us to aim high, it is nevertheless a decision-making error. Consequently, many economists argue that the winning strategy ought to be one that sees the world exactly as it is, coldly calculating our capabilities and picking only fights that we are sure to win. This Homo economicus model still dominates economics and other corners of the social sciences.

11   How can we **adjudicate** between these two alternative views? An evolutionary perspective is useful here because it forces us to think through how these alternative strategies would fare in direct competition with each other—which ones would survive Darwin's mill of natural selection? Imagine a world in which there are three types of individuals: economists (who are unbiased), Muhammad Alis (who are overconfident—okay, he was the greatest, but it's a good label), and Woody Allens (who are underconfident). If these guys are competing for food, the Woody Allens will shy away from conflict, which helps them avoid costly confrontations. But it also means they might starve. The economists will have a better idea about which conflicts they can win, and so they won't be quite so scrawny. But uncertainty about the outcome of any one conflict means they will occasionally leave food on the table that they could have claimed and won. In contrast, the Muhammad Alis of the world rarely back down from a fight, and therefore they always have a shot at eating and surviving. As long as the value of eating is sufficiently greater than the cost of conflict, the Muhammad Alis will win the day.

12   Hence, a degree of overconfidence can be beneficial on average, even if it causes occasional disasters. As long as the prize at stake sufficiently exceeds the cost of competing for it, fortune favors the bold.

13   There is, however, going to be some **optimal** margin of overconfidence: Unbounded overconfidence will be detrimental. Blind willingness to fight—especially when two such strategies meet—can lead to so much conflict that no gain will be worth it. Napoleon's attack on Waterloo in 1815 and the banks' subprime-lending practices in 2008 both eventually pushed the limits of confidence too far. In fact, if the costs of competition become extreme, outweighing the potential gain, underconfidence becomes the best strategy (even Ali would leave the ring if his opponent pulled out a machine gun). Although this situation may be rare (people usually compete precisely because a prize is greatly valued), Woody Allens may be better suited to a world in which technology changes the odds and a miscalculation can mean the collapse of the global banking system or the unleashing of a mushroom cloud.

14   So how can we use these ideas to raise ambitions while reining in disaster? The problem is that it's never obvious how much confidence is the right amount. In life, love, finance, and politics, there's a fine line between losing out when we could have won and getting burned by pushing too hard.

15   But there is one general lesson from evolution that helps us identify when overconfidence is likely to lead us astray. Our judgment and decision-making mechanisms evolved to deal with the adaptive problems of our evolutionary past, not with the problems of our modern social and physical world. Our brains developed over millions of years, during much of which we lived in small kin groups of hunter-gatherers. It is only in the past 10,000 years that we began living with strangers in large urban societies, organizing ourselves into hierarchical political units, and operating complex machines and lethal weapons. Although overconfidence may often continue to help us just as evolution intended—in relevant contexts and settings—it has a powerful and pervasive evolutionary legacy that continues to dominate our judgment and decision-making, even in complex political, social, or technological settings when such overconfidence is far less likely or able to bring any advantages and simply increases the chance of disaster.

16   We can predict, therefore, that overconfidence is most likely to help in "evolutionarily **salient**" contexts that are similar to the adaptive challenges of our past, such as individual combat like boxing. It is least likely to help in "evolutionarily novel" contexts—such as sitting at a desk in a bank guessing the behavior of 100 million strangers, or commanding thousands of invisible troops from an underground bunker.

17   The good news is that evolutionary reasoning suggests ways to avoid the most dangerous situations in which overconfidence is likely to arise. First, we can make sure that overconfidence is nurtured in settings where a go-getting attitude helps performance (such as sports), and suppressed in settings where accurate assessment is more important than will (such as global climate change). Second, we can target the underlying contexts that make or break overconfidence. For example, notice that we exhibit overconfidence only when we are not sure who will win a fight. This suggests that we should be encouraging as much information sharing as possible—the more interaction we have with our opponents, the more likely we are to agree on the strengths and weaknesses of each side. This is precisely the reasoning underlying recent calls for mutual inspections of nuclear arms facilities between Russia and the US.

18   There are also implications for the way we design our decision-making institutions. The lesson from the banks is that, left unchecked, overconfidence can become self-reinforcing and almost immune to correction—only confident personalities get the jobs, only big risk-takers make big returns, and only those with big returns move up the ladder to the top of the firm. And the bonuses are back already! As much as one may like free markets, the only sure way to counter strong incentives for risk-taking is getting external regulation right.

19   We all benefit from the ambition that populates the world with Michael Jordans and Muhammad Alis—what crazy guy hatched the idea of flying, or going to the moon? Human achievement is a thing of great beauty.

20   But overconfidence is an increasingly dangerous strategy today. The modern world is very different from the one in which we evolved, and to which our decision making and behaviors adapted via natural selection. The big decisions of today are dependent on multiple and complex interacting bureaucracies and stakeholders, in which accurate assessments and painstaking planning may be boring but are critical to success—an evolutionary novelty we are not "designed" for. Political and economic overconfidence are therefore all the more important because they are more likely to be misplaced and yet also to have implications for millions. We may not be able to eliminate this bias in our decision-making, but it is crucial that we understand it and reset our institutions accordingly if we are to shake our long record of self-imposed disasters.

4. Use context clues and/or a dictionary to define the following words (marked in bold in the reading).

   a. Racked (para. 1): _____

   b. Fiasco (para. 3): _____

   c. Cognition (para. 7): _____

   d. Adjudicate (para. 11): _____

   e. Optimal (para. 13): _____

   f. Salient (para. 16): _____

5. Identify the claim and the evidence of the argument given by the authors.

   _____

   _____

   _____

   _____

6. Choose two pieces of evidence and identify what kinds of evidence they are.

   _____

   _____

7. Do the authors give any counter-evidence? Explain.

   _____

   _____

8. Do you agree or disagree with the authors' claims about overconfidence? Critically write an essay in which you explain your reasoning.

   _____

   _____

   _____

   _____

SECTION TWO

Evaluating Assumptions

After you've judged the reliability of the evidence of an argument, you need to evaluate the assumptions made by the author of the argument. As you learned on pp. 138–139 of Chapter 4, assumptions are beliefs that an author takes for granted as being true. They often serve as the underlying basis for an argument. Once you've identified the assumptions of an argument, you need to decide if the assumption is *warranted* or *unwarranted*. A warranted assumption is an assumption that is likely to be true, often because it has evidence or reasons supporting it. An unwarranted assumption is an assumption that has no support and that the author has no good reason to hold.

You need to be aware that sometimes assumptions are a matter of worldviews (as you read about on p. 159 of Chapter 5), and someone who has been raised in a certain culture might find an assumption warranted that a person from another culture would judge as unwarranted. In certain cases, this conflict can't be resolved, and no agreement can be reached. For example, when it comes to abortion, some people are pro-life and some are pro-choice. People on both sides of this issue fundamentally disagree, because they hold different, irreconcilable assumptions, none of which can be adequately proven or disproven. This is why two people, starting with different assumptions, can both think critically about an issue and arrive at different conclusions.

Tips for Critical Thinkers: Evaluating Assumptions

- **Look for backing for the assumption.** Can any evidence be gathered in support of the assumption? Don't forget that this evidence will also need to be evaluated.
- **Try to determine if the assumption is the result of a bias.** Is it an unfair judgment that is not based on evidence?
- **See if the assumption is internally consistent.** Some assumptions—such as the belief that every statement should be doubted—contradict themselves and should be considered unwarranted.
- **Determine whether the assumption can be proven true or false at all.** Some abstract statements (such as certain political or religious claims) often can't be proven true or false; one accepts them based on how well they seem to explain the world. Such judgments are by nature very personal and generally have to be either accepted or rejected based on personal choice.

PRACTICE 7-8   Judging Assumptions

Directions: On another sheet of paper, determine the assumptions underlying the following arguments, then decide if each assumption is warranted or unwarranted. Explain your decision. You may need to use your school's library or the Internet to see if you can uncover backing for an assumption.

1. Because a fetus is not a person, abortion should be legal.
2. Since scientific evidence indicates that the earth is 4.5 billion years old, you should ascribe to that belief.
3. Phillip showed signs of guilt when questioned by the police, so he probably stole the money.
4. Patti spanked her children, and they grew up to be productive adults, so spanking children is a good idea.
5. Crop circles were found in a field in England. Aliens visit earth!

Evaluating Logic

Once you've checked the reliability of an argument's evidence and evaluated the assumptions underlying it, it's time to appraise the logic of the argument. The source can be absolutely credible, the evidence true, and the assumptions warranted, but if the connection between the evidence and the conclusion of the argument—the logic—is faulty, the argument will fail.

Evaluating Deductive Arguments

As you learned in Chapter 6, *deductive arguments* are arguments that draw specific conclusions from generalizations. When the fact that the premises are true means that the conclusion absolutely has to be true, the argument is *valid*. Some deductive arguments have true premises but false conclusions, so they are not valid. For a deductive argument to work logically, it must be valid. A valid deductive argument that has true premises (i.e., good evidence) is *sound*. Soundness is what you hope for in a deductive argument, but to determine if the argument is sound, you have to make sure it's valid. Here is an example of a valid deductive argument:

All mothers have children. Therefore Leslie, who is a mother, has at least one child.

Premise: All mothers have children.
Premise: Leslie is a mother.
Conclusion: Therefore Leslie has at least one child.

There is simply no way that Leslie could not have a child if it's true that all mothers have children and Leslie is a mother. The conclusion of this argument has to be true.

Some deductive arguments might appear valid at first glance, but you need to look at them carefully. Knowing the above argument is valid, decide if the following argument is valid:

All mothers have children. Therefore Leslie, who has a child, is a mother.

This argument is invalid. Do you understand why it is invalid? Fathers also have children, and for all we know, Leslie is a man, so we can't conclude from the argument above that Leslie is a mother. The premises could be true and the conclusion could still be false.

Truth and validity are not the same thing. The premises of an argument could be true but the conclusion could be false if the deductive argument is not valid. Or, the conclusion of an argument could be true but the argument invalid; in that case, the author of the argument got lucky. Figure 7-2 illustrates the possible combinations of truth and validity. Notice that only the first column—true premises and valid logic—represents a sound deductive argument.

Determining validity can be challenging. Try the following four examples on your own, and then check your answers afterwards. Be sure to read the accompanying explanations for *why* each example is either valid or invalid.

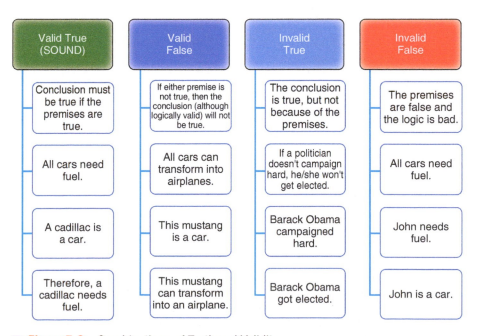

■ **Figure 7-2** Combinations of Truth and Validity

Examples

_____ 1. All people who are on Twitter also use Facebook.
Eden frequently uses Twitter to communicate and express her opinion online.
Eden also uses Facebook.

_____ 2. All people who are on Twitter also use Facebook.
Michaela uses Facebook.
Therefore, Michaela must also be on Twitter.

_____ 3. Warren posts a lot of photos to Instagram. We can conclude he is a talented photographer.

_____ 4. Everyone who uses the website Pinterest has red hair.
Dom uses Pinterest, so we can conclude that Dom has red hair.

Answers and Explanations

___V___ 1. All people who are on Twitter also use Facebook.
Eden frequently uses Twitter to communicate and express her opinion online.
Eden also uses Facebook.

Explanation: This syllogism is valid because the conclusion (that Eden uses Facebook) *must* be true if it is true that ALL people who are on Twitter use Facebook, and we are told that Eden uses Twitter.

___I___ 2. All people who are on Twitter also use Facebook.
Michaela uses Facebook.
Therefore, Michaela must also be on Twitter.

Explanation: While the major premise of questions 1 and 2 are identical, notice how the minor premise (the second statement) has been switched here, making the argument invalid. We are told in the major premise that people on Twitter also use Facebook, but we are NOT told that all people on Facebook also use Twitter (and we cannot logically switch the two social media sites). The minor premise only tells us that Michaela uses Facebook. We cannot logically conclude that she is on Twitter because we are never told that people on Facebook all use Twitter (we are told the other way around—that all people on Twitter use Facebook).

___I___ 3. Warren posts a lot of photos to Instagram. We can conclude he is a talented photographer.

Explanation: This example is invalid and can be referred to as *no certainty* or *no guarantee*. We are never given a major premise that states "All people who post photos to Instagram are talented photographers" (*if* we were given such a major premise then we could, indeed, conclude that Warren is a talented photographer). Remember that in a valid argument, there is a guarantee that the conclusion is true if the premises are true. Here, there is no guarantee because we cannot assume a major premise that has not been provided to us, so the argument is deemed invalid.

___V___ 4. Everyone who uses the website Pinterest has red hair.
Dom uses Pinterest, so we can conclude that Dom has red hair.

Reminder

Syllogisms are a specific type of deductive argument that contain a major premise, a minor premise, and a conclusion (see Chapter 6, p. 203).

Explanation: If it is true that everyone who uses Pinterest has red hair, and it is true that Dom uses Pinterest, then it must be true (we are guaranteed) that Dom has red hair. Granted, in the real world we know that this is not true because blondes and brunettes also use Pinterest, but in the realm of logic and deductive arguments, this is a valid argument.

| **Determining Validity** | **PRACTICE 7-9** |

Directions: Determine whether the following deductive arguments are valid by figuring out if there is any way their conclusions could be false if their premises are true. In the blank provided, write V if the argument is valid or I if it is invalid. Remember that validity and soundness are different; an argument can be valid but have a false conclusion. (Note: Some of the items are deductive arguments you first encountered in Chapter 6.)

_____ 1. All things that walk have four legs.
  Humans can walk.
  Humans have four legs.

_____ 2. All animals need to eat.
  Reggie needs to eat.
  Reggie is an animal.

_____ 3. Everyone who eats too much will get sick.
  John is sick.
  He ate too much.

_____ 4. People who love you hug you. He hugged you, so he must love you.

_____ 5. Those who commit a crime will be found guilty. John was found guilty, so he must have committed the crime.

_____ 6. Students who regularly attend their college classes get passing grades. Oliver never skips a class (he attends regularly). Therefore, we can conclude that Oliver will get passing grades.

_____ 7. Stealing is wrong, but Britta's friends have been shoplifting from local stores. Therefore, Britta should try to dissuade her friends from stealing.

_____ 8. Since the fact that germs cause illness is well-founded, and since Carl is ill, doctors ought to find germs in his body.

_____ 9. Students who plagiarize get sent to the Dean. Johan plagiarized, so he will get sent to the Dean.

_____10. Bullies need to be punished. Nelson bullies Bart; therefore, Principal Skinner should give him a detention.

As you learned in Chapter 6, syllogisms are common forms of deductive arguments. Many syllogisms begin with a conditional statement (a statement where the second part of the sentence is true if the first part is true). In a conditional statement, the actual condition that needs to be fulfilled is known as the **antecedent,** and the thing that happens if the condition is fulfilled is known as the **consequent**. Here's an example with the parts labeled.

antecedent   consequent
If it is raining, the ground gets wet.

Simply speaking, there are two ways that deductive arguments built from conditional statements can be valid: **Modus ponens** and **Modus tollens**. In a Modus ponens argument, the antecedent is, indeed, true, so it logically follows that the consequent is true. In a Modus tollens argument, the consequent is not true or did not happen, so we can conclude that the antecedent also did not happen. The following syllogism is valid and is an example of Modus ponens:

If it is raining, the ground gets wet. It rained. Therefore the ground is wet.

Modus ponens can be written out as a logical notation in the following manner:

P ⟶ Q (you can read this as "If P, then Q")
P (so you know that P, the antecedent, did occur)

_____ or ∴ (you can read the line or the three dots as "therefore")
Q (so you conclude that Q, the consequent, did occur)

This next syllogism is also valid, and it is an example of Modus tollens:

If it is raining, the ground gets wet. The ground isn't wet, so it must not be raining.

Modus tollens can be written out as a logical notation in the following manner:

P ⟶ Q (you can read this as "If P, then Q")
-Q (so you know that Q, the consequent, did **not** occur)

_____ or ∴ (you can read the line or the three dots as "therefore")
-P (so you conclude that P, the antecedent) did **not** occur)

Often the validity of a deductive argument is compromised in one of two ways. The first way is known as _affirming the consequent_ and the second one is known as _denying the antecedent._

The next syllogism commits the mistake of _affirming the consequent_, which means assuming that if the consequent is true, it makes the antecedent true. This assumption makes the syllogism invalid.

If it is raining, the ground gets wet. The ground is wet. Therefore it rained.

Just because the ground is wet doesn't mean it rained. The ground could have gotten wet when someone sprayed it with a hose, for example.

The next syllogism is invalid because it _denies the antecedent_, meaning that it makes the mistake of assuming that if the antecedent is false, the consequent must be false.

If it is raining, the ground gets wet. It didn't rain. Therefore the ground isn't wet.

Again, the ground could still be wet even though it didn't rain. So just because the antecedent is false, you can't assume that the consequent is automatically false.

Figure 7-3 should help you to understand and differentiate among the valid and invalid forms of syllogisms that use conditional statements.

Valid form 1: Modus ponens	Valid form 2: Modus tollens
P ⟶ Q P _____ Q	P ⟶ Q -Q _____ -P
Example	Example
If it is raining, then the ground will get wet. It's raining, so therefore the ground is wet.	If it is raining, then the ground will get wet. The ground isn't wet, so therefore it must not be raining.

Affirming the Consequent	Denying the Antecedent
P ⟶ Q Q _____ P	P ⟶ Q -P _____ -Q
Example	Example
If it is raining, then the ground will get wet. The ground is wet, so therefore it rained.	If it is raining, then the ground will get wet. It didn't rain, so therefore the ground can't be wet.

■ **Figure 7-3** Valid and Invalid Forms of Syllogisms that Use Conditional Statements

Antecedents and Consequents

PRACTICE 7-10

Directions: Determine whether the following deductive arguments are valid or invalid. Write V if the argument is valid (remember if it is either Modus ponens or Modus tollens then it is valid). If the argument is invalid, write AC if it makes the mistake of *affirming the consequent* and write DA if it makes the mistake of *denying the antecedent.*

_____ 1. If you feed your dog table scraps, it'll get really fat. I see that your dog is fat, so you must have been feeding it off the table.

_____ 2. When you do the crime and get caught, you have to face the consequences. You jaywalked and a cop saw, so now you are going to get a ticket.

_____ 3. Your t-shirt has a stain on it, so you must have eaten spaghetti, since people who eat spaghetti stain their shirts.

_____ 4. If your eyes are red, you must have been cutting onions. Luckily, your eyes aren't red, so I know you haven't been cutting onions.

_____ 5. Since playing video games for three hours a day leads to eyestrain, and you play far more than three hours a day, you can expect to get eyestrain.

_____ 6. If the sky is blue, it's a nice day out. There's not a cloud in the sky and it's blue, so we should go for a walk, because it's a nice day.

_____ 7. If you don't change your oil regularly, your car's engine is bound to seize. You haven't changed your oil in 3 years, so you'd better get ready to start shopping for a new car (since the engine is going to seize).

_____ 8. If you don't change your oil regularly, your car's engine is bound to seize. Your car's engine has seized, so you must not have changed your oil regularly.

_____ 9. All children cry when they get hurt (you can think of this as the conditional statement, *If a person is a child, then he or she will cry when hurt*). Elaine cried hysterically when she fell off her bike, so that tells us Elaine is a child.

_____ 10. All children cry when they get hurt. Elaine isn't a child, so we know she didn't cry when she fell off her bike.

Evaluating Validity in a Passage

PRACTICE 7-11

Directions: Read the following passage, then fill in the argument map using the underlined statements. Finally, answer the questions that follow.

Illegal downloading is free advertising for the artists, and any recording artist that has a lot of his or her music illegally downloaded is bound to get more popular. Lady Gaga has definitely gotten more popular, so her music must have been illegally downloaded a lot. I bet if you asked Lady Gaga if she supported illegal downloading, she'd say "yes," since she owes her popularity to it. And if one of the most popular artists around supports illegal music sharing, why wouldn't you?

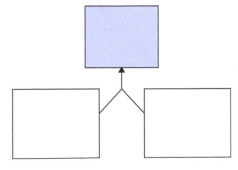

1. There is a syllogism buried in the passage. What is the major premise of the syllogism (the generalization)?

   _____

   _____

   _____

2. What is the minor premise of the syllogism (the application of a specific case)?

   _____

   _____

   _____

3. What is the conclusion of the syllogism?

   _____

   _____

   _____

4. Does the syllogism use valid logic? If not, what mistake does it make?

   _____

   _____

   _____

5. What inference does the author of the argument draw from the conclusion of the syllogism, and does he have a good reason to make this inference?

   _____

   _____

   _____

6. Do you think Lady Gaga's rise in popularity was due mostly to illegal downloading? What are some other possible reasons for her popularity?

   _____

   _____

   _____

Evaluating Inductive Arguments

Informal Fallacies

Informal fallacies are fallacies that affect inductive arguments. Formal fallacies (such as the fallacy of Affirming the Consequent), are fallacies that affect deductive arguments.

Inductive arguments are harder to evaluate than deductive arguments, primarily because the conclusion of a good inductive argument is only probably true. If there is any way that the conclusion of a deductive argument could be false while the premises are true, you know that argument uses bad logic. But the chance always exists that the conclusion of an inductive argument, even a *cogent* one (an argument with a high degree of probability) might be false, so no simple test exists to figure out if an inductive argument is good.

Instead, you need to check to see if the evidence sufficiently supports the conclusion. There needs to be enough accurate, relevant evidence that the conclusion seems highly probable. You have already learned to evaluate evidence in that regard. Another major thing you need to look out for are informal fallacies, which often compromise the logic of inductive arguments. A **fallacy** is a mistake in the reasoning of an argument. The problem with fallacies is that they are superficially convincing; unless you know about the most common types, you might be fooled into thinking an inductive argument is good when it isn't.

Recognizing Informal Fallacies If you recognize any of the informal fallacies listed below in an inductive argument, you will know that the argument is probably not cogent or probable. An example of each fallacy is given after the definition of the fallacy.

Ad Hominem

Ad hominem literally means "against the man." This fallacy consists of an attack on the person making the argument rather than on the argument itself. People who commit this fallacy hope that if they can get you to dislike the person making the argument, you will conclude that the argument is bad. Of course, who makes an argument doesn't have much to do with the quality of the argument:

> **Example:** "I see your evidence that if whaling continues at the current rate, whales will become extinct, but I don't believe it. Aren't you a member of that crazy PETA group? They are nothing but domestic terrorists, and so are you."

A specific type of the ad hominem fallacy is called the *You Too fallacy*. This fallacy is committed when one person tries to deflect an accusation by accusing the accuser of being guilty of the same offense. You might think of it as the "Two Wrongs Don't Make a Right" fallacy.

> **Example:** "I don't think you should be warning me about the dangers of binge drinking. Didn't I see you double-fisting beers at a party last weekend?"

Appeal to Force

When someone tries to convince you that an argument is correct by threatening you in some way, he or she has engaged in the *Appeal to Force fallacy*. Sometimes the threat is direct, but most times in the real world it is veiled or takes the form of political or economic pressure.

> **Example:** "Senator, I'm sure that you'll find my pro-choice argument convincing. As a side note, the donations that my Pro-Choice group usually makes to your campaign are under consideration at this very moment, and I hope I can argue in good conscience that they should be made at the same level this year."

Appeal to the Masses

If you argue that a claim is true because lots of people believe it, you've committed the fallacy of *Appeal to the Masses*. But how many people believe a claim has nothing to do with whether it's actually true. At one time most people believed the sun revolved around the earth, but of course that didn't make it so.

> **Example:** "You don't believe in Bigfoot? How could thousands of people who believe in Bigfoot be wrong?"

Arguing from Ignorance

The fallacy of *Arguing from Ignorance* happens when an arguer asserts that a claim is true because you can't prove it false (or less often, that it's false because you can't prove it true).

As you've learned, though, you need good evidence before you accept a claim. How could a lack of evidence prove a claim? Of course it can't.

Example: "I know ghosts exist, because no one has proved that they don't."

Begging the Question

Begging the Question means that the conclusion of the argument is simply a restatement of the premise. This kind of fallacy is tricky, because there are many different ways to say the same thing, and so therefore you might not realize right away that the evidence is just the conclusion in different words.

Example: "Jennifer Lawrence is the most beautiful woman alive. I know that's true, because she's incredibly pretty."

A particular subtype of this fallacy is called circular reasoning. *Circular reasoning* occurs when the conclusion is dependent on premises for its support, and the premises are in turn dependent on the conclusion for their support.

Example: "We know that Mayor Richardson is an honest person. His autobiography says he never told a lie as an adult, and we can be sure his autobiography is reliable, because he's so honest."

Burden of Proof

The *Burden of Proof fallacy* is committed when someone makes a claim and then says that it's up to you to prove him or her wrong. The burden of proof, however, is rightfully on the person making the claim; if you want other people to believe something, you have to give evidence.

Example: "The Greek god Zeus actually exists. Prove that he doesn't."

Complex Question

The *Complex Question fallacy* means asking two questions but disguising them as only one question, and assuming that the first question has been answered when it hasn't.

Example: "When did you start stealing things?"

Either-Or

The *Either-Or fallacy* happens when an arguer artificially narrows choices or consequences of an argument down to two options. In fact, there are usually many more than two possible choices in the real world.

Example: "Either the soul can be scientifically detected, or it doesn't exist."

False Analogy

A *False Analogy* occurs when someone tries to use an analogy as evidence in an argument (see p. 227) when the similarity between the two things being compared is only superficial. A good analogy, one that would carry weight in an argument, compares two things that have essential similarities.

Example: "Since my car is red and can go really fast, your car, which is also red, must be able to go really fast as well."

False Authority

As you learned, expert testimony can be a reliable form of evidence. The fallacy of *False Authority* is committed when someone tries to use the testimony of an expert to support his or her argument, when the expert's proficiency lies outside of the area about which he or she is testifying. The person committing the fallacy hopes that you will be wowed by the fact that the person is an expert in one field, without noticing that he or she is not actually an expert in the field under question and therefore the endorsement is irrelevant.

> **Example**: "Bill Gates says that the foreign policy of Pre-emptive War is bad, so therefore you shouldn't support it."

False Cause

False Cause, also called *Post Hoc*, happens when one assumes that because one event happened after another event, the first event had to have caused the second event. Often, events are purely coincidental, and causation must be demonstrated.

> **Example**: "Several of the people who discovered King Tut's tomb later died tragic deaths. His tomb must be cursed."

Many superstitions arise from this fallacy. For example, if you see a black cat and then later have bad luck, did seeing the black cat cause your bad luck?

A subtype of this fallacy is *Mistaking Correlation for Causation*. This fallacy is committed when someone assumes that because two events occur together, one must have caused the other. Of course, it could be a coincidence, or a third event could be the root cause of the other events.

> **Example**: "The economy always seems to go south whenever a Republican president is in the White House. It seems that Republican presidencies cause economic downturns."

Guilt by Association

When someone attempts to discredit an argument or belief by pointing out that someone who is widely disliked also held that belief, he or she is engaging in the fallacy of *Guilt by Association*. Who believes a claim has nothing to do with the truth value of that claim.

> **Example**: "You oppose animal experimentation? You know who else opposed animal experimentation? Hitler."

Hitler also believed in working hard to accomplish his goals, but that doesn't automatically discredit the idea that you need to work hard; this should help you understand why the person holding an idea is not as important as the evidence and logic supporting the idea.

Hasty Generalization

Hasty Generalization is one of the key fallacies of inductive arguments, because it involves jumping to a conclusion based on too little evidence. If your sample size is not large enough, but you draw a conclusion from it anyway, you have committed the fallacy of Hasty Generalization. Sufficient evidence is needed for a good argument (p. 230). In one of the practices in Chapter 6, you identified this argument as inductive: "I looked at 100 sheep, and they were all white. All sheep are white." Given the huge number of sheep in the world and knowing what you know now about hasty generalization, can you logically conclude that "All sheep are white"?

> **Example**: "A person of a certain ethnicity stole my identity, so all people of that ethnicity are thieves."

© Jerry Sharp/Shutterstock.com

Moving the Goalposts

Moving the Goalposts means asking for evidence from your opponent that fits certain criteria, and then when your opponent provides that evidence, changing the criteria. In this way, your opponent is never able to prove her argument, even though she met the criteria you yourself set.

Example: "Amanda is a very stingy person. Do you have any evidence that she gives to charity? Oh, she gave to the American Cancer Federation last year? Well, that was only one charity. Oh, she also gave to the MS Foundation? Well, she didn't give more than $5,000.00, so she is definitely stingy."

Naturalistic Fallacy

The *Naturalistic fallacy* is committed when an arguer assumes that because something is natural, it must be good. Of course, many human-made substances are good, and many naturally occurring substances (like uranium) are harmful.

Example: "Chemotherapy shouldn't be used to treat cancer; it's just shooting chemicals into your body. Instead, cancer should be treated with all-natural herbs."

Red Herring

Red Herring means including irrelevant details in an argument to distract an opponent's attention. In this way, the person committing the fallacy hopes that the irrelevant material will be taken as evidence supporting the unrelated conclusion. On p. 227, you learned how important it is for evidence to be relevant.

> **Example:** "Perhaps passing the healthcare reform bill is an ethical necessity, but are we spending enough money on national defense? Do we want Iran attacking our troops while we are debating healthcare?"

Slippery Slope

The *Slippery Slope fallacy* occurs when an arguer suggests that taking an action will inevitably give rise to a chain of events that will lead to undesirable consequences, when the chain of events is not very likely, and the arguer makes no attempt to prove that it is likely.

> **Example:** "If we cut taxes, the government will go bankrupt, and the United States will become a Third World country."

Straw Man

When a person misrepresents his opponent's argument to make it sound ridiculous so that he can refute the ridiculous argument instead of the real one, he has committed the *Straw Man fallacy*. The arguer hopes that the mischaracterized argument will be mistaken for the real argument, and he probably also hopes that the ridiculous characterization will make his opponent look ludicrous.

> **Example:** "You believe that the drinking age should be lowered? Why would you argue that it is a good idea to have thousands of drunken teenagers running around?"

A final word on fallacies: Just because an argument contains a fallacy doesn't automatically mean that the conclusion of the argument is false. It just means that the argument is bad, although by pure luck the conclusion could still be true. If an argument does contain a fallacy, you need to reserve judgment on the conclusion, neither believing or disbelieving it, until you've heard logical arguments that use good evidence that support the conclusion, or until good counter-arguments are offered against it.

| Fallacies | PRACTICE 7-12 |

Directions: On another sheet of paper, make a chart detailing the above fallacies. Label the columns "Fallacy," "Definition," and "Example." Then fill in the chart.

| Fallacies | PRACTICE 7-13 |

Directions: Identify the logical fallacy best exemplified by each statement and write it in the blank. No fallacy is used more than once, but not all fallacies are used.

Here's a model

Organic foods are always better for you than other types of foods, regardless of vitamin content, simply because they are natural. _____naturalistic fallacy_____

Now you try

1. If you buy the new GM Courageous, you can be certain you'll be buying a wonderful automobile, because the GM Courageous is a great car. _____

2. No one has ever proven that aliens don't abduct people, so it's logical to believe that they do. _____

3. I took zinc last week and my cold went away. It worked for my mother too, and her best friend. Zinc cures colds! _____

4. I don't like your friend Joe because he has brown eyes. The serial killer Jeffrey Dahmer had brown eyes! _____

5. There is no way Socrates could have been right about morals. After all, Socrates was ugly. _____

6. You have the right to dispute your ticket in court, but if you dispute it and lose, you will gain points on your driver's license. No, I'm sure you don't want to dispute this ticket. _____

7. If we don't put prayer back in our schools immediately, then society will crumble.

_____

8. You know Brad Pitt's newest movie is a great film. It's number one at the box office.

_____

9. When you were skipping class, did you do something productive? _____

10. The World Bank is a terrible institution. After all, George Clooney testified to this very point in a press conference last night. _____

11. Every time I say a little magical saying, I find whatever I have lost. My little magical saying actually works to recover lost objects. _____

12. It's not up to me to do your work for you. If you think I'm wrong about chiropractors being able to cure heart disease, show me the evidence against it. _____

PRACTICE 7-14 | **Fallacies in a Short Passage**

Directions: Look back at Practice 7-2 on page 224. In the blanks below, identify the sentence or sentences where the author commits the indicated fallacy, then explain why it qualifies as an example of the indicated fallacy.

Straw Man _____

_____

_____

Explanation _____

Ad Hominem _____

Explanation _____

Begging the Question _____

Explanation _____

PRACTICE 7-15 | **Fallacies in Real Life**

Directions: Read some political blogs or newspaper opinion columns. Find a piece of writing that commits one or more of the fallacies you just learned about. Bring your findings in to share them with the class.

Using Argument Maps in Evaluation

This is where the *argument maps* you learned to make in Chapter 6 come in handy—visually showing the logic of inductive and deductive arguments and helping you determine which evidence goes with which conclusion will make it far easier for you to evaluate arguments. Consider the argument from p. 206 of Chapter 6, reprinted below in Figure 7-4. The argument map allows you to determine:

- The primary argument, circled in green (the circles on the map are just explanatory—you don't need to make them on your argument maps).
- The total number of arguments in this passage, four.

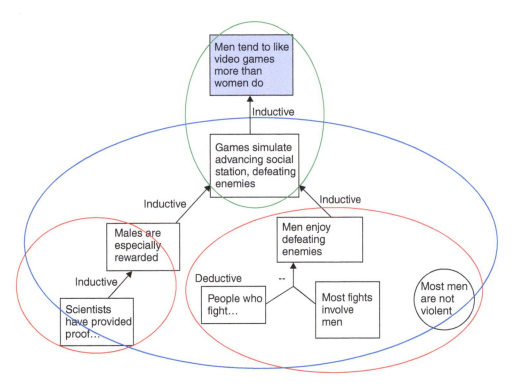

■ Figure 7-4   Evaluating an Argument Using an Argument Map

- That the evidence for the primary argument comes from the sub-argument, circled in blue, and that the evidence for the blue sub-argument comes from the red sub-arguments.
- That almost all of the arguments are inductive, but one of the sub-arguments is deductive.

Having figured out these things, you now know exactly which evidence you need to evaluate (possibly including evaluating the source of the evidence). You also now know exactly which logical relationships you need to judge to make sure they don't contain any fallacies or that they are valid. You can more easily put to use the skills of evaluation you just learned.

Real-World Mistakes of Evaluation and Their Consequences

Failures in evaluation that take place on a large scale can cost thousands of lives and billions of dollars. The Iraq War was at least partially the result of a failure to evaluate. The Bush administration rightfully wanted to protect the people of the United States from weapons of mass destruction (WMDs) in the hands of rogue nations, and they received intelligence indicating that Saddam Hussein, dictator of Iraq, possessed such weapons. The source of the information was an Iraqi defector codenamed "Curveball." Curveball testi-fied that Iraq possessed banned biological weapons, and he claimed that he had worked at a plant that manufactured mobile weapons labs. He insinuated that he was an important person in Saddam's Iraq and that he had proof positive of the existence of the WMDs. Colin Powell, Secretary of State, used Curveball as his primary source for a presentation to the United Nations, a presentation that was instrumental in justifying the war in Iraq.

It turned out that Curveball wasn't a credible source. Although his initial reports were believed long enough to contribute to the war, it was soon discovered that he was a habit-ual liar. For example, he claimed that he had graduated first in his class at the university he attended, when in fact he had graduated at the bottom of his class. He was also fired from his job at a television station for theft. Moreover, he seemed to be an alcoholic, often showing up for intelligence-related briefings drunk or hung-over. All of these were red flags, warning signs that Curveball was not to be trusted. Yet no one discounted the evidence he gave to support his claim that Iraq had WMDs, even though he was an unreliable source for such evidence.

It's not clear who's to blame for this failure of evaluation—the CIA seems to have had a hand in the mistake, having taken note of some of the warning signs, but the German intelligence service were the ones dealing directly with Curveball, so they also seem to bear part of the blame. Still, it's clear that a major failure of evaluation led to the president of the United States having faulty information concerning a threat to his country—faulty information that in large measure caused him to authorize a war he might not have otherwise approved.

For Discussion

1. Explain how the above discussion details a failure of evaluation.
2. How could the CIA and/or the Bush administration have avoided these mistakes of evaluation?

Real-World Successes of Critical Thinking

The Environmental Movement

You just read about the cost of failing to successfully employ the skills involved in critical thinking, but thinking critically can also produce great results. During the 20th and 21st centuries, the Environmental Movement successfully identified and called attention to the effects of pollution and other dangers facing our planet.

Directions: Using the internet or a library, research the Environmental Movement in depth. Prepare a detailed description of the successes of the Environmental Movement, including an explanation of any skills, character traits, and standards of critical thinking that contributed to its success. Get ready to share your findings with the class.

Chapter Summary

- When you *evaluate* something, you see if it is good or if it works.
- *Fair-mindedness* means treating other's views as you would treat your own. You can practice being fair-minded by restating the opponent's position in neutral language, looking for what is good about the position, trying to get into your opponent's mindset, remaining humble, and finally evaluating it.
- When you *evaluate arguments,* you check to see that they use good evidence, employ good logic (deductive arguments must be sound and inductive arguments must be cogent), and are not refuted by counter-arguments.
- When you *evaluate the evidence of an argument,* check to see that it is relevant, sufficient, non-opinionated, and accurate. Accuracy can often be judged by checking the *credibility of the author or source.* To check credibility, make sure that the author or source is current, accessible, verifiable, unbiased, and knowledgeable.
- *Assumptions* can be evaluated by checking to see if they are supportable, unbiased, and consistent.
- To *evaluate the logic of an argument,* determine whether it is inductive or deductive. A deductive argument is *valid* when its conclusion must be true if its premises are

true. It's *sound* when it is valid and has good evidence. An inductive argument is *cogent* if it commits no fallacies and has good, sufficient evidence.

- *Argument maps* help you evaluate arguments by visually illustrating them.

READ, WRITE, AND THINK CRITICALLY: SECTION TWO

Directions: Survey the following text and answer the questions below. Then, read and annotate the selection and answer the questions that follow.

1. What is your prior knowledge of this topic?

   _____

   _____

   _____

2. Read the title and first paragraph and make a predication about the content of the article.

   _____

   _____

   _____

"Crack Baby" Study Ends with Unexpected but Clear Result

Susan Fitzgerald

Susan Fitzgerald is a freelance journalist and college journalist instructor. She has published several books as well as articles in The Philadelphia Inquirer, *where the following piece appeared in 2017.*

1 Jaimee Drakewood hurried in from the rain, eager to get to her final appointment at Children's Hospital of Philadelphia.

2 Ever since her birth 23 years ago, a team of researchers has been tracking every aspect of her development—gauging her progress as an infant, measuring her IQ as a preschooler, even **peering** into her adolescent brain using an MRI machine.

3 Now, after nearly a quarter century, the federally funded study was ending, and the question the researchers had been asking was answered.

4 Did cocaine harm the long-term development of children like Jaimee, who were exposed to the drug in their mother's womb?

5 The researchers had expected the answer would be a resounding yes. But it wasn't. Another factor would prove far more critical.

6 A crack **epidemic** was raging in Philadelphia in 1989 when Hallam Hurt, then chair of neonatology at Albert Einstein Medical Center on North Broad Street, began a study to evaluate the effects of in-utero cocaine exposure on babies. In maternity wards in Philadelphia and elsewhere, caregivers were seeing more mothers hooked on cheap, smokable crack cocaine. A 1989 study in Philadelphia found that nearly one in six newborns at city hospitals had mothers who tested positive for cocaine.

7 Troubling stories were circulating about the so-called crack babies. They had small heads and were easily **agitated** and prone to tremors and bad muscle tone, according to reports, many of which were anecdotal. Worse, the babies seemed aloof and avoided eye contact. Some social workers predicted a lost generation—kids

with a host of learning and emotional deficits who would overwhelm school systems and not be able to hold a job or form meaningful relationships. The "crack baby" image became symbolic of bad mothering, and some cocaine-using mothers had their babies taken from them or, in a few cases, were arrested.

8   It was amid that climate that Hurt organized a study of 224 near-term or full-term babies born at Einstein between 1989 and 1992—half with mothers who used cocaine during pregnancy and half who were not exposed to the drug in utero. All the babies came from low-income families, and nearly all were African Americans.

9   Hurt hoped the study would inform doctors and nurses caring for cocaine-exposed babies and even guide policies for drug prevention, treatment, and follow-up **interventions**. But she never anticipated that the study, funded by the National Institute on Drug Abuse, would become one of the largest and longest-running studies of in-utero cocaine exposure.

10 One mother who signed up was Jaimee's mom, Karen Drakewood. She was on an all-night crack binge in a drug house near her home in the city's West Oak Lane section when she went into labor. Jaimee was born Jan. 13, 1990, weighing an even 7 pounds.

11 "Jaimee was beautiful when she was born. A head full of hair. She looked like a porcelain doll," Karen Drakewood, now 51, said recently in her Overbrook kitchen. "She was perfect."

12 But Drakewood knew looks could be deceiving.

13 "My worst fear was that Jaimee would be slow, mentally retarded, or something like that because of me doing drugs," she said. She agreed to enroll her baby in the cocaine study at Einstein. Drakewood promised herself that she would turn her life around for the sake of Jaimee and her older daughter, but she soon went back to smoking crack.

14 Hurt arrived early at Children's Hospital one morning in June to give a talk on her team's findings to coworkers. After nearly 25 years of studying the effects of cocaine and publishing or presenting dozens of findings, it wasn't easy to summarize it in a PowerPoint presentation. The study received nearly $7.9 million in federal funding over the years, as well as $130,000 from the Einstein Society.

15 Hurt, who had taken her team from Einstein to Children's in 2003, began her lecture with quotations from the media around the time the study began. A social worker on TV predicted that a crack baby would grow up to "have an IQ of perhaps 50." A print article quoted a psychologist as saying "crack was interfering with the central core of what it is to be human," and yet another article predicted that crack babies were "doomed to a life of uncertain suffering, of probable deviance, of permanent inferiority."

16 Hurt, who is also a professor of **pediatrics** at the University of Pennsylvania, is always quick to point out that cocaine can have devastating effects on pregnancy. The drug can cause a problematic rise in a pregnant woman's blood pressure, trigger premature labor, and may be linked to a dangerous condition in which the placenta tears away from the uterine wall. Babies born prematurely, no matter the cause, are at risk for a host of medical and developmental problems. On top of that, a parent's drug use can create a chaotic home life for a child.

17 Hurt's study enrolled only full-term babies so the possible effects of prematurity did not skew the results. The babies were then evaluated periodically, beginning at six months and then every six or 12 months on through young adulthood. Their mothers agreed to be tested for drug use throughout the study.

18 The researchers consistently found no significant differences between the cocaine-exposed children and the controls. At age 4, for instance, the average IQ of the cocaine-exposed children was 79.0 and the average IQ for the nonexposed children was 81.9. Both numbers are well below the average of 90 to 109 for U.S. children in the same age group. When it came to school readiness at age 6, about 25 percent of children in each group scored in the **abnormal** range on tests for math and letter and word recognition.

19 "We went looking for the effects of cocaine," Hurt said. But after a time "we began to ask, 'Was there something else going on?'"

20 While the cocaine-exposed children and a group of nonexposed controls performed about the same on tests, both groups lagged on developmental and intellectual measures compared to the norm. Hurt and her team began to think the "something else" was poverty.

21 As the children grew, the researchers did many evaluations to tease out environmental factors that could be affecting their development. On the upside, they found that children being raised in a nurturing

home—measured by such factors as caregiver warmth and affection and language stimulation—were doing better than kids in a less nurturing home. On the downside, they found that 81 percent of the children had seen someone arrested; 74 percent had heard gunshots; 35 percent had seen someone get shot; and 19 percent had seen a dead body outside—and the kids were only 7 years old at the time. Those children who reported a high exposure to violence were likelier to show signs of depression and anxiety and to have lower self-esteem.

22 More recently, the team did MRI scans on the participants' brains. Some research has suggested that **gestational** cocaine exposure can affect brain development, especially the dopamine system, which in turn can harm **cognitive** function. An area of concern is "executive functioning," a set of skills involved in planning, problem-solving, and working memory.

23 The investigators found one brain area linked to attention skills that differed between exposed and nonexposed children, but they could not find any clinically significant effect on behavioral tests of attention skills.

24 Drug use did not differ between the exposed and nonexposed participants as young adults. About 42 percent used marijuana and three tested positive for cocaine one time each.

25 The team has kept tabs on 110 of the 224 children originally in the study. Of the 110, two are dead—one shot in a bar and another in a drive-by shooting—three are in prison, six graduated from college, and six more are on track to graduate. There have been 60 children born to the 110 participants.

26 The years of tracking kids have led Hurt to a conclusion she didn't see coming.

27 "Poverty is a more powerful influence on the outcome of inner-city children than gestational exposure to cocaine," Hurt said at her May lecture.

28 Other researchers also couldn't find any devastating effects from cocaine exposure in the womb. Claire Coles, a psychiatry professor at Emory University, has been tracking a group of low-income Atlanta children. Her work has found that cocaine exposure does not seem to affect children's overall cognition and school performance, but some evidence suggests that these children are less able to **regulate** their reactions to stressful stimuli, which could affect learning and emotional health.

29 Coles said her research had found nothing to back up predictions that cocaine-exposed babies were doomed for life. "As a society we say, 'Cocaine is bad and therefore it must cause damage to babies,'" Coles said. "When you have a myth, it tends to linger for a long time."

30 Deborah A. Frank, a pediatrics professor at Boston University who has tracked a similar group of children, said the "crack baby" label led to **erroneous** stereotyping. "You can't walk into a classroom and tell this kid was exposed and this kid was not," Frank said. "Unfortunately, there are so many factors that affect poor kids. They have to deal with so much stress and deprivation. We have also found that exposure to violence is a huge factor."

31 Frank said that cocaine—along with other illicit drugs, alcohol, and cigarettes—"isn't good for babies," but the belief that they would "grow up to be addicts and criminals is not true. Some kids have stunned us with how well they've done."

32 Jaimee Drakewood came to her last visit at Children's with her 16-month-old son KyMani in tow. It was the 31st time she had met with the researchers.

33 "We do appreciate everything you've done, because it's not easy to get to all these appointments," said team member Kathleen Dooley, as she handed Drakewood a framed certificate of appreciation. "We are proud of you and we feel you are family, because you are."

34 The team plans to stay in touch with study participants each year. They have started a new study that uses MRI and other tools to explore the neural and cognitive effects of poverty on infant development.

35 "Given what we learned," Hurt said, "we are invested in better understanding the effects of poverty. How can early effects be detected? Which developing systems are affected? And most important, how can findings inform interventions for our children?"

36 The team considers Jaimee and her mother, Karen, among their best success stories. Jaimee is heading into her senior year at Tuskegee University in Alabama and hopes to become a food inspector. She is home for the summer with her son and working as a lifeguard at a city pool.

37 After a few starts and stops, including a year in jail, Karen Drakewood is off drugs and works as a residential adviser at Gaudenzia House. Her older daughter just received a master's degree at Drexel University; her son is

a student at Florida Atlantic University. Even in the worst moments, Karen Drakewood said she tried to show her kids "what their future could hold." "If a child sees the light, they will follow it."

38 Jaimee Drakewood credits her big sister and mother for keeping her on track. "I've seen my mom at her lowest point and I've seen her at her highest. That hasn't stopped me from seeing the superwoman in her regardless of where she was at," Jaimee said.

39 Despite her family's history, Jaimee believes she and her siblings are "destined to have accomplishments, to be greater than our parents."

3. Use context clues and/or a dictionary to define the following words (marked in bold in the reading).

   a. Peering (para. 2): _____

   b. Epidemic (para. 6): _____

   c. Agitated (para. 7): _____

   d. Interventions (para. 9): _____

   e. Pediatrics (para. 16): _____

   f. Gestational (para. 22): _____

   g. Cognitive (para. 22): _____

   h. Regulate (para. 28): _____

   i. Erroneous (para. 30): _____

4. What is the claim of the article? Put it into your own words.

   _____

   _____

   _____

5. What evidence does the author give to support her claim? Identify the type of each evidence you cite.

   _____

   _____

   _____

6. In paragraphs 7 and 15, people made predictions and arrived at conclusions about "crack babies." Did the people doing so commit any fallacies? If so, which ones?

   _____

   _____

   _____

   _____

7. On another sheet of paper, write a journal entry in which you reflect on stereotypes and what this article has to say about them.

8. Write a critical analysis (see instructions in Chapter 8) in which you carefully evaluate this article.

CHAPTER 8

Explanation

Learning Goals

In this chapter you will learn how to

➤ Explain Your Thoughts
➤ Trust Your Reasoning
➤ Develop Your Writing Using the 5 Es
➤ Use Patterns of Organization in Writing
➤ Write about Reading through Three Types of Writing Assignments
➤ Communicate Orally
➤ Adhere to Grammatical Standards

PREVIEW OF TERMS

Explanation p. 263

Reasoning p. 264

Graphic organizer p. 265

Communication p. 265

Prewriting strategies
   p. 266

Brainstorming p. 266

Questioning p. 266

Freewriting p. 266

Mapping p. 266

Thesis statement p. 266

Paraphrasing p. 267

Critical response p. 272

Critical analysis p. 276

Journal p. 283

Common knowledge
   p. 285

Plagiarism p. 285

Oral communication
   p. 286

See glossary, pp. 391–397

What Is Explanation?

In the 1950s sitcom "I Love Lucy," Desi Arnaz's character Ricky Ricardo would frequently say to his wife, "Lucy, you got some explainin' to do!" This was his typical response to some mischief Lucy had caused. What Ricky wanted was an **explanation**—a clear account of the reasoning used by Lucy that somehow resulted in a funny situation for the characters. Like Lucy, you will often need to explain yourself so that your logic can be followed by others.

© Tony Baggett/ Shutterstock.com

Explanation is the skill of putting ideas (your own or someone else's) into words. When you explain something, your goal is to be clear and understandable so that others can recognize your evidence and follow your logic. This chapter focuses on explanation, both written and oral. You already learned how to write a summary and a paraphrase (see Chapter 3, pp. 86–91), so you have already had some experience with writing to explain what you've read. In this chapter, you will develop the ability to respond to a reading by practicing three types of writing exercises frequently assigned by instructors:

1. Critical response
2. Critical analysis
3. Journal

In addition, you will review the patterns of organization from the standpoint of an author (you learned about these patterns in Chapter 6 from the perspective of a reader). As you know, critical readers identify an author's pattern of organization to help them make sense of the information they are reading. Writers are conscientious about choosing the pattern of organization that best suits their topic and purpose and makes explanation easier.

This chapter focuses on *critical writing*—using the skills of a critical thinker (comprehension, interpretation, inference, monitoring, analysis, evaluation, explanation, and problem-solving) to explain ideas in written format, usually while creating an argument. Critical writing differs from *creative writing* in that the creative authors of poems, novels, and short stories use writing as a means of expressing their feelings and making a personal connection. Out of the three common writing assignments listed above, the journal is the most creative and original. The others (the critical response and the critical analysis) will require you to stick closely to the tenets of critical thinking and reading.

Before you take on the task of explaining yourself through writing, however, let's review the attitude of trust in reasoning.

Reviewing the Critical Thinker's Traits: Trusting Your Reasoning

Reasoning is the process of using the information available to you to come to logical conclusions and decisions. Using what you have learned so far in this book to approach an issue or a problem will lead you to a justifiable conclusion.

Have you ever had the experience of doubting a decision you have made? That uncomfortable feeling often results from approaching an issue quickly and carelessly or by reacting emotionally (and not logically). For example, say you have to make a big decision in your life such as whether or not you should move to a different state for a good job opportunity. If you quickly decide not to move because you will miss your friends and because your current job isn't that bad, then you might doubt yourself and always wonder if you made the wrong decision. On the other hand, if you make the decision by approaching the issue carefully and systematically the way a critical thinker would approach it, you are more likely to be satisfied with the result. Instead of making an emotional decision based on what your friends are doing and what you're comfortable with, you can make a logical decision by identifying your career goals, by researching the company, by visiting the towns and cities in close proximity to the job site, by speaking to other people already working for the company, by analyzing how your financial situation would be affected by the new opportunity, and by cautiously weighing the pros and cons of the available options. Careful consideration may convince you to move or it may persuade you to stay in your current job in your current town, but as long as you have arrived at the decision logically rather than emotionally, you can trust that you made the right decision. You will not be as likely to doubt yourself later: you will trust that your reasoning led to the best outcome for you.

> " I think, therefore I am. "
> —René Descartes

Trusting in reason also involves having the courage to follow your reasoning where it leads. Have you ever begun to investigate an issue and then said to yourself, "I don't know if I like where this is going"? A critical thinker who trusts in reason will nonetheless continue on, for truth is what matters most to him.

Thinker to Emulate: Rachel Carson

© Everett Collection/Newscom

Rachel Carson (1907-1964) was a biologist and writer best known for her book *Silent Spring* (1962), a ground-breaking indictment of the use of pesticides. Prior to writing full-time, she worked as an aquatic biologist with the U.S. Bureau of Fisheries and U.S. Fish and Wildlife Service, which gave her opportunities to research and publish articles and books about sea life. Through this work, Carson came to recognize the dangers DDT (dichlorodiphenyltrichloroethane) posed to marine life and birds. As DDT had been used with great success during WWII to control the spread of malaria and typhus, Carson knew that there would be resistance to her findings, especially by people in the agricultural and chemical industries. She spent years researching pesticides both in the United States and in Europe and found a tremendous amount of documentation to support her claim that they caused cancer in people and serious harm to the environment. Carson argued that scientists should find an alternative to DDT and that other pesticides should be more fully researched and more carefully used. The publication of *Silent Spring* had a tremendous impact. Carson testified before a Congressional committee and, eventually, DDT was banned. Carson is a thinker to emulate because she trusted her reasoning enough to go where the evidence led her—even if that meant inciting controversy—and to explain her logic so that others could understand her concerns and take action.

By taking the extra time and effort to think systematically through an issue and to write about it thoroughly, you can be confident that your reasoning is good. When faced with a big decision or an intellectual challenge, approach the situation with the following tips in mind.

Tips for Critical Thinkers: Trusting Your Reasoning

- **Remind yourself of the power of reason**. Think of what people have been able to accomplish solely with the power of their minds.
- **Think of your past intellectual successes**. Recall times that you solved a challenging problem, successfully wrote a paper, or skillfully handled a controversial topic. At the same time, remember it is important to be humble, to recognize when you don't have all the answers and when you need to consult references or experts in the field.
- **Get organized**. Take the time to use or develop a **graphic organizer** (a visual of the information) or a pro/con list. The more organized your thinking is, the more likely it is that you can trust it.
- **Be intellectually brave.** Have the courage of your convictions and be willing to follow your reasoning where it leads.
- **Know that effort (and not how much intelligence you are born with) is what leads to success.** In the next chapter, you will learn more about persistence (working toward a goal in spite of challenges and set-backs). As a critical thinker you will use your intelligence to approach challenges, but it is important not to give up even when a task seems difficult. If you think that you aren't "smart enough," then you might just need to do some additional research to get the information you need to work through a problem. Trust that focusing on your goal and working diligently to reach it can result in great success.

Discussion Questions

1. Can you think of a time that you had to make a big decision? How did you approach it? Did you doubt yourself? Did you base your decision mostly on logical reasons or emotional ones? How did your approach to making the decision affect how much you trusted your reasoning? Explain.

2. It is often harder to trust yourself when popular opinion is against you (as was the case with some of Rachel Carson's findings). What advice would you give someone who has to face a hostile or critical audience?

EXPAND YOUR UNDERSTANDING

Learning More about DDT While Writing Critically

Directions: Visit the following websites to research DDT for yourself. Then, on another sheet, answer the questions that follow.

- http://toxics.usgs.gov/definitions/ddt.html
- www.chem.duke.edu/~jds/cruise_chem/pest/pest1.html
- www.eco-usa.net/toxics/chemicals/ddt.shtml

THINK AND WRITE CRITICALLY

1. DDT was credited with saving lives and increasing crop production. How do you think Rachel Carson weighed these benefits against the negatives her research exposed?
2. How would she answer critics who were in favor of using DDT?

THINK
AND WRITE
CRITICALLY

Writing to Explain Using the 5 Es

Throughout this book, you have become skilled at recognizing both effective **communication** (such as a paragraph with a clear topic sentence and useful supporting details or a clearly executed speech) and ineffective communication (such as a paragraph filled with ambiguous language and logical fallacies or a confusing speech filled with jargon). The skill of explanation requires you to find ways to effectively communicate your reasoning to others, typically through written or oral communication. Many of the concepts you have learned so far about critical reading will come in handy as you focus on writing effectively in response to a text. When you write to explain, keep these five Es in mind: Explore, Express, Expand, Evaluate, and Enhance. See Figure 8-1 on p. 267 for a visual representation of this process.

The Five Es for Writing to Explain

1. **Explore.** First, you need to explore the topic or text. It's hard to write anything of substance if you don't know much about the topic or if you barely skimmed the reading! If you are responding to a specific reading, then you should explore it by reading it several times and annotating it thoroughly. Use graphic organizers and prewriting strategies to help focus your thinking. **Prewriting strategies** involve thinking about and organizing your ideas about a topic prior to writing. Prewriting helps you get started, often the hardest part of writing. Common prewriting strategies include the following:

   - **Brainstorming** is thinking of and writing about whatever comes to mind. When you brainstorm, simply write down words or short phrases; at this stage, you do not have to write complete sentences. The important thing to remember is to avoid censoring yourself; in other words, don't stop yourself from writing down or saying something because you don't think it is good enough.

   - **Questioning** is a prewriting strategy in which you pose questions about the topic or reading that you would like to have answered. When you ask questions of the topic, you want to steer away from questions that would generate one-word or "yes/no" answers, as those will not be complex enough to explore further. Instead, you should ask more sophisticated questions that give you the opportunity to learn more about the subject as you seek answers.

   - **Freewriting** is exactly what it sounds like: You write freely without worrying about the mechanics of writing (such as grammar and spelling). Some writers will set a timer and write until the timer goes off (with the option of continuing to write if they wish). Through freewriting, you get your thoughts onto paper, and it can also get you past your initial reluctance to start writing. Another advantage of freewriting is that it can show you how much you know (or don't know!) about a subject.

   - **Mapping**—creating a visual representation of what you want to say—helps you identify your topic, major details, and minor details. In the center of your map, put the topic in a large circle or box. Draw lines out from the topic as you think of major details that you want to cover. From those major details, draw additional lines to minor details (often in smaller boxes or circles). As a prewriting strategy, mapping can encourage you to get visually focused on the writing task.

2. **Express.** Once you have read and annotated the text completely, start to form an opinion about it. Ask yourself how you feel about the issue: do you agree or disagree with points you came across during your reading? Do you have strong reactions or emotions? If you had a conversation about this subject, what would you say about it? In other words, what is your opinion? Even if you change your opinion several times as you work on the assignment, you should still try to write it out in the form of a **thesis statement**—a single sentence that expresses the topic and your opinion about it. An *explicit thesis*, one that is clearly expressed (rather than an implied thesis), will serve as a clear guide to you as you write about what you have read.

3. **Expand.** This step is probably the most time-consuming, because you will need to expand upon your reasons for holding your opinion. This is where evidence comes into play. An unfounded opinion (an opinion that lacks solid grounds for holding it) is weak and unconvincing. Therefore, when you write to explain, you need to elaborate on the reasons behind your opinion. As you detail the reasons you have for expressing your thesis, you might need to conduct some research or reread the original passage. Consider the types

of evidence covered in Chapter 6, and try to address a variety of evidence in your writing.

Whether you are writing a critical response, critical analysis, or journal entry, one of the best ways to expand on your ideas is to incorporate some of the ideas of the author you have been reading through paraphrasing and quoting (be sure to cite using proper documentation style according to your instructor's requirements). Most of your paper should be in your own words, so you will rely more on paraphrasing than on quoting. As you learned in Chapter 3 (p. 89), **paraphrasing** is rewording an author's original text to make it easier to understand. When an author writes something particularly well or if a passage is difficult to paraphrase without losing some of the author's message, then you should quote directly from the text. If you use a direct quotation, then you cannot change anything from the original unless you use brackets (to show a word has been changed or added for clarity) or an ellipsis (three spaced dots to show that words have been omitted).

Spotlight on Standards: Clarity

Clarity, one of the standards of critical thinkers (in addition to accuracy, completeness, fairness, relevance, and significance), means the state of being clear or lucid. If information is cloudy, it could lead to misunderstandings and confusion. Therefore, critical thinkers will make every effort to ensure that their own writing or speech is clear. In addition, they will attempt to clarify other writer's or speaker's information if it is misleading or vague (see Chapter 3 for a review of deciphering unclear language). Sometimes information is unclear simply because you might not have enough prior knowledge to process it; for example, if you were reading a research study that cites statistics, but you never took a math course in statistics, then you might be able to find somebody to help explain the unclear information to you. When you are writing, the final step is to enhance your product, and, ideally, you will focus on clarity. You should read out loud or have a classmate read your work to identify potential troublesome spots. If you or a peer editor says something like "this doesn't make sense" or "this isn't clear" or "this is vague," then it is likely you need to work on clarity. Try to keep your explanations simple: Often clear, precise, everyday language is better than trying to impress your readers with unusual word choices and unnecessarily complex sentence structure.

4. **Evaluate.** Once you have expanded upon your reasoning, you can evaluate your logic and how well you expressed yourself. Ask yourself some tough questions: Did I cover the topic adequately? Did I research (if necessary) or reread the original work several times? Are my reasons to support my opinion convincing? Are there any logical fallacies? Did I evaluate and measure my work against the standards of a critical thinker? Does my tone suit the audience and the subject matter? Did I communicate clearly and effectively? Did I come to a conclusion that I trust? When you evaluate, you might find that a section of your paper is not well supported; if that is the case, then you may need to go back and reread the original passage(s) and add more support in the form of paraphrases or quotes. An essential component of evaluation is revision (literally meaning to see again). Upon honest evaluation, you will probably find that your draft is lacking in some areas. Perhaps you need to reorganize a section or add details. If any passages are boring, include an amusing anecdote or compelling evidence. You should

Explore	Express	Expand	Evaluate	Enhance
• Use prewriting strategies • Read the text several times • Annotate • Fill out graphic organizers	• Determine your opinion about topic • Formulate a thesis statement • Use paraphrases and quotations from the reading	• Detail the reasons for holding your opinion • Provide responses to anticipated objections to your opinion • Add more paraphrases and quotes	• Make sure your logic is sound • See if you have thoroughly and fairly covered topic • Consider the appropriateness of your tone • Assess whether or not you trust your reasoning • Evaluate organization, word choices, and details • Revise: achieve the standards of a critical thinker	• Proofread and edit • Improve upon sentence structure • Add (or change) transitions • Verify the correctness of references and citations (if necessary) • Adhere to publication requirements (font, spacing) • Prepare to submit to audience

■ **Figure 8-1**   Writing to Explain: Explore, Express, Expand, Evaluate, and Enhance

focus on organization, word choices, and content during a thoughtful revision process. Revising well should help you and your paper get closer to the standards of a critical thinker: accuracy, clarity, completeness, fairness, relevance, and significance.

5. **Enhance.** Last, you will enhance the final product by editing it. Put it aside for a day or two before you reach this stage, and then pretend you are reading it for the first time. If any sections are still confusing even after revising during the last step, make improvements to your sentence structure and add well-chosen transitions. In addition, double-check that you have properly cited all references (if you used other research in your paper). Verify that you have complied with all publication and submission requirements such as font size, spacing, and documentation guidelines. Good points and logical reasoning can become muddled by grammatical errors or punctuation mistakes. Editing, the final step in the writing process, is your chance to change and improve your writing to make it more effective, and it will greatly enhance your paper.

Patterns of Development in Writing

As you learned in Chapter 6, patterns of development (or "thought patterns") are employed by writers to organize their ideas. In that chapter, you learned how identifying the pattern of development could help you with comprehension, inference, analysis, and other skills.

Pattern of Development	How to Use	Transitions
Cause and Effect	Brainstorm list of causes that led up to an event; brainstorm list of effects that occurred as results of a cause; because this pattern can lead to a complex array of causes and effects, it is best to focus your writing on one or the other	*because, cause, leads to, results in, as a consequence, therefore, reasons, happens, since*
Chronological	Tell a narrative or describe a process in time order; explain a historical event or period using chronological order	*first, second, now, then, later, during, after, before, until, finally, last, soon, next, subsequently, consequently, at the same time, dates/times*
Classification	Categorize, classify, or order assorted topics and discuss how and why they belong in a particular class (and don't belong in another class)	*order, category, classify, groups, traits, types, classes*
Comparison and Contrast	Compare and/or contrast two or more people, events, places, writing styles, theories, arguments, etc.	Comparison: *Similar to, similarities, in comparison, like, both, in common* Contrast: *In contrast, differences, different from, unlike, however, instead*
Definition	Define a term and develop the qualities inherent to the term with specific images	*defined as, is, termed, means*
Example	Give ample examples/evidence to develop a thesis	*for example, for instance, in this case, specifically, one reason, such as, some, few, many, especially, to illustrate*
Listing	Provide a list of ideas that are ranked similar in importance to support a thesis	*and, also, another, besides, in addition, moreover, furthermore*
Mixed	Use two or more patterns of development that work together to explain your ideas	Variety of transitions

■ **Figure 8-2** Uses of Patterns of Development in Writing

In this chapter, you will learn how to select the pattern of development that best suits the needs of your writing assignment. In addition, you will learn how to incorporate graphic organizers into the planning stages of writing.

If necessary, quickly review the patterns of development covered in Chapter 6 (p. 208) as well as the transitions covered in Chapter 3 (pp. 66–67). What you probably remember from those chapters is that most authors do not pick a pattern of development just for the heck of it ("Today I think I'll write a cause and effect essay."); nor do they randomly decide to insert transitions. Instead, their purpose and content drive the organization and use of transitions. Sometimes the pattern of development can help you generate ideas if you are stuck with writer's block. Figure 8-2 details how you can incorporate the patterns of development and corresponding transitions into your own writing.

Use Graphic Organizers to Organize Your Ideas

To help you organize your ideas, use graphic organizers to focus your thoughts before and during the writing process. The following graphic organizers (Figures 8-3 to 8-9) are available from your instructor, so you can ask for full-size copies, draw your own, or adapt them as necessary for your particular writing needs.

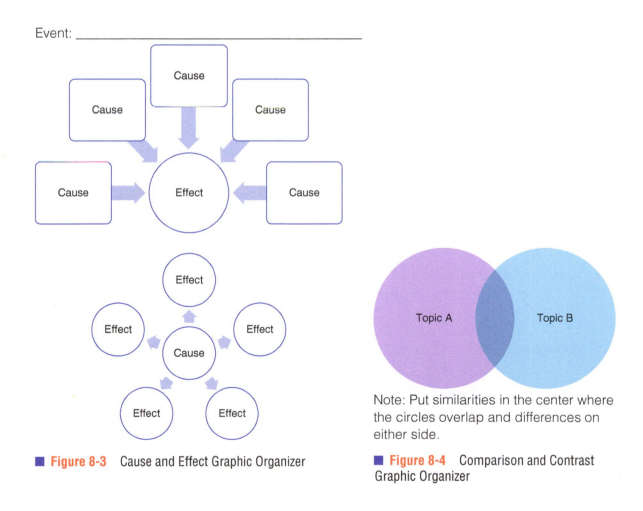

■ **Figure 8-3**   Cause and Effect Graphic Organizer

Note: Put similarities in the center where the circles overlap and differences on either side.

■ **Figure 8-4**   Comparison and Contrast Graphic Organizer

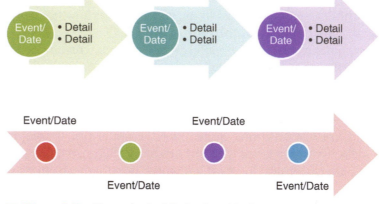

■ **Figure 8-5**   Chronological Order Graphic Organizers

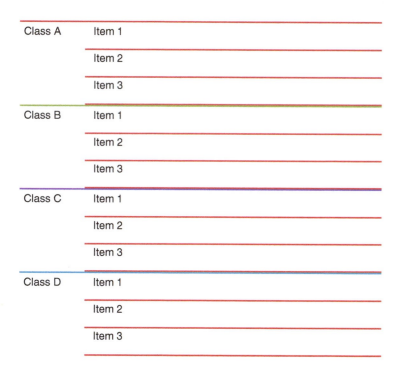

■ **Figure 8-6**   Classification Graphic Organizer

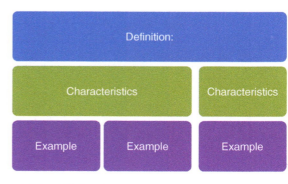

■ **Figure 8-7**   Definition Graphic Organizer

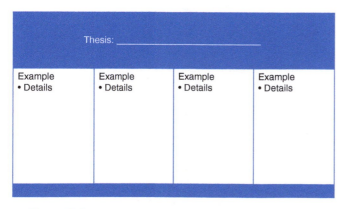

■ **Figure 8-8**   Example Graphic Organizer

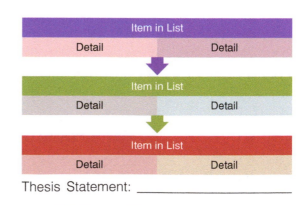

■ **Figure 8-9**   Listing Graphic Organizer

Directions: Plan an essay about an important decision you made in which it was vital that you trusted your reasoning (for example, where to live, which college to attend, what major to pick, how to spend your money, how to handle relationship trouble). Use at least two of the graphic organizers to generate ideas and organize your essay.

Writing about Reading

While we cannot possibly anticipate every type of writing assignment you will work on throughout your college years, we can give you the skills to tackle three of the most common types of writing assignments: *critical responses, critical analyses, and journals*. You will practice each of these types of writing in this chapter, and to help you write them, we have provided models for you throughout the chapter using the following reading, "Mouthing Off in America" by Stephen Randall.

Mouthing Off in America

Stephen Randall

Stephen Randall is a journalist and Deputy Editor of Playboy. *He is also the articles editor of the* Los Angeles *magazine and has written articles for* Los Angeles Times. *His novel* The Other Side of Mulholland *was a* Los Angeles Times *Book Review Best Book of 2001. He has also edited several editions of* The Playboy Interviews. *This article appeared in the* Los Angeles Times *on January 16, 2011.*

When it comes to opinions, we're all living in an intellectual Costco, where it's volume, volume, volume.

1   You think too much. And you're not alone. Everybody's thinking too much. We live in an era in which it is important to have opinions. Not necessarily smart or original ones; almost any opinion will do as long as it's forcefully expressed. When it comes to opinions, we're all living in an intellectual Costco, where it's volume, volume, volume.

2   It wasn't that long ago that opinions were something carefully considered and weighed, so that they'd stand the test of time and reflect well on the author. Thinkers were like gourmet chefs laboring over an elaborate meal they wanted to be perfect. But today, opinions are Big Macs—thrown together hastily, served by the billions and not very good for you.

3   You probably don't want to have as many opinions as you have. But everyone around you has them. There's cable news, of course. Keith Olbermann and Glenn Beck each have plenty of opinions. When you sell opinions for money, the way Keith and Glenn do, it doesn't take you long to catch on that the more opinions you have, the more money you make. So, like radish farmers who grow more radishes in order to get rich, Keith and Glenn create dozens of new opinions per night.

4   But here's the problem: They're not very smart opinions. And they're forcing everyone around them, including you, to also have far too many opinions. We post them on Facebook; we tweet them; we express them in comments on Huffington Post. We've become junior-grade cable goons—but paid much less.

5   We get angry too, just like Keith and Glenn. What's the point in having an opinion if it's not an angry opinion? If something upsets us—like a member of Congress and a bunch of innocent bystanders being shot in Tucson—we don't mourn, we fulminate. We assign blame. Or we deflect blame—angrily. It's hard to find the good guys when one side is self-righteously accusing the other side of lacking civility as if that were any more likely to spark violence than movies or video games, and the response is, weirdly, to defend a lack of civility as if it's a good thing.

6   Opinion inflation has invaded every aspect of our lives. It causes us to post our opinions about our dry cleaner on Yelp. Did you used to have an opinion about your dry cleaner, or was he just sort of there, like a shrub or a parking meter? Did you even notice what George W. Bush wore on his feet? Probably not, but half the country

wanted to weigh in on President Obama's wearing of flip-flops to the beach. If the Gap or Starbucks changed their logos a few years ago, would you have noticed? And more important, would you have run to Facebook (if it had existed) to cast your vote for the old Gap logo, as if it had always been a meaningful part of your life?

7 The Internet is a Petri dish of opinion inflation, breeding commentary like bacteria. Because few people do anything interesting or have anything factual to report, they toss off a short opinion. That, in turn, leads to opinion hyperinflation; just look at the comments sections on any blog. Opinions quickly devolve from Big Macs into rat poison. Civility makes only a rare appearance, and facts are no longer facts. Evolution, climate change, gravity—it's all one point of view against another. Everyone gets a vote, even the people who aren't particularly sane.

8 There was a time when thoughtful people tried to be balanced. The old-style political columnists were famous for saying nothing. They presented both sides of any given issue in an "on the one hand/on the other" fashion, pretty much allowing readers to form their own opinions, which—lacking proper guidance—readers rarely did. Walter Cronkite voiced so few opinions that when he uttered one—about the Vietnam War—it changed the course of history.

9 Of course, those days were boring. Today's onslaught of nonstop commentary everywhere you look is significantly more entertaining. Walter Lippmann was boring; Arianna Huffington is not. Eric Sevareid could put you to sleep faster than Ambien; Sean Hannity is a shot of double espresso (with the new, not the old, Starbucks logo).

10 Now we're hooked. We don't go to a new restaurant to eat a meal; we go there to dissect it and then tweet about it. We can't post a link to an article without giving it some sort of grade. We criticize the music we listen to and the TV we watch. Awards shows have been reduced to weird Joan Rivers screeds about what celebrities are wearing on the red carpet. Each dress has to be deconstructed by a panel of experts and found wanting. It's all turning us into surly teenagers who disagree with everything.

11 There's a certain irony, I realize, to expressing an opinion about opinions. And perhaps I should be grateful. Not only am I more entertained these days, but when I'm feeling lazy, I can switch from thinking too much to not thinking at all. I am so surrounded by opinions that I don't need any of my own. I can turn on Fox or MSNBC and adopt an entire political philosophy without knowing a thing. Of course, the problem is that when I share that philosophy, I don't sound intelligent, I sound like a drunk at a bar arguing with an empty barstool.

12 On his old HBO show, Dennis Miller used to end his trademark rants with, "Of course, that's just my opinion. I could be wrong." He was right. I could be wrong too. But he was also way too opinionated.

Critical Response Writing

A **critical response** is your reaction to a text after you have reflected on it and considered your own perspective on the issue being discussed. While it is expected that you will share some of your own experiences and opinions in a critical response, the original text must remain the focus of the work. Do not stray too far from the author's points in your attempt to interject your own ideas; your ideas must be in direct and close relation to the text itself. Think of the critical response as a discussion between you and the author or between you and other readers interested in the passage.

The length of a critical response varies, so you would do best to consult with your instructor. Sometimes a few well-developed paragraphs are sufficient; other times you need to devote several pages to your response. As with anything you write, you should identify the author, title, and copyright date within the first few sentences. Don't assume that your readers are as familiar with the text as you are: Summarize it.

Because the critical response includes personal reactions, you are encouraged to use first-person voice ("I feel . . . " or "In our country we tend to believe. . . . "). In addition, the critical response is not highly structured and does not require you to write a formal thesis statement; in fact, you can move spontaneously from one observation to the next so long as the critical response remains closely connected to the original text. To help you gather and organize your reactions, use an organizer such as this Planning Form for Critical Response.

Planning Form for Critical Response

Title of Reading: _____

Author: _____

Copyright date: _____

Explore
Annotate the reading then answer the following questions.

1. What idea(s) do you agree with?	
2. What idea(s) do you disagree with?	
3. What do you have questions about?	
4. What are some ideas you found intriguing and wish to explore further?	

Express

5. Briefly summarize the entire text in your own words (in 1-5 sentences).	
6. Select the points from #4 that you want to develop in your response.	

Expand	
7. Locate 3-5 quotes from the original that might help to support your point(s). List them here. Note: You do not have to use them all; once you start your draft, you might find that they are not all needed. Remember to include quotation marks and citation.	

Tips for Critical Thinkers: How to Write a Critical Response Using the 5 Es

- **Explore.** *Read the text. Read it again. Again. And again.* In other words, you need to be extremely familiar with the original text if you expect to have anything meaningful to add to the discussion. As you read, you should annotate. In particular, mark places where you either strongly agree or disagree. You should also mark places where you have questions or concerns about what the author has written. Use prewriting strategies (brainstorming, questioning, freewriting, mapping) to generate ideas to develop later in your paper.

- **Express.** *First off, identify the author, title, and copyright date, and briefly summarize the work. Look back over your annotations, think about what the text meant to you, and write about it.* Try to address some pertinent questions: Did the text affect you on a cultural level? Did the text touch you emotionally? Did it hurt or offend you in some way (if so, remember what you learned about defense mechanisms in Chapter 1)? What would you say to the author if you had the chance? Also, consider whether you should employ a specific pattern of development such as comparison/contrast as you reflect on the passage and explain your reaction to it.

- **Expand.** *Locate some particularly meaningful quotes from the author and integrate them into your critical response* using attributive tags ("The author argues. . ."). Expand upon your initial reaction (which might have been emotional and spontaneous) to include some logical connections to the original text.

- **Evaluate.** *Perhaps the most important consideration to evaluate is whether you digressed from the text and spent too much valuable time and space on your own experience.* If your response is no more than a personal narrative that is loosely connected to the reading (which might be more appropriate for a journal entry), then you need to revisit the text and pull in some quotes and examples of the author's to round out your response. As you evaluate how well you responded to the author's work, remember that the critical response is a discussion or dialog between you and the author or between you and other readers (not a monologue!).

- **Enhance.** *Read out loud for clarity.* If you have classmates who read the same reading, then you could utilize peer editing. Don't forget to make an appointment at your campus's Writing Center, especially if writing is not your strongest subject, to enhance your critical response. Refer to the grammar primer at the end of this chapter.

Sample Critical Response: "Mouthing Off in America" by Stephen Randall

In Stephen Randall's "Mouthing Off in America" in the *Los Angeles Times* (January 16, 2011), the author brings attention to the sheer number and poor quality of opinions in this country. He explains that people used to think about concepts cautiously so that when they actually expressed an opinion, it was thoughtful and important. Now, however, people throw opinions around carelessly, and they get bonus points if they can express them loudly, angrily, or obnoxiously. Randall gives special attention to political pundits who get paid well to express their half-baked opinions, and then he explains that the average TV viewer doesn't have to think anymore but simply has to repeat what was on TV.

Randall (2011) writes this crucial point about spreading our opinions: "We post them on Facebook; we tweet them; we express them in comments on Huffington Post" (p. 271). His point makes me wonder if part of the problem is how our society expects (and gets) instant gratification and feedback. One hundred years ago, if you expected anyone to read and respond to your opinion, you had to write it up and get it published in a newspaper, journal, or book. That would take time, so you could carefully formulate an air-tight opinion that would stand up to inspection. Today, however, social media sites, blogs, and YouTube make it possible for everyone to see your average Joe's words, photos, and videos on the computer screen instantly; this kind of power can be intoxicating for people who normally wouldn't stand a chance at getting their ideas published in a more traditional format.

Randall (2011) also writes, "Opinion inflation has invaded every aspect of our lives. It causes us to post our opinions about our dry cleaner on Yelp. Did you used to have an opinion about your dry cleaner, or was he just sort of there, like a shrub or a parking meter?" (p. 271). Randall's statements about "Opinion inflation" and what people are apt to rant about on Facebook and Twitter gave me the idea to do a quick scan of my Facebook friends and see if they are expressing the same type of empty and useless opinions Randall hates:

> "Four hours in the ER last night is too long."
> "Old Navy has the best sales ever!"
> "Even if you can get FREE candy bars with coupons, it is not worth having them in the house—too much temptation!"
> "Watched all the 'Harry Potter' movies over vacation. . . . Harry Potter Book 7/ Part 2 is by far the best!!!"
> "Why is Conan O'Brien so horrendously homely? I can barely look at him."

Perhaps most alarming about this trend in our culture is what it is turning us into: "surly teenagers who disagree with everything" (Randall, 2011, p. 272). He makes a valid point about the effects so many sub-par opinions have on us. Whereas it used to be that experts would weigh in on restaurant meals, music, and movies, now we all operate under the misconception that we are qualified to critique anything and everything. People will even take photographs of their meals and post them later on Facebook and Instagram! We can't enjoy a meal, song, or TV program without coming up with ways to shoot it down later online.

Finally, the author acknowledges that "there's a certain irony . . . to expressing an opinion about opinions" (Randall, 2011, p. 272). I wonder if he wrote that sentence in order to head off the many critics who were bound to write immediately to the *Los Angeles Times* that Randall sure has some nerve complaining about all the opinions out there!

PRACTICE 8-2   Writing a Critical Response

Directions: Select one of the readings you have read in this class this semester. On a separate piece of paper, write a critical response to it.

Critical Analysis Writing

A **critical analysis** is an evaluation or a critique of how well an author met the goals of a text. Perhaps a better name for the critical analysis would be a *critical analysis and evaluation*. You are using many skills as you write a critical analysis—but, most importantly, you are analyzing and evaluating. When you write a critical analysis, you analyze (break down) the elements of the text in order to put yourself in a good position to evaluate it. Because evaluation is a higher-order thinking skill, you will draw on much of what you learned throughout this textbook to write an effective critical analysis. In particular, review the following chapters and concepts prior to attempting your first critical analysis:

- **Chapter 4—Inference.** Carefully read the sections on purpose and audience. In a critical analysis, you will draw inferences about the author's purpose and then try to determine how successful the author was in reaching his or her target audience.
- **Chapter 5—Self-regulation.** As you write the analysis, you should take into consideration the author's worldviews and biases (as well as your own).
- **Chapter 6—Analysis.** Remember that analysis involves breaking down a text in order to scrutinize how well the components work together to form a unified piece. You will spend a large part of the critical analysis looking at evidence.

- **Chapter 7—Evaluation**. In many cases, your instructors will want you to evaluate an author's use of logic. A huge part of evaluation involves determining validity (if the argument is a deductive one) or identifying fallacies (if it is inductive).

Like the critical response, the critical analysis requires the writer to identify the author, title, and copyright date and to summarize the original piece. However, the crucial distinction between the two types of writings is this: In the critical response, *the student's personal experiences matter,* but in the critical analysis, *the focus is entirely on the original passage.*

While "critique" and "evaluate" might make you think of nit-picking or being highly critical, in reality your critical analysis could be positive and complimentary. The point is to analyze and evaluate the author's ability to get his or her point across effectively: Some authors are successful; some are not; some fall somewhere in between these two extremes. In a critical analysis, your job is to figure out where the author rests on this imaginary scale of success. You will be considering such factors as author's tone, use of language, biases, assumptions, logic, and evidence. A large part of your critical analysis should be devoted to the author's evidence. You should identify types of evidence and determine if the evidence is relevant, sufficient, made up of facts/opinions/reasoned judgment, and accurate (see Chapters 6 and 7).

Because a critical analysis is more complex than a critical response, you should expect it to be much longer. Your task is to write a thesis statement and then spend the remainder of the critical analysis trying to support that thesis. While the organization of a critical response is flexible, a critical analysis should be more tightly organized and focused on developing your explicit thesis statement. One way to organize it would be to devote one section to each component that you need to address (i.e., tone, evidence, purpose, and so on). You also need to devote some space to identifying the author, title, and date and to summarizing the original work, so expect to write several pages depending on the length of the passage and your instructor's requirements.

Due to the complexity of writing a critical analysis, you may want to consider using the following organizers: the evidence evaluation form and the inference form. These forms serve to strengthen your organization and help you focus your thoughts about a reading's strengths and weaknesses. Below, we have filled in both forms using our sample article "Mouthing Off in America," but you can ask for blank forms from your instructor for other assignments.

Critical Analysis: Evidence Evaluation Form

Title of Reading: _____ *"Mouthing Off in America"* _____
Author: _____ *Stephen Randall* _____
Copyright date: _____ *January 16, 2011* _____
Claim: _____ *The author claims that Americans express too many hasty, ill-formed* _____
_____ *opinions.* _____

Evidence	Page #/ paragraph #	Type of evidence
"Intellectual Costco"	1	Analogy
"Opinions are Big Macs"	2	Analogy
Cable news hosts	3, 5, 9, 10	Testimony
Facebook, Tweets, Huffington Post comments	4, 6	Testimony
"Internet is a Petri dish"	7	Analogy
Walter Cronkite	8	Fact

Does evidence appear sufficient, relevant, and accurate? Explain.

Yes, the evidence does appear to be sufficient (he gives lots of specific examples). It's entirely relevant because every piece of evidence is directly related to opinions expressed in America. Finally, his evidence is accurate and verifiable—anyone can check out cable news and Facebook and verify what Randall uses as support.

Does the author use mostly fact, opinion, or reasoned judgment? Explain.

Mostly, Randall uses facts and opinions. He has strong opinions about what he sees on cable TV and on the internet. He also uses facts that can be verified by other people who are familiar with his examples.

Does the author present an effective mix of different types of evidence? Explain.

Randall does use a good mix of evidence, though he probably relies more on analogies and testimony (his own opinion) more than the other types. It would help if he had gotten some statistics—like if he had the number of tweets that were sent out about some minor episode (like about what Obama was wearing on his feet while on vacation).

Are there any failures in logic? Explain.

One failure in logic might be in his hasty generalization that most Americans are like cable news hosts who get paid to spread their opinions.

What other evidence would you have expected to see?

It would have helped if he had gotten other experts to weigh in on if they, too, believe that Americans throw around their opinions too much. Some more statistics and facts would also help balance his argument.

What is your overall evaluation of the evidence as a whole? Does it adequately support the claim?

Overall, I believe the evidence fits together nicely to support his claim. If I didn't already agree with his claim, however, then I might need more evidence like statistics and expert testimony.

Critical Analysis: Inference Evaluation Form

Title of Reading: _____ *"Mouthing Off in America"* _____

Author: _____ *Stephen Randall* _____

Copyright date: _____ *January 16, 2011* _____

Does the author state his or her purpose? If so, write it on the lines below and cite page number. If not, what do you infer to be the purpose? Explain.

The author's implied purpose is to persuade readers that we have the tendency to share our sloppy opinions too readily with the rest of America.

What can you infer about the intended audience?

The audience includes Americans, specifically readers of the Los Angeles Times, and people who are familiar with the internet, Facebook, tweets, cable TV (specifically hosts like Glenn Beck), and who are familiar with such establishments like Costco and McDonalds.

Annotate the reading. List emotive words (superlatives, aesthetics, judgment, or recommendation) in the space below:

"You think too much" (para. 1) -superlative

"Not necessarily smart or original ones" (para. 1) - judgment

"Gourmet....elaborate" (para. 2) - aesthetic

"Should" (para. 10) - recommendation

What image(s) or feeling(s) do the words convey? Explain.

Most of Randall's word choices have a negative connotation related to how many poor opinions are out there. When he writes about people from the past who thoughtfully and carefully weighed all the evidence before expressing an opinion, he sounds more positive and admiring.

How would you define the author's tone?

The author seems irritated throughout the article.

How does use of language contribute to this author's tone?

Randall's strong use of words like "rat poison" (para. 7) shows that he has very little patience for people who constantly feel the need to share their unimportant opinions.

What is your perception of the author (his or her credibility, expertise, and education)? If necessary, do a quick Internet search to determine the author's background.

Stephen Randall is a journalist and is the deputy editor of Playboy magazine. He has an long list of published articles as well as several non-fiction books listed on his website www.stephenrandall. com. Some of his other articles criticize contemporary American obsessions such as Facebook and reality shows. While I could not find information about his education, his career as a journalist and deputy editor suggests formal education and considerable expertise in the field of writing.

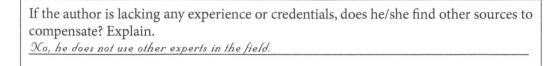

If the author is lacking any experience or credentials, does he/she find other sources to compensate? Explain.

No, he does not use other experts in the field.

Does the author express any bias or unwarranted assumptions? Explain.

Yes, he does seem biased against cable news hosts, and his annoyance with them seems to spread out to include average Americans who want to share their opinions maybe out of a need to connect with other people.

What do word choices suggest about the audience (level of education, familiarity with topic, relationship with author)? Does the author use any jargon? Explain.

The author's choice of language is sophisticated but not too overwhelming. I believe your average American reading the newspaper could understand his article without any trouble. Any jargon he uses is related to the internet (Yelp, tweets, Facebook, etc.).

Can you draw any inferences about the writing situation?

It seems that he wrote this soon after the mass shooting in Arizona by Jared Loughner on 1/8/11 (which sparked political opinions from all sides). The article also seems to be a reaction to the popularity of cable news programs.

Do you think the author achieved the intended purpose? Why or why not? Explain.

Yes, I do think he fulfilled his purpose. His writing was persuasive and should make every audience member think twice before posting some silly opinion on Facebook or expressing an opinion in public without giving it serious consideration first.

Tips for Critical Thinkers: How to Write a Critical Analysis Using the 5 Es

- **Explore.** *You must read the passage several times before you can expect to write a thoughtful critical analysis. Annotate.* Mark with an asterisk or exclamation point any ideas that need to be examined more closely in your analysis. Fill out the Evidence Evaluation form and Inference form. Begin to formulate an opinion about the author's strengths and weaknesses.
- **Express.** *Write a thesis statement and then develop it in an organized fashion.* One way to do this would be to devote a paragraph or section to each point you intend to discuss. For example, you could have sections on evidence, audience, tone, use of language, and author's credibility. Another way to organize the paper would be to have one section on strengths and one on weaknesses. Be specific. If you write a general statement ("The author uses more opinions than facts"), then be sure to follow up with specific examples that support your statement.
  Remember that a thesis statement is a single sentence that expresses your opinion about the topic or passage. The thesis statement will guide you as you write the rest of your critical analysis, so keep these ideas in mind in order to write an effective thesis:
  - **Be clear and concise.** Don't get fancy; be direct and simple. Think to yourself, "If I had to explain my opinion to someone who doesn't know much about this subject,

author, or reading, what would I say?" Literally, say it out loud and listen to hear if it sounds easy to understand. Better yet, try it out on a friend and see if he or she understands your point.

- **Avoid making an announcement**. You should not declare to your audience what you are doing. Announcing "I am going to write about the author's strengths and weaknesses" or "This paper will be about an article I read" cannot work as thesis statements because they don't include your opinion about the topic.
- **Don't be vague or clichéd**. A statement such as "This article is important" does not add much to any discussion about the topic. Avoid vague generalities and clichés.
- **Be flexible**. As you work on your critical analysis, you might find evidence that contradicts your thesis statement. You will need to be open to these other ideas and fair-minded enough to incorporate them into your understanding of the topic. Your goal in writing a critical analysis is not to "prove" your thesis by looking for and finding only those points that confirm your beliefs; rather, the goal is understanding and truth. Having a tentative thesis statement allows you to look at different viewpoints honestly and fairly without letting a stubborn adherence to your thesis get in your way. You might need to revise your thesis several times as you work on the critical analysis.
- **Expand.** *Add an introduction and conclusion.* Both the introduction and the conclusion should include your overall impression of how strong the reading is and how successful the author was in achieving his or her purpose. The introduction should include the identifying information (author, title, and copyright date), your thesis statement, and each of the points you plan on covering in the body of the critical analysis (in the same order in which they are addressed). Include some carefully selected quotes throughout the body of the paper that illustrate your points effectively, and introduce these quotes with your own words and an attributive tag.
- **Evaluate.** *How did you do? Did you nit-pick without adequate support, or did you thoughtfully analyze the author's work?* Did your thesis effectively convey your opinion? Did you support your thesis with thoughtful evidence from the text? Make sure you included identifying information (author, title, copyright date) and focused entirely on the author's work without distracting personal insight. Also, because this type of paper is more complex, make sure you are well organized and that you used appropriate transitions; evaluate and then revise accordingly.
- **Enhance.** *If possible, utilize peer editing, your campus's Writing Center, or an individual conference with your instructor.* Most instructors are happy to provide assistance if you make an appointment or come prepared to scheduled office hours.

Sample Critical Analysis: "Mouthing Off in America" by Stephen Randall

Note: The thesis statement is underlined.

Stephen Randall's article in the *Los Angeles Times* (January 16, 2011), "Mouthing Off in America," might hit a nerve with some Americans and will certainly annoy the cable news hosts he criticizes. Randall asserts his opinion that people have too many opinions and that they are not well-formed. He also believes that many people simply repeat the opinions they hear on cable news; this conveniently allows them to sound politically savvy without doing any original thinking whatsoever. Finally, he points to the vast number of opinions spread on the Internet that make average people think that they, too, have something important to add to the opinion-of-the-minute when in reality they don't. While Randall's evidence is persuasive and eye-opening, his tone and references to political figures on TV may prevent some readers from accepting his claim despite such solid evidence.

His goal—to get readers thinking about this glut of opinions—is certainly met. He uses ample evidence to make his case that we are, indeed, "living in an intellectual Costco, where it's volume, volume, volume" (Randall, 2011, p. 272). Some of his pieces of evidence are hypothetical: "We don't go to a new restaurant to eat a meal; we go there to dissect it and then tweet about it. We can't post a link to an article without giving it some sort of grade" (Randall, 2011, p. 272). These hypothetical examples are ones we can all relate to, so they work. Most of his evidence involves specific and verifiable examples that make them more convincing. He contrasts the ridiculous number of opinions spewed each night by the likes of Glenn Beck with the carefully expressed opinion cited by Walter Cronkite in 1968 regarding the Vietnam War, and clearly Randall has a much greater level of respect for Cronkite.

In addition to hypothetical examples and specific examples of opinions spouted on TV, Randall uses clever and thought-provoking analogies that give readers distinct and unappealing images to associate with opinions. His Costco analogy works with shoppers who know that they can go to Costco and see huge aisles of bland soup and cereal, but they are not likely to find special, gourmet ingredients—much like how we hear so-so opinions all day long but rarely come across any unique blends of thought. Randall (2011) uses another food-related analogy when he writes, "Thinkers were like gourmet chefs laboring over an elaborate meal they wanted to be perfect. But today, opinions are Big Macs—thrown together hastily, served by the billions and not very good for you" (p. 271). Most readers will instantly relate to the contrast between an "elaborate meal" from the past and a "Big Mac" quickly consumed today. We recognize that the energy and passion that goes into a gourmet meal (or a critical thought) is superior to the quality of a Big Mac (an empty opinion). He uses a simile to express his disdain for certain news commentators: "So, like radish farmers who grow more radishes in order to get rich, Keith and Glenn create dozens of new opinions per night" (Randall, 2011, p. 271). Again, readers get an image that is not very flattering regarding how many opinions (or radishes) get thrown around with very little thought or research behind them. Randall (2011) establishes yet another unflattering image with this metaphor: "The Internet is a Petri dish of opinion inflation, breeding commentary like bacteria" (p. 272). Even non-scientists can picture a festering Petri dish and recognize how harmful these opinions can be if they overtake our culture.

While Randall's evidence is largely strong and specific, his weaknesses include his tone and his references to certain political commentators. Randall's aggravated tone does not do enough to win over the population that thinks expressing your opinion is a wonderful thing. Most readers of the *Los Angeles Times* live in the entertainment hub of the country, so they might not take too kindly to Randall's criticism of people who post their opinions on Facebook and Twitter because it is likely that many of them do the very activity that Randall critiques, and they might even closely follow their favorite entertainers' tweets. Randall's tone is sometimes grouchy, such as when he writes, "Everyone gets a vote, even the people who aren't particularly sane" (Randall, 2011, p. 272). Readers who are strongly in favor of expressing their opinions might be put off by Randall's inference that some opinions are not worth much, and that those who put forth a lot of opinions might be less than sane.

In addition to his tone, Randall's references to specific media figures might count against him. Many of his examples hinge on the audience's familiarity with pundits such as Keith Olbermann, Glenn Beck, and Sean Hannity. If readers never heard the rants that Randall refers to, then his point may fall flat. However, curious readers could easily search for archived news programs and see these men turn red in the face as they passionately argue a point. It is more likely, however, that some members of Randall's audience are huge fans of these commentators, and they will not be receptive to Randall's criticism of them. If either Randall's tone or his references to

TV personalities offends some readers, they might discount everything he says, not learn from his evidence, and post a link to his article with a scathing review!

Despite these weaknesses, Randall's opinion is thoughtful and well-supported. He develops it using clear examples and analogies that most readers will appreciate. While his tone and references to political analysts can be off-putting to certain readers, many people will recognize the truth in his frustration. Overall, Randall's article "Mouthing Off in America" appeals to critical thinkers who are, like Randall, irritated by the number of opinions they are forced to endure on a daily basis.

Writing a Critical Analysis	**PRACTICE 8-3**

Directions: Select one of the readings you have read in this class this semester. Fill out the Evidence Evaluation Form and Inference Form. On a separate piece of paper, write an organized and well-developed critical analysis.

THINK AND **WRITE** CRITICALLY

Journal Writing

Instructors often require students to keep a **journal,** an informal collection of ideas written down over a period of time (usually one semester). Journals have many benefits, notably the following:

- **Journals are "nonthreatening."** You can be more creative and less formal in your journal writing. As mentioned at the beginning of the chapter, you can use your journal to practice your creative writing abilities and get in touch with your emotions.
- **Journals can reveal progress**. It is exciting for you to see your progress in your journal. Many teachers grade journals, in fact, based on whether a student shows progress from the beginning of the semester to the end.
- **Journals provide you with a record of your thoughts**. Writing in a bound journal makes it easier to hold on to a record of your thoughts (individual sheets of paper can easily get lost), so you can keep them for future reference.

Even if your instructor does not assign a journal, there is no reason for you not to keep one on your own! *Why would I make work for myself and keep a journal if it isn't assigned*, you might be asking yourself this very minute. Well, in addition to the benefits listed above, here are two more:

- **A journal can provide you with ideas for future writing assignments**. It can be a goldmine of ideas and inspiration.
- **Keeping a journal can be a "test" to see whether you have mastered the material**. If you struggle to write anything in response to what you are learning (a reading, a current event, a scientific study, a court case, a geometry proof), then you need to work harder, reread, or ask questions in class. Then, try to write a journal entry about what you did not understand at first and how you eventually mastered it.

As part of your grade, sometimes teachers will allow you to submit your journal in an electronic format (such as on a blog site), so verify the guidelines required for your class. Some instructors prefer you to respond to a particular writing prompt (i.e., "Recount a time when you felt disappointment like Langston Hughes did as a boy in his short story 'Salvation'"); other instructors allow students more freedom for you to be creative (i.e., "Write a journal entry about Langston Hughes' 'Salvation'"). Whatever your instructor's preference is, however, know that your job is to show that you have thought about the topic, organized a response, and written something of substance.

Tips for Critical Thinkers: How to Keep a Journal Using the 5 Es

- **Explore.** If your instructor does not give you a specific prompt to follow, then be creative! Prewriting activities can help you find something new and fresh to write about.

- **Express.** Connect with the topic in a way that is meaningful to you and then find the best way to organize it. The patterns of development can give you an idea about how to approach the topic. For example, if you were writing a journal entry about Barbara Ehrenreich's "The Unbearable Lightness of Breast Cancer," you could compare and contrast Ehrenreich's attitude with the attitude your aunt had when she battled the disease, or you could write about the effects of the pink ribbon marketing that Ehrenreich did not mention.

- **Expand.** Don't be skimpy in your journal. Expand each journal entry so that it becomes a meaningful record of your thinking. Commit to writing for a set amount of time, say, 30 minutes, and then write for 10 minutes more and see if your response become clearer and more sophisticated. Bring in biographical information and experiences if that helps get your ideas across, but do not forget to stick to the prompt (if required) and frequently refer back to the topic or reading.

- **Evaluate.** How did you do? Do you need to summarize the information first in order for your response to make better sense? Did you shed new light on the material? Did you organize it well? Do you need to add or delete transitions to improve clarity? Would you be proud to share your journal entry with your instructor or your classmates?

- **Enhance.** Due to the less formal nature of a journal, you do not need to spend as much time enhancing your writing as you would if you were submitting a critical response or analysis. However, keep in mind that small errors add up to a big, negative impression. As always, proofread and edit. You should still submit high-quality work, even if that means writing a rough draft on scrap paper and then transferring it to your journal later. If your journal is electronic, then that makes enhancing it even easier.

Sample Journal Entry: "Mouthing Off in America" by Stephen Randall

Stephen Randall makes some excellent points in "Mouthing Off in America." Not only does he make the point that people have too many opinions, but he makes it clear that these opinions aren't that good. It was as if he was reading my mind after spending time with my relatives! Most of the people in my family have strong opinions, and it seems like whoever can state his (or her) opinion with the loudest voice or with the reddest face is the winner.

I've been guilty of doing the exact same thing. Randall writes, "Not only am I more entertained these days, but when I'm feeling lazy, I can switch from thinking too much to not thinking at all. I am so surrounded by opinions that I don't need any of my own. I can turn on Fox or MSNBC and adopt an entire political philosophy without knowing a thing." Again, it is like he is reading my mind. I've watched Bill O'Reilly, Sean Hannity, and Greta Van Susteren, and then gone out with my friends who watch stuff like "Dancing with the Stars" and "The Voice" and don't bother with political shows, so I can impress them with my political knowledge. However, it's not my knowledge at all—it's Bill's or Sean's or Greta's, and I barely understand it but can make it sound convincing if I pound the table with my hand for emphasis or yell in my buddy's face if he tries to disagree with me.

Randall's article has made me think about what I can do differently. Tonight, I am going to watch different political shows and see how they compare with the ones I usually watch. Then I'm going to pick one or two topics to learn about in depth, and I'll do some research on the internet and in the college library. I won't have as many opinions that way, but I might have deeper, better opinions.

Writing a Journal Entry   PRACTICE 8-4

Directions: Select one of the readings you have read in this class this semester. On a separate piece of paper (or in your journal), write a journal entry about it. You can pick from the following prompts or be creative and think of your own way to respond.

- Which point does the author make that you strongly agree or disagree with? Why? Explain. You could start this journal entry by explaining where you fall on the "Measure of Belief" scale.
- If you could have lunch with the author, what would you want to discuss about the passage? Be specific.
- How does the author's text reflect worldview and bias? How do your own worldview and biases compare or contrast with the author's?
- What do you suppose caused the author to write about this topic?
- Pick an image that the author's text evokes. Draw a picture of what you envision when you read the text, and then write to explain it.

THINK
AND **WRITE**
CRITICALLY

Using Sources and Avoiding Plagiarism

Your critical responses, critical analyses, and journal entries may be made up of only your own ideas, citations from the original passage, or **common knowledge,** information that many people know just from living in this world or information that could be easily found in common reference books such as general encyclopedias. However, depending on your instructor's requirements, you may need to develop your points further by doing some more reading and researching about your topic (if necessary, review how to evaluate sources from Chapter 7). For example, the author of the model critical analysis used only her own ideas and some common knowledge to develop her opinion about Randall's article. In several places, she speculates and uses hypothetical examples of what she believes *might* happen if readers are offended by Randall's opinion about opinions. Specifics drawn from actual research would make the critical analysis more interesting, accurate, and convincing. Citing other sources (using your instructor's preferred mention of citation, usually APA or MLA) would give the student's ideas more weight. By doing some in-depth reading and research, she could incorporate new material into her critical analysis to improve it greatly; however, check first with your instructor or professor to see if outside research is encouraged. If you do need to conduct additional research, be sure to stay on target with your thesis and remember to be open-minded and flexible if you come across information that might require you to revise your thesis statement.

> ### APA or MLA Documentation Styles
>
> Find out whether your instructor requires you to use APA (American Psychological Association) or MLA (Modern Language Association) format (or another format), and learn the rules for proper citations. You can get instructions from your college's English department or library, both of which should have copies of the latest editions of the APA and MLA handbooks, or refer to these websites:
> http://owl.english.purdue.edu
> www.apastyle.org
> www.mla.org/style

You will also need to give credit to your sources. **Plagiarism** is a serious breach of academic honesty in which you take credit for words or ideas that are not your own (either by accident, by sloppy note-taking, or through deliberate dishonesty). To cite sources accurately, get in the habit of carefully recording the author's name, title of the work, publication information, page number (when applicable), and copyright date. Whenever possible, check out the item from the library or print out the document from the Internet so that you can refer frequently to the publication information. When you quote or paraphrase from a source, use the author's or organization's name so that readers are clear about who owns the ideas and words.

Oral Communication

You will not always have the luxury of time to prepare a well-written critical response, critical analysis, or journal entry that details your reasoning. Instead, people frequently have to explain themselves through oral communication. **Oral communication** can be as informal as simply telling someone what you were thinking about or as formal as preparing a speech to deliver to an audience. Many of the points you learned about communicating effectively on paper will also apply to oral communication. Before we talk about oral communication, however, answer the following questions.

Discussion Questions

Directions: In pairs or small groups, discuss the following questions. Be prepared to share your points with the entire class.

1. Brainstorm about some public figures that you believe are effective communicators (think about politicians, sports figures, actors, newscasters, and others). What are some traits they exhibit that make them effective at communicating their messages?

2. Think of some public figures who are less successful at communicating. What are they doing or not doing that makes them ineffective?

3. Brainstorm some examples of facial expressions and body language that result in effective communication without written and/or spoken words.

4. Try to come up with an example of a time that you felt that you communicated effectively. Try to identify what you did that worked particularly well.

5. Come up with an example of a time when you felt that you were not communicating effectively. How could you tell your message was not coming across well? What would you try differently the next time?

EXPAND YOUR UNDERSTANDING

Learning More about Public Speaking While Writing Critically

Search the Internet for videos of speeches by leaders known for their communication skills: Martin Luther King, Jr., John F. Kennedy, Jr., Barack Obama, and the people you discussed in Discussion Question 1 above, and answer the following questions on a separate sheet of paper.

1. What are they doing that works well?
2. Do you see something that would suggest they trust their own reasoning?

After you discussed what effective oral communication looks like, you probably noticed some similarities between writing and speaking. Effective writers and speakers are

© Evan Meyer/Shutterstock.com

organized and direct, and they use plenty of good reasons to support their opinions. Good writers and speakers keep their audience and purpose in mind. The tips below highlight ways for you to be an effective communicator.

Tips for Critical Thinkers: How to Be an Effective Communicator

- **Know your audience.** If your audience is already receptive to your ideas, then you don't have to provide as many in-depth details to convince them of your logic as you would if your audience is unreceptive to your argument.
- **Be clear and concise.** Much like a well-written explanation, a good oral explanation is clear and concise. State your claim clearly in one simple sentence. Provide the most important pieces of evidence in a logical order.
- **Jot down notes ahead of time.** Depending on the formality of the occasion, your notes might be as informal as a few words in the margin of a spiral-bound notebook or as formal as a PowerPoint presentation. Do not rely entirely on your memory! Explaining yourself to an audience can be stressful, so your notes can serve as useful reminders of important points you wish to cover.
- **Anticipate questions and rebuttals.** Especially for an audience who might dislike some of your points, you should be well prepared. Do your homework and figure out what are some likely questions and how you will rebut them so that you won't be blindsided by tough counterarguments.

| **Preparing an Oral Presentation** | **PRACTICE 8-5** |

Directions: Using the critical analysis you wrote for this chapter, prepare a short, 5 to 10-minute presentation to give to your instructor and classmates.

Real-World Mistakes of Explanation and Their Consequences

Occurring March 27, 1977, the Tenerife plane crash that killed 583 people maintains its title as the worst aviation disaster in history. Flights KLM 4805 and Pan Am 1736, both 747s, crashed at takeoff. In part, the plane crash was a consequence of failing to communicate effectively.

Other factors contributed to the crash; notably, there were two major problems that could not have been avoided. First, there was dense fog that greatly hampered visibility. Second, the site of the crash, Los Rodeos Airport on the Spanish island of Tenerife (in the Canary Islands), was overcrowded due to a terrorist bombing at a nearby airport. Neither of the planes involved in the deadly crash were originally supposed to be at Los Rodeos, but they were rerouted there after a bomb detonated at Gran Canaria International Airport.

The problem that *could* have been avoided, however, was poor communication. Both the KLM and Pan Am aircrafts were waiting to taxi down the runway and turn in preparation for takeoff. The transcript of the accident indicates that the overcrowding at Gran Canaria International Airport was making it difficult for the planes to get into position, and due to the fog, air traffic controllers could not see the planes and had to rely on verbal communication.

Several conversations proved to be problematic. There was some confusion over which exit the Pan Am aircraft should take; Robert Bragg, the Pan Am first officer who survived the crash, said that air traffic control (ATC) wanted them to take the fourth exit as opposed to the third one, and transcripts relay attempts to clarify this point. The fatal misunderstanding, however, occurred when the pilot on the KLM airplane, Captain Jacob

Veldhuyzen van Zanten, advanced the throttles for takeoff despite not having clearance from ATC. First officer Klaas Meurs questioned his superior about not having takeoff clearance and then contacted ATC. Although ATC gave the KLM aircraft some additional instructions about takeoff, it did not formerly and explicitly release the plane for takeoff. ATC believed that KLM was at the takeoff position (but not actually going ahead with takeoff) and said, "Okay." This word, "okay" is not a standard response, and it unfortunately was followed by radio interference that made the communication about the Pan Am flight taxiing down the runway hard to hear within the KLM cockpit. Moments later, KLM flight engineer Willem Schreuder questioned whether the Pan Am flight was cleared for take-off. Perhaps reluctant to question the senior pilot Veldhuyzen van Zarten yet again, both Meurs and Schreuder accepted the pilot's answer, and the crash happened seconds later.

This crash is an especially tragic example of failure to explain; most misunderstandings do not result in almost 600 fatalities. Even so, there are some valuable lessons to take from this incident. First, you need to explain yourself clearly and anticipate when you might confuse your audience so that you can add more information as necessary. Second, you should not hesitate to ask for clarification when someone tells you information that does not seem to fit with your own understanding of the situation. Finally, if your profession utilizes standard words and phrases, you should use them so that other professionals in the field will know what you mean and will respond appropriately.

For Discussion

1. Explain how the mistakes discussed above qualify as a failure of explanation.

2. What actions could the participants have taken to avoid these mistakes?

Real-World Successes of Critical Thinking

Stephen Hawking

You just read about a tragic failure of critical thinking, specifically explanation, but thinking critically can also produce great results. The world-renowned physicist Stephen Hawking has explained complex truths about the universe so that even nonscientists can understand them. In addition to writing such books as *A Brief History of Time* (1988), *The Universe in a Nutshell* (2001), and *The Grand Design* (2010), Hawking explains concepts through oral communication, despite his considerable physical and vocal challenges.

Directions: Using the Internet or a library, research Stephen Hawking in depth. Prepare a detailed description of the successes of this scientist, including an explanation of any skills, character traits, and standards of critical thinking that contributed to his success. Get ready to share your findings with the class.

Chapter Summary

- *Explanation* is the skill of providing reasons for a belief or a decision.
- *Trusting your reasoning* is a trait of critical thinkers that means feeling confidence in the research and thought given to an intellectual challenge.
- Use the *5 Es* to explain yourself through writing: (1) Explore, (2) Express, (3) Expand, (4) Evaluate, and (5) Enhance.
- The *patterns of organization* (as covered in Chapter 6 and reinforced in this chapter from a writer's perspective) focus the writer's thoughts about the topic or reading so that he or she can write in a thoughtful and organized manner. The patterns

of organization include the following: Cause/Effect, Chronological, Comparison/ Contrast, Classification, Definition, Example, Listing, and Mixed.

- Respond to a variety of readings through three types of *writing assignments* typically given by college instructors and professors: (1) Critical Response, (2) Critical Analysis, and (3) Journal Entry. Each of these assignments requires you to read carefully, annotate, organize your ideas, and write thoughtfully.

- Another way to explain your thoughts is through *oral communication*. As with writing, oral communication requires you to know your audience and to prepare for audience members who might not readily agree with you unless you provide ample evidence.

READ, WRITE, AND THINK CRITICALLY: EXPLANATION

Directions: Reread "Mouthing Off in America" (p. 271) and on a separate piece of paper answer the questions that follow. What is your prior knowledge of this subject? Write a short letter to Stephen Randall to express your own opinion about opinions.

1. Look up information about Walter Cronkite. Write a brief biography about him and explain how his opinion regarding the Vietnam War changed the course of that conflict.
2. Watch one of the cable news shows that Randall references. Would you recommend that your classmates and instructor watch the show? Why or why not? Explain.
3. Go on Facebook, Twitter, and Yelp and make a list of five to 10 opinions you see. Do you find these opinions to be helpful and valuable or, like Randall, do you think they are "not necessarily smart or original"? Explain.
4. Locate another article, essay, or blog post about opinions and complete the following writing assignments. Be sure to provide your instructor with a copy of or link to the new text you find.
   a. Write a critical response to the text.
   b. Write a critical analysis of the text.
   c. On a separate piece of paper (or in your journal), write a journal entry about the text using one of the prompts below. First, be sure to organize your thoughts using an appropriate graphic organizer.
      i. Compare and contrast the new opinion you find with Randall's opinion in "Mouthing Off in America."
      ii. What are the positive and negative effects of expressing your opinion online, according to both authors?
      iii. How has your experience highlighted what both Randall and the other author have to say about opinions?
      iv. Will you be more or less likely to express your opinion after reading these texts? Develop your answer.

Adhering to the Standards: Grammar

In a chapter about explaining your ideas, you may wonder if grammar really matters. As a critical thinker, you certainly understand that grammatical errors can affect a reader's ability to understand a text. Effective grammar, spelling, and punctuation contribute to the overall quality of the work. Yes, grammar *does* matter—largely because good grammar contributes to the standards of excellence embraced by critical thinkers: significance, clarity, accuracy, completeness, fairness, and relevance. Review the following rules and suggestions, and keep the standards in mind at all times. While it is beyond the scope of this textbook to cover grammar in depth, mastering these particular concepts should improve your writing. If you need additional practice or instruction, see a tutor in your college writing center.

Standards of critical thinkers	How the standards relate to grammar
Significance	Make **significant** words (subjects and verbs) the stars of your sentences, and correctly use **dependent and independent clauses** to show your readers which of your ideas are most **significant**.
Clarity	Use **clear** and direct **subjects** and **verbs** to help your readers comprehend your message. Use active (not passive) voice. In addition, make certain that all **pronouns** have **clear antecedents** to ensure that your message is not vague or ambiguous.
Accuracy	Use appropriate **punctuation** in the correct place in a sentence to show your concern for **accuracy**, and you will also eliminate run-ons and comma splices.
Completeness	Avoid **fragments** in order to express your ideas **completely**.
Fairness	Avoid **absolute terms** so that your writing is **fair** and balanced (absolutes suggest exaggeration or bias on the part of the writer).
Relevance	Know particular rules that are **relevant** to academic writing.

Significance

*Make **significant** words (subjects and verbs) the stars of your sentences, and correctly use **dependent and independent clauses** to show your readers which of your ideas are most significant.*

The most **significant** parts of speech in a sentence are **subjects** and **verbs.** As a result, they deserve center stage as the stars of your sentences—in the independent clauses!

© anthonycz/Shutterstock.com

© Makkuro GL/Shutterstock.com

© Panda Vector/Shutterstock.com

Subject	Verb	Common Linking Verbs
• Person • Place • Thing • WHO or WHAT? • Noun or pronoun	• What the sentence says about the subject; what is going on in the sentence • Action verbs (run, jump) • Helping verbs establish tense ("to be" or "to have" plus can, should, must, will, and so on) • Linking verbs ⟶	• is • am • are • was • were • be • been • become • seem • feel • appear • taste • smell • look • sound

Nouns can be **subjects** or **objects** in the sentence. The **subject** is the noun or pronoun (person/place/thing/who/what) that does the action in the sentence. The subject is never in a prepositional phrase; the noun in the prepositional phrase is the **object**. ("Selma jumped on the table" has two nouns—*Selma* and *table*, so which one is doing the action? *Selma*! *Table* is in the prepositional phrase "on the table" which makes the noun "table" the *object* of the preposition. An *object* is never the *subject*!)

Crossing out prepositional phrases can help you identify the main parts of the sentence (the subject and the verb) since the subject and verb will NEVER be in a prepositional phrase. So how do you recognize a prepositional phrase? Well, a phrase does NOT contain a verb (notice how "on the table" lacks a verb), and a prepositional phrase typically starts with a preposition that is a "little" word and indicates a **time** or **location** relationship between the noun/pronoun in the prepositional phrase and another word in the sentence (see list of common prepositions). In addition, you can use this little trick to help identify the prepositional phrase: **Think of a prepositional phrase as showing *when* a squirrel is going to jump off a tree OR *where* the squirrel is in relation to the tree!**

Common Prepositions

© evgenia kislyakova/Shutterstock.com

Time/When The squirrel will jump . . . *after* the storm. *during* the storm. *until* the storm. *before* the storm.	About Across Along Around Aside from Before Beneath Beyond Despite During Excepting	Above After Along with As At Behind Beside By Down Except For	According to Against Among As for Because of Below Between Concerning Due to Except for From
Location/Where The squirrel is . . . *behind* the tree. *between* the trees. *on top of* the tree. *next to* the tree.	In Inside Into Next to On Onto Outside Regarding Throughout Toward Unlike With	In addition to Inside of Like Of On account of Out Over Since Till Under Until Within	In spite of Instead of Near Off On top of Out of Past Through To Underneath Up Without

A **clause** is a group of words that contains a verb (as opposed to a **phrase** which is a group of words that does not contain a verb).

There are two kinds of clauses (verbs are double-underlined below):

Independent Clauses (IC)	Dependent Clauses (DC)
An IC is a clause that can stand by itself; it could stand alone as a sentence because it has a subject and a verb, and it expresses a complete thought:	A DC, on the other hand, **cannot** stand by itself. Instead, it must be connected to an independent clause in order to make sense.
• *I went to see my academic counselor.* • *I decided to major in culinary.* • *I arrived on time for the first day of classes.*	• *as I made decisions about my future* • *because my school counselor gave me some good advice* • *even though my alarm did not ring*

	Common Subordinating Conjunctions			
Dependent clauses will begin with a subordinate conjunction or a relative pronoun:	After Although As As if As long as As though Because Before	Even if Even though If If only In order that Now that Once Provided	Rather than Since So that Than Though Till Unless	Until When Whenever Whereas Whether While
	Relative Pronouns			
	Who Whomever Whose Whom That		Which Whichever What Whatever Whoever	

Well-written sentences will direct your readers to the most **significant** ideas. Good writers will put the most important ideas in the *independent* clause!

- *As I made decisions about my future, I went to see my academic counselor.* [DC, IC.] Significant idea = *I went to see my academic counselor.*
- *I decided to major in culinary because my school counselor gave me some good advice.* [IC DC.] Significant idea = *I decided to major in culinary.*
- *Even though my alarm did not ring, I arrived on time for the first day of classes.* [DC, IC.] Significant idea = *I arrived on time for the first day of classes.*

Note: You will want to pay attention to the correct punctuation.

IC DC. (You do not need a comma whenever you *end* the sentence with a dependent clause.)

DC, IC. (Whenever you *start* the sentence with a dependent clause, you need a comma. Review the section on commas.)

NOW YOU TRY!

Significance Practice #1 Directions: For each of the following sets, identify the group of words as a dependent clause (DC) or an independent clause (IC). Be ready to explain why you identified the group of words the way you did.

1. _____ Provided that my credits will transfer.
2. _____ Whereas my last school was in another state.
3. _____ The Registrar's office will review my college transcript.
4. _____ Because I must be careful about financial aid funds.
5. _____ Transferring to another educational institution is not always easy.
6. _____ While I was watching television last night.
7. _____ I stopped at the bank on my way to work.
8. _____ Enrollment has increased steadily each year.
9. _____ Now that the semester has started.
10. _____ As they talked about the future.

Significance Practice #2 Directions: In each of the following sentences, underline the independent clause, and put parentheses around the dependent clause.

1. My back felt much better after I started doing yoga.
2. Cats never come when you call them.
3. As they walked through Central Park, the couple held hands.
4. The audience remained silent while the orchestra played.
5. Ever since I was little, I wanted to study archaeology.

Significance Practice #3 Directions: Add an independent clause to the following dependent clauses.

1. Although the game was rained out, _____.
2. Because the quarterback was injured, _____.
3. _____ after you check the score from last night's game.
4. When we arrived at the ballfield, _____.
5. _____ before the inning begins.

Significance Practice #4 Directions: Add a dependent clause to the following independent clauses.

1. Cybil will go for a long walk *after* _____.
2. *Before* _____, Ahmed will make a list.
3. *Although* _____, Yolanda went to the mall.
4. I couldn't go to work *because* _____.
5. *Now that* _____, we can put away our winter clothes.

Significance Practice #5 Directions: Write three original sentences incorporating dependent and independent clauses. Be sure to put most significant idea in the independent clause.

1. _____
_____
_____
2. _____
_____
_____
3. _____
_____
_____

Clarity

*Use **clear** and direct **subjects** and **verbs** to help your readers comprehend your message. Use active (not passive) voice. In addition, make certain that all **pronouns** have **clear antecedents** to ensure that your message is not vague or ambiguous.*

Often when you explain your reasoning, you need to make clear *who* or *what* is doing the action (and what, exactly, that action *is*). Review what you learned about significance, subjects, verbs, independent clauses, dependent clauses, and prepositional phrases in the last section. Remember that the subject of a sentence is never in a prepositional phrase; the noun in a prepositional phrase is the *object* (and a phrase never contains a verb).

Clarity Practice #1 Directions: In each of the following sentences, cross out the prepositional phrase, circle the subject, and underline the verb. Remember to ask *who* or *what* is doing the action to determine the subject. As you figure out the verb, recall that the verb could have more than one part (action verb, helping verb, and/or linking verb). Tip: not every sentence will have a prepositional phrase.

1. A spider made an impressive web in the corner.
2. Mosquitoes are a nuisance.
3. Swiftly and completely, the rising river flooded the town.
4. He has been moody lately.
5. Dr. Lankford retired from private practice.

Clarity Practice #2 Directions: Review the practices in the last section on significance. In each one, cross out the prepositional phrase (if applicable), circle the subject, and underline the verb.

You may have a pronoun stand in for a noun, as is the case in item #4 in the first practice ("He"). Part of being clear and direct is making sure your pronoun has a clear antecedent (the word or phrase that the pronoun refers to). In addition, the pronoun and antecedent must agree in person (gender—he/she/it, as well as first person, second person, and third person) and number (singular or plural). Pronouns and their antecedents have been underlined in the following examples:

Incorrect: *My coworkers are overworked, underpaid, and stressed out. He has been moody lately.* (Who? Which one of your coworkers? "Coworkers" is plural whereas "He" is singular. Perhaps you need to add another sentence in between the two sentences to clarify your message: *Out of all of my coworkers, Dylan has had the toughest time dealing with the change in leadership.*)

Correct: *Dylan is overworked, underpaid, and stressed out. He has been moody lately.*

Incorrect: *Bike riders must be careful on the road. People driving cars might not see you.* ("You" is second person, but the pronoun refers to the third person subject "riders.")

Correct: *Bike riders must be careful on the road. People driving cars might not see them.*

You learned in Chapter 3 that grammatical mistakes might result in ambiguous or vague language. Perhaps you have even had teachers write on your papers, "Vague pronoun reference." Be clear about which noun your pronoun is standing in for, and read your sentences aloud to check for clarity. In the examples below, the pronoun is underlined.

Incorrect: *In spite of the fishing boat hitting the dock, it was not damaged.* (What exactly wasn't damaged? The boat or the dock?)

Correct: *In spite of the fishing boat hitting the dock, the boat was not damaged.* (As you can see, sometimes you will need to eliminate the pronoun entirely in favor of clarity.)

Incorrect: *In 1991, Anita Hill provided testimony accusing U.S. Supreme Court nominee Clarence Thomas of sexually harassing her, yet the Senate still confirmed his life-time appointment to the bench. This will be debated in history books for generations to come.*

(What exactly does "this" refer to? What is being debated? Anita Hill's testimony or the Senate confirmation of Clarence Thomas?)

Correct: *In 1991, Anita Hill provided testimony accusing U.S. Supreme Court nominee Clarence Thomas of sexually harassing her, yet the Senate still confirmed his life-time appointment to the bench. This confirmation will be debated in history books for generations to come.*

(Adding the word "confirmation" to the pronoun "this" clarifies the message.)

Clarity Practice #3 Directions: Each of the sentences below contains an error related to pronoun use. Rewrite each sentence to make the message clear.

1. Brandon finished fourth in the cold and rainy marathon; it was disappointing.

_____

_____

2. Each college applicant should proofread their essays carefully.

_____

_____

3. Grandma wanted to take her grandchildren to a farm to pick strawberries, but they were not available.

_____

_____

As you are striving to be clear and direct, write in *active* voice rather than *passive* voice. In other words, be sure that your subject is the prominent place in the sentence (in the independent clause) rather than in a prepositional phrase. Observe the difference in the following examples:

Active voice: *A spider made an impressive web in the corner.*
Passive voice.   *An impressive web in the corner was made by a spider.*

Passive voice is wordy; it puts the subject toward the end of the sentence, and it creates an unnecessary prepositional phrase.

Clarity Practice #4 Directions: Each of the following sentences is in passive voice. Change to the more direct and clear active voice.

1. Roast beef was served at our dinner last night by Uncle Larry.

_____

_____

2. The garden is being tilled by the 4H club.

_____

_____

3. Working until 8:00 p.m., the lab report was finally printed by the senior researcher.

_____

_____

Clarity Practice #5 Directions: Look for incidents of passive voice in one of your recent papers. Tip: a form of the verb "to be" (is/was/were/been) plus the past tense of a verb often signifies passive voice. Revise each passive voice sentence using the active voice construction.

Accuracy

Use appropriate **punctuation** in the correct place in a sentence to show your concern for **accuracy**, and you will also eliminate run-ons and comma splices.

When to Use Commas		Examples
In between elements in a series (three or more words, phrases, or clauses)		I plan to run three miles, visit my grandmother, and relax with my friends later today.
In between independent clauses joined by coordinating conjunctions	*FANBOYS:* For And Nor But Or Yet So	I plan to run three miles, so I hope my knee does not bother me. (NO COMMA: I plan to run three miles and place first in my age group. Notice that you do not have an independent clause after the "and" which makes the comma unnecessary.) IC, and IC.
In between coordinate adjectives (not usually adjectives referring to size, age, or color); if you can switch the order of the adjectives and put an "and" in between them, then you should use comma		My book club is reading an intriguing, complex novel next month. (NO COMMA: My book club is made up of little old women. Notice that if you switch the order and add "and," it does not work: My book club is made up of old and little women.)
Before and after interrupting elements		Did you consider, for example, your work schedule when you registered for classes?
Before and after words of direct address, interjections, and "yes" and "no"		Thank you, Mrs. Sanders, for your efforts on my behalf. Yes, I did turn off the dryer before leaving the house. Well, once again we are meeting at the coffee shop.

After introductory phrases and clauses	After a prepositional phrase: Around the corner**,** you should find the store you need. After a dependent clause: After going to the store**,** you might want to run to the bank.
Within dates, numbers, addresses, titles, correspondence, and direct quotations	Lincoln was assassinated on April 14**,** 1865**,** much to the dismay of the entire country. We spend holidays in Atlantic City, New Jersey. Judd Davenport**,** PhD**,** is one of our history professors. Dear Sally**,** Thank you for the lovely gift. Sincerely**,** Anna Lu Jacklyn called out**,** "Police!"

When to Use Semicolons		Examples
In between closely related independent clauses (use it like a period when the second independent clause helps to explain or illustrate the first)		People are reluctant to get the flu vaccine**;** some studies have shown it is not always effective.
In a compound sentence when using an adverbial conjunction/ transition (must also use a comma *after* the adverbial conjunction)	*Adverbial Conjunctions* also consequently currently finally hence however indeed likewise moreover nevertheless next overall primarily rather similarly then therefore thus	Maxine was frustrated with her low grades in algebra**;** nevertheless, she continued studying and practicing problems.

When to Use Colons	Examples
Following an independent clause when you can substitute the words "which is/are as follows" (i.e., what comes *after* the colon illustrates or explains what comes *before* the colon)	New college students face one major challenge: time management. (Notice how you could substitute the words *which is* in place of the colon—New college students face one major challenge which is time management.)
After a greeting in business correspondence	Dear Senator Ortiz:
In time and ratios	8:30 a.m. class 2:1 ratio

Errors that can be elminated with correct punctuation:

Run-ons

When there is no punctuation between independent clauses	Incorrect: IC IC. The computer system was down no one knew what to do.

Comma Splices

When there is a comma in between two independent clauses—a comma is not strong enough to hold together two independent clauses!	Incorrect: IC, IC. The computer system was down, no one knew what to do.

Fix run-ons and comma splices one of five ways:

1. Put a period in between the independent clauses (be sure to capitalize the second sentence). IC. IC.
   The computer system was down. No one knew what to do.

2. Use a comma and a coordinating conjunction (FANBOYS: for, and, nor, but, or, yet, so). IC, FANBOYS IC.
   The computer system was down, and no one knew what to do.

3. Use a semi-colon IF the two independent clauses are closely related. IC; IC.
   The computer system was down; no one knew what to do.

4. Change one of the independent clauses to a dependent clause. IC DC. or DC, IC.
   No one knew what to do because the computer system was down.
   Because the computer system was down, no one knew what to do.

5. Use a semi-colon, transitional element, and comma to combine the two independent clauses. IC; transitional element, IC.
   The computer system was down; as a result, no one knew what to do.

NOW YOU TRY!

Accuracy Practice #1 Directions: Identify each group of words as a run-on (RO), a comma splice (CS), or a correct sentence (C).

1. _____ June is my favorite month it is the beginning of summer.
2. _____ After working three weekends in a row, Armando was happy to have off.
3. _____ I thought I texted you yesterday, I had hoped you would visit.
4. _____ Mia is my black cat Mason is the white one.
5. _____ Last year we went snowboarding, this year we will try skiing.

Accuracy Practice #2 Directions: Select one run-on or comma splice from the above practice. Correct it using each method for fixing run-ons and comma splices.

1. Put a period in between the independent clauses (be sure to capitalize the second sentence). IC. IC.

   _____

2. Use a comma and a coordinating conjunction (FANBOYS: for, and, nor, but, or, yet, so). IC, FANBOYS IC.

   _____

3. Use a semi-colon IF the two independent clauses are closely related. IC; IC.

   _____

4. Change one of the independent clauses to a dependent clause. IC DC. DC, IC.

   _____

5. Use a semi-colon, transitional element, and comma to combine the two independent clauses. IC; transitional element, IC.

   _____

Accuracy Practice #3 Directions: Each of the following items is missing punctuation. Add commas, semicolons, and colons as needed.

1. The professor said "Our chemistry lab will be closed on Thursday, January 10 2019 for maintenance."
2. Critical thinkers evaluate information based on six standards accuracy clarity completeness fairness relevance and significance.
3. When you evaluate a source of information you should determine if it is current and unbiased.
4. Wise brave Socrates encouraged people to ask questions and search for truth.
5. Campus security monitor the buildings and grounds their priority is the safety of the entire college community.
6. Women have contributed to science for instance Marie Curie and Rachel Carson changed history with their discoveries.
7. In our most recent history class we learned about ancient Rome Italy.
8. Tell me please what you are planning on doing after graduation.
9. The class that usually meets at 1030 a.m. will meet in the library.
10. Lydia have you considered changing your major?

Completeness

*Avoid **fragments** in order to express your ideas **completely**.*

A fragment is a group of words posing as sentence when it actually is not! It may look like a complete sentence because it begins with a capital letter and ends with a period, but it is not a complete sentence for one of these reasons:

1) Missing a subject	*Should have a professional look at it.*
2) Missing a verb	*Calling my former employer for a reference.*
3) Doesn't express a complete thought (is a dependent clause)	*Once you finish your resume.*

To express your ideas **completely**, you must learn how to identify and fix fragments. Fortunately, the fixes are easy: combine the fragment with another sentence or add a subject, verb, or independent clause as needed.

Correct:

- *Micah should have a professional look at it.* (added subject "Micah")
- *Calling my former employer for a reference **was uncomfortable but necessary**.* (added verb "was" and expressed a complete thought)
  OR make the -ing word a verb by adding a helping verb and subject: **I am** calling my former employer for a reference.
- *Once you finish your résumé, **you should have a professional look at it**.* (combined with independent clause)

NOW YOU TRY!

Completeness Practice #1 Directions: For each of the following sets, identify the group of words as a fragment (F) or a complete sentence (C). Be ready to explain why you identified the group of words the way you did.

1. _____When trying to sound funny.
2. _____Hoping to do better on the next test.
3. _____If the student finishes the project on time.
4. _____Although the bus was late.
5. _____Talking to her mother on the phone.
6. _____Nicholas was sure he would pass the class.
7. _____Practicing the saxophone takes up a lot of Keyana's time.
8. _____Because Brian never actually read the directions.
9. _____Exercise is essential for good health.
10. _____Quickly threw the ball to her teammate.

Completeness Practice #2 Directions: Select five fragments from the above practice and fix them. Remember the two strategies to fix them: add missing elements to the fragment to make it complete -OR- combine the fragment with a sentence/independent clause.

1. _____
2. _____
3. _____
4. _____
5. _____

Fairness

*Avoid **absolute terms** so that your writing is **fair** and balanced (absolutes suggest exaggeration or bias on the part of the writer).*

Which sentence below is a fair and unbiased account of your contributions to the household chores?

I always do the dishes and take out the trash.
I often do the dishes and take out the trash.

In the first sentence, the use of the word "always" does not allow for any exceptions; it is too strong (and probably exaggerated). Even if your brother did the dishes one time and your sister took out the trash once, those contributions to the household chores prevent you from honestly using the word "always." The second sentence is a fair and unbiased explanation of how much you do at home. Words like "always" are **absolute terms**, and they should be used sparingly, if at all, in academic writing. Some absolute terms could result in your expressing an unfair and untrue stereotype ("All women are terrible drivers"). Instead, you should use a **qualifier** that best captures the degree, strength, or quantity that you are trying to express. Qualifiers help you explain your ideas more appropriately, honestly, and fairly.

Common ABSOLUTE TERMS	Common QUALIFIERS
• Always	• Most
• Never	• Some
• Every	• Few
• All	• Usually
• None	• Frequently
	• Rarely
	• Might
	• May
	• Could

Similarly, some authors will use adjectives and adverbs for rhetorical effect (to persuade a particular target audience). In that case, the word choice may be too strong and, therefore, not fair:

Strong Adjectives	Strong Adverbs
Constant	Constantly
Continuous	Continuously
Total	Totally
Complete	Completely
Perfect	Perfectly
Utter	Utterly

I am <u>totally</u> annoyed by my coworkers' <u>constant</u> interruptions.

However, sometimes you *do* want to use strong word choices! If the situation and the context require it, you can state your position in strong terms: <u>*All*</u> *animals deserve kind and ethical treatment.* Just be sure that you are not opening yourself up to allegations of being unfair, biased, or untruthful: *I am frustrated because I perform my job <u>perfectly</u>, yet my coworkers are <u>completely</u> incompetent.*

NOW YOU TRY!

Fairness Practice #1 Directions: For each of the following sentences, circle any absolute terms, underline any qualifiers, and highlight any strong adjectives or adverbs. Write an appropriate term, qualifier, or adjective/adverb in its place.

1. Every single college student I know uses a cell phone constantly.
2. My college instructor never answers my email.
3. Some of my textbooks are a total waste of money.
4. My friend always picks me up late; she is a constant disappointment.
5. I am continuously amazed by the utter lack of manners exhibited by today's youth.

Relevance

*Know particular rules that are **relevant** to academic writing.*

Finally, you should familiarize yourself with a few rules that are especially relevant to academic writing. When in doubt, check with your instructor or with tutors in the writing center on your college campus.

Titles: Italics or Quotation Marks?

Italicize long works such as books, movies, plays, and magazine titles; put quotation marks around short works—article titles, poems, and short stories.

Quotations: Where to Put Punctuation?

The answer is, it depends! Commas and periods go within the quotation marks:

> *"Damon, call home," his mother said.*
> *Later, she admonished him, "I meant for you to call home today."*

Semicolons and colons go outside of the quotations: *To underscore her feelings, Damon's mother resorted to a cliché: "Home sweet home."*

If you have a quote within a quote, the usual double quotation marks indicate the words taken from a source or spoken in dialogue, but then you must place single quotations around the words that the source or person quoted:

> *Damon's mother told him, "I keep thinking about that line from The Wizard of Oz when Dorothy said, 'There is no place like home.'"*

First, Second, or Third Person Point of View?

First person (I, me, my) point of view is appropriate in assignments that call for personal reflection such as a journal entry. Second person (you, your) point of view is appropriate in directions but only if you are actually addressing your specific reader(s) on how to do something or make something. Most of the time in academic writing, you will use third person point of view (he, she, they, researchers, readers, Americans, patients, personnel). Third person is professional and results in an objective, academic tone. Whichever one is appropriate for a given assignment, be sure to use the same point of view consistently within an assignment.

Contractions and Abbreviations?

Avoid using contractions in formal, academic writing. Don't = do not; they're = they are; won't = will not, and so on (notice we did not write "etc." as you should avoid both "et cetera" and its abbreviation "etc." in all formal writing).

Some institutions and organizations are well known by their abbreviations, but you should write out each word and put the abbreviation in parentheses the first time you use it in a paper:

> *Consult the Center for Disease Control (CDC) for more information.*

You are free to use the abbreviation in all subsequent references to the organization.

CHAPTER 9

Problem-Solving

Learning Goals

In this chapter you will learn how to

➤ Solve Problems
➤ Understand Reading and Writing as Problem-Solving
➤ Be Persistent
➤ Describe Problems
➤ Break Down Problems
➤ Construct Solutions
➤ Evaluate Solutions

PREVIEW OF TERMS

Problem p. 303
Problem-solving p. 303
Wicked problems p. 304
Persistence p. 305
Sub-problem p. 312
Hypothetical deductive method p. 317
Hypothesis p. 317
Satisficing p. 320
Optimizing p. 320
See glossary, pp. 391–397

What Is Problem-Solving?

A **problem** is a challenge that needs to be overcome but that requires a series of steps to overcome it. So **problem-solving** means using all the skills you've learned as a critical thinker and strategically applying them to the challenges at work, school, or in your personal life in order to surmount them.

Being able to solve difficult problems is one of the primary benefits of critical thinking. You encounter numerous problems every day, from finding out that a class you need is full, to having to figure out a new route to work when an accident closes down the road you normally take, to reading a difficult passage and constructing a written response to it. Inference, analysis, evaluation, and indeed all the skills you've mastered so far in this book will help you solve problems, and the more complex the problem, the more these skills will help you solve it. Although every problem is different and needs to be approached differently, Figure 9-1 illustrates a basic strategy you can use when you approach a challenge that will make you better at overcoming it.

Reading and Writing as Problem-Solving

We just defined a problem as a challenge that needs to be surmounted but that will require you to follow a series of steps to be successful. By this definition, both reading and writing are also forms of problem-solving. This is true on several levels; after all, what student hasn't struggled to comprehend a difficult reading or to write a complex essay?

Critically reading a complicated text is a form of problem-solving, because your challenge when you read is to fully comprehend the text, extract the information contained

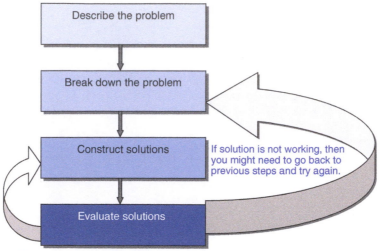

■ Figure 9-1 Problem-Solving Strategy

within it, evaluate that information, and use it. As you learned earlier, you have to take multiple steps and apply various skills to overcome the challenge of reading critically. The strategy explained in this chapter for solving problems can further help you to make sense of difficult reading passages.

- **Describe the problem**. Preview the selection to get a sense of the topic and the main point the author makes about it; ensure you understand important elements like the author's purpose and audience; identify obstacles like difficult or technical vocabulary; and take note of the resources you have available (such as dictionaries, reference works, or teachers) to help you understand the reading.
- **Break down (analyze) the problem.** Identify the structural elements of the text—the title, introduction, thesis, headings, if any, and conclusion—as well as rhetorical elements such as tone. Then determine the argument(s) the author is making, including the parts of that argument(s,) and think about whether you have read any similar arguments before.
- **Construct a solution.** Use skills like inference and analysis to ensure you understand the author's argument(s).
- **Evaluate the solution.** Monitor yourself, including your understanding of the author's argument(s) and your biases and preconceptions, and evaluate the author's assumptions and biases and the validity of his or her reasoning and conclusions.

Explaining your ideas in writing is also a form of problem-solving. The challenge in writing critically is to express yourself clearly, in an organized fashion, so that your readers understand you. As you learned in the last chapter, writing also often involves creating and defending arguments. Again, the problem-solving strategy you will learn in this chapter works well with the writing process.

- **Describe the problem.** Decide on your topic, figure out what you want to say about it (your main point), set your goals (such as what you need to have accomplished by a certain time or date), identify the sources you will use, and pre-write to generate ideas.
- **Break down (analyze) the problem**. Plan your writing, deciding what ideas and supporting details to use to support your thesis and organizing them logically using an outline.

Real Problems

This chapter will give you a strategy for solving problems that you can use on academic problems, such as reading, writing, and math problems, as well as on personal problems, which this chapter will focus on. But problems in the real world may be far more complex. Some problems are even known as **wicked problems**, because they are so convoluted that they are nearly impossible to solve or because solving them would create problems just as bad. Many social problems, such as poverty or racism, are wicked problems. Still, this problem-solving strategy can help even with these difficult social problems. Of course, it doesn't guarantee success, and, like, critical thinking, it can't be used mechanically. You've got to be careful, use all of your knowledge and experience, and be persistent if you hope to make progress.

- **Construct a solution**. Write your first draft. Focus on getting your ideas on paper in an organized, logical fashion. Pay attention to grammar and spelling, but don't try to make your writing perfect.
- **Evaluate the solution.** Evaluate your writing based on how well you've accomplished the goals you set for yourself in the first step of the process. Where necessary, revise, making content and organizational changes, and edit, correcting grammar and mechanics.

In this chapter, you will learn to solve real-world problems, as well as how to approach reading and writing challenges, by implementing the strategy laid out above. One of your best tools for solving problems, though, will be your critical thinker's attitude of persistence, so let's review it first.

Reviewing the Critical Thinker's Attitude: Being Persistent

Persistence means not giving up when things get difficult. It's easy to keep at a task when it's enjoyable, but when the task starts to get tedious, you need to do your best to keep at it until the job is done, no matter how long it takes or how difficult it gets. Studies have shown that intelligence and creativity each only account for about 25 percent of success; perseverance accounts for a whopping 50 percent! In fact, "overnight success" is a myth. For almost all the overnight success stories you can think of—from performers like Mozart or Beyoncé to inventors like Thomas Edison—the reality is that each person spent an average of 10 years working single-mindedly in obscurity before his or her breakthrough occurred.

> I know the price of success: dedication, hard work, and an unremitting devotion to the things you want to see happen.
> —Frank Lloyd Wright

Being persistent is important in the short term because it allows you to accomplish things and solve problems in your daily life; it will help you get your homework done, stay in shape, or complete jobs at work. Here are some tips to help you remain persistent in the short term.

Tips for Critical Thinkers: Maintaining Short-Term Persistence

- **Set a goal.** Decide what task you need to accomplish in the current situation.
- **Avoid procrastination.** Get started on accomplishing your goal right away; don't put it off.
- **Reward yourself.** If and only if you accomplish your goal (or reach a point in your task that you set for yourself), engage in an activity you enjoy as a reward for your hard work. Play a game, listen to music, have a snack, or do something else you like doing.
- **Push past your limits.** When you are ready to quit, work for a few more minutes, read a few more pages, exercise for longer, or do a few more parts of the task.

While the above tips will help you day to day, using persistence to accomplish long-term goals requires a slightly different approach. You can increase your chance of becoming a lifelong success (like an expert scientist, company CEO, or accomplished musician, for example), by following these tips.

Tips for Critical Thinkers: Maintaining Long Term Persistence

- **Find a passion.** You won't be able to be persistent in the long term if you don't enjoy what you are working at. Whether it's your job, a hobby, a sport, or an activity like singing or woodworking, in order to be committed to it and persist in learning and perfecting the necessary skills you have to really want to do it.
- **Make a realistic plan.** Decide what steps you need to take to become good at your chosen occupation.

- **Practice**. Work hard to get better at your passion. Practice on a regular basis, every day if necessary.
- **Specialize**. Resist the urge to "branch out" or "try other things." An accomplished expert is rarely a jack-of-all-trades. For example, you don't see expert musicians "dabbling" in physics and discovering new theories any more than you see physicists "giving music a try" and coming up with hit songs.
- **Don't get discouraged and don't give up**. There will be times when the work you put in to your chosen occupation doesn't seem like it's being rewarded, so keep your goal in mind, envision the rewards of your ultimate success, and keep at it; if your goal was realistic in the first place, persistence will get you to it.

PRACTICE 9-1	Persistence

Directions: Respond to the following prompts on a separate sheet of paper.

THINK AND **WRITE** CRITICALLY

1. Decide on a task you need to accomplish in the next week. Explore how you could use short-term persistence to accomplish this task by doing the following:

   a. clearly identifying your goal

   b. deciding on a reward you could give yourself if you accomplish it

   c. explaining how you could push past your limits while trying to accomplish it.

2. Consider how you could use long-term persistence to become successful in a particular area of your life. What are you passionate about? Could this passion be turned into a career? What steps would you need to take to make this passion into a career?

A great example of someone who displayed incredible short and long-term persistence is Barbara McClintock, a Nobel Prize–winning scientist. McClintock discovered early in her life that she had a talent and a passion for science, and she pursued it tenaciously from then on. She applied to Cornell University, despite discouragement from her mother, who believed that a woman's main goal should be to marry. In 1921, she was accepted at Cornell and began studying botany but soon switched to genetics, which she would study for more than 50 years. While in the graduate program at Cornell, she published several breakthrough studies on the genetic makeup of maize.

Thinker to Emulate: Barbara McClintock

Barbara McClintock was born in 1902 in Hartford, Connecticut and died in New York in 1992 at the age of 90. During her life, she worked tirelessly in the field of genetics, studying how chromosomes affect the development of maize (a kind of corn). She made breakthroughs in her field, being the first to create a genetic map of maize. She was also a pioneer in the area of genetic recombination, and although other scientists resisted, she never gave up on the idea. Eventually her ideas were vindicated, and, in 1981, her persistence was awarded with the Nobel Prize in Physiology and Medicine.

Courtesy of the Barbara McClintock Papers, American Philosophical Society.

McClintock next took a position at the University of Missouri, but she grew unsatisfied, feeling excluded by many of the other faculty, and took a position at Cold Spring Harbor Research Laboratory. In 1944, she was made a member of the National Academy of Sciences, and in 1954, she became the Genetics Society of America's first female president. None of these honors distracted her from her studies, though, and she made several more breakthroughs over the coming years, identifying genetic regulatory mechanisms well before other scientists did.

Even though her discoveries were at first resisted, the scientific community eventually came to realize that McClintock's ideas about genetic regulation were correct. She received many prizes for her work, among which were the National Science Medal and the Nobel Prize.

McClintock was also an expert problem-solver, partially because of her persistence. When she needed to solve a problem, "she worked in spurts, night and day for weeks.... She was so good at it that she often found herself solving problems for her peers, teachers, and seniors of her profession" (Tang, 2006, p. 49).

Biographers disagree about whether McClintock was a victim of gender discrimination. Some believe her career in science was more difficult because she was a woman; others think she wasn't mistreated because of her sex. One thing is clear, though: Barbara McClintock set her sights on a goal and displayed great persistence until she became a legend in her field.

Discussion Questions

1. Is Barbara McClintock's story admirable to you? Why or why not?

2. Have you ever persisted in an interest or activity that other people have discouraged? Explain.

Describe the Problem

Persistence combined with an effective problem-solving strategy will allow you to solve many problems. The first step in solving a problem is to describe it, and this involves three elements: You need to make sure that you acknowledge that a problem exists; make sure you fully understand the problem, including the context of the problem; and get your desired goal or outcome clear in your mind. This is detailed in Figure 9-2.

Acknowledge the Problem

Acknowledging a problem exists can be difficult, especially if the challenge has to do with your personal life. Think back to what you learned about denial (Chapter 1, p. 23). Often, people avoid addressing problems by refusing to admit they exist. Of course, problems can never be solved if you don't acknowledge them. If a problem concerns you personally, you will need to admit that it is yours and that you have the responsibility for solving it. If it doesn't concern you personally, it will probably be easier to acknowledge the problem, but you will still need to take responsibility for solving it, if that is your job.

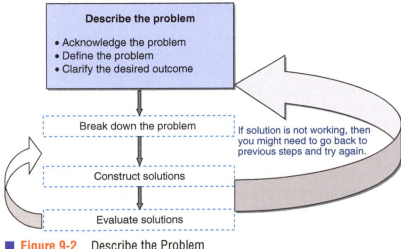

■ **Figure 9-2** Describe the Problem

Define the Problem

Once you have acknowledged a problem or challenge exists, you have to make sure you fully understand it by defining it, using the following steps:

1. **Clearly and explicitly state the problem**. Avoid generalities. For example, if you need to buy a car so that you can get a job, don't say, "I need money"; that's too general. State specifically how much money you need and why you need it. How you characterize the problem will greatly affect your success at solving it. For example, if you say "I'm always broke and never have enough money for anything," you have already hurt your chances of finding a solution; by using words like *always* and *never*, you haven't so much defined the problem as defined *yourself*. But if you define the problem as "I am temporarily short on cash and need to raise enough to pay for a car so that I can get a job," you have clarified the problem and indicated that it can be solved.

2. **Note the problem's context, including the circumstances that surround it and those that led up to it.** In the car example, you would have to clearly explain why you face the specific problem, why you do not have the money to buy a car. For instance, perhaps you have been involved in a demanding unpaid internship and all the money you have earned from work study has gone to college expenses. You also need to indicate why you need the car so badly by showing how a part-time job would ease your financial situation.

3. **Note time constraints and other conditions or obstacles**. How long do you have to solve the problem, and what could hinder you from solving it? Perhaps you need the car by the end of the month; that's the time constraint. You also need to continue to do well in your classes, so you can't devote all your time to making money or shopping for a car.

4. **Note what resources are available to help you solve the problem**. What tools or assets do you have at your disposal to help you overcome the challenge? Maybe your parents could help you, and your friends might be willing to give you rides on a limited basis while you try to earn the money for a car.

Clarify the Desired Outcome

The final part of describing the problem is stating clearly what would qualify as a solution. List all possible resolutions to the problem; be creative. Perhaps you could buy a used car, car pool, buy a motorcycle, or ride a bike.

Describing Reading and Writing Problems

In a general sense, the information above relates to how you should begin to solve reading and writing challenges. When it comes to reading, in order to comprehend a difficult text you need to figure out why you are reading it, what your goal is. You can then begin to define the problem and clarify your desired outcome by previewing, noticing hindrances like difficult vocabulary, figuring out the context of the reading, including the author's purpose and his or her audience, and, finally, taking stock of anything you have available to help you understand the text (like reference books, reading centers, or professors).

In writing, you can begin to meet the challenge—creating a complex essay that effectively communicates your thoughts and argument to your readers—by choosing your topic, deciding on your purpose, setting your goals, gathering your resources, and, perhaps most importantly, pre-writing to generate ideas.

Describing Problems

Directions: Begin to solve the following problems by describing them. Define them (state the problem in clear, specific words; note its context; and note time constraints, obstacles, and resources available) and clarify the desired outcomes.

Here's a model

I need transportation so I can accept a part-time job I've been offered. There isn't any public transportation around, so that's out. I need a car. The thing is, I don't have much money at the moment. Last semester I had a really busy schedule, wasn't able to work, and now I have almost nothing in the bank. My school schedule is still challenging this semester, but it isn't quite as bad, so I think I can manage a part-time job; I just can't devote all my time to it. The job offer only lasts until the end of the month, so I need to solve this problem soon. My parents said they'd do what they could to help me (short of buying me a car), and my friend Jim said he'd be able to drive me there and back for the next couple of weeks.

Statement of Problem: He needs transportation so he can accept a part-time job.

Context: He hasn't been working because of his course load. He's had more money going out than coming in and is almost broke. He's had an offer for a part-time job he needs to help pay his bills.

Time constraints and obstacles: He needs the car by the end of the month, his bank account is low, no public transportation exists, and he can't devote all his time to solving the problem.

Resources available: Friends, parents

Desired outcomes: acquire new or used car, enter into some sort of car-sharing arrangement

Now you try

1. Evelyn has been doing poorly in college. She attends all her classes, but when it comes time to take tests or quizzes, things fall apart. She failed the first round of exams in all her classes. It's not that she is partying too much or anything, either; it's just that she can't seem to efficiently learn all the material covered in class. In high school, she was never taught a good study method or even how to study at all. She needs to pass her midterms—about five weeks from now—or her status as a full-time student will be jeopardized. Her friends and professors have offered her help, and she knows they have lots of tutors on campus, but she's starting to despair.

Statement of Problem: _____

_____

Context: _____

_____

Time constraints and obstacles: _____

_____

Resources available: _____

_____

Desired outcomes: _____

_____

2. Stephen was traveling overseas. While staying in Paris, he went out with some new French friends, and when he woke up the next morning, discovered he had lost his passport. He tried to retrace his steps, but his friends had taken him places in the city that he didn't recognize; he also didn't have any way of contacting those friends. He needed to solve the problem quickly, as his money wouldn't last long, and he needed to get back to the States because he was going to be best man for his brother who was getting married in two weeks. He called his parents, and they suggested talking to the local police or perhaps visiting the U.S. embassy.

Statement of Problem: _____

_____

Context: _____

_____

Time constraints and obstacles: _____

_____

Resources available: _____

_____

Desired outcomes: _____

_____

3. Pick a problem you are currently facing in your life and describe it.

Statement of problem: _____

_____

Context: _____

_____

Time constraints and obstacles: _____

_____

Resources available: _____

_____

Desired outcomes: _____

_____

4. This strategy will work, in slightly modified form, on academic challenges too. The following somewhat difficult reading selection could be considered as a problem to be solved, with the problem being to fully comprehend the author's meanings and implications. Read the selection and perform the problem-solving tasks that follow. Answer on another sheet of paper.

The Purpose of Education

Dr. Martin Luther King Jr.

Dr. Martin Luther King Junior was born on January 15, 1929. He was a Baptist minister and famous leader in the African-American Civil Rights Movement. He combated racism and racial inequality using peaceful civil disobedience. King was assassinated on April 4, 1968. He had a national holiday created for him, and his legacy lives on.

As I engage in the so-called "bull sessions" around and about the school, I too often find that most college men have a misconception of the purpose of education. Most of the "brethren" think that education should equip them with the proper instruments of exploitation so that they can forever trample over the masses. Still others think that education should furnish them with noble ends rather than means to an end.

It seems to me that education has a two-fold function to perform in the life of man and in society: the one is utility and the other is culture. Education must enable a man to become more efficient, to achieve with increasing facility the legitimate goals of his life.

Education must also train one for quick, resolute and effective thinking. To think incisively and to think for one's self is very difficult. We are prone to let our mental life become invaded by legions of half truths, prejudices, and propaganda. At this point, I often wonder whether or not education is fulfilling its purpose. A great majority of the so-called educated people do not think logically and scientifically. Even the press, the classroom, the platform, and the pulpit in many instances do not give us objective and unbiased truths. To save man from the morass of propaganda, in my opinion, is one of the chief aims of education. Education must enable one to sift and weigh evidence, to discern the true from the false, the real from the unreal, and the facts from the fiction.

The function of education, therefore, is to teach one to think intensively and to think critically. But education which stops with efficiency may prove the greatest menace to society. The most dangerous criminal may be the man gifted with reason, but with no morals.

The late Eugene Talmadge, in my opinion, possessed one of the better minds of Georgia, or even America. Moreover, he wore the Phi Beta Kappa key. By all measuring rods, Mr. Talmadge could think critically and intensively; yet he contends that I am an inferior being. Are those the types of men we call educated?

We must remember that intelligence is not enough. Intelligence plus character—that is the goal of true education. The complete education gives one not only power of concentration, but worthy objectives upon which to concentrate. The broad education will, therefore, transmit to one not only the accumulated knowledge of the race but also the accumulated experience of social living.

If we are not careful, our colleges will produce a group of close-minded, unscientific, illogical propagandists, consumed with immoral acts. Be careful, "brethren!" Be careful, teachers!

Eugene Talmadge

Eugene Talmadge (1884–1946) was a democratic politician and governor of Georgia. Apparently a right-wing segregationist, Talmadge expressed racist views. He was known for opposing the Supreme Court Decision that black people should be allowed to vote in Democratic primaries in Georgia.

© StampGirl/Shutterstock.com

a. Indicate your goal for reading this selection.
b. Preview the reading, noticing any elements like text boxes. List and define unfamiliar vocabulary words.
c. Make a list of resources you can use to help you understand this piece.
d. Note the audience and how you determined it.
e. Specify the author's purpose.

5. Writing can also be considered a form of problem-solving. Imagine that you need to convey Dr. Martin Luther King's speech to a classroom of eighth-graders. Your task is to write a one-page paper in which you clearly and concisely explain the speech in a way that students of that grade level could easily understand and relate to. Begin to solve this problem by setting your goal, taking stock of any available sources that you will draw on, and pre-writing to generate ideas (as you learned to do in the last chapter). Work on a separate sheet of paper.

THINK AND WRITE CRITICALLY

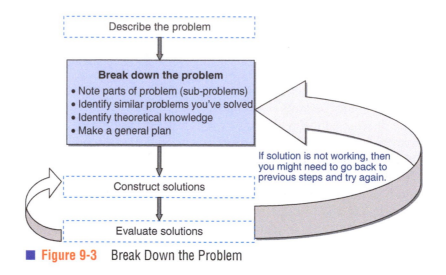

Break Down the Problem

After you've described the problem, it's time to analyze it; break it down into its constituent parts. This step of the problem-solving strategy has four parts, shown in Figure 9-3.

Note the Parts of the Problem

Start breaking down the problem by seeing if it consists of **sub-problems**, lesser problems that together make up the major problem. If so, these problems will have to be solved first. For each smaller problem, you should employ this problem-solving strategy, working persistently and methodically on each problem in the order that they need to be solved until you have solved the overall problem.

Continuing our car example, the main problem of getting transportation actually consists of several sub-problems. The first sub-problem is determining if buying a car or engaging in some sort of car-sharing situation is the better option. The second sub-problem depends on the solution to the first one. If a car seems like the better option, then two more sub-problems need to be solved. A suitable car needs to be located, and money needs to be raised to purchase it. At the same time, decent grades need to be maintained. Each of these sub-problems needs to be solved before the overall challenge has been overcome.

Identify Similar Problems You've Solved in the Past

Critical thinkers make good use of all the resources they have available, including prior knowledge and past experience. Therefore, the next part of breaking down the problem involves thinking back to similar problems you may have encountered in the past and remembering how they were solved, in case you can use this knowledge to solve the present one. In our example, perhaps you helped a friend look for a used car in the classifieds last year, so you have some experience with one of the sub-problems involved in your problem.

Identify Theoretical Knowledge

After you've thought about similar problems, consider whether you might have any theoretical knowledge that could help you solve the current problem. Theoretical knowledge means knowledge you have been told or taught as opposed to knowledge that you have gained through practical experience. You use theoretical knowledge all the time when solving problems in subjects like math or physics. For example, if you need to discover the length of the hypotenuse of a triangle, knowing the Pythagorean Theorem will allow you to figure it out. In the car example, if you have read about how to use body language to persuade people, this could be theoretical knowledge that you could use when trying to haggle for a used car.

Make a General Plan

The last part of breaking down the problem is making a general plan. You have to determine in what order you need to solve the sub-problems and when you need to solve them by. You don't need to figure out solutions to the sub-problems at this point (that's the next step). Here's a possible plan for the car problem:

1. I'll need to decide in two days whether I should buy a used car or try to work out a car-sharing arrangement.
2. If I decide to buy a used car, I need to decide what type of used car I want by next week.
3. By the end of the month, I need to earn enough money to buy a car.
4. By the start of next month, I have to locate a suitable car, haggle for it, and buy it.

Breaking down Reading and Writing Problems

You can break down reading and writing problems using the same basic problem-solving method described above. In reading, identifying sub-problems, identifying similar problems you've had experience with, identifying theoretical knowledge, and making a plan will involve noting the structural elements of the text, like the introduction and conclusion, and the rhetorical elements, like tone and mood. These are all sub-problems that need to be figured out in preparation for decoding the author's overall meaning. You will also need to identify any arguments the author is making, including premises and conclusions, to prepare to understand and evaluate those arguments.

In writing, you accomplish the breakdown step by planning carefully and being clear what ideas you are trying to convey. Creating an outline (see p. 99) is an effective way to plan your writing.

Breaking Down Problems	PRACTICE 9-3

Directions: Continue solving the following problems by breaking them down. Note sub-problems, note similar problems solved in the past, identify theoretical knowledge, and make a plan.

Here's a model

Continuing to try to find transportation, I thought more about my problem. I have to figure out if I should buy a used or new car or try to go in with my buddy Tom on a car we can share. But Tom's and my schedules don't mesh well. I might have to buy a used car. Thinking ahead, I remember the *Kelley Blue Book* was pretty useful when I helped Jim find his old clunker last year, so maybe that could give me a vague idea of what kind of used cars are out there and how much they cost. Of course, I'm going to need to somehow earn the money for it, but maybe I can at least get a decent deal on the car if I can haggle well. I know we talked about how to drive a good bargain in my psychology class this semester. I am also going to need to come up with a way to pay for insurance, registration, gas, and maintenance.

Sub-problems: The first sub-problem is determining which is the better option: buying a car or car-sharing. If a car seems like the better option, then a suitable car needs to be located, and money found to purchase it, insure it, and upkeep it. Decent grades also need to be maintained.

Similar Past Problems: Used KBB to help a friend find a used car last year.

Theoretical Knowledge Available: Psychology knowledge about bargaining

General Plan: 1. Decide whether to buy a used car or try to work out a car-sharing arrangement, 2. if I decide to buy a used car, research the type I want, 3. earn enough money to buy a car, 4. locate a decent car, haggle for it, and buy it, and 5. do this on evenings and weekends, so I do not miss classes.

Now you try

1. Evelyn has been working on her problem. She's not sure which of her study skills are weakest, but she knows she'll have to find out quickly. If she can figure it out, she's then going to have to do something about it, probably by developing some kind of a study system. Her roommate is always in her dorm room, playing loud music and talking on the phone, so it's not the quietest place to study. She has started to make use of some of her resources, and she did read about a certain technique called the Harvard System. Luckily, she doesn't feel entirely alone, since she watched her boyfriend struggle with and overcome a study skills problem during his first semester.

   Sub-problems: _____

   _____

   _____

   Similar Past Problems:_____

   Theoretical Knowledge Available: _____

   General Plan: _____

   _____

   _____

2. Stephen continues to struggle to get out of France. He hasn't ever experienced anything like this, and he's feeling anxious, but he's determined to solve the problem. He knows he'll have to visit available agencies like the police or the embassy. He's certain that these agencies will tell him he'll have to fill out all sorts of paper work and visit multiple government offices to apply for another passport. His hotel did give him a pamphlet called *Passport Problems: Where to Start*, so that might help. Alternately, he figures that he could work harder to locate the friends he met in Paris so they might be able to help him recover his lost passport.

   Sub-problems: _____

   _____

   _____

   Similar Past Problems:_____

   Theoretical Knowledge Available: _____

   General Plan: _____

   _____

   _____

3. Breakdown the problem from your life that you described in Practice 9-2.

Sub-problems: _____

_____

_____

Similar Past Problems: _____

Theoretical Knowledge Available: _____

General Plan: _____

_____

_____

4. Continue working through your comprehension of the speech by Dr. Martin Luther King (on p. 310) by analyzing (breaking down) the selection. Write your answers on a separate sheet of paper.

THINK AND WRITE CRITICALLY

a. Annotate the selection, indicating the introduction, body, and conclusion.
b. Identify the author's tone and how you determined it.
c. Identify the premises and conclusion of the author's argument.
d. Note any similar arguments you've encountered in the past.

5. Continue your work of explaining Dr. King's speech to an eighth-grade class. Organize the material you came up with during the pre-writing step by producing a preliminary outline. Finalize it into a formal outline.

Construct Solutions

The next step in solving the problem is coming up with solutions. Of course this is one of the most difficult parts of problem-solving (after all, if the problem had an easy solution, it wouldn't be much of a problem), and no single best method exists for coming up with solutions. You have to draw on all of your critical thinking skills, your knowledge of the subject, your creativity, and your intuition to come up with possible solutions. Creativity and knowledge of the subject matter are especially important; you need to be able to come up with original solutions, but each solution is specific to each unique problem, so knowing about the subject of the problem will be vital. There are four things you need to do when constructing solutions, as illustrated in Figure 9-4.

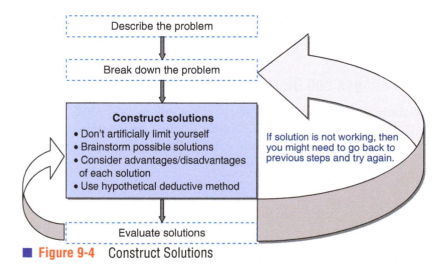

■ **Figure 9-4**   Construct Solutions

Do Not Artificially Limit Yourself

When you described the problem, you noted any conditions or constraints that could limit you. However, *be careful not to artificially limit yourself* by giving yourself constraints that don't really exist. Try the problem in Practice 9-4.

PRACTICE 9-4	**Thinking Outside the Box**

Directions: Connect all nine dots with only four straight lines and without lifting your pencil from the paper.

    If you had difficulty with this puzzle, it was probably because you were giving yourself artificial limitations. You have to literally "think outside the box" to complete this task (look at Figure 9-6 on p. 325 for the solution, but don't look until you've genuinely tried to complete it). In real life, you can artificially limit yourself too; for instance, in our transportation example, if you decide you will only look for used cars with a single previous owner because you think you stand a better chance of getting a car that's in good shape, you might be missing out on some great deals.

Brainstorm Possible Solutions

Again, since each problem is different, there's no single best way to solve each one. But generally you should *brainstorm alternative methods to solve a problem*. Be creative and don't censor your ideas until you've got them down on paper. Think of any method that will get you closer to a solution. For instance, when seeking to raise money for a used car, you might consider delivering pizzas on the weekends, selling some old possessions on eBay, playing the lottery, taking out a loan from a bank, or borrowing money from your parents and friends. You should also consider combining possible alternatives.

Consider Advantages and Disadvantages of Solutions

Once you've come up with some possible solutions, you should *consider their respective advantages and disadvantages*. For each possible solution (or combination of solutions), actually write down a list of pros and cons. After brainstorming your solutions above, for example, you might make the following chart:

Deliver Pizzas		Play the Lottery	
Pros	Cons	Pros	Cons
Make good money	Less time to study	Quick and easy	Costs money
Meet people	Have to borrow a car	Huge payoff	Very unlikely to win
	Pay for gas		Have to check numbers

After you've listed your pros and cons, weigh them in your mind, because some disadvantages will outweigh some advantages, and vice versa. In the chart above, the fact that playing the lottery could give you a huge payday is far outweighed by the fact that you are more likely to get struck by lightning than you are to win the lottery, so this is a huge con. Weighing the advantages and disadvantages of playing the lottery allows you to reject it as a solution to your problem.

Use the Hypothetical Deductive Method

Some (but not all) problems can be solved by the **Hypothetical Deductive Method.** This method involves coming up with a **hypothesis** (an educated guess) about the cause of your problem, making a prediction based on your hypothesis, and then figuring out whether your hypothesis is right or wrong by testing your prediction. If your prediction is proven wrong when you test it, it means that your hypothesis is probably not true.

> **Reminder**
>
> On p. 212 of Chapter 6, you learned about science and the scientific method.

The Hypothetical Deductive Method probably wouldn't work in helping you get transportation, but it would help you figure out what's wrong with your new ride when it breaks down. For example, if your used car won't start, you could guess that the battery is dead. From that hypothesis, you would make the prediction that if you jump-start the car, it should start. If it fails to start even after you jump it, that means that the problem is probably not the battery, and your hypothesis was wrong. As you probably noticed, the Hypothetical Deductive Method is closely related to the scientific method, because both involve making predictions and testing them.

Constructing Solutions for Reading and Writing Problems

"Solving" reading problems means coming up with a full understanding of what an author is saying and getting a solid grasp on the argument an author is making. Equally importantly, it means noticing any implications an author is making or inferences you should draw from the ideas an author has expressed.

In writing, the solution phase is where you actually do the work—produce a draft of your piece. It is, however, a rough draft, so while you should pay some attention to grammar and mechanics, you can mostly leave that for the next step. You should focus here on getting your ideas on paper.

The Hypothetical Deductive Method	PRACTICE 9-5

Directions: On another sheet of paper, respond to the following:

- Have you ever used the Hypothetical Deductive Method to solve a problem?
- If not, consider a problem in your life that it could help you solve, and explain how you could use it to solve that problem.

THINK
AND WRITE
CRITICALLY

PRACTICE 9-6 — Constructing Solutions

Directions: Continue solving the following problems by constructing solutions. Brainstorm possible solutions to the indicated problem or subproblem, then pick one of the solutions you came up with and write the pros and cons in the chart. Think outside the box; if you can think of or research realistic solutions not mentioned in the passage, feel free to list them.

Here's a model

Okay, so I have decided I need to buy a used car, and I've even figured out the basic kind of car I want and how much I want to spend. Now I just need to earn $3500.00 for the car.

Possible solutions to earn the money: Deliver pizzas on the weekend, play the lottery, sell some old possessions on eBay, take out a loan from a bank, borrow money from parents and friends

Solution being considered: _____ Take out a loan from a bank _____	
Pros	**Cons**
Get the money quickly	Needs to be paid back
Could get extra money	No credit means higher interest rate
Won't take away from my studying	Have to pay back more than was lent
Could help me build up credit	
Can pay back with job car lets me get	

Now you try

1. Evelyn discovered that most of her problems lie in her note-taking abilities. She isn't taking notes efficiently, so she doesn't have the material she needs to study and she can't remember to focus on it. She needs to learn how to take better notes, and she hopes that the resources available to her will help her do that.

   Possible solutions to learning to take better notes:

   _____

   _____

Solution being considered: _____	
Pros	**Cons**

2. Stephen decided that before he tries to get a new passport, he's going to use all his persistence to find his old passport. He's going to try to track down the people he was hanging out with so that he can find out if one of them found it or get them to help look for it.

Possible solutions for finding Stephen's friends: _____

_____

_____

Solution being considered: _____	
Pros	**Cons**

3. Construct a solution to the problem from your life that you have been working on solving.

    Possible solutions to your problem: _____

_____

_____

Solution being considered: _____	
Pros	**Cons**

4. Strengthen your comprehension of the speech by Dr. Martin Luther King (on p. 310). On a separate sheet of paper, complete the following tasks.
   a. Identify the assumptions underlying Dr. King's argument.
   b. Explain what you can infer about Dr. King himself from reading this selection.
   c. Note any implications you might draw from the author's arguments.
5. Continue explaining Dr. King's speech to an eighth-grade class. Write the first draft of your paper. Pay special attention to clarity, and try to use good grammar and spelling, but don't try to make your draft perfect.

THINK AND WRITE CRITICALLY

Evaluate the Solution

The problem-solving strategy doesn't end when you've found a potential solution. Now you need to evaluate the solution you have chosen, as shown in Figure 9-5.

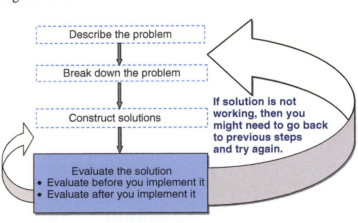

Describe the problem

Break down the problem

Construct solutions

Evaluate the solution
• Evaluate before you implement it
• Evaluate after you implement it

If solution is not working, then you might need to go back to previous steps and try again.

■ **Figure 9-5** Evaluate the Solution

Evaluate the Solution before Implementing It

Before you put your solution into action, you need to do the following:

1. **Check if it achieves your goal, or if it's the solution to a subproblem, if it gets you closer to your ultimate goal.** Revisit the goal you identified back when you described the problem and make sure your solution will actually accomplish it or get you closer to accomplishing it. It is sometimes easy to lose track of your eventual objective when you are working on a complex problem that involves many subproblems. In our example, you've decided that getting a loan from the bank is the main solution in solving your transportation problem. This solution will definitely help you get transportation, because it gets the necessary money for the vehicle fast.

> **Reminder**
>
> On page 22, you learned how easy it is to give in to wishful thinking.

2. **Make sure your solution is realistic.** Is it something that you can actually do, or is it the product of wishful thinking? Do you have the resources, support, and ability necessary to implement it? Continuing with the car problem, do you have the necessary credit to get a loan, or do you have someone who is willing to co-sign for you? Do you have enough money to pay the monthly payments? If so, then your potential solution has passed two checks.

3. **Make sure your solution is consistent with your values, so that you don't regret it later.** You learned about values and worldviews in Chapter 5 (pp. 159–160); since values are the moral guidelines by which you live your life, if you violate your own values to solve a problem, you may find out that you've only created a bigger problem for yourself. In our example, taking out a loan, as long as you fill out the application honestly, shouldn't violate any of your values, so that's not an issue.

4. **Decide if your solution is optimal or if you are simply settling for the first one you thought of.** Just settling for a solution is called **satisficing**, or choosing a response that satisfies the requirements and suffices to solve the problem but doesn't solve it in the best possible way. This isn't a bad strategy necessarily—if the decision isn't very important, or if the payoff to devoting more work to solving the problem isn't very large, then settling for a response that is good enough is a rational decision. We do this all the time in our daily life. When you go out to a restaurant, rather than studying the menu carefully, trying to remember times you had each entrée and weighing the taste of one against another in your memory, you might glance at it quickly to see if a dish that you know you've liked in the past is available. And in this case, that's good enough. Considering that we each make thousands of small decisions a day, we settle for most of the things we choose, and that's okay.

   But in other circumstances, settling isn't good enough; you need to come to the best decision that you possibly can. This is called **optimizing**. If you are choosing a life mate, settling probably isn't a good idea. It's likely worth the extra time, or even the heartache, to find the person who suits you best. Or if you are the president and have to make a decision about national security, you would be wise to gather all the information you can, discuss it with all of your expert advisors, spend a great deal of energy, and arrive at a decision that is as close to optimal as possible (it is often impossible in the real world to arrive at a truly optimal decision, but you can avoid settling on the first one that seems to work). In both these cases, the common dominators are *importance*, *payoff*, and *consequence*. If the decision being made is very important and will likely affect your life a great deal, the reward for success is great, and the penalty for being wrong is extreme. In situations that have these characteristics, looking for the best possible solution, rather than satisficing or settling for a solution, is the best choice (you can only look for the optimal solution if you have enough time). In the transportation problem, getting a loan probably isn't satisficing—it might truly be the ideal solution, considering that you'll probably be able to pay it back quickly with the good job the new vehicle will enable you to get.

Evaluate the Solution after Implementing It

If your potential solution doesn't pass your early evaluations, you will have to modify it or discard it completely and go back to early steps of the problem-solving strategy. You might need to describe the problem again, break it down further, or come up with more potential solutions. But if it passes the initial tests, it's time to put it into action. Even after you've implemented it, you should continue to evaluate it. Basically, you will need to ask yourself "Does my solution look like it's working?"

Monitor the solution to make sure it is actually succeeding at getting you closer to your goal. Sometimes a solution will look good before you implement it, but once you start putting it into action, you find out that you lacked some sort of key knowledge. Lacking important information while you constructed your solution will likely mean that the solution you came up with isn't going to work. In our example, if you didn't know that someone had stolen your identity, that could quickly ruin your credit and cause your loan to get rejected. You'll have to keep tabs on your loan process, and if your loan hits a snag, you will need to find out why.

Also, *monitor the situation.* You might find that the situation has changed and you can no longer realistically carry out your solution. You might have heard the expression, "the best laid schemes of mice and men. . . ." This old adage means that events in the world have a way of wrecking even the best-formulated plan by changing the circumstances under which it was devised. In the sample problem, you would need to keep your eye on any budding financial crisis. For example, since the last economic downturn, banks have made it more difficult to borrow money.

Monitor your performance as well. Look back at Chapter 5 and the three-phase self-monitoring process. Make sure you are using the process to ensure that you have put in your maximum effort and used all your skills effectively.

If you determine after you've implemented the solution that it doesn't appear to be working, that the changing situation is reducing its effectiveness, or that you didn't work to your capacity, you will need to go back to earlier phases of the problem-solving strategy to see if you can come up with a solution that will work better.

Evaluating Solutions for Reading and Writing Problems

Just as with general problems, when you evaluate solutions to reading and writing problems, you have to check to see if you've done what you need to do. When reading, check that you have fully understood the author's point. Monitor your comprehension, double-checking to make sure that you fully understand the reading. Identify any assumptions or biases you hold or the author seems to hold. Last, judge the author's writing. Did he or she make a good, well-reasoned argument and express him- or herself clearly and effectively?

In terms of writing, this is when you revise and edit your piece to make sure that you have expressed yourself well and provided clear, logical, and valid support for your point. You may add or delete content and fix grammatical, mechanical, and stylistic issues.

Evaluating Solutions	PRACTICE 9-7

Directions: Finish solving the following problems by evaluating the solutions. Choose the most promising solution for each problem from the ones you brainstormed in Practice 9-6 and evaluate it by considering if it achieves the ultimate goal, if it is realistic, if it is consistent with your values, and if it is optimal.

Here's a model

Solution to transportation problem: <u>Take out a bank loan</u>

How does it achieve the goal? <u>It gets me the money to buy a used car</u>

Is it realistic? <u>Probably, as long as my parents are willing to co-sign if the bank requires it</u>

Is it consistent with your values? <u>Yes. I won't be dishonest with anyone when seeking the</u> <u>loan, and I will make sure to repay it on time.</u>

Is it optimal? <u>It appears to be. I'll probably be able to pay it back quickly with the job my</u> <u>new car will let me get.</u>

Now you try

1. **Solution to study skills problem**: _____

   How does it achieve the goal? _____

   _____

   Is it realistic? _____

   _____

   Is it consistent with your values? _____

   _____

   Is it optimal? _____

   _____

2. **Solution to passport problem**: _____

   How does it achieve the goal? _____

   _____

   Is it realistic? _____

   _____

   Is it consistent with your values? _____

   _____

   Is it optimal? _____

   _____

3. **Solution to the problem from your life**: _____

   How does it achieve the goal? _____

   _____

   Is it realistic? _____

   _____

   Is it consistent with your values? _____

   _____

   Is it optimal? _____

   _____

4. Evaluate Dr. Martin Luther King's argument (on p. 310) and your comprehension of it. On another piece of paper, complete the following tasks.
   a. Consider if you have a full understanding of Dr. King's piece or if you are still unclear about any part of it. If you are unclear, revisit earlier steps or make use of further resources to fill in the gaps in your comprehension.

THINK
AND **WRITE**
CRITICALLY

   b. Identify any biases the author seems to have. Identify any biases within yourself. Write down a strategy to counterweight your own biases so that you can fairly evaluate the author's argument.

   c. Evaluate the author's argument, noting if it commits any fallacies and if it is plausible and compelling in general.

5. Finalize your paper in preparation to present it to the imaginary eighth-grade class. Proofread your paper, checking it carefully for mistakes in grammar, mechanics, spelling, or sentence structure. Try to judge how you've succeeded at making Dr. King's speech clear and accessible to eighth-graders. If necessary, make content and organization changes. Proofread it one final time.

Solving Problems   PRACTICE 9-8

Directions: Consider the following challenges. With a partner, use the problem-solving strategy from this chapter to solve each problem. Answer on another sheet of paper.

1. Your close friend is involved in an abusive relationship. Consider how you could help him or her.
2. Your student senate is running low on funds for student programs such as social clubs and recreation. Come up with a way to raise money for your student senate.
3. You are having a conflict with a co-worker. You can't agree on how to divide the work that needs done each day. Devise a way to resolve this conflict.
4. Pick a reading selection from another class you are taking and use the problem-solving steps from this chapter and this textbook to critically read it and gain full understanding of it.
5. Pick a writing assignment you need to complete for this or another class and use the problem-solving steps from this chapter and this textbook to produce a quality piece of critical writing.

Having begun to master the problem-solving strategy, you are now in a position to tackle academic and real-world problems in an effective way—using the traits and skills of a critical thinker and reader. And once again, being able to solve problems more effectively is one of the greatest benefits in becoming a critical thinker.

Real-World Mistakes of Problem-Solving and Their Consequences

On August 29, 2005, Katrina, a hurricane of incredible strength, made landfall on the Gulf Coast of Louisiana. With winds in excess of 120 miles per hour and heavy, sustained rain, the storm wreaked havoc. The Federal Emergency Management Agency (FEMA) most definitely had a problem on its hands. It failed to respond to the problem effectively.

Its failures came in all stages of the problem-solving process. During its preparation for the storm, FEMA didn't adequately prepare for the scope of the disaster. An investigative report by Congress declared that the federal government and FEMA's "biggest failure was in not recognizing Katrina's likely consequences as it approached." FEMA had advance warning of how severe the hurricane was likely to be, but it didn't get ready for the storm.

After the storm hit, the problems continued and even got worse. FEMA failed to identify which areas had been impacted the worst, and they weren't aware of the places refugees were congregating. The most egregious example of this failure was the fiasco at The Superdome in New Orleans. For four days, 25,000 people were left on their own, with no food, water, or medical supplies. The FEMA director at the time, Michael Brown, learned about the people stranded in The Superdome by watching the news.

Reports also came in that FEMA was turning away aid in places where it was desperately necessary. Walmart donated three trailer trucks full of water, but FEMA refused to accept them and instead sent them away. The Coast Guard tried to deliver thousands of gallons of fuel to the people of the Gulf Coast, but FEMA prevented them from doing so. Fearing liability issues, they failed to make good use of the resources available: They gave mops to doctors who traveled south to donate their time and expertise. These doctors mopped floors in frustration while hurricane victims suffered and died around them. Worse, FEMA didn't realize for days and days how badly they were doing at managing the situation.

The Federal Emergency Management Agency wanted to help the people of the Gulf Coast by solving the problems created by Hurricane Katrina, but poor problem-solving strategies stopped them from doing so. The billions of dollars in damage, 1300 dead, and hundreds of thousands left homeless in the wake of Katrina make it excruciatingly clear how important effective problem-solving skills can be.

For Discussion

1. Explain how the above discussion details a failure of evaluation.
2. How could FEMA have more effectively solved the problems caused by Katrina?

Real-World Successes of Critical Thinking

Peter Pronovost

You just finished reading about the cost of failing to employ critical thinking, but people who do think critically can be very successful. Peter Pronovost, a doctor who specializes in intensive care, created an intensive care checklist that detailed five things all doctors should do before inserting a central venus catheter. This checklist is credited with saving thousands of lives.

Directions: Using the internet or a library, research Dr. Peter Pronovost and his intensive care checklist protocol. Prepare a thorough description of the successes of the checklist protocol and the issues it was intended to address within intensive care units. Include an explanation of any skills, character traits, and standards of critical thinking possessed by Dr. Pronovost that contributed to his success in this area. Get ready to share your findings with the class.

Chapter Summary

- A *problem* is a challenge that that requires a series of steps to overcome. *Problem-solving* means using all your critical thinking skills and strategically applying them to problems in order to solve them.

- *Critical reading and critical writing are both forms of problem-solving,* because they both involve using a series of steps to overcome a challenge.

- *Persistence*—not giving up when things get difficult— is one of the most important traits to have when solving problems.

- The first step in problem solving is *describing the problem.* This step includes acknowledging the problem, clarifying the problem, and describing the desired outcome.

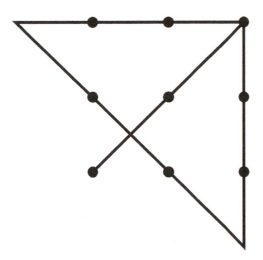

■ **Figure 9-6**   Solution to Practice 9-4

- The second step is *breaking down the problem*. This step includes noting sub-problems, identifying similar problems you've solved in the past, identifying theoretical knowledge, if available, and making a general plan.
- The third problem-solving step is *constructing solutions*, which includes not artificially limiting yourself, brainstorming solutions, considering the advantages and disadvantages of each solution, and possibly using the *Hypothetical Deductive Method*.
- The final step is *evaluating the solution*, both before and after you have implemented it.

READ, WRITE, AND THINK CRITICALLY: SECTION ONE

Directions: Skim through the following text and answer questions 1-3. Then, read the selection and answer the questions that follow.

1. What do you think the selection will be about? *Answers will vary.*

   _____

   _____

2. What is your prior knowledge of this topic?

   _____

   _____

3. The title of the selection is "Homophobia doesn't just oppress gay people, it affects us all." What does this suggest about what the author will claim about homophobia?

   _____

   _____

Homophobia Doesn't Just Oppress Gay People, It Affects Us All

To be thought of as gay still elicits a fearful response in far too many people.

David Hudson

David Hudson has worked for 20 years as a writer and journalist in the UK. He is the editor of a digital magazine, Out in the City, *and he often writes about issues concerning the gay community. The following essay was published in the* Independent *in 2014.*

1   A few years ago, on a trip to Vancouver, I found myself sat at the back of a sightseeing trolley tour. The driver was an amiable older man, who reeled off the history of the city with knowledge and affection: dropping in the occasional insight and story from his own life as he pointed out the famous sights and local landmarks. It turned out that he had the little finger missing from one of his hands. He explained that he had been involved in an accident, and the finger had been violently bent backwards. When healed, the finger was still bent at an awkward angle backwards. Not only was this an inconvenience, but—he chuckled "people thought I was... ahem, you know?"

2   The occupants of the trolley laughed. Even I smiled. We all knew what people must have thought. If a man's pinky finger sticks out backwards, he might be gay. Eventually, the driver decided it would be easier to have the near-useless finger cut off: hence the missing **digit**.

3   The trolley tour came to an end. Its occupants disembarked, entertained and educated by our history tour and the amusing anecdotes. The driver had meant no harm. It was only later, when I reflected upon his story that the significance of what he had said sunk in. Apparently he had had a part of his body **amputated** because he didn't like people thinking he might be gay. Yes, that was only part of the reason, but still, it seems to have been a factor in his decision.

4   I was reminded of this when I read a recent article by Graeme La Saux. In *The Times* at the beginning of the month, the former Chelsea football player—who, like the driver on my trolley tour, is heterosexual—reflected on how, in the early 1990s, he found fellow players and fans questioning his sexuality. The **taunting** began after it was discovered that he read *The Guardian* and had been on a touring holiday around Europe with a fellow footballer friend.

5   "The **homophobic** taunting and bullying left me close to walking away from football. I went through times that were like depression. I did not know where I was going. I would get up in the morning and would not feel good and by the time I got into training I would be so nervous that I felt sick."

6   Le Saux stuck things out, but the memories of his experiences—in particular, the vicious taunting he received from some other players on the pitch, have not dimmed.

7   "The abuse I had to suffer would be multiplied a hundredfold for a player who was openly gay. The burden would be too much."

8   This weekend, London's Southbank will be hosting a three-day cultural festival entitled 'Being a Man'. I have been invited to participate in a panel discussion on 'Being a Gay Man', in which one of the subjects for discussion will be 'the level of oppression felt by gay men.' That gay men—and women—continue to be oppressed is without doubt. Were this event to take place in Russia, I could be arrested for publicly discussing my sexuality. Was it Uganda or Nigeria, I could face a lynching or several years' imprisonment. I consider myself fortunate to live in the UK, where laws exist to protect me from such persecution. However, although homophobic oppression may be less visible in the United Kingdom, like environmental pollution, it remains in the atmosphere. And, as the examples I offered at the beginning of this piece, I don't believe homophobia just **oppresses** gay men: it affects straight men too.

9   You think those examples were extreme? Have you ever modified your behaviour—perhaps opted to wear something different, or chosen not to reveal you like a certain song or film—purely because you didn't want people to think... 'Well, you know'. If so, then you have reacted to—and become a victim of—homophobic oppression. To be revealed as gay, or thought of as gay, still elicits a fearful response in far too many people. It's a fear that we pass on to the next generation when we tell our children what toys they can or can't play with, or what colour possessions they can own. When little boys are told to 'be a man'... there is only one type of man that the rebutter has in mind.

10   When so many gay people are the victims of truly vicious homophobic oppression, why should I be bothered to highlight that suffered by straight people? It's because the 'them' and 'us' mentality around homophobia is part of the problem. Homophobia affects everyone – not just gay people.

11   Those who introduce homophobic laws believe such laws affect only 'them'—the LGBT community. If you are heterosexual, it can be so easy to think that such laws are nothing to do with you—that they're something

happening to other people in another country. But the suffering faced by a section of society will **inevitably** affect society as a whole.

12   Three years ago, I interviewed Roger Crouch, who had just won a 'Hero of the Year' award from Stonewall, at the LGBT charity's annual Equality Awards ceremony. Roger's son, Dominic, aged 15, killed himself after experiencing bullying at schools— some of it homophobic in nature. In the months after his son's death, Roger talked at schools about the dangers of homophobic bullying, but he remained devastated by his loss. A few days after our interview, he took his own life—a double tragedy for his surviving wife and daughter.

13   If you think homophobia and homophobic oppression have no effect on you, think again.

4. Use context clues, word parts, and/or a dictionary to define the following words.
   a. digit (para. 2): _____
   b. amputated (para. 3): _____
   c. taunting (para. 4): _____
   d. homophobic (para. 5):_____
   e. oppresses (para. 8): _____
   f. inevitably (para. 11): _____

5. Summarize the selection.

   _____
   _____
   _____
   _____

6. In paragraph 1 and 2, the author recounts how a tour guide made a homophobic joke and a group of people smiled or laughed. What is your view on this issue? Are such jokes okay or not?

   _____
   _____

7. What is the author's tone? Why did he choose this tone when writing this piece?

   _____
   _____
   _____
   _____
   _____
   _____

8. Use the problem-solving method to devise a solution to curb the use of homophobic language and to help combat homophobia at your college.

   _____
   _____

9. Use the problem-solving method to evaluate the solution you constructed in number 8. What challenges might you face in implementing your solution?

_____

_____

_____

_____

_____

PART II

Thinking Critically about Current Issues

Putting It All Together   331

Gun Violence and Gun Control   331

    1. "We Can't Stop Mass Murder" *Shikha Dalmia*   332

    2. "Ban Guns" *Paul Waldman*   335

    3. "What Explains U.S. Mass Shootings? International Comparisons Suggest an Answer" *Max Fisher and Josh Keller*   338

Technology Addiction   343

    1. "Why You Can't Stop Checking Your Phone" *Leon Neyfakh*   344

    2. "Does Social Media Addiction Really Exist?" *Catherine Knibbs*   348

    3. "Google's Former Ethicist Says Better Design Is Key to Tackling Our Tech Addiction" *Jenny Anderson*   350

Peace and War   353

    1. "Humans Evolved to Have an Instinct for Deadly Violence, Researchers Find" *Ian Johnston*   354

    2. "On Peace" *Daniel Zajfman*   356

    3. "On the Perils of Indifference" *Elie Wiesel*   359

Self-Driving Cars   363

  1. "Who's Making Sure That Self-Driving Cars Are Safe?" *Ruth Reader*   364

  2. "Here's How Self-Driving Cars Could Catch On" *David Roberts*   368

  3. "To Get the Most out of Self-Driving Cars, Tap the Brakes on Their Rollout" *Jack Barkenbus*   372

Women's Issues   375

  1. "Julia Pastrana: A Monster to the Whole World" *Bess Lovejoy*   376

  2. "A Shortage of Women" *Terry L. Jones*   380

  3. "Why We Still Need Feminism" *Casey Cavanagh*   382

Putting It All Together

At this point, you've learned all the traits and skills of a critical thinker. You've learned how to be curious, humble, open-minded, organized, skeptical, fair-minded, confident in your reasoning skills, and persistent; and you've discovered how important it is to approach your life with these traits. You've also learned and practiced comprehending, interpreting, inferring, self-monitoring, analyzing, evaluating, explaining, and problem-solving. We've focused on the traits and skills one at a time, isolating them so that you could practice and master them.

In the real world, however, you won't use any of these skills or traits alone. They go together and complement each other, and when you approach a difficult text or a tough problem, you will need to use all of the skills and habits at the same time to be successful. Your ability to comprehend will help you interpret, which will aid you when you infer and draw conclusions, for example. When you analyze and break an argument into its component pieces, you will also evaluate how well those parts of the argument are doing their job. Your ability to explain your thinking will be helped by the fact that you've arrived at your conclusions by using all of the skills and traits. And of course when you problem-solve, you'll continuously use all of the skills and mindsets you've mastered. Similarly, you won't just be intellectually humble when you are using the skill of interpretation and skeptical while self-monitoring. The character traits, like the skills, are also used continuously and all together.

You've also learned the importance of accuracy, completeness, fairness, clarity, relevance, and significance and can use your skills to find out what is most likely to be true and to reach a good conclusion rather than to just win arguments. By now, you should also be aware of the value of having intellectual integrity. So if you put together all of the skills, traits, and standards you've learned, you will have become a critical reader, writer, and thinker. Congratulations!

Critical Reading, Writing, and Thinking Skills Practice

This part of the text is divided into five topical readings. Each theme contains three texts, each of which is followed by a series of questions designed to provide further practice with the critical reading, writing, and thinking skills you have learned. We recommend that you continue your study of a topic by doing your own research to enhance your understanding of important issues facing us.

Topic: Gun Violence and Gun Control

When you evaluate, you examine the evidence that supports a claim and determine if it makes a good argument. Often you have to evaluate conflicting arguments or arguments that make sophisticated, nuanced points that do not lend themselves to a tidy "this side or that side" approach. The topic of gun violence (and gun control) sparks diverse opinions, and these opinions can become political and heated. Once that happens, our defense mechanisms and emotions kick in, and we lose the chance to have a productive debate. The best way to deal with such controversial topics is to examine evidence as well as biases as objectively as possible. Evaluating a controversial topic through the lens of a critical thinker can help you achieve understanding and allow you to propose possible solutions to this complex problem.

Keep reading as various authors share their opinions about gun control. You will answer questions at each skill level (comprehension, interpretation, inference, and so on), and then you will write about this controversial topic yourself. Use additional paper when necessary.

Measure of Belief

How likely is it that a particular belief is true?

How true is the belief?

	1	2	3	4	5	
Definitely NOT true	○	○	○	○	○	Definitely true

What do YOU think? Measure your current belief on the Likert scale.

Write a **journal entry** about your level of belief in the following claim: *Gun control can solve the complex problem of gun violence.*

_____

_____

_____

_____

_____

_____

Read and annotate each of the following articles and answer the questions that follow.

Reading #1: "We Can't Stop Mass Murder" by Shikha Dalmia

Reading #2: "Ban Guns" by Paul Waldman

Reading #3: "What Explains U.S. Mass Shootings?" by Max Fisher and Josh Keller

Reading #1: "We Can't Stop Mass Murder"

Shikha Dalmia

A senior analyst with the nonprofit Reason Foundation (a think tank advocating for free minds and markets), Shikha Dalmia writes for multiple publications, including Forbes, Bloomberg View, The Week, Reason *magazine,* The Wall Street Journal, Time, *and* Times of London. *She appears on various news programs on television and radio, and she has degrees in chemistry, biology, mass communication, and journalism. In 2009, she was a co-winner of the Bastiat Prize for Online Journalism.*

October 6, 2017

1   In the wake of massacres like the Las Vegas mass shooting, many Americans reflexively demand gun control. The instinct is understandable. But that doesn't mean such initiatives will be effective beyond the margins.

2   So what should we do instead? How about focusing less on preemptively thwarting prospective attackers and instead boosting the defensive capacities of prospective victims.

3   There is no doubt that Stephen Paddock was a gun nut. Police found 23 firearms in his hotel room and 19 more in his home. Even more chillingly, he converted his semi-automatic rifles that shoot only once when the trigger is pulled into something resembling automatic guns that shoot multiple times by using "bump stock"—a device that uses the recoil energy of the gun to partially reload. (This contraption basically **eviscerated** the existing laws that make it exceedingly difficult and expensive for private citizens to buy automatic weapons.)

4   All of this is boosting calls for more **stringent** gun regulations, especially since Paddock, who had no history of mental illness or crime, would have cleared every background check. And even Republicans and the NRA are jumping on board with plans to at least ban conversion kits that include "bump stock." No mass killer seems ever to have deployed this device before, but given the danger of copycats, banning its sale may make some difference at the margins. Or it may not. It's hard to predict.

5   But anyone who thinks that this—or similar measures—would significantly deter motivated shooters like Paddock, who meticulously planned his grisly attack, is fooling themselves.

6   There are about 300 million guns in this country—nearly one for every man, woman, and child. Congress can pass all the regulations it wants—and even declare an outright ban on guns. Anyone who wants a gun badly enough would still be able to get one. Substantially reducing America's stockpile of guns might make it more difficult for a potential killer to get a firearm undetected, but accomplishing that won't require a ban on guns, but a *war* on guns, whose constitutional implications are identical to those of the conservative war on terrorism. Indeed, it won't just require liberals to end their "truce with the Second Amendment"—as *The New Yorker*'s Adam Gopnik wants—but also **eviscerate** other aspects of the Constitution.

7   There is no good or easy way to get Americans to voluntarily surrender their guns. Asking them nicely won't do the trick.

8   Liberals like to tout Australia's "buyback" programs as a possible model, but the success of that program in actually reducing the number of guns—and gun-related homicides—is deeply disputed. Indeed, one indication that the program wasn't all that it is cracked up to be is that illegal gun ownership in Australia is up again, necessitating yet another amnesty initiative by the country this year.

9   Besides, Australia's love affair with guns is nowhere as strong as America's—which is why Australia doesn't have the Second Amendment to begin with and America does. That, combined with the greater number of guns in this country, might make any buyback program prohibitively expensive for taxpayers.

10 So what is the alternative? Basically, forcing people to give up their guns. But the kind of intrusive searches of the homes and property of gun owners this would entail would make the Bush administration's warrantless surveillance of telecommunications look positively restrained. Nor are Americans likely to simply lie down and take it. They will likely resist and fight back, which would require the government to crack down even more— or, in other words, declare war on its own people.

11 No matter how much liberals want a gun-free paradise, they can't simply wish away a deeply entrenched gun culture. If they truly want to reduce the number of firearms, they need to be prepared to get **draconian**.

12 But would that even be worth it? I am highly skeptical that reducing the number of guns will actually result in fewer mass killings. Paddock took 59 lives—including his own. But look at the worst mass murders in modern American history: 9/11, in which thousands were killed by hijacked airplanes crashing into buildings; the 1995 Oklahoma City bombing that killed 168 people with a homemade bomb and a truck. Meanwhile, the Nice attacker in France managed to kill 87 people—and injure 434—by simply mowing them down with his truck.

13 The grim lesson is this: There is nothing we can do to completely stop all killers at all times. The possibilities for mayhem are infinite. A society's means to stop them are finite. Psychotics and terrorists will always find ways to exploit the cracks. No government can create an entirely foolproof system.

14 So what can be done?

15 Employ modest firearm restrictions that can be enforced, sure. But also, encourage private entities to step up their own lines of defense. It is really quite amazing that Paddock could sneak in so much weaponry— and install security cameras in his room to monitor police activity outside—completely undetected by the Mandalay Bay. As I have written previously, that kind of thing would never happen in my home country of India, where after the 2011 Mumbai attack, every hotel runs every car, every piece of luggage, and every hand bag through a metal detector. Ditto for movie theaters and malls. Neighborhoods have installed their own private guards.

16 One reason Indians are taking security into their own hands is that their government is so **inept** that Indians have no illusions that it will protect them. But even where the government is more functional, it can't be omnipresent—and protect everyone from every single threat.

17 The American Hotel & Lodging Association declared after the Las Vegas shooting that it will re-evaluate the industry's security protocols. That's good. Other industries should follow suit.

18 The only way killers like Paddock—or Islamist terrorists, for that matter—have a prayer of being **thwarted** is if we fundamentally rethink our security strategy and build millions of points of resistance. Trying to go after their means (as liberals want to do) or targeting them by their motives (as conservatives want to do) won't cut it.

1. Indicate which of the following topics is too broad (TB), too specific (TS), and just right (JR).

   a. _____Gun violence in America

   b. _____Las Vegas shooter Stephen Paddock

   c. _____Increasing defense of potential gun victims

2. Define these words from the selection using context clues or a dictionary. For your convenience, words are in bold font in the article.

   a. Eviscerate (paras. 3, 6) _____

   b. Stringent (para. 4) _____

   c. Draconian (para. 11) _____

   d. Inept (para. 16) _____

   e. Thwarted (para. 18) _____

3. Reread para. 12. Which sentence below is the main idea?

   a. I am highly skeptical that reducing the number of guns will actually result in fewer mass killings.

   b. But look at the worst mass murders in modern American history: 9/11, in which thousands were killed by hijacked airplanes crashing into buildings; the 1995 Oklahoma City bombing that killed 168 people with a homemade bomb and a truck.

   c. Meanwhile, the Nice attacker in France managed to kill 87 people—and injure 434—by simply mowing them down with his truck.

4. Put the main idea (claim) of the article in your own words.

   _____

   _____

5. Draw inferences about the audience, purpose, and tone of this article.

   a. Audience: _____

   b. Purpose: _____

   c. Tone: _____

6. Examine your biases and worldview. Do you have a bias for/against the topic of gun control? How does your own opinion of gun ownership contribute to potential bias? Write a brief explanation.

   _____

   _____

   _____

7. Identify three pieces of evidence from the article. Determine what type of evidence each one is.

   a. Evidence: _____

      Type: _____

   b. Evidence: _____

      Type: _____

   c. Evidence: _____

      Type: _____

Reading #2: "Ban Guns"

Paul Waldman

Paul Waldman writes for The Week, The American Prospect, *and* The Washington Post. *He has written several books:* The Press Effect: Politicians, Journalists, and the Stories That Shape the Political World *(2000, with Kathleen Hall Jamieson);* Fraud: The Strategy Behind the Bush Lies and why the Media Didn't Tell You *(2004);* Being Right is Not Enough: What Progressives Must Learn From Conservative Success *(2006); and* Free Ride: John McCain and the Media *(2008, with David Brock). As a senior researcher, he worked at Annenberg Public Policy Center and Media Matters for America.*

October 6, 2017

1   Whenever America has one of its periodic mass shootings, you can count on seeing this particular exchange played out on cable news and in conversations across the country. The advocate for guns will say to the promoter of restrictions, "You just want to ban all guns!" to which it is replied, "No, I don't! I just want some common-sense regulation!" In anticipation of this criticism, Democratic politicians will regularly begin their remarks on gun control by saying, "I support the Second Amendment, and I'm not trying to ban guns. I just believe. . ."

2   So since no one else wants to say it, I will: Yes, I'd like to ban guns. Almost all of them, at least the ones in private hands.

3   Now before you begin penning your angry, threatening email to me (and so you know, you won't be the first or even the hundredth to communicate your friendly sentiments), let me be completely clear about what I'm *not* saying. First and most important, I know that guns are not going to be banned. And I know that with around 300 million of them already in circulation, collecting them would be an impossible task even if we tried (which we won't). I am fully aware of the Second Amendment, and of how the Supreme Court decided for the first time in 2008 that it **confers** an individual right to own a gun. This isn't a realistic proposal for legislation.

4   At times, however, it's worthwhile to step back from the concrete debates we're having, as important as those are, and spend a moment contemplating what kind of society we'd prefer if there were no practical **impediments** to radical change. If we could snap our fingers and create any situation we wanted, to start over, what would we do?

5   I'd suggest that if we were able to do that, we'd be much better off if we abandoned the **absurd** fetishism around guns that leaves us awash in so much blood and gore. America would simply be safer if we constructed our gun laws like one of our peer countries in Europe or Asia, in which private gun ownership is relatively rare and strictly regulated.

6   To gun owners, let me make something else clear: I get it. I get that the hunting rifle your grandfather passed down to you gives you a strong and meaningful connection to him. I get that guns are fun, and that just holding one, let alone firing it, can give you an intoxicating feeling of power and potency. I get that tricking out your guns with all kinds of cool accessories and reading about them and talking about them and thinking about them is hugely enjoyable for you. I'm a gearhead too, just about different hobbies. I'll even grant that you're one of the responsible ones, that you take safety seriously and that it burns you up that people who are less careful than you give gun owners a bad name.

7   But no matter how trustworthy you might be, you have to reckon with the price we all pay for the thing you enjoy: Over 30,000 Americans dead every year, and tens of thousands more **maimed** and paralyzed. Can you imagine how many restrictions on our rights we'd welcome if terrorists were killing 30,000 of us a year?

8   Oh, but you say, society has to pay that price, because this isn't just a hobby, it's my family's safety. Would you deprive people of the ability to defend themselves, even in their own homes? Well, if we're imagining what it would be like to start over, then yes, I would. You wouldn't be able to shoot an intruder, but he probably wouldn't have a gun either.

9 We don't have to imagine the horror such a society would produce, because we have examples all over the world. Do you think defenseless homeowners in England or Japan or Singapore have to fend off a daily stream of home invaders breaking down their doors with homicide in mind? No, they don't. They have crime, and even murders. What they don't have is the kind of body count that we do. It's not because Americans are an inherently violent people, it's because guns are so easily available here.

10 Yet many on the political right continue to make the ludicrous argument that even if you took away everyone's guns, people would still have evil in their hearts, and if they really wanted to kill they'd find a way. Sen. John Thune (R-S.D.) recently suggested that instead of passing restrictions on guns, "people are going to have to take steps in their own lives to take precautions," and if you find yourself in a mass shooting, you should "get small" to make yourself less of a target. It's like the weather—it's not like you can do anything about it, right?

11 But the fact is that the easier it is to get guns, the easier it is to kill many, many people. To take just one vivid example, on December 14, 2012, the very same day that Adam Lanza murdered 20 children at Sandy Hook Elementary School, a man named Min Yingjun entered the Chenpeng Village Primary School in China with equally murderous intent. He attacked 23 children. But since he was wielding a knife instead of a gun, every one of those children survived.

12 Imagine if we could save all those lives, the 11,000–12,000 gun homicide victims and the 20,000 gun suicides we have every year, a number that researchers tell us would be far smaller if the means to so surely and easily complete a suicide attempt weren't available. Imagine if we didn't have to pay the billions of dollars we spend every year treating gunshot victims. Imagine if police didn't kill 1,000 or so Americans every year, which they do in large part because they're trained to believe that anyone who looks at them funny might be about to shoot them. Imagine if our country could have that much less fear, that much less misery, that much less grief.

13 We may not often think about it in these terms, but if you're a gun advocate (or a member of the party that supports **unfettered** gun rights), you're saying that all this is just the price we have to pay for the joy some people take in their guns. No other developed country pays it, but we must.

14 So yes, if I had my way, there would be little private ownership of guns, and what there was would be highly regulated, with strict requirements on licensing, training, and record-keeping. You might be able to get an instrument whose very purpose is to kill, but you'd have to jump through some pretty serious hoops, and there would be lots of things that could disqualify you from that privilege. You could keep a small number of bolt-action hunting rifles, but anything else you'd have to go to a range to use, unless there were some extraordinary circumstance that absolutely demanded you keep a different kind of gun in your home. I realize that to some people that sounds like a nightmare.

15 No matter what legislation we might pass, even in liberal states that have increased restrictions in recent years, we won't get anywhere near banning guns. In particular, we won't address the biggest gun problem we have, which is not mass shootings but the daily **carnage** that claims around 90 Americans lives every day—and that means handguns, not military-style rifles or accessories like bump stocks. Precisely because we can't start from scratch, all we can do is trim around the edges, try to find ways to reduce the unending slaughter a little bit here and a little bit there.

16 Those things are absolutely worth doing—if there's a **compelling** reason why we shouldn't have universal background checks or why someone has a constitutional right to a magazine that holds 30 rounds or a device that turns their semiautomatic rifle into an automatic one, I've yet to hear it. Those are the questions we're actually going to debate, and we should.

17 But when you talk to people from other countries about America and guns, you always get the same incredulous questions. Are you people crazy? How can you tolerate this? And the answer is that while we might not be crazy, our gun reality is.

18 We may not be able to change the two centuries that brought us to where we are. But it wouldn't hurt to imagine something less awful.

1. Reread para. 4, and explain what the author wants readers to consider or imagine.

   _____

   _____

2. Define these words from the selection using context clues or a dictionary. For your convenience, words are in bold font in the article.

   a. Confers (para. 3) _____

   b. Impediments (para. 4) _____

   c. Absurd (para. 5) _____

   d. Maimed (para. 7) _____

   e. Unfettered (para. 13) _____

   f. Carnage (para. 15) _____

   g. Compelling (para. 16) _____

3. Clarify what the author means when he uses the phrase "jump through some pretty serious hoops" in the following sentence from para. 14: *You might be able to get an instrument whose very purpose is to kill, but you'd have to jump through some pretty serious hoops, and there would be lots of things that could disqualify you from that privilege.*

   _____

   _____

4. Explain the comparison the author makes in para. 11 about what happened on December 14, 2012, in China vs. America.

   _____

   _____

5. The author uses several words that have strong negative connotations. Select one of the words below, and write a brief paragraph to explain what image or impression the word evokes in you. What do you picture when you hear/read the word?

   Impediments (para. 4)

   Absurd (para. 5)

   Maimed (para. 7)

   Carnage (para. 15)

   _____

   _____

   _____

   _____

6. Paraphrase the hypothetical scenario the author establishes in para. 8.

   _____

   _____

   _____

7. Summarize the statistics the author provides in para. 12. Are these statistics likely to convince the reader of the author's claim? Why or why not?

_____

_____

_____

Reading #3: "What Explains U.S. Mass Shootings? International Comparisons Suggest an Answer"

Max Fisher and Josh Keller

Max Fisher writes for The Interpreter, The New York Times, The Washington Post, _and_ The Atlantic _about a variety of countries, political movements, and world events. Josh Keller writes for_ The New York Times, The Chronical of Higher Education, _and_ The Interpreter. _As deputy international editor at_ The New York Times, _Keller focuses on international news._

Nov. 7, 2017

1 When the world looks at the United States, it sees a land of exceptions: a time-tested if noisy democracy, a crusader in foreign policy, an exporter of beloved music and film.

2 But there is one **quirk** that consistently puzzles America's fans and critics alike. Why, they ask, does it experience so many mass shootings?

3 Perhaps, some speculate, it is because American society is unusually violent. Or its racial divisions have frayed the bonds of society. Or its citizens lack proper mental care under a health care system that draws frequent **derision** abroad.

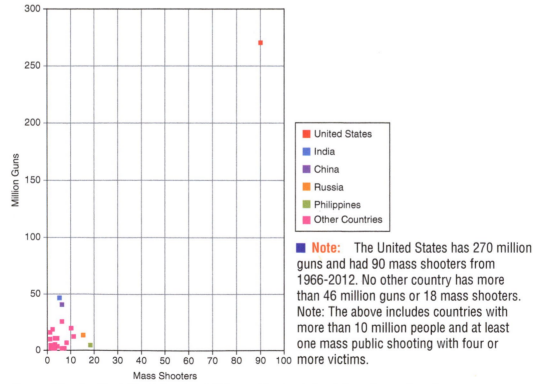

Note: The United States has 270 million guns and had 90 mass shooters from 1966-2012. No other country has more than 46 million guns or 18 mass shooters. Note: The above includes countries with more than 10 million people and at least one mass public shooting with four or more victims.

Source: Adam Lankford, The University of Alabama (shooters); Small Arms Survey (guns).

4   These explanations share one thing in common: Though seemingly sensible, all have been debunked by research on shootings elsewhere in the world. Instead, an ever-growing body of research consistently reaches the same conclusion.

5   The only variable that can explain the high rate of mass shootings in America is its astronomical number of guns.

A Look at the Numbers

6   The top-line numbers suggest a correlation that, on further investigation, grows only clearer.

7   Americans make up about 4.4 percent of the global population but own 42 percent of the world's guns. From 1966 to 2012, 31 percent of the gunmen in mass shootings worldwide were American, according to a 2015 study by Adam Lankford, a professor at the University of Alabama.

8   Adjusted for population, only Yemen has a higher rate of mass shootings among countries with more than 10 million people—a distinction Mr. Lankford urged to avoid outliers. Yemen has the world's second-highest rate of gun ownership after the United States.

9   Worldwide, Mr. Lankford found, a country's rate of gun ownership correlated with the odds it would experience a mass shooting. This relationship held even when he excluded the United States, indicating that it could not be explained by some other factor particular to his home country. And it held when he controlled for homicide rates, suggesting that mass shootings were better explained by a society's access to guns than by its baseline level of violence.

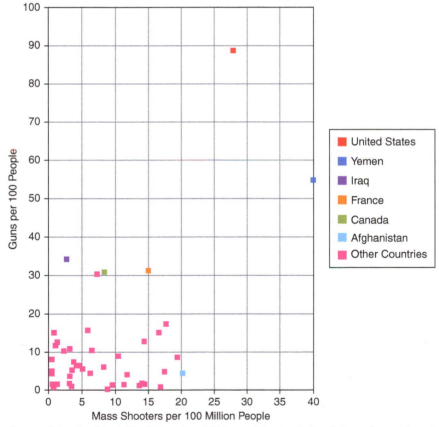

Source: Adam Lankford, The University of Alabama (shooters); Small Arms Survey (guns).

Factors That Don't Correlate

10   If mental health made the difference, then data would show that Americans have more mental health problems than do people in other countries with fewer mass shootings. But the mental health care spending rate in the United States, the number of mental health professionals per capita and the rate of severe mental disorders are all in line with those of other wealthy countries.

11 A 2015 study estimated that only 4 percent of American gun deaths could be attributed to mental health issues. And Mr. Lankford, in an email, said countries with high suicide rates tended to have low rates of mass shootings—the opposite of what you would expect if mental health problems correlated with mass shootings.

12 Whether a population plays more or fewer video games also appears to have no impact. Americans are no more likely to play video games than people in any other developed country.

Racial diversity or other factors associated with social **cohesion** also show little correlation with gun deaths. Among European countries, there is little association between immigration or other diversity metrics and the rates of gun murders or mass shootings.

A Violent Country

13 America's gun homicide rate was 33 per million people in 2009, far exceeding the average among developed countries. In Canada and Britain, it was 5 per million and 0.7 per million, respectively, which also corresponds with differences in gun ownership.

14 Americans sometimes see this as an expression of deeper problems with crime, a notion ingrained, in part, by a series of films portraying urban gang violence in the early 1990s. But the United States is not actually more prone to crime than other developed countries, according to a landmark 1999 study by Franklin E. Zimring and Gordon Hawkins of the University of California, Berkeley.

15 Rather, they found, in data that has since been repeatedly confirmed, that American crime is simply more lethal. A New Yorker is just as likely to be robbed as a Londoner, for instance, but the New Yorker is 54 times more likely to be killed in the process.

16 They concluded that the **discrepancy**, like so many other **anomalies** of American violence, came down to guns.

17 More gun ownership corresponds with more gun murders across virtually every axis: among developed countries, among American states, among American towns and cities and when controlling for crime rates. And gun control legislation tends to reduce gun murders, according to a recent analysis of 130 studies from 10 countries.

18 This suggests that the guns themselves cause the violence.

Comparisons in Other Societies

19 Skeptics of gun control sometimes point to a 2016 study. From 2000 and 2014, it found, the United States death rate by mass shooting was 1.5 per one million people. The rate was 1.7 in Switzerland and 3.4 in Finland, suggesting American mass shootings were not actually so common.

20 But the same study found that the United States had 133 mass shootings. Finland had only two, which killed 18 people, and Switzerland had one, which killed 14. In short, isolated incidents. So while mass shootings can happen anywhere, they are only a matter of routine in the United States.

21 As with any crime, the underlying risk is impossible to fully erase. Any individual can snap or become entranced by a violent **ideology**. What is different is the likelihood that this will lead to mass murder.

22 In China, about a dozen seemingly random attacks on schoolchildren killed 25 people between 2010 and 2012. Most used knives; none used a gun.

23 By contrast, in this same window, the United States experienced five of its deadliest mass shootings, which killed 78 people. Scaled by population, the American attacks were 12 times as deadly.

Beyond the Statistics

24 In 2013, American gun-related deaths included 21,175 suicides, 11,208 homicides and 505 deaths caused by an accidental discharge. That same year in Japan, a country with one-third America's population, guns were involved in only 13 deaths.

25 This means an American is about 300 times more likely to die by gun homicide or accident than a Japanese person. America's gun ownership rate is 150 times as high as Japan's. That gap between 150 and 300 shows that gun ownership statistics alone do not explain what makes America different.

26 The United States also has some of the weakest controls over who may buy a gun and what sorts of guns may be owned.

27 Switzerland has the second-highest gun ownership rate of any developed country, about half that of the United States. Its gun homicide rate in 2004 was 7.7 per million people—unusually high, in keeping with the relationship between gun ownership and murders, but still a fraction of the rate in the United States.

28 Swiss gun laws are more stringent, setting a higher bar for securing and keeping a license, for selling guns and for the types of guns that can be owned. Such laws reflect more than just tighter restrictions. They imply a different way of thinking about guns, as something that citizens must affirmatively earn the right to own.

The Difference Is Culture

29 The United States is one of only three countries, along with Mexico and Guatemala, that begin with the opposite assumption: that people have an inherent right to own guns.

30 The main reason American regulation of gun ownership is so weak may be the fact that the trade-offs are simply given a different weight in the United States than they are anywhere else.

31 After Britain had a mass shooting in 1987, the country instituted strict gun control laws. So did Australia after a 1996 shooting. But the United States has repeatedly faced the same calculus and determined that relatively unregulated gun ownership is worth the cost to society.

32 That choice, more than any statistic or regulation, is what most sets the United States apart.

33 "In retrospect Sandy Hook marked the end of the US gun control debate," Dan Hodges, a British journalist, wrote in a post on Twitter two years ago, referring to the 2012 attack that killed 20 young students at an elementary school in Connecticut. "Once America decided killing children was bearable, it was over."

1. Reread paras. 18 and 32. Why do you suppose the authors wrote these single-sentence paragraphs?

_____

_____

_____

2. Define these words from the selection using context clues or a dictionary. For your convenience, words are in bold font in the article.
   a. Quirk (para. 2) _____
   b. Derision (para. 3) _____
   c. Cohesion (para. 12) _____
   d. Discrepancy (para. 16) _____
   e. Anomalies (para. 16) _____
   f. Ideology (para. 21) _____

3. Fisher and Keller develop their main idea (that Americans endure more gun-related deaths because of the large number of guns in the county and the lax restrictions on gun ownership) by comparing/contrasting data with other countries. Paraphrase the major details the authors provide about these other countries:
   a. Yemen

_____

_____

b. Canada

_____

_____

c. Britain

_____

_____

d. Switzerland

_____

_____

e. Finland

_____

_____

f. China

_____

_____

g. Mexico

_____

_____

h. Guatemala

_____

_____

4. Infer the authors' purpose. Determine both the general purpose (inform, persuade, or entertain) as well as the specific purpose. There may be more than one correct answer; just be sure you could support your choices with evidence from the text.

To inform	To persuade	To entertain
• To explain	• To convince	• To be funny
• To clarify	• To recommend	• To tell a story
• To show	• To suggest	• To frighten
• To introduce	• To argue	• To inspire
• To provide background	• To express an opinion	• To shock
• To describe	• To take a political stance	• To connect emotionally
• To give directions	• To sell	• To excite
• To define		• To reminisce

General purpose: _____

Specific purpose: _____

5. Explain the American worldview as it relates to guns (para. 29–33). You may want to look up the Second Amendment to the United States Constitution and incorporate it into your explanation.

_____

_____

_____

6. Fisher and Keller use multiple statistics in their article. Write a brief paragraph that explains why the strength of an argument such as this one depends on the standard of accuracy.

_____

_____

_____

7. What is the assumption that the authors identify in para. 29? What are its possible implications?

_____

_____

_____

Writing about Gun Violence and Gun Control

Now that you have read three different articles on the topic, you will develop your own ideas through writing and solving problems. Use a separate sheet of paper to develop your ideas completely.

Explanation (Ch. 8)—Revisit your measure of belief in the claim: _Gun control can solve the complex problem of gun violence._

1. Write a **journal entry** about how your individual beliefs evolved after reading a variety of perspectives.
2. Optional: Write either a **critical response** or a **critical analysis** using your choice of the articles on gun violence/gun control.

Problem Solving (Ch. 9)—Think about how gun violence has affected students and staff in American schools. School administrators have increased security and legislators have proposed various solutions in hopes of keeping people safer. Go through the four steps of the problem-solving process to come up with an original solution to the problem of school shootings.

Topic: Technology Addiction

Critical thinkers strive to form beliefs that are likely to be true and to make good decisions. Some people (often parents and educators) worry that Americans' current level of dependence on technology will have detrimental effects. As critical thinkers, we can read a variety of opinions about tech dependence and determine if, indeed, we should believe that Americans have a problem, and, if so, consider how to solve the problem. You will answer comprehension, interpretation, inference, analysis, and evaluation questions after each article, and then you will write about technology in the form of journal entries, critical responses, and critical analyses.

Measure of Belief

How likely is it that a particular belief is true?

How true is the belief?

	1	2	3	4	5	
Definitely NOT true	○	○	○	○	○	Definitely true

What do YOU think? Measure your current belief on the Likert scale.

Write a **journal entry** about your level of belief in the following claim: *People are addicted to technology.* You could also explore your level of belief in the following secondary claim: *Technology addiction is serious and requires intervention.*

_____

_____

_____

_____

_____

Read and annotate each of the following articles and answer the questions that follow.

Reading #1: "Why You Can't Stop Checking Your Phone" by Leon Neyfakh

Reading #2: "Does Social Media Addiction Really Exist? by Catherine Knibbs

Reading #3: "Google's Former Ethicist Says Better Design Is Key to Tackling Our Tech Addiction" by Jenny Anderson

Reading #1: "Why You Can't Stop Checking Your Phone"

Leon Neyfakh

Leon Neyfakh hosts the podcast Slow Burn *about the Watergate scandal and the impeachment of former President Bill Clinton. A Harvard University graduate, Neyfakh wrote for his college newspaper,* The Harvard Crimson. *He worked for newspapers* Boston Globe *and* New York Observer.

October 6, 2013

1   Drive for long enough in America, and you're bound to see someone texting behind the wheel. Maybe it'll be the guy ahead of you, his head bobbing up and down as he tries to balance his attention between his screen and his windshield. Or maybe it'll be the woman weaving into your lane, thumbing at her phone while she holds it above the dashboard. Maybe it'll be you.

2   A recent study by the Virginia Tech Transportation Institute showed that drivers who are texting are twice as likely to crash, or almost crash, as those who are focused on the road. It's a disturbingly common habit: According to a survey analyzed by the Centers for Disease Control and Prevention, nearly one-third of American adults had e-mailed or texted on their phones while driving at least once during the previous month. And while most get away with it **unscathed**, many do not. The National Safety Council estimates that 213,000 car crashes in the United States in 2011 involved drivers who were texting, up from 160,000 the year before.

3   Concerned Americans have taken up the fight against this "national epidemic," as US Transportation Secretary Ray LaHood called it: Forty-one states, including Massachusetts, have outlawed texting while driving, and police are experimenting with increasingly aggressive enforcement strategies. Meanwhile, advocacy groups are taking a page from past public-safety successes, like the push to get people to wear seat belts and the anti-drunk-driving movement. AT&T has released an **array** of ads based around the slogan "It can wait," and commissioned a documentary film by Werner Herzog, in which people who have lost loved ones to texting-and-driving accidents join those who have caused such crashes in begging viewers to abstain.

4 But there's a problem with treating the texting and driving threat as simply a matter of public awareness: Most people already know they shouldn't do it. One federal survey showed that 94 percent of Americans think it should be illegal to text while driving. Yet they persist. Among teens, who are twice as likely as adults to have extended text conversations while driving, the problem is particularly worrisome. According to one analysis, a state antitexting law barely reduces the likelihood a teenager will text and drive.

5 It seems clear something powerful is at work, overriding people's knowledge that what they're doing behind the wheel is dangerous. To figure out what that something might be, psychology and communications researchers around the world have started studying what exactly is happening in our heads when we reach for a phone in the car. What their research so far suggests is that texting and driving is unlike any public safety issue we've dealt with before. It's not like the judgment error of drinking too much and deciding to drive home anyway; it's not like neglecting to put on your seat belt. That's because at the center of the problem, the experts say, is an entirely new kind of object—the modern smartphone—that has become **embedded** in our consciousness in a way that's changing our behavior on a massive scale.

6 In this light, the deadly phenomenon of texting and driving is just one **manifestation** of a broader affliction facing society: Our phones have effectively programmed us with new habits, including a powerful urge to pull them out when we're not supposed to. That urge—to check our e-mail, to glance at Facebook, to see who just texted us—can be as intense when we're standing in line or at dinner with our families as it is when we're driving a car. But it's only in a car that resisting it becomes a matter of life and death. In order to fight the problem, we need to understand how that urge works—and acknowledge that merely telling people texting and driving is dangerous, and punishing them for doing it, might not be enough.

7 "You have to start with the question of why it happens," said Scott Campbell, a communications professor at the University of Michigan who studies compulsive cellphone use. "Once you have a grasp on why it happens, then you can start to attack the actual mechanisms that lead to the behavior. Without that, you're just experimenting."

8 Driving is hard. A lot can go wrong as you operate a two-ton vehicle in a parking lot, never mind at highway speed. Not surprisingly, paying attention to a small computer at the same time makes it much more likely you'll mess up. And while sending or reading a text message might only take a few seconds, that can be an eternity when you consider how little time it takes for a child to run into the street or for traffic to suddenly slow in front of you. In a car, getting distracted even briefly can be catastrophic: In 2011, official reports listed 387,000 people injured and 3,331 people killed as a result of distracted driving.

9 The remedy seems simple: Drivers should just decide to ignore their phones in the car. But as cellphone researchers look more deeply into the practice, they are concluding that decision-making may only be part of the story. For many people, they say, using a smartphone may be less a decision than a habit—a move they make without initially thinking about what they are doing or why.

10 Habits form when we do something so often that it becomes automatic, sometimes even compulsive or involuntary. Researchers who study the psychology of habit formation are finding that for many people, cellphone use fits this category perfectly. In a recent paper, researchers reported the results of an experiment in which 136 test subjects were given smartphones equipped with software that kept track of their usage for six weeks. The subjects pulled out their devices for very brief periods up to 60 times per day, according to lead author Antti Oulasvirta, a senior researcher at the Max Planck Institute for Informatics, and tended to interact with them in ways that met several definitions of habitual behavior. In diary entries, subjects indicated they were moved to pull up certain applications under the same circumstances over and over: Those who repeatedly checked their e-mail or looked at the news, for instance, said they consistently did so when they got bored.

11 People whose cellphone use is driven by such automated habits are more likely to text and drive, according to a paper published earlier this year by Scott Campbell and his student Joseph Bayer. In the paper, Campbell and Bayer asked 441 college students a series of questions—adapted from a more general questionnaire used by psychologists to assess habit formation—aimed at determining the extent to which their phone use was habitual. Those who scored high on the scale tended to be the same people who admitted to texting while driving on a regular basis.

12 The tricky thing about fighting habitual behavior is that the brain's ability to form habits is actually one of its strengths. A habit is a powerful shortcut that helps us stay more productive: If we learn to react automatically to

things in our environment, we preserve mental energy for the harder decisions. You don't want to have to think about it every time you turn out the lights and lock the front door in the morning.

13   Phones, however, may hold a power over our habitual behavior that we haven't fully appreciated yet. Psychologists believe habits tend to revolve around triggers: **Trundling** down the stairwell of a T station, we pull out our Charlie Cards; settling into our desks at work, we automatically check for messages. But Campbell and Bayer, as well as other researchers who have looked closely at the way we use our mobile phones, say the habits people form around the "everything boxes" in our pockets are fundamentally different: Because we use them in so many different situations, and to accomplish so many different tasks, we develop a vast range of triggers and cues associated with pulling them out and looking at them.

14   These triggers can be quite basic—the phone ringing or buzzing with a message—and they can come from inside as well as out. One's desire to reach for the phone might be rooted in complex emotions like loneliness and curiosity, for instance. Humans crave resolution, and smartphones offer it: It's hard to resist seeing whether a crush has texted back, or a co-worker has sent a reply to a crucial e-mail. By connecting us to everybody we know, all the time, smartphones present a **novel** way to scratch all kinds of itches.

15   At the heart of the texting and driving problem, according to researchers, is that people who habitually use their cellphones in daily life have a hard time stopping themselves from reacting to that multitude of triggers when they're behind the wheel. "The idea that you can just turn off all those associations when you get into the car—I just don't think it's realistic," said Stephen O'Connor, a psychologist at Western Kentucky University who recently coauthored a paper linking compulsive cellphone use to a heightened rate of crashes.

16   Worse yet, driving itself may **exacerbate** the problem. According to Paul Atchley, a psychologist at the University of Kansas who studies texting and driving, drivers are at a disadvantage when it comes to resisting temptation, because their prefrontal cortex, the part of the brain responsible for inhibition, is engaged by the task of driving. "The part of your brain that would say, 'Don't do this, this is bad for you,' is occupied," he said.

17   If smartphone use has become more automatic than conscious for a broad swath of the population, it suggests a complete solution to the problem will require more than laws and ad campaigns: What people who text and drive must do is change their behavior in a way that's akin to kicking a compulsion. One approach to these kinds of compulsive behaviors is to simply remove the temptation, the way a smoker might throw away his lighter and avoid hanging out with other smokers. An idea that's been floated recently is to have phones automatically shut off when they detect they're being used in a moving car—in fact, one can already download apps that do this. But until it becomes possible to teach a phone to distinguish between a driver and a passenger, such solutions are unlikely to gain traction.

18   Atchley argues for a campaign inspired by the "friends don't let friends drive drunk" approach to reducing drunken driving. "If it's a social problem, the solution has to be a social solution," Atchley said.

19   That could include abstaining from contacting people we suspect are driving (though, obviously, much of the time we have no idea), or getting passengers to crack down on drivers. But it could also involve drawing lines about phone use in other contexts as well, essentially training ourselves to distinguish between situations where it is and isn't OK. "If we think it's socially unacceptable to have one person in a group constantly playing with their phone," said Atchley, "it's our responsibility as a friend to say, 'Can you put the phone down and just hang out with us?'"

20   Another idea suggested by the new research is that we might fight habit with habit. The goal would be to develop a new trigger for turning the phone off, or even stashing it in the trunk, before getting into the driver's seat.

21   Ultimately, the researchers agree, figuring out how to stop grabbing for our phones will depend on recognizing that we're relating to this new technology with some very ancient instincts—and that we'll need to take those into account, not just fight them. "It is a new kind of problem," said Campbell, "and in a way it's the same old problem we've always faced as human beings: that underlying need to connect, to overcome those boundaries between self and other. What I'd call the human condition."

1. In your own words, answer the question posed in the title: Why can't we stop checking our phones?

_____

_____

_____

_____

2. Define these words from the selection using context clues or a dictionary. For your convenience, words are in bold font in the article.
   a. Unscathed (para. 2) _____
   b. Array (para. 3) _____
   c. Embedded (para. 5) _____
   d. Manifestation (para. 6) _____
   e. Trundling (para. 13) _____
   f. Novel (para. 14) _____
   g. Exacerbate (para. 16) _____

3. Explain why ads and laws have not been successful in getting people to stop texting while driving.

_____

_____

_____

_____

4. Paraphrase the point the author makes about how forming habits is largely beneficial (para. 12).

_____

_____

5. Draw inferences about the audience, purpose, and tone of this article.
   a. Audience: _____
   b. Purpose: _____
   c. Tone: _____

6. Examine your biases and worldview. Do you have a bias for/against the topic of texting while driving? Do your own habits and experiences concerning cellphone use affect your ability to think critically about this topic? Write a brief explanation.

_____

_____

_____

7. Identify three pieces of evidence from the article. Determine what type of evidence each one is.

    a. Evidence: _____

       Type: _____

    b. Evidence: _____

       Type: _____

    c. Evidence: _____

       Type: _____

Reading #2: "Does Social Media Addiction Really Exist?"

Catherine Knibbs

Catherine Knibbs works as CEO and Director of PEER Support Yorkshire CIC. A writer, public speaker, and researcher, Knibbs is trained in psychology and psychotherapy. Her specialty is as a child trauma psychotherapist. She has been a guest on multiple podcasts and wrote the book Cybertrauma: The Darker Side of the Internet for Children and Young People *(2016). The following text appeared on the Psychreg.org website in 2017.*

August 13, 2017

1 It seems there is a lot of media focus at the moment on the sensationalisation of the 'impact of social media' (without rigorous and robust research to support these claims), how screens and the apps are 'addictive' (again using **layman** terms rather than an academic perspective). However, I take a very different view of this topic. Does social media addiction really exist?

2 I see smartphones, laptops and any 'internet-ready device' as a tool and a medium, intertwined and inseparable. This means we use it to help us achieve something, in the same way we use a kettle to boil water. Furthermore, we can also use it to create a connection with someone, like having a conversation. Therefore these devices have an overlapping function and form—and this is where the research and media can be at loggerheads.

3 For example terms like 'Facebook addiction' are far more complicated than first appears. This seems to be a term devoted to people who use Facebook a lot. What would need to be explored to define this as an addiction in the true sense of the word is the same motivational factors as a person who is addicted to substances. We would need to explore the negative consequences that result from this behaviour. What we do know is that some people are more likely to check their Facebook account more often than other people for a large number of varying reasons, such as accessibility (internet or busyness), availability, whether they access on a laptop or smartphone and even so much as boredom levels (e.g., those days in the office when there is a gap in the activity levels), however these are only a few examples.

4 Let's take a look at some of the reasons a person may check Facebook numerous times a day. They range from wanting, needing, and hoping for connection with others. This could be about a supportive network. This could be about flirting, dating, or sharing an event such as a holiday, and so on (either one you have been to, or are going to), with those people whom you will/have attended with, perhaps even discussions about new productivity items for your workplace. The list goes on. Yet, in these instances the connection is about connection with other human beings who are (most likely) not in the same **vicinity** or room as you. It means you can connect with your friends, family. and colleagues in short interactions, rather like an email exchange or phone call during the day/night. We called this progress when the telephone was invented? However, I'm not so sure that I have really read much research around the addictive nature of phone calls, or perhaps emails and good old fashioned letters such as pen pals.

5 This brings me to my view about the word 'addictive' when relating to anything digital. I see that this is about attachment (in the sense of the theory) and also is about relationships through cyberspace. As far as I know we don't tell our children to come in from playing because they're addicted to their friends? We might suggest that

certain friendships are unhealthy or unhelpful for them, but we don't use these terms associated with, often the same relationship behaviours carried out through social media.

6 So what would an addictive behaviour be or mean in relation to social media or devices? Again this would need a number of really rigorous pieces of research because I suggest it's far more complicated that the actual time spent 'physically' on the device. There is a fair amount of research appearing in regards to behaviours where people have been classified as addicted due to their lack of interaction with real life people, yet I consider the motivation behind this. Perhaps they are too shy, withdrawn, depressed, or have anxieties about people, or have a behavioural difficulty that makes real life interactions uncomfortable?

7 Some time ago the link between violent media (TV shows at the time) attempted to suggest that violent TV shows would result in violent behaviours in those who watched, due to a number of factors (Social learning theory would suggest this was we 'copy' other behaviours), yet we are still struggling to say that this is a direct cause effect link. Recently there has been further research around the violent computer games showing less of a cause-effect link.

8 The main reason for this is human beings have a brain that is wired for connection, learns from previous behaviours, can predict and alter new behaviours, and also likes it when we are both rewarded and motivated. We can choose.

9 I'm suggesting the 'addictive' behaviours of anything smartphone-related could be considered to be an actual addiction, when you use the definition from Gabor Mate which is:

Addiction is any behaviour where a person craves and finds temporary relief in something, but suffers negative consequences as a result of and is unable to give up, despite those negative consequences.

10 If checking your Facebook account hundred times a day causes you negative consequences and you don't stop this behaviour then by this definition you are addicted, however if you check your account hundred times a day and do not have negative consequences then you would not be considered addicted. It's all dependent upon the consequences, how they affect you and your life (and perhaps brain activity or focus). How do we qualitatively or quantitatively measure this without the high degree of variables giving us subjective and varying answers? Technically, I think this is where the research can help, yet we are only in the first 10 years of social media as a construct and concept. We have much to observe and measure before we really can say this causes that (highly unlikely), or as I suspect, this may result in this or that behaviour in future.

11 Which brings me onto terms such as digital **dementia**, digital overload and digital outsourcing, digital **amnesia**; vague yet possibly our new domain of social and media sensationalisation? I need to research more before commenting on these terms. Watch this space for that in the future.

---

1. Comprehending Knibbs's article depends on a complete understanding of the word *addiction* as it is used in psychology. See how the word is defined by either the American Psychological Association, the National Institutes of Health, or the Center for Disease Control, and write the definition below.

    _____

    _____

    _____

2. Define these words from the selection using context clues or a dictionary. For your convenience, words are in bold font in the article.

    a. Layman (para. 1) _____

    b. Vicinity (para. 4) _____

    c. Dementia (para. 11) _____

    d. Dementia (para. 11) _____

3. Clarify unclear language in para. 2. The phrase "at loggerheads" originated in the United Kingdom. Do a brief Internet search to see what you can learn about this phrase. Then, explain how Knibbs uses it in her article.

_____

_____

_____

4. Read the following potential conclusions, and label each one either A (Appropriate), I (Inappropriate), or M (More information needed).

   a. _____ The majority of people (over 50%) would agree with this statement from the article: "I see smartphones, laptops and any 'internet-ready device' as a tool and a medium, intertwined and inseparable" (para. 2).

   b. _____ People in the United Kingdom are addicted to social media in much larger numbers than in America.

   c. _____ Social media's potential for addiction is a topic that needs further research.

5. Paraphrase the Facebook example the author gives in para. 10.

_____

_____

_____

6. Explain the hypothetical evidence in paras. 3 and 4 as well as the analogy in para. 5.

_____

_____

7. Evaluate the author's evidence in terms of sufficiency.

_____

_____

_____

Reading #3: "Google's Former Ethicist Says Better Design Is Key to Tackling Our Tech Addiction"

Jenny Anderson

A reporter for The New York Times, *Jenny Anderson won the prestigious Gerald Loeb award for her coverage of Merrill Lynch. She frequently writes about Wall Street and educational issues, and she co-wrote the book* Spousonomics: Or How to Maximize Returns on the Biggest Investment of Your Life *(2011). The following piece was published on Quartz.*

February 8, 2018

1 People who talked about how too much technology was bad for kids used to be labeled **luddites** and alarmists. Now the problem of tech addiction is so widely accepted that the people who helped create the problem are banding together to try and fix it.

2   At "The Truth about Tech: How Kids get Hooked," a day-long conference in Washington, DC, sponsored by Common Sense, a nonprofit organization that reviews and rates media, Tristan Harris, a former in-house **ethicist** at Google, said tech has to change its design—for the sake of humanity.

3   "I see this as game over until we change course," Harris said. "We have to redesign all of it with a different, more compassionate view of human nature."

4   Harris, who recently founded the Centre for Humane Technology, said we should think of ourselves as residents of a digital city, from the moment we wake up and dive into our phones. "That environment is designed by Apple and Google," he said. "That city is completely unregulated—it's the Wild West—it's build a casino wherever you want, maximize developer access to do whatever they want to people."

5   As he explains in a 2014 TED talk, in order to manage the endless stream of notifications and information we receive on our phones, we need zoning laws like cities have, with designated places for kids and shopping, and stronger **demarcation** between tools that help us interact with the world outside our phones (calendars, text messages) and those that suck us into them (social media).

6   He suggested a few immediate actions companies like Apple could take to make smartphones less addictive, including a default grey home screen rather than a color one. As Nellie Gray wrote recently for the New York Times, "Companies use colors to encourage subconscious decisions" about which apps we open, and how often we do so. Greyscale home screens give users more control over how they distribute their attention.

7   Harris also suggested that changing vibrations and notifications, so that direct messages from people we know are prioritized over Beyonce's latest Instagram update. The uncertainty of not knowing what might be coming can make us more compulsive about checking—perhaps because phone notifications follow the model of "random reinforcement" (essentially, reward at irregular intervals), which is known in psychology to be far more difficult to break free of than regular, expected rewards.

8   The Center for Humane Technology is teaming up with Common Sense Media to lobby for legislation to study the effects of technology on kids and to educate parents and children about technology's effects. (The group has $7 million in funding, and another $50 million in donated media and airtime from partners including Comcast and DirecTV.) Jim Steyer, CEO of Common Sense said the impact of tech on our kids was one of the "most important cultural issues facing everyone in the room, but also our entire nation and the globe."

9   Harris expressed hope that Apple, Samsung, and Google may change their phone designs to help us cope with our vulnerabilities to tech addiction, rather than to take advantage of them. It would be harder to change Facebook and YouTube, he noted, because these kinds of companies' business models depend on keeping us hooked.

10   "When you wake up in the morning, you have certain goals for your life or for your kids," he said. But when you open YouTube, "it doesn't know any of those goals, it has one goal: To make you forget your goals and to keep you watching as many YouTube videos as possible."

11   The drumbeat of complaints against tech is reaching a fever pitch, as other high-profile technologists join in to warn about its dangers to children and society at large.

12   Roger McNamee, an early Facebook investor, also joined the Center for Humane Technology—in part because he was terrified at the site he helped create. "I contributed to creating something that created great harm," he said. "I want them [Mark Zuckerberg and Sheryl Sandberg] to join me in fixing this." (So far, no such luck, he noted.)

13   Last year, Sean Parker, one of Facebook's original investors and its first president, said of Facebook, "God only knows what it's doing to our children's brains." Chamath Palihapitiya, a venture capitalist who was an early employee at Facebook, said in November that the social network was "ripping apart the social fabric of how society works." Apple CEO Tim Cook told The Guardian in January that he would not let his nephew on social media.

14   Also in January, two giant investors sent a letter to Apple asking the company to address how technology affects its youngest users, suggesting that the company increase funding for research on the subject and change its design to help better parents limit kids' screen time. Pediatric and mental health experts recently called on Facebook last week to **abandon** Messenger Kids, a service introduced for kids as young as 6.

15 Harris said developers have to think big to help address the social crisis. "It's not about making this an individual choice, about how to make the design work for you," he said. "It's how make defaults work for everybody in the shortest possible time."

---

1. What is the "just right" topic of the article?

   _____

2. Define these words from the selection using context clues or a dictionary. For your convenience, words are in bold font in the article.
   a. Luddite (para. 1) _____
   b. Ethicist (para. 2) _____
   c. Demarcation (para. 5) _____
   d. Abandon (para. 14) _____

3. What word choices suggest that the author has concerns about technology addiction and its effects on society?

   _____

   _____

4. Explain the "digital city" comparison in paras. 4 and 5.

   _____

   _____

5. Select one of the ideas that tech developers have for decreasing the addictive properties of technology. Paraphrase the idea, and then write a brief evaluation of how helpful you believe it could be.

   _____

   _____

   _____

   _____

6. Anderson references several people who have been heavily involved in technology development. Select one of the people she mentions, and conduct a brief internet search on him/her. List a few biographical highlights below.

   _____

   _____

   _____

7. How do Anderson's expert opinions contribute to her credibility?

   _____

   _____

   _____

Writing about Technology Addiction

Now that you have read three different articles on the topic, you will develop your own ideas through writing and solving problems. Use a separate sheet of paper to develop your ideas completely.

Explanation (Ch. 8)—Revisit your measure of belief in the claim: *People are addicted to technology.* Also, revisit your response to the secondary claim: *Technology addiction is serious and requires intervention.*

1. Write a **journal entry** about how your individual beliefs evolved after reading a variety of perspectives.
2. Optional: Write either a **critical response** or a **critical analysis** using your choice of the articles on technology addiction.

Problem Solving (Ch. 9)—Think about how technology dependence has negatively affected you or a friend, perhaps by damaging a relationship, resulting in a car accident, or lowering one's ability to focus on school. Select one of those specific problems (or think of one on your own), and then go through the four steps of the problem-solving process to come up with a solution.

Topic: Peace and War

Human violence toward other humans is an ongoing problem and has been so throughout the history of our species. The question is, how do we promote peace? In the following three articles, you will explore the roots of human violence and read about the necessity to curb it. Prompts that follow each piece will guide you in using the skills and character traits of critical thinkers as you learn and eventually write about the subject. Use additional paper when you need to.

What do YOU think? Measure your current belief on the Likert scale.

Write a **journal entry** about your level of belief in the following claim: *It is possible for the human race to eventually eliminate violence.*

_____

_____

_____

_____

_____

_____

Measure of Belief

How likely is it that a particular belief is true?

How true is the belief?

	1	2	3	4	5	
Definitely NOT true	○	○	○	○	○	Definitely true

Read and annotate each of the following articles and answer the questions that follow.

Reading #1: "Humans Evolved to Have an Instinct for Deadly Violence, Researchers Find" by Ian Johnston

Reading #2: "On Peace" by Daniel Zajfman

Reading #3: "The Perils of Indifference" by Elie Wiesel

Reading #1: "Humans Evolved to Have an Instinct for Deadly Violence, Researchers Find"

Ian Johnston

Ian Johnston is a freelance journalist who works out of London in the United Kingdom. He regularly publishes in the Independent, *which is where the following article appeared.*

September 28, 2016

1   Humans have evolved with a **propensity** to kill one another that is six times higher than the average mammal, according to new research.

2   Scientists calculated that when we first developed into modern humans about two per cent of deaths were caused by fellow Homo sapiens, according to an article about the research in the journal *Nature.*

3   While this rate is well below the highest figure—found among meerkats where nearly 20 per cent of deaths are caused by other meerkats—many mammals kill each other only rarely or not at all.

4   For all their ferocious reputation, tigers are much less likely to fight each other to the death—with a rate of 0.88 per cent.

5   And we are also prone to periods of extreme violence that can put even meerkats in the shade. Between about 1200 and 1500 in the Americas more than 25 per cent of the people there were killed by other humans.

6   The researchers **compiled** information about more than four million deaths among more than 1,000 mammals from 80 per cent of the mammalian families, including some 600 human populations from the Palaeolithic era to the present day.

7   They then used this information to create an evolutionary tree of different mammals' propensity towards violence.

8   Humans, they found, were closely related to mammals who were more likely to kill each other than most.

9   Writing in Nature, the researchers said: "Lethal violence is considered by some to be mostly a cultural trait."

10   "However, aggression in mammals, including humans, also has a genetic component with high **heritability**. Consequently, it is widely acknowledged that evolution has also shaped human violence."

11   "From this perspective, violence can be seen as an adaptive strategy, favouring the perpetrator's reproductive success in terms of mates, status or resources."

12   The researchers found that lethal violence was used by nearly 40 per cent of mammals, but suggested this was probably an under-estimate.

13   The average percentage of deaths caused by members of the same species was about 0.3 per cent.

14   But, about 160,000 to 200,000 years ago, the same figure for humans was estimated to be about two per cent, more than six times higher than the average.

15   The Nature paper said there analysis "suggests that a certain level of lethal violence in humans arises from the occupation of a position within a particularly violent **mammalian** clade, in which violence seems to have been ancestrally present".

16   "This means that humans have inherited their propensity for violence," it added.

17   "We believe that this effect entails more than a mere genetic inclination to violence. In fact, social behaviour and **territoriality**, two behavioural traits shared with relatives of Homo sapiens, seem to have also contributed to the level of lethal violence."

18   The researchers stressed this inherited tendency towards violence did not mean humans were unable to control themselves.

19   "This prehistoric level of lethal violence has not remained invariant but has changed as our history has progressed, mostly associated with changes in the socio-political organization of human populations," they wrote.

20   "This suggests that culture can **modulate** the inherited lethal violence in humans."
And, in an email to *The Independent,* the lead author of the paper, Dr José María Gómez, of Granada University in Spain, said: "Do not fall into the trap of. . . making over-simplifications.
"Humans are moral animals and we cannot escape from that."

21   The researchers compared their estimate for the 'murder' rate among the earliest Homo sapiens—made using comparative methods developed by evolutionary biologists—with studies on observed levels of human-on-human killings.

22   The Paleolithic era was quite peaceful in human terms and close to the researcher's estimate.

23   In the 'Old World', there were spikes during the Mesolithic, about 10,000 to 5,000 years ago, and Mediaeval age, about 500 to 1500 AD, when about 10 per cent of humans died at the hands of their own species.

24   But things were significantly worse at times in the New World.

25   During a period from 3,000 to 1,500 years ago, more than 15 per cent of deaths were caused by humans, the study found.

26   Then came the astonishing surge to more than 25 per cent in the run-up to the arrival of Christopher Columbus in 1492, when millions more people died as they were exposed to European diseases for the first time.

27   In the modern world, there are some remarkably low rates of death from violence.

In the UK, which has one of the lowest levels in the world, 0.9 out of every 100,000 people (0.0009 per cent) is intentionally killed by someone else, according to the United Nations Office on Drugs and Crime.

28   Professor Mark Pagel, commenting on the research in an article in Nature, wrote that the question of whether humans were naturally violent had been long debated with philosopher Thomas Hobbes suggesting humans lived in "continual fear and danger of violent death" in the 17th century.

29   Others, such as French thinker Jean-Jacques Rousseau, suggested we were more the product of our environment.

30   "The work by Gómez and colleagues opens up a new approach to uncovering the origins of human violence, giving good grounds for believing that we are intrinsically more violent than the average mammal," Professor Pagel wrote.

31   "Their findings fit well with anthropological accounts that describe hunter–gatherer societies as being engaged in 'constant battles'."

32   "But societies can also modify our **innate** tendencies. Rates of homicide in modern societies that have police forces, legal systems, prisons and strong cultural attitudes that reject violence are, at less than 1 in 10,000 deaths (or 0.01%), about 200 times lower than the authors' predictions for our state of nature."

---

1. According to the author, is violence innate to our species? Support your answer.

   _____

   _____

   _____

   _____

2. Define these words from the selection using context clues or a dictionary. For your convenience, words are in bold font in the article.

   a. Propensity (para. 1) _____

   b. Compiled (para. 6) _____

    c. Heritability (para. 10) _____

    d. Mammalian (para. 15) _____

    e. Territoriality (para. 17) _____

    f. Modulate (para. 20) _____

    g. Innate (para. 32) _____

3. Identify three major details and three minor details from the article.

_____

_____

_____

_____

4. Which of the following statements is an appropriate inference to draw from para. 32?

_____

    a. Ancient peoples were less violent that modern, developed societies.

    b. There is reason to hope we can reduce violence further.

    c. Genetic research has nothing to contribute to our understanding of the human propensity toward violence.

5. Find two pieces of evidence that gives facts and figures. What point does the author use this evidence to establish?

_____

_____

_____

6. In para. 11, the author states, "From this perspective, violence can be seen as an adaptive strategy, favouring the perpetrator's reproductive success in terms of mates, status or resources." In your opinion, can violence be a successful evolutionary strategy? Why or why not?

_____

_____

_____

Reading #2: "On Peace"

Daniel Zajfman

Professor Daniel Zajfman, an Israeli physicist, is the President of the Weizmann Institute of Science. He holds several patents relating to small molecules and outer space and has won multiple awards, including the Guttwirth prize and the Minerva Award Lecture. The following text appeared in Seed.

January 21, 2011

1 Since the first humans began experimenting with new designs for spears, scientific research has held the potential to change not only the way we live, but also how long we live. Human and animal labor has been replaced by the work of levers and machines. Distances have shrunk as new means of travel have been invented, and

communication across these distances has become **instantaneous**. Modern drugs now cure many lethal diseases. In short, the quality of life and its span have improved for most, unfortunately not all, people on this planet.

2 Though we sometimes imagine it takes place in isolation from the rest of human activity, science continuously updates our understanding of who we are, the reality of the world we live in, and our place in that world. Science has given us the insight that in a universe not unlike a set of Russian matryoshka dolls, the doll that represents us is smaller than a dust mote—with even smaller ones nesting inside. Developments such as satellite television and the internet are changing both the speed at which we receive information from halfway across the planet and our access to the means of **disseminating** that information. This technology has had a direct impact on politics in both democratic and non-democratic countries around the world. In truth, few human activities influence our daily lives as much as those resulting from scientific research.

3 Of course, warfare has been a powerful motivator for scientific invention since ancient times. Archimedes, for instance, was the first to lay out the physical principles of the lever. He also applied those principles in the design of bigger and better catapults for the Greek army. The inventions of pulleys and torsion springs in the classical world allowed soldiers to fling heavier weights over walls and shoot projectiles farther with crossbows. Often, armies quickly adopt and improve technologies that were not specifically intended for waging war. A new method for casting iron led to the invention of the cannon; in the past century, airplane, submarine, and radar technologies were first put to use to fight wars. Yet where would we be today without levers or pulleys, metal casting or airplanes?

4 It's true that science has enabled some to apply its potential for destruction to **heinous** goals. Wars have become increasingly technology-based and weapons more destructive, and thus scientific research has also excelled in developing better defense systems.

5 But can scientific research be used as a **catalyst** for peace?

6 Consider this: The results of scientific research are universal. The formula for the velocity of a falling object will always apply, whether that object is dropped from the Great Wall of China or the Empire State Building. The proof of a mathematical theorem is either valid or it's not, and that validity exists independent of any cultural, religious, or national context. Our wireless communications systems are based on electromagnetism research conducted in just a few countries, yet they work the same way wherever we take them. And just one vaccine can protect all the world's people from smallpox, even those on opposing sides of a conflict.

7 Technically, peace between two warring countries is achieved through lengthy negotiations and the signing of complicated agreements by the rival nations' leaders. But true peace cannot be attained or sustained until the citizens of both sides get to know each other and develop a basic dialogue that leads to tolerance, and later to understanding and respect, for their ethnic and national differences.

8 Peace treaties, tied to a particular time and place, become history the moment they're signed. Science, on the other hand, by the very universality of its language, is the ideal format for opening channels of communication between people, even before a conflict officially ends. In no sense does science belong to any "side," and when two scientists meet, they do so as equals. They may disagree in their discussions, but their differing opinions will be dictated not by politics or **nationalism**, but rather by the different approaches they have used to solve a scientific problem. Because science is universal, it provides an integral basis for open discussion and, by extension, an ideal platform for communication.

9 Possibly the best example of the power of scientific collaboration is one that's not well known by the public, though it has been documented extensively. After WWII, when hatred and distrust still ran high on both sides, the first contact between Germans and Israelis took place between scientists of the Weizmann Institute in Israel and the Max Planck Society in Germany. The meetings and scientific collaborations of the 1950s opened the door to the establishment of diplomatic relations between the two countries in 1965. The year 2009 marked the 50th anniversary of the historic visit of Professor Otto Hahn, former president of the Max Planck Society, to Israel.

10 What can be learned from the German-Israeli example? Why was it so successful, and why does that success continue today?

11 Almost certainly the initial basis of collaboration—mainly basic science involving fundamental questions in physics, chemistry, biology, and mathematics—created an open environment in which scientists could use another universal commodity, curiosity, to drive cooperation. Here we can see the value of creating the

opportunity (through funding) and establishing a broad scientific framework in which a scientist is allowed to freely choose partners, as well as the mode of cooperation.

12 Such scientific cooperation, when it becomes firmly established, can spawn further collaborative projects between scientists in other countries where relations are tense. For instance, the scientific ties between Germany and Israel laid the groundwork for the SESAME project: a **decommissioned** German particle accelerator that is in the process of being upgraded and moved to a site in Jordan. A number of Israeli scientists are deeply involved in the project; when it's finished it will be used by researchers from Israel and other countries in the region ranging from Tunisia and Egypt to Pakistan.

13 But even before the first particle beam was deployed, SESAME provided a forum for scientists from the different countries to meet and discuss science. In November 2009, 50 years after the first German visit to Israel, Professor Ada Yonath of the Weizmann Institute attended a meeting of researchers in Petra, Jordan. She was surprised to find that those most eager to speak with her and be photographed with her were a group of young Iranian scientists. Not a word of politics passed between them, but if there is to be real peace, it might begin with something as simple as a discussion between a few scientists speaking a common language.

14 Ultimately, once scientific cooperation is established, along with a certain level of trust, additional messages can be passed through these channels and the issues moved to a higher level. Clearly, scientific collaboration cannot bring about peace on its own. But it can be a useful tool for bridging cultural gaps. By providing a common, universal language, it can open the door to all sorts of communication.

1. Label the following topic choices for the article as too broad (TB), too specific (TS), and just right (JR).

   Cooperation between the Max Planck and Weizmann institutes _____

   Peace _____

   Using science to promote peace _____

2. Define these words from the selection using context clues or a dictionary. For your convenience, words are in bold font in the article.
   a. Instantaneous (para. 1) _____
   b. Disseminating (para. 2) _____
   c. Heinous (para. 4) _____
   d. Catalyst (para. 5) _____
   e. Nationalism (para. 8) _____
   f. Decommissioned (para. 12) _____

3. What is the author's claim in the article? What major details does the author give to support the claim?

   _____

   _____

   _____

4. Is the purpose of the article to inform, persuade, or entertain? How do you know?

   _____

   _____

   _____

5. Knowing that the author is a scientist, do you detect any bias in the article? If so, give examples. If not, how do you think the author managed to avoid being overly biased?

_____

_____

_____

6. Is the author's argument primarily inductive or deductive? How do you know?

_____

_____

7. Evaluate the author's argument? Is it strong? Why or why not? What counter-argument might someone make against it?

_____

_____

_____

Reading #3: "On the Perils of Indifference"

Elie Wiesel

Elie Wiesel (b. 1929) was born in Romania. Imprisoned in Auschwitz in 1944, Wiesel eventually wrote Night *(1958) and* Jews of Silence *(1966) about the Holocaust. In 1963, he became a U.S. citizen. He was appointed chair of the Presidential Commission on the Holocaust in 1978, was awarded the Congressional Gold Medal of Achievement in 1985, and won the Nobel Peace Prize in 1986. The following is a speech (1999) in which he asked Congress and President Clinton to avoid indifference in the face of human suffering.*

1999

1 Mr. President, Mrs. Clinton, members of Congress, Ambassador Holbrooke, Excellencies, friends:

2 Fifty-four years ago to the day, a young Jewish boy from a small town in the Carpathian Mountains woke up, not far from Goethe's beloved Weimar, in a place of eternal **infamy** called Buchenwald. He was finally free, but there was no joy in his heart. He thought there never would be again. Liberated a day earlier by American soldiers, he remembers their rage at what they saw. And even if he lives to be a very old man, he will always be grateful to them for that rage, and also for their compassion. Though he did not understand their language, their eyes told him what he needed to know—that they, too, would remember, and bear witness.

3 And now, I stand before you, Mr. President—Commander-in- Chief of the army that freed me, and tens of thousands of others—and I am filled with a **profound** and abiding gratitude to the American people. Gratitude is a word that I cherish. Gratitude is what defines the humanity of the human being. And I am grateful to you, Hillary, or Mrs. Clinton, for what you said, and for what you are doing for children in the world, for the homeless, for the victims of injustice, the victims of destiny and society. And I thank all of you for being here.

4 We are on the threshold of a new century, a new millennium. What will the legacy of this vanishing century be? How will it be remembered in the new millennium? Surely it will be judged, and judged severely, in both moral and metaphysical terms. These failures have cast a dark shadow over humanity: two World Wars, countless civil wars, the senseless chain of assassinations (Gandhi, the Kennedys, Martin Luther King, Sadat, Rabin), bloodbaths in Cambodia and Nigeria, India and Pakistan, Ireland and Rwanda, Eritrea and Ethiopia, Sarajevo and Kosovo; the inhumanity in the **gulag** and the tragedy of Hiroshima. And, on a different level, of course, Auschwitz and Treblinka. So much violence; so much **indifference**.

5   What is indifference? Etymologically, the word means "no difference." A strange and unnatural state in which the lines blur between light and darkness, dusk and dawn, crime and punishment, cruelty and compassion, good and evil. What are its courses and inescapable consequences? Is it a philosophy? Is there a philosophy of indifference conceivable? Can one possibly view indifference as a virtue? Is it necessary at times to practice it simply to keep one's sanity, live normally, enjoy a fine meal and a glass of wine, as the world around us experiences harrowing upheavals?

6   Of course, indifference can be tempting—more than that, seductive. It is so much easier to look away from victims. It is so much easier to avoid such rude interruptions to our work, our dreams, our hopes. It is, after all, awkward, troublesome, to be involved in another person's pain and despair. Yet, for the person who is indifferent, his or her neighbors are of no consequence. And, therefore, their lives are meaningless. Their hidden or even visible **anguish** is of no interest. Indifference reduces the Other to an abstraction.

7   Over there, behind the black gates of Auschwitz, the most tragic of all prisoners were the "Muselmanner," as they were called. Wrapped in their torn blankets, they would sit or lie on the ground, staring vacantly into space, unaware of who or where they were—strangers to their surroundings. They no longer felt pain, hunger, thirst. They feared nothing. They felt nothing. They were dead and did not know it.

8   Rooted in our tradition, some of us felt that to be abandoned by humanity then was not the ultimate. We felt that to be abandoned by God was worse than to be punished by Him. Better an unjust God than an indifferent one. For us to be ignored by God was a harsher punishment than to be a victim of His anger. Man can live far from God—not outside God. God is wherever we are. Even in suffering? Even in suffering.

9   In a way, to be indifferent to that suffering is what makes the human being inhuman. Indifference, after all, is more dangerous than anger and hatred. Anger can at times be creative. One writes a great poem, a great symphony. One does something special for the sake of humanity because one is angry at the injustice that one witnesses. But indifference is never creative. Even hatred at times may elicit a response. You fight it. You denounce it. You disarm it.

10 Indifference elicits no response. Indifference is not a response. Indifference is not a beginning; it is an end. And, therefore, indifference is always the friend of the enemy, for it benefits the aggressor—never his victim, whose pain is magnified when he or she feels forgotten. The political prisoner in his cell, the hungry children, the homeless refugees—not to respond to their plight, not to relieve their solitude by offering them a spark of hope is to **exile** them from human memory. And in denying their humanity, we betray our own.

11 Indifference, then, is not only a sin, it is a punishment.

12 And this is one of the most important lessons of this outgoing century's wide-ranging experiments in good and evil.

13 In the place that I come from, society was composed of three simple categories: the killers, the victims, and the bystanders. During the of times, inside the ghettoes and death camps—and I'm glad that Mrs. Clinton mentioned that we are now commemorating that event, that period, that we are now in the Days of Remembrance—but then, we felt abandoned, forgotten. All of us did.

14 And our only miserable consolation was that we believed that Auschwitz and Treblinka were closely guarded secrets; that the leaders of the free world did not know what was going on behind those black gates and barbed wire; that they had no knowledge of the war against the Jews that Hitler's armies and their accomplices waged as part of the war against the Allies. If they knew, we thought, surely those leaders would have moved heaven and earth to intervene. They would have spoken out with great outrage and conviction. They would have bombed the railways leading to Birkenau, just the railways, just once.

15 And now we knew, we learned, we discovered that the Pentagon knew, the State Department knew. And the illustrious occupant of the White House then, who was a great leader—and I say it with some anguish and pain, because, today is exactly 54 years marking his death—Franklin Delano Roosevelt died on April the 12th, 1945. So he is very much present to me and to us. No doubt, he was a great leader. He mobilized the American people and the world, going into battle, bringing hundreds and thousands of valiant and brave soldiers in America to fight fascism, to fight dictatorship, to fight Hitler. And so many of the young people fell in battle. And, nevertheless, his image in Jewish history—I must say it—his image in Jewish history is flawed.

16   The depressing tale of the St. Louis is a case in point. Sixty years ago, its human cargo—nearly 1,000 Jews—was turned back to Nazi Germany. And that happened after the Kristallnacht, after the first state sponsored **pogrom**, with hundreds of Jewish shops destroyed, synagogues burned, thousands of people put in concentration camps. And that ship, which was already in the shores of the United States, was sent back. I don't understand. Roosevelt was a good man, with a heart. He understood those who needed help. Why didn't he allow these refugees to disembark? A thousand people—in America, the great country, the greatest democracy, the most generous of all new nations in modern history. What happened? I don't understand. Why the indifference, on the highest level, to the suffering of the victims?

17   But then, there were human beings who were sensitive to our tragedy. Those non-Jews, those Christians, that we call the "Righteous Gentiles," whose selfless acts of heroism saved the honor of their faith. Why were they so few? Why was there a greater effort to save SS murderers after the war than to save their victims during the war? Why did some of America's largest corporations continue to do business with Hitler's Germany until 1942? It has been suggested, and it was documented, that the Wehrmacht could not have conducted its invasion of France without oil obtained from American sources. How is one to explain their indifference?

18   And yet, my friends, good things have also happened in this traumatic century: the defeat of Nazism, the collapse of communism, the rebirth of Israel on its ancestral soil, the demise of **apartheid**, Israel's peace treaty with Egypt, the peace accord in Ireland. And let us remember the meeting, filled with drama and emotion, between Rabin and Arafat that you, Mr. President, convened in this very place. I was here and I will never forget it.

19   And then, of course, the joint decision of the United States and NATO to intervene in Kosovo and save those victims, those refugees, those who were uprooted by a man, whom I believe that because of his crimes, should be charged with crimes against humanity.

20   But this time, the world was not silent. This time, we do respond. This time, we **intervene**.

21   Does it mean that we have learned from the past? Does it mean that society has changed? Has the human being become less indifferent and more human? Have we really learned from our experiences? Are we less insensitive to the plight of victims of ethnic cleansing and other forms of injustices in places near and far? Is today's justified intervention in Kosovo, led by you, Mr. President, a lasting warning that never again will the deportation, the terrorization of children and their parents, be allowed anywhere in the world? Will it discourage other dictators in other lands to do the same?

The Kosovo Conflict

In 1999, NATO and the United States undertook a joint bombing campaign and then a ground invasion to stop the ethnic cleansing of Serbs being carried out by Albanians in the territory of Kosovo.

22   What about the children? Oh, we see them on television, we read about them in the papers, and we do so with a broken heart. Their fate is always the most tragic, inevitably. When adults wage war, children perish. We see their faces, their eyes. Do we hear their pleas? Do we feel their pain, their agony? Every minute one of them dies of disease, violence, **famine**.

23   Some of them—so many of them—could be saved.

24   And so, once again, I think of the young Jewish boy from the Carpathian Mountains. He has accompanied the old man I have become throughout these years of quest and struggle. And together we walk towards the new millennium, carried by profound fear and extraordinary hope.

---

1. Identify the topic of Wiesel's speech. What strategies did you use to figure it out?

_____

_____

_____

2. Define these words from the selection using context clues or a dictionary. For your convenience, words are in bold font in the article.

   a. Infamy (para. 2): _____

   b. profound (para. 3): _____

   c. gulag (para. 4): _____

   d. indifference (para. 4): _____

   e. anguish (para. 6): _____

   f. exile (para. 10): _____

   g. pogrom (para. 16): _____

   h. apartheid (para. 18): _____

   i. intervene (para. 20): _____

   j. famine (para. 22): _____

3. Summarize the article.

_____

_____

_____

_____

_____

4. Identify Wiesel's audience and purpose.

_____

_____

_____

_____

5. What do you learn about Franklin Delano Roosevelt in paras. 15–16? How does this information help shape Wiesel's worldview?

_____

_____

_____

6. Wiesel mentions many atrocities that occurred during the twentieth century. Pick one and explain what you already know about it. Where could you find more information about it?

_____

_____

_____

7. What argument does he make in para. 9?

_____

_____

_____

8. Wiesel poses very difficult questions that do not have easy answers and that are not formerly answered within his text. Reread the difficult questions he poses in paras. 4, 5, 16, 17, 21, and 22, choose one, and attempt to answer it.

_____

_____

_____

Writing about Peace and War

Now that you have read three different articles on the topic, you will develop your own ideas through writing and solving problems. Use a separate sheet of paper to develop your ideas completely.

Explanation (Ch. 8)—Revisit your measure of belief in the claim: *It is possible for the human race to eventually eliminate violence.*

Write a **journal entry** about how your individual beliefs evolved after reading a variety of perspectives.

1. Optional: Write either a **critical response** or a **critical analysis** using your choice of the articles on peace and war.

Problem Solving (Ch. 9)—What are some other options for reducing the amount of violence in the world? How do we establish more peace? Go through the four steps of the problem-solving process to come up with a solution to the problem you chose.

Topic: Self-Driving Cars

Self-driving cars may be on the horizon, but whether or not they are a good idea remains an open question. Recent accidents involving such vehicles may make you wonder if they're safe. Reading and researching about the topic of self-driving cars will allow you to develop and support an informed opinion on the subject. You'll read three pieces on the subject, respond to questions that prompt you to use the skills of critical thinkers (comprehension, interpretation, up through evaluation and problem solving), and ultimately write about the subject. Use additional paper when you need to.

Measure of Belief

How likely is it that a particular belief is true?

How true is the belief?

 1   2   3   4   5

Definitely NOT
true   ○   ○   ○   ○   ○   Definitely true

What do YOU think? Measure your current belief on the Likert scale.

Write a **journal entry** about your level of belief in the following claim: *Self-driving cars are a good idea.*

_____

_____

_____

_____

_____

_____

_____

Read and annotate each of the following articles and answer the questions that follow.

Reading #1: "Who's Making Sure That Self-Driving Cars Are Safe?" by Ruth Reader

Reading #2: "Here's How Self-Driving Cars Could Catch On" by David Roberts

Reading #3: "To Get the Most out of Self-Driving Cars, Tap the Brakes on Their Rollout" by Jack Barkenbus

Reading #1: "Who's Making Sure That Self-Driving Cars Are Safe?"

Ruth Reader

Ruth Reader writes for Fast Company *magazine, an American business periodical that specializes in design and technology. Ms. Reader has written for various outlets and has also worked in radio and television. The following article was published in* Fast Company *Magazine.*

March 27, 2018

1   The self-driving future may be closer than you think. There are already plenty of **autonomous** cars cruising the streets in California, Michigan, Florida, Arizona, Nevada, and Massachusetts. And those fleets are poised to grow exponentially, with Waymo, Uber, General Motors, and others promising to have tens of thousands of them on the road by 2020. These phantom rides have been largely greeted with excited curiosity. But in the wake of a high-profile death in Arizona, new questions are being raised about their safety, and both techies and regulators are being pressured to come up with some answers.

On Sunday, March 21, a woman named Elaine Herzberg was wheeling a bicycle across a two-lane road known as Mill Avenue in Tempe, Arizona, when she was struck by one of Uber's self-driving cars. She was transported to the hospital, but ultimately died of her injuries. The tragic accident has many people asking what went wrong and who's responsible.

2   "Who will be charged in her death, this is why I'm against these," remarked a Twitter user named Cha's Dad shortly after the incident made headlines. He was one of many outraged people demanding that someone take responsibility for her death. Much is still unknown about the accident and Uber is currently cooperating with police as they continue to investigate. But there are lots of little points of confusion. For instance, it was late at night when the accident happened, but the lack of light should not have stopped the car's sensors from detecting Herzberg. Velodyne, the company that makes the Lidar sensor used in Uber's cars, rushed to tell Bloomberg that its technology was not responsible for stopping the vehicle. Another company, Aptiv, which supplies advanced assisted driving systems for Volvo, also **deflected** responsibility, saying its technology had been disabled at the time of the accident.

3 The law is murky when it comes to who is ultimately responsible in the event of a self-driving accident. In general, there aren't a lot of rules governing how cars that drive themselves should be rolled out onto public streets and what happens when they fail. Furthermore, regulators have not forced companies to provide insight into how their vehicles think and make decisions.

4 Instead, they've taken an extremely light touch when it comes to creating rules for self-driving startups. Last fall, the National Highway Traffic Safety Administration issued "a vision for safety." The 36-page report is a **paean** to open markets, encouraging state governments to "support industry innovation" by becoming more "nimble" in order to keep up with the speed of technological change. The voluntary guidance stays pretty nonspecific and tells states not to get in the way.

5 As a result, states are largely left to come up with their own sets of rules for self-driving cars and how they should be validated and introduced to public roads. That can be problematic, because it creates a gulf in standards between states. California, for example, requires companies and individuals operating autonomous vehicles on its streets to obtain a permit and report certain data like collisions and disengagements. By comparison, Arizona is among the most permissive states when it comes to self-driving technology, though the state has now barred Uber from testing self-driving vehicles in the state.

6 In 2015, the state's governor, Doug Ducey, issued the state's first autonomous car rules. They called for an oversight committee for self-driving activity and required self-driving cars to be insured and have safety drivers with a drivers license; someone who could take the wheel if needed. In the weeks before Uber's accident in Tempe, Ducey updated those rules in an executive order. The state now asks companies with self-driving vehicles without a driver in the front seat to have a system in place wherein if the car fails, it can achieve a "minimal risk condition." Secondly, it **mandates** the state Department of Transportation to develop a protocol for how law enforcement should interact with a self-driving car in the event of an accident, one which the agency says is still in development. It's unclear how the state plans on validating these criteria are met.

7 In addition to the fact that the current administration is anti-regulation, the federal government has in part been lax about rule making because the protocol for building safe cars in general is well-established. Manufacturers are responsible for designing and testing their own vehicles against safety standards set out by government agencies and, of course, individual cars have to pass certain mechanical safety and emissions tests every year. Plus, the driver is a built-in fail-safe. This is true even in the case of a software glitch. "There are bugs in software of the most basic things in the car," says Nathan Aschbacher, CTO of Polysync, a self-driving car startup. "The way that is mitigated is, at the end of the day, you have a human behind the wheel."

8 Tesla has been able to roll out its autopilot feature, a sort of faux self-driving experience, and update it over time, because there's a human in the car who's able to take the wheel in case of emergency. Even the most recent iteration, which promises to keep the car in pace with traffic and lane change as necessary, comes with this disclaimer, "Autopilot should still be considered a driver's assistance feature with the driver responsible for remaining in control of the car at all times."

9 Fully self-driving cars will change that **paradigm**.

What Went Wrong in Tempe

10 There are inherent difficulties to making a human the back-up to a car that drives itself. Once people have had the experience of being a passive driver, they have a hard time stepping back into the role of driver. According to a study conducted last year, people also need time to adapt to different kinds of driving conditions and behavior.

11 In the case of Uber's accident in Tempe, there was a safety driver monitoring the car as it drove. It

© Associated Press

appears from a new video of the accident that the driver was looking down rather than at the road, though the footage is inconclusive. It does show that the victim, who was walking across the road, wasn't visible until the car was within striking distance. Investigators are still trying to determine what went wrong here, but the incident serves as an opportunity to examine more closely what sorts of tests self-driving cars should have to pass before being allowed onto public roadways.

12   Car companies working on self-driving are very focused on eradicating the driver, the longstanding safety mechanism. Waymo is currently testing cars with empty driver's seats in Arizona. California recently passed rules allowing self-driving car companies to test their cars to drive around like drones, with no safety driver upfront. General Motors has announced it will produce cars without steering wheels and brake pedals as early as 2019. Roughly 40,000 people in the U.S. die from automotive crashes every year, notes Aschbacher, "Once you **cede** control, what will you accept as safe enough?"

13   This is a big question among those tinkering on the future of mobility. Many advocates of self-driving technology say that these cars will reduce vehicle-related death. While it may reduce driver error, it may also introduce a whole new spectrum of problems–none of which is currently regulated.

Fears of a "Flash Crash" in the Autonomy Space

14   One of the existing examples of algorithms taking over for humans provides some insight into what happens when algorithms take over for humans. In the case of high-frequency trading algorithms, there is something called a "flash crash." You may remember the one that happened in 2010 when the stock market bottomed out before quickly rebounding. In these cases, money can go missing, but banks and bankers are responsible for balancing out inequity. "If there's a flash crash in this autonomy space," says Polysync CPO, David Sosnow, describing a software or hardware bug might cause all makes of a certain car model to behave erratically, "There is no reset button the following day–likely a lot of people have died or been seriously injured."

15   Some people in the industry are calling for software safety standards. "Every 1,000 lines of code in a car contains an average of 50 errors," says Zohar Fox, CEO and cofounder of Aurora Labs. "Standard QA testing misses about 15% of those errors, far too high a number given the growing importance of software reliability."

16   The International Organization for Standardization's guidelines for electrical systems in cars, a set of guidelines for electric systems in cars, is currently making way for self-driving technology. Historically, the standard has set rules for how automotive components should be tested individually and as integrated into a vehicle. As cars have become more computerized, the organization has embraced some software, though the most complicated code it's dealt with doesn't come near the intricacy of that of a self-driving car.

17   "The difficulty they are facing is in repairing system errors once they are on the road already and in detecting system errors before they result in malfunctions," says Fox. System errors aren't the only challenges self-driving cars will have to overcome to be safe. They'll also have to become proficient in understanding and responding to the kind of cues human drivers signal to each other while on the road.

18   At their most competent they'll have to be able to interact safely with humans in the car and humans outside of the car. It's the latter that presents a bigger challenge. "The autonomous vehicle or the self-driving vehicle could be safe, but what if somebody else does something?" asks Srikanth Saripalli, an associate professor in mechanical engineering at Texas A&M University. How does the car respond if someone jaywalks? What about when a motorcycle weaves in and out of traffic lanes? What if the car enters a situation it's never encountered before?

19   There are some who believe that the answer to making self-driving cars more safe is in **vetting** them within simulated environments. This way, the car can test how it would react to errant pedestrians and dogs and kids on bicycles without having to worry about injuring anyone. Simulated environments will train cars to behave better, but perfecting these systems won't give regulators insight into how to govern them.

20   Saripalli believes that regulation should be minimal to encourage innovation, but he thinks that the cars should have to pass a series of mandated tests, tests that standards organizations and the government will ultimately have to agree on. But he also thinks, there should be more transparency in the process, much the way California already requires self-driving car companies to test on their streets and to share data on disengagements. He believes that as car companies are required to test their technology more vigorously, those results should be posted "somewhere that everybody can check," he says. It's through transparency he believes, that self-driving cars will ultimately be made safer–or at the very least something all people can better understand.

21 "Before autonomous cars are on the road, everyone should know how they'll respond in unexpected situations," writes Saripalli in a new article addressing how self-driving car safety should be quantified. He says self-driving car companies should undergo specific tests and that the data from those tests should be shared with federal regulation boards like NHTSA. As it stands, the federal government has largely relied on states to come up with their own rules regarding self-driving cars.

1. Having surveyed and then read the article, what is the state of regulations on self-driving cars at the time the article was written?

   _____

   _____

   _____

   _____

2. Define these words from the selection using context clues or a dictionary. For your convenience, words are in bold font in the article.

   a. Autonomous (para. 1) _____

   b. Deflected (para. 2) _____

   c. Paean (para. 4) _____

   d. Mandates (para. 6) _____

   e. Paradigm (para. 9) _____

   f. Cede (para. 12) _____

   g. Vetting (para. 19) _____

3. Paraphrase para. 12.

   _____

   _____

   _____

   _____

4. What assumptions about simulated environments underlie para. 19?

   _____

   _____

   _____

   _____

5. Examine your biases and worldview. Do you have a bias for/against the topic of self-driving cars? Why do you think you feel the way you feel? Write a brief explanation.

   _____

   _____

   _____

6. In your opinion, does the article make an argument for or against self-driving cars, or does it do some combination of both? Explain your answer.

_____

_____

_____

Reading #2: "Here's How Self-Driving Cars Could Catch On"

David Roberts

David Roberts, originally from Tennessee, is a prolific writer who has produced pieces for CNN, Reuters, The Atlantic, The Chicago Tribune, *and other outlets. The following text appeared in* Vox.

May 9, 2018

1 There's been a string of stories in the past year or so about fatalities involving self-driving cars. The latest, from March, was about a pedestrian run down in Arizona by a self-driving Uber vehicle, which apparently saw her but deemed her a "false positive" (shudder).

2 Of course, as fans of the technology will rush to tell you, none of the vehicles involved were actually "self-driving"—they are vehicles with driver-assist features, which can take over for human drivers in limited circumstances. (Level 2 autonomy, in the jargon.)

3 The public, however, is unlikely to track such distinctions. The casual news consumer can be forgiven the impression that self-driving vehicles are being **deployed**, and killing people, at random—that we're just winging it, using public streets as live experiments.

4 Predictably enough, there's been blowback, leading Arizona to suspend its testing program (as has Toyota). It seems that simply tossing autonomous vehicles into the wild is not going to work.

A Program in Texas Aims for a Gentler Debut for AVs

5 Happily, a self-driving vehicle experiment planned for Texas shows a better and more realistic path to public acceptance.

6 A Silicon Valley startup called Drive.ai announced yesterday that it will launch a ride-hailing service using autonomous vehicles in Frisco, Texas, in July. It's not the first company to offer such a service — there's one in Phoenix, Arizona—but it's the first one in Texas.

7 If you want a deep dive into the details, Cade Metz at the New York Times has one. I'll just focus on one aspect: the pains the program has taken to introduce autonomous vehicles in a safe and nonthreatening way, aimed at winning public support and growing incrementally.

8 If shared autonomous vehicles are going to catch on—if they're going to ease congestion and eliminate parking like their enthusiastic fans promise—it's not going to be through uncontrolled experiments on public roads. It's going to look something like what Drive.ai is doing.

The Key Challenge for AVs Is Incremental Introduction

9 As I've written before, autonomous vehicles have always faced a chicken-and-egg problem. If cities and infrastructure could be designed *around* autonomous vehicles (AVs), containing only AVs, the difficulties facing AVs would be negligible. All vehicles would be smart and would respond in standard, predictable ways to one another and to pedestrians.

10 But new cities are the exception. In most places, AVs will have to enter a market dominated by old infrastructure and human drivers. Those are enormous challenges, given their unpredictability and enormously variable features. (Pesky humans. . .)

11 The last 10 percent of AVs will be easy; it's the first 10 percent that's the problem.

12 The answer will be incrementalism in all aspects: in autonomy, range, scope, and usage. That's the direction the Drive.ai pilot points; everything about it is geared toward slow, incremental introduction, focused on the comfort and confidence of the human beings involved.

Drive.ai's Program Will Serve Limited, Fixed Routes, with Clearly Marked Vehicles

13 To begin with, Drive.ai vehicles will operate only on fixed routes in a limited part of Frisco (a northern suburb of Dallas with 175,000 residents), which boasts wide streets, speed limits of under 45 mph, and an average of 230 sunny days a year. They will connect a Dallas Cowboys facility with two nearby retail and **residential** centers and be open only to the roughly 10,000 employees or residents of those buildings (for free, at least for the first six-month trial). The vehicles will stop at set pickup points.

© Mopic/Shutterstock.com

14 The company is closely coordinating with the city and private partners to stay abreast of any construction or changes on the route.

15 Drive.ai's passenger vans, modified Nissan NV200s, will be bright orange and clearly marked "self-driving." (The **bristling** array of equipment on the roof, including multiple cameras, radar, and sensors that triangulate using pulses of light, is another clue.)

16 And here's a cool twist: The vans will be able to communicate with pedestrians via LED screens on the front and both sides, which will feature messages like, I assume, "Out of my way, flesh sack."

17 Initially, each van will have a human in the driver's seat, ready to take over if needed. If the complexity of a situation overwhelms the vehicle's ability to navigate it, it will ping the driver in. Over time, Drive.ai hopes to move to a "chaperone" in the passenger's seat (mainly there to help the people using the service) and eventually to full autonomy.

AVs Need to Learn and They Need to Keep Humans Happy

18 The Drive.ai project has two features I think are going to be crucial to the successful introduction of AVs.

19 The first is a focus on deep learning. The chair of Drive.ai's board is Andrew Ng, a legend in artificial intelligence and deep learning circles. He was a professor of computer science at Stanford, then directed the Stanford Artificial Intelligence Lab, then directed the Google Brain Deep Learning Project, then directed Baidu's AI research, and so on.

20 He's helping the Drive.ai team, which came out of the Stanford lab, focus on deep learning, which means every vehicle will learn from every interaction and all incoming data and share what it learns with the rest of the fleet. In that way, the vans are meant to become more and more confident, not only in these particular routes but in the vagaries of human interaction generally.

21 In terms of deep learning, starting with a fixed, limited set of routes is like establishing a clean experiment. Complications, in the form of pedestrians, road features, or more congested routes, can be introduced in a deliberate, controlled way, allowing the scope of the program and its learning to rise together, **incrementally**. It can master one set of challenges before taking on more.

22 The second important feature is the focus on human-machine interaction (HMI—yes, there's always an acronym). Drive.ai seems to be taking a broad view of HMI.

23 Narrowly, HMI involves interactions between vehicles and their passengers. More broadly, it involves the safe interaction of vehicles with pedestrians, cyclists, and other vehicles.

24 More broadly still, it involves the interaction of the ride-hailing system with the public and public institutions. That's the part Silicon Valley types are not always the best at: getting buy-in and support from local officials, businesses, and civic groups, not by promising "disruption" but by offering a service that is tangible, useful, and safe.

25 If AVs are like a scary new species, the modest service Drive.ai is offering will effectively put them in a zoo, a "geofenced" area, rather than releasing them into the wild. Here's how Ng puts it:

> Self-driving cars have different strengths and weaknesses than human drivers. They are always attentive, have <100 ms reaction times, and have no blind spots. On the flip side, they don't understand certain complex situations, such as a construction worker communicating using hand gestures. By choosing geofenced regions and working with partners, we can take advantage of self-driving cars' strengths while diminishing their weaknesses.

26 If these first 10,000 AV users are excited about their new ability to hop from home to work to shopping without lugging a car around; if they are charmed on their evening walk when the van stops, makes some cute ding-dong noise, and says, "Go ahead and cross, friend!" on its LED; if they give glowing quotes to the journalists who are certain to be swarming the area—well, then, confidence will build. The service could add new routes and stops; it could start operating at night as well; it could open up to the public at large.

27 What's likely, if the program succeeds, is that other cities will begin thinking about limited areas or routes of their own where AVs might prove useful—or even limited areas where all vehicles except AVs could be banned.

28 As that kind of thinking starts, it will be important for advocates of livable **urbanism** to engage, to make sure that AVs are used to enhance transit and multi-modal urban transportation systems, rather than seeking to replace them.

29 On that score, Drive.ai is saying all the right things. It will "aim to unlock access to areas underserved by traditional mass transit and improve connectivity to existing transit lines," Ng writes. "Thoughtful self-driving deployments can increase mass transit ridership and reduce individual car usage, thus driving down a city's transportation costs."

30 Silicon Valley cynics (and who has better earned their cynicism?) may see this as lip service. But one way or another, autonomy is going to creep into the transportation system, likely through limited, geofenced programs like Drive.ai's. Advocates for good urbanism would do well to engage with early experiments like this and try to guide them to uses that enhance urban livability rather than adding to urban congestion.

31 AVs won't transform the transportation system in one big sci-fi flash. They will do so incrementally, step by step. It's up to the rest of us to ensure that those steps move in the right direction.

1. How does the word "incrementally" relate to the title of the article? Explain your response.

   _____

   _____

   _____

2. Define these words from the selection using context clues or a dictionary. For your convenience, words are in bold font in the article.

   a. Deployed (para. 3) _____

   b. Residential (para. 13) _____

   c. Bristling (para. 15) _____

   d. Incrementally (para. 21) _____

3. What example of unclear language is the word "chaperone" in para. 17? What word or phrase could the author have used to make the point more clearly?

   _____

   _____

   _____

4. Identify the audience of the article. How did you figure it out?

   _____

   _____

   _____

5. In para. 30, the author says, "Silicon Valley cynics (and who has better earned their cynicism?). . . ." What do you infer the author feels about Silicon Valley, and how do you know?

   _____

   _____

   _____

6. The author outlines an argument for how self-driving cars could be successfully introduced. What evidence does the author give in support of his argument? In your opinion, is it an effective argument? Why or why not?

   _____

   _____

   _____

Reading #3: "To Get the Most out of Self-Driving Cars, Tap the Brakes on Their Rollout"

Jack Barkenbus

Jack Barkenbus conducts research for Vanderbilt University in the capacity of Visiting Scholar. He was formerly the director of the University of Tennessee's Energy, Environment and Resources Center. The following piece was published in The Conversation.

February 8, 2018

1 Every day about 100 people die in car crashes on U.S. roads. That death toll is a major reason why both Congress and the Trump administration are backing automotive efforts to develop and deploy self-driving cars as quickly as possible.

2 However, officials' eagerness far exceeds the degree to which the public views this as a serious concern, and overestimates the public's willingness to see its driving patterns radically altered. As those of us involved in studies of technology and society have come to understand, **foisting** a technical fix on a skeptical public can lead to a backlash that sets back the cause indefinitely. The backlash over nuclear power and genetically modified organisms are **exemplary** of the problems that arise from rushing technology in the face of public fears. Public safety on the roads is too important to chance consumer backlash.

3 I recommend industry, government and consumers take a more measured and incremental approach to full autonomy. Initially emphasizing technologies that can assist human drivers—rather than the abilities of cars to drive themselves—will somewhat delay the day all those lives are saved on U.S. roads. But it will start saving some lives right away, and is more likely to avoid mass rejection of the new technology.

Not so Fast

4 Most Americans are indifferent to what officials and safety **advocates** see as a serious problem. They react in horror to the deaths of even a few dozen passengers in a relatively infrequent airline crash but think little about the 100 lives lost daily from driving. The rewards from driving, such as personal freedom and convenience, overwhelm fears. In fact, most people believe their driving skills are better than average, making them more likely to think they'll avoid the tragedies that befall others.

© mato181/Shutterstock.com

From *The Conservation, January 3, 2018* by Jack Barkenbus. Copyright © 2018 by Jack Barkenbus. Reprinted by permission.

5 As a result, the push for autonomous driving on the basis of improved safety is a solution to a situation the public doesn't consider a serious problem. We know from the studies of psychologist Paul Slovic that the public is very uncomfortable with novel technologies that cede human control to machines. This is particularly true, in a phenomenon called "betrayal **aversion**," when the benefits of technologies are overpromised and reality doesn't appear to be consistent with those expectations. Unless self-driving cars can dramatically reduce fatalities, the public may remain skeptical.

Serious Safety Concerns

6 Surveys show the American public is far from sold on the safety benefits of autonomous vehicles. A recent survey by the Pew Research Center revealed that more than half of the American public would be worried about riding in an autonomous vehicle due to concerns over safety and the lack of control.

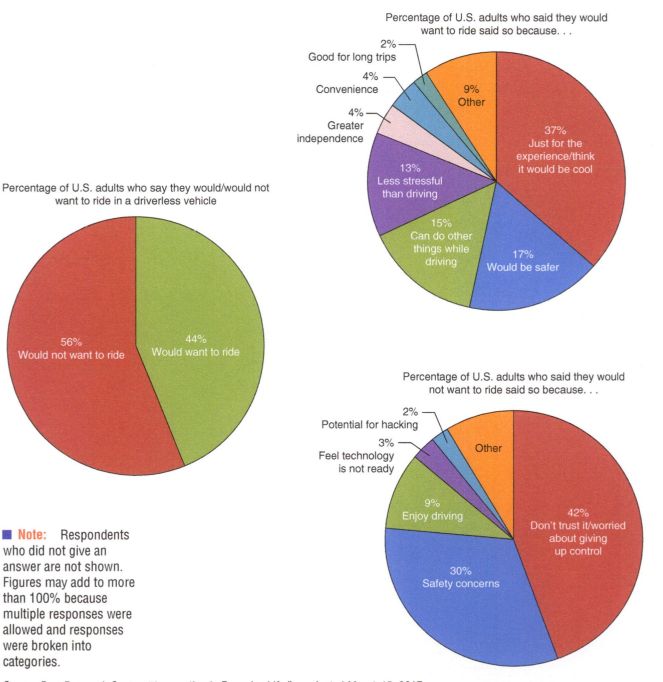

Percentage of U.S. adults who said they would want to ride said so because. . .

- 2% Good for long trips
- 4% Convenience
- 4% Greater independence
- 9% Other
- 37% Just for the experience/think it would be cool
- 13% Less stressful than driving
- 15% Can do other things while driving
- 17% Would be safer

Percentage of U.S. adults who say they would/would not want to ride in a driverless vehicle

- 56% Would not want to ride
- 44% Would want to ride

Note: Respondents who did not give an answer are not shown. Figures may add to more than 100% because multiple responses were allowed and responses were broken into categories.

Percentage of U.S. adults who said they would not want to ride said so because. . .

- 2% Potential for hacking
- 3% Feel technology is not ready
- Other
- 9% Enjoy driving
- 42% Don't trust it/worried about giving up control
- 30% Safety concerns

Source: Pew Research Center, "Automation in Everyday Life," conducted May 1-15, 2017

7 Another survey found that only 15 percent of people would prefer autonomous vehicles to traditional human-driven cars. It's true that some groups (men, people with more education and people under 45) are less worried than others, but these differences of opinion are less significant than the overall public view. Aside from simply the fear of being in these vehicles without the option of control, much of the American public still **relishes** the joy of the driving experience.

8 Public fears may ease as people become familiar with self-driving cars, but this experience needs to be gained gradually over time. The mental chasm between having complete control over the vehicle to the complete absence of control is huge. Consumer advocates are already warning public officials that federal laws and rules designed to hasten the movement to autonomy are too permissive, and risk triggering a public backlash.

9 A steady stream of crashes, both serious and minor, would simply reinforce public fears that self-driving cars are not safe. The media, sensitive to these fears, will be eager to cry betrayal when there is a contradiction between these accidents and the technology's rationale. And politicians, wanting to be seen as protectors of public health, may promote a new "Make America Drive Again" movement.

10 To avoid public backlash or overreaction, industry and government should not rush, but rather move more deliberately toward deploying fully autonomous cars on U.S. roads. There is still much the industry can do in terms of cutting-edge technology to assist drivers. Innovations such as adaptive cruise control and automatic emergency braking already have considerable public support and will work to **acclimate** the public to more advanced stages of driver autonomy.

11 Government and industry are right to continue inventing and innovating technologies that can contribute to autonomous vehicles. But rather than racing to get self-driving cars on U.S. roads, they should slow the rollout down to a pace the public can adjust to. That way, the safety benefits can be both real and long-lasting.

1. What is the "just right" topic of the article?
   _____

2. Define these words from the selection using context clues or a dictionary. For your convenience, words are in bold font in the article.
   a. Foisting (para. 2) _____
   b. Exemplary (para. 2) _____
   c. Advocates (para. 4) _____
   d. Relishes (para. 7) _____
   e. Acclimate (para. 10) _____

3. Identify two major details from the article.
   _____
   _____

4. Draw inferences about the audience, purpose, and tone of this article.
   a. Audience: _____
   b. Purpose: _____
   c. Tone: _____

5. What is the author's general view on new technology? Is it a good or bad thing? How do you know?
   _____
   _____
   _____
   _____

6. Identify the argument the author makes. What is the claim? What is the evidence, and what kind of logic does it use?

_____

_____

_____

7. Evaluate the author's argument. Is the evidence sufficient? If it is deductive, is it valid and sound? If it is inductive, is it cogent?

_____

_____

_____

Writing about Self-Driving Cars

Now that you have read three different articles on the topic, you will develop your own ideas through writing and solving problems. Use a separate sheet of paper to develop your ideas completely.

Explanation (Ch. 8)—Revisit your measure of belief in the claim: *Self-driving cars are a good idea.*

1. Write a **journal entry** about how your individual beliefs evolved after reading a variety of perspectives.
2. Optional: Write either a **critical response** or a **critical analysis** using your choice of the articles on self-driving cars.

Problem Solving (Ch. 9)—If you believe that self-driving cars should be implemented, what is the most effective way to get society to be more accepting of them? Or if you believe they are a bad idea, how do we prove this to prevent their implementation? Go through the four steps of the problem-solving process to come up with a solution to the problem you chose.

Topic: Women's Issues

Historically, women have faced many problems and issues, and they still do. The issues are complicated and multifaceted, ranging from suffrage, to domestic violence, to economic justice. In this section, you will read three articles that bring some of these issues to the fore, both in a historical and modern context. The questions that follow each article will encourage you to use the character traits (like curiosity, humility, open-mindedness, and so forth) as well as the skills of critical thinkers (like comprehension, interpretation, and inference), and ultimately you'll write about women's issues. Use additional paper when you need to.

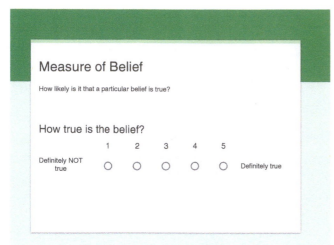

Measure of Belief

How likely is it that a particular belief is true?

How true is the belief?

	1	2	3	4	5	
Definitely NOT true	○	○	○	○	○	Definitely true

What do YOU think? Measure your current belief on the Likert scale.

Write a **journal entry** about your level of belief in the following claim: *Women and men deserve equal rights.*

_____

_____

_____

_____

_____

_____

_____

Read and annotate each of the following articles and answer the questions that follow.

Reading #1: "Julia Pastrana: A Monster to the Whole World" by Bess Lovejoy

Reading #2: "A Shortage of Women" by Terry L. Jones

Reading #3: "Why We Still Need Feminism" by Casey Cavanagh

Reading #1: "Julia Pastrana: A Monster to the Whole World"

Bess Lovejoy

Bess Lovejoy is an author who often writes about history. Her work has appeared in The Wall Street Journal, The New York Times, The Smithsonian, Time, *and* The Boston Globe, *among others. She is the author of* Rest in Pieces: The Curious Fates of Famous Corpses. *The following article appeared in* The Public Domain Review.

2015

World History Archive/Newscom

1   When Julia Pastrana was born, in the mountains of Western Mexico in 1834, her mother worried that her looks were the result of supernatural interference. The local native tribes often blamed the *naualli*, a breed of shape-shifting werewolves, for stillbirths and deformities, and after seeing her daughter for the first time, Julia's mother is said to have whispered their name. She fled her tribe—or was cast out—not long after.

2   Two years later, Mexican herders searching for a missing cow found Julia and her mother hiding in a mountain cave. They took them to the nearest city, where Julia was placed in an orphanage. Sweet, intelligent, and almost totally covered in black hair, she became a local celebrity. After hearing of her unusual looks and charming **disposition**, the state governor adopted Julia to serve as a live-in amusement and maid. She stayed with the governor until she was twenty, when she decided to return to her own tribe. But she never completed the trip home: an American showman known as M. Rates met her somewhere on her journey back to the mountains, and persuaded her to take up a life onstage.

3   Julia would go on to become one of the most famous human curiosities of the nineteenth century, variously known as "the Ape Woman," "the Bear Woman," or "the Baboon Lady." She made her debut in December 1854, at the Gothic Hall on Broadway in New York City. She wore a red dress, sang Spanish folk tunes, and danced the Highland Fling. Huge, appreciative crowds flocked to see her, although it wasn't really the singing and dancing they were after: they came to gawk at her hairy face and body, her jaw that jutted forward, her unusually large lips, and her wide, flat nose. In his book *A Cabinet of Medical Curiosities*, Jan Bondeson records a **contemporary** newspaper account:

> The eyes of this *lusus natura* beam with intelligence, while its jaws, jagged fangs and ears are terrifically hideous . . . nearly its whole frame is coated with long glossy hair. Its voice is harmonious, for this semi-human being is perfectly docile, and speaks the Spanish language.

4   It's worth noting that the idea that Julia was half-human didn't originate with the press. Physician Alexander B. Mott, son of renowned New York surgeon Valentine Mott, examined her during a private back-room viewing and declared her a hybrid, half-human and half-orangutan. Other doctors agreed. At the time, orangutans were the biggest and most fearsome primate most Americans knew, a symbol of wild, primitive nature and dangerous sexuality. The rampaging orangutan of Poe's 1841 story *The Murders in the Rue Morgue*, who slits a beautiful woman's throat with a straight razor, helped cement the associations of these creatures with horror, fascination, and sex. But the link wasn't new: two hundred years earlier, Dutch doctor Jacob Bontius wrote that orangutans were "born from the lust of Indian women, who mix with apes and monkeys with detestable sensuality."

5   And while Julia's promotional material emphasized her femininity, in keeping with other representations of nineteenth century bearded women, it also underlined her animalistic, racialized otherness. Her promotional material referred to her tribe of "Root-Digger Indians" as "spiteful and hard to govern," living in animal caves and enjoying intimate relations with bears and apes. The implications were clear: Julia was both a symbol of our **repressed** animal natures and the literal product of sex with beasts.

6   In England, where Julia ventured with a new **impresario** after successful tours of the eastern US and Canada, this otherness continued to be a useful promotional strategy. A poster advertising Julia's show at London's Regent Gallery, where she appeared three times a day in 1857, portrayed her with exaggerated, reddened lips and a large nose, much like contemporary racialized images of African-Americans. (This despite the fact that at least one doctor declared she had "no trace of Negro blood.") The twelve-page promotional booklet that Theodore Lent, Julia's new showman, prepared advertised her as "the Baboon Lady," and again described her parents' close contact with wild animals. But it also assured audiences that in Julia "the nature of woman predominates over the ourang-outang's," and described her as sociable, clever, and kind.

7   While Julia's promotional package included certificates from scientists **attesting** to her hybrid nature, from the start there were those who knew she was entirely human. Anatomist Samuel Kneeland Jr, former curator of comparative anatomy for the Boston Natural Historical Society, examined Julia and declared her all human, and "a perfect woman, performing all the functions of her sex." In 1857, the zoologist Francis Buckland visited her and stated, I believe that her true history was that she was simply a deformed Mexican Indian woman."

8   The most famous English scientist of the day, Charles Darwin, did not go to see her in London, but learned of her existence and of a cast taken of her teeth, which was supposed to show an irregular double set in both upper and lower jaws. In his *Variation of Animals and Plants Under Domestication*, Darwin compared Julia to hairless dogs, theorizing that skin disease in the animal world could be connected to excess teeth. Julia, however, didn't have extra teeth, just thickened gums that made misleading impressions on the casts. Had anyone bothered to ask her about her mouth, she would have explained that she had the usual number of teeth. But almost all the doctors who examined her directed their questions to Lent, while Julia kept silent.

9   Silent but lucrative, which was how Lent liked it. Exhibiting Julia had made Lent a wealthy man, but by then rival showmen, possibly even including P.T. Barnum, began to take an interest in her. Lent decided to make the arrangement with his living, breathing, investment more permanent; he proposed to Julia.

10 We don't know exactly what Julia thought of Lent, although Bondeson believes she was in love and "touchingly devoted" to him. Certainly, Julia's entire world revolved around her showman: she was not allowed to go out during the day, in case being seen on the street would diminish her earning power, and only travelled to the circus at night wearing veils. She had very few friends, although she did develop a rapport with the Viennese

actress and singer Friederike Gossman, who later said that a "light fog of sadness" always hung over Julia. Nevertheless, Julia accepted Lent's proposal. She once told Gossman, "[my husband] loves me for myself."

11   Aside from Gossman, one of the few who took Julia seriously as a person was German circus owner Hermann Otto. He visited Julia in Vienna and had a long conversation with her, later recording his impressions in his book *Fahrend Volk (Travelling People)*. He wrote that Julia seemed:

> a monster to the whole world, an abnormality put on display for money, someone who had been taught a few artistic turns, like a trained animal. [But] for the few who knew her better, she was a warm, feeling, thoughtful, spiritually very gifted being with a sensitive heart and mind. . .and it affected her very deeply in her heart with sadness, having to stand *beside* people, instead of *with* them, and to be shown as a freak for money, not sharing any of the everyday joys in a home filled with love.

12   In the winter of 1859, the couple travelled to Moscow, where crowds flocked to their exhibition at the Circus Salomansky. That August, Julia discovered she was pregnant. The baby, which arrived in March 1860 after a difficult birth, was unusually large, covered in hair like his mother, and had the same pronounced lower facial features. Julia was said to have held him and cried.

13   The baby lived only thirty-five hours, and Julia, who had been lacerated with forceps during the birth, survived for just a few more days after that. The official cause of death was metro-peritonitis puerperalis (inflammation of the peritoneum about the uterus), but more romantic sources say she died of a broken heart.

14   By impregnating his wife, Lent's plan to secure his investment through marriage had backfired—or so it seemed. At the hospital where Julia gave birth, Lent met a Professor Sokolov of Moscow University. Sokolov was an expert on embalming, and had recently pioneered a technique that blended mummification with **taxidermy**, creating corpses that still looked rosy and alive. He and Lent struck a deal, in which Sokolov would buy the bodies of Julia and her son, preserve them, and put them on display at the university's Anatomical Institute.

15   Her body stayed at the Anatomical Institute's museum for only six months, before Lent, hearing how good she and her son looked, took advantage of an escape clause in his contract and returned to take them back. Evidently he realized that Julia could be a money-maker dead as well as alive.

16   Lent put the bodies on display in London in 1862, where they could be seen for a shilling—less than he charged when Julia could sing and dance, but at least now he could display her for longer periods of time. Again the scientists weighed in: Buckland visited and said "the face was marvelous, exactly like an exceedingly good portrait in wax," while *The Lancet* declared the embalming "completely successful." The bodies went on to tour, and when they visited Vienna, Hermann Otto described seeing his old acquaintance in a "red, silk-like harlot's dress with a frightening rictus across her face."

17   In 1921, Haakon Lund, manager of Norway's then-biggest carnival, purchased the bodies of Julia and her son from an American in Berlin. The bodies toured through Norway in the 1920s with the slogan "Humanity, know thyself."

18   By then, however, the culture around exhibiting human oddities had started to change. As the nineteenth century progressed, "freak" exhibitions fell more and more out of favor, and Lund took pains to present his exhibition under the guise of popular education. He hired medical students wearing white lab coats to serve as guides, and displayed posters that at least gave the pretense of providing medical and scientific background information.

19   The bodies went into storage in the 1950s. By the 1970s, when the bodies emerged for small tours, they were frequently greeted by outrage in the newspapers. In 1973 Sweden banned their presence, saying corpses could no longer be exhibited for profit. This marked the end of their touring days, and Lund stashed the mummies in the carnival's storehouse near Oslo. Three years later, teenagers broke in and ripped off Julia's arm, thinking she was a mannequin. The police later recovered the bodies, but Julia's infant was damaged beyond repair. He ended up in the trash.

20   Julia's body re-emerged in the public consciousness in 1990, when journalists at the Norwegian magazine *Kriminal Journalen* discovered her languishing in the basement of Oslo's Institute of Forensic Medicine. From then on, the fate of Julia's body became a fixture of Norwegian newspaper reports and government committees. Journalists, academics, and other officials spilled a great deal of ink debating the merits of burying her versus keeping her body above ground so that scientists might one day study her conditions. In the end, Norway's

Ministry of Church, Education and Research decided to keep the remains above ground, and they were moved to the Institute of Basic Medical Science at the University of Oslo in 1997.

21 In 2005, Laura Anderson Barbata, a Mexico City-born, New York-based visual artist then on a residency in Oslo, began petitioning the university for the **repatriation** of Julia's body.

22 While the initial replies from the university were disappointing, Barbata persisted, placing a death notice for Julia in an Oslo newspaper and arranging for a Catholic Mass to be said for her.

23 In February of 2013, Julia's body—encased in a white coffin covered in white roses—was finally buried in a cemetery in Sinaloa de Leyva, a town near her birthplace. Despite all she endured, Julia's story had something of a happy ending. It's a pity she wasn't alive to see it—and to know she was remembered as more than a monster.

1. What was Julia Pastrana's background and heritage?

_____

_____

_____

_____

2. Define these words from the selection using context clues or a dictionary. For your convenience, words are in bold font in the article.

   a. Disposition (para. 2) _____

   b. Contemporary (para. 3) _____

   c. Repressed (para. 5) _____

   d. Impresario (para. 6) _____

   e. Attesting (para. 7) _____

   f. Taxidermy (para. 14) _____

   g. Repatriation (para. 21) _____

3. Identify a major detail and two minor details in para. 6.

_____

_____

_____

_____

4. In para. 8, the author details how doctors who visited Julia Pastrana asked Lent questions about her instead of asking Julia herself. What are the implications for the status of women at this time?

_____

_____

_____

_____

5. In your opinion, was Lent wrong to marry Julia Pastrana? Why or why not?

_____

_____

_____

6. Julia Pastrana faced exploitation both for her appearance and for being a woman. How do you think she felt about this? Cite evidence in the text to support your response.

_____

_____

_____

7. Why do you feel Laura Anderson Barbata (paras. 21–23) went to such lengths to get Julia Pastrana's body returned to Mexico? Explain in detail.

_____

_____

_____

Reading #2: "A Shortage of Women"

Terry L. Jones

Dr. Terry L. Jones is a professor at the University of Louisiana at Monroe. He has published several books and articles about the Civil War and the outdoors in general, and he has received awards relating to those publications. The following article was published in Country Roads *magazine.*

August 16, 2017

1   In Louisiana's early days the French population was entirely male because the colony fell under the **jurisdiction** of the navy department, and conditions were considered too dangerous for women and children. When Louisiana was established in 1699 the population was just 82 men and boys, 13 of whom listed their occupation as buccaneer.

2   Most of the men were *coureurs de bois* ("runners of the woods") who engaged in the fur trade with Indians. In 1704, acting governor Sieur de Bienville became concerned that the *coureurs de bois* were losing their Christianity by spending so much time with the Indians and marrying Indian women. He also worried about their loyalty. If an Indian war erupted, on whose side would the *coureurs de bois* fight?

3   Bienville's solution was to bring good Christian women to Louisiana for the men to marry. Thus, in 1704 the ship *Pelican* arrived at the capital Fort St. Louis de la Mobile (in modern-day Alabama) with twenty-three women. Some were as young as fourteen, but French law allowed a girl to marry at age twelve.

4   The so-called Pelican Girls volunteered to come but were no doubt misled by officials who portrayed Louisiana as a Garden of Eden filled with eligible young bachelors. What they found were half-wild *coureurs de bois* and crude shacks with dirt floors and deer skins stretched over the windows. Even the French Marines who **garrisoned** the colony wore animal skins instead of uniforms.

5   The Pelican Girls found husbands, but Bienville's experiment failed. The women quickly became **disillusioned** because their new husbands continued to spend much of their time in the woods (often with their Indian wives) and refused to plant gardens. Food became so scarce that some girls survived by eating acorns.

6   To force their husbands to build better homes, the Pelican Girls launched the Petticoat Rebellion and denied their husbands "bed and board" until better homes were built. The **ploy** worked, but it also angered Bienville because he blamed the women for creating unnecessary problems. Bienville claimed the young women were pampered city girls who did not want to work and asked his superiors to only send hard working country girls in the future.

7   Unfortunately, the *Pelican* also brought Yellow Fever to Fort St. Louis and many of the Pelican Girls died within a short time. Thus, Louisiana continued to suffer from a shortage of settlers, and John Law's Company of the West took drastic steps to populate the colony in 1717—1721 after it became proprietor. In addition

to sending volunteers who wanted to come to Louisiana to start a new life, Law convinced the government to deport thousands of criminals as well.

8   During this four-year period, more than one-half of the women who arrived in Louisiana had been convicted of prostitution and branded on the face with the *fleur de lys*. Five of them became the first French women to reside in Natchitoches. As it turned out, the men there did not seem to care if the women were branded because four of them quickly married and the fifth had two proposals. Her suitors agreed to fight a duel to settle the matter, but the commandant stopped them. It is assumed that the woman was then allowed to choose the man she wanted.

9   The Natchitoches District, which included all of North Louisiana, continued to suffer a shortage of women for years to come. According to researcher Elizabeth Shown Mills, in 1740 approximately 50 percent of all native-born girls in the district were married before reaching age fourteen, usually to a soldier or trader in his mid-20s. When the Louisiana Purchase was made in 1803, more than 1 in 5 of the people living in northwest Louisiana were descended from female convict **deportees**.

10   Thanks to John Law's efforts, Louisiana's population soared to about 8,000. Among the arrivals were six Ursuline nuns who landed in New Orleans in 1727. The Ursulines were dedicated to education and opened the colony's first school for girls and later operated Louisiana's first charity hospital. They also took in orphans and helped care for unmarried women. Today, the Ursulines are still active in New Orleans, and several schools can trace their **origins** to the nuns. Saint Mary's Catholic Church is located on the site of the original Ursuline Convent.

11   In 1728, another ship arrived in New Orleans with 88 eligible young women. Each girl's belongings were stuffed in a small chest that resembled a casket so the girls became known as *les filles a la cassette*, or "the casket girls." The Ursuline nuns cared for and watched over the Casket Girls until they were married. Records indicate that all found husbands, even one who "looked more like a soldier on guard duty than like a young lady."

___

1. Why was there initially a shortage of women in Louisiana's early days?

   _____

   _____

   _____

2. Define these words from the selection using context clues or a dictionary. For your convenience, words are in bold font in the article.

   a. Jurisdiction (para. 1) _____

   b. Garrisoned (para. 4) _____

   c. Disillusioned (para. 5) _____

   d. Ploy (para. 6) _____

   e. Deportees (para. 9) _____

   f. Origins (para. 10) _____

3. Find the euphemism in para. 6. What is it a euphemism for?

   _____

   _____

   _____

4. What is the purpose of the article? How do you know?

   _____

   _____

   _____

5. Do you have any bias about gender issues? For example, do you feel men and women should have certain domestic roles? Why or why not? If you find you have preconceptions, where do you believe you got them? If you don't have any preconceptions, how did you avoid them?

6. The women who arrived in Louisiana were often disadvantaged because of their backgrounds. What disadvantages did they have? How did they use what little power they had to better their situation? Explain in detail.

7. Did the arrival of more women in Louisiana make the situation there better or worse? Explain your answer in detail, using evidence from the text to support your response.

Reading #3: "Why We Still Need Feminism"

Casey Cavanagh

Boston-born Casey Cavanagh holds a Bachelor's Degree in writing. She is the content manager at an online advertising agency and a freelance writer and editor. She has written numerous pieces for publications like Elite Daily *and the* Huffington Post, *where the following essay appeared in 2014.*

2014

1 Feminists are not angry lesbians who hate men. Feminists do not believe women are better than men, or that women deserve special privileges. They do not believe women are victims.

2 In order to be considered a feminist, you only need to be on board with one idea: All humans, male and female, should have equal political, economic and social rights.

Although more and more people are beginning to understand the true definition of feminism and openly identifying with it, there has always been a negative **stigma** attached to it. Part of this problem is the way our media **sensationalizes** things, trying to pass the most radical and extreme versions as the standard which, in this case, depicts a feminist as a man-hater who hates lipstick, crinkles her nose at stay-at-home moms, and unapologetically supports abortions on demand.

3 It's these false assumptions that cause anti-feminist campaigns, such as the recent "Women Against Feminism," which consists of people posting photos of themselves with statements such as: "I don't need feminism because I don't choose to ignore the fact that men have issues too" and "I don't need feminism because I already have equal rights." Reading through the majority of these posts quickly brings forth a glaringly obvious problem: how misguided too many people still are about what being a feminist actually means.

4 As Lena Dunham pointed out, "Feminism isn't a dirty word. It's not like we're a deranged group who think women should take over the planet, raise our young on our own and eliminate men from the picture."

5   Being a feminist has nothing to do with how you look, what you wear, who you date, or how often you have sex. Being a feminist doesn't mean you think women deserve special rights; it means you know we deserve equal ones.

6   While a primary purpose of feminism is to **empower** women, it does not mean feminists view all women as weak and oppressed. Feminists are not aiming to make women stronger; they already know they're strong. They just want society to see that too.

7   Empowering women does not mean belittling or punishing men. Men, too, suffer from gender role assumptions that place expectations upon them to live and act a certain way. Feminists believe each person should be viewed based on their individual strengths and capabilities as a human being, not the strengths and capabilities assumed of their gender. They believe every person should be treated equally—not because of gender, but in spite of it.

Why We Still Need Feminism

8   There are some people who believe that feminism is a thing of the past—that we don't need it anymore because the **patriarchal** system no longer exists. After all, we can vote, right? That's true. In fact, in all demographics, females vote more than men do. Yet, women still hold less than 20 percent of seats in Congress, even though they make up more than half the population. Some believe the patriarchal system doesn't exist because we have equal employment opportunities. But if this were really the case would there still be a 23 percent pay gap?

9   It is great so many women today feel like they have equal opportunities as men. If it wasn't for past feminist movements, who knows where we would be today. But we still need feminism, and will continue to need it, until every other woman in the world feels this way as well.

10   We still need feminism because when people get married it is assumed the woman will take the man's last name. Because when women are assaulted, they are often the ones who feel ashamed.

11   We still need feminism because we teach women how to prevent rape, instead of teaching people to not view women as objects. Because women are told that walking alone at night makes them "an easy target." Because, sometimes, a movie's rating (PG-13 versus R) depends on how much a female appears to be enjoying sex in a certain scene.

12   We still need feminism because our bodies are still being legislated, because McDonald's still asks us if we want a girl or boy toy, because we use terms like "bitch" and pussy" to imply weakness.

13   We need feminism because FGM (Female Genital Mutilation), the act of cutting off and restitching female genitals to prevent pleasurable sex—and it can happen to girls as young as 5 months old—is still practiced in 29 countries. Because more than 120 countries don't have laws against marital rape, and still allow child brides—some as young as 6 years old.

14   We need feminism because infanticides, the act of killing children within a year of birth, can be attributed to millions of fewer females than males in Middle Eastern countries, and because in Afghanistan women going to college can be considered justifiable grounds for disfiguring.

15   Being a feminist does not mean you think women can't speak for themselves, it means you realize that, even though some may be lucky enough to, there's still many who can't.

It is not a gender issue—it is a humanity issue.

16   It isn't about telling women what to do, it is giving them the ability and freedom to be able to choose to do whatever they want to do—whether that be a stay at home mom, electrical engineer, or business CEO. The purpose is to create a society of equal say, to provide people with the freedom of choice, rather than limited choices of assumption.

17   Feminists don't believe women should look or behave a certain way, it means they want women have to have the freedom to look and behave however they want—unapologetically. It is not about telling women what they need.

18   While reading through Women Against Feminism posts that say things such as, "I don't need it because I already feel equal" and "I don't want feminism because I don't need special treatment, and don't support

sleeping around," I can't help but think it isn't about our personal wants and needs, though they are all relevant, but rather what we—as a society—needs.

19 If you are a feminist, you believe women should be treated the same as men, not because we're better, but because we're human.

20 As Joseph Gordon-Levitt so **eloquently** worded it, "I'm a believer that if everyone has a fair chance to be what they want to be and do what they want to do, it's better for everyone. It benefits society as a whole."

21 The idea that there are still people, let alone women, proudly declaring they don't need feminism is alarming and frightening—at best.

22 We need feminism because people are still blindly agreeing that women don't need to be paid for the same work as men, that they are okay with the indifference and injustices so **ingrained** in society that they have accepted it as a way of life. That they are not only looking the other way to these issues, but they are also entirely and genuinely convinced they are doing the world a favor by hushing feminist attempts.

23 Some people don't feel the need to voice their thoughts on the matter at all, and that's okay. But there is a big difference between being indifferent and being ignorant. And that difference is speaking out about an issue when your opinion is based on misguided information and false assumptions.

24 Why do we need feminism? For the same reason screenwriter John Whedon gave when asked why he writes such strong female characters, "Because you're still asking me that question."

---

1. According to the article, what is the definition of feminism?

   _____

2. Define these words from the selection using context clues or a dictionary. For your convenience, words are in bold font in the article.

   a. Stigma (para. 2): _____

   b. Sensationalizes (para. 2): _____

   c. Empower (para. 6): _____

   d. Patriarchal (para. 8): _____

   e. Eloquently (para. 20): _____

   f. Ingrained (para. 22): _____

3. Annotate the essay.

4. Identify the main idea of the essay. If it is explicit, quote it below. If it is implied, write a sentence that states it.

   _____

   _____

5. Do you have any visceral reactions to this article? Before you read it, what was your view on feminism? How did you develop this view?

   _____

   _____

   _____

6. What is the author's argument for the necessity of feminism? Identify the claim, the evidence, and the logic of the article.

_____

_____

_____

7. In your opinion, does the author give a compelling argument? Why or why not? Explain in detail.

_____

_____

_____

Writing about Women's Issues

Now that you have read three different articles on the topic, you will develop your own ideas through writing and solving problems. Use a separate sheet of paper to develop your ideas completely.

Explanation (Ch. 8)—Revisit your measure of belief in the claim: _Women and men deserve equal rights._

Write a **journal entry** about how your individual beliefs evolved after reading a variety of perspectives.

1. Optional: Write either a **critical response** or a **critical analysis** using your choice of the articles on women's issues.

Problem Solving (Ch. 9)—Does the state of gender equality still require improvement? If not, why not? If so, how could it be improved? Go through the four steps of the problem-solving process to come up with an answer/solution to the problem you chose.

Appendix: Word Parts

Common Root Words		
Root	**Meaning(s)**	**Example(s)**
Auto	Self	Autocratic
Ben(e)	Good	Benefit
Biblio	Book	Bibliophile
Bio	Life	Biosphere
Chron(o)	Time	Chronological
Corp	Body	Corporeal
Cred	To believe	Credible
Dict	Say, tell	Dictate
Fact	Make or do	Factory
Graph	Writing	Graphic
Heter(o)	Different	Heterosexual
Homo	Same	Homogenous
Hydr(o)	Water	Hydroplane
Log	Speech, words, or the study of	Dialogue, Terminology, Psychology
Macro	Large	Macroeconomics
Micro	Small	Microscope
Multi	Many	Multitalented
Negat	Make nothing, none	Negative
Path	Feeling, suffering	Sympathy
Ped	Foot, child	Pedestrian, Pediatrician
Phil(o)	Love of	Philanthropist
Phobia	Hate, fear of	Agoraphobia
Phon(o or e)	Sound, voice	Phonics
Photo	Light	Photograph
Poly	Many, much	Polygon
Pseudo	False	Pseudoscience
Scop	Seeing	Periscope
Tel(e)	Far off	Telescope
Viv	Life	Viable

Common Prefixes		
Prefix	**Meaning(s)**	**Example(s)**
Ab, abs, a	Away from, down, not	Abnormal
Bi	Two, double	Biweekly
Cent	Hundred	Centennial
Circum	Around	Circumvent
Contra	Against, opposite to	Contradict
De	Opposite of, away from; down	Decline
Dec(a)	Ten	Decade
Dis	Not	Disable
Equi	Equal	Equator
Extra	Outside of	Extramarital
Hemi	Half	Hemisphere
Hyper-	Over, above	Hyperactive
Inter	Between	Intercoastal
Mal	Bad	Malpractice
Mis	Wrong, bad	Mistreat
Mono	Single, one	Monocle
Non	Not	Nonessential
Peri-	Around	Perimeter
Pre	Before	Preview
Re	Back, again, anew	Revert
Retro	Backwards	Retrograde
Semi	Half or partial	Semicircle, Semiconscious
Sub	Under	Subpar
Tri	Three	Triple
Uni	Single, one	Unicycle

Common Suffixes			
Part of Speech	Suffix	Meaning(s)	Example(s)
Adjective	able, ible	Able to _____	Edible
Adjective	ish, like	Like a _____	Boorish, Ladylike
Adjective	less	Without	Loveless
Adjective	ward	In the direction of _____	Wayward
Adjective	ous	Having, full of, characterized by _____	Harmonious
Adjective	ly	Having the qualities of _____	Princely
Adverb	ly	Perform in the manner of, showing manner or degree	Quickly
Noun	ability, ibility	Able to be or to do	Accessibility
Noun	cide	Killing, killer	Suicide
Noun	ation, tion, sion	The act of _____	Subtraction
Noun	ee	A person who is _____	Referee
Noun	er, or	One who does _____	Teacher, Doctor
Noun	ic	The art or science of _____ or actions or qualities of _____	Economics
Noun	onym	Name or word	Pseudonym
Verb	fy	To make or cause	Horrify

Source: *Building an Active College Vocabulary* by Licklider.

GLOSSARY

Accuracy: The condition of being true or correct

Ambiguity: Displaying two or more meanings where the intended meaning is unclear

Ambiguous language: A word, phrase, or sentence in which one can determine two or more specific meanings and it isn't clear which meaning is intended

Analogy: A comparison between two subjects

Analysis: The skill of taking something apart, looking at the pieces that make it up, and determining how they work, separately and together

Anger: The defense mechanism that involves getting angry in order to avoid confronting disconcerting information

Annotating: The act of marking up documents that you read, noting what's important

Antecedent: In a conditional statement, the actual condition that needs to be fulfilled

Antonym: A word that has the opposite meaning to another word

Apathy: Indifference, or a lack of interest

Appropriate conclusion: An inference that is logical and likely to be accurate based on prior knowledge and the information provided

Argument: A claim backed up by one or more reasons offered in its support

Argument mapping: A way to visually analyze an argument so that the relation between the evidence and conclusions is clear

Assumptions: Beliefs that an author takes for granted as being true

Attribution mistake: Unfairly attributing a person's behavior to the wrong cause

Audience: The group of people that the author (or speaker) has in mind to address

Avoidance: The defense mechanism that involves avoiding people or media that might provide disconcerting information

Bias: An unfair judgment; one-sidedness

Bloom's Revised Taxonomy: A system developed for teachers so that they can test to see if their students have mastered a concept and so that they can make sure they are teaching on a deep level

Brainstorming: A pre-writing strategy in which you think of and write down whatever comes to mind; also, a problem-solving strategy wherein you generate possible solutions

Cause and effect: A pattern of organization based on reasons and consequences

Character traits: Dispositions of critical thinkers (curiosity, humility, open-mindedness, flexibility, organization, skepticism, fair-mindedness, trust in reason, and persistence) that motivate them to use their skills to think critically

Chronological: A pattern of organization based on time

Claim: a statement that someone declares is true and that might be open to challenge or disagreement

Clarifying meaning: Making something more clear by resolving vagueness, ambiguity, euphemism, doublespeak, or other obstacles hindering communication

Classification: A pattern of organization based on organizing into categories

Cogent: A term describing an inductive argument with a conclusion that is highly probable

Cognitive dissonance: Anxiety that results from trying to hold two contradictory ideas at the same time or from trying to deny what you have already admitted to yourself is true

Common knowledge: Information that many people know just from living in the world or information that can be easily found in common reference books such as general encyclopedias

Communal reinforcement: The tendency of people to believe what they hear, often repeatedly, within their communities

Communication: The act of conveying information to others, typically through speech or writing

Comparison/contrast: A pattern of organization based on showing what is similar or different about a subject

Completeness: Whether something is finished and contains all necessary information

Comprehension: The skill of making basic sense of a message

Conclusion: 1. A claim of an argument that is supported by evidence. 2. Another word for *inference*; a reasonable judgment based on evidence

Conditional statement: A statement where the second part of the sentence is true if the first part is true

Confirmation bias: The human tendency to only pay attention to the evidence that supports what you already believe, while ignoring or downplaying information that might prove you wrong

Conformity: The human desire to fit in that causes people to believe mistaken things because others in their community believe those things

Connotation: The feelings or images associated with a word beyond its dictionary definition

Consequences: Another word for *implications*; the effects of assumptions and ideas

Consequent: In a conditional statement, the thing that happens if the condition is fulfilled

Context clues: Hints within the sentence a word appears in, or in surrounding sentences, that suggest its meaning

Counter-argument: An argument used to refute another argument

Counter-evidence: A particular type of evidence given in opposition to the claim of an argument

Critical analysis: A writing assignment that requires the reader to analyze and evaluate the text

Critical reading: Using the skills of a critical thinker on a text in order to determine if the text is credible, to decide if it makes a good argument or presents a good case, and to avoid being taken in by rhetorical tricks and emotional manipulation

Critical response: A writing assignment that focuses on the reader's feelings and reactions to the text

Critical thinking: A reflective, rational process used to make good decisions or to form beliefs that are more likely to be true

Critical writing: Writing to explain

Curiosity: Trait of critical thinkers that makes them intellectually hungry for knowledge and information

Deductive reasoning: A type of logic that involves drawing a specific conclusion from a generalization

Defense mechanisms: Protective strategies used to avoid thinking about ideas that cause us anxiety or challenge our beliefs.

Definition: A system of organization based on meanings of terms or ideas

Definition clue: A definition of a word placed close to an unfamiliar word that provides its meaning

Denial: The defense mechanism that involves denying that information or a problem exists at all

Denotation: The dictionary definition of a word

Details: Elements in a text that support, expound upon, or explain main ideas or other details

Dictionary: A print or online list of words and their meanings organized alphabetically

Doublespeak: A special form of euphemism that is used to disguise or distort meaning

Emotive words: Words that express opinion, judgment, or emotion

Empirical evidence: A type of evidence that can be directly observed, measured, or tested scientifically

Equivocation: A situation in which a speaker or writer uses different meanings for the same term in the middle of an argument

Ethnocentric: Having the attitude that one's own ethnicity is superior to others' ethnicities; judging the world based solely on the viewpoint of one's own ethnicity

Etymology: The origin and history of a word

Euphemism: A word that is used to replace another more offensive or disagreeable word

Evaluation: The skill of judging something on its merits in order to determine if it is effective or useful

Evidence: Support for the claim of an argument

Examples: Context clues that provide you with an idea of what a word means by giving you examples of things that could fall into the class to which the word refers

Example pattern: A pattern of organization based on cases or illustrations

Expert testimony: An expert's interpretation of facts that relate to his or her field of expertise

Explanation: The skill of putting your own or someone else's thoughts into words so that they are clear and understandable

Extraordinary claim: A dubious claim; a claim that involves the supernatural or that is overly far-reaching, too good to be true, or primarily intended to frighten

Fact: A direct or documented observation of the world; something that can be easily checked by independent observers

Fair-mindedness: Trait of critical thinkers that involves treating our own and other's viewpoints equally when evaluating them

Fairness: The quality of having impartiality and honesty

Fallacy: A mistake in the reasoning of an argument that is superficially convincing

Flexibility: Trait of critical thinkers that involves being willing to change one's mind

Formal outline: A structured outline that makes use of letters, numbers, and indentation according to a set style

Framing: The act of casting an issue in a certain light in order to influence the way you or someone else thinks about it

Freewriting: A prewriting strategy in which you write freely without worrying about mechanics or grammar in order to get your ideas on paper

Glossary: A concise list of key words and their definitions as they are used in the textbook or field of study, usually found in the back of the book

Graphic organizer: A visual that condenses and presents information

Guide words: Words at the top of each page of a print dictionary that indicate the range of words located on that page

Humility: Trait of critical thinkers that involves understanding that they don't know everything and could be wrong in any particular situation

Hypothesis: An educated guess arrived at for the sake of testing

Hypothetical example: A piece of evidence that is based not on hard facts but on imagined possibilities

Hypothetical Deductive Method: In problem-solving, a method that involves coming up with a hypothesis about the cause of the problem, making a prediction based on the hypothesis, and then figuring out whether the hypothesis is right or wrong by testing the prediction

Images: Mental pictures associated with a word

Implication: The consequence or possible effect of assumptions and ideas

Implied main idea: A main idea that an author never directly states; also known as an implicit main idea

Imply: To hint or suggest something

Inductive reasoning: A type of logic that involves drawing a general conclusion from specific pieces of evidence

Inference: The skill of drawing conclusions from available information

Informal outline: An outline that is casual in terms of style

Informed opinion: An opinion resulting from the research and experience of an expert in the field; also called reasoned judgment

Interpretation: The skill of noticing details, identifying relevant information, and clarifying ideas

Irony: A situation in which what seems to be the case and what is actually the case are sharply different; the use of words to convey the opposite of their literal meaning

Irrelevant: A term characterizing information or evidence that does not pertain to the claim of the argument or issue under discussion

Jargon: Technical language specific to a field

Journal: An informal collection, often in a notebook or blog, of a person's thoughts and reactions

Listing: A pattern of organization employed when a writer wants you to know that multiple points are important or that there is more than one factor to be considered in the issue under discussion.

Loaded language: When a writer uses word choice in an attempt to persuade the reader without evidence or argumentation

Logic: In an argument, the reasoning that links the evidence to the conclusion

Main idea: The most significant idea in a paragraph, article, or textbook chapter

Major detail: A specific ideas that supports, explains, and elaborates on a main idea and that is significant to the passage as a whole

Mapping: 1. Using geometric shapes and lines to indicate the organization of material. 2. A prewriting strategy in which you create a visual representation of what you want to say to help you identify your topic, major details, and minor details

Meaning: What is intended or referenced by language

Memory errors: Mistakes such as forgetting something, combining two or more memories into one, or actually creating false memories

Metacognition: Thinking about thinking; being aware of your mental processes throughout a mental task

Metaphor: Comparison that does not use the words *like* or *as*

Minor detail: A specific idea that supports, explains, and elaborates on a main idea or on a major detail but that is not overly significant to the passage as a whole

Mixed pattern: A pattern of organization using more than one other pattern of organization

Mnemonics: Techniques for improving the memory

Modus ponens: A valid form of a deductive argument in which the antecedent occurs so, therefore, the consequent occurs

Modus tollens: A valid form of a deductive argument in which the consequent has been shown not to occur so, therefore, the antecedent must not have occurred

Monitoring: The practice of checking your thinking throughout any mental task (see *self-monitoring*)

Natural selection: In the theory of evolution, the idea that traits acquired through genetic mutation that make it more likely for an organism to survive and produce offspring become widespread throughout a population of animals

Obstacles: Things that hinder one's ability to think critically

Open-mindedness: Trait of critical thinkers that involves being willing to consider new ideas

Opinion: A judgment about something

Optimizing: In problem-solving, trying to find the best possible solution (compare to *satisficing*, p. 395)

Oral communication: Explaining your ideas through speech

Organization: Trait of critical thinkers that involves approaching problems and life according to a system

Outline: A method of organization used to indicate the different levels of importance and relationships between ideas on a given topic

Paraphrasing: Recounting an author's words; using different phrasing than the original passage

Pattern of organization: The method the author uses to present the evidence and to arrange it logically so as to support his or her claim most effectively

Persistence: Trait of critical thinkers that involves not giving up when things get difficult

Personal opinion: A statement that other people might disagree with and to which others may apply their own personal interpretations and come to different conclusions about based on the same information; often involves matters of taste

Plagiarism: A breach of academic honesty in which you take credit for words or ideas that are not your own

Predicting: An active mental process that requires you to speculate and hypothesize about what might happen next in a reading

Prefix: A word part placed at the beginning of a root word to make a new word with a different meaning

Premise: In an argument, a proposition offered as support for a claim

Previewing: Another word for surveying; the act of looking over a reading selection to get an overview of it

Prewriting strategies: Strategies for generating ideas for writing and for organizing those ideas

Prior knowledge: The information you already know through learning and experience

Problem: A challenge that needs to be overcome but which requires a series of steps to overcome it

Problem-solving: The skill of overcoming challenges by using all the other skills of critical thinking and applying them according to a system

Process Pattern: A sub-pattern of organization used to show how to complete a task, or how a task was completed, and when the order of the steps matters

Proof: Evidence for a claim

Pseudoscience: A theory or system that claims to be scientific but is not

Purpose: The aim or goal an author (or speaker) wants to accomplish or achieve; general purposes include to inform, to persuade, or to entertain

Questioning: A pre-writing strategy in which you pose questions about a topic and look for answers to them as you read

Rationalizing: The act of coming up with seemingly credible reasons to believe a conclusion when those reasons are actually false

Reasoned judgment: An opinion resulting from the research and experience of an expert in the field; also called *informed opinion*

Reasoning: The process of using rational thought, evidence, and logic to come to a justifiable conclusion

Relevance: How closely related specific information is to the issue at hand

Rhetorical question: Question with an obvious answer or that is simply used for effect

Root word: The most basic form of a word

Satisficing: In problem-solving, choosing a response that satisfies the requirements and suffices to solve the problem but doesn't solve it in the best possible way (compare to *optimizing*, p. 395)

Science: A system by which we discover truths and laws about the material world; uses the scientific method

Scientific fact: The results of experimental testing

Scientific method: A method of analysis used in science; has six steps, namely observation, questioning, proposal of hypothesis, prediction, experimental testing, and revision or acceptance of hypothesis

Scientific theory: A wide-ranging explanation of scientific observations and/or scientific facts

Self-monitoring: The skill of keeping tabs on your thinking to see if it is effective

Significance: How important something is to a discussion, a text, an issue, or an argument.

Simile: Comparison using the words *like* or *as*

Skepticism: Trait of critical thinkers that involves doubting a claim until evidence for it is provided

Skills of critical thinkers: Things that critical thinkers can do while thinking critically (namely comprehend, interpret, infer, analyze, evaluate, monitor, explain, and solve problems)

Social constructions: Ideas that we develop because of the influence of our society and culture

Sound: A term describing a valid deductive argument that has true premises

Standards of critical thinking: Values that critical thinkers care about (namely, accuracy, completeness, fairness, relevance, clarity, and significance). The component of intellectual integrity involved in being a critical thinker

Stated main idea: A main idea that an author says directly in the text; also known as an explicit main idea (compare to *implied main idea*, p. 394)

Statistics: Numbers calculated from sets of data.

Status quo bias: A preference for the existing state of affairs (the way things are)

Strong critical thinker: A thinker who thinks critically about his or her own cherished beliefs as well as about other's beliefs (compare to *weak critical thinker*, p. 397)

Subject: Another word for *topic*; what the reading is about

Sub-problems: Lesser problems that together make up a larger problem

Subtopics: Smaller topics within a larger, general topic

Sufficiency: Having enough evidence to support a particular conclusion

Suffixes: Word parts added to the end of a root word to create a new word by changing its part of speech or tense

Summarizing: Giving a comprehensive but succinct overview of a reading

Summary: A concise overview of the main points of a selection, chapter, article, or essay

Surveying: A strategy that involves looking over a reading selection prior to reading it in order to get an overview of it; also known as *previewing*

Syllogism: The classic form of a deductive argument; it has two premises and a conclusion; the first premise is the generalization, and the second premise is a specific fact or observation to which the generalization is to be applied

Synonym: A word that has a meaning identical to or close to that of another word

Testimonial: A personal story about events that happened to someone

Textual features: Items used by authors (such as introductions or historical notes) that aid readers in understanding the material

Thesis: The main idea of a longer piece of writing

Tone: The attitude or feeling conveyed in a piece of writing

Topic: The subject of a passage or longer piece of writing

Topic sentence: The main idea of a paragraph

Transition: A word that suggests the level of importance of what is being discussed or indicates an author's shift in direction or focus

Trust in reason: Trait of critical thinkers that involves believing that reason can improve lives and advance the human race

Truth value: In an argument, a term describing the ability of a proposition to be judged true or false

Vague language: Language that does not have a precise meaning

Vagueness: The quality of having no clear, precise meaning

Valid: A term describing a deductive argument wherein the truth of the premises guarantees the truth of the conclusion

Visual clues: Text features that aid in comprehension (such as headings in bold or larger font and visual aids such as charts or tables)

Voice: The individual writing style of an author

Warrant: A reason to believe that an assumption is true

Weak critical thinker: A thinker who does not think critically about his or her own cherished beliefs and who is primarily concerned with proving him or herself correct (compare to *strong critical thinker*, p. 396)

Webbing: One method of mapping that involves putting the topic in the center of the page in a circle and then branching off with smaller circles in order to devise an organizational scheme

Wicked problem: A real-world problem that is incredibly convoluted or that may not have a good solution at all

Wishful thinking: The mistaken belief that wanting something to be true makes that thing more likely to actually be true

Word parts: Smaller components that make up a word; prefixes, roots, and suffixes

Working vocabulary: The words a person understands and is comfortable utilizing on a daily basis

Worldview: The framework we use to understand the world and our relationship to the world

Writing situation: The relationship between the circumstances that led an author to write, who the author is, what the author wants the text to do, and whom the author is writing for

BIBLIOGRAPHY

Chapter 1

Carroll, R. T. (2005). *Becoming a critical thinker: A guide for the new millennium.* Boston: Pearson Custom Publishing.

Carroll, R. T. (2009). *Skeptic's dictionary.* Retrieved from www.skepdic.com

Darwin, C. (1900). *The origin of species by means of natural selection.* New York: D. Appleton and Company.

Ennis, Robert H. (1996). *Critical thinking.* Upper Saddle River, NJ: Prentice Hall.

Ennis, R. H. (2000, October 18). *An outline of goals for a critical thinking curriculum and its assessment.* Retrieved from www.criticalthinking.net/goals.html

Facione, N.C., & Facione, P.A., (1996). Externalizing the critical thinking in clinical judgment. *Nursing Outlook, 44,* 129–136.

Facione, P. A. (2007). *Critical thinking: What it is and why it counts.* Retrieved from www.insightassessment.com

Facione, P. A., Sánchez, (Giancarlo) C. A., Facione, N. C., & Gainen, J. (1995). The disposition toward critical thinking. *Journal of General Education. 44*(1), 1–25.

Fundamental attribution error. (2009). Retrieved from http://viswiki.com/en/Fundamental_attribution_error

Haskins, G. R. (2006, Aug. 15). *A practical guide to critical thinking.* Retrieved from www.skepdic.com

Quammen, D. (2006*). The reluctant Mr. Darwin: An intimate portrait of Charles Darwin and the making of his theory of evolution.* New York: W. W. Norton & Company.

Paul, R. W. (1995). *Critical thinking: How to prepare students for a rapidly changing world.* Santa Rosa, CA: Foundation for Critical Thinking.

Schacter, D. L. (2001). *The seven sins of memory: How the mind forgets and remembers.* New York: Houghton Mifflin.

Tavris, C., & Aronson, E. (2007). *Mistakes were made but not by me: Why we justify foolish beliefs, bad decisions, and hurtful acts.* Orlando, FL: Harcourt.

Wright, R. (1994). *The moral animal: Why we are the way we are: The new science of evolutionary psychology.* New York: Vintage Books.

Chapter 2

Language can hinder proper Rx dosage. (2003, April 28). *Drug Store News.* Retrieved from www.cedrugstorenews.com/userapp/

Ferner, R. E., & Aronson, J. K. (2006, August). Clarification of terminology in medication errors: Definitions and classification. *Drug Safety, 29*(11). Retrieved from http://adisonline.com/drugsafety

Franklin, D. (2005, October 25). The consumer: And now, a warning about labels. *New York Times.* Retrieved from www.nytimes.com

Miller, W. (1997). *Richard Wright and the library card.* New York: Lee & Low Books.

Paul, M. (2007, January 25). *Many patients misinterpret directions on medicine bottle labels.* Retrieved from www.northwestern.edu/observer/issues/2007/01/25/labels.html

Richard Wright (American Writer). (2010). In *Brittanica Online Encyclopedia.* Retrieved from www.britannica.com/EBchecked/topic/649552/Richard-Wright

Chapter 3

Carroll, R. T. (2005). *Becoming a critical thinker: A guide for the new millennium* (2nd ed.). Boston: Pearson Custom Publishing.

Kirchhoff, S., & Keen, J. (2007, April 25). Minorities hit hard by rising costs of subprime loans. *USA Today.* Retrieved September 27, 2009, from www.usatoday.com

Lutz, W. (1997). *The new doublespeak: Why no one knows what anyone's saying anymore.* New York: HarperCollins.

Plain Language Association. (2009). *Your portal to clear writing.* Retrieved from http://plainlanguagenetwork.org

Van Gelder, T. J. (2005). Teaching critical thinking: some lessons from cognitive science. *College Teaching,* 53, 41–46.

Chapter 4

Brooklyn College English Department. (2009). *Literary terms.* Retrieved from http://academic.brooklyn.cuny.edu/english/melani/lit_term.html

Clymer, A. (2010, June 28). Robert C. Byrd, a pillar of the Senate, dies at 92. *The New York Times.* Retrieved from www.nytimes.com/2010/06/29/us/politics/29byrd.html

Definition of *communal reinforcement.* (2010). *The skeptic's dictionary.* Retrieved from www.skepdic.com/comreinf.html

Holley, J. (2010, June 28). Sen. Robert Byrd dead at 92; West Virginia lawmaker was the longest serving member of Congress in history. *The Washington Post.* Retrieved from www.washingtonpost.com

Jones, E. A. (Ed.). (1996). *Preparing competent college graduates: Setting new and higher expectations for student learning.* San Francisco, CA: Jossey-Bass, Inc.

Paul, R., & Elder, L. (2001). *The miniature guide to how to study and learn.* Dillon Beach, CA: Foundation for Critical Thinking.

Chapter 5

Associated Press. (2008, March 28). *Girl's death probed after parents rely on prayer: Wisconsin child, 11, received no medical treatment for undiagnosed illness.* Retrieved from www.msnbc.msn.com/id/23832053

Bartlett's Familiar Quotations Online. (n.d.) Retrieved from www.bartleby.com.

Beck, J. (Oct., 1985). Removing four roadblocks to bias-free reading and writing. T*he English Journal, 7,* 56–58.

Benoit, W. L. (1994). The genesis of rhetorical action. *Southern Communication Journal, 59,* 342–355.

Bitzer, L. F. (1968). The rhetorical situation. *Philosophy and Rhetoric, 1,* 1–14.

Caplan, A. (2008, March 31). Children's health can't be left to faith alone: When parents won't seek medical care, they must be punished by law. *MSNBC.* Retrieved from www.msnbc.msn.com/id/23885944

Carroll, R. T. (2005). *Critical thinking. Becoming a critical thinker: A guide for the new millennium.* Boston: Pearson Custom Publishing.

Carroll, R. T. (2007, March 28). *Teaching critical thinking.* Retrieved from www.skepdic.com

Carroll, R. T. (2008). *The skeptic's dictionary.* Retrieved from www.skepdic.com

Consigny, S. (1974). Rhetoric and its situations. *Philosophy and Rhetoric, 7,* 175–186.

Dweck, C. S. (2002). Beliefs that make smart people dumb. In R. J. Sternberg (Ed.), *Why smart people can be so stupid.* New Haven, CT: Yale University Press.

Eagleton, T. (1991). *Ideology: An introduction.* London: Verso.

Facione, P. A. (2007). *Critical thinking: What it is and why it counts.* Milbraw, CA: California Academic Press. Retrieved June 15, 2008, from www.insightassessment.com

Facione, P. A., Sánchez, C. A., Facione, N. C., & Gainen, J. (1995). The disposition toward critical thinking. *Journal of General Education, 44*(1), 1–25.

Fleming, D. B. (1979–80, Winter). A neglected critical thinking skill: Recognizing bias. *Indiana Social Studies Quarterly, 32*(3), 53–56.

Halverson, W. H. (1981). World views. *A concise introduction to philosophy* (4th ed., pp. 411–442). New York: Random House.

Girl's death probed after parents rely on prayer: Wisconsin child, 11, received no medical treatment for undiagnosed illness. (2008, March 28). *Health on msnbc.com*. Retrieved from www.msnbc.msn.com/id/23832053

Kurland, D. (2000). *What is critical reading?* Retrieved from criticalreading.com

Martinez, M. (2006, May). What is metacognition? *Phi Delta Kappan, 87*, 696–699.

Phan, H. P. (2010, May). Critical thinking as a self-regulatory process component in teaching and learning. *Psicothema, 22*(2), 284–292.

Pirozzi, R. (2003). *Critical reading, critical thinking: A contemporary issues approach* (2nd ed). New York: Addison-Wesley Educational Publishers, Inc.

Sonia Sotomayor. (2010, October 4). Retrieved from http://judgepedia.org/index.php/Sonia_Sotomayor

The White House. (2009, May 26). *Judge Sonia Sotomayor*. Retrieved from www.whitehouse.gov/the_press_office/Background-on-Judge-Sonia-Sotomayor

Vatz, R. E. (1973). The myth of the rhetorical situation. *Philosophy and Rhetoric, 6*, 154–161.

Walters, K. S. (1989, Spring). On world views, commitment, and critical thinking. *Inform Log, 11*(6), 75–89.

Chapter 6

Bloom, B. S. (1956). *Taxonomy of educational objectives, handbook I: The cognitive domain*. New York: David McKay Co, Inc.

Bunge, M. (1984). What is pseudoscience? *Skeptical Inquirer, 9,* 36–46.

Carroll, R. T. (2005). *Becoming a critical thinker: A guide for the new millennium*. Boston: Pearson Custom Publishing.

Chiles, J. R. (2001). *Inviting disaster: Lessons from the edge of technology*. New York: HarperBusiness.

Clark, D. (2009, May 26). *Bloom's taxonomy of learning domains: The three types of learning*. Retrieved from http://nwlink.com/~Donclark/hrd/bloom.html

"I am not a professional." (2004). *Chess Mate*. Retrieved from www.chess-mate.com/xiejunn.htm

Lau, J., & Chan, J. (2009). Argument analysis. *Critical thinking web*. Retrieved from http://philosophy.hku.hk/think/arg

The problem of induction. (2009, Sept. 8). *Stanford encyclopedia of philosophy*. Retrieved from http://plato.stanford.edu/entries/induction-problem

Seech, Z. (2009). *Writing philosophy papers*. Belmont, CA: Wadsworth.

Twardy, C. R. (2004). Argument maps improve critical thinking. *Teaching Philosophy, 27*(2), 95–116.

Van Gelder, T. (2002). Argument mapping with Reason!Able. *The American Philosophical Association Newsletter on Philosophy and Computers*, 85–90.

Xie Jun. (2010, Nov. 8). In *Wikipedia*. Retrieved from http://en.wikipedia.org/wiki/Xie_Jun

Chapter 7

Carroll, R. T. (2005). *Becoming a critical thinker: A guide for the new millennium*. Boston: Pearson Custom Publishing.

Criteria for evaluating internet sources. (2009, February 19). The University of British Columbia Library. Retrieved from www.library.ubc.ca/home/evaluating

Criteria for evaluating print sources. (2009, October 29). The University of British Columbia Library. Retrieved from www.library.ubc.ca/scieng/PrintEval.html

Driscoll, D. L., & Brizee, A. (2010, January 8). Evaluating print vs. internet sources. *Purdue Online Writing Lab.* Retrieved from http://owl.english.purdue.edu/owl/resource/553/04

Follath, E., Goetz, J., Rosenbach, M., & Stark, H. (2008, March 22). The real story of "Curveball": How German intelligence helped justify the US invasion of Iraq. *Spiegel Online International.* Retrieved from www.spiegel.de/international/world/0,1518,542840-4,00.html

Lau, J., & Chan, J. (2009). Argument analysis. *Critical Thinking Web.* Retrieved from http://philosophy.hku.hk/think/arg

Specter, M. (2009). *Denialism: How irrational thinking hinders scientific progress, harms the planet, and threatens our lives.* New York: The Penguin Press.

Warrick, J. (2006, June 25). Warnings on WMD "fabricator" were ignored, ex-CIA aide says. *Washington Post,* A01. Retrieved from www.washingtonpost.com/wpdyn/content/article/2006/06/24/AR2006062401081_pf.html

Chapter 8

Alvermann, D. E. and Phelps, S. F. (2005). *Content reading and literacy: Succeeding in today's diverse classrooms* (4th ed). Boston: Pearson Education.

Henderson, E. (2008). *The active reader: Strategies for academic reading and writing.* New York: Oxford University Press.

Henry, D. J. (2008). *Writing for life: paragraph to essay.* New York: Pearson Education.

Hirschberg, S., & Hirschberg, T. (2007). *Arguing across the disciplines.* New York: Pearson Education.

Lear, L. (1996–2010). *The life and legacy of Rachel Carson.* Retrieved from www.rachelcarson.org

On this day: 27 March. (n.d.). *BBC.* Retrieved from http://news.bbc.co.uk/onthisday/hi/dates/stories/march/27/newsid_2531000/2531063.stm

Public Broadcasting Service. (n.d.). *Nova: The final eight minutes.* Retrieved from www.pbs.org/wgbh/noval/planecrash/minutes.html

Ramage, J. D., Bean, J. C., & Johnson, J. (2009). *Allyn & Bacon guide to writing.* New York: Pearson Education.

Randall, S. (2011, January 16). Mouthing off in America. *Los Angeles Times.* Retrieved from www.latimes.com

Strong, R. W., Perini, M. J., Silver, H. F., & Tuculescu, G. M. (2002). *Reading for academic success: Powerful strategies for struggling, average, and advanced readers, grades 7–12.* Thousand Oaks, CA: Corwin Press.

Tierney, R. J., Readence, J. E., & Dishner, E. K. (1995). *Reading strategies and practices: A compendium* (4th ed.). Boston: Allyn & Bacon.

Topping, D., & McManus, R. (2002). *Real reading, real writing: Content-area strategies.* Portsmouth, NH: Heinemann.

U.S. Fish & Wildlife Service: Rachel Carson National Wildlife Refuge. (2009). *Rachel Carson biography.* Retrieved from www.fws.gov/northeast/rachelcarson/carsonbio.html

Chapter 9

Associated Press. (2006, February 15). Chertoff: 'Katrina' overwhelmed us. *MSNBC.* Retrieved from www.msnbc.msn.com/id/11355684

Barbara McClintock: A brief biographical sketch. (n.d.). *Cold Spring Harbor Laboratory Archives.* Retrieved from http://library.cshl.edu/archives/archives/bmcbio.htm

Duckworth, A. L., & Seligman, M. E. P. (2005). Self-discipline outdoes IQ in predicting academic performance of adolescents. *Psychological Science, 16*(12), 939–944. doi: 10.1111/j.1467-9280.2005.01641.x

Eugene Talmadge. (2010). In *New Georgia Encyclopedia*. Retrieved from www.georgiaencyclopedia.org/nge/Home. jsp

Jones, E. A. (Ed.). (1996). *Preparing competent college graduates: Setting new and higher expectations for student learning*. San Francisco: Jossey-Bass Publisher.

Lehrer, J. (2009, August 2). The truth about grit. *Boston Globe*. Retrieved from www.boston.com/bostonglobe/ideas/articles/2009/08/02/the_truth_about_grit/?page=1

McClintock, B. (1983). Autobiography. *The Nobel Foundation*. Retrieved from http://nobelprize.org/nobel_prizes/medicine/laureates/1983/mcclintock-autobio.html

Reif, F. (2008). *Applying cognitive science to education*. Cambridge, MA: MIT Press.

Research and Development of the U.S. Department of Science. (n.d.). *Barbara McClintock and transposable genetic elements*. Retrieved from www.osti.gov/accomplishments/mcclintock.html

Ross, B. (2005, Sept. 5). FEMA director takes heat for Katrina response. *ABC News*. Retrieved from http://abcnews.go.com/WNT/HurricaneKatrina/story?id=1099765

Shane, S. (2005, Sept. 5). After failures, government officials play blame game. *The New York Times*. Retrieved from www.nytimes.com

Tang, J. (2006). *Scientific pioneers: Women succeeding in science*. Lanham, MD: University Press of America.

Tierney, J. (2005, Sept. 17). Going (down) by the book. In *The New York Times*. Retrieved from www.nytimes.com

INDEX

A

Abbreviations, 302
Accuracy, 6, 196, 232–233, 296–298
Advanced argument mapping,
    206–208
AIM, 117
Ambiguous language, 92–93
Ambiguous, terms and statements,
    94–95
American Psychological Association
    (APA), 285
Analogies, 198, 227
Analysis, 15, 187–188
    argument mapping, 204–208
    arguments, 192–194
    critical thinker's traits, 188–192
    evidence, 195–199
    logic, 202–204
    patterns of organization, 208–212
    scientific method, 212–215
    and their consequences, real-world
        mistakes of, 215–216
Anderson, Jenny, 350–352
Anecdotes, 196, 197
Anger, 113
Annotating, 84–86
Antecedents, 247, 249
Antonym clues, 50–51
Appropriate conclusion, 117–118
    drawing, 118–120
Argument maps, in evaluation,
    256–257
Arguments
    cue words and phrases, 193
    evaluating, 226
    identifying, 192–194
    mapping, 204–208
Assumptions, 199
    evaluation of, 243–244
Attribution mistakes, 22
Audience, inferring an author's,
    120–121, 128–134
Author credibility, evaluation of,
    233–239
Avoidance, 113

B

Barkenbus, Jack, 372–374
Begley, Sharon, 200–201
Being skeptical
    about claims, 190
    about texts, 190–191
Biases, 180
    recognizing, 166–170
Bigfoot exists argument, 204
Bloom's Taxonomy, 155, 156
Brainstorm, 114, 316
Byrd, Robert, 113

C

Carr, Nicholas, 27–30
Carson, Rachel, 264
Cause and effect pattern, 208
Cavanagh, Casey, 382–384
Character traits, 5, 12–13
Chronological order graphic
    organizers, 270
Chronological/process pattern,
    208–209
Claim, 65
    extraordinary, 188–189
Clarify meaning, 86–87
Clarity, 6, 267, 294
Classification pattern, 209
Cogent, 202
Cognitive dissonance, 177
Common knowledge, 285
Communal reinforcement, 113, 114
Communication, 265
Comparison/contrast pattern, 209–210
Completeness, 6, 117, 299–300
Comprehension, 14, 31–32, 34, 101
    becoming a better reader, 34–35
    critical thinker's traits, 32
    real-world mistakes of, 55–56
    survey and predict, 41–44
    topic, identification of, 37–41
    vocabulary (See Vocabulary)
Confirmation bias, 19–20, 223
Conformity, 23

(C continued)

Connotation, 125
    effect of, 126
    noticing, 127–128
Consequents, 247, 249
Construct solutions for
    problem-solving, 315–319
Context clues, 47–48
Contractions, 302
Control phase of self-monitoring, 171
Counter-argument, 226
Counter-evidence, 199
Critical analysis writing, 276–281
Critical reading, 4
Critical response writing, 272
Critical thinker, 111, 178
    analysis of, 188–192
    attitude toward the world, 8–10
    evaluation of, 222–225
    inference, 112–115
    portrait of, 15, 16
    self-monitoring, 154–158
    skills of, 13–16
    traits, 32, 61–64, 264–265
Critical thinking, 5
    benefits of, 6–7
    facts about, 5–6
    meaning of, 3–4
    profiles in, 11–12
    real-world successes of, 56, 102, 145,
        179, 216, 258, 288, 324
    way of, 18–20
Critical writing, 4
Curiosity, 8, 32

D

Dalmia, Shikha, 332–333
Daniels, Mitch, 17–18
Darwin, Charles, 11–12
Deductive arguments, evaluation of,
    244–248
Deductive reasoning, 14, 203
Defense mechanisms, 18, 23–25,
    113, 114
Definitions, 48–49
Denial, 113

Denotation, 125
Details, 65–80
Dictionaries, 54–55
Doublespeak, 96
Dunning, Brian, 217–219

E

Easterbrook, Gregg, 236–238
Ehrenreich, Barbara, 146–149
Emotive words, 68–69
Enumeration, 210
Equivocation, 94
Euphemisms, 96
Evaluation, 15, 221–222
    arguments, 226
    assumptions, 243–244
    critical thinker's traits, 222–225
    evidence, 226–233
    logic, 244–256
    source and author credibility,
       233–239
    and their consequences, real-world
       mistakes of, 257–258
    using argument maps in, 256–257
Evidence, 195–199
    evaluation of, 226–233
    kinds of, 196–199
    logic and, 203–204
    recognizing conclusion and, 196
    spotting, 195–196
Example clues, 51–52
Example pattern, 210
Expert testimony, 197, 231
Explanation, 15, 263–264
    real-world mistakes of, 287–288

F

Facts, 197, 230
    characteristics of, 231
    identifying, 232
    and statistics, 227
Fair-mindedness, 10, 222
    detecting problems with, 224–225
    practicing, 224
Fairness, 6, 171, 300–302
Fallacies, 251, 255–256
    in real life, 256
    in short passage, 256
Federal Emergency Management
      Agency (FEMA), 323–324
Fisher, Max, 338–341
Fitzgerald, Susan, 259–262
5 Es, 265–266, 275
Flexibility, 9, 113, 114
Formal outline, 99, 100

Fossils, 38
Fowler, James, 240–242
Frame, 96

G

Glossaries, 54
Grammar, 289–302
Graphic organizer, 269–270
Gun control, 331–343
Gun violence, 331–343

H

Hall, Harriet, 103–105
Hayward, John, 236–238
"Healing" shrines, 157
Heuristics, 134
Hierarchy of Needs (Maslow), 45
Histrionic personality disorder, 210
Houdini, Harry, 189
Hudson, David, 325–327
Human sexuality, hormones' complex
      role in, 81–83
Humility, 8–9, 61–64
Hypothetical Deductive Method, 317
Hypotheticals, 198, 227

I

Implied main idea, 73–74, 77–80
Inductive arguments, evaluation of,
    250–256
Inductive reasoning, 14, 202
Inference, 14, 111–112
    author's audience, 120–121, 128–134
    author's purpose, 121–123, 128–134
    author's tone, 123–125, 128–134
    critical thinker's traits, 112–115
    making, 115–120
    recognizing assumptions, 138–141
    recognizing implication, 141–143
    and their consequences, real-world
      mistakes of, 143–145
    word connotation, 125–134
Inferring word connotation, 125–134
Informal fallacies, 250
    recognizing, 251–255
Informal outline, 100
Intellectual humility, 114
Interaction with Peers, 45
Internet, 34
Interpretation, 14, 61
    ambiguous language, 92–93
    ambiguous, terms and statements,
      94–95
    annotating, 84–86

    clarify meaning, 86–87
    language, clarification of, 97–98
    main ideas and details,
      identification of, 65–80
    mapping, 100–101
    outlining, 99–100
    real-world mistakes of, 101
    significance, 64–65
    unclear communication, 98

J

Johnson, Dominic, 240–242
Johnston, Ian, 354–355
Jones, Terry L., 380–381
Journal writing, 283–284

K

Keller, Josh, 338–341
Khosla, Proma, 135–136
King, Martin Luther Jr., 310–311
Knibbs, Catherine, 348–349

L

Language
    clarification of, 97–98
    to determine bias, 168–169
Listing pattern, 210–211
Loaded language, 168, 169
Logic, 202
    evaluation of, 244–256
    and evidence, 203–204
Lovejoy, Bess, 376–379

M

Main idea, 65–80
Major details, 65, 71–73
Managers, 6
Mapping, 100–101
McClintock, Barbara, 306–307
Medication mistakes, 56
Memory errors, 20
Memory test, 21–22
Metacognition, 170–172
Metaphors, 93
Miner, Horace, 162–164
Minor details, 65, 71–73
Mixed pattern, 211
Modern Language Association
      (MLA), 285
Modus ponens, 247
Modus tollens, 247
"Mouthing Off in America" (Randall),
      271–272, 275–276, 281–283, 284

N

Neyfakh, Leon, 344–346

O

Obstacles, 18–19
  to critical thinking, 24–25
  by emotions, 22–23
  way we think, 19–22
Offit, Paul, 103, 106
Online sources, evaluation of, 234
Open-mindedness, 9, 113, 114
Opinion, 230
  identification of, 232
Oral communication, 286
Organization, 9, 154–156
Organization's credibility, evaluation
  of, 239
Outlining, 99–100

P

Paraphrasing, 86, 89–92
Patterns of organization
  cause and effect pattern, 208
  chronological/process pattern,
    208–209
  classification pattern, 209
  comparison/contrast pattern,
    209–210
  definition of, 210
  example pattern, 210
  identifying, 211–212
  listing pattern, 210–211
  mixed pattern, 211
Peace and war, 353–363
Peer interaction, 45
Perlman, David, 81–82
Persistence, 10, 305, 306
Personal opinion, 230
  characteristics of, 231
Pierrehumbert, Ray, 103, 105–106
Plagiarism, 120, 285
Planning phase of self-monitoring, 171
Portrait of critical thinker, 15, 16
Predicting, 43–44
Previewing, 41–42
Print sources, evaluation of, 233–234
Prior knowledge, 41, 43
Problem-solving, 15
  acknowledge, 307
  breaking down, 312–315
  clarify desired outcome, 308
  construct solutions, 315–319
  critical thinker's attitude, 305–307
  define, 308

  describing, 309–310
  evaluate the solution, 319–323
  reading and writing as, 303–305, 308
  and their consequences, real-world
    mistakes of, 323–324
Pseudoscience, 214–215
Purpose, inferring an author's,
  121–123, 128–134

R

Randall, Stephen, 271–272
Rationalization, 19
Reader, Ruth, 364–367
Reading and writing problems,
  303–305, 308
  constructing solutions for, 317
  evaluating solutions for, 321
Reading, writing about, 271–272
Real-world mistakes of
  analysis, 215–216
  comprehension, 55–56
  evaluation, 257–258
  explanation, 287–288
  inference, 143–144
  interpretation, 101
  problem-solving, 323–324
  self-monitoring, 178
Reasoned judgment, 231
Reasoning, 19
  trust in, 10, 264–265
Recognizing assumptions, 138–139
  in longer passages, 139–140
  in short passages, 139
  in visual, 140–141
Reflection phase of self-monitoring,
  171–172
Relevance, 6, 302
  determine, 227–229
Rhetorical questions, 193
Roberts, David, 368–370

S

Sample critical response, 275–276
Science, 212, 214
Scientific facts, 213
Scientific method, 212–215
Scientific theory, 213
Self-driving cars, 363–375
Self-monitoring, 14–15, 153–154
  changing your mind, 177–178
  and controversial issues, 175–176
  critical thinker's traits, 154–158
  monitoring your thinking, 170–176
  recognizing biases, 166–170
  recognizing worldviews, 159–161

  and their consequences, real-world
    mistakes of, 178–180
Seligman, Katherine, 180–184
Shermer, Michael, 103–104
Shostak, Seth, 103, 106–107
Significance, 6, 64–65, 290–293
Similes, 93
Skeptical attitude, adoption of, 189–190
Skepticism, 9–10, 188
Sotomayor, Sonia, 222
Source credibility, evaluation of,
  233–239
Stated main idea, 73–77
Statistics, 197, 232
Status quo bias, 113–114
Student–student interaction, 45
Subject, 37
Sufficiency, 229
Summarizing, 86
Surveying, 41–42
Syllogisms, 203, 248
Synonym clues, 49–50

T

Talmadge, Eugene, 311
Technology addiction, 343–353
Testimonials, 227, 232
Testimony, 196–197
  expert, 197
Text features, 42
Theoretical knowledge, identification
  of, 312–313
To Kill a Mockingbird (Lee), 31
Tone, inferring an author's, 123–125,
  128–134
Topic, identification of, 37–41
Topic sentence, 65
Transitions, 66–67
Truth, 245

U

Unclear communication, 98

V

Vagueness, 93
Valid, 203
Validity
  determination of, 245, 247–248
  evaluation of, 249–250
Visual cues, 42
Visual learning, 58–59
Vocabulary, 47
  antonym clues, 50–51
  context clues, 47–48

Vocabulary (*Continued*)
   definitions, 48–49
   dictionaries, 54–55
   example clues, 51–52
   glossaries, 54
   synonym clues, 49–50
   word parts, 52–54

W

Waldman, Paul, 335–336
Wallace, Lane, 88–89
Webbing, 100

Wiesel, Elie, 359–361
Wishful thinking, 22–23
Women's issues, 375–385
Word connotation, inferring, 125–134
Word parts, 52–54
Wright, Richard, 32–33
Writing
   about reading, 271–272
   critical analysis, 276–283
   critical response, 272–276
   journal entry, 283–285
   patterns of development in, 268–270
Writing situation, 168, 169

X

Xie Jun, 155

Z

Zajfman, Daniel, 356–358